The Arab-Israeli Conflict

The Arab-Israeli Conflict

Two Decades of Change

EDITED BY
Yehuda Lukacs
and Abdalla M. Battah

Westview Press
BOULDER & LONDON

Copyright © 1988 by Westview Press, Inc.

Published in 1988 in the United States of America by Westview Press, Inc., 5500 Central Avenue, Boulder, Colorado 80301

Library of Congress Cataloging-in-Publication Data
The Arab-Israeli conflict: two decades of change/
   edited by Yehuda Lukacs and Abdalla M. Battah.
     p.   cm.
   Based on a conference held at American University, Apr. 3-4, 1987.
   Includes index.
   ISBN 0-8133-7516-9 (sc)
   ISBN 0-8133-0841-0 (pbk)
   1. Jewish-Arab relations—1973-   .—Congresses.   2. Israel-Arab War,
1973-   .—Influence—Congresses.   3. Israel—Politics and government—
Congresses.   4. Palestinian Arabs—Politics and government—
Congresses.   5. Middle East—Politics and government—1945-   —
Congresses.   I. Lukacs, Yehuda.   II. Battah, Abdalla M.
III. Series.
DS119.7.A67234   1988
973'.048—dc19

88-15375
CIP

Printed and bound in the United States of America

(∞)   The paper used in this publication meets the requirements of the American National Standard for Permanence of Paper for Printed Library Materials Z39.48-1984.

10   9   8   7   6

For Professors
Yusuf Ibish and Alan R. Taylor,
our teachers, friends, and colleagues

Contents

Acknowledgments   ix

1   Introduction, *Abdalla M. Battah and Yehuda Lukacs*   1

PART ONE
REGIONAL ACTORS

Israel

2   Israeli Foreign Policy Since the Six Day War,
     Avner Yaniv   11

3   Israeli Policies Toward the Arab States and the
     Palestinians Since 1967, *Don Peretz*   26

4   From Political Nationalism to Ethno-Nationalism:
     The Case of Israel, *Yoram Peri*   41

5   The Impact of the Six Day War on the Israeli Right:
     A Second Republic in the Making? *Ilan Peleg*   54

The Palestinians

6   Palestinian Nationalism Since 1967: An Overview,
     Naseer H. Aruri   71

7   The West Bank Palestinians and the Politics of
     Marginalization, *Emile F. Sahliyeh*   83

8   The Structural and Political Context of the PLO's Changing
     Objectives in the Post-1967 Period, *Cheryl A. Rubenberg*   93

9   The PLO in Retrospect: The Arab and Israeli Dimensions,
     Aaron David Miller   120

The Arab States

10   The June 1967 War: A Turning Point? *L. Carl Brown*   133

11   Structural and Ideological Change in the Arab Subsystem
     Since the Six Day War, *Bassam Tibi*   147

12   The Dialectics of Inter-Arab Relations, 1967–1987,
     Bahgat Korany   164

13   Egypt, Syria, and the Arab State System,
     Raymond A. Hinnebusch   179

PART TWO
THE SUPERPOWERS' POLICIES

The United States

14   American Middle East Policy Since the Six Day War,
     Steven L. Spiegel   199

15   Entanglement: The Commitment to Israel,
     Duncan L. Clarke   217

16   Jewish and Arab Diasporas in the United States and Their
     Impact on U.S. Middle East Policy, Andrea Barron   238

The Soviet Union

17   Moscow and the Arab-Israeli Conflict Since 1967,
     Robert O. Freedman   263

18   The Soviet Union and the Arab States Since 1967,
     Yahia H. Zoubir   293

19   The Economic Factor in Soviet Middle Eastern Policy,
     Walter G. Seabold   308

PART THREE
THE PEACE PROCESS

20   The "Peace Process" Twenty Years Later: Failure Without
     Alternative? Johan Galtung   321

21   The Palestinianization of the Arab-Israeli Conflict,
     Herbert C. Kelman   332

22   Paradigms of Reality: The Art and Science of Evaluating
     the Middle East Peace Process, Ofira Seliktar   344

23   Psychological Considerations in the Peace Process,
     Joseph V. Montville   364

24   Arabs and Israelis: Changing Perceptions and Political
     Attitudes, Erika G. Alin and Abdul Aziz Said   370

About the Contributors   387
Index   392

Acknowledgments

In preparing this volume we benefited from the assistance of numerous organizations and individuals.

Major funding for this project was made by American University's Kennedy Political Union and School of International Service. Other assistance was made by AU's Graduate Student Council and Women's Forum.

Louis W. Goodman, Dean of the School of International Service, deserves highest credit for providing moral and intellectual encouragement. Mary Eager, Assistant to the Dean, and the work-study students at the dean's office are to be thanked for their support and tolerance of our sometimes excessive demands.

Scott Wilson and Brian Keane, respectively the former and present presidents of the Kennedy Political Union, must be acknowledged for their efforts and contributions. Our sincere thanks are also due to the following individuals for their invaluable help: Kamel Abdallah, Cheryl Badra, Elizabeth Barker, Bret Bierer, Pua Chupak, Marla Clayton, Rob Connallon, Kathy Harman, Kamel Husseini, Lisa Haws, Deborah Horowitz, Laurie Houseknecht, Elliott Jones, Nail Al-Jubair, Eric Kennedy, Ghaleb Al-Khaldi, R. Scott Mantsch, Kathy McCall, Fadi Mudarres, Marty Ostertag, Bill Panzer, John Parks, Ursula Parks, Peter Scholl, and Todd Wilkenson.

We are grateful to Patricia and John Dockham, Linda Butler, and Andrea Barron for their meticulous and creative copy-editing, and to Mark Steinberg for his last-minute efforts in preparing the volume for typesetting.

Barbara Ellington and Sarah Tomasek of Westview Press deserve our special thanks for their patience and support. To Adil Battah, Jim Bigus, Munther Damin, Tzipi and Avi Goldberg, Ella and Shukey Weiss, and Lindsay and Aaron Miller, thank you for your years of friendship.

Finally, to the women in our lives, Debra J. Battah, little Anisa and Nadia Battah, and Louise Noakes, our love and appreciation.

Yehuda Lukacs
Abdalla M. Battah

1

Introduction

Abdalla M. Battah and Yehuda Lukacs

The year 1987 marked the twentieth anniversary of the Six Day War. The war was a turning point in the Arab-Israeli conflict, bringing in its wake numerous changes in the domestic and foreign policies of the actors involved. It also altered the regional balance of power, and led to an increase in superpower involvement in the Middle East.

This volume, which grew out of a conference organized at American University, focuses on these changes. The contributors do not provide a narrative of events, but rather offer new interpretations on the changes and processes set in motion during the last two decades.

The organization of the volume is based on our assumption that the study of the Arab-Israeli conflict has to incorporate the dynamic interaction of three levels of analysis: domestic, regional, and international. We believe that processes of conflict and conflict resolution derive their momentum from the interplay among domestic politics, regional considerations and global developments. For example, Sadat's trip to Jerusalem and the ensuing Egyptian-Israeli peace treaty cannot be fully understood unless one examines domestic politics in Egypt and Israel, inter-Arab politics, and the superpowers' strategic posture *vis-à-vis* the Middle East.

It is thus that the essays presented here, taken as a whole, provide a macro-perspective that reflects the complexity and dynamism of the Arab-Israeli conflict.

A second assumption is that there are two dimensions to the Arab-Israeli conflict. The first—the interstate conflict—involves Israel and the Arab states. The second, the intercommunal conflict, which has been much less recognized, involves two ethnic communities, the Israelis and the Palestinians, struggling over part of, or the whole of historic Palestine. (Whether the focus of the conflict is on the whole of Palestine or only on part of it—the West Bank, Gaza, and East Jerusalem—is, of course, a function of one's political perspective.)

The intercommunal conflict has two subsidiary dimensions: the conflict between Israelis and Palestinians in the occupied territories, and the conflict between Israel and the Palestine Liberation Organization (PLO) taking place also in adjacent Arab countries, namely Lebanon and Jordan. It is worth mentioning that unlike many other intercommunal conflicts, the leadership of one of the antagonists (the Palestinians) resides outside the disputed territory and, hence, regional and international dynamics also play an important role.

Prior to 1948, the intercommunal dimension had predominated, but this active struggle between the *Yishuv* (the Jewish community in pre-1948 Palestine), and the Palestinian community came largely to an end with the establishment of the state of Israel. This is not to suggest that the Palestinians gave up their claim to Palestine, but merely to indicate that the character of the conflict transformed into an interstate one.

From 1948 to 1967, the Arab-Israeli conflict could be described mainly as an interstate conflict. The occupation of the Sinai Peninsula and the Golan Heights in 1967 added new elements to the interstate dimension and insured its continuation. With the 1967 war, the Israeli-Palestinian inter-communal conflict was revived and inextricably linked developments in the interstate dimension to those in the intercommunal dimension of the conflict.

Moreover, the post-1967 period bore witness to the beginning of a gradual transformation of the foci of the conflict from the interstate dimension to the intercommunal. This development resulted from the occupation of East Jerusalem, the West Bank and Gaza Strip, with a Palestinian population over a million, as well as from the fact that the defeated Arab states were discredited in their claim to champion the Palestinian cause, the PLO's rise to center stage. The role of the PLO was formally recognized by the 1974 Arab Summit in Rabat which proclaimed it as the "sole legitimate repre-sentative of the Palestinian people." This declaration attested to the Arab states' formal recognition of the intercommunal dimension of the conflict by emphasizing the centrality of Palestinian participation in any negotiated settlement.

The post-1967 era could be divided into two periods: 1967–1982, and 1982–present. During the first period, the interstate dimension predominated and several eruptions occurred: the 1969–1970 Egyptian-Israeli War of Attrition; the 1973 October War, fought between Egypt and Syria, and Israel; and the 1982 Israeli invasion of Lebanon. In addition, several agreements were signed between Israel and its neighbors, such as the 1974 Israeli-Syrian disengagement agreement; and several Israeli-Egyptian agreements: Sinai I and II, signed in 1974 and 1975; the 1978 Camp David Accords; and the 1979 Peace Treaty. Notwithstanding these agreements, during this period there were no attempts at directly addressing the intercommunal conflict, excepting the Autonomy Plan in the Camp David Accords. This plan, however, was deemed inadequate by the Palestinians who argued that it would not lead to the realization of their demands for self-determination.

The first period ended with the 1982 Israeli invasion of Lebanon. This war is a prime example of how the two dimensions of the conflict coalesced. The first Israeli-Palestinian war, while taking place in Lebanon, was fought over the ultimate control the West Bank and Gaza. Although there were instances of interstate conflict during the 1982 war (between Israel and Syria, albeit in a limited manner), the focus of the war clearly demonstrated Israel's resolve to cement its control over the West Bank and Gaza. The PLO, by virtue of the support and popularity it enjoyed in the West Bank and Gaza, was in a position to prevent Israel's implementation of the Autonomy Plan called for by the Camp David Accords. The Lebanon invasion was thus an attempt to crush the PLO and to prevent it from interfering in Israel's attempt to impose the Autonomy Plan.

The second period, which began in the aftermath of the Lebanon war, culminated in late 1987 in the Palestinian uprising in the occupied territories. While the intercommunal conflict began to escalate following the 1982 war, the interstate dimension of the conflict remained dormant. Israel and Egypt have signed a formal peace treaty; Israel and Jordan, albeit in a formal state of war, have managed to reach a *modus vivendi*, while Israel and Syria continued to be in a strategic stalemate. The future of the interstate conflict, however, is linked to the resolution of the intercommunal conflict. Should the Israeli-Palestinian conflict remain unresolved, escalation of the interstate conflict into open warfare cannot be ruled out.

It is because of all these factors that a retrospective analysis of the Arab-Israeli conflict during the last two decades must take into account the transformation of the two dimensions of the conflict as well as an understanding of the linkage and interdependence between these two dimensions.

The centrality of the Arab-Israeli conflict in contemporary world politics has led to an inordinate number of studies and books that have attempted to cover all aspects of the dispute. The conflict has been taking place not only on the battle field, but also in the halls of academia, on editorial pages, and on television. Even among scholars who are supposed to be objective observers, the conflict has engendered emotional intensity which has often led to confusion.

First is the disagreement among scholars on the basic facts of the conflict. Scholars are not immune to the passions that animate the belligerents, who adhere to differing versions of history to support their respective claims. This tug-of-war between scholars has led to a lack of consensus and has manifested itself in contradictory arguments along the same lines which the belligerents themselves use. In addition, this lack of consensus has led some scholars to hold certain factors as causes, while others see these same factors as effects. For instance, is terrorism a cause or an effect?

Second, the conflict lends itself to differing characterizations. Some see it as a clash of nationalism, others as either a territorial dispute, an ethnic or religious strife, imperialist intrusion, an extension of the East-West conflict, and so on. While different perspectives are essential in any scientific inquiry, lack of agreement on the nature of the Arab-Israeli conflict has the effect of dispersing energies in many directions.

Third, is the tendency to explain the conflict in terms of a single cause. This is often due not only to political bias but to disciplinary loyalty. For example, political psychologists overemphasize psychological factors, econ-

omists economic factors, and so on. Similarly, disciplinary compartmental-
ization causes many researchers to overlook the dynamic interaction between
all levels of the conflict. Political psychologists and anthropologists, for
example, focus on individual and group behavior often at the exclusion of
everything else. Domestic considerations are often overemphasized by so-
ciologists, economists, and political scientists, and global strategic considerations are the preoccupation of international relationists.

Fourth, like other protracted conflicts, the Arab-Israeli conflict is fraught
with periodic crises such as the present uprising in the territories. While
there is an urgency to diffuse the situation, often enough policymakers and
analysts become too consumed by the crisis at the expense of the overall
process of the conflict. The danger is that energies become misdirected and
the fundamental causes ignored, and instead of a major surgery a local
anaesthetic is prescribed.

A closer examination and realistic assessment requires us to take into
consideration the multiplicity of causes, the multilevel aspect, and the
protracted nature of the conflict. Consequently, the analyst should look at
the simultaneous interplay between the actors (individual, state, non-state,
regional, international) and the factors or issues involved (economic, political,
social, cultural, religious, etc).

*   *   *

The twentieth anniversary of the Six Day War offered an opportunity
to reflect upon the current status of the conflict and to assess the state of
knowledge in the scholarly community that deals with the Arab-Israeli
conflict. Consequently, we convened a conference at American University
entitled *Twenty Years After the Six Day War: Assessments and Perspectives.*
We were fortunate enough to have assembled an impressive array of scholars
and policymakers who were generous enough to share their views with us.

Care has been taken to represent the various viewpoints. Scholarship
was the sole criterion in the selection process, which needless to say, implied
that participants—irrespective of their political inclination—analyze their
subject matter as objectively as possible. We were pleased with the results.

The book is divided into three parts. The first covers the regional actors,
Israel, the Palestinians, and the Arab states, and deals with issues such as
domestic and foreign policy processes, the role of nationalism, religious
fundamentalism, interstate relations, and changes within the regional subsystem. Part two examines the international dimension—specifically the role
of the two superpowers. The third part analyzes the "peace process" from
a number of different perspectives. All chapters were written prior to the
uprising on the occupied territories. Publication deadlines prevented us
from asking the authors for updates. However, on their own initiatives,
Professors Kelman and Sahliyeh submitted chapter postscripts, and Andrea
Barron provided a revised version of her chapter.

The first section deals with Israel. Avner Yaniv provides an overview of
the evolution of Israeli foreign policy since 1967; Don Peretz analyzes Israeli
policies toward the Arab states and the Palestininans; and Yoram Peri and

Ilan Peleg, respectively, examine the changing nature of Israeli nationalism, the dichotomy between political nationalism and ethno-nationalism on the one hand, and the impact of the Six Day War on the Israeli right on the other.

The role of the Palestinians is discussed in the second section. Naseer Aruri provides a macro-perspective on Palestinian nationalism since 1967; Emile Sahliyeh discusses the process of "marginalization" of the West Bank elites, while Cheryl Rubenberg addresses the structural transformation within the PLO. Finally, Aaron Miller focuses on the relationship between the Palestinians, the Arab states, and Israel.

The third section deals with the Arab states. L. Carl Brown challenges the prevailing view of the Six Day War as a turning point in the history of the Middle East. Bassam Tibi elaborates on the dynamics of the Arab states subsystem and the changes resulting from the 1967 war. Bahgat Korany examines the dialectics of Arab nationalism, the two prevailing modes of nationalism, *raison d'état* versus *raison de la nation*; and Raymond Hinnebusch discusses Egyptian-Syrian relations and its impact on the Arab-Israeli conflict.

The second part of the volume shifts the focus to superpower policies and rivalries. Steven Spiegel provides an overview of American Middle East policy since 1967; Duncan Clarke evaluates the formal American commitment to Israel and its implications for both countries. Andrea Barron examines the role of domestic factors in the American foreign policy process, comparing the activities of the American-Jewish and Arab-American diasporas and their impact on United States policy *vis-à-vis* the Middle East.

Soviet policy in the Middle East is the subject of the next section. Robert Freedman and Yahia Zoubir, respectively, offer differing perspectives on Moscow's role and position in the Middle East. Walter Seabold looks at Soviet military transactions and their role in Soviet policy in the Middle East.

The "peace process" is addressed in the last part of the book. Johan Galtung argues that what is termed the "peace process" has not been a genuine quest for peace. Herbert Kelman analyzes the changing nature of the Arab-Israeli conflict and argues that the conflict since 1967 has been "Palestinianized." Ofira Seliktar examines the state of scholarship with regard to the study of the Arab-Israeli peace process; Joseph Montville addresses psychological factors that exacerbate the Israeli-Palestinian conflict. Finally, changes in perceptions and political attitudes among Israelis, Palestinians, and Arabs, are analyzed by Erika Alin and Abdul Aziz Said.

PART ONE

Regional Actors

Israel

2

Israeli Foreign Policy
Since the Six Day War

Avner Yaniv

One of the anomalies of Israel is the wide disparity between its minuscule size and the preponderant place it occupies in world affairs. With a surface area of less than 20,000 square miles and a population of barely four million (five million if the Arab population of the occupied territories is included), the Jewish state is sometimes considered the world's fourth largest military power. It is at the center of one of the world's most intractable conflicts. It is engaged in an acrimonious dispute with the Soviet Union. At certain periods, it succeeded in establishing a significant presence on the African continent, has often loomed inordinately large (not always in positive and flattering terms) in Latin America, despite the geographical distances involved, and has figured prominently in the affairs of Europe. Finally, Israel has for decades now been among the closest allies of the United States, so much so that many governments in the developing world, and even in an odd way the Soviet Union, have come to regard their relations with Israel as an important factor impinging on their relations with the United States.

Israel's international visibility did not spring out of nowhere, but evolved gradually over the state's forty years in existence. While the foundations of this salience were laid during the decade of relative prosperity and stability between the 1956 Sinai campaign and the 1967 Six Day War, it is only during the past two decades that Israel has truly impinged on the world's consciousness. The main reason for this, obviously, has been the ever escalating drama of the Arab-Israeli conflict—the spectacular Israeli military victory in June 1967, the hostilities that brought the superpowers to near collision in the Suez Canal zone during 1968–1970, the gripping drama of the Yom Kippur war with the quadrupling of oil prices that accompanied it, the agony of the Israeli invasion of Lebanon, the sudden and quite unexpected rise of Shi'ite militancy in Lebanon. Then, too, there has been Israel's never ending string of daring military exploits, such as the raid on Beirut airport, the lifting of the Soviet radar system, the rescue of hostages from Entebbe, and the raid on Iraq's nuclear reactor. Israel's visibility has further increased with the rise of Palestinian nationalism which, by constantly vying for international attention, inevitably drew attention to its adversary.

Israel's increased prominence has been accompanied by a number of critical changes of emphasis in its foreign policy agenda. Broadly speaking, Israel's foreign policy since June 1967 has undergone six important shifts:

1. It has moved from a mainly European orientation to a decisively American one;
2. It has shifted from a careful maintenance of cordial relations with the Soviet bloc to, on occasion, near open conflict with it;
3. It has upgraded significantly relations with white South Africa while relegating the public dimension of relations with Black Africa to a secondary role;
4. It has developed significant though still largely covert relations with a number of critical Asian countries;
5. It has shifted its priorities in Latin America while experiencing an erosion in its status and prestige there; and
6. It has begun a shift from tacit alliances with non-Arab Middle Eastern countries such as Iran and Ethiopia to accommodation with major Sunni Arab states such as Egypt and Jordan.

Crossing the Atlantic

Israel has been actively searching for some sort of great power security guarantee ever since its inception. Rebuffed by the United States in the early 1950s, the Israelis settled for a series of "rainy day" solutions, first with France under the Socialist government of Guy Molet,[1] and then, as France became increasingly aloof under the enigmatic leadership of Charles de Gaulle, with the Federal Republic of Germany.[2] Toward the end of the Eisenhower administration, there were signs of greater United States willingness to treat Israel more sympathetically. This tendency gathered momentum under the Kennedy administration and matured during the presidency of Lyndon Johnson.[3]

On the eve of the Six Day War, France imposed an arms embargo on Israel (in fact, on the entire Middle East, but Israel was its only arms client) as part of its attempt to prevent the use of force against Nasser's Egypt. Fortunately for Israel, however, the action coincided with a major switch in Washington, where the Johnson administration, increasingly bogged down in Vietnam, was impressed and gratified by Israel's spectacular defeat of Soviet allies Egypt and Syria. As an added benefit of the June war, the Soviet naval supply route for North Vietnam through the Suez Canal was blocked.

When the Nixon administration took over in January 1969, the shift in American policy toward Israel from aloofness to patronage accelerated. With the Middle East now viewed as an arena of East-West competition, the objective became to eject the Soviets from the region. Making Israel dependent on United States military and economic aid was seen as a means of providing the United States with important leverage: the United States would thereby become the only world power capable of delivering Israeli territorial concessions to the Arabs.

From the Israeli point of view, it was a happy coincidence of perceived interests. There were indications that the United States would go as far as offering Israel a formal treaty of alliance, a major objective of Israeli foreign policy before the Six Day War, if it agreed to return all the territories occupied in 1967. But Israel was not prepared to commit itself to such a transaction, viewing the territories as a more valuable security asset than a formal treaty with the United States. Moreover, the governments of Eshkol, Meir, and Rabin (1967–1977) increasingly came to the conclusion that most of the fruits of an alliance with the United States, especially military and economic aid, could be accrued irrespective of the status of the occupied territories. The goal of a formal and public defense treaty with the United States was thus tacitly dropped.[4]

With the advent of the Likud to power in 1977, however, the search for a formal treaty with the United States resumed. The treaty idea was actively encouraged by President Carter as an inducement for Prime Minister Begin to make substantial concessions in the Sinai and the West Bank, but no territorial quid pro quo was forthcoming. In any case, the objective was seemingly attained in the fall of 1981 by Defense Minister Sharon in what came to be known as the Memorandum of Strategic Understanding. But the document was stillborn. It aroused a great deal of opposition both in the United States and in Israel, where critics charged that its designation of the Soviets as adversaries was against Israel's interests. It is thus not entirely surprising that the Reagan administration seized the first opportunity (the passage of the Knesset law annexing the Golan in mid-December 1981) to suspend the ill-fated document.

Since then, Israeli-United States cooperation in military and strategic matters has developed so extensively that the Israeli objective of a security alliance with the United States has to all intents and purposes been achieved. Tightening of relations has proceeded despite the strains caused by the Lebanon war, when the United States seemed intent on denying Israel a decisive defeat of the PLO. Other tensions centered on Washington's apparent desire to reach an understanding with Syria concerning Lebanon that involved bringing a "political," disarmed PLO into an Israeli-Jordanian-Palestinian dialogue. But the dismal failure of this United States policy on the one hand and the replacement of the controversial Ariel Sharon by the far more congenial (though equally hardline) Moshe Arens as Israel's defense minister on the other brought about a dramatic change.[5] This trend was reinforced when Shimon Peres became prime minister under the Labor-Likud power-sharing agreement following the Israeli general elections of 1984. From then until the time of writing, Israel's relations with the United States have become so intertwined—as manifested by economic aid, military assistance, intelligence sharing, offering Israel the status of a NATO ally, the free trade agreement, and the agreement concerning a Voice of America relay station in the *Arava* area—that even such bones of contention as the Iran-*Contra* affair, the Pollard spy case, and the revelations about the scope of Israel's trading with South Africa seem unable to reverse the trend.

Israeli relations with Western Europe have undergone a parallel eclipse. From 1967 to 1973, France tirelessly pressed its fellow Europeans to adopt a pro-Arab stance so as to bring their Middle East policies to some elusive middle point between the United States and Soviet positions. Launched by General de Gaulle and upheld by his immediate successor, Georges Pompidou, French policy focused mainly on a restrictive interpretation of UN Resolution 242, in effect requiring Israel to commit itself in advance to a return to the 1967 lines. Notwithstanding resistance from the Federal Republic of Germany and Holland, the main guardians of support for Israel within the EEC, the policy met with a certain degree of success for reasons having less to do with the specifics of the Middle East situation than with intra-EEC relations and jockeying for position in the world arena. As of 1970, when the impact of the oil price rise began to be felt, and the prestige and influence of the United States in Europe was on the wane owing to the ripples of the Vietnam war, French pressure increasingly bore fruit. Not surprisingly, the Yom Kippur war and the oil crisis of 1973 sealed the trend. In the decade that followed, all the members of the EEC—France under Giscard d'Estaing, Britain under Heath and Callaghan, Italy under Moro and Craxi, the Federal Republic (already under Willy Brandt but even more so under Helmut Schmidt), as well as all the smaller states— responded to the oil crisis by adopting increasingly pro-Arab positions. Often this was a policy more of verbal stunts aimed at assuaging Arab sensibilities than of substantive moves with any real impact. Just as often it was an easy way of presenting a common front in meetings of the EEC Council of Ministers where no consensus could be reached on anything else.

The main landmarks in this process were the statement of the Council of Ministers meeting in Brussels on 6 November 1973, the statement of the same body meeting in London 17 June 1977, and the Venice Declaration of the Council of Ministers on 13 June 1980. In their ensemble these declarations added up to a shift of emphasis not only concerning the meaning of UN Resolution 242 but also the status of the Palestinians. The 1973 declaration, for example, was the first clear EEC recognition of "legitimate rights" of the Palestinians, not as "refugees" but as a distinct national identity. This set the tone for other EEC statements over the next decade, including support of the Palestinian claim for a "homeland" (as in the 1977 statement) and, above all, endorsement of the special status of the PLO as the representative of the Palestinians (as in the Venice Declaration of 1980).

Such a trend in Europe's position concerning the Arab-Israeli conflict, especially given the obvious rapport with oil interests, would have elicited a sharp response from any Israeli government, whatever the political climate in the country. But it happened to coincide with the hardening of attitudes that accompanied the advent of Menachem Begin to power. The European-Israeli exchange became a veritable dialogue of the deaf. Begin lashed out at prominent European leaders for what he claimed was a "Munich" type appeasement, while the European leaders either replied with similar acrimony or simply ignored the Israeli position.

What incensed the Israelis most was Europe's lukewarm reaction to Sadat's peace initiative, Camp David and the Egyptian-Israeli peace treaty of March 1979, not to mention its seeming indifference to the French decision to provide Iraq with nuclear infrastructure. Such positions implied to Israelis that while Israel should continue to cultivate economic ties with the European Community, especially the long-standing agreement of association under article 238 of the Treaty of Rome, no hope for any political understanding was realistic any longer. In Israeli perceptions, what distinguished Europe's political positions from those of the Soviets was more a matter of style than substance. Against this background of Israeli bitterness, Shimon Peres alone worked hard both as prime minister and subsequently as foreign minister trying to repair these deteriorating relations. But while successful in reopening a dialogue between Jerusalem and various European capitals, he did not try (and most probably would not have succeeded if he had) to reverse the trend that since 1967 has relegated Europe to a secondary role in Israel's overall foreign policy picture.[6]

Moscow and Jerusalem

The Six Day War was also a critical watershed in Israel's relations with the Soviet bloc. During Israel's darkest hour in 1947–1948, when the new state was fighting for its very survival, the U.S.S.R. had been the only world power to offer military and political support. (The United States, in contrast, had imposed an embargo on all arms shipments to the country.) Thus, despite the Soviets' subsequent shift to become the major arms supplier of Israel's most powerful and implacable Arab foes, a deeply felt sense of gratitude to the Soviet Union lingered throughout the 1950s and 1960s, and may have survived even to the present.[7]

Be that as it may, on the eve of the 1967 war the Soviet Union was perceived in Israel as a dangerous and pernicious spoiler. After having informed Egypt of alleged Israeli troop concentrations on the Syrian border, the Soviets refused to accept Israeli denials of warlike intent. Israeli officials, including Prime Minister Eshkol, then offered to escort Soviet Ambassador Chuvakhin for an inspection of the border area, where the forces were supposedly amassed, but the Soviet diplomat declined.[8]

During the war itself, the Soviets sided with the Arabs, and when Israel launched its attack on the Syrian Golan they severed diplomatic relations with the Jewish state. All the Soviet bloc countries except Rumania followed suit, and then proceeded to refurbish the defeated Arab armies with enormous quantities of the latest models in their arsenals.

A few years later, during the war of attrition with Egypt along the Canal, direct Soviet involvement in the fighting forced Israel to compromise one of the most important maxims of its national security doctrine—namely, that no encounter with a superpower on the battlefield should ever be countenanced. But when Soviet pilots flying MiG fighters with Egyptian markings began to elbow Israel Air Force jets flying over Egyptian airspace, Israel had to choose between yielding—and thus exposing its greatly inferior ground forces in the Canal zone—and challenging the Soviets. It chose the latter path. The result was a deliberate Israeli air ambush in which four Egyptian MiGs flown by Soviet pilots were shot down and two more were severely hit. Israel did not make the story public for more than a decade.[9]

Not illogically, this incident was followed by heavy Soviet involvement on the side of Syria and Egypt. But while the Soviet arming of the Arabs was a cause of grave concern in Israel, policymakers also did not fail to see certain advantages that it entailed: Israelis were convinced, for example, that the Soviets did not want a full-blown war with its attendant risks, but preferred the "no war no peace" situation so advantageous in consolidating their position in the region. It is true that the Soviets were not sufficiently secure in their Middle East position to dictate to their Arab clients if, when, and on what scale to launch wars, which explains why they could not stop Sadat from ejecting the Soviet technicians from Egypt in July 1972. It also explains why the Soviets could not stop Egypt and Syria from resorting to force in 1973, and why Premier Kosygin was unable (despite the fact that he rushed to Cairo in person) to persuade Sadat to accept a ceasefire when Egypt had the upper hand in the Sinai fighting. Nonetheless, a certain restraining element remained. Moreover, there was an advantage—albeit fraught with risk—in what the Israelis perceived as the U.S.S.R.'s weak bargaining position *vis-à-vis* its Arab allies. The massive airlift of arms to the Arabs during the 1973 fighting—the direct result of this weakness—could have had disastrous consequences for Israel, but the other side of the coin was that it left a reluctant United States virtually no choice but to come down in a similar way on the side of Israel. It thus gave Israel something approaching an American security guarantee, a kind of insurance policy against direct Soviet intervention in the fighting. Thus, when Egypt's Third Army was nearly surrounded by Israeli forces and the Soviets spread rumors that they were about to launch a military action to bail Egypt out of this near catastrophe, Israel's decision makers deduced that the Soviets were bluffing to protect their credentials as allies in the eyes of the Arabs.[10]

The U.S.S.R.'s relations with the PLO were similarly marked, in Israeli thinking, with ambiguities and contradictory calculations. The Soviets had supported the PLO since 1969, and following the 28 October 1974 Rabat summit had adopted in their public statements the Arab formula designating the PLO as the "sole legitimate representative of the Palestinian people." They also trained PLO personnel, supplied the organization with large quantities of mainly light arms, and lent their support for the PLO in the international arena—a key consideration given the importance in PLO strategy of the accumulation of international support.

At the same time, however, the Soviets were persistently cajoling the PLO to change its approach to the question of a settlement. Moscow had never altered its insistence on the return to the pre-1967 lines as the basis for a solution, and consequently, consistently rejected the PLO covenant and the "secular and democratic state in Palestine" idea. It was also unenthusiastic about terrorism, and kept pressing the PLO to show greater flexibility.[11]

Another important element in Israeli attitudes toward the U.S.S.R. was the question of Soviet Jewry, the handling of which was linked to the vagaries of the situation in the Middle East. As long as formal diplomatic relations had been maintained between the two countries, the issue was restricted to quiet diplomacy through official channels. Even after diplomatic relations were broken in 1967, Israel avoided any discussion of this vexatious issue, especially when immigrants from the Soviet Union began arriving in large numbers. The acrimonious public campaign for Soviet Jewry only began to gather momentum in the aftermath of the Yom Kippur War, when Soviet-American detente and pressure for a Geneva peace conference with Soviet and PLO participation came to the fore.

A peace conference along such lines would confront Israel with a formidable coalition of forces and compel it either to accept the unacceptable—a settlement imposed by the superpowers and based on a Palestinian state on the West Bank—or to walk out of the conference and face a major crisis with the United States. From the standpoint of the Rabin-Allon-Peres foreign policy-making team, this kind of a conference thus had to be prevented. One way of doing so was to bar Soviet participation by laying down terms they could not accept without severely damaging their interests. These included the restoration of diplomatic ties with Israel and the opening of unrestricted emigration for Soviet Jews.

The advent of Carter only reinforced this direction in Israeli policy. President Carter was (usefully from the Israeli perspective) adamant on human rights. At the same time, he doggedly emphasized (less usefully for the Israelis) the centrality of the PLO, the need to cooperate with the Soviet Union in the search for peace in the Middle East, and the importance of the Geneva conference as both the venue and the means of seeking peace. Thus, from the Israeli point of view, Carter's human rights agenda could be used to push the issue of Soviet Jewry not only for its own sake but also as a means of preventing a Geneva conference in which Israel would face a superpower condominium pressing it to embrace the PLO.

But while Israel saw no need for overlooking the Soviets' negative impact on the Arab-Israeli conflict and adamantly opposed Soviet participation in a peace conference, it was careful to avoid a strident and public presentation of the Soviet bloc as formal enemies; as already mentioned, it was this that accounted for a large part of the widespread Israeli opposition to the Memorandum of Strategic Understanding Ariel Sharon had negotiated in Washington in 1981. Moreover, throughout this entire period, intermittent exchanges with the Soviets at various levels were going forward under both the Rabin and Begin governments. Channels of communication included Israeli Communist Party (Rakah) delegations to Moscow; visits to the Soviet Union of Israeli academics; visits to Israel of Soviet journalists and low-level party apparatchiks; a dialogue through clergy of the Orthodox Church; continuous contacts between Israeli and Soviet diplomats at the UN; a series of talks between the Israeli and Soviet ambassadors to Washington; and occasionally meetings between the foreign ministers of both countries.[12]

With the establishment of the National Coalition government in Israel on the one hand, and the advent of Mikhail Gorbachev in Moscow on the other, the stage was set for a new phase. Gorbachev launched a far more dynamic policy in the Middle East and quickly attained a diplomatic prominence the Soviet Union had not enjoyed in the region for many years. On the Israeli side, Shimon Peres took a number of steps that contributed to the thaw.

Among these was an Israeli move on the international peace conference. From Peres' point of view, a true international conference of a multinational nature was as unthinkable in the 1980s as it had been in the 1970s, and for the same reasons. But the unofficial negotiations Israel had been conducting with Jordan ever since 1967 had reached a kind of stalemate: while Peres apparently believed that there was enough common ground to risk public dialogue, King Hussein needed a semblance of an international conference to shield him from charges of a bilateral deal. At some point, Peres decided he could accept the idea of a conference as a calculated risk. The main risk was that the Soviet Union would accept the invitation offered them, which carried the same preconditions as had been demanded by Rabin, Allon, and Peres in the mid-1970s (i.e., free Jewish emigration and the restoration of full Soviet-Israeli diplomatic ties). If Peres was correct in his calculation that they could not accept both terms, he would still have the semblance of an international conference, without the Soviet Union, but with sufficient participation to meet Jordan's precondition for formal and public peace talks. At the time of writing, it appears that Peres did not miscalculate insofar as the Soviets were concerned, but rather misjudged his ability to force the hands of his partners and rivals in Israel itself. The positive result of the enterprise is that it did contribute something to reducing tensions between Moscow and Jerusalem.

African Dilemmas

Israel's relations with Black Africa during the 1956-1967 period were extensive in scope, exemplary in achievement and gratifying to Africans and Israelis alike. The Israelis who became involved in this part of their country's foreign policy shared a deep sense of mission and were further motivated by the enthusiasm with which they were received. Most of them were engaged in actual instruction and assistance programs. Their relatively small salaries and simple lifestyles were contrasted by the Africans with the patronizing, distant and condescending approach of officials of other assistance programs.

Following the Six Day War, however, this exhilarating experience lost its splendor. Israel's image as an innocent and courageous little David gave way to that of a formidable military Goliath occupying Arab lands. The Palestinian issue offered many Africans a focal point of identification which, though often based (with Arab encouragement) on a racial misrepresentation, exerted significant influence. But the most important factor affecting Israel's relations with Africa was the emergence of Arab economic power, especially as of 1970, when oil prices began to rise.

Likewise, after the 1967 war, Israel's trade and security-related cooperation with South Africa underwent a substantial increase. South Africa supplied a wide range of commodities from coal, raw diamonds, and (reportedly) uranium to spare parts for French-made weapon systems France was selling to South Africa but withholding from Israel following its 1967 arms embargo.

The growing tensions in Israel's relations with Black African states on the one hand, and the simultaneous expansion of relations with South Africa on the other, made Israel's Africa policy as a whole increasingly untenable. This built-in tension surfaced on the eve of the Yom Kippur War during the Addis Ababa conference of the Organization of African Unity (OAU), when the participating African heads of state pressed Israel to contribute to a pan-African fund whose main purpose was to help finance guerrilla operations against South Africa. Hoping to avoid offending either side, Israel made a symbolic contribution of $10,000. In so doing, it offended both, Black Africa by the modesty of the sum and South Africa by the very fact that it contributed to a fund directed against them. In retrospect, this incident appears to have accelerated the breach with Black Africa and thus ultimately to have paved the road to a great expansion of Israel's South African connection.

But it was the Yom Kippur War that actually precipitated Black Africa's wholesale severance of ties with Israel. The move was, at least in part, the fruit of a concerted and sustained campaign begun in the 1960s by leading Arab states, particularly Egypt and Saudi Arabia, which had become concerned about the implications of Israel's highly successful African program and the positive image it projected. Pressures by the Arab states in their efforts to cultivate closer relations with the Africans and dislodge Israel from the continent initially led to African statements of support for the Arabs in their conflict with the Israelis. The campaign accelerated with rising oil revenues, culminating in the Africans' 1973 decision to break off relations on the grounds that Israel was occupying African (Egyptian) territory.

The Israelis were shocked and outraged. The idealism that had guided policy previously (and even the more pragmatic notion that supporting Black Africa was a good way of obtaining African support at the United Nations) gave way to a deep cynicism concerning the Africans and the view that Israel should concentrate on maximizing business opportunities instead of spending good will, much less resources, trying to cultivate friends and influence in the continent. The number of Israelis working in Africa as government officials plummeted, while the scope of private Israeli business operations substantially increased. The business opportunities offered by Africa's raw materials and development needs became the main focus of Israeli attention.[13]

Not unrelated to this was the upgrading of Israeli relations with white South Africa. Israeli hopes in Black Africa had acted as a restraint on its relations with Pretoria. Despite the economic ties (which although expanding were not seen as indispensable) and the importance of a 100,000-strong Jewish community (mainly in Johannesburg, Durban, Port Elizabeth, Pretoria, and Capetown), the diplomatic profile had remained low. The small Israeli diplomatic delegation was headed by a consul general, in contrast to the Israeli missions in the Black African countries with which it maintained relations, all of which were headed by a ranking ambassador.

By the mid-1980s, Israel's volume of sales to South Africa reached close to a half-billion dollars annually. Much of this was taken up with arms transfers: Israel's decision in the wake of the 1967 French arms embargo to seek self-sufficiency in weapons production created a need for foreign markets in the interest of economics of scale. South Africa's anticipated long-term struggle with its black majority and black neighbors, meanwhile, made it a ready customer for the products developed by such Israeli firms as *Ta'as* (IMI), *Tadiran*, *El Op*, IAI, and RAFAEL.

But even while Israeli trade with South Africa was expanding, Israel not only maintained an extensive (and very beneficial) network of contacts (through assistance missions of variable size) in numerous Black African capitals but its trade with these countries continued to grow. The same African regimes that maintained these unpublicized relations with the Jewish state would ritually condemn Israel in forums of the UN, OAS, and Non-Aligned bloc. However, aside from outrage at the African backing of the 10 November 1975 UN resolution condemning Zionism as a form of racism, Israel came to ignore African criticisms of its relations with the apartheid regime and paid only scant attention to the criticism of liberals, especially Jewish ones, in the West.

At the time of writing, these trends in Israel's relations with Africa showed important signs of change. Congressional pressures in the United States forced a reappraisal of relations with South Africa leading to a lower diplomatic profile but not necessarily to a reduction in the financial scope of transactions, official Israeli protestations to the contrary notwithstanding. At the same time, the decline in Arab oil power, Egypt's peace with Israel, and a dynamic Israeli campaign have led to the resumption of full diplomatic relations between Israel and Zaire, Liberia, and Cameroon. Israel's relations with Africa, then, may be moving back to their state on the eve of the Six Day War.[14]

Asian Opportunities

The same factors that affect Israeli relations with Black Africa hold true in Asia as well. From a shining example of development in its most exalted form, Israel has become in the eyes of many developing countries a pariah supplying arms and counter-insurgency expertise. Its knowhow and assistance are keenly desired, but not the normal, public relations that could compromise dealings with the oil-rich Arab states. Meanwhile, the growth of Israel's productive capacity in weapons-related technologies has created a new basis for an expansion of relations with a certain category of Asian countries, notably Singapore, South Korea, and Taiwan. Sri Lanka is another example of a country that has resumed substantive dealings with Israel without admitting as much in public. Since Israel needs the trade outlets, it cannot be too pedantic in its insistence on normal, publicized relations. Its pariah status is thus enhanced.

In the long run, however, Israel's low-profile relations with these Asian countries may turn into an advantage. With the death of Mao and the consolidation of the new, liberal regime of his successors in the People's Republic of China (PRC), Israel's earlier assumption that relations with Beijing were unattainable may prove to be false. The PRC, to be sure, is cautious and not too keen to be recognized as a close partner of the Jewish state. But this caution about the public face of relations is increasingly at odds with China's strong interest in cultivating extensive, multidimensional contacts with Israel. In the technology realm, China has a large but outdated inventory of Soviet weapons it can scarcely afford to replace, while Israel (driven by the same economic factors to develop expertise in overhauling antiquated weapons) has become the world's most important center for the ingenious renovation and modernization of Soviet weapons systems. Israel's expertise in agro-technologies, especially methods of cost saving and multiplying productivity, is another area of immense importance to the Chinese. Meanwhile, in the diplomatic and political sphere, the Peres initiative for an international conference has suddenly aroused Chinese interest because it suggests an opportunity for the PRC as a permanent member of the UN Security Council to become a party to a critical international diplomatic process.

The PRC may have to pay for Israeli assistance with the hard currency of full diplomatic recognition, and at the time of writing there were already strong signs that it is willing to comply. For the Israelis, this would be a priceless gain both from the material point of view (given Israel's limited productive capacity versus the huge scale of PRC needs) and as an inestimable boon to Israel's international status, which has suffered such an eclipse since the Six Day War. Given this emerging opportunity, it was just as well that Israel had not, in the meantime, developed full diplomatic relations with Taiwan and South Korea.[15]

The Latin American Tightrope

On the face of it, Israel's relations with Latin America invite comparison with its relations with Western Europe. Diplomatic recognition came almost immediately after independence and has been maintained ever since in all

Latin American countries except Cuba (which broke off relations on the eve of the Yom Kippur War after the death of its Jewish Ambassador to Israel). The presence of substantial Jewish communities in most larger states in the region has made it easier for Israel to establish useful channels of communication. Beneath this reassuring surface, however, Israel's position in Latin America is riddled with complexities.

The roots of the difficulties lie in fundamental changes both in Israel and in Latin America, as well as in their various relations with the United States. Israel was initially favorably perceived in Latin America. It is true that conservative Catholic and militaristic/fascist elements were dubious about the new state, but the intelligentsia, the left, and the bulk of the middle class tended to see it as an incarnation of their own values. This attitude was reinforced by Israel's successful assistance programs in the continent in which the emphasis—as in Africa during the same period—was largely on education, irrigation, and the modernization of depressed rural areas in general.

But this image rapidly eroded after the Six Day War. Latin America, far removed from the Middle East and basically ill-informed about it, saw Israel's victory in traditional militaristic terms. Meanwhile, Israel's growing emphasis on arms sales and military training programs in its dealings with these countries entailed a shift in partners from the relatively progressive elements to the mainly conservative and often corrupt, inept, and tyrannical regimes. From being hailed as an agent of hopeful change, Israel came to be seen as a tool of reaction.

These tendencies were greatly enhanced by Israel's growing dependence on the United States at a time when most Latin American countries— under the impetus of Cuba and more recently the *Sandinistas* in Nicaragua— were increasingly challenging the United States' political hegemony in the Western Hemisphere. The two trends were in no way causally related, but their coincidence greatly damaged Israel's standing in the continent. It left the Jewish state no choice but to go along with the policies of the United States, not out of conviction but out of the inescapable political necessity born of an excruciating dependency.

This regrettable twist of political fortunes, in turn, created another problem for Israeli policy. The Jewish communities in countries such as Argentina, Brazil, Uruguay, Chile, and Venezuela, themselves split between left and right, were caught in a precarious position between conservative regimes and their domestic opponents. For the conservative regimes, the Jews represented a mainstay of support for left-wing opposition. For the left, their relative affluence and strong ties to Israel (increasingly seen as supporting the regime) made them suspect of complicity with the intolerable status quo. Israel was thus forced to walk an uneasy tightrope between all these conflicting pulls. The exercise has so far led to no great disasters, but it also reinforced the process of Israel's decline in the mind of Latin America.

Finally, as Israel's arms industry has grown in importance, so too has the role of Latin American markets. But arms sales have brought it into a competitive situation with the United States, which, protecting its own interests, generally opposes Israeli arms deals in Latin America except in cases where the purchasing regime is so unpopular in the United States that Washington prefers that Israel make the sale. Hence, the so-called surrogate accusation. This restrictive United States policy faces Israel with the disagreeable choice of selling arms in Latin America against the wishes of the United States government or trading in arms with despotic regimes such as Pinochet's Chile, the Colonels in Argentina, or Somoza in Nicaragua, thereby grievously compromising the generally liberal American Jewish community. Either way, Israel's standing in Latin America suffers.[16]

Israel's Foreign Policy in the Middle East

Close functional cooperation in the absence of "normal" diplomatic ties was also the hallmark of Israel's foreign relations closer to home, in the Middle East. During the 1950s and 1960s, Israel established close relations with Turkey, Iran, and Ethiopia. These countries—which the Israelis labeled the "periphery states"—were either non-Arab or non-Moslem. Turkey and Iran, for instance, were in almost chronic tension with their Sunni Muslim neighbors (Syria and Iraq in particular) in the heartland of the Arab world surrounding Israel. Ethiopia was at odds with Sudan. Building on this basis, Israel developed extensive relations with Iran and Ethiopia beginning just after the 1956 war and accelerating following the 1967 war. Even at the peak of these relations, however, Israel's partners insisted—to Israel's great chagrin—on keeping the contacts low-keyed and based on security apparatuses rather than full diplomatic representation.

A combination of Israel's apparent weakness in the 1973 war, the oil crisis, and the rise of Arab influence did much to erode these peripheral alliances. Moreover, as Israel moved toward peace with Egypt, the balance-of-power concept of holding the Sunni Arabs at bay through alliances with their regional foes increasingly lost its clear-cut validity. Indeed, following the rise of the tyrannical regime of Mengistu Mariam in Ethiopia and the fanatical ayatollahs in Teheran, it often appeared as if Israel and some of its erstwhile foes in the Arab world had a common cause against these powers—especially against Iran.

This, to be sure, is not as simple a proposition as it was sometimes presented in the heat of the debate in America concerning the infamous Iran-Contra scandal. Pan-Arabism of the Nasserist variety may well be dead. The Sunni Arab bloc that haunted Israel's foreign policymakers in the years preceding the Six Day War has clearly given way to far more powerful particularist tendencies leading to the progressive rise of distinct Syrian nationalism, Iraqi nationalism, Palestinian nationalism, certainly Egyptian nationalism, to a lesser extent even Jordanian nationalism, and (problematic but nonetheless real) Lebanese nationalism. These emerging Arab particularist entities are motivated by a pursuit of their own state interests, which are often as conflicting as their declared overriding conflict with Israel, or for that matter, Iran.

Recognizing this, however, it may still be premature to argue that the Arab will and ability to stand together either against Israel or Iran has irrevocably dissipated. In moments of extreme tension—such as the 1973 war or, more recently, the Iranian advance on Basra—the Arab world has shown clear signs of willingness to unite against a common foe. But to note this is not the same as to uphold the validity of a harsh dichotomy dividing the Middle East into (from the Israel point of view) bad guys (Sunni Arabs) and good guys (non-Sunni and/or non-Arabs). The road toward more open relations between Israel and some of its neighbors may be slowly opening. If this is the case, as the *de jure* Israeli-Egyptian peace and the *de facto* Israeli-Jordanian peace suggest, it would be without doubt an outstanding result of the gigantic process of change set in train by the Six Day War.[17]

Notes

1. The most comprehensive history of Israel's relations with France is Sylavia Kowitt-Crosbie, *The Tacit Alliance*. (Princeton N.J.: Princeton University Press, 1974).

2. For a detailed history of German-Israeli relations see Lily Gardner Feldman, *The Special Relationship Between West Germany and Israel*. (Boston: George Allen & Unwin, 1984).

3. For the latest history of United States relations with Israel see Steven Speigel, *The Other Arab-Israeli Conflict*. (Chicago: Chicago University Press, 1985).

4. This aspect of Israeli policy is discussed at great length in this author's own study, Avner Yaniv, *Deterrence Without the Bomb: The Politics of Israeli Strategy*. (Lexington: D.C. Heath & Co., 1987), pp. 48–54, 88–92, 152–157, 214–220.

5. For details see Avner Yaniv, *Dilemmas of Security: Politics, Strategy and the Israeli Experience in Lebanon*. (New York: Oxford University Press, 1987), pp. 137–147, 206–216.

6. For details see Avner Yaniv. "The European Community and Israel Since October 1973." Avigdor Levy ed, *The Arab-Israeli Conflict: Risks and Opportunities*. (Tel Aviv: Stratis, 1975), pp. 37–50; Avner Yaniv, "Dutch Middle East Policy Since 1973." *The Wiener Library Bulletin*, vol. xxx, Nos. 41–42 (1977): pp. 47–57; Avner Yaniv, "The European Community and the Middle East: The Politics of Ambiguity." (Haifa: University of Haifa—Institute for Middle Eastern Studies, Occasional Papers, No. 8, 1976); Avner Yaniv, "The European Community and the Palestinians." Gabriel Ben-Dor ed, *The Palestinians and the Middle East Conflict*. (Ramat Gan: Turtledove, 1978), pp. 291–320; David Allen and Aflred Pijpers eds, *European Foreign Policy-Making and the Arab-Israeli Conflict*. (The Hague: Martinus Nijhoff, 1984).

7. On this period in Soviet-Israeli relations see Arnold Krammer, *The Forgotten Friendship: Israel and the Soviet Union, 1947–53*. (Chicago: University of Illinois Press, 1974).

8. The details are amply provided in Michael Brecher (with Benjamin Geist), *Decisions in Crisis: Israel, 1967, 1973*. (Berkeley: University of California Press, 1980), pp. 46–7, 110–11.

9. On the Soviet role in the 1968–1970 military encounter along the Suez Canal see Lawrence L. Whetten, *The Canal War*. (Cambridge: The M.I.T. Press, 1974).

For details on the Israeli air ambush see Yaniv, *Deterrence Without the Bomb*, pp. 174-177.

10. A concise statement of such an Israeli interpretation is available in Efraim Karsh, *The Cautious Bear: Soviet Military Engagement in Middle East Wars in the Post-1967 Era*. (Boulder: Westview Press, 1986).

11. See Galia Golan, *The Soviet Union and the Palestine Liberation Organization*. (New York: Praeger, 1980).

12. For an up-to-date survey of Israeli-Soviet relations see Arthur Jay Klinghoffer with Judith Apter, *Israel and the Soviet Union*. (Boulder: Westview Press, 1985).

13. For a perceptive analysis of Israel's relations with Black Africa see Naomi Chazan, "Israel in Africa." *The Jerusalem Quarterly* 18 (Winter 1981), pp. 29-45.

14. A factually rich, well-written but contentious analysis of Israel's relations with South Africa is offered in James Adams, *The Unnatural Alliance: Israel and South Africa*. (London: Quartet Books, 1984). For an update by critical but less contentious Israeli journalists see Yossi Melman and Dan Raviv "Has Congress Doomed Israel's Affair with South Africa?" *Washington Post* 22 February 1977.

15. On Israel and China see Y. Shichor, *The Middle East in China's Foreign Policy*. (Cambridge: Cambridge University Press, 1980), pp. 21-29; also Yossi Melman and Dan Raviv "Israel's Other Arms Deal: Selling Weapons to China." *Washington Post*, 30 November 1986. Also *Ha'Aretz*, June 19, 21, 1987.

16. For a comprehensive analysis of this issue in Israeli foreign policy see Yoram D. Shapira, "External and Internal Influences in the Process of Latin-American-Israeli Relations."Michael Curtis, ed. *Israel in the Third World*. (New Brunswick: Transaction Press, 1976), pp. 147-181. For a grossly contentious but factually valuable update see Bishara Bahbah. *Israel and Latin America: The Military Connection*. (New York: St. Martin's Press for the Institute of Palestine Studies, 1986).

17. The historical, conceptual and political evolution of Israel's peripheral alliances is traced in some detail in Yaniv, *Deterrence Without the Bomb*, pp. 88-97; 157-8; 220-223.

3

Israeli Policies Toward the Arab States and the Palestinians Since 1967

Don Peretz

In the twenty years since the Six Day War of June 1967 Israeli policies toward the Arab states and the Palestinians have been transformed several times, as a result of political changes within the country and because of changes beyond the borders.

Israel's defeat of Egypt, Syria, and Jordan radically altered the Middle East balance of power. Previously, Israel was perceived as one of several militarily strong regional powers, albeit the strongest (with the possible exception of Turkey). Nevertheless, Israel's power was seen as limited, less than that of combined Arab might. After all, Egypt, Syria, and Iraq were recipients of massive quantities of modern Soviet military equipment and their leaders all demonstrated excessive confidence in the capacity to use this power against Israel. Not only international opinion but the average Israeli perceived Arab might and the rhetoric emanating from it as a mortal threat. Israel's miliary commanders had far greater confidence in their ability to cope with the situation than the public at large. Consequently, the defeat of the Egyptian, Jordanian, and Syrian armies in addition to the Iraqi air force was a stunning surprise. So taken aback were Arab leaders at the 1967 disaster that many blamed their defeat on a secret conspiracy between the United States and Israel rather than on the superiority of Israel's military machine.

Israel's political leaders were initially unprepared for the consequences of such a decisive victory; at first their policies were ambivalent toward the defeated states and the hundreds of thousands of Arabs, mostly Palestinians, in the conquered territories. It was certain, however, that no Israeli politician would countenance return to the pre-June *status quo.* Within a week of the war Prime Minister Levi Eshkol proclaimed: "The position that existed until now shall never return again."[1] Later he explained, however, that if the Arab states "will agree to discuss peace with us and will forego their war against us there is no problem I hope that we will not be able to solve in direct negotiations. . . ."[2] Implicit in Eshkol's remarks was the assumption that occupied territories could be bargaining cards for peace. On the other hand, the situation was regarded by those opposed to any territorial concessions as fluid enough to justify their continued participation in the wall-to-wall coalition government formed on the eve of the war.

Thus Menachem Begin and his *Gahal* (*Herut* plus Liberal Party) colleagues, militant opponents of any territorial concessions, remained in the cabinet until 1970. Their perceptions of Israeli policy toward the Arab states and Palestinians was that it was malleable enough for them to leave their imprint, or at worst to prevent advocates of territorial concession from leaving theirs.

From 1967 until 1970 a status quo policy prevailed, for both domestic and foreign policy reasons. At home all members of the wall-to-wall coalition wanted to preserve internal tranquility, and thus neither hawks nor doves attempted to disrupt the strange *Gahal*-Labor Party (plus Liberals and religious parties) combination that had brought about the 1967 victory. This meant that during the 1969 election for the Seventh Knesset there were few differences among the major parties on matters of security and foreign policy, although there was extended discussion about the future of the occupied territories. During the election, the territories (Sinai, Golan, Gaza and the West Bank) were still regarded as bargaining cards by the non-nationalist centrist and Labor Parties. Even the orthodox National Religious Party (NRP) had not yet developed the strong annexationist tendencies that were later to move it into the *Herut*-dominated nationalist camp.

On the other hand, neither the newly formed Peace List nor the Jewish faction of the divided Israeli Communist Party (*Maki*) called for departure from the occupied territories without a final peace agreement. Only *Rakah*, formed in 1965, the largely Arab wing of the once unified Communist Party, demanded immediate evacuation. Before the election *Mapam* accused Defense Minister Moshe Dayan of adventurist and expansionist ambitions, and its leaders called for "peace without annexation," but it abandoned its dovish policies after joining with the Labor Party to form the new Labor Alignment.

By election time it was difficult to differentiate between policies of the Alignment and its right-wing partners in the coalition. Since there was a consensus among nearly all parties that there would be no evacuation before peace, the question of remaining in the territories was becoming more and more theoretical. As the possibilities of entering direct negotiations with the defeated Arab states grew more remote, any necessity for definitive policies about the future of the occupied territories became less immediate.

Within the government, discussions focused more on transition arrangements within the territories than over their ultimate and final status. And increasingly it was the *de facto* arrangements imposed by Defense Minister Dayan rather than the consensus of the cabinet that determined day-to-day policies within the territories. Indeed, for all practical purposes Dayan became the sovereign authority, especially in the West Bank and Gaza. He emphasized creation of "new facts" in the territories which, he proclaimed, Israel held by "right and not on sufferance."[3] Creating new facts meant not only imposition of Israeli law on Arab Jerusalem, but establishment of two score Jewish settlements in the occupied territories. The new settlers represented all wings of the Labor movement, including *Mapam*, which agreed to assist in settlement of the Golan, although it refrained from establishing its collectives in the West Bank or Gaza.

Establishing "new facts" also meant attempts to freeze the post-war demography of all the occupied territories; the hundreds of thousands of Arab residents and refugees from the 1947 war who had moved to the West Bank and the Golan and who fled during June 1967 were not permitted to return to the newly occupied territories. Only *Rakah* advocated permitting the more than 100,000 formerly Syrian residents of the Golan Heights to return. Prior to development of extensive plans for Jewish settlement in Golan a few Israelis were attracted to a proposal of Yigal Allon to establish a semi-autonomous "Druzistan," or Druze vassal state in Golan.[4] The "new facts" doctrine reinforced *de facto* annexation of Jerusalem by extensive construction of Jewish housing developments in formerly Jordanian Jerusalem, revamping of the interior of the Old City, and confiscation of several thousand acres of land within greatly extended municipal boundaries of Jerusalem, to which were added large tracts of land on the West Bank.

Under the doctrine the West Bank and Golan road network was extended, numerous military bases and outposts were set up, the electricity grid and water system were integrated with those of Israel, and government assistance was offered to Jewish investors in the territories. Among the benefits received by Jewish entrepreneurs were cheaper prices for raw materials, lower interest rates on loans, and government securities in regard to security and tax relief.

Despite pressures from Likud members of the coalition to permit un-restricted Jewish settlement in the West Bank, there were initial efforts to direct it according to a plan devised by Deputy Prime Minister Allon. At first semi-fortified settlements were established in the Jordan Valley to form a security grid against penetration from across the river. The Allon plan called for creation of a ring of Jewish settlements around the Arab inhabited regions of the West Bank with the large Arab towns of Jenin, Nablus, and Ramallah as their center.[5] Although the plan was never officially adopted as government policy, it was followed quite closely during the ten years of Labor's hegemony over the territories. A basic premise was that the West Bank Arab population would govern itself with as little interference as possible from occupation authorities, but that all strategic points would remain under Israeli military control.

Additional aspects of Dayan's policy included removal of barriers between the occupied territories and pre-1967 Israel facilitating free movement of Arab labor from the West Bank and Gaza to employment centers in Israel where there were shortages of unskilled, cheap labor, especially in con-struction, agriculture, and services. Dayan's "open bridges" policy made possible visits by thousands of Arab residents from the occupied territories to Jordan and the Arab world beyond; it also facilitated return visits by Arabs from Jordan and other countries, although security controls imposed on these visits greatly limited the number of entries. The rationale for "open bridges" was that the policy would make possible reunion of Arab families separated by the war, extend Israel's influence and economic potential into the Arab world, and help dispose of West Bank agricultural produce.

Not all members of the Labor Alignment were enthusiastic about the "new facts" doctrine or Dayan's other Arab policies. Finance Minister Pinhas Sapir was concerned about the detrimental impact of the large Arab work force on Israel. Although only five percent of Israel's total labor force, workers from Gaza and the West Bank provided some twenty percent of those in construction and agriculture by 1969. Even many of the left-wing collective settlements had resorted to Arab labor for their expanding economies. What would happen in the event of a severe economic recession, asked Sapir? When these workers became the first to lose their jobs, they could easily become embittered and hostile. To preserve the Jewish State it was not enough to maintain political separation; the economic bonds that were rapidly binding the two peoples together had to be severed. Sapir perceived Dayan's "open bridges" as a threat rather than a boon, as the opening wedge to "de-Zionization."[6]

Effects on International Community

By 1970 it was apparent that Israel's continued occupation of the territories was the focus of policies toward the Arab states and the Palestinians. All parties to the conflict, the Arab states, the United States, the Soviet Union, and the international consensus perceived these policies as central in the Arab-Israeli conflict.

Israel and the United States envisaged continuation of the *status quo,* i.e., continued Israeli occupation for the indefinite future, as offering the greatest prospect for regional stability.

In view of continued Arab rhetoric about no negotiations, no recognition, and no peace with Israel, the status quo seemed the least troublesome of policies. Within Israel the mainstream of public opinion supported continuation of the status quo; it was the least disruptive policy to follow in a government that included both Labor and *Gahal.*

The United States, however, was subjected to pressures from a variety of sources unwilling to settle for the status quo, including the Soviet Union, America's moderate Arab friends, the European community, and the Third World. Furthermore, the new Nixon administration which replaced President Johnson in 1969 was determined to undertake new Middle East initiatives. The result of this combination of international factors and President Nixon's decision to restart the peace process was the 1969 Rogers Plan, a more detailed outline of proposals based essentially on U.N. Security Council Resolution 242.[7] Since the Soviet Union and Israel rejected the plan it disappeared from the negotiating agenda. In 1970 a new Rogers plan was offered following escalation of hostilities between Egypt and Israel in artillery duels and air combat across the Suez Canal.[8] The situation was exacerbated by increased Soviet support for Egypt through provision of large-scale military aid and arrival of Soviet officers to advise and train Egyptian armed forces. The second Rogers plan was essentially a three-month cease-fire agreement rather than a broad-based peace scheme. Nevertheless, it caused internal dissension in the coalition; when it was accepted by the cabinet majority, Begin resigned and *Gahal* left the government.

The return of Begin and *Gahal* to the opposition was a major deterrent to greater flexibility by the Labor-led government between the 1970 cease-fire and the 1973 war with Egypt and Syria. Characterized by William Quandt as a period of "standstill diplomacy," there were no new Israeli initiatives nor was heavy American pressure exerted to alter the status quo.[9] Beneath the apparently calm surface, however, both Israel and the Arab states were preparing for a new round of warfare, Israel with increased assistance from the United States, and Syria, Egypt, and Iraq with new infusions of weapons from the Soviet Union. Between 1968 and 1971 U.S. military credits to Israel increased from $25 million to $545 million. After the 1970 crisis in Jordan, when King Hussein defeated attempts by Palestinian guerrilla factions to disrupt his government, there was a quantum leap in American military assistance to Israel, which had played an important behind-the-scenes role in supporting the king.

The October 1973 war, Egyptian President Anwar Sadat's attempt to break the diplomatic impasse and alter the status quo policies of Israel and the United States, led to a new phase of Israeli and American policy. The war again focused attention on the potentially destabilizing effects of the Arab-Israeli conflict, opened a wedge between the United States and Israel on Middle East issues, and caused political dissension within the Israeli establishment. The extremely high costs of the war for Israel in lives and resources had not been anticipated, nor was the shift in the regional balance of power caused by the emergence of Saudi Arabia as financier of the Arab confrontation states foreseen. The sudden escalation of oil prices following the war greatly increased the economic power of the oil-producing states, especially Saudi Arabia, while costs of the war and the rise of imported oil prices seriously undermined Israel's position as the dominant regional power.

Israel was no longer in a position to resist appeals to change the status quo. Under American pressure, it made small territorial concessions in both Sinai and Golan following U.S. Secretary of State Henry Kissinger's 1974 and 1975 Disengagement Agreements between Israel and Egypt and Syria.

The setbacks sustained by Israel in the October 1973 war shook up the election campaign for the eighth Knesset, which had been postponed until December 1973 because of the war. The Labor government was opposed by the new Likud bloc, formed from a wide coalition of nationalists favoring annexation of the occupied territories; it included *Gahal* (*Herut* and Liberals) in addition to the Land of Israel Movement, the State List, and Free Center, the latter two splinters from larger parties.

The Labor platform now called for "peace and cooperation" with peoples of the region, and welcomed the international peace conference scheduled for December.[10] Although the platform stated that "Israel will not return to the lines of June 4, 1967, which were a temptation to aggression," it called explicitly for "territorial compromise." References in previous pronouncements to Israel's role in the territories were toned down. No mention was made of large investments or land acquisition by government or private sources. Instead, Israel's position in the territories until peace treaties or an interim agreement would give priority to security considerations. A major change was specific reference to Palestinian "self-identity" in Jordan, a distinct change from the position taken by Prime Minister Golda Meir a year earlier that "there is no such thing as a Palestinian."[11]

Although the Alignment emerged as victor, the gap between Labor and the nationalists was closer than ever before. From 1969 to 1973 the *Herut*-led opposition (*Gahal* in 1969, Likud in 1973) increased in strength from 21.7 to 30.2 percent of the votes (from 26 to 39 seats) while the Labor Alignment decreased from 46.2 to 39.6 percent (from 56 to 51 seats). As a result of this setback and growing public dissatisfaction with consequences of the October war, the Alignment replaced its traditional leadership with a new generation of politicians in the hope that public opinion would shift back in its favor.

The new Labor triumvirate, Prime Minister Yitzhak Rabin, Defense Minister Shimon Peres, and Foreign Minister Yigal Allon, did little to alter traditional Labor domestic or foreign policies. Other than the second disengagement agreement negotiated by Kissinger between Israel and Egypt in 1975 there were no new developments in policy toward the Arab states. The occupied territories remained the focus of discussion in attempts to restart the peace process, but Labor's policy remained as ambivalent as ever.

A new phenomenon emerged on the domestic scene after the 1973 war to influence policies toward the Arab states and Palestinians. Formed as a faction within the National Religious Party during the spring of 1974, *Gush Emunim* (Bloc of the Faithful) soon extended its membership to include non-Orthodox nationalists opposed to the return of the occupied territory. Although relatively small in numbers, *Gush Emunim's* patriotic fervor and dedication to Jewish settlement of the West Bank soon won it extensive influence, especially in Likud. The organization pursued its program with militant activism, frequently confronting the Labor government with establishment of illicit West Bank settlements. While the government insisted that all Jewish settlement in the territories be undertaken with its approval as part of a unified plan, the reaction to *Gush Emunim's* activities was usually a mild reproach. As a result, Jewish settlement areas were extended beyond those envisaged in the Allon plan.

The Alignment's failure to deal decisively with Gush Emunim's infractions in the West Bank seemed to characterize its overall approach to policy toward Arab problems. Not only was there the Likud opposition and *Gush Emunim* to deal with. In the government coalition the NRP (National Religious Party) had become more militantly nationalist after 1974 and also opposed withdrawal from the West Bank. Within the Alignment, the controlling triumvirate of Rabin, Peres, and Allon differed among themselves.

During the mid-1970s Peres took the position that the West Bank was an integral part of *Eretz Yisrael*, Allon was inclined to discuss a peace settlement in terms that might include substantial Israeli withdrawals, and Rabin was somewhere in between. To further undermine Labor, Rabin resigned as prime minister a few months before the election after revelations of his involvement in an illegal financial transaction. The most serious blow came during the election campaign with formation of a new electoral list, the Democratic Movement for Change (DMC). Many of its leaders and supporters, former members of the Labor establishment, were disaffected with the inability of the Alignment to deal with the country's domestic and foreign problems. A large percentage of the votes cast for the DMC were drained from former supporters of Labor, resulting in a loss of nineteen Knesset seats and the emergence of Likud as the dominant party, the first time that the government was to be headed by a party other than Labor.

As Likud took over the government and Menachem Begin became Israel's new prime minister, apprehensions about Israel's foreign policy increased abroad. But Begin soon disappointed his most militant admirers. Not only did he fail to annex all the occupied territories, but initially he even attempted to restrain *Gush Emunim*, the organization which before the election he had praised for its patriotism. Any fears or hopes of a more militant foreign policy were short-circuited by President Sadat's precipitous announcement in November 1977 that we was prepared to visit Jerusalem for direct negotiation of peace with Israel. Although a few members of Begin's cabinet were reluctant to follow through on the Sadat initiative, the euphoria generated by the Egyptian president's announcement was so pervasive that Begin had to respond favorably.

Sadat's Visit and the Camp David Talks

Sadat's visit started a new process in Israel-Arab affairs; it required a symmetric response if Israel were to maintain its good name in the international community and continue the special relationship with the United States. More subtle means than outright annexation were required to achieve Likud's goal of reunifying historic *Eretz Yisrael*. Begin's answer was his "peace plan" presented to the Knesset in December 1977.[12]

The twenty-six-point plan called for termination of military government in the West Bank and Gaza and its replacement by administrative autonomy of the Arab residents. An eleven-member elected administrative council with headquarters in Bethlehem would be responsible for local Arab affairs, to include education, religion, finance, transportation, construction and housing, industry, commerce and tourism, agriculture, health, labor and social welfare, refugee rehabilitation, local police supervision, and admin-istration of justice. Overall security, however, would remain the responsibility of Israeli authorities. Residents of the territories would have the right to choose between Israeli and Jordanian citizenship. Those choosing Israeli citizenship would be entitled to vote in Knesset elections while Jordanian citizens would be eligible to vote for the Jordanian parliament. Free movement between the territories and Israel would be permitted. Residents of Israel and the territories could acquire property on either side of the former border.

While offering autonomy to the Arab inhabitants of the territories, Begin did not abandon loyalty to unification of historic *Eretz Yisrael*. A key provision of his plan stated that "Israel stands by its right and its claim to sovereignty over Judea, Samaria, and the Gaza district."[13] Within Likud, it was understood that the plan did not vitiate the fundamental objective of permanently incorporating the territories into Israel.

While continuing negotiations with Egypt which led to the 1978 Camp David agreements and the 1979 Israeli-Egyptian peace treaty, the Likud government made every effort to preempt future decisions about the West Bank. Jewish settlement was extended and intensified and all pretense that it would be confined to areas uninhabited by Arabs was abandoned. Relationships between *Gush Emunim* and the government were transformed from confrontation to cooperation, and for all practical purposes, *Gush Emunim*, or its leaders, became the government in Jewish settlement areas. Within the next decade there was more than a threefold increase in the number of Jewish settlements and more than a tenfold increase in settlers, many of them in the midst of heavily populated Arab regions and towns. Land acquisition and control of West Bank water resources was greatly extended with the primary purpose of developing Jewish settlement rather than increasing the productivity of the indigenous Arab population.[14]

Begin denied any incompatibility between his autonomy scheme and plans for Jewish settlement. "Full autonomy" in the Camp David agreements in no way implied separation of the territories from Israel. "The Green Line," separating pre-1967 Israel from Jordan, "no longer exists—it has vanished forever. There is no line any more," he stated.[15] He avoided the issue of annexation, asserting that such a measure was unnecessary because "Judea and Samaria are an integral part of our sovereignty. It is our land. It was occupied by Abdullah against international law, against our inherent right. . . . You annex foreign land. You don't annex your own country. It is our land. You don't annex it."[16]

Begin's peace plan became the basis for the 1978 Camp David framework agreement for the West Bank and Gaza. It too avoided the question of annexation by providing for a five-year transitional arrangement during which the Arab inhabitants would be granted full autonomy and Israel's military government and civilian administration would be withdrawn. The final status of the West Bank and Gaza would be determined at the end of the five-year transitional period in a peace treaty to be signed between Israel and Jordan.

Although Israel, the United States, and Egypt accepted provisions of the Camp David agreements leading to the 1979 Israeli-Egyptian peace treaty, it was never possible to implement the autonomy scheme. Neither Jordan nor the Palestinian inhabitants of the territories accepted the autonomy proposals or the peace treaty. To further complicate matters, soon after negotiations began for implementation of autonomy, it was evident that Egyptian and U.S. interpretations differed greatly from Israel's. Begin perceived autonomy as applying to the Arab residents of the territories rather than to the territory itself. His conception was similar to that of "autonomism," a term designating Jewish national autonomy in pre-World War II Europe. Under this concept Jews elected representatives to Eastern European parliamentary bodies and were authorized to govern their own affairs in religion, social, and cultural matters, a system similar to the millet system in the Ottoman empire.[17]

Begin perceived autonomy as an interim measure to arrange a settlement with Egypt. Peace with Egypt would ultimately give Israel greater freedom of action in the West Bank and Gaza. Both the autonomy arrangement and the return of Sinai were the price Israel had to pay to achieve a normal relationship with Egypt. The five-year transition period would provide opportunity to create many more "new facts" and persuade the United States to accept Israel's integration of the territories.

The Likud government's true intentions toward the Palestinian inhabitants were indicated in military government policies after 1977. While Jewish settlers were treated with greater leniency and given a free hand to extend their influence, restrictions on the indigenous Arab population were applied with greater severity. Policies toward the Arab population were institutionalized during November 1981 in a measure that allegedly would move toward implementation of the autonomy plan. The measure, Military Order 949, established a "civilian" administration to provide for affairs of the local population. The order supposedly separated military and security matters from those of a civilian nature. Nevertheless, the "Head of the Civilian Administration" was a reserve officer appointed by the Israeli army's area commander. The government explained that civil administration would be taken over by local Palestinians who would absorb tasks formerly undertaken by the military. The new scheme supposedly complied with the Camp David autonomy plan calling for "withdrawal" of Israeli military and civilian administration, but in effect it merely changed the labels or titles of those controlling affairs of the Arab inhabitants.[18]

The new "civil" administrator, Menachem Milson, justified the arrangement as a strategy for making peace with the Palestinians on their terms, according to the "rules" of Middle East diplomacy. The previous Labor government had failed in its policies, Milson argued, because it did not "play by the rules" of Arab politics. Dayan's non-interventionist policies in local affairs had encouraged the PLO to seize political domination of the West Bank and Gaza. The PLO became firmly entrenched and thus captured most posts in the 1976 local elections authorized by the Labor government. With the majority of Arabs silenced by intimidation, it was necessary to remove PLO control and replace it with more "moderate" local influences. The best strategy for removing the PLO, Milson believed, was to capitalize on traditional inter-Arab divisiveness. Since most PLO support came from the urban elite, it could be undermined by support for rural notables hostile to the urban bourgeoisie. Israel would support an organization of Village Leagues in a rural resurgence against the PLO-dominated urban middle class.[19]

According to the "rules of the game" Israeli authorities would reward those who cooperated, with financial patronage, priority in employment, and new housing. Funds would be allocated to the Village Leagues for distribution through a Regional Development Fund. Every "encouragement" would be offered to "cooperative" elements while pressures would be intensified against those unwilling to "play the game." The new policy led to Israel's manipulation of funds from abroad sent to the West Bank, harsher methods to "pacify" militant nationalists, and exercise of more severe censorship over Arab newspapers sympathetic to the PLO. Within a few months the mayors of the largest West Bank Arab towns and cities were dismissed, expulsions for infractions of military ordinances were increased, curfews were more frequent, and demolition of houses, seizure of property, and imprisonment without trial occurred more often.

But the new policy failed to achieve Milson's desired goals; it led to increased civil unrest, to sharp criticism by much of the Israeli press and public, and to widespread international condemnation. Many critics perceived the policy as a move toward annexation rather than an extension of civil authority to the inhabitants. The four West Bank universities, Bethlehem, Hebron, al-Najah, and Bir Zeit, became centers of opposition and were closed for weeks or months at a time. Municipal Councils refused to deal with the new "civil" officials and were accordingly replaced, usually by Israeli army officers. With increased rioting and intensification of the army's countermeasures, civil unrest became greater than in any previous year of occupation. To help the army, the Chief of Staff (against the advice of Milson) issued directives to increase both personal and collective punishments and to authorize Jewish settlers (mostly *Gush Emunim*) to assist in combatting the unrest.

West Bank civil unrest now overshadowed Israel's policies *vis-à-vis* the Arab states and the occupied territories, leading to deterioration of relations with Egypt and a near halt in negotiations for normalization. Negotiations with Egypt were also threatened by Begin's attempts to demonstrate Israel's strategic superiority through an air attack on Iraq's nuclear reactor in 1981, as well as the annexation of East Jerusalem in 1980 and of the Golan Heights in 1981. For all practical purposes the peace process was grinding to a halt.

War in Lebanon

Within Likud attention now focused on the PLO as the principal obstacle to achieving the party objectives. The PLO was perceived by Begin's chief military advisor, Ariel Sharon, now Minister of Defense, as the primary cause of West Bank unrest, the troublemaker in Lebanon, and a threat to Israel's northern settlements.

During 1980 and 1981 Palestinian guerrilla attacks had increased across the northern border and Israeli retaliations were more frequent, leading many observers to predict another invasion of Lebanon, on a larger scale than the 1978 invasion undertaken in retaliation for a commando raid on the Tel-Aviv–Haifa road. To head off an outbreak of major hostilities, President Reagan sent his personal emissary, Philip Habib, to negotiate a cease-fire. The cease-fire along the border lasted nearly a year, but Likud, determined to destroy the PLO, was awaiting an opportunity to terminate the agreement and drive all manifestations of the organization from Lebanon.

Defense Minister Sharon also sought to broaden Israel's objectives with the strike into Lebanon, forcing a peace settlement on the Lebanese government and causing Syrian military units to leave the country. Although the Israeli government under former Prime Minister Rabin had reached an understanding with the United States in 1975–76 to authorize Syrian "peace-keeping" forces to enter Lebanon, Sharon was concerned that much of the country had fallen under Syrian control.

The occasion for terminating the 1981 cease-fire was presented when a dissident Palestinian terrorist faction shot Israel's ambassador to Great Britain in June 1982. Israel responded with artillery fire at PLO bases in south Lebanon. Within hours, the PLO responded, providing the excuse for a massive invasion with the stated objection of driving Palestinian forces north of the Litani River. But Israeli forces continued to advance northward to Beirut, laying siege to the non-Christian western sector of the city. Sharon also seized the opportunity to attack Syrian forces, inflicting heavy losses.

The siege of West Beirut lasted far longer than anticipated, causing extensive damage to the city, large numbers of civilian deaths, and heavier Israeli casualties than were militarily or politically acceptable. International pressure was building up to bring a halt to the fighting while on the home front public dissatisfaction was causing political tremors within Likud and providing fuel for the Labor opposition. Scores of soldiers refused to fight, and overt public opposition was expressed in Israel—the first such events in any Israeli war.

Before Israel withdrew, the Lebanese parliament elected a new president, the leader of the right-wing Maronite Phalangist militia, Bashir Gemayel. But before he took office, Gemayel was killed in an explosion with more than two dozen of his colleagues at Phalangist headquarters. The assassination led to the re-entry of Israeli troops into Beirut and the authorization by Israel authorities for Phalangist militia forces to "cleanse" Palestinian refugee camps of any remaining PLO guerrillas. The Phalangists massacred several hundred men, women, and children at the Sabra and Shatila refugee camps, raising a storm of protest throughout the world and in Israel where Sharon and army leaders were held accountable. Later, Sharon was removed as defense minister although he remained in the cabinet. The far-reaching military-political strategy for replacing Syria as the dominant power in Lebanon was aborted. Within a few months Israel began a slow withdrawal from the areas around Beirut, gradually moving southward. Mismanagement and the high costs of the war became a principal campaign issue in the 1984 election.

Results of the 1984 election were so close that neither Likud or Labor was able to form a new government. A compromise was reached by formation of a second National Unity Government, one of whose principal tasks was to complete withdrawal from Lebanon. Most troops left within a year, leaving only a narrow border strip under Israeli control. This "security" zone was held by the South Lebanese Army, a small militia armed, trained, and largely directed by the Israel defense forces.

North of the SLA-controlled border area Syria again reestablished its predominant influence as the major military and political force. The Phalange, which had maintained a close de facto alliance with Israel for several years, cut its ties and turned toward Damascus. The hoped-for peace treaty between Israel and Lebanon, although drafted and prepared for signature, was rejected by the Lebanese parliament and denounced by Syria. Within months after their retreat from Beirut, PLO forces began to return. Three years after the June 1982 invasion all of Israel's principal objectives were lost and its position vis-à-vis the PLO, Lebanon, and Syria was less secure than before the war.

Israel suffered another setback as a result of alienating Lebanon's Shiite population. Initially many Shiites had not opposed the invasion. However, by 1985 relations between Israeli forces and the Shiite population of South Lebanon became so strained that there were frequent armed clashes between the two. The situation was exacerbated early in 1985 when Defense Minister Rabin imposed an "iron fist" policy on South Lebanon, applied mostly to Shiite regions from which the withdrawing Israeli forces were attacked. Subsequently, all Shiite factions became engaged in a vendetta with Israel. The situation was destructive to Israel's hopes of establishing a special relationship with the Shiites, who had become the largest community in numbers and second to none in military power and political influence.

A major diplomatic consequence of the 1982 war was President Reagan's Middle East peace plan, focusing on resolution of the Palestine conflict. The plan was built on provisions of U.N. Security Council Resolution 242 and the Camp David proposals for the West Bank and Gaza. To maintain the appearance of even-handedness, the proposal stated that the United States would support neither establishment of an independent Palestinian state in the West Bank and Gaza, nor their annexation and permanent control by Israel. Several members of the 1982 Labor opposition expressed cautious approval, but the Likud-dominated government rejected the plan

as a "serious danger" to the country's security; it was rejected in the Knesset
by a vote of 50 to 36.

The difficulty in altering policies toward the Arab states and the Palestinians
with the Likud in government was made clear in the principles adopted
by the National Unity Government formed in September 1984, which
diluted indications of Labor willingness to make concessions for peace.
True, the agreement called for continued withdrawal from Lebanon, but
withdrawal had been initiated earlier by Likud under pressure from public
opinion at home and abroad. While appealing to Egypt and Jordan to revive
the peace process, the agreement skirted the issues that were obstacles to
a more active role by the two countries. Furthermore, the agreement
guaranteed inaction on the issue that was most crucial, the future of the
West Bank and Gaza, where the status quo was to be maintained: no
annexation and no change in sovereignty. In any event, no Palestinian state
was to be formed in the occupied territories, nor would Israel negotiate
with the PLO.[20]

Jewish settlement was to continue, although the number of settlements
would have to be agreed upon by both Labor and Likud. Rather than
increasing the number of settlements, existing ones were "thickened" so
that Jewish population in the territories continued to grow. During the
next three years there were few changes in administration of the Palestinian
population in the territories. The rhetoric of control was modified, and
when Shimon Peres became prime minister, the government announced
that it would comply with recommendations by the United States to
"improve the quality of life" in the territories. This meant permission for
more private investment from abroad, removing certain financial restrictions,
and indirect discussions with Jordan for a hypothetical development scheme
to cost several hundred million dollars. On the other hand, restrictions on
political activity and organization continued as during the previous twenty
years.

Shimon Peres, first as prime minister and later as foreign minister,
attempted several peace explorations in the face of vehement opposition
from Likud members of the government. In a speech to the U.N. General
Assembly during October 1985 he laid the framework for direct negotiations
with Jordan based on U.N. Resolutions 242 and 338, agreeing that Palestinians
could participate in the Jordanian negotiating team and that the Soviet
Union could play a role. While Jordan's King Hussein and Egypt's President
Mubarak responded favorably, Peres was severely criticized by his Likud
cabinet colleagues.

Peres continued his peace initiatives even after he rotated positions with
Likud leader Yitzhak Shamir, who became prime minister when Peres became
foreign minister. Before the rotation, Peres improved relations in the "cold
peace" with Egypt at a summit conference with Mubarak in Alexandria.
The two leaders agreed to resolve remaining border issues and declared
that "a new area in bilateral relations between Egypt and Israel as well as
in the search for a just and comprehensive peace in the Middle East" was

about to start. In support of the declaration, Egypt upgraded its *chargé d'affaires* to full ambassador, replacing the previous envoy to Israel withdrawn in 1982. Peres also opened secret talks with King Hassan II of Morocco, a contact perceived as the most important with an Arab leader since the 1977 visit of Sadat. Appraisals of the meeting differed; Peres called it a great success, Hassan, an expose of differences with Israel. Several members of Likud called it a betrayal of Israeli interests. Differences between Peres and Shamir, and between Labor and Likud, over Arab policies continued through 1987 when the critical issue became whether or not Israel should support a new international Middle East peace conference. There seemed to be little if any coordination on foreign policy within the government, with Foreign Minister Peres undertaking initiatives on his own while Prime Minister Shamir attempted to subvert them, even categorizing his foreign minister's efforts as dangerous and subversive of Israel's security. The idea of an international conference, he stated at a *Herut* conference, is "suicide and surrender. . . . As long as the Likud is in the government there will be no international conference."[21]

Conclusion

Before its conquest of the West Bank, Gaza, Golan, and Sinai, Israel had little room for maneuver in its policies toward the Arab states and the Palestinians. Its cards in terms of territory were few, and there was little else that the country could offer at the bargaining table. Certainly public opinion would not have countenanced the return of numerous Palestinian refugees, payment of massive amounts of compensation, or evacuation of territory, with every square mile considered of vital strategic importance.

After 1967 there was greater room for diplomatic maneuver. The Arab territories under Israeli control were so extensive that large areas could be used as bargaining cards without jeopardizing national security. Indeed, Prime Minister Begin did agree to return Sinai to Egypt in exchange for a peace treaty and, in Begin's mind, in return for Israel's continued hold on the West Bank, Gaza, and Golan. The 1967 conquests also strengthened Israel's bargaining position in the international community, with the Arab states, and with the Palestinians by considerably diminishing their terms for a settlement. Before 1967 there was pressure to give up territory within the 1949 armistice frontiers in exchange for peace. After 1967 no major party to the conflict, neither front-line Arab state, mainstream Palestinian group, nor interested outside powers demanded more than withdrawal from the 1967 occupied territories. In recent years the major parties seem to have dropped the pressure for return of Palestine refugees to their homes within the pre-1967 frontiers. None of the confrontation states, Egypt, Jordan, Syria, Lebanon, nor the PLO mainstream calls for a settlement in which Israel would have less territory than it held in 1967 or an Arab population within its borders other than indigenous Israeli Arabs.

Consequently, the focus of attention and concern has been the Arab territory remaining in Israeli hands since the 1979 peace treaty. The West

Bank, Gaza, and Golan have become the bargaining cards that Israel holds for reaching a final settlement.

The principal obstacle to a settlement is the division in public opinion over the use of the bargaining cards. While there is support for use of the territorial cards in the bargaining process, there is also strong opposition. The Likud mainstream refuses to consider "surrender" of any part of the West Bank, Gaza, and Golan—a refusal that has become the glue holding together the Likud bloc. With public opinion so divided, with the Likud as the second largest political grouping, and with the growing strength of the militant nationalist right, it is unlikely that Israeli policies toward the Arab States and the Palestinians can be substantially altered in the near future.

Notes

1. Bernard Reich, *Quest for Peace: United States–Israeli Relations and the Arab-Israeli Conflict* (New Brunswick: Transaction Books, 1977), p. 82.

2. Ibid., pp. 82–83.

3. *Jerusalem Post Weekly* (JPW), No. 470, October 27, 1969, pp. 6–7.

4. *Jewish Observer and Middle East Review*, Vol. 18, No. 40, Oct. 3, 1969, pp. 14–15.

5. Yigal Allon, "Israel: the Case for Defensible Borders," *Foreign Affairs*, October 1976, Vol. 55, No.1.

6. Don Peretz, "The War Election and Israel's Eighth Knesset," *Middle East Journal*, Spring 1974, Vol. 29, No. 2.

7. Yehuda Lukacs, ed., *Documents on the Israeli-Palestinian Conflict, 1967–1983* (Cambridge: Cambridge University Press, 1984), "The Rogers Plan, 9 December 1969," p. 18.

8. Reich, pp. 159–161.

9. William B. Quandt, *Decade of Decisions: American Policy Toward the Arab-Israeli Conflict, 1967–1976* (University of California Press, 1977), Chapter V.

10. *New Outlook*, December 1973–January 1984, Vols. 16–17, Nos. 9,1 (146,147), pp. 44–45.

11. Ibid.

12. Aryeh Shalev, *The Autonomy Problems and Possible Solutions*, Paper No. 8, Jan. 1980, Center for Strategic Studies, Tel Aviv University.

13. Ibid., Point 24.

14. See Don Peretz, *The West Bank: History, Politics, Society, and Economy* (Boulder: Westview Press, 1986), Chapters 4 and 5.

15. *Jerusalem Post*, April 30, 1979.

16. Comments during *Issues and Answers*, May 22, 1977, cited in Bernard Reich, "Israel's Foreign Policy and the Elections," in Howard R. Penniman (ed.), *Israel at the Polls: The Knesset Election of 1977*, (Washington, D.C.: American Enterprise Institute, 1979), p. 272.

17. See *Encyclopedia Judaica*, Vol. 3, Jerusalem, McMillan Co., 1972, article on "Autonomism."

18. Peretz, *The West Bank*, pp. 83–86.

19. See Michael Oren, "A Horseshoe in the Glove, Milson's Year in the West Bank," *Middle East Review*, Fall 1983, Vol. XVI, No. 1, pp. 17–29.

20. JPW, No. 1, 246, October 16–22, 1985.

21. JPW, No. 1, 394, week ending July 25, 1987.

4

From Political Nationalism to Ethno-Nationalism: The Case of Israel

Yoram Peri

Introduction

Those who study Israeli politics and society are of the opinion that two distinct periods can be differentiated in the history of Israel since its institutional and cultural arrangements were crystallized, following independence in 1948.[1] The view that the transition from the first period to the second occurred in the mid-1960s is also widely shared. Nevertheless, opinions differ as to the cause of that change.

One group ascribes the change to Israel's post-revolutionary stage. The change may be marked by a crisis stemming from the partial realization of the Zionist revolution or the passage from the generation of the founding fathers to that of the sons.[2] Another school attributes the political and cultural change to the demographic shift in Israel, from a society in which most of the Jews are *Ashkenazi* to one in which the majority are of Asian or African origin.[3]

Yet another approach emphasizes the cultural plane. Proponents of this view point to the decline of the dominant Zionist-socialist ethos and its replacement by a nationalistic "New Zionism."[4] Alternatively, the transition is from a secular civil religion to a traditional religious approach; in other words, a process of religionization.[5]

These three approaches deal exclusively with the Jewish components of the Israeli population, almost completely ignoring the non-Jews who in 1987 comprised almost one-third of the 5.8 million people living in areas controlled by the State of Israel. Karl Deutsch rightfully pointed at the "blind spot of Israeli social scientists" and claimed that the interactions between Jews and Arabs in this binational society must be taken into account.[6]

Deutsch's comment is important, particularly in light of insights derived from research of nationalist movements generally. For a long time, social scientists believed that what characterized the modern era is, in the words of Clifford Geertz,[7] the process of reducing primordial sentiments to civil order, or "the transfer of primary trust from the ethnic group to the state," a harmonious entity.[8] However, for more than a dozen years, they acknowledged the importance of the intrinsic conflict between the two components of the term nation-state. In addition, they recognize a process of primordialization and ethnic renaissance which occurs in many societies, both industrialized and developing.

This process has far-reaching social significance since it changes the basis of legitimation for political systems. If, in the past, this base was political, now the emphasis is placed on ethno-nationalism. In this respect, the Israeli case is not exceptional. What makes it special is that, for certain historical reasons, the process was greatly accelerated. Within a short period, and as a result of the war that lasted six days in June 1967, the state's political borders collapsed, the Israelis became reacquainted with their historical homeland and the societal composition of the population was revamped. With the addition of more than one million Palestinians from Israeli-occupied territories, Israel was transformed into a *de facto* binational society.

The Six Day War brought about a change in the definition of the Israeli collective identity, and it is this transformation that best explains the changes in the political, social and cultural systems in Israel.[9] Before substantiating this claim, the relevant terminology and definitions prevalent in Israel regarding the collective identity should be reviewed.

Man's need to define his identity is an existential one. For example, Apter claims that identity, together with a sense of immortality and meaning, are the truly deep individual needs that some institution—religion or, in a non-religious society, politics—must provide.[10] This need for defining identity exists both at the individual level and at the collective level.[11] The definitions of who we are, what differentiates us from others, who belongs to us and who does not, and what our relationship is to our surroundings are all essential. This is because the collective identity legitimizes the social order and determines the essence of political authority. It justifies the distribution of power in society and clarifies the boundaries of political mobilization. The collective identity clarifies the correct and just role of the authorities, and prescribes the intensity of loyalty to the political regime.

The collective identity is a product of dynamic interaction between individuals and select cultural components, and is created by a continuous process of selecting specific elements from a cultural repertoire and loading them with symbolic value. Because the process is continuous, the collective identity is not static; it is a cluster of symbols in dynamic relation to one another, such that each of the symbols is differentially emphasized over time.

The collective identity in modern societies is based primarily on nationalism. In the words of Ya'akov Talmon: "The death of God in the 18th century caused many to seek focal points of group identity outside the church. A substitute was found in the image of the nation." The intelligentsia play the main part in shaping the collective identity,[12] but they are not alone. The political elites constitute a direct, creative, and manipulative force in the development of national identity no less than the intelligentsia.

The political elites are those who respond to the question "Who are we?" with decisions regarding the political order. Since political elites aspire to create a social and political order that will grant them a power advantage or that will legitimize their privileged position in society, nationalism can be perceived as rational political strategy used by elite groups in order to gain for themselves certain political goals.

This is especially true regarding particular poly-ethnic societies, societies that have deep social cleavages, and visionary—as opposed to service— societies. In the case of visionary societies, it is expected that the state will educate the citizens with ideal values and mold them into a moral community that has a sense of mission and purpose. In the case of service societies, the aim of the state is to provide its citizens with material services only. In such a society, it is enough for a competing elite to claim power based on the fact that it is better able to provide the goods. In contrast, in a visionary society, the elite will claim legitimacy based on the fact that it reflects more authentically the components of the collective identity.

In summary, the collective identity is a cluster of components in dynamic relation to each other. In defining the collective identity, various combinations are created which give different weight to certain components. Defining collective identity is an ongoing problem with which the political system must deal, and through which political elites attempt to make their attributes more central in the society in order to gain power and legitimacy.

The history of the Jewish people is characterized by ceaseless efforts to deal with the problem of Jewish collective identity. That identity has always been shaped by different and opposing elements: primordial-tribal, national, historical, religious, universalist, and others. "Jewish society has always possessed various elements of identity; moreover, the attempts to crystallize the content of the identity have been focused around several dimensions that could not easily be combined and organized together."[13]

This problem of Jewish self-definition persisted through the birth of the Zionist movement and the establishment of the Jewish state. Among the various definitions of the new Israeli collective identity—and this paper deals only with the period since the establishment of the state—two were especially prominent. They are the national-political definition, namely statism or tatism (Mamlachtiyut, in Hebrew), and the ethno-nationalist definition. The following analysis, dealing with the two terms as ideal types in the Weberian sense, presents them as a dichotomy. In fact, it is difficult to find extreme, clear-cut, and inclusive expressions; the concrete historical examples are more complex and gray.

It should also be remembered that, although it is possible to identify attachments or inclinations of political movements and parties to one of two definitions, there is no direct congruence between the various national approaches on the one hand and the political movements on the other.

Thus, we shall limit our discussion of the two nationalist schools of thought to the theoretical level.

The State Versus the Nation

The statist thesis holds that the boundaries of the Israeli collective are fixed by the political dimension, and a congruence exists between the social collective and political citizenship. In other words, the state's boundaries are those of the collective, and whoever belongs to the state also belongs to the collective. Because the state is central to the definition of collective identity, it is not only a means, but a supreme value in and of itself. It is an "abstract system of roles and operational rules which have a continuous and independent existence, and the authorities' legitimacy is not conditioned by any public factors."[14]

Statism, particularly in its extreme expressions, demands that individuals direct their total faith to the state in such a way that any additional focus of faith must be of secondary importance. From this it cannot be inferred that the state negates a national collective identity. Rather, it defines that identity in terms of civil membership in a political entity. According to this approach, nationality is identical to legal citizenship[15] and the state is accepted as the supreme arbitrator in human affairs. Furthermore, in many cases, statism sanctifies the state and its executive branch in particular. Raising statism to the level of a civil religion is not peculiar to Israel. This is an often-used strategy for nation- or state-building in developing societies seeking political and social integration and suffering from deep social cleavages and traditional loyalties.

As regards Israel, the use of a civil base, i.e., the state's political boundaries, to define the collective is quite problematic. It suggests that there is no difference between Jews and non-Jews within the Israeli collective, since both are citizens of the state. On the other hand, Israel is defined as a Jewish state, and as such it has strong relations with Jews who are not its citizens. Accordingly, the statist approach has found it difficult to deal with the Jewish-Arab domestic matters as well as Israel-Diaspora relations, displaying an inconsistent approach in its institutional treatment of the issues. While the Arabs of Israel are ostensibly citizens with equal rights, as stated in the Declaration of Independence, they nevertheless suffer from institutional discrimination. At the same time, Diaspora Jews, who are not citizens of the state, nevertheless belong to the collective, to a certain degree, more so than others. This is evidenced by Israel's Law of Return, which grants Diaspora Jews, and only them, almost automatic citizenship if and whenever they desire.

In contrast to the political underpinning of statism, it is the socio-cultural dimension that is used as a basis for the ethno-national definition of collective identity. While the framework that determines the collective boundaries and its identity for the statist approach is civil and political, the boundaries of the collective, according to the second approach, are primordial (or those viewed as primordial), of the nation, blood relations, language, culture, and tradition.

There are a number of principles common to the various ethno-nationalist approaches, the most important of which are: the perception that human society is naturally divided into nations and the assumption that each nation has its own particular character. Thus, it is claimed that the values and interest of the nation come before all other values and interest of groups or individuals. Because the nation can only express itself completely within a political framework, it requires a state. Accordingly, while ethno-nationalism is based on the social sphere it also extends the ethnic community into economic and political spheres. The state serves as the tool of the ethnic community—a tool that serves it, and not the power that directs it. Political expression is intended to ensure conditions that enable the existence and growth of a distinctly separate cultural identity.

According to an ethno-nationalist definition, citizenship alone is not enough for one to belong to the national collective because it is limited only to the political arena. Membership in the collective is possible only for those who belong to the nation. And since there is no Israeli nation, but only a Jewish people, only Jews and not members of other ethnic groups are members of the Israeli collective.

Furthermore, according to the ethno-nationalist approach, the collective's boundaries are not necessarily congruent with the state's borders and, in the case of Israel, there are people who are outside the state and are members of the collective, namely Diaspora Jews. Also, there are citizens of the state—the non-Jews—who are not members of the collective. Therefore, the latter are not entitled to participate in the shaping of the collective Israeli identity.

Two examples of this differentiation will suffice. In 1981, when there were a number of terrorist attacks against the Jews of Brussels and Paris, Prime Minister Menachem Begin warned that if these actions did not cease, the government of Israel would have to guarantee the safety of the Jews there. Even if there was no intent to follow through on this warning, its ideological basis is significant. It supposes that intervention by the government of Israel to defend the Jews of France or Belgium is legitimate despite political boundaries. For while the Jews of France and Belgium are citizens of those countries, they nevertheless belong first and foremost to the Jewish people. Therefore, the government of the Jewish people is responsible for them.

On the other hand, in 1984, when it appeared that the Labor Alignment might establish a government supported by Arab members of the Knesset, the Tehiya Knesset members took the position that such a government would not be legitimate, since a majority would be achieved by the support of non-Jewish parliamentarians. The fact that the Israeli Arabs are entitled to civilian and judicial equality, and are represented by members of parliament, did not in the eyes of the ethno-nationalists suffice to give them the right to determine the composition of the government of Israel.

Participation in the Collective

Since the bases of the two nationalist approaches differ, there are also different criteria for membership in the national collective. The principal difference is between voluntary and organic membership.[16] In the statist approach, citizenship is generally perceived as similar to a civilian alliance based on a contract. Membership is not intermediated and it is rationally based on convenience; thus, citizenship is primarily a question of subjective conscience. Even under statist approaches that grant the state a more sacred position, it is still possible to enter and exit the collective by becoming a citizen or losing one's citizenship. In contrast, ethno-nationalism is based on primordial attachments, making it virtually impossible to enter or leave the collective except by birth or death. The individual has no significance except within the framework of the community. There is no room at all here for volunteerism.

The concept of participation in the Israeli collective, based on the ethno-nationalist approach, is simpler, more crystallized and coherent, than the statist approach. Ethno-nationalists regard belonging to the Jewish people as a sufficient basis for membership in the collective. The difference between the two bases of participation in the collective was manifested several times during the last two decades when Jewish citizens of foreign countries who were accused or convicted of criminal offenses found shelter in Israel and extradition was sought. In many of these cases, ethno-nationalists demonstrated opposition to extradition in spite of international agreements to which Israel is signatory. The usual argument is that a Jew cannot be abandoned to foreign peoples.[17]

The Territorial Component

A different significance is attached to the territorial component in the definitions of the collective identity. According to the statist approach, the orientation regarding the geographic sphere is primarily instrumental; it is the physical area in which the state exists and in which its citizens reside. The territory is a stage for operations, a source of resources and aids for national integration, but it is not a goal in and of itself.

In contrast, ethno-nationalism attributes intrinsic significance to the nation's territory. In the past, the land influenced the original shaping of the people's character, and thus it had a supreme value in and of itself. The extreme expression of ethno-nationalism holds that the national existence cannot be completely realized if there is no identification between the place of residence of the people and the homeland. Ethno-nationalism tends to grant the land the status of sanctity, even in cases where there is an absence of institutional religion. Generally, in order to strengthen the ties between land and nation, use is made of the fact that blood was spilled on the land by members of the nation. This, in effect, deepens the land's sacred character.

A consequence of the land being linked to the cosmic order and not to the political order may well result in decisions relating to the land being

determined not by governmental authority but by a "higher authority."
Indeed, it is easy for religious ethno-nationalists to base claims of this sort
on religious sources and holy writings. Even non-religious ethno-nationalists
are likely to cast doubt on the right of the political institutions to render
decisions regarding the future of the land. The relationship to the land
supersedes and becomes superior to all other relationships. In Israel, this
approach is taken many times by supporters of the ethno-national school
who say that, should it become necessary to choose between Greater Israel
and democracy, they will not hesitate to choose the former.

The universalist-particularist sphere is illustrated in the question of the
collective's relation to its environment. A term such as "family of nations"
is used in statist terminology. In contrast, the ethno-nationalists divide the
world into two: "us" and "them," the Jews against everyone else—the
"Gentiles."

Political symbols can clarify this matter effectively. The Israeli Labor
Party, for many years the dominant party, used two flags on festive occasions:
the blue and white national flag, and the red flag, which symbolized the
working class and its ties to the socialist international. Other parties also
emphasized, in various degrees, participation in international organizations;
the left in the socialist camp; and the liberals in the international liberal
movement. In contrast, the ethno-nationalist stream has but one flag, the
national flag. Their national approach is monistic and tends to accentuate
the hostile relationship between Jews and all other peoples throughout
history.

This basic difference in approach also influences attitudes toward the
Arab-Israeli conflict. While the political nationalists see it as a political
conflict, the ethno-nationalists view it as a deeper expression of the ongoing
hostility between Jews and Gentiles, yet another incarnation of the anti-
Semitism that has plagued the people of Israel for generations. Therefore,
the conflict requires caution and no chance-taking, and it is basically not
solvable.

The Religious Component

The religious component also differentiates in most cases between the
ideal types of statist nationalism and of ethno-nationalism. The question is
whether or not the social order is explained as the reflection of the cosmic
order or is disconnected from it. Do the basic suppositions on which the
social and political institutions are based derive from religion, or do they
have a secular, legal, rational, or traditional basis?

The religious component takes on great significance in the collective
identity when there is a national religion, when a nation has only one
religion and all members of that religion belong to the nation.[18] Judaism
is an ideal example, and in fact religion was the central component in
defining Jewish identity throughout history.

The religious component of the Jewish identity was central for so long
that even the secular Zionist revolutionaries found it difficult to exclude

religion entirely from the new collective identity. Thus it was the leaders of the Labor movement who initiated the inclusion of a course of religious studies, called "Jewish heritage," into the school curricula.

The sharpest dispute in Israel between the statist school and the ethno-nationalist school regarding religion is the question of the status of religious law as opposed to state law. The statist enacted a secular, Western judicial framework in which the Knesset is the highest authority determining the law. In contrast, the purpose of the ethno-nationalist school is to strengthen the position of the *Halacha*, the traditional religious law. The idealists would base state law only on the *Halacha*, while more pragmatic thinkers would integrate the secular law with the *Halacha*.

Universalism and Particularism

One of the prominent characteristics of political Zionism is that it strove to integrate two contradictory value premises: Jewish particularism on the one hand, and universalism as modern Western culture on the other. The two national schools in Israel—political nationalism and ethno-nationalism—put different emphases on these two contradictory value premises. The former emphasizes the importance of the universalist dimension, without totally ignoring the particularist, and occasionally attempts to blend the two. Ethno-nationalism accentuates particularism and demands total rejection of universalism, claiming that it opposes and contradicts Judaism, and that it stems from Athens and not Jerusalem. Thus one can find in a left-wing newspaper a headline emphasizing international brotherhood and solidarity, while Rabbi Meir Kahane, of the ultra-nationalist party *Kach*, claims that democracy, humanism, pluralism, and tolerance are Western values that oppose and contradict the spirit of Judaism.

The universalist dimension enables the statist school of thought to overcome the difficulties stemming from the existence of a non-Jewish minority in Israel. The Arab citizens need not identify with the Jewish components of Israeli culture, as long as they identify with the state's universalist dimension. In contrast, the absence of a universalist component enables the ethno-nationalists to claim that it is impossible to consider equal rights between Arabs and Jews in the State of Israel since the two ethnic groups have no common ground.

As has been mentioned, what is presented here is a dichotomy of ideal types of national attitudes. In the field of nationalism, there is often a confusion of terms and definitions which stems not only from disagreement between researchers and thinkers, but also, to a great extent, from the lack of a common language. Accordingly, it is worth mentioning several similar terms that express the differentiation being made here. Smith distinguishes between bureaucratic nationalism, and romantic, or ethnic, nationalism. Elsewhere, instead of the term "bureaucratic nationalism," he uses the term "nationalism inspired by the state." In contrast, integral or organic nationalism is closer to the term ethno-nationalism although it is not identical to it.

The most extreme expression of the statist model is political, Jacobin messianism—"totalitarian democracy," in the words of Ya'akov Talmon, or as referred to by Apter, "the mobilizing system," in which politics encompasses all areas of life: The state is the source of morals, and individuals are required to sacrifice themselves for the goals of the collective. In contrast, integral nationalism, organic nationalism, or folk-nationalism are the most extreme expressions along the spectrum of ethno-nationalism. They are characterized by ethnocentrism, xenophobia, or, to use Morris Barrah's phrase, "national egoism," and the belief that self-determination is accomplished by a political struggle in blood and fire. Except in the case of very small and extreme factions, it is difficult to find expressions of these two polar approaches in Israel. However, at various times, nationalist manifestations close to the ideal types can be discerned.

Collapse of the Political Boundaries

During the first period, from the establishment of the state until the first half of the 1960s, statism was the dominant ethos in Israel, its civil religion. Competing perceptions posed no threat to statism, but the Six Day War greatly weakened the statist ethos and made the ethno-nationalist ethos more popular. First and foremost, the war resulted in reestablishment of contact with areas of the ancestral homeland and awakened the realization of a dream nurtured for two thousand years. With the territories under Israeli control, the importance of land, among the variables of the collective identity, increased to such an extent that a new school of territorial nationalism has developed.

The territorial factor gained special influence among certain religious groups such as Gush Emunim, whose approach to the land of Israel is religio-messianic. According to their belief, the holiness of Eretz Yisrael means that non-Jews who live there are by no means entitled to rights equal to those held by Jews. Since the land is holy the secular political institutions do not have the authority to determine its future and most certainly have no authority to hand over parts of it to non-Jewish sovereignty. Liberating the holy lands from foreign hands is the first part of the process of realizing the messianic prophecy, and this process must be accelerated in order to establish a theocracy.[19]

Another effect of the Six Day War was the collapse of the collective's political boundaries. The borders of the state, which gained international recognition and internal legitimation in Israel after the war of independence in 1948, were replaced by new boundaries, i.e., the cease-fire lines of 1967 (along with modifications agreed upon later regarding the Syrian and Egyptian borders). There is no international consensus regarding these lines. In fact, the opposite is true: there is international consensus that these will not be Israel's permanent political borders. More significantly, there is no internal agreement in Israel itself regarding these borders.

While the territories were not formally annexed by the state (with the exception of the Golan Heights and the Jerusalem region), as Jewish settlement has spread, Israeli municipal and regional councils have been established and, in many legal aspects, have become part of the Israeli administrative system. Other Israeli actions, in the fields of land, water, construction, roads, agriculture, etc., brought about the *de facto* annexation of the West Bank. In addition, there is the Israeli demand to annex—at the time of a political settlement—parts, or all, of the territories. In other words, while the territories are not yet an integral part of the State of Israel, neither are they external to it.[20] This is precisely the meaning of the absence of political borders.

The collapse of the political boundaries completely weakened the civilian definition of the collective identity. If there are two judicial systems in a territory controlled by the state, one in Israel itself and one in the territories, and if there are two judicial systems in the territories, one for Arabs and one for Jews, how is it possible to define the Israeli collective with a civil-universalist definition?

The collapse of the political boundaries weakened the state's component in the collective identity cluster. If the administered territories, which do not formally belong to the state, are no less meaningful than the area under Israeli jurisdiction, and if the state's political institutions are limited in their authority to deal with issues central to the nation's future, then the state's position is not what it was prior to 1967. Accordingly, primarily since the early 1960s, the use of the term *Eretz Yisrael* instead of "the State of Israel" has become widespread. This nomenclature is not accidental and is used intentionally by those who support the ethno-nationalist approach, who frequently use the term "the people of Israel."

The limited legitimacy granted to the state's political institutions, the Knesset and the government by the ethno-nationalists who advocate annexation justifies, in their view, their illegal settlements in the territories. This attitude found its most extreme expression in the establishment of the Jewish underground in the territories. Its members have carried out violent operations against Arabs, which they justify not only on the basis of their claim that the state neglects their security, but also on the grounds that they are entitled to determine the future of the nation, particularly because of the state's limited authority. This underground might have been considered an insignificant phenomenon had it not been supported by major segments of the political, religious, and secular establishment that adhere to the ethno-nationalist approach.

In addition to renewing contact with the territories of the ancestral homeland and bringing about the collapse of the collective's political boundaries, the Six Day War also caused a change in the social structure of the population. Within Israel's pre-1967 borders, one out of five people was a non-Jew. Following the occupation, the ratio became approximately 1:3.5. In 1987, there were 700,000 Arabs and other minorities living in Israel, more than a million Palestinians in the territories, and 3.8 million Israeli Jews. In social terms, Israel has become a *de facto* binational society.

The change in the social composition created a situation familiar to other polyethnic states.[21] In the case of conflict between ethnic groups, the ruling group tends to emphasize its primordial attributes, its ethnicity, as the central basis for defining the national collective. By doing so, it is able to make the other ethnic groups appear more peripheral and insignificant. Use of this strategy is more widespread if the minority ethnic group is supported by a neighboring society that has the same ethnic roots. By contrast, the deployment of civil universalist and political principles for the purpose of defining the collective identity will emphasize equality between the two ethnic groups, and cause the ruling group to lose its relative advantage.

As the conflict between the two ethnic groups worsens, it can be expected that the differences that separate them will become increasingly sharp, leading to further discrimination. Thus it is not surprising that during the first half of the 1980s, a member of the Knesset suggested changing the criminal law so that a Jew who kills an Arab for nationalist reasons would not be prosecuted according to the existing criminal law, but dealt with preferentially.

An additional factor, in combination with these changes that occurred in 1967, contributed to a decrease in the centrality of the statist definition of the collective identity. As was previously stated, these various definitions are not necessarily harmonious, and may contain internal contradictions resulting from the tensions between the various components of the collective identity. There was more internal tension in the statist definition than in the ethno-national one. We have made reference to the tension between the pluralism and universalism of secular Western culture and Jewish particularism, two principles that co-exist in the statist approach.

The same is true for the religious dimension. In spite of the fact that the statist approach is civil and secular, it has made much use of religious symbols deriving from the bible and the Second Temple period and, in fact, the bible itself served as the central ceremonial symbol within the framework of the Ben-Gurion statist version of civil religion. These symbols were adopted along with secular symbols and values stemming from socialist ideology or from other secular sources.

One example of the internal tension in the statist definition is the relation between Israel and other nations. The statist approach vacillates between isolationism and the belief that Israel is part of the family of nations. Israeli foreign policy reflected the deeper tension between the two cultural orientations; between the approach that emphasizes the national exclusive belief that "Israel is a light unto the nations," and the approach that considers establishment of the state of Israel as the normalization of the Jewish people and its transformation into a "nation like all other nations."

In contrast, the ethno-nationalist definition of the collective identity is more harmonious, both within each of the components themselves and in the relations between the components as well. By emphasizing the primordial, the particular, and the exclusive, ethno-nationalism grants legitimacy to the differentiation, self-evident to many, between the various ethnic groups, and justifies discrimination in its own favor.

This matter can be clarified by referring to the example discussed above of the flag and its color. By waving the national flag along with the red flag, adherents of the statist approach are sending a rather complicated message. They represent international solidarity together with national exclusivity. They speak of national unity while accentuating class conflict. In contrast, the ethno-nationalist school appeals only to national imagery; to national exclusiveness against a hostile world; and to internal national unity without class or other social division. Thus, during the 1981 election campaign, one could observe Menachem Begin creating an artificial rift between Israel and the western world through a verbal war with the Chancellor of West Germany, Helmut Schmidt, the U.S. Secretary of Defense, Caspar Weinberger, and other Western leaders.

Simultaneously, the self-confidence of the statist school collapsed. After the Likud's rise to power in 1977, the heads of the Labor Party decided not to use the red flag and color in the 1981 election campaign, but rather to use the national blue and white. The Party did so not only to blur its social-democratic orientation, but primarily to turn its back on internationalism and universalism, which lost popularity as ethno-nationalist attitudes became more widespread. During the elections, the Labor Party leaders asked their European colleagues not to express solidarity with their Israeli friends, as is customary among political parties that are members of the Socialist International.[22]

During the 1980s, the struggle between the two schools of thought to define the collective identity has intensified. The ideological rift, however, does not quite overlap the lines that divide the various parties, and in each of the major political movements different interpretations of the dominant approach can be discerned. It is difficult to predict what may happen in the future. However, it can be assumed that, as long as the social conflict continues and intensifies, the ethno-nationalist ethos will become increasingly powerful. On the other hand, it is difficult to predict a return to the situation that prevailed in the 1950s—one dominant approach and all others insignificant. What is clear is that the tension and conflict between the two primary schools of thought will intensify, and the struggle to define the collective identity in Israel may even reach crisis proportions.

Notes

1. This article is based on a segment from an extensive study that deals with the processes of change in national identity, and compares Israel 1967–1987 to Poland of 1919–1939. Parts of it were first presented on August 5, 1984 at a symposium at Tel Aviv University to analyze the 1984 elections. Other parts were delivered at a colloquium on April 10, 1987 at the Center for Jewish Studies at Harvard University.

2. For example, Amos Elon, The Israelis: Founders and Sons (New York: Holt, Rinehart & Winston, 1971).

3. For example, Eric Cohen, "Ethnicity and Legitimation in Contemporary Israel," The Jerusalem Quarterly, No. 28, Summer 1983, pp. 111–124.

4. Lily Weisbrod, "From Labour Zionism to New Zionism," *Theory and Society* Vol. 10(5), 1981, pp. 777–803.

5. Charles Liebman and Eliezer Don-Yechieh, *Civil Religion in Israel: Traditional Religion and Political Culture in the Jewish State* (Berkeley: University of California Press, 1983).

6. Karl Deutsch in Ernest Kraus, ed., *Politics and Society in Israel* (New Brunswick and Oxford: Transaction Books, 1985).

7. Clifford Geertz, ed., *Old Societies and New States* (London: The Free Press of Glencoe, 1963).

8. Walker Connor, "Nation-Building or Nation-Destroying," *World Politics*, Vol. 24(3), 1972, pp. 319–355.

9. Baruch Kimmerling, "Between Primordial and Civil Definition of the Collective Identity: *Eretz Yisrael* or The State of Israel," in Erik Cohen, Moshe Lissak and Yuri Almagor, eds., *Comparative Social Dynamics* (Boulder: Westview Press, 1985).

10. David Apter in Clifford Geertz, ed., *Old Societies and New States* (London: The Free Press of Glencoe, 1963).

11. A.D. Smith, *Theories of Nationalism*, (London: Duckworth, 1971).

12. A.D. Smith, *The Ethnic Revival* (Cambridge: Cambridge University Press, 1981); *Nationalism* (Oxford: Martin Robertson, 1979); *Nationalist Movements* (London: Macmillan, 1976).

13. S.N. Eisenstadt, "Some Remarks Concerning the Problem of the Continuity of Historical Jewish Patterns in Israeli Society," in Kahana, Reuven, Kupstein, Simcha, eds., *Problems of Identity and Legitimacy in Israeli Society* (Jerusalem: Akademon, 1980) (in Hebrew).

14. Dan Horowitz and Moshe Lissak, *Origins of Israeli Polity: Palestine Under Mandate* (Chicago and London: University of Chicago Press, 1978).

15. A.D. Smith, *Theories of Nationalism* (London: Duckworth, 1971).

16. Ibid.

17. In 1987, the Supreme Court ruled against the decision of the Minister of Justice who chose not to extradite a French (Jewish) citizen who was charged by French authorities with murder.

18. As with other components, the similarity here between the Israeli and the Polish cases is striking. The significance of Catholicism as a component of the Polish national identity was evident not only during 1919–39 but in the Poland of the last decade as well.

19. Uriel Tal, "Foundation of a Political Messianic Trend in Israel," *The Jerusalem Quarterly*, No. 35, 1985.

20. Meron Benvenisti, *The West Bank Data Project* (Washington, D.C.: American Enterprise Institute, 1984).

21. The number of states in the world that are uni-ethnic are few and far between. In only ten percent of the states does one ethnic group constitute 90 percent of the population. In 1971, in no less than 30 percent, the dominant ethnic group accounted for more than 50 percent of the population. Connor, Walker, "The Politics of Ethno-Nationalism," *Journal of International Affairs*, Vol. 27, No. 1, 1973, pp. 1–21.

22. During the subsequent election campaign in 1984, the red color returned to the Labor Party's campaign.

5

The Impact of the Six Day War
on the Israeli Right:
A Second Republic in the Making?

Ilan Peleg

The Six Day War brought about important changes *within* Israel's political system, changes that may now be evaluated, twenty years after the decisive victory over the Arab states, with greater clarity than previously. Such an evaluation of *domestic* political changes in Israel could utilize various methodologies and focus on numerous aspects of Israel's political process. This article examines the effect of the war on the Israeli political right, with particular emphasis on: (a) the *historical dynamics* that brought the Israeli right from a weak, even peripheral, political force only a few years before the war to quick legitimation and then power through open elections; (b) the 1967 war's *ideological consequences*, characterized by the emergence of a new belief system and a radicalized psycho- ideological framework; (c) the impact of the war on the Israeli political system as a whole, particularly in its approaches to the Arab-Israeli conflict and the character of the Israeli political system itself. Are we seeing now, twenty years after the war, an evolution of a different system, a Second Republic of sorts?*

From Legitimacy to Power:
The Historical Rise of the Right

When the State of Israel was established in 1948, the Israeli right was in shambles. The two important right wing parties that ran in the elections for the First Knesset in 1949—the General Zionists and the Herut—failed even to mount a serious challenge to Mapai, the dominant labor party. The General Zionists, representing the middle and upper middle class and

---

*The Second Republic analogy refers to a series of successive regimes in France during the nineteenth and twentieth centuries.

supportive of a *laissez-faire* economy, received only seven seats and soon joined the government of David Ben-Gurion. Herut won fourteen seats in 1949 and a mere eight in 1951, a performance that led its leader, Menachem Begin, to seriously contemplate withdrawal from political life altogether.[1]

Herut's poor showing was due partly to the suspicion in which many Israelis held it for its close association with Begin's *Irgun Zvai Leumi* (IZL). Indeed, the birth of Herut in 1948 had marked the victory of the IZL, the Revisionist movement's military branch, over the more moderate, "civilian" branch. Many of the veteran Revisionists were removed from power and denied influence in favor of the young *Irgunists.*[2] Meanwhile, the party continued to hold ideological positions—such as its demand for Jewish control of both the East and the West Banks of the Jordan River—that placed it beyond the limits of the Israeli national consensus.

Even after the armistice agreements with the Arabs were signed, *Herut* refused to join in the general acceptance of the agreed-upon lines of demarcation (the Green Line). In April 1949 Begin, now in the Knesset, called for a no-confidence vote in the Ben-Gurion government for having signed an agreement with (and thereby bestowed recognition on) the Hashemite Kingdom of Jordan. The motion was easily defeated, demonstrating *Herut's* isolation, not to say irrelevance, regarding the territorial question and foreign policy in general.

Throughout the 1950s the party had a superhawkish stance on all foreign policy matters: it supported the extension of Israel's military reprisals and condemned any restraint; it not only enthusiastically supported the 1956 attack on Egypt but demanded an attack on Jordan as well and called for new elections when Ben-Gurion ordered the Israeli army to withdraw from the Sinai. The positions created a serious image problem for the party that continued well into the 1960s. Between 1949 and 1961, the *Herut* decisively lost five consecutive elections.

Toward Legitimation: 1963–1967

The relatively long peace along Israel's borders prior to the Six Day War enabled *Herut* to gain a measure of respectability in the eyes of the public. Although *Herut* remained verbally militant, the absence of major foreign policy disagreements in Israel during this period[3] enabled it to erase the memory of its belligerent past.

More importantly, Ben-Gurion's resignation as Israel's prime minister in 1963 gave Herut an opportunity for political recovery. Ben-Gurion had been involved in a long-term, often personal battle with the Revisionists since the 1920s. He sharply condemned IZL terror and personally faced Begin on bitter issues such as the *Altalena* affair and German reparations. As the preeminent leader of Mapai, Ben-Gurion was committed to denying even minimal legitimacy to *Herut;* in forming all his governments he began with the assumption that all parties could be included "with the exception of *Herut* and *Maki* [the Communists]." In 1963 he wrote to Moshe Sharett that if Begin ever became prime minister, he would lead Israel to destruction.[4]

Another factor in *Herut's* legitimation was the political realignment within Israel's Left that followed Ben-Gurion's departure. Though not widely known at the time, Ben-Gurion's unexpected resignation was the result of internal dissension within *Mapai*, Israel's ruling party. But as the Left began to move toward a restructuring and unity, with *Mapai's* new leadership under Levi Eshkol negotiating with a smaller Labor party, *Ahdut Ha'avoda*, ultimately to form a new Labor party, the right, too, began to consolidate its forces. Thus, in April 1965, even before the 1965 agreement that created the Labor Alignment (*Ha'maarach*), *Herut* and the Liberals, including the General Zionists, announced the creation of *Gahal*, the *Herut*-Liberal bloc.

In order to maintain a measure of autonomy, the two components of the new *Gahal* bloc agreed to maintain independent political organizations. Yet it was clearly understood that the leadership of the new bloc would be in the hand of Menachem Begin.

The establishment of *Gahal* may well represent Begin's most important political victory. His *Herut* party, long shunned for its ultranationalist positions and annexationist zeal, had finally gained legitimacy and acceptance by the respectable middle class as represented by the Liberals and General Zionists. By starting to build bridges with other parties, Herut diffused its own controversial image without actually giving up its long-held ideological positions. Article 2 of the preface to the *Gahal* agreement, for instance, reads: "The *Herut* Movement will continue to bear aloft in the midst of the nation the principle of the integrity of the homeland, the right of the Jewish people to Eretz Israel in its historic completeness as an eternal right which accepts no denial." Moreover, while there was no specific reference to Transjordan for the first time since 1948, Herut still supported revision of the armistice lines and continued to hope for territorial expansion, a position regarded in Israel as extremely radical before the Six Day War.

Gahal failed badly at the polls in the November 1965 elections for Israel's Sixth Knesset, receiving only twenty-six seats. The hawkish *Rafi* (Israel Workers' List), established by Ben-Gurion and six of his former Mapai disciples (including Dayan and Peres) when the Labor Alignment was formed in May 1965, also lost credibility. The Alignment won handily, indicating general approval of the practical, moderate policies of Eshkol and his team.

Despite *Gahal's* setback at the polls, Begin's stance after the 1965 elections remained as radical as ever. In March 1966 he published a comprehensive analysis of Israel's foreign policy in *Ha'uma* (The Nation), a journal read almost exclusively by his disciples.[5] At a time when almost everyone else saw the 1949 armistice lines as Israel's final borders, Begin began his article by assuming the existence of an eternal war of annihilation waged by the Arabs against Israel.[6] He clearly rejected any association with the Arab world—"We better call Israel not a *Middle Eastern* state but a *Mediterranean* state"[7]—and supported a policy of alliance and non-neutrality.[8] Foreshadowing the policy that was to lead to the Strategic Understanding he was to conclude with the United States more than fifteen years later, he wrote: "Being a *Mediterranean* state we can be a link beyond our own limited area, where we are surrounded by enemies: we have an opportunity to establish alliances in different places . . . we have to look in different directions."[9] The article ends ominously: "One cannot play with the right on a land: either you have it or not . . . one cannot divide the land either. . . . Any partition is temporary. Therefore it is so important that our people and the world know and perceive that we have a right to our entire homeland."[10]

To sum up, the condition of the radical right in Israel on the eve of the 1967 war did not appear promising. It continued to adhere to ideological positions widely unacceptable to the majority of the Israeli public. Although *Herut* was successful in gaining a measure of legitimacy through the creation of *Gahal*, the elections of 1965 revealed that this was, in political terms, far from sufficient.

The Crisis of May–June 1967 and After

The dramatic events of May and June, 1967 reinforced the legitimation of *Herut* begun with the establishment of *Gahal* in 1965 and helped the party achieve acceptance not only among Israel's right wing voters and middle class but, for the first time, nationally. When the crisis erupted in May 1967 with the Egyptian troop movement into the Sinai, Begin enhanced his popularity across the spectrum of Israeli public opinion by working diligently and publicly for the establishment of a National Unity Government. Then, as calls for Eshkol's resignation as prime minister mounted, he earned considerable applause by proposing that his long-time rival, David Ben-Gurion, head a new government. When *Gahal* was invited to join a National Unity Government, Begin insisted that the defense minister portfolio should go to Moshe Dayan, Ben-Gurion's protegé. Thus, an unplanned but enormously important side effect of the crisis was the enhancement of Menachem Begin's status in wide circles of the Israeli body politic and the attenuation of his image as an ambitious, unrestrained, and irresponsible politician. The seeds of the 1977 revolution that brought Begin to power were thus sown a decade earlier, in the summer of 1967.

While the 1967 crisis initially looked like a great victory for the political leadership of the Alignment (*Mapai* and *Ahdut Ha'avoda*), in fact it was a victory for the right. First, the hawkish elements within the historical *Mapai* elite, now represented by Dayan, returned to power, with the active assistance of the Herut leadership under Begin. Second, the Six Day War gave much needed credibility to *Herut's* position on foreign policy matters and proved that total war could have quick, handsome rewards. Moreover, Hussein's decision to join Nasser in the war against Israel gave *Herut's* claim to the West Bank at least a measure of credibility for the first time since 1949. The appearance of the PLO prior to the Six Day War was also a God-sent gift to *Herut* insofar as it signified the radicalization of the Arab position toward Israel.

Begin made the most of his brief service (1967–1970) in the National Unity Government. As a Minister without Portfolio, he was unburdened with the management of a ministry and could devote all his energy to issues of real importance for him, foreign policy and especially the future of the occupied territories. And, while he was outwardly deferential and conciliatory in his dealings first with Prime Minister Eshkol and then with Prime Minister Golda Meir, Begin stuck to his maximalist positions, even though, according to the Rabin memoirs, Begin and his fellow ministers all subscribed to a 19 June 1967 agreement that Israel would withdraw to its international borders with Egypt and Syria in exchange for a peace treaty and that the future of the West Bank would be dealt with separately.[11]

Thus, while still a member of the National Unity Government, Begin argued in the Knesset for setting up Jewish quarters in the Arab cities of the West Bank in order to create, as he put it, "an atmosphere of mutual trust" between the native Arabs and their Jewish neighbors.[12] Within the government, he routinely sided with the hawks, especially General Dayan; some referred to him as "Abba Eban's watchdog."[13] He protested when Israeli officials met with Ambassador Gunnar Jarring, the UN-designated mediator, as he did when Israel accepted Resolution 242 (on May 1, 1968),[14] and when plans to hold Rhodes-style negotiations were discussed.[15] Finally, when the government decided in August 1970 to accept an American diplomatic initiative calling for Israeli-Arab discussions through Ambassador Jarring, Gahal withdrew from participation in the Government at Begin's insistence.

The Revived Opposition, 1970–1977

The decisive Israeli victory of 1967 allowed Begin not only to maintain his leadership of Gahal but also to bring about what might be called the Herutization of the right-of-center political bloc. A comparison between the 1969 party platform, written before the elections for the seventh Knesset, and the 1965 Gahal agreement makes this evolution clear: while the 1965 agreement committed Herut alone to annexationist policies, the 1969 platform unambiguously associated Gahal as a whole to such policies at a time when they had actual political meaning, since Israel now had physical control over the territories. Thus, the preface to the 1969 platform stated that: "we will maintain the integrity of the land; Eretz Israel will never be divided again." Chapter 1 of the platform called for extending Israeli legal sovereignty to the liberated territories, a position that even Begin's Government did not adopt when it came to power in 1977. Another clause called for large-scale Jewish agricultural and urban settlements in Judea, Samaria, Gaza, the Golan Heights, and the Sinai.

Begin's resignation from the Meir Government in August 1970 gave Herut (and him personally) much greater freedom of action in the political arena. The party and its leader soon became pillars of Israel's annexationist forces, which included, in addition to a few small political factions, Gush Emunim and the Greater Israel Movement.

Despite the growing strength of the movement, it was clear to Begin, a seasoned politician, that unless all the nationalist forces were politically united, they would not be able to control the fate of the occupied territories. This was the thinking behind the 1974 establishment of the Likud ("Unity"), a coalition that included Gahal (*Herut* and the Liberals), *La'am* ("State List," composed of individuals close to Ben-Gurion and Dayan), the Free Center of Shmuel Tamir,[16] and the Greater Israel Movement. The Likud was created through the efforts of General Ariel (Arik) Sharon, an ultra-nationalist paratrooper with a long and controversial history of radical involvement in the Arab-Israeli conflict. It was on this coalition that Begin finally rode to power.

As had been the case with *Gahal*, it was clear from the very beginning that the Likud would be dominated by *Herut*. The political program of the new body was identical to *Herut's* traditional ideological perspective. The Likud platform for the 1973 election declared that the Jewish people had an inalienable right to all of Biblical Palestine and opposed any withdrawal from the West Bank. It stated that formal peace treaties between Israel and its Arab neighbors must recognize Israel's right to control the areas from which the Arabs had launched attacks before the 1967 war, namely, the West Bank, the Gaza Strip, the Golan Heights, and possibly the Sinai. The territorial message of the Likud was simple: "not an inch!"[17] Finally, it called for intensifying the settlement campaign, particularly in Judea and Samaria, as a step toward annexation; the "local inhabitants," would be allowed to choose between Israeli citizenship or the citizenship of another country.

Although the Likud failed to defeat the labor parties in the 1973 elections, the establishment of an ultranationalist coalition for the first time in Israel's history indicated the movement of the entire political system to the right. Begin was now not only the head of the "fighting family," as the IZL veterans were called, but the recognized leader of a large bloc of political parties unified around the concept of "Greater Israel."

The Ballot Box Revolution

Begin's electoral victory in 1977 is possibly the single most important event that grew out of the Six Day War of 1967, for even if a direct link between the war and the election cannot be demonstrated, an indirect link is clear. Many observers were surprised by the results of the elections, which, by giving Likud a twelve seat edge in the Knesset, ended more than a half-century of Labor party dominance. In fact, the electoral upset came at the end of a long period of political realignment in Israel,[18] and data from the preceding elections demonstrate a steady erosion in the Labor coalition's standing.[19]

Demographic changes in the Israeli voting public in terms of age, socio-economic status and ethnic origin help explain the ballot box revolution of 1977. The electorate was becoming younger and younger, and the Likud clearly led the Alignment among voters under thirty (it tied the Alignment among the middle-aged and trailed among older voters). Moreover, the elections marked the emergence of what was known in the country as

Israel Hashnia—the Second Israel: Jews from non-European countries who had immigrated after the establishment of the State (or their descendants), the relatively poor classes, blue-collar workers. While most of these people had hardly even heard of Jabotinsky, they felt closer to the Likud than to the Alignment leadership and were sensitive to Begin's superhawkish message, rich in emotionalism, symbolism and mysticism. The Alignment represented for them the First Israel: wealthy, educated, secular, and *Ashkenazi* (European). Begin, forever the man in the opposition, represented the Second Israel, even though he was not one of them in terms of ethnic affiliation.

Yet there was another, more fundamental reason for the 1977 revolution. The 1967 and the 1973 wars, both traumatic for the Israelis, brought about an ideological radicalization, a clear movement to the right of the entire political system. Continuing Arab hostility had ended by creating the climate for the victory of the radicals. The myth of the egalitarian, just society had lost its attraction, and for the first time the electorate was eager to adopt Begin's annexationist alternative. After more than fifty years, the Israeli body politic had caught up with the Revisionists.

To some extent, the 1977 shift also reflected a new confidence in Israel's ability to dictate conditions to the Arabs. Israel's overwhelming military superiority had been clear for at least a decade, and increasing numbers now believed that it should be used to impose a new political order, a new territorial design, on the region. Begin became the clear choice of those who adopted this line of thinking.

Many, although not necessarily all, of those who elected Begin understood the implications of their choice. Begin had a lifelong record of commitment to ultranationalist principles, and the Likud's 1977 platform was even more forthright than its 1973 platform had been. Its categorical position that "between the sea and the Jordan there will be Jewish sovereignty alone" closed the door not only on a Palestinian state, but also on the return of the West Bank to Jordan, though it did leave room for some sort of nominal autonomy for the Palestinians.

With Begin's victory, the ideology could become policy. A man who thoroughly understands symbols, the new prime minister lost no time in differentiating himself from the non-religious, matter-of-fact attitude of the Labor leaders who had preceded him as prime minister. Through a series of public gestures, he made clear with full pomp and circumstance that a new Israel was being ushered in. Thus, his first act upon learning of his party's victory was to don a yarmulke and pronounce the *Sheheheyanu*, the traditional Jewish prayer of thanksgiving. When President Katzir asked him to form the new government, he proceeded directly to the Western Wall in the Old City of Jerusalem. He then visited with Rabbi Zvi Yehuda Hacohen Kook, mentor of *Gush Emunim*, thereby sanctioning the actions of the ultranationalist organization and making it, in a sense, Israel's officially designated avant-garde. During his first visit to the United States as prime minister, he again departed from the style of previous Israeli leaders by holding highly visible meetings with religious leaders such as Rabbi Soloveichik and Rabbi Schneerson (the Lubavicher Rabbi). Most important, immediately after the 17 May elections, he visited *Gush Emunim's* illegal settlement at Kaddum. His announcement that there would be many more settlements in Judea and Samaria received worldwide coverage. It was an omen for the future.

Though it is possible to find similarities between the Likud and the Alignment,[20] Likud's rise to power, to a large extent brought about by the 1967 war, represented a dramatic change in Israeli foreign policy. A new set of actors emerged, a new ideology was announced, new symbols were emphasized. In 1977 it looked as if Israel's second republic had come into being, different from the one conceived by Zionism's founding fathers, and different from the Israel existing prior to 1967.

From a Model Society to a Neo-Revisionism: The Ideological Rise of the Right

The foundations for the ideology of the Israeli right were laid in the pre-State era by the Revisionist Zionist leader Vladimir Jabotinsky (1880–1940). The prevailing ideology during the Mandate years had been that of the traditional labor Zionists, who offered the Jewish community in Palestine the myth of the establishment of a *Model Society*: egalitarian, democratic, participatory, economically self-sustaining, agricultural, and progressive. The labor group believed that physical-agricultural work is the supreme personal and collective value and that Zionism through hard work would establish its right to legitimate existence on the land. The Revisionists, under Jabotinsky, offered an *alternative myth* of national grandeur, military might, and territorial expansion.

Under Jabotinsky's disciple, Menachem Begin, the Revisionist ideology witnessed further radicalization. Begin, leader of the *Irgun*, represented an entire generation of persecuted East European Jews for whom the dream of total redemption and unlimited power was emotionally attractive. He demanded tougher language and action than even Jabotinsky himself was willing to endorse. After Jabotinsky's death in 1940, Begin was able to crystalize the Revisionist ideology into a coherent whole, which might be called *Neo-Revisionism*. Neo-Revisionism went through a crucial stage of development as a result of the Six Day War. With the 1977 elections, Begin and his associates had an opportunity to *implement* the movement's ideology.

The Neo-Revisionist camp in contemporary Israel is far more diversified than the Zionist right of the 1920 and 1930s ever was. It embraces both secular and religious segments of the society, including the veteran *Herut* leadership, the Revisionists and *Betarists*, the remnants of the radical Jewish undergrounds *Irgun* and *Lechi*, the secular Tehiya Party, as well as such messianic groups as *Gush Emunim*, the Faithful of the Temple Mount, and even Meir Kahane's *Kach* Party. Politically and ideologically, the Six Day War significantly broadened the support base of the radical right.[21]

The following are some of the most important components of the Neo-Revisionist belief system, along with some brief remarks as to how each was affected by the Six Day War:

1. The Jews have the right to *exclusive control* over Eretz Israel in its entirety. The traditional Zionist position is that there should be a Jewish *presence* in Eretz Israel. This leaves no room for compromise over land, which is rejected by the Neo-Revisionists as unachievable and undesirable. The Six Day War transformed this radical rightist position from a theoretical claim to a real one, intensifying the insistence on the "integrity" of the land.

2. The Jews are "people who dwell alone," who will never be allowed to achieve a normal existence within the family of nations. Yehoshafat Harkabi believes that this principle gives the right license to deviate from the norms of accepted international behavior,[22] something that surely characterized Begin's foreign policy. The Six Day War reinforced the conviction that abnormality is the natural, existential condition of the Jewish people (and hence Israel).[23]

3. Anti-Semitism is a permanent condition, a cosmic reality, and a dominant fact-of-life for the Jewish people. The outside world is not merely attitudinally hostile but *actively* involved in efforts to destroy Israel and the Jewish people. Although this is a deeply held conviction, the right used it instrumentally during the Begin years: every time Likud policies were attacked by non-Jews, particularly Europeans, Begin accused them (often by name) of being anti-Semites (while Jews who opposed the right were called "self-haters").

The link between the Six Day War and the perception of anti-Semitism by right wing elements in Israel is straightforward. Thus, while much of the criticism of Israeli policies and actions over the past twenty years has focused on its control of the occupied territories, the Neo-Revisionists see this criticism as fundamentally motivated by anti-Semitism.

4. The Holocaust is the *center of gravity*, an analytical device applied with little discrimination to every aspect of the relationship between Jews and the world.

When Ben-Gurion as prime minister decided to accept war reparations from West Germany in 1952, he was vehemently attacked by Begin, who called the negotiations with Germany "the ultimate abomination, the like of which we have not known since we became a nation," and *Hilul Hashem* (the defamation of God's name).[24] In trying to obtain reparations, Ben-Gurion was not motivated solely by economic and political considerations. Rather, he realized that by *not* creating a visible link with Germany, Israel would forever be Holocaust-centered, in essence *controlled* by the tragic past of the Jewish people.

The Neo-Revisionists, on the other hand, developed a *Holocaust-fixation* that saw any conflict between Jews and others in apocalyptic terms. When, in the middle of the Lebanese War, Reagan sent Begin a cable congratulating him on his birthday, Begin cabled a surprising response, drawing parallels between Beirut of 1982 and Berlin of 1945:

I feel as a prime minister empowered to instruct a valiant army facing Berlin where, among innocent civilians, Hitler and his henchmen hide in a bunker deep beneath the surface.[25]

On the whole, the Neo-Revisionist Holocaust-fixation deepened as a result of the 1967 war and further intensified as a result of the trauma of 1973. For the radical right, both wars served as yet new proof that the world was about to annihilate the Jews, although both wars can be seen as evidence of an objective change for the better in the condition of the modern Jew.

5. The Arabs are the modern carriers of the anti-Semitic germ and are increasingly referred to as *Amalek*, the Biblical nation identified as Israel's mortal, eternal enemy. While Labor leaders have been known to maintain close ties with Arab leaders in Israel through the years, among the Neo-Revisionists there is a pronounced tendency to see them in terms of the anti-Semitic experience in general and the Holocaust in particular.

The implications of applying the anti-Semitic, Holocaust, *Amalekite* terminology to the Arab-Israeli conflict are far-reaching. First, while the Jewish-German "conflict" was artificially manufactured by the Nazis, the Arab-Israeli conflict is a genuine dispute between two national movements. Second, if the Arabs are anti-Semites, Nazis and Amalekites, if their anti-Israeli feelings are merely a new form of the anti-Semitic germ, and if the PLO is the "Arab SS," as Begin has called it, then no solution to the Arab-Israeli conflict is ever possible. Third, if the Arabs are Amalekites, then they should be dealt with using the methods recommended by Rabbi Meir Kahane, or worse.

The experience of the 1967 war and the close, daily contact that it led to between Arabs and Jews (especially in the occupied territories) caused significant radicalization in the position of the right toward the Arabs.

It is important to realize that the philosophy of the right is by no means nihilistic. In addition to the negative message outlined above, it has a positive message which organically complements the negative one.

Within the belief system of the right, the negative perception of victimization, powerlessness, vulnerability, and dependence that characterized the conditions of the East European communities is balanced by an equally strong positive image that constitutes a *monumental overcompensation* for the Jewish conditions in the *Galut* (Diaspora). From the reality of total insecurity emerged the demand for total security. The content of the positive image was unlimited power, national grandeur, and territorial expansion as national goals, overwhelming superiority over adversaries, total independence from powerful allies, and, in the final analysis, total collective redemption. Psychology and theology are forever mixed in the attitudinal prism of the Israeli right. The link between the Old Right (Begin's secular Herut) and the New Right (*Gush Emunim's* religious zealots) is thus *not* accidental or unnatural; it is organic. This organic link is the glue that holds the Neo-Revisionist camp together.

This belief system has led to self-proclaimed geostrategists on the right (such as Yuval Ne'eman, Oded Yinon, and Zvi Shiloah) calling for Israeli domination of the entire Middle East and offering such plans as the creation of a "new order" in Lebanon, the dismemberment of the Hashemite Monarchy in Jordan, the division of Iraq, Syria, and Egypt into mini-states, and so forth. Ariel Sharon, Begin's minister of defense, said in one of his speeches:

> We must broaden the domain of our strategic and security interests beyond that of Middle Eastern states and the Red Sea so that in the 1980s this domain will include such states as Turkey, Iran, and Pakistan, and regions such as the Persian Gulf and Africa, particularly northern and central Africa.[26]

It was Sharon's removal from office as a result of the first stage of his plan—the invasion of Lebanon—that prevented the implementation of these grandiose schemes. But prior to Sharon's departure, a new attitude toward foreign policy had emerged in the political elite around Begin emphasizing narrow national interests, military solutions to pressing political problems, and force as the way to deal with the Arabs. The invasion of Lebanon was a logical conclusion of the Neo-Revisionist *Weltanschauung*.

Toward a Second Republic?

There can be no doubt that the Six Day War helped the Israeli right in terms of relative strength within the political system. The spokesmen of the Neo-Revisionist camp skillfully used the 1967 crisis and those that followed (especially the 1973 war) to enhance their political power and finally take over the government. It is more difficult to assess the impact of the war on the Israeli political system as a whole, but a series of generalizations could nevertheless tentatively be reached:

1. It seems likely that the war strengthened the Israeli right politically and ideologically not only in the short run, but possibly permanently. Thus, Begin's first and surprising electoral victory in 1977 was followed by a second victory in 1981. Even without Begin, under the uninspired leadership of Shamir and following the highly unpopular war in Lebanon, the right has performed impressively. All in all, ongoing conflict with the Arabs tends to reinforce the nationalistic perceptions and outlooks that are intimately linked to the Neo-Revisionist world view.

2. Needless to say, the Six Day War made possible the whole issue of annexation through the territories it captured. The right has been in the forefront of the annexation drive, and although the number of Israelis supporting the return of all territories has actually *risen* (from 1 percent in 1969 to 8 percent in 1984, according to data collected by the Israeli Institute of Applied Social Research[27]), 41 percent of all Israelis in 1984 supported total annexation, with another 5 to 6 percent supporting the annexation of most of the territories. What these figures mean in political terms is that a genuine territorial compromise, even if the Arabs were to agree, has become almost impossible.

Meanwhile, the right has succeeded, through legal and extralegal actions, in leading Israel toward a *de facto* annexation of the occupied territories without bestowing the necessary rights on the Arab population. These actions included a large-scale settlement effort in the occupied territories,[28] the implementation of new policy of land seizure and control,[29] and expansion of the economic domination of the occupied territories.[30]

New legal and administrative procedures were introduced, such as six regional councils established by the Begin government in the occupied territories to create a formal, legal, and administrative separation between the Israeli settlements and settlers and the local Arab municipal and regional system. Controlled from the start by hawkish settlers, the councils quickly became the means of effecting Begin's *de facto* annexation and instruments of political control.[31] They supplied state services and became involved in practically all high-level decisions (planning and infrastructure, land and water use, security, and legal issues). Above all, through their central organization, the councils became a powerful political lobby, making certain that no territorial compromise could ever be achieved.

The November 1981 establishment of a civilian administration in the occupied areas was a further step toward annexation. As an attempt by the Begin government to predetermine the outcome of the autonomy talks, it was a violation of the spirit of Camp David and even of Israel's own position in the talks, since the powers given to the administrator were exactly those foreseen for the self-governing authority proposed at Camp David. According to Benvenisti, "The civilian administration constituted the transformation from a temporary to a permanent system."[32]

Over the years, an impressive machinery of control over the unwilling, restive population has been erected in the occupied areas, a *bizarre appendix to the lively, functioning Israeli democracy.* With the accumulation of thousands of orders issued by the military government, the existing Jordanian law was almost suspended, in itself a violation of international law. The Defense Emergency Regulations of the British Mandate, which in the past were used harshly against the Jews of Palestine, have been adopted by Israel's military government in the West Bank. These 120 sweeping orders allow the authorities to act arbitrarily and without due process. Persons accused of violating the regulations or the orders of the military government, are tried by a military court whose judges are officers appointed by the military government. No regular system of judicial review exists for decisions of the military courts.

The annexation of the West Bank and Gaza, undoubtedly the central objective of Begin-Shamir's foreign policy (1977–1984), has created fundamental, long-term changes in Israel's political system, although it may be yet too early to assess the extent of these changes and their precise character.

3. The Six Day War was also responsible for the emergence of a number of radical parliamentary and extraparliamentary groups in Israel. some of which were successful in achieving not only notoriety but genuine political importance. Thus, Tehiya, a party which supports outright annexation and

whose leaders have hinted on occasion that loyalty tests should be administered to Arabs, has outflanked Likud on the right, attracting many Likud
supporters and emerging as the country's third largest political party. On
the religious side of right-wing extremism, likewise created by the conditions
produced by the Six Day War, there has been the meteoric rise of *Gush
Emunim* (established in 1974) and a decade later the electoral success of
Rabbi Kahane's *Kach* party, "a quasi-fascist movement" that has benefited
from the intense interaction between Arabs and Jews and the continuing
atmosphere of acute crisis.[33]

The appearance of *Tehiya, Gush Emunim, Kach,* and the Jewish underground in the territories, and particularly their great impact on the young,[34]
raises the question of whether we may witness in Israel of the 1980s the
emergence of a Second Republic. Although the answer to that question is
by no means clear, and full-fledged analysis will require a wider historical
perspective than we can hope for at the present time, preliminary observations
suggest that we are indeed witnessing today a new reality, a phenomenon
that may be called "the emergence of Israel's Second Republic."

On the one hand, Israel in the post-1967 era, and even after a seven-
year rule of what was generally perceived as an ultranationalist regime, has
remained faithful to the democratic principles on which it was founded.
Moreover, the political process within the country continues to be lively
and democratically effective. Thus, the huge demonstrations following the
invasion of Lebanon in 1982 ultimately led (albeit indirectly) to the resignation
of Prime Minister Begin, and the highly critical report of a commission of
inquiry (The Kahan Report) brought about the fall of his powerful defense
minister, Ariel Sharon.

On the other hand, it is undeniable that a series of fundamental changes
have occurred within Israel that in their totality could change the very
nature of Israeli democracy. First, for twenty years now, Israel has controlled
an alien people against their will, and a political solution is not yet in
sight. Second, the nature of the Israeli control over the West Bank and
Gaza Palestinians is not, nor can it be, democratic and it is possible that
lack of democracy there would affect Israel proper. Third, the continued
occupation has caused a growing polarization within the Israeli body politic,
leading to the emergence of many radical right-wing groups openly supportive
of harsher policies against Israel's Arab minority.

It remains to be seen how Israel will solve the dilemma of the occupation.
So far, Israel's democratic institutions and, above all, the long-standing
humanitarian foundations on which Judaism itself is based have been able
to withstand the pressure from the right. Although the right's mythology
has spread to a public far beyond the traditional nationalist circles, the
alternative liberal and humanitarian belief system continues to prevail. When
the Sabra and Shatila massacres occurred, 400,000 Israelis demonstrated.

Yet, the perpetuation of the Arab-Israeli dispute, and particularly the
close and hostile daily contact between the Israeli and the Palestinian
populations (on the West Bank and in Israel proper), has put the future

of the Israeli democracy in grave danger. The emergence of the Jewish underground on the West Bank and a racist party in the Knesset are merely warning signs.

Notes

1. Interview of author with Dr. Yochanan Bader, July 2, 1985.
2. Among them Eri Jabotinsky, H. Rosenbloom, R. Weinstein, H. Segal, Sh. Junichman, A. Grossman, A. Altman, B. Lubatzki, E. Shostak. Begin also forced out a few potential competitors from the IZL.
3. Although the Lavon affair began as a foreign policy (in fact, intelligence) issue, it was fought as a domestic political matter. This section of the article and others draw heavily on Ilan Peleg, *Begin's Foreign Policy 1977–1983: Israel's Move to the Right*, (Westport, CT: Greenwood Press, 1987), ch. 2.
4. Ben-Gurion to Sharett, May 21, 1969; see Yehoshafat Harkabi, *Fateful Decisions*, (Tel Aviv: Am Oved, 1986), p. 177 (in Hebrew).
5. Menachem Begin, "Concepts and Problems in Foreign Policy," *Hauma* 16, March 1966, pp. 461–487 (in Hebrew).
6. Ibid., p. 461.
7. Ibid., p. 464.
8. Ibid., p. 465.
9. Ibid.
10. Ibid., p. 488.
11. Yitzhak Rabin, *Pinkas Sherut*, Sifriat Poalim, Tel-Aviv, 1979, Vol. 1, p. 227 (in English); *Rabin Memoirs*, (Boston: Little, Brown, 1979).
12. *Jewish Observer and Middle East Review*, January 1, 1969.
13. Benko Adar, "Majesty Without Grandeur," *Al Hamishmar*, June 17, 1977 (weekly supplement), pp. 3–4 (in Hebrew). Eban was the Foreign Minister in the governments of Eshkol and Meir. He was and remains a leading Israeli dove.
14. "Coalition Under Strain," *Jewish Observer and Middle East Review* 17 (May 24, 1968), pp. 5–6.
15. Armistice agreements between Israel and four of its neighbors were signed in 1949 on the Mediterranean island of Rhodes.
16. A former IZL commander and a Herut member.
17. Gertrude Hirschler and Lester S. Eckman, *From Freedom Fighter to Statesman: Menachem Begin* (New York: Shengold Publishers, 1979), p. 267.
18. A. Arian, "Conclusion," in Howard R. Penniman, ed., *Israel at the Polls: The Knesset Elections of 1977* (Washington, DC: American Enterprise Institute, 1979), pp. 284–86.
19. Data from Uri Ra'anan, "Putting the Israeli Election Under a Microscope," *New York Times*, June 4, 1977.
20. See, for example, Noam Chomsky, *The Fateful Triangle: The United States, Israel, and the Palestinians* (Boston: South End Press, 1983).
21. The literature on the radical right is extensive. It includes testimonies of the Neo-Revisionists themselves (e.g. Ben-Ami, A., ed., *The Greater Israel Book*, (Tel-Aviv, 1977); Yuval Ne'eman, *A Policy of Sober Perspective*, (Tel-Aviv, Revivim, 1984); Moshe Shamir, *Facing the Tough War*, (Tel-Aviv, Shikmona, 1974); Zvi Shiloah, *A Great Land for a Great Nation*, (Tel-Aviv, Otpaz, 1970), biographies of Begin (e.g. Silver or Hirschler and Eckman), Sharon (e.g. Benziman) and Kahane (e.g. Kottler), literature on Gush Emunim (e.g. books by Danny Rubinstein and Zvi

Ra'aman, articles by Rubinstein-Peleg in *Reconstructionist*, Oct. 1986, a series of analyses by Ehud Sprinzak: "Gush Emunim, the Iceberg Model of Political Extremism," *Medina, Mimshal Veyachasim Binleumiim* 17, Spring 1981, pp. 36–39; *Gush Emunim: The Politics of Zionist Fundamentalism in Israel*, the American Jewish Committee, 1986); on-going commentaries in publications such as *Ha'uma* or *Nekuda* (positive), or *New Outlook* (negative); analyses of the policy on Lebanon (of special importance are the books by Na'or, Schiff-Ya'ari, and Shiffer), and much more.

22. Harkabi, ibid., p. 209.

23. For the idea of abnormality see, for example, Ya'acov Herzog, *People Who Dwell Alone*, (Tel-Aviv: Sifriat Ma'ariv, 1975), or Eliezer Livneh, *Israel and the Crisis of Western Civilization*, (Tel-Aviv: Shocken, 1972), as well as publications such as *Ha'uma, Zot Ha'aretz*, and *Nekudah*. The fact that people like Herzog and Livneh, both of whom were quite remote from traditional Revisionism, adopted with such fervor the idea of Israel's "abnormality" indicates, as already mentioned, the wide spread of Neo-Revisionist ideas within the Israeli Society, a new phenomenon that was brought about by the shock of the Six Days.

24. Howard M. Sachar, *A History of Israel: From the Rise of Zionism to Our Time* (New York: Knopf, 1979), p. 372.

25. Michael Jansen, *The Battle of Beirut*, (Boston: South End Press, 1982), p. 71.

26. For Sharon's speech, see *War by Choice*. Tel-Aviv, Kibutz Meuchad, 1985; for Yinon's view, see his piece in *Kivunim*, No. 14, February 19, pp. 49–59; for Shiloah, see note 21.

27. Reported in Asher Arian, *Politics in Israel: The Second Generation* (Chatham, NJ: Chatham House, 1985), p. 251.

28. The settlement effort was fully documented by Meron Benvenisti, *The West Bank Data Project: A Survey of Israel's Policies* (Washington DC: American Enterprise Institute, 1984). The Begin governments increased the number of Jewish settlements in the territories from 24 to 106, and the number of residents from 3,200 to 28,400, in six short years. More important, the settlement occurred in the populated areas of Samaria in order to prevent any future territorial compromise.

29. In 1983, when Begin resigned his premiership, Israel controlled about 42 percent of the land on the West Bank (Benvenisti, ibid., p. 19). Under the legal guise of claiming "state land" the Likud government initiated a process of almost unlimited Jewish expansion into the territories.

30. See, for example, Danny Rubinstein, "Annexation Deluxe," *New Outlook*, June 1981, pp. 16–20 and 48.

31. Benvenisti, ibid., p. 49.

32. Ibid., p. 44.

33. Ehud Sprinzak, "Kach and Meir Kahane: The Emergence of Jewish Quasi-Fascism," *Patterns of Prejudice*, Vol. 19, No. 3, 1985.

34. The right's impact on the Israeli youth was documented by the Van Leer Institute of Jerusalem.

The Palestinians

6

Palestinian Nationalism
Since 1967: An Overview

Naseer H. Aruri

The period of the past twenty years is not a new departure for the Palestinians; it is a continuation of a nationalist struggle which spans the largest portion of this century.[1] The Palestinian nationalist struggle did not begin in 1967 or in 1948.

History of the Movement

As early as 1891 Palestinian leaders urged the Ottoman government not to facilitate land transfers to Jewish settlers in Palestine. They also pressed their concerns about Jewish immigration and land alienation after the coup by the Young Turks in 1908, using the local press and central parliament among other vehicles. They insisted that Palestine remain an Arab country and not be used to solve the plight of European Jewry. The General Syrian Congress, which included a Palestinian delegation, declared after the Paris Peace Conference of 1919 its opposition to the mandate systems, to the concept of a "Jewish commonwealth" in Palestine, and to the separation of Palestine "from the mother country." The Congress resolutions demanded that "the determining considerations of the settlement of" the Palestinians' "own future" be the "real desire" of the "people":

> We would not have risen against Turkish rule, under which we enjoyed civic and political privileges, as well as rights of representation, had it not been that the Turks denied us our rights to *national existence*.

As to the rights of the Jewish minorities, the resolution stated: "Our Jewish fellow citizens shall continue to enjoy the rights and to bear the responsibilities which are ours in common."

Palestinian resistance to British mandatory rule and the Zionist movement peaked in the 1930s: the six-month general strike in 1936 was followed by a thoroughgoing rural uprising which engaged displaced and landless peasants

71

and unemployed urban workers, supported by urban professionals and merchants, who gathered under the umbrella of the Arab Higher Committee.[2] The nationalist movement resisted the principle of territorial partition or merger with Transjordan. But despite broad support for its nationalist aims, the movement could not achieve the cohesion and strength to withstand the continued pressure.

The struggle was re-ignited in 1947–1948, a period which the Zionist movement refers to as Israel's war of independence. For the Palestinians, it was a colonial war of conquest, which ended in the destruction of Palestinian society and institutions. For them it was the era of the catastrophe (*al-Nakba*). The people of Palestine suddenly found themselves refugees with all the human, legal, economic, social, and psychological liabilities which that naked status implied. Under those conditions, the active pursuit of political sovereignty was not the priority of the day. Existence itself was the priority—to find shelter and a source of livelihood, to readjust and get over the trauma, to provide for their children and their children's education.

The activists among them integrated their struggle into the Arab nationalist movement, while some went underground. Other, more conservative elements, unaccustomed to a Hobbesian world and refusing to accept dispossession and dispersal as final, hoped against hope that the combined force of Arab armies, Arab diplomacy and international goodwill would achieve their deliverance and bring them redress.

Given these antecedents, the rise of the Palestinian national movement in 1967 was a re-emergence, for which the Arab defeat served as impetus. It did not come as a new departure for the Palestinians but a mere reawakening in response to what the Arabs now called the setback (*al-Naksa*).

The re-emergence of Palestinian resistance was more than a reawakening. On the positive side, it has assumed different forms of struggle: non-violent resistance inside Palestine and a militant armed struggle outside, combined with diplomacy. It produced a new type of leadership, and a new class base. The elite families who presided over the Arab Higher Committee were replaced by professionals and intelligentsia from the Palestinian mainstream. The new social backbone consisted of the internal refugees in crowded Gaza and the West Bank, the uprooted peasants in Galilee and the West Bank, the merchants and small manufacturers victimized by the occupation, the students and intellectuals under occupation, and the external refugees in Lebanon, who manned the infrastructure of a state-in-formation.

Finally, the conditions created by the 1967 war had enabled the Palestinian national movement to evolve into a broadly based, widely representative, political body with a sophisticated organizational structure suitable for a nation-building strategy.[3] A military apparatus which dwarfed every single militia in pre-1982 Lebanon stood side by side with a civilian infrastructure which provided health, educational and social services that rivaled those of any state in the area. Possessed with extensive administrative and diplomatic machinery, Arab and international legitimacy, and broad Palestinian support, the PLO was developing from a virtual government-in-exile to a real state.

The Challenge and the Reaction

The re-emergent Palestinian nationalism in the aftermath of the 1967 war was destined to collide with the interests of the dominant powers in the region. The defeat of the Arab state system in but six days would undermine its legitimacy as a viable and credible agent of liberation. Israel's stunning victory would place it face to face with the direct party to the conflict. The United States would have to cope with a post-Nasserite period of turbulence in an area which it had come to regard as its own turf. The nature of the challenge presented by Palestinian nationalism to each of these forces as well as their responses to the challenge will be discussed under separate headings.

Palestinian Nationalism and the Arab State System

From the Palestinian perspective, the Arab defeat in 1967 was an indictment of Arab ideologies, institutions, political parties, armies, and diplomacy. The Arab state system could no longer sustain the guardianship role it had assumed over the Palestinian cause since 1947. The Arab-Israeli conflict was to be de-Arabized and Palestinianized. The relationship between the Palestinian Nationalist Movement (PNM) and the Arab order evolved in several phases that paralleled the ideological transformation of Arab politics.[4]

The First Period, 1967–1973. The 1967 war produced two political currents, in the Arab world: an accommodationist current pursuing the re-establishment of a stable political order, and seeking integration into the world economy and state system; and a revolutionary current spearheaded by the Palestinian resistance, which sought to create a brave new world and topple the Arab order. The Arab masses who rallied around the resistance believed that a revolutionary situation created by the 1967 war would launch a post-Nasserite brand of Arab revolution that would not only liberate Palestine but also confront Western domination and create a new, politically independent, socially and economically autonomous Arab society.

The potential role of the Palestinian resistance in this anticipated transformation was the main catalyst during the first phase of the post-1967 period. But the Arab order was on the rebound by 1970, reasserting control and no longer feeling defensive about the crushing defeat it suffered in 1967. It had recovered from the shock, and between 1970 and 1973 proceeded to draw new parameters for an Arab strategy. By 1973, the Arab populace, which had experienced the euphoria of the Palestinian armed struggle, was pacified by a new euphoria, that of the October war. The anticipated Arab revolution and the vanguard role of the Palestinian resistance proved quite illusory. Far from creating the long-awaited revolutionary situation, the 1967 war had set the stage for a second phase of Palestinian-Arab relations in which cooperation and co-optation replaced the use of force.

The Second Period, 1973–1977. The October war of 1973 ushered in a new order and a new era in Palestinian-Arab relations. It was expected that the Palestinians, represented by the PLO, would march together with the Arab state system to reap the benefits to be derived from a limited Arab-Israeli war. The struggle for Palestine was to be incorporated into an Arab diplomatic strategy which aimed at "erasing the consequences of aggression." The PLO, as sole legitimate representative of the Palestinian people, was to march together with the Arab state system toward a political solution confined to the West Bank and Gaza only. Yet Palestinian-Arab relations were characterized during this period by a pattern of antagonistic collaboration. In one sense, the elevation of the Palestinian question to a new prominence was the price paid by the Arab state system for containment of social revolution.

The Third Period, 1977–1982. The third period, extending from 1977 to 1982, witnessed a distancing from the PLO by Arab states, evident in the Camp David affair and the Arab failure to deal effectively with its consequences. The Arab states no longer treated the Palestinian question as central to the Middle East conflict. And when Israeli measures calculated to end the stalemate produced by Camp David culminated in the invasion of Lebanon, the PLO found itself alone in facing Israel. The conflict was once more de-Arabized and regained its 1948 setting: a conflict between natives and settlers.

The Fourth Period, 1982 to the Present. From 1982 on, the Palestinians have been disunited, caught between the regional strategies of various Arab states, each with its own priorities, which transcend the liberation of Palestine or even the West Bank.

On the whole, the Palestinian experience with the Arab states has been an unhappy one. A consistent pattern has prevailed: in 1936 Arab regimes helped smother the first major Palestinian revolution of this century; in 1948 they acquiesced in Palestinian dispossession and dismemberment; in 1970–1971 the Jordanian army was unleashed against the resistance and its domestic backers; in 1976 Syria entered Lebanon to clip the wings of the Palestinian movement and its Lebanese allies; in 1982 the Arab states sought to confine the damage resulting from Israel's war in Lebanon to the Palestinians; and in 1985–1987 Syria and Jordan competed for control of the Palestinian movement. Other Arab states have their own priorities which range from the war in the Gulf to the civil war in Sudan, Chad, the Sahara and elsewhere.

Palestinian Nationalism and Israel

Apart from exposing the Arab state system as corrupt, inefficient and incapable, the 1967 war also brought Israel face to face with the direct party to the conflict. The re-emergence of the Palestinian movement, in control of its own destiny, threatened Israel with moral and political isolation in the international community. Having revived the centrality of the Palestinian factor in the Middle East conflict, the Palestinians, as freedom fighters and members of an organized body, presented Israel and the Zionist movement with a moral dilemma.[5] Their demands were not unlike those of Jews in the Western world—demands for secular, non-racial, pluralistic societies. Yet the ideal of Zionism in Israel is racial and exclusionist. The very concept of a Jewish state precludes the notion of pluralism and coexistence.

Discriminatory laws actually enabled Israel to consolidate its Jewish character beginning in 1948, but they were little noted until after 1967, when they were reinjected into the public discourse on the Middle East. The Law of Return, which establishes automatic citizenship for Jews in Israel while denying the same to indigenous Arabs, and the law of citizenship which classifies Arabs as having "Arab nationality," and Jews as having "Jewish nationality," are but two examples of a system based on legal discrimination. Together with the World Zionist Organization/Jewish Agency status, which makes it possible to render a wide range of social services by Zionist institutions (such as the Jewish National Fund) *only* to holders of "Jewish nationality," these laws and corresponding practices negate the unexamined claim of a democratic Israel.

Thus, confronted with Palestinians seeking to return home, the Israelis could no longer claim that they were in danger of being pushed into the sea. The rise of the Palestinian resistance was the single most important factor that exposed Israel as a colonialist oppressor, its enterprise based on legal discrimination between Jews and non-Jews. The refugees in Gaza and Lebanon, the Palestinian workers inside the so-called Green Line, the demolished homes, the barbed wire, the interrogation centers, the military orders now numbered in four digits are a stark reminder of a bitter reality— the reality that many favorable assumptions about Israel as a democracy, a refuge, a land of freedom, are beginning to wear thin as the PNM forces it to reveal its true face.

The re-emergence of the Palestinian national movement in 1967 and the worldwide recognition of the right to self-determination for the Palestinians have created a national obsession in Israel. The predominant conceptions of the state—geographic and biblical—dictated a fight with the PLO to the finish. There was no room for both. Hence, Israel's zero-sum solution which has inevitably led to the war not only against Palestinian nationalism in Lebanon but also against every single component, symbol, reminder, and embryo of that nationalism in the West Bank, Gaza, and in Israel proper. Israel's war against "terrorism" has been extended to Arab mayors, students, electric companies, flags, water, research centers, and even symbolic herbs like sage and thyme. Israeli attempts to consolidate the occupation in the early 1970s triggered a non-violent resistance in the West Bank leading to the formation of the Palestinian National Front on August 5, 1973. The PNF employed various means of non-violent resistance ranging from setting up a legal defense fund for dissidents and landowners facing expropriation to organizing boycotts, strikes, and public rallies to protest the occupation. It struggled against the regime's effort to subordinate the Palestinian economy to Israel, and encouraged businessmen not to pay taxes. When the crackdown finally came in April 1974, most of the PNF leaders were in prison while others had been expelled across the Jordan River. Evidence of ill-treatment including torture against PNF members was documented by the Insight team of the *London Sunday Times.*[6] Wide-ranging violations were documented by Amnesty International and the United States *State Department Reports on Human Rights Practices.*[7]

But the resistance continued in the occupied territories deriving support from the impact of the October 1973 war, the Rabat summit conference defining Palestinian authority, and Yasir Arafat's invitation to the United Nations. It gained broad momentum when the nationalist bloc achieved a sweeping victory in the Israeli-sponsored municipal elections of 1976 in the occupied territories, and when the Nazareth Democratic Front, led by Tewfiq Zayyad, ended a long reign of Arab "moderates" on the Nazareth City Council.[8] Observance of the Day of the Land on March 30th became an annual Palestinian event not only in the Galilee, where 10,000 demonstrators from 32 Arab villages protested the killing of six Arabs by the police, but in the West Bank, Gaza, Lebanon and elsewhere. The resistance was further intensified by the Sadat visit to Jerusalem and the Camp David affair (1979). It was reorganized under the umbrella of the National Guidance Committee, which followed in the footsteps of the banished PNF and impelled the Begin Government to institute the "Iron Fist" policy, culminating in the ouster of all mayors elected in 1976 except Bethlehem's Elias Freij. By 1982, Palestinian nationalism had forced Israel to govern the West Bank and Gaza directly. Having dealt a crippling blow to the Hashemite establishment by rejecting its mayoral candidates in 1976, and having stood effectively against the Village League quislings which Israel tried to impose, the PNM put Israel in the position of having to run the local municipalities through its own army officers as part of the ill-named civil administration.

These developments have coincided with the ascendancy of the radical right in Israel's politics, a fact which itself is related to Israel's inability to cope with a combination of economic, social, security and political problems, which, in part, are related to the confrontation with Palestinian nationalism. Thus the Israeli establishment's orientation toward brute force, repression, and discrimination against Arabs, as well as the religious establishment's justification of extra-judicial executions carried out by the army and by West Bank settlers, have undermined the claim that Israel is a bastion of democracy created for the oppressed and the downtrodden. More than that, Israel's presumed raison d'être has been seriously challenged by the re-emergence of Palestinian nationalism. Contrary to its claims to establish a home for the "stateless," Israel continues to rule over 1.2 million stateless people living in their own home while another two and a half million stateless people are denied the right to return home.

The Palestinians have thrown yet another challenge at Israel. The very existence of an organized Palestinian presence, which derived its power from Palestinian and Arab public support, was the single most important barrier to a political settlement in 1967 on Israeli terms. When the Arab states refused to recognize Israel on its own terms, contrary to widely held Israeli expectations that the "long siege" was over, a grandiose militaristic sentiment began to replace all reason. Xenophobic chauvinism, religious extremism, and arrogance became widespread phenomena, and are leading to moral decadence and corrosion of the society. Prime Minister Shamir, unable to advance legal arguments for retaining the occupied territories, resorts to the word "because." The *Sephardic* Chief Rabbi Mordechai Eliahu thus ruled that the person who shot and killed an Arab girl in Nablus was "not to be considered a murderer." Examples of this sort abound. Suffice it to say that the proximity of the political and religious right to the fascist conception of the state has become a disturbing phenomenon to those Israelis who still believe in some form of coexistence.

Palestinian nationalism during the past two decades has thus challenged Israel to reveal its true character, making it impossible for it to go on flaunting democracy and humanism. Hence it brands Palestinian nationalism as terrorist, while Israel itself commits some of the worst acts of state terrorism, not only in the Middle East but in other areas as well. It also assisted repressive regimes in Central America.

Palestinian Nationalism and the United States

For the United States, the re-emergence of Palestinian nationalism constituted a new factor, which forced the United States into a close alliance with Israel.[9] The revolutionary potential of the Palestinian movement reinforced Washington's fear of communism, and the more Cold War-orientated the Presidents who occupied the White House, the closer the special relationship grew between the United States and Israel, and the less credible the United States became as a conciliator.

America's peace proposals, from the Rogers Plan to the Reagan Plan, which span two decades, have a common aim: containment of Palestinian nationalism. These plans have not brought the region closer to peace; in fact, peace is farther away now than at any previous time.

The Palestinian national movement has challenged the United States to assume responsibility as a superpower in the region and to endorse the global consensus on a political settlement. Not only did the United States fail to associate itself with that consensus, it has stood alone with Israel against an international peace conference since 1974. The setbacks to US diplomacy in 1978–79 and in 1982–83 are directly attributed to Palestinian nationalism. Just as Israel suspends all reason when it deals with Palestinian nationalism, so does the United States. Its policy and demeanor in that respect have become Israelized. Israel was allowed to subvert two U.S.-sponsored cease-fires brokered by Philip Habib in 1981 and 1982 and to veto the September 1, 1982 Reagan Plan. In short, America's inability to distinguish between Israeli objectives in the Middle East and its own has compromised its credibility as a responsible superpower.

So the Palestinian encounters with the Arab states, Israel, and the United States have been very unpleasant. The only difference in their attitudes towards the PNM is that while the two latter forces wanted to decimate the PNM, the former worked to clip its wings. Now that the PLO has been uprooted and stands divided, these forces have accounts to settle: the Arab states must share the allegiance of their citizenry with the PLO; Israel has to contend with the direct party to the conflict; and the United States must contend with a spoiler of its efforts to rearrange the Middle East. Perhaps it is testimony to the vitality of this movement, even during its weakest hour, that such an impressive combination of forces would coalesce to bring about its destruction.

Alternative Courses

The foregoing posits that the Palestinian national movement has had its successes and failures, constraints and opportunities during the past two decades. Since the re-emergence of Palestinian nationalism, the interests of the Palestinian movement have collided with those of the dominant powers in the region: the Arab state system, whose defeat in the June 1967 War undermined its legitimacy as a viable and a credible agent of liberation; Israel, whose stunning victory in 1967 placed it face to face with the direct party to the conflict; and the United States, which has had to cope with a post-Nasserite period of turbulence in an area which it had come to regard as its own turf. The challenge which Palestinian nationalism presented to each one of these three forces, as well as their responses to the challenge, generated a relationship which imposed certain constraints, yet promised opportunities for Palestinian nationalism.

As the PLO grew dangerously dependent on external support and its future was inextricably linked to the varying interests of the Arab states, its effectiveness in trying to realize its own raison d'être of changing the status-quo was seriously curtailed. The Arab state system would not tolerate any fundamental changes which ran counter to its interests, as the experiences with Jordan, Syria, and Egypt demonstrated since 1970. Given these constraints, the PLO was in danger of becoming more answerable to the Arab state system than to its own constituents. The diplomatic campaign which the Arab states and the PLO waged jointly after the 1973 war failed to bring the Palestinians nearer to achieving their goals. And during the 1982 invasion of Lebanon, the diplomatic successes of the 1970s counted for very little during the siege of Beirut. That invasion has in fact resulted in the ongoing impasse and the fragmentation of the PLO.

The question now is whether the next few years are likely to witness further erosion in the Palestinian position or a turning of the tide. The answer will depend largely on the nature of the constraints facing the movement and the opportunities open to it. It will also depend on the extent to which it may become possible for the restraints and problems at the local, regional, and global levels, to be overcome.

The chief local problem has, of course, been the disunity of the movement and the fragmentation of the PLO. Without unity, there can be no remedy for the impasse, no cure for the paralysis, no clearly defined strategy and hence no hope of success. The split in the movement had enabled several

Arab forces—regular and irregular alike—to attack Palestinian communities and undermine their cause. While Amal militias laid siege to refugee camps in Lebanon, Syria continued to atomize the Palestinian struggle in an attempt to establish hegemony over the movement. Jordan openly coordinated with Israel against the PLO, even as Israel applied the "Iron Fist" policy with great contempt. Meanwhile, Egypt and Morocco lobbied Palestinian leaders to recognize Israel, which itself rejected recognition.

Against this background, the 18th Palestine National Council (PNC) convened in Algiers in April 1987, and the far-reaching consequences of this unity session cannot yet be calculated. The meeting came at a time when serious impediments faced not only the Palestinians but various regional actors and the superpowers as well. In Israel, the crisis of leadership and governance have seriously impaired any efforts to put forth a coherent position that would end the political stalemate, ongoing since the Lebanon invasion. The contemplated Syrian design for a new order in Lebanon was dealt a severe blow as the Amal proxy proved to be a weak instrument for that order. Although Jordan and Egypt had undertaken various initiatives, they came to nothing in face of opposition by the US Congress to arms shipments and the reluctance of a disappointed Secretary of State to remove the Middle East from the bottom of the diplomatic agenda. Moreover, American credibility reached an all-time low in the wake of revelations about arms shipment to Iran with excess profits going to the Nicaraguan *Contras.* It is hardly an accident that the European Economic Community foreign ministers, on 13 February 1987, called for an international peace conference under the auspices of the United Nations, a position which runs counter to Washington's agenda. As for the Soviet Union, its exclusion from the Middle Eastern diplomacy has ensured the persistence of stalemate and the resultant condition of the Israeli occupation.

By emphasizing a more independent posture and a unified position, the 18th PNC has placed the PLO in a less vulnerable situation *vis-à-vis* the Arab states and their conflicting aims. Jordan, for example, with its long-standing eagerness to present its own Palestinians at a peace forum, represents a frail challenge to the PLO as the legitimate representative. Syria, with its aspiration for the role of principal power broker, clashes with Palestinian insistence on an independent role, and Egypt's second-class relationship with the United States has presumably given it an indispensable role in preparing an international peace conference.

The reconciled PLO could now insist on pursuing the objectives outlined in the 1974 Rabat and 1982 Fez summit meetings without having to cater to the narrower dimensions of Arab strategies or having to be burdened by their particularistic exigencies. The pursuit of political and national independence from the disparate Arab states and from Israel can now be simultaneous. The opportunities which may open up for the Palestinians in the aftermath of the 18th PNC will be inextricably linked to the extent of independence and the quality of the unity which the movement maintains. A unified and independent PLO could offer Syria an enhanced role in the regional politics of the area, just as Syria could enhance the PLO's own role in a peace process. By the same token, a heightened Soviet posture in the Middle East could become more manageable with the cooperation of a PLO reconciled with Syria. The PLO would benefit greatly from an enhanced Soviet role in Middle East diplomacy and an expiration of the U.S. monopoly of it. The more cohesive the PLO, the more mutual its relations will be with Syria and the USSR and the less vulnerable it will be to U.S. prescriptions regarding Arab cooperation and to Israeli coercion.

The 18th PNC session has terminated the post-1983 regional and global alignment, paving the way for a restructuring more in consonance with a reconstituted PLO. This is not to say that the centrifugal forces that rejoined the movement will impose their terms on the majority. Both factions moved toward reunification, implicitly admitting that previous strategies were flawed: that is, the assumptions of the 17th PNC in 1984 and those of the Amman accord in February 1985 that Cairo and Amman were capable of advancing the Palestinian cause, as well as the assumption that a junior partnership with Syria's Assad would administer eventual redress. By declaring the dissolution of the National Salvation Front, which was to be Assad's instrument for challenging Arafat's leadership, the leftist factions elevated the cause of unity to new heights and served notice to Assad that their faction is not a puppet. By the same token, Arafat's adoption of a platform closer to that of the leftists—his agreement to abrogate the Amman accord and the categorical rejection of Washington's arbitrary conditions for PLO recognition—signaled an important shift towards realignment in closer proximity to Syria's declared position. That endeavor, however, entailed neither acceptance of Syrian leadership nor repudiations of relations with Egypt. The overriding concern was the preservation of the PLO as an independent national body within the Arab world.

Needless to say, this independence has traditionally been the single most disturbing element for the disparate Arab states. Their eagerness to carve out the Palestinian cause among themselves and to control one or another faction has inflicted severe damage on the movement, the people, and the cause. It is no wonder that—despite careful efforts by the 18th PNC to avoid a break with Egypt and despite acceptance by the official Egyptian delegation of the PNC formulation—the Mubarak government impulsively moved toward closing PLO offices in Egypt, just as Hussein's government closed those in Amman a year earlier upon sensing PLO inclinations against a Jordanian diktat. For the past few years, those Arab states that purported to know the realistic requisites for peace have urged the Palestinians to speak with one voice; ironically the emergence of that one voice in Algiers has already caused consternation in Palestinian-Arab relations: the Saudis were unhappy with the admission of the Communist Party to the PLO Executive Committee, Morocco was upset with the presence of a *Polisario* representative, Jordan had already flirted with Peres about the convening of a so-called international peace conference, and Syria had sent word to the leftist leadership not to return to Damascus for the time being.

Such problems are not without precedent, and it is not likely that these negative effects will undermine the PLO, even though its hard-won cohesion confronts the Arab regimes on both sides of the spectrum with a serious dilemma. The reunified Palestinian movement has relations with Syria, Jordan, the various Lebanese factions, the Soviet Union, and Egypt. The new regional game is not zero-sum any more. Anyone of these groups would be risking reproach were it to pursue peace without the PLO. And the road to the Soviet Union is not necessarily through Damascus.

In the final analysis, the true test of the PLO's reconstituted cohesion will come if and when the hard choices have to be made: whether the international peace conference will be shaped by Peres and Mubarak, in which case it would provide nothing more than what Shultz describes as "supportive international context," with "geographic subcommittees" serving as the new euphemisms for direct negotiations; or whether it will be shaped by the Soviet Union, Syria, and a united PLO, in which case conditions would not be imposed. The true test will also come when the hard question has to be answered as to whether or not success can be achieved on the basis of cooperation with an Arab system whose very survival is considered a vital American interest.

The platform for the new political landscape implies that Palestinian redress cannot emerge from the present constraints embedded in the local, regional, and global environments. When these are overcome, under conditions of national unity, they may be turned into opportunities. That means a decision to redefine the terms of discussion, to redraw the rules of the game, and to recapture the initiative. A longer-range investment may have to take priority over short-term returns.

Notes

1. See Ann M. Lesch, *Arab Politics in Palestine 1917–1939.* (Ithaca, N.Y.: Cornell University Press, 1979); Pamela Ann Smith, *Palestine and the Palestinians, 1876–1983* (London: Croom Helm, 1984); Adbul Wahab Kayyali. *Palestine: A Modern History* (London, 1978).

2. On the 1936 revolt, see Ghassan Kanafani, *Palestine: The 1936–1939 Revolt,* trans. The Tricontinental Society (London, 1980).

3. See Cheryl Rubenberg, *The Palestine Liberation Organization: Its Institutional Infrastructure* (Belmont, MA: Institute of Arab Studies, 1983); Helena Cobban, *The Palestine Liberation Organization: People, Power, and Politics* (Cambridge: Cambridge University Press, 1984).

4. Naseer H. Aruri, "Palestinian Impasse: Constraints and Opportunities," *Scandinavian Journal of Development Alternatives,* Vol. VI, No. 1 (March 1987), pp. 61–85.

5. For a discussion of the status of national liberation movements under international law, see W. Thomas and Sally V. Mallison, *The Palestine Problem in International Law* (London: Longmaur, 1986).

6. "Israel Tortures Arab Prisoners: Special Investigation by Insight" *Sunday Times* (London) June 17, 1977.

7. See *Country Reports on Human Rights Practices* for 1985, 1986, 1987: Submitted to the Committee on Foreign Affairs, House of Representatives, and the Committee on Foreign Relations, U.S. Senate, by the Department of State; See *Amnesty International Report 1987* (London: Amnesty International, 1987), pp. 348–352.

8. See Naseer H. Aruri, ed., *Occupation: Israel Over Palestine* (Belmont, MA: AAUG Press, 1984); Rosemary Sayigh, *Palestinians: From Peasants to Revolutionaries* (London: Zed, 1979).

9. For a discussion of U.S. policy and Israel, see Noam Chomsky, *The Fateful Triangle* (Boston: South End Press, 1983); Naseer Aruri, et al., *Reagan and the Middle East* (Belmont, MA: AAUG Press, 1983).

7

The West Bank Palestinians and the Politics of Marginalization

Emile F. Sahliyeh

The evolution of West Bank Palestinians' political attitudes has over the years been affected by political developments in the external environment. As such, periods of cleavage and rivalries among the Arab countries were accompanied by a mood of demoralization among West Bank Palestinians. Following the establishment of Israel in 1948, the physical dispersion of the Palestinians was accompanied by the political fragmentation among rival Arab leaders. With the annexation of the West Bank by Jordan, many of the West Bank urban elite accepted integration into the Jordanian polity. This process of integration had a dual effect of making Jordan the custodian of the Palestinian question and of relegating the West Bank urban elite into marginal status. Still other Palestinians were attracted to Nasser's pan-Arabism, the Ba'th Party, and the Islamic Brotherhood movement in the 1950s.

With the abrupt dismemberment of the West Bank from Jordan as a result of the 1967 June war, it seemed likely that West Bank Palestinians would develop their own indigenous leadership and initiatives for ending the Israeli military occupation. However, the political position of the local elite became more vulnerable to the pressures and counterpressures of three external actors which had developed high stakes in the unfolding of political developments inside the occupied territories. These three actors were Jordan, the PLO, and Israel. These outside players shared a common interest, though for different reasons, in discouraging the emergence of a local leadership among the Palestinian inhabitants of the occupied territories. As a consequence of their policies, an external leadership for Palestinians developed. In the process the role of the local elite was undermined, thus preventing the emergence of an all-West Bank political leadership.

This chapter was updated in March 1988 in order to incorporate a postscript which deals with the Palestinian uprising in the occupied territories.

Yet, the pressures of Jordan, the PLO, and Israel were not the only factors responsible for the reliance of West Bank Palestinians on outside actors for leadership and ideological guidance. More precisely, West Bank Palestinians felt a deep sense of psychological, political, and physical vulnerability *vis-à-vis* Israel, a condition that discouraged the development of political self-confidence. In addition, the Palestinians were economically dependent on outside assistance—whether from Jordan, the PLO, or Arab countries. Such a dependency was inevitable since after 1967, Israel avoided any large investment in the West Bank's economic infrastructure. Such considerations led to the growth of a tradition of political resignation and helplessness among West Bank urban politicians.

Before further analysis of the impact of these factors on the evolution of political behavior in the West Bank, key concepts and terms that are used in this chapter will be defined. The term "political resignation" refers to the general reluctance of the West Bank elite and other political and social movements to develop their own autonomous leadership. In addition, such political players were reluctant to advance their own initiatives that would address the specific concerns of Palestinians in the West Bank and Gaza Strip. Political resignation defined in such a manner does not presuppose political passivity on the part of the local population toward Israel's military authority. Rather, the local population looked for outside help in order to put an end to the military occupation.

The term "elite" refers to those members of the West Bank population who, because of their economic status, social prestige, profession, education, and political linkages, have articulated the political interests and demands of the local population. More precisely, the West Bank urban elite can be categorized on the basis of social and economic composition, as well as political orientation, identification, and allegiance. The elite has traditionally consisted of the administrative, elected elite (including municipal council members and representatives of various unions and associations), the professional elite (including doctors, engineers, and lawyers), the communications elite (including journalists and writers), the business elite (including merchants and landlords), religious dignitaries, and members of the academic community.

Finally, the term "political and social movements" refers to existing mass organizations and groups in the West Bank. More specifically, the term denotes the student movement, the labor union movement, women's organizations, and professional associations. Both Islamic and communist trends are incorporated within the definition of political and social movements.

The External Actors

Between 1949 and 1967, the Jordanian government adopted a number of policies to ensure the incorporation of the West Bank into the kingdom.[1] Three such policies—co-optation, political fragmentation, and political control—hindered the emergence of an all-West Bank political leadership and the formation of area-wide political frameworks. Concerning the policy of co-optation, the government assigned fifty percent of the seats in the Jordanian Parliament to West Bank Palestinians. The key members of prominent West Bank families were also given cabinet posts. The Jordanian government divided the West Bank region into seven self-autonomous districts that were directly linked to Amman. The government, for the most part, banned the formation of political parties and associations.

The PLO as an external actor contributed further to diminish the incentives of local politicians to develop an autonomous leadership. The emergence of the PLO in the mid-1960s and its elevation to the position of ideological and exclusive political representative of the Palestinian people by the mid-1970s served to maintain the local elite's peripheral status. The organization gradually offered itself as a reference point for political allegiance and ideological inspiration, thus presenting itself as a credible alternative to Jordan within the West Bank.

In addition to its ideological and political appeal, the PLO mobilized both instrumental and coercive resources in order to further widen its power base and legitimacy. The organization utilized Arab financial assistance to buy influence within the occupied territories. In this context, it distributed economic benefits and political rewards among the West Bank local elite, institutions, and groups. It occasionally employed intimidating techniques, including threats and assassination attempts, against its opponents within the occupied territories.

Fluctuations in the PLO's political influence at the regional and international levels, its cooperative or conflictual relationships with Jordan and Syria, and the cohesion or dissension within its ranks all had a direct bearing upon the unity or fragmentation of the urban elite. Moreover, the fact that the PLO was an umbrella organization of multiple sub-actors further complicated the process of elite formation and contributed to differences among West Bank political forces.

While the roles of Jordan and the PLO are not to be underestimated in the unfolding of political developments, Israel, by virtue of its military control, also exerted significant influence on the West Bank. The occupation has left a deep impact on the political composition, orientation, and roles of the local elite and various groups. To begin with, the occupation of the West Bank rallied local political forces behind the goal of resisting Israel. In this regard, members of the West Bank urban elite formed a number of political structures and frameworks for the expression of grievances and for the articulation of the local population's interests. Between 1967 and 1970, the urban elite established the Higher Committee for National Guidance and the Islamic Supreme Council to organize opposition against Israel's occupation. Between 1973 and 1977, the Palestine National Front was formed and between 1978 and 1982, the National Guidance Committee (the coalition of pro-PLO politicians) was established. The primary task of these two institutions was to generate support for the PLO and to resist the Israeli presence.

Aside from the military aspect of its occupation, the Israeli government's economic policy between 1967 and 1977 also affected the configuration of political power at both the elite and mass level. More precisely, Israel's decision to allow a significant portion of the West Bank labor force to seek employment opportunities inside Israel weakened the power base of traditional conservative politicians. Such a work force was no longer dependent for its economic subsistence upon employment by the West Bank large landowners and business class. The decline in the traditional politicians' influence was caused by two additional developments. Israel's policy of deportation took a heavy toll on conservative politicians during the initial years of occupation. Between 1967 and 1971, 469 West Bank Palestinians, including prominent pro-Jordanian figures, were deported. The decline in the position of power of the older politicians also resulted from the Israeli government's amendment of Jordan's municipal election law. According to the modified law, women and men who did not own property were allowed to vote in the 1976 municipal elections.

Israel's economic and liberalization policies in the first half of the 1970s facilitated the formation of a nucleus of politicians who were younger, better educated, and employed in white collar professions. Despite such a liberal policy, the military administration did not allow the crystallization of a viable political leadership for the Palestinians in the occupied territories.[2] Between 1978 and 1982, the Israeli government removed from office 14 out of 24 West Bank mayors who were elected in 1976. Though the Jordanian law calls for conducting municipal elections every four years, the Israeli government has refused to authorize elections since 1976. The end result of Israel's policy served to reinforce the process of creating an external leadership for the Palestinians.

The PLO, Israel, and Jordan sought to play a dominant role in the occupied territories. Thus, their relationship with each other was one of competition and conflict, demonstrated by habitual attempts to penetrate and weaken each other's sphere of influence. In this regard, Jordan exploited the rising Islamic trend to contain pro-PLO groups while the PLO utilized the radicalized student movement to undermine the influence of Jordan and its supporters. During the late 1970s and early 1980s, there was also competition between the communists and followers of various PLO factions for control of the student movement, labor unions, and women's and professional organizations.[3] The Israeli government during the Likud rule, 1977–1984, made systematic efforts to contain the PLO's influence within the occupied territories. During those years, many West Bank political activists were placed under town arrest and the majority of the mayors were removed from office. In its attempt to create a more collaborative local leadership, the Israeli military authorities formed six village leagues in West Bank rural areas.[4] These leagues tried unsuccessfully to create for themselves a political presence among the youth.

Competition among the three outside players also took place with regard to the allocation of resources. For instance, while Jordan was the primary vehicle for the allocation and distribution of economic aid in the West Bank, by the late 1970s the PLO also became a principal distributor of economic rewards. Similarly, Israel's policy of absorbing the West Bank labor force generated economic prosperity at the individual level, thus undermining Jordan's traditional pivotal economic role.

The competitive and conflictual nature of the relationship among Jordan, the PLO, and Israel did not preclude the possibility of implicit or even explicit bilateral cooperation against the interests of the third actor. For instance, tacit cooperation took place between Jordan and Israel against the PLO during the 1972 municipal elections. Likewise, following the ascension of the Likud coalition to power in 1977 and its intensified settlement drive in the occupied territories, Jordan and the PLO together established the Joint Jordanian-Palestinian Economic Committee to distribute financial assistance inside the occupied territories. Moreover, Jordan and the PLO combined efforts to frustrate Israel's attempt to create a rural-based alternative leadership in the West Bank.

In its attempt to control the West Bank, each actor was not only concerned with arresting the rise of an autonomous local leadership; each desired also to foster a client or satellite elite to promote its interests and to broaden its political legitimacy. Political backing of satellite leadership, however, was ensured only so long as those leaders did not attempt to develop their own autonomy. The movement of several West Bank elite groups toward greater degrees of independent political thinking and initiatives prompted the relevant external actor to halt the flow of resources and to apply pressure in order to check nonconformist political behavior. In this regard, the quest by the Palestine National Front (a coalition for the West Bank new nationalist elite, particularly the communists) was disquieting to the PLO.[5] Likewise, Israel eventually hindered the activities of the village leagues when several leaders began to deviate from the guidelines prescribed by the military administration. Similarly, the Jordanian government often withheld economic assistance and political privileges from opposing West Bank politicians and institutions.

Although the West Bank's elite groups relied on outside forces for leadership, their dependency did not amount to automatic and unquestionable loyalty. Such dependency did not imply complete identification with the interests of these external actors, nor with their local constituents in the occupied territories. Some West Bank politicians (including the mayor of Bethlehem) repeatedly urged the external organization to make the occupied territories its primary constituency. In addition, members of the West Bank urban elite utilized existing municipal structures to advance their own interests. They manipulated their external linkages to buttress their own positions and to contain the political influence of rival politicians and movements.

Changes in the power positions of Jordan, the PLO, and Israel not only affected elite formation and loyalties; their interaction also had a similar impact on West Bank youth. In particular, both the prolongation of Israel's occupation and the emergence of the PLO radicalized the youth. By the late 1970s, two opposing political trends surfaced among West Bank students.[6]

The first trend was secular in orientation. It took the form of an intense ideological identification with Palestinian nationalism and Marxism/Leninism mixed with elements of Palestinian nationalism. The second trend was religious in nature. It took the form of an Islamic resurgence.

Like the urban elite, students looked for leadership in the external environment. By doing so, they not only contributed to the process of promoting a diaspora leadership for Palestinians, but also relegated West Bank politicians to a marginal status. As such, the secular branch of the student movement became the PLO's most ardent supporter and one of its primary vehicles for influence and legitimacy within the occupied territories. In contrast, the Islamic branch of the student movement was manipulated by Jordan despite an ostensible non-Jordanian component to its political thinking. Moreover, because of the PLO's divisive nature, the student movement became an arena for power struggles among rival PLO groups.

Phases in the Political Situation

As a result of the policies, pressures, and power relationships among Jordan, the PLO, and Israel, six distinct political phases emerged in the evolution of political trends in the West Bank. During the first phase, from 1967 to 1970, an overwhelming majority of West Bank politicians advocated the return of the West Bank to Jordanian sovereignty. Leaders of the protest against occupation were drawn from the ranks of the traditional politicians, including former Jordanian officials, members of the Islamic religious establishment, and leaders of the political opposition during the Jordanian regime. The PLO was not as evident, for it had not yet developed an interest in the occupied territories. The leaders of the organization were then contemplating the liberation of all of Palestine and the idea of a West Bank/ Gaza Strip state was anathema to them.

In the second phase, from 1970 to 1973, political paralysis engulfed the Arab world in the wake of the death of President Nasser of Egypt and the outbreak of the Palestinian-Jordanian civil war in 1970. This paralysis was accompanied by political resignation on the part of the West Bank urban elite. This feeling of resignation was attested to by a lack of interest in the 1972 municipal elections on the part of many West Bank local politicians and the mass public.

Despite such conditions, however, the outbreak of the 1973 October war ushered in a new third phase which affected the political composition and orientation of West Bank leaders. The new elite derived its political legitimacy and influence by identifying politically with the PLO, and by espousing the formation of a Palestinian state in the West Bank and Gaza Strip. Unlike the conservative elite, the economic power of the new leaders did not flow from a linkage with Jordan, but was based on their own independent economic base. The shift in the West Bank urban elite's posture from a pro-Jordanian to a pro-PLO stance was accelerated by the PLO's diplomatic gains in the mid-1970s. In particular, West Bank Palestinians were impressed by the PLO's increasing tendency to consider a diplomatic solution to the Palestinian question and to view the occupied territories as the site for a future Palestinian state. As a result of these developments, the power and influence of the pro-Jordanian conservative elite was significantly reduced, reaching a low ebb in the 1976 municipal elections when the traditional leaders lost most of their seats to the new nationalist politicians.

The fourth phase, from 1976 to 1978, saw a further evolution in the political activities of West Bank politicians. During this period they became increasingly demoralized by the political disarray which swept the Arab world in the wake of Egypt's decision to embark upon a unilateral political settlement with Israel. Further, the PLO's political predicament following Syria's intervention in the Lebanese civil war on the side of the Christian forces and the emergence of the Likud bloc to power in Israel in 1977 exacerbated such demoralization. In addition, it was during this phase that more signs of the latent power struggle between the PLO and West Bank politicians—particularly the communists and independent leftists—began to surface. This phase of subdued political activism came to an end with the signing of the Camp David accords in the fall of 1978.

The fifth phase was marked by three major events: the normalization of relations between Jordan and the PLO, the formation of the Palestinian-Jordanian Joint Economic Committee to advance steadfastness within the occupied territories, and the reconciliation between Syria and the PLO. These developments induced the West Bank urban elite to overcome their differences and unite their political stands in order to counter the common danger stemming from both the signing of the Camp David accords and the intensified construction of Jewish settlements by the Likud government.

At the start of phase six in the late spring of 1980, the political activism, composition, and resolve of the West Bank urban elite was seriously threatened. More specifically, on May 2, 1980, three of the West Bank's leading politicians, the mayors of Hebron and Halhoul and Shaikh Rajab al-Tamimi (a religious leader in Hebron), were deported to Lebanon on charges of inciting the local population. A month later, Israeli settlers attempted to assassinate the mayors of Nablus, Ramallah, and Al-Bireh. The Israeli offensive against the West Bank's new elite accelerated with the appointment of Ariel Sharon as Minister of Defense. Further, in early March 1982, the National Guidance Committee, which grouped many West Bank politicians together, was outlawed. Moreover, during the following months, eight mayors were removed from office.

At the same time, the Israeli government intensified its search for a rural-based leadership as a substitute for the pro-PLO urban elite. Its offensive against the Palestinians reached a climax in the summer of 1982 when the army dismantled the PLO's political headquarters in Beirut and its military infrastructure in southern Lebanon by expelling most Palestinian troops from the country. The PLO's exodus from Beirut and the split within its ranks further reduced the political influence of pro-PLO leaders in the West Bank.

Such developments led to the rise of a different brand of pro-PLO politicians and to the reemergence of the pro-Jordanian conservative elite.[7] The rise of such a group of politicians was the result of the diplomatic alliance between Jordan and the PLO that developed in the wake of the Lebanon war. Many West Bank politicians began to articulate political positions that showed dual loyalty to both Jordan and the PLO, as they recognized that only through a joint Jordanian-Palestinian diplomatic initiative could West Bank Palestinians hope to extricate themselves from Israel's military occupation. Members of this new pragmatic camp also displayed a greater degree of flexibility and willingness to deal with the Israeli military government and to engage in a dialogue with the Israeli peace camp. They also believed that military force was no longer relevant and useful for a resolution of the Palestinian question. The pragmatic politicians urged both Israel and the PLO to recognize their mutual rights.

In the second half of the 1980s, the political future of the pragmatic camp seems to be uncertain. The rift in the relationship between Jordan and the PLO placed the pragmatic politicians on the defensive. In view of the absence of diplomatic opportunities to resolve the Palestinian question and the deep-seated hostilities within the Arab world, a strong mood of frustration is sweeping the occupied territories. This political frustration is manifested in a growing tendency among the youth toward violence, radicalism, and fundamentalism.

Postscript

The increase in the activism of the youth was attested to by the frequency of demonstrations and strikes after 1985. An annual average of 3,000 violent demonstrations and strikes occurred in the second half of the 1980s. The youth's activism culminated in the 1987–1988 popular uprising.

This uprising was characterized by a high degree of intensity and a willingness on the part of the youth to endure considerable suffering and pain. Unlike previous waves of unrest, the Palestinians in 1987–1988 demonstrated that they were determined to end Israeli occupation of their land.

This unprecedented wave of protest was caused by the growing political frustration and desperation of the Palestinians. The relegation of the Palestinian problem to a marginal status, as the Arab states were occupied with the Iran-Iraq war, and the bitter rivalries and divisions among the Arab countries convinced many of the youth to take matters into their own hands. After all, it is their land and their lives that are at stake.

The youth's uprising presented a serious challenge to many of the players (Jordan, the PLO, and Israel) that traditionally had a strong interest in West Bank/Gaza developments. By waging the demonstrations, the youth further undermined the role of the local elite and placed them more on the defensive. In contrast to the moderation of those politicians, the new generation is uncompromising in its political stands. The youth insist upon establishing a secular democratic state in the whole of Palestine and believe that the use of violence is justifiable in the Palestinians' struggle for self-determination. In this context, the youth's attitude is more militant than the PLO's mainstream.[8]

The uprising gave the PLO leaders additional legitimacy and credentials to buttress their position *vis-à-vis* their rivals (Jordan and Syria). The militancy of the youth would compel the leaders of the PLO to adopt hardline positions. This is likely to be the case if the diplomatic solution to the Palestinian problem is not forthcoming.

While reinforcing the position of the PLO, the 1987–1988 uprising seriously undermined Jordan's relevance to West Bank Palestinians' aspirations. The overwhelming majority of Palestinians in the territories are opposed to any linkage of the West Bank and Gaza with the East Bank of Jordan. They emphatically insist that an independent Palestinian state be established. Their opposition to Jordan is evidenced in their unequivocal demand that the PLO should only represent West Bank interests in any diplomatic negotiations.

The intensity, the duration, and the pervasiveness of the uprising have serious implications for Israel. Despite the killing of one hundred Palestinians and the wounding of several thousand others, the West Bank/Gaza inhabitants are determined to continue their uprising. The youth in particular, prove to be daring and unafraid of the Israeli army.

The uprising surpassed in its significance the political activities of the Arab countries and the PLO since 1967. In Israel, it shocked the public and perplexed the leaders of both the Labor and Likud parties. Despite the presence of a large number of Israeli troops, the Palestinians did not give any sign of yielding to Israel's military pressure. Suppression of the Palestinian demonstrators caused worldwide criticism. The reaction of the American Jewish community and the American public to the manner in which the Israeli government dealt with the protest created tension in American-Israeli relations. The Reagan administration, after many years of diplomatic negligence activated its search for a political solution to the Palestinian-Israeli problem.

Lack of progress toward a peaceful resolution of the conflict and the prolongation of Israel's military occupation would certainly increase the levels of political frustration and desperation of the Palestinians in the West Bank and Gaza Strip. Under such conditions there would be no room for moderation and flexibility. The cycle of violence and counter-violence on both sides of the conflict would intensify. This situation threatens to transform the conflict into an inter-communal civil war for the exclusive control of Palestine.

Notes

1. For a detailed treatment of the West Bank under Jordanian rule, see Shaul Mishal, *West Bank/East Bank: The Palestinians in Jordan, 1949–1967* (New Haven, CT: Yale University Press, 1978).

2. For the evolution of political attitudes among West Bank Palestinians, the reader is referred to: Ann Mosley Lesch, *Political Perceptions of the Palestinians on the West Bank and Gaza Strip* (Washington, D.C.: Middle East Institute, 1980); Mark A. Heller, "Politics and Social Change in the West Bank," *Palestinian Society and Politics*, ed. Joel Migdal (Princeton, NJ: Princeton University Press, 1980); and Moshe Ma'oz, *Palestinian Leadership on the West Bank* (London: Frank Cass & Co., Ltd., 1984).

3. For further elaboration of these trends, see Emile Sahliyeh, *In Search of Leadership: West Bank Politics Since 1967* (Washington, D.C.: Brookings, 1988), especially chapters 4–7.

4. See Salim Tamari, "In League With Zion: Israel's Search for a Native Pillar," *Occupation: Israel Over Palestine*, ed. Nasser H. Aruri (Belmont, MA: Association of Arab-American University Graduates, Inc., 1983), pp. 377–390.

5. Ibrahim Dakkak, "Back to Square One: A Case Study in the Reemergence of the Palestinian Identity in the West Bank, 1967–80," *Palestinians Over the Green Line: Studies in the Relations Between Palestinians on Both Sides of the 1949 Armistice Line Since 1967*, ed. Alexander Schoelch (London: Ithaca Press, 1983), pp. 20–21.

6. See chapters 6 and 7 concerning the emergence of Islam and the student movement in Emile Sahliyeh, *In Search of Leadership: West Bank Politics Since 1967* (Washington, D.C.: Brookings, 1988).

7. See Emile Sahliyeh, "The West Bank Pragmatic Elite: The Uncertain Future," *Journal of Palestine Studies* 15 (Summer 1986): pp. 34–45.

8. These observations about the militancy of the youth are sustained by a survey conducted by Mohammed Shadid and Rick Seltzer in the summer of 1986 in which they interviewed 1,024 Palestinians. "Political Attitudes of Palestinians in the West Bank and Gaza Strip," *Middle East Journal* 42 (Winter 1988): pp. 16–32.

8

The Structural and Political Context of the PLO's Changing Objectives in the Post-1967 Period

Cheryl A. Rubenberg

The two most salient aspects of the Palestine Liberation Organization (PLO) in the post-1967 period are the tenacity of its structural framework and the profound alterations that have occurred in its fundamental objectives. This paper will examine the relationship between the two and will illustrate the extraordinary impact historical circumstances have had on the Palestine national movement, especially in the transformation of its goals.

Structural Characteristics of the PLO

The PLO is an umbrella organization consisting of some eight resistance groups (see Table 8.1) of varying strength.[1] However, it has been dominated since 1969 by one group, Fateh.[2] Fateh is the oldest of the resistance groups and its present leaders, who are also the dominant leaders in the PLO, were its founding fathers. They include Yasser Arafat, Salah Khalaf, Khalil Wazir (assassinated by Israel on April 16, 1988), Faruq Qaddumi, Khaled Hassan, and Hani Hassan. Fateh is characterized by an absence of ideology (except as nationalism is considered an ideology) and an exclusive focus on the question of Palestine.[3]

Also important with regard to structure are the political institutions of the PLO: the Palestine National Council (PNC), the Central Council (CC), and the Executive Committee (EC). These institutions were established with the founding of the PLO in 1964 and have remained viable since that time despite the PLO's transformation in 1969 from a political organization

Thanks are due to Naseer Aruri and Abbas Alnasrawi for their careful reading and helpful comments on early drafts of this chapter.

TABLE 8.1   Main Resistance Groups Under the PLO Umbrella

Group	Date of Emergence	Ideology/ Orientation	Sponsor	Leader
Fateh	1959	Nationalist	Independent	Yasser Arafat
Popular Front for the Liberation of Palestine (PFLP)	1967	Pan-Arabist/ Neo-Marxist	Independent	George Habash
Democratic Front for the Liberation of Palestine (DFLP)	1969	Marxist	Independent	Nayef Hawatmeh
Saiqa	1966	Pro-Syrian/ Ba'athist	Syria	Isam al-Qadi (replaced Zuhair Mushin, who was assassinated in 1979)
Popular Front for the Liberation of Palestine--General Command (PFLP--GC)	1968	Pro-Syrian/ anti-Fateh	Syria	Ahmed Jibril
Arab Liberation Front (ALF)	1969	Pro-Iraqi/ Ba'athist	Iraq	Abdel-Rahim Ahmed
Palestinian Popular Struggle Front (PPSF) *	1967	Anti-Fateh/ Pro-Syrian	---	Samir Gosheh
Palestine Liberation Front (PLF) *	1977	Pro-Iraqi/ anti-Fateh	---	Talat Ya'qub

NOTE: The Palestinian Communist Party, based mainly in the West Bank, was not given seats on the PNC or representation on the Executive Committee until the 18th PNC in 1987.

* The PPSF and the PLF have usually had seats at the PNCs but the PPSF has never had a seat on the Executive Committee; however, the PLF has had a seat on the Executive Committee since the 16th PNC in February 1983.

serving as an appendage to Egyptian diplomacy to an independent Palestinian nationalist organization with military, civilian, and political components.

There is a dialectical relationship in the structure and functions of PLO institutions that will be explored below but it is necessary to know something about the institutions at the outset. The PNC is a parliamentary body that is vested by the Basic Constitution as the PLO's supreme policy-making authority. In practice it has usually acted to set broad policy guidelines of sufficient ambiguity to allow the EC flexibility in their implementation. Too, the policy guidelines have typically been shaped by the leadership and presented to the PNC for discussion and ratification. (Not unlike the American political system wherein the President sets the agenda and Congress reacts to Executive initiatives.) According to the constitution, PNC members are to be elected by the Palestinian people though in practice this has never been possible. Instead, participation has normally been the result of negotiations between the leaders of the various resistance groups prior to each PNC session with representation reflecting the relative strength of each group. Between May 1964 and April 1987 the PNC held 18 regular

TABLE 8.2   Dates and Venues of Palestine National Councils

First	May 28-June 2, 1964	Jerusalem
Second	May 31-June 4, 1965	Cairo
Third	May 20-24, 1966	Gaza
Fourth	July 10-17, 1968	Cairo
Fifth	February 1-4, 1969	Cairo
Sixth	September 1-6, 1969	Cairo
Seventh	May 30-June 4, 1970	Cairo
Extraordinary Session	August 27-28, 1970	Amman
Eighth	February 28-March 5, 1971	Cairo
Ninth	July 7-13, 1971	Cairo
Tenth	April 11-12, 1972	Cairo
Eleventh	January 6-12, 1973	Cairo
Twelfth	June 1-9, 1974	Cairo
Thirteenth	March 12-20, 1977	Cairo
Fourteenth	January 15-23, 1979	Damascus
Fifteenth	April 11-19, 1981	Damascus
Sixteenth	February 14-22, 1983	Algiers
Seventeenth	November 22-28, 1984	Amman
Eighteenth	April 20-25, 1987	Algiers

NOTE: Most of the data in this chart is from Alain Gresh, *The PLO, The Struggle Within: Towards an Independent Palestinian State* (London: Zed Press, 1983), pp. 252-23. Helena Cobban, *The Palestine Liberation Organization: People, Power and Politics* (New York: Cambridge University Press), p. 270, provides a similar though less accurate list. It is quite remarkable that the PLO was able to convene the PNC 18 times in 23 years; this is certainly one mark of the PLO's distinctiveness among liberation movements.

sessions and one extraordinary session (see Table 8.2) with between 100 and 450 delegates in attendance.[4]

In addition to establishing the framework of PLO policy, the PNC is charged with electing the Executive Committee. However, in actuality the PNC essentially ratifies a list of EC members presented to it after lengthy behind-the-scenes negotiations among resistance group leaders. (Similar to the U.S. Congress approval of presidential nominations for Executive officers.) The Executive Committee typically consists of between twelve and fifteen members and is the *de facto* ruling and decision making body of the PLO. Its composition also reflects the relative strength of the resistance organizations. The Executive Committee elects the PLO chairman who, since 1969, has been Yasser Arafat.[5] As the strongest resistance organization, Fateh has dominated each of the political institutions from 1969 through the present.

The PLO's Changing Objectives

At the same time that the PLO has maintained this structural continuity (i.e., the leadership of Fateh and the persistence of the political institutions), it has radically transformed itself from a national liberation movement to a conservative nationalist organization. Originally, Fateh leaders espoused objectives similar to those of other twentieth-century anti-colonialist liberation movements: they intended to free their homeland from foreign oppression and colonialism, and armed struggle was to be the means to that end.[6] However, by the latter part of 1967 Fateh's Central Committee changed its goal from the liberation of Palestine to the establishment of a "secular, democratic state of Palestine" in which Jews, Muslims and Christians would live together with equal access to human, civil and political rights. Fateh's first public statement on the secular, democratic concept was made on January 1, 1968, and it was formally adopted at the third Fateh General Congress in October 1968. At the 5th PNC session in February 1969, the new objective became official PLO policy.[7]

Subsequently, at the 12th PNC in June 1974, the PLO again fundamentally altered its goals, abandoning the idea of a democratic secular state in all of Palestine, and calling instead for the establishment of "a Palestinian national authority in any Palestinian areas liberated from Israeli control."[8] This was the first formulation of the idea of an independent Palestinian state alongside Israel. A further point in the PNC program stated that the PLO would use "every means" to achieve its ends, implying the retreat from armed struggle.[9] (During the October 1973 war Arafat had written to U.S. Secretary of State Henry Kissinger declaring the PLO's willingness to take part in a post-war political settlement.)[10]

At the 13th PNC in March 1977, the two-state idea was further refined and clearly articulated as policy, and the PLO formally declared its willingness to participate in negotiations for a political settlement.[11] Official PLO policy from 1977 through the present has centered on the objective of securing an independent Palestinian state in any part of Palestine (understood to mean the West Bank and Gaza) that could be freed from Israeli occupation, and the PLO has consistently sought to engage in a diplomatic process that would lead to such an end.

By 1978 PLO guerrilla activity had declined significantly and in March of that year, in the aftermath of Israel's invasion of Lebanon, Arafat agreed to co-operate with a United Nations peace-keeping force (the UNIFIL) in South Lebanon. As such, the PLO chairman was, by implication, endorsing Security Council Resolution 425 which created UNIFIL's mandate and specifically mentioned Israel. In the words of one analyst, this "marked a turning-point in the history of the Palestinian resistance movement . . . It constituted the first open acceptance by the leader of the PLO of a cease-fire agreement with Israel, and his decision to co-operate with UNIFIL was subsequently endorsed by all the official PLO bodies."[12] Again in July 1981, the PLO accepted a cease-fire agreement, this one mediated by U.S. envoy Philip Habib, which it scrupulously honored for eleven months (in spite of repeated Israeli provocations)[13] until Israel invaded Lebanon in June 1982.

Following a 1983 split in the PLO and the convening of the 17th PNC in November 1984 by Fateh without most of the other resistance organizations, Chairman Arafat signed an accord with King Hussein of Jordan (in February

1985) in which the concept of an independent state was reduced to the notion of a homeland and self-government in a confederation with Jordan.[14] The agreement also contained the idea of a joint Jordanian-PLO negotiating team and, in effect, compromised the status of the PLO as the sole representative of the Palestinian people.[15] The Jordanian-PLO accord remained operational for a year until King Hussein abrogated it in February 1986.[16] In 1985 Arafat made a formal pronouncement in Egypt known as the "Cairo Declaration" in which he stated the PLO's condemnation of "all operations outside [Palestine] and all forms of terrorism."[17]

At the 18th session of the PNC in April 1987, the various resistance groups were reunited and the PLO restated the objective of national self determination in an independent state in part of Palestine. The emphasis on diplomacy was also reiterated with the PLO calling for an international conference under the auspices of the Security Council as the means to facilitate a solution to the question of Palestine.[18] During this session the Executive Committee declared the Jordanian-PLO agreement "null and void."[19]

The fundamental transformation of its basic aim from national liberation to an independent state in part of its native homeland distinguishes the PLO in the annals of liberation movements. Its relinquishing of armed struggle in favor of diplomacy is also unusual among such nationalist drives.[20] In addition, the perpetuation of Fateh's dominance and of the leadership of Arafat, Khalaf, Wazir, Qaddumi, and the Hassan brothers are remarkable, particularly considering the numerous setbacks the PLO sustained, e.g. the 1970 "Black September" battle in Jordan and the 1982 Israeli invasion of Lebanon, plus the failure to achieve any of the PLO's goals including the liberation of any part of Palestine, recognition by Israel (or by the U.S.) of the Palestinian right to self-determination, or Israeli (or United States') recognition of the PLO as the representative of Palestinian nationalist aspirations.

The following is an attempt to analyze and explain these aspects of the PLO. Major emphasis is placed on four elements: (1) The PLO is a nationalist movement without a territorial base of its own. (The reemergence of Palestinian nationalism—after the creation of Israel—occurred among the communities of displaced Palestinian refugees.[21] Those Palestinians who remained and became Israeli "citizens" did not participate in the resistance nor did they even provide a "sea" in which the resistance could "swim.") Thus since the resistance was not based on its native soil it was at an inherent disadvantage plus being dependent on Arab "host" states. (2) The PLO was severely constrained by the environment in which it had to function, i.e., the nature of the Arab state system. (3) The Soviet Union's position on the Palestine/Israel conflict significantly restricted the policy options of the PLO. And, (4) the PLO was further constrained by the unique characteristics of Israel as a colonial power: the ideology it espoused as a "national liberation movement" itself, the successful linking of political Zionism with the legacy of the Holocaust and historic anti-Semitism, as well as the linkage of biblical images and symbols with concepts of "restoration" and "return." In addition, the nature of the alliances the Zionist movement/Israel was able to forge with the Western powers *and* the Soviet Union was highly unusual. In the post-1967 period, Israel enjoyed the full moral, diplomatic, economic, and military support of the United States, the most powerful state in the international system. Indeed, the PLO was not struggling against an "ordinary" colonial-settler, imperialist regime.[22]

To a lesser extent, the nature of the PLO leaders themselves is considered. But regardless of the conclusions that may be drawn about the group of individuals who have directed the PLO since 1969, it seems unlikely that persons with different socio-economic and ideological dispositions would have been able to achieve more than this group in terms of national liberation, given the combination of objective structural and environmental impediments confronting Palestinians.

Dialectics of Structure and the Nature of the Arab State System

In considerable measure the structural characteristics of the PLO derive from the circumstance of Palestinian dispersion and displacement. As a result of the establishment of Israel as a "Jewish state" and the policies of Zionist leaders to rid the area of as many Palestinians as possible, more than 770,000 Palestinians, over half the indigenous population, were driven from or fled Palestine between November 1947 and January 1949.[23] The majority of these individuals were confined to refugee camps in Lebanon, Syria, Jordan, the West Bank, and Gaza. Some Palestinians eventually made their way out of the camps, into universities, and migrated to professional jobs in the Gulf states, Saudi Arabia, and other places in the Middle East as well as scattering across the globe. In addition, after the conclusion of the armistice accords in 1949, the total Palestinian national patrimony was under foreign domination.[24] Israel seized and occupied one-quarter more land than it had been allotted in the 1947 U.N. partition plan; Jordan illegally occupied the West Bank (subsequently "annexing" it); and Egypt illegally occupied and administered the Gaza Strip.[25] Following the 1967 war Israel occupied all of historic Palestine.

Without any independent territorial base and with Palestinians geographically fragmented, it is highly unlikely that one "party" capable of dominating resistance activities could have developed. The situation was further complicated by the fact that the resistance constituency was socio-economically diverse, ranging from the destitute camp population to middle and upper class teachers, bureaucrats, educated professionals, and wealthy businessmen working in Jordan, the Gulf states, and elsewhere, and of course it included Christians among the Muslim majority. The class and religious variations as well as the divergent life experiences of Palestinians in the diaspora were reflected in ideological differences and disagreements regarding the appropriate strategy and tactics of Palestinian resistance. Thus some Palestinians supported Fateh, others the PFLP, still others the DFLP, and so on.

When Fateh became the dominant force in the PLO, it concluded that in order to strengthen the organization's legitimacy, independence, and influence the PLO needed to maintain the support of all Palestinian constituencies. At the same time, Fateh did not want to alienate the Arab governments—especially Syria—and it feared that if those groups supported by Arab states (notably Saiqa) were excluded from the PLO, the regimes might act against the organization.[26] Thus the structure of the PLO as an "umbrella" for all the Palestinian and Arab-sponsored groups was established and institutionalized.

The diversity of the groups that were subsumed within the PLO made it essential that the PLO pursue a politics of "unity" and "consensus." The emphasis on unity and consensus added to the PLO's legitimacy and mass support, which in turn contributed to the institutionalization of the PLO as the organizational embodiment of Palestinian nationalism. Subsequently, this institutional legitimacy precluded any other group from unilaterally claiming to represent Palestinian interests or from pursuing an independent policy. The failure to establish legitimacy by those groups that did split from the organization serves to illustrate this point.[27] On the other hand, the politics of unity and consensus constrained the PLO's strategy and tactics to the lowest common denominator that was acceptable to *all* the factions—Palestinian and Arab-sponsored—and ultimately allowed the Arab regimes (in conjunction with several other factors) to determine Palestinian politics.

In addition, the absence of an independent territorial base necessitated that the resistance organize in and operate from the Arab states, and thus mandated that the resistance maintain good relations with the Arab regimes. This situation also made the resistance susceptible to Arab state interference; and Arab regimes, seeking to maximize their own state interests, acted in every possible way to dominate resistance politics. For instance, they created and supported groups such as Saiqa and the ALF that functioned to serve the Arab states rather than Palestinian interests; they attempted to coopt genuine Palestinian groups; and they engaged in overt repression of the resistance (e.g., Jordan in 1970, Syria in 1976, Syria's sponsorship of the Fateh dissidents in 1983 and of Amal in the "camp wars" in 1985–87, and so on).[28] Indeed, the use of force against the resistance by Arab governments plus the refusal of any Arab regime (except the Lebanese) to permit guerrilla activity from its territory after 1967 emphasizes the negative impact of the Arab states on the freedom of the resistance to determine its objectives, strategy, and tactics.[29] Thus, while the PLO maintained its independence from any one Arab government in the post-1969 period, it has been, in essence, dependent for its very existence on the grace of the Arab regimes.[30] This situation was a major determining factor in the transformation of fundamental PLO goals and methods.

In the aftermath of Nasser's defeat in 1967 (and the defeat as well of Jordan and Syria) the locus of power in the Arab world shifted to the conservative states, led by Saudi Arabia.[31] After the 1973 war the dominance of the conservative order was fully established and that order involved the recognition, at least *de facto*, of Israel's permanence in the region.[32] Even Syria, which regularly presented itself as a "radical" state, was prepared to conclude an accord with Israel—as testified to by the 1974 Syrian-Israeli disengagement agreement. After the Arab regimes acquiesced in Israel's existence, they exerted strong pressure on the PLO to do likewise. To a considerable extent they did so out of fear that a PLO committed to a democratic, secular state in Palestine might enmesh the Arab states in an undesired war with Israel. But in addition the "logic" of the Arab state system mandated the PLO's abandonment of the democratic secular state concept since such an idea directly threatened the Arab regimes whose political authority did not rest on the consent of the governed.[33] Moreover, the "lesson" of the Jordanian repression against the Palestinians in September 1970, implemented by King Hussein but sanctioned by Nasser and the entire Arab state order, was that the Arab regimes were prepared to annihilate the Palestinian resistance if it transgressed the parameters set by the system.[34]

It is also the case that the PLO's success in establishing institutional legitimacy was not only a reflection of Palestinian sentiment. It derived as well from the October 1974 Arab summit decision at Rabat that granted the PLO the status of "sole legitimate representative" of Palestinians. At the same time, the Arab regimes advocated recognition for the PLO at the United Nations, and as a result Arafat was invited to address the General Assembly (in November 1974) and the PLO was accorded the status of an observer-member. This international recognition further enhanced the PLO's legitimacy. But the willingness of the Arab states to confer the Rabat mantle and to lobby the General Assembly only came after the 12th PNC in June 1974 when the PLO altered its objectives and brought them into line with what was acceptable to the Arab regimes, i.e., the acceptance of an independent Palestinian state alongside Israel, plus the declared willingness to engage in diplomacy.[35]

The transformation in PLO objectives and the organization's accommodation to the policies prescribed by the Arab regimes was facilitated through Fateh's leadership.[36] As noted above, Fateh began with the goal of liberating Palestine but altered that in 1968 to the concept of a democratic, secular state. On November 4, 1973 Fateh issued a position paper (which it further clarified in early January 1974), supporting the idea of a "national authority" in part of Palestine.[37] Fateh then worked to establish the two-state idea as official PLO policy, resulting in the adoption of the national authority proposal by the PNC in June 1974 and the institutionalization of the partition concept at the 13th PNC in 1977.

It is of significance that by 1973–74 Fateh was the most powerful and best organized of all the resistance organizations. It had many thousand more men in its armed forces than the other groups; it dominated most of the mass organizations; and it dominated all three PLO political institutions.[38] It also had a solid alliance with Syrian-sponsored Saiqa and the Marxist DFLP (which owed its existence to Fateh's support for its split from the PFLP).[39] Fateh's control of the PLO political apparatus—the EC, the CC, and the PNC—made possible its imposition on the organization of policies it supported. Indeed, in the final analysis, whether policies were the result of the "conservative" world view of Fateh leaders,[40] the imperatives of the Arab state order, or were determined by other factors such as the Soviet position and the post-1967 U.S.-Israeli alliance, is less important than the fact that the organizational dominance of Fateh and its decision to pursue certain policies assured that those goals and tactics became official PLO policy.

It is possible to speculate that even had George Habash and the PFLP been in a position of institutional preeminence in 1973-74, the mandates of the Arab system (as well as the objective facts of Israel's military superiority, its sponsorship by the United States, and the tepid support offered the PLO by the Soviet Union) would have forced them, if not at that particular moment, then later, to adopt the two-state line. Indeed, the PFLP's acceptance of the two-state formulation at the 13th PNC in 1977 lends credence to the argument that PLO policies were more determined by environmental factors than by the personal politics of Fateh leaders. Of additional relevance in this regard is the DFLP's public advocacy of the national authority/two-state idea in 1973, before Fateh articulated it, and the DFLP's alliance with Fateh to secure the proposal's adoption at the 12th PNC and later at the 13th.

In any case, the wealthy, conservative Arab states "rewarded" Fateh leaders for their promotion of "acceptable" policies by making financial contributions to the PLO *through* Fateh, which allowed Fateh to increase its control over the mass organizations, recruit more fighters, and develop the civilian institutions in Lebanon (which Fateh dominated, and which in turn contributed to Fateh's organizational power).[41] Thus, in the post-1974 period Fateh's position in the PLO was strengthened simultaneously with the growing domestic (i.e. among Palestinian constituencies), regional, and international legitimacy of the PLO as the organizational embodiment of Palestinian nationalism. This convergence also enhanced Fateh's legitimacy and its dominant position; and, as a result, its ability to determine policy increased even further. Significantly, even during Fateh's weakest period, after the December 1983 departure from Tripoli and the PLO split, none of the other groups or alignments was able to establish a legitimate organizational alternative to the PLO, or to alter Fateh's status as the resistance group with the greatest mass support.[42] Moreover, when the dissident groups were reunited in April 1987, they came together under the PLO umbrella with Fateh still dominant and with the objective of a two-state settlement through diplomacy intact as policy.

The intention in the foregoing is not to suggest that the structure of the PLO determined the policy transformations the organization underwent. Given the variety of forces impinging on the Palestinian resistance including the interests of the Arab states, the dependence of the resistance on the Arab regimes in the absence of an independent territorial base (plus the Soviet factor and the U.S. role as discussed below), it seems likely that any Palestinian organization confronting the same set of circumstances would have made similar choices. The intention is rather to emphasize the magnitude of the policy transformations and to illustrate how the existing structure functioned to implement changes and to perpetuate the leadership of Fateh.

The Uniqueness of the Enemy and the Positions of the Great Powers

As important in altering and determining fundamental Palestinian objectives as the elements in the preceding discussion were factors uniquely related to Israel—the power occupying Palestine.

Israel's Position on Palestinian Nationalism

Israel, including the Labor Alignment and the Likud Party as well as the post-1984 "national unity government," has been clear and constant on its policy toward the Palestinians. Israel's position can be categorized as absolute rejectionism, expressed in three "nos": no recognition of the Palestinian right to self determination; no Palestinian state; and no negotiations with the PLO.

In 1969 Labor Prime Minister Golda Meir denied the existence of the Palestinian people, stating: "It was not as though there was a Palestinian people in Palestine considering itself as a Palestinian people and we came and threw them out and took their country away from them. They did not exist."[43] Israeli leaders portrayed the PLO objective of a democratic, secular state as implying the physical destruction of Israel and its people. There were no debates in Israel (or in the United States) on the merits of a democracy in Palestine in which all citizens would have equal rights versus the concept of a "Jewish state" in Arab Palestine. Moreover, when the PLO abandoned the idea of a secular democracy and proposed to accept an independent state alongside Israel, Israel categorically rejected that too and continued to refuse to participate in negotiations with the PLO. In 1975 Prime Minister Yitzhak Rabin explained why Israel would never negotiate "with any Palestinian element . . . [stating that to do so would provide] the basis for the possibility of creating a third state between Israel and Jordan," which Israel would never accept: "I repeat firmly, clearly, categorically: it will not be created," he declared.[44] In 1982 Rabin spoke in support of Menachem Begin's Likud government, again declaring that the PLO could never be a partner to any negotiations, "even if it accepts all of the conditions of negotiations on the basis of the Camp David agreements [including Resolutions 242 and 338], because the willingness to speak with the PLO is the willingness to speak about the establishment of a Palestinian state, which must be opposed."[45]

It should also be noted that it was the Labor Party that began the settlement and colonization of the West Bank—within four months after the 1967 war—though the Likud, which came to power in 1977, carried forward the program with considerable zeal. On the question of settlements and Palestinians, Raphael Eitan, Chief of Staff under Menachem Begin, told the Knesset's Foreign Affairs and Defense Committee in April 1983, that many more Jewish settlements had to be built on the West Bank: "When we have settled the land," Eitan declared, "all the Arabs will be able to do about it will be to scurry around like drugged roaches in a bottle."[46] Shimon Peres, leader of the Labor Party and prime minister in the first half of the national unity coalition, is more tactful than Begin and Eitan, but on the basic issues of self determination, a Palestinian state, and negotiations with the PLO, he and his Labor Party colleagues are just as rejectionist as the Likud leaders. Peres' 1986–87 advocacy of an "international conference" should not be misunderstood as evidencing any substantive change on these matters.[47]

It is also important to consider the basis for this Israeli rejectionism which, in spite of official Israeli pronouncements, has nothing to do with PLO "terrorism," Israeli security, or any of the other reasons usually cited. In fact, several prominent Israeli analysts such as General (res.) Mattityahu Peled, an architect of the June War and currently a Member of the Knesset, and Major General (res.) Yehoshafat Harkabi, former Chief of Israeli Military Intelligence and former head of Strategic Research for the Ministry of Defense, have argued that Israel's security would be best served by the establishment of a Palestinian state.[48] Ideological factors play a part in explaining certain aspects of Israel's position on the Palestinians, but in the view of this writer, Israeli rejectionism stems primarily from psychological imperatives, i.e., the fear that recognition of Palestinian rights in part of Palestine would delegitimize and weaken Israel's claim of the "right" to a Jewish state anywhere in Palestine. The psychological perspective affords some insight into the seemingly irrational fact that as the PLO increasingly moderated its objectives and tactics, Israel became increasingly rejectionist on the Palestinian issue. Israeli analyst Avner Yaniv explained Israel's reaction to the PLO's transformations:

> Given its rise to international political stardom [in 1973–75], a moderate—political rather than terrorist—PLO . . . could become far more dangerous than the violent PLO of the previous years. With such a moderate posture the PLO could be far more successful in making significant inroads into European and American public opinion, gradually changing government policy in these traditional strongholds of support for Israel . . . Hence, military action against the PLO could perhaps be employed not only for military ends but also for the purpose of weakening PLO moderates and strengthening their radical rivals. . . .
> . . . persistently and skillfully, he [Arafat] seemed to be inching his complex and divided organization toward an indirect acceptance of UN Resolution 242. By 1977 Arafat had . . . pushed the PLO toward acceptance, in a March 1977 meeting of the Palestine National Council (PNC), of the notion of a

Palestinian state "in the territories from which Israel withdraws." Another year or two of maneuvering, many Israeli policy makers feared, and Arafat would come close enough to an acceptance of UN Resolution 242 to convince the Carter administration that the time had come to deal with the PLO directly. If it ever came to that, Israel would either have to yield—which would mean the eventual establishment of a Palestinian state on the West Bank—or face a major breach with the United States. The former alternative was perceived as . . . unacceptable. . . .

. . . by 1977 the emphasis was shifting implicitly to the macro-political ramifications of the battle of South Lebanon. Exposing the PLO to the fiercest military pressures would not only limit its danger in the Galilee but also undermine the position of the moderates within its ranks. . . . In turn President Carter's maneuver to coopt the PLO into the search for peace in the Middle East would be foiled too. . . .

. . . [By 1981 Israel reasoned that] if the PLO were to "go political" and gradually renounce military action . . . it would increase the political menace (from the Israeli point of view) of a Palestinian state. To escape this trap without running the risk that a political settlement with the PLO would entail, Israel could do only one thing—go to war. [i.e., the rationale for the 1982 war in Lebanon][49]

The Soviet Union and Imperialism

That Zionism was a colonial-settler movement sponsored by British imperialism is a historic fact (though one that is often unstated or severely distorted).[50] That Israel is itself imperialist is also indisputable—having extended and imposed its power both by direct territorial acquisition (i.e., in 1948 seizing one-quarter more land than it was granted in the partition resolution; in 1967 occupying Egypt's Sinai, Syria's Golan Heights, and the remainder of historic Palestine; in the settlement and colonization program that was begun in the West Bank in September 1967 and continues unabated; in the 1967 "reunification" of Jerusalem and its 1980 "annexation" as well as the 1981 "annexation" of the Golan Heights; and in the 1982–85 occupation of South Lebanon) and through gaining indirect control over the political and economic life of other areas (e.g., the control over South Lebanon that was established after 1978 through Saad Haddad, and the attempt to dominate Lebanon through the imposition of the Phalange in 1982).[51]

Nevertheless, and in spite of its backing by the Western imperial powers, the Soviet Union has consistently supported Israel. The 1947 U.N. resolution calling for the partition of Palestine received a majority vote in the United Nations only because of the cooperation between the Soviet Union and the United States in securing its passage. Moreover, Moscow provided Zionist forces their heavy weapons in the fighting in 1947–49, granted the new state immediate *de jure* recognition, and consistently maintained its support for Israel's right to exist as a Zionist state within the pre-1967 boundaries. Even after Israel's massive territorial expansion in 1967 and its subsequent occupation of the land of neighboring Arab states, the Soviet Union (though it broke formal diplomatic relations following the 1967 war) continued to support Israel's integrity as an independent nation state.

Moscow backed Security Council Resolution 242; cooperated with U.S. Secretary of State William Rogers in "two-power" and "four-power" talks on the Middle East in 1969; jointly wrote and supported Security Council Resolution 338 after the October 1973 war; participated in the December 1973 Geneva Conference arranged by Kissinger; issued a "joint-statement" in 1977 on the Middle East with President Carter; and, moreover, made not a move to assist the PLO during the siege of Beirut in the summer of 1982, watching placidly as Israel, with the full support of the U.S., drove the PLO from Lebanon. Indeed, no other liberation movement in the international system has confronted a regime backed by both the Western powers *and* the Soviet Union.[52]

Since Israel enjoyed this unusual global power support, Fateh leaders initially looked to the Peoples' Republic of China for assistance. In 1964 Arafat and Wazir went to China under Algerian auspices. Between 1965 and 1969 China provided Fateh with arms estimated at approximately $5 million and Chinese leaders publicly supported the objective of liberating Palestine from "Zionism, imperialism, and 'Soviet revisionism.'"[53] Significantly, the Chinese strongly favored Fateh despite the absence of ideological affinity.[54] However, after the 1970 Black September crisis in Jordan, Chinese support for the resistance declined markedly.[55] In 1971 Henry Kissinger made his first visit to China as the United States sought to normalize relations with Peking, and in the same year the Chinese were reinstalled in their seat as a permanent member of the U.N. Security Council.[56] Once reestablished at the United Nations China never used the veto this seat afforded it to block resolutions opposed by the PLO.[57] Chinese support for the resistance increased somewhat beginning in late 1974 but the 1971–74 hiatus was a blow to the PLO, and as a result it was compelled to rely on Moscow. In turn, Soviet influence was a determining factor in the transformation of Fateh's (and the PLO's) objectives.

Fateh leaders initially met Soviet officials in Moscow under Egyptian auspices in 1968. In 1970 Arafat headed the first independent PLO delegation to the Soviet Union although the PLO did not receive Soviet arms until July 1972. Moscow's decision to supply the PLO with weapons appears to have been related to the move by Egyptian President Anwar Sadat to expel all the Soviet advisors from Egypt. The day following Sadat's announcement (on July 8, 1972), Moscow hosted a PLO delegation headed by Arafat during which the arms agreement was concluded. Shortly thereafter the PLO began receiving Soviet weapons, but via Syrian ports.[58] Moscow did not recognize the PLO as the sole, legitimate representative of Palestinians until 1978.[59]

From the outset of Soviet-Palestinian contacts, Moscow urged Fateh leaders as well as leaders from other resistance groups to consider a settlement based on two states as called for in the original partition resolution.[60] The Soviet Union never supported the liberation of Palestine nor did it support the concept of a democratic, secular state in Palestine. By May 1971 Moscow was applying explicit pressure both for a two-state objective and for a political settlement.[61] On October 29, 1973, the Soviet ambassador in Beirut handed urgent letters to Arafat, Habash, and Hawatmeh "recommending" to them the idea of pushing for a Palestinian state in the West Bank and Gaza.[62] With the Soviet position added to the pressure that was being exerted by the Arab states (and in the absence of Chinese support), the acceptance by the PNC in June 1974 of the two-state formula was probably inevitable.

The U.S.–Israeli Relationship

In addition to the Soviet factor, the PLO had to confront Israel's alliance with the United States in the context of America's preeminent position in the Middle East (and globally). Moreover, apart from its relationship with Israel, the United States was innately opposed to the Palestinian nationalist movement as it has been to all Third World revolutionary nationalisms.[63] For instance, Henry Kissinger worked tirelessly to keep the Palestinian question off the Middle East political agenda and to exclude the PLO from participation in the "peace process" he directed between 1973 and 1976. However, had it not been for the special U.S.-Israeli relationship, it seems likely that the PLO's transformation from a revolutionary nationalist movement to a conservative nationalist organization would have resulted in the PLO's recognition by the United States and its achievement of the re-defined, limited goals.[64]

While support for a movement/state such as Zionism/Israel by an imperialist power is certainly not unusual, the magnitude of U.S. support for Israel in the post-1967 period is unique. After the June War Washington provided Israel *unqualified* diplomatic, military, and economic backing. Given the strength of the U.S.-Israeli alliance and the impact of U.S.-Israeli rejectionism on Palestinian nationalism, it is important to consider the nature of the U.S.-Israeli relationship.

Washington's special partnership with Israel is based on beliefs about Israel's strategic utility to American interests in the Middle East. The concept of Israel as a "strategic asset" is predicated on the idea that Israel promotes American interests by: acting as a counter to Arab nationalist movements; fostering and exacerbating the divisions and weaknesses in the Arab world; stabilizing the region through its absolute military superiority; containing the spread of Soviet expansionism; and ensuring the survival of pro-American Arab regimes. There is considerable room for debate concerning how effectively Israel contributes to the realization of these objectives;[65] nevertheless, the actual extent to which Israel fulfills the strategic role it has been assigned is less significant than the *perceptions* held by American policymakers about its usefulness as a surrogate, and the fact that such perceptions became institutionalized as objectively existing reality in American political culture.

The main factors that contributed to the institutionalization of the beliefs about Israel's strategic efficacy include: (1) Israel's stunning military performance in the June 1967 war, defeating three major Arab states in six days; (2) the 1969 Nixon Doctrine, postulating the reliance on certain states in crucial areas acting as substitutes for direct U.S. intervention in the defense of American interests; (3) Israel's mobilization (at the request of Henry Kissinger) for possible intervention on the side of Jordan in the September 1970 crisis between King Hussein and the Palestinians. (It should be noted here, though, that Israel performed no function other than the mobilization at that time. Jordan, by itself, crushed the Palestinians and repulsed a Syrian tank force. Nevertheless, the mobilization alone has been used as the primary legitimation for the argument that Israel is protecting pro-American Arab regimes.)

A fourth factor involves the intensity with which Henry Kissinger was committed to the strategic asset/surrogate power concept, and includes the contributions he made to its legitimation in American political culture as well as to the concretization of the idea through massive transfers of military and economic assistance to Israel. Kissinger, of course, was the most influential individual in the foreign policy-making elite for eight critical years from 1968 to 1976. (5) Pro-Israeli forces in American society—which themselves became far stronger and more important in the post-1967 period—contributed time, money, passion, organizational and other skills to reinforcing the strategic asset thesis.[66] (6) A subtle transformation in the nature of policy-making on Middle Eastern issues in which Congress came to play an increasingly important role plus the ability of pro-Israeli forces to interface with the electoral process, and thus to strongly influence Congress, also contributed.[67] And, (7) ideological factors, including beliefs about Israel's role in the cold war anti-Communist consensus that dominates American foreign policy, played a critical part in the institutionalization of the strategic asset perception. During the Reagan Administration, Israel's contribution to the "anti-terrorist" dimension of the American ideological construct was particularly significant.

As important as any of these elements, independently or collectively, is the fact that the idea of Israel as a strategic asset to U.S. interests was repeated so often, by so many sources, and the legitimations were so manifold, that the process of institutionalization was extremely rapid.[68]

The major "source" for "knowledge" about foreign affairs in American society is official Washington. Journalists—and the media in general—typically take their cues from the government. Scholars and the intelligentsia also usually maintain an uncritical posture about foreign policy, contributing little more than restatements of official positions.[69] Thus, the primary sources of "knowledge" about Israel's strategic utility were government officials such as Henry Kissinger, Alexander Haig, Henry Jackson (former Democratic Senator from Washington), and several others who reiterated the concept with great frequency. Then, reflecting the opinions of such officials, a secondary source of "knowledge" was the media, popular commentators, and scholars who widely repeated the idea. For instance, op-eds in the *New York Times*, the *Washington Post*, and elsewhere endlessly discussed Israel's alleged strategic value. The pro-Israeli lobby was also a source of "knowledge" about Israel, continuously producing documents and studies on Israel's supposed surrogate utility. Eventually the "knowledge" about Israel's strategic importance to the United States became part of the paramount reality, or the reality of everyday life, for the majority of Americans dealing with the Middle East. In other words, Israel's role came to be taken for granted as objectively existing reality.

The "legitimations" that served to institutionalize the strategic asset thesis were numerous and complex. They ranged from "self-evident truths" to "theoretical propositions" and sophisticated "theories," and within a re-markably short time the concept became integrated into the symbolic universe that sustains U.S. foreign policy. One important level of legitimation is language—itself a subjective formation of human activity. Linguistic typifications such as America's "moral commitment" to Israel's "survival"; the only "democracy" in the Middle East (indeed, not just a democratic state, but "a light unto nations"); America's sole "reliable ally" in the region; the "restoration" of the "chosen people" to the "promised land"; courageous "pioneers" that made "the desert bloom"; Israel's "Western" orientation as well as its "strategic utility" and others were so habitually repeated, externalized, objectified, and finally internalized in the collective American social psyche that what began as an opinion about one possible policy for maximizing American interests in the Middle East, was transformed into an unquestionable pillar of the social order.

The importance and intricacy of the various types of legitimations in the process of institutionalizing Israel's strategic role are apparent in but one example: the United States never merely "supported Israel," or engaged in "relations" with it, as Washington does with other states; rather, the United States undertook a "moral commitment" to Israel's "right to exist" and to its "security and survival" (despite the fact that in reality the security and survival of Israel were *never* in danger[70]). The concepts of "moral commitment" and the "right to exist" involve subtle propositions about America's "obligations" to the survivors of the Holocaust and the alleged relationship between that event and modern political Zionism. In addition, despite Israel's spectacular military performance in June 1967, the "self-evident truth" of an embattled, mortally threatened state was sustained, and despite the contradiction between a beleaguered underdog and the concept of a surrogate power, this image, combined with the propositions just suggested, contributed powerfully to the legitimation and institutionalization of the U.S.-Israeli strategic relationship.

With the process of institutionalization came new explanations and justifications, e.g., elaborate portrayals of Israel's alleged role in the global fight against Communism, and later, its status as the leading eradicator of "international terrorism." In addition, mechanisms of control were necessary to insure that the institutional definition of situations was maintained. Those who questioned the strategic asset thesis were labeled "anti-Semitic," "pro-PLO" (in a context wherein "PLO" had already been delegitimated), com-munist sympathizers, fellow-travelers, and so on. This resulted in considerable "spontaneous" self-censorship. In addition, deviant ideas were ignored or systematically delegitimized: discussions about Palestinian rights or the legitimacy of the Palestinian quest for self-determination were virtually unheard of in the media, scholarship, or other establishment venues in the United States. Moreover, the very existence of the institution was a controlling mechanism in that by setting up pre-defined patterns of behavior that were channelled in one direction, i.e., U.S.-Israeli strategic co-operation, other possible avenues of policy or conduct were excluded. Thus, U.S. recognition of the PLO or its acknowledgement of or support for any Palestinian goal became virtually impossible. Eventually, sophisticated "scholarly" theoretical legitimations (such as Nadav Safran's *Israel the Embattled Ally*[71]) appeared which further institutionalized the idea. The result was that within a few short years an entire institutional history was created, an idea was objectified, and the institution—Israel as a strategic asset—was internalized within major sectors of the policy making elite and informed Middle East observers.

As a consequence, subsequent to the completion of the institutionalization process, it was no longer possible for the United States to pursue policies that Israel strenuously opposed, and denying Palestinian nationalism is, as discussed above, a fundamental Israeli objective. Moreover, since institutions possess an inherent inertia and claims to legitimacy based on historicity as well as involving controlling mechanisms, and since in the case of Israel, additional claims of morality, commitment, etc., reinforced institutional legitimacy, for the United States to have recognized the PLO or the Palestinian right to self-determination would have involved the much more complex process of deinstitutionalization. But because of the nature of institutions in general *and* because of the domestic component of this particular institution, such a process would have been extremely difficult. In other words, the institutionalization of the strategic asset concept *and* the fact that pro-Israeli forces in the domestic political system were able to interface with the electoral process together inhibited U.S. decision-makers from pursuing policies that supported Palestinian interests.

It is also true that Israel enjoys a position of special regard in the minds of many Americans as a result of the Holocaust and the guilt and obligation associated with that event as well as for centuries of Christian anti-Semitism. Zionists successfully constructed a linkage between the persecution of Jews in Europe and the creation of a Jewish state in Palestine which greatly contributed to the support for Israel in the United States. In addition, the Judeo-Christian religious tradition inclined a number of Americans to a favorable disposition toward Israel since they saw in the establishment of the state the fulfillment of biblical prophecy. And, finally, the Western cultural orientation of Israel's *Ashkenazi* elite predisposed many Americans to sympathize with Israelis against Palestinians who were perceived as culturally dissimilar as well as religiously infidel. The net effect of all these circumstances was the full weight of the United States marshalled against the Palestine national movement—even after its complete transformation.

The PLO, however, did not understand the nature of Israel's institutional position and special status within the United States. PLO leaders believed that if the organization became sufficiently "moderate," the United States would recognize it and support the Palestinian right to self-determination in the reduced territorial parameters of the West Bank and Gaza. In turn, they expected the United States to exert pressure on Israel to accept an accommodation with the PLO. This misperception also contributed to the transformations in the PLO's objectives and tactics. In fairness to the PLO, it must be noted that the United States occasionally sent "mixed" signals about its position. For instance, President Carter chose March 15, 1977, a time when the 13th PNC was in mid-session, to make his first public pronouncement about the Palestine issue. At a town meeting in Clinton, Mass., Carter spoke of the necessity to secure a "homeland" for Palestinians. It was the first time any American president had addressed the Palestine issue and undoubtedly the delegates at the PNC considered both the timing and the substance of the statement significant.

Conclusion

In 1987, twenty years after Israel completed its occupation of historic Palestine, the PLO retained a remarkable structural continuity including the continuity of its leadership. However, it had undergone substantive transformations of enormous magnitude. In 1967 Fateh was a guerrilla group fighting for the liberation of its homeland. In 1987 Fateh directed a complex political organization that engaged in international diplomacy in a manner similar to established territorial states—though without sufficient military force or other power capabilities to induce its Zionist adversaries to participate in a negotiated settlement. The transformations in the PLO were the result of a combination of unique historical and environmental factors including the absence of a Palestinian territorial base and the consequent dependence of the resistance on Arab regimes; the fragmented, dependent, state-centric nature of the Arab state system; the Soviet Union's position on Israel; and the institutionalized role Israel enjoys in American political culture both as a "strategic asset" to U.S. interests and as restitution for 2,000 years of Christian persecution.

Yet, in spite of the enormity of the transformation in the PLO from a revolutionary national liberation movement to a political organization that proposed a settlement based on securing a state in a fraction of its native homeland, the Palestinian condition did not improve. Indeed, in the twenty years after the 1967 war it worsened considerably. Palestinians remained stateless, homeless, dispersed, repressed, and with no visible prospect of achieving even their most minimal objectives. The Palestinian situation is surely one of the greatest anomalies—and tragedies—of contemporary international politics.

Notes

1. The PLO was originally a creation of the Arab states. At an Arab summit conference in 1964, the Arab regimes, responding to Egyptian President Gamal

Abdul Nasser's leadership, established the mandate for a separate Palestinian organization. Ahmed Shuqairy organized the group which held its founding conference
in May 1964. Some 422 individuals from various parts of the Palestinian diaspora
met in East Jerusalem (then under Jordanian occupation) and wrote the Palestinian
National Charter as well as the Basic Constitution (which set out the PLO's political
structure). However, the PLO was under the control of Egypt, and functioned
entirely as a political organization in inter-Arab politics to serve Egyptian national
interests. Its military wing, which consisted of three Palestinian contingents under
the control of Arab countries, had no independence and was not involved in guerrilla
activities. Shuqairy headed the organization until 1969 when (after a brief period
of leadership by Yahya Hammouda) at the fifth PNC, Fateh emerged as the dominant
party in the PLO. With the ascension of Fateh, the PLO became an independent
organization—that is, independent of Egyptian control or of the control by any
single Arab state. For good general introductions to the PLO see William B. Quandt,
Faud Jabber, and Ann Mosely Lesch, *The Politics of Palestinian Resistance* (Berkeley,
University of California Press, 1973); Paul A. Jureidini and William E. Hazen, *The
Palestinian Movement in Politics* (Lexington, MA: D.C. Heath, 1976); Helena Cobban,
The Palestine Liberation Organization: People, Power and Politics (New York: Cambridge
University Press, 1984); and Abdallah Frangi, *The PLO and Palestine* (London: Zed
Press, 1983).

    2. For a variety of reasons Fateh has been by far the most popular group among
the Palestinian masses. The DFLP and the PFLP also have mass bases of support
but neither have the extensive popular backing that Fateh does. The other five
groups have little or no mass support being essentially creations of Arab governments.
The only exception is the Palestine Communist Party which, as noted, originated
in the West Bank as a mass organization. Still, compared to Fateh, the PFLP, and
the DFLP, its mass base is relatively small, though among trade unionists in the
West Bank it enjoys wide support.

    3. Fateh eschewed pan-Arabism and instead took the position that since its task
was the liberation of Palestine, it could not wait for the unity of the Arab world.
In part this stand was related to the Fateh leaders' conviction that if they were to
survive in the Arab world and receive support from such countries as Kuwait, Saudi
Arabia, and Syria they could not pursue or advocate policies that were threatening
to the established regimes. They also understood quite clearly that the Arab regimes,
even such allegedly progressive ones as Nasser's, were not going to risk their national
interests in order to liberate Palestine. In addition, the Fateh leaders shared a number
of characteristics that seem to have shaped their world view including the following:
they were all Sunni Muslims and most, including Arafat, had close ties with the
Moslem Brotherhood in Egypt; they came from middle class or better families (with
the possible exception of Wazir); they were educated and lived in Egypt for an
important period in the early 1950s (with the exception of the Hassan brothers);
they spent their early years as professionals in Kuwait and Saudi Arabia as well as
other places in the Arabian peninsula. For a detailed portrait of these individuals
see John W. Amos II, *Palestine Resistance: Organization of a National Movement*
(New York: Pergamon Press, 1980), pp. 43–67.

    Fateh leaders were influenced by the Algerian revolution and initially believed
that armed struggle was the only means to achieve their objective of liberating
Palestine. Indeed, at the outset they seem not to have considered any other possible
tactics beside armed struggle. However, later they abandoned armed struggle without
a coherent program for achieving their goals. To some extent their lack of a formal
ideology contributed to this. However, so did the nature of the PLO as an organization

as well as a number of external environmental factors that strongly impinged on the PLO and constrained its ability to develop policies independently. Fateh's mass organization is its General Conference (or General Congress) which is supposed to be the ultimate decision-making body but there have only been five General Conferences/Congresses (1959, 1965, 1968, 1971, and 1980). Thus the institution remains only theoretically powerful. *De facto* power is in the hands of the Central Committee. (There is also an intermediate body, the Revolutionary Council.) To understand Fateh's power it is necessary to examine the workings of Fateh's Central Committee (not to be confused with the PLO's Central Council). It is also useful to analyze the debate within Fateh and the various positions of Fateh leaders over time.

4. Seats at PNC meetings are distributed among resistance groups, mass organizations (e.g., the General Union of Palestinian Students, the General Union of Palestinian Workers, the General Union of Palestinian Writers, the General Union of Palestinian Women), Palestinian communities in the diaspora (e.g., the United States, Kuwait, etc.), independents, prominent Palestinian personalities, and others. Individuals who are not formally identified with one of the resistance groups are usually nevertheless affiliated with one in some way ("independents" are typically pro-Fateh).

5. For further analysis of PLO political institutions see Cheryl A. Rubenberg, *The Palestine Liberation Organization: Its Institutional Infrastructure* (Belmont, MA: Institute for Arab Studies, 1983)—available from the Association of Arab-American University Graduates, Belmont, MA. Also see Cobban, *The Palestine Liberation Organization*, pp. 3–18.

6. On Fateh's early objectives see Cobban, *The Palestine Liberation Organization*, p. 16; Amos, *Palestinian Resistance*, p. 56.

7. On the "democratic secular state" concept, see Cobban, *The Palestine Liberation Organization*, p. 16; Abu Iyad (Salah Khalaf) with Eric Rouleau, *My Home, My Land* (New York: Times Books, 1981), pp. 65 and 139; and Alain Gresh, *The PLO Struggle Within: Toward an Independent Palestinian State* (London: Zed Press, 1983),particularly pp. 17–18 and pp. 9–57 in general. There is far too little appreciation of this concept in the U.S., especially in how progressive and innovative it was.

8. On the 12th PNC and the "national authority" concept see Gresh, *The PLO: The Struggle Within*, pp. 129–175; Cobban, *The Palestine Liberation Organization*, p. 17; and Amos, *Palestine Resistance*, p. 320 for the text of the ten-point program reprinted from *al-Nahar*, June 3, 1974.

9. See Gresh, *The PLO: The Struggle Within*, p. 168 and passim.

10. Henry Kissinger, *Years of Upheaval* (Boston: Little Brown, 1982), p. 503.

11. On the significance of the 1977 PNC and the clear formulation of the "two-state" solution see Gresh, *The PLO: The Struggle Within*, pp. 177–210.

12. Cobban, *The Palestine Liberation Organization*, p. 96.

13. For a discussion of Israel's attempts to provoke the PLO to break the cease-fire agreement see Avner Yaniv, *Dilemmas of Security: Politics, Strategy, and the Israeli Experience in Lebanon* (New York: Oxford University Press, 1987), pp. 107–110.

14. In the context of the split within the PLO an attempt was made to reform the structure of the PLO and to introduce a system of checks and balances to govern the functioning of the political institutions. In March 1984 a coalition known as the Democratic Alliance (made up of the PFLP, the DFLP, the PLF, and the Palestine Communist Party) met in Aden, South Yemen, and produced a "working paper" that advocated a system of collective leadership including a redistribution of the balance of power among the resistance groups within the EC and greater

power for the Central Council. In response to the Democratic Alliance's proposals, Fateh's Central Committee submitted a plan of its own for "reform" and for PLO reconciliation. After lengthy meetings an accord was signed on June 27, 1984 known as the "Aden-Algiers Agreement." It contained a number of proposals designed to democratize the PLO, including the limiting of Arafat's power and authority, a collective chairmanship, a general secretariat for the EC, and so on. See "Aden-Algiers Agreement between Fateh Central Committee and the Palestinian Democratic Alliance, Aden, June 27, 1984," excerpts, *Journal of Palestine Studies*, Vol. 14, no. 1 (Fall 1984), pp. 200-04. However, within weeks of the signing the agreement began to come apart and as a result the Democratic Alliance called for a postponement of the PNC. Arafat then seized the opportunity to reassert Fateh's dominance and convened the PNC without the participation of the Democratic Alliance (members of the National Alliance and the Fateh "dissidents" did not participate either). See note 42 of this chapter. For one (though flawed) analysis of this period see Emile F. Sahliyeh, *The PLO After the Lebanon War* (Boulder, CO: Westview Press, 1986), pp. 189-202.

15. For a text of the Jordanian-PLO accord (released February 23, 1985) see *Journal of Palestine Studies*, Vol. 14, no. 3 (Spring 1985), p. 206. For an excellent analysis of Jordanian-PLO relations historically see Naseer Aruri, "The PLO and the Jordanian Option," *MERIP Reports*, no. 131 (April 1984), pp. 3-9. (Several other articles in this issue are also relevant.)

16. For a text of Hussein's speech on the abrogation of the Jordanian-PLO accord see the *Journal of Palestine Studies*, Vol. 15, no. 4 (Summer 1986), pp. 206-32.

17. For the text of Arafat's statement see "Cairo Declaration on the PLO and Terrorism as read by Chairman Yasser Arafat, Cairo, 7 November 1985," *Journal of Palestine Studies*, Vol. 15, no. 2 (Winter 1986), pp. 214-16.

18. See "Resolutions of the Political Committee of the Eighteenth Session of the PNC, Algiers, 26 April 1987"; "Final Statement of the Eighteenth Session of the PNC, Algiers, 26 April 1987" in *Journal of Palestine Studies*, Vol. 16, no. 4 (Summer 1987), pp. 195-204. For an analysis of the 18th PNC see *Middle East International*, no. 299 (May 1, 1987), pp. 3-5 and Naseer Aruri, "Can the PLO Now Seize Its Opportunities," *Middle East International*, no. 301, (May 29, 1987), pp. 12-13. Also see Naseer Aruri, "Interview," *Al Fajr* (Jerusalem), August 30, 1987 for his analysis, which disagrees in fundamental ways with the analysis in this paper, of past opportunities missed by the PLO and what he considers future opportunities to be. For an analysis of the issue of an international conference (and General Assembly Resolution 38/58 which sets out the framework for such a conference) see Cheryl A. Rubenberg, "U.S. Policy Toward the Palestinians: A Twenty Year Assessment," *Arab Studies Quarterly*, Vol. 10, no. 1 (Winter 1988).

19. See "Cancellation of the Amman Agreement, Algiers, 19 April 1987," *Journal of Palestine Studies*, Vol. 16, no. 4 (Summer 1987), pp. 195-96.

20. India, of course, stands out as an exception to this generalization, since it won its independence from Britain based on a strategy of non-violent resistance. But the Palestinian situation is unique both because of the lack of a coherent strategy and tactics and because the political situation consistently and explicitly excluded the possibility for the PLO to realize any of its fundamental objectives through diplomacy regardless of how much it altered the objectives or made changes in its strategy and tactics.

21. For an excellent analysis of Palestinian nationalism before the creation of Israel see Ann Mosely Lesch, *Arab Politics in Palestine 1917-1939: The Frustration of a Nationalist Movement* (Ithaca: Cornell University Press, 1979). Also see Yehoshua

Porath, *The Emergence of the Palestinian Arab National Movement, 1918–29* (London: Frank Cass, 1974) and Yehoshua Porath, *The Palestinian Arab National Movement: From Riots to Rebellion, 1929–1939* (London: Frank Cass, 1977).

22. For an analysis of Israel as a colonial-settler state see the French-Jewish writer Maxime Rodinson, *Israel: A Colonial-Settler State?* (New York, Monad Press, 1973). Also see Ibrahim Abu-Lughod, ed., *The Transformation of Palestine: Essays on the Origin and Development of the Arab-Israeli Conflict* (Evanston, Ill: Northwestern University Press, 1971).

23. For works by Israeli Jewish writers describing the Zionist policy of driving Palestinians out of Palestine in order to have an exclusive Jewish state see Tom Segev, *1949: The First Israelis* (New York: The Free Press, 1986); Benny Morris, "The Causes and Character of the Arab Exodus from Palestine: The Israeli Defense Forces Intelligence Branch Analysis of June 1948," *Middle Eastern Studies*, (London, January 1986); Benny Morris, "Operation Dani and the Palestinian Exodus from Lydda and Ramle in 1948," *The Middle East Journal*, Vol. 40, no. 1 (Winter 1986), pp. 82–109; Benny Morris, "The Harvest of 1948 and the Creation of the Palestine Refugee Problem," *The Middle East Journal*, Vol. 40, no. 4 (Autumn, 1986), pp. 671–85; Simha Flapan, *The Birth of Israel: Myths and Realities* (New York: Pantheon Books, 1987); Shabtai Teveth, *Ben-Gurion and the Palestinian Arabs: From Peace to War* (New York: Oxford University Press, 1985); and Menachem Begin, *The Revolt* (London: W. H. Allen, 1951). Much of the relevant material was expunged from the revised edition Begin published in 1977 with Nash Publishing Co. in New York. For several important works by Palestinians who express what it meant to be dispossessed, transformed into refugees, and consigned to exile as a result of the creation of Israel see: Iyad, *My Home, My Land*; Nafez Nazzal, *The Palestinian Exodus from Galilee, 1948* (Beirut: Institute for Palestine Studies, 1978); Fawaz Turki, *The Disinherited: Journal of a Palestinian Exile: With an Epilogue 1974* (New York: Monthly Review Press, 1974); Sami Hadawi, *Bitter Harvest: Palestine 1914–1979* (New York: The Caravan Books, 1979); Mohammad Tarbush, *Reflections of a Palestinian* (Washington D.C.: American-Arab Affairs Council, 1986); Rosemary Sayigh, *Palestinians: From Peasants to Revolutionaries* (London: Zed Press, 1979); Leila Khaled, *My People Shall Live: The Autobiography of a Revolutionary* (London: Hodder and Stoughton, 1973). For analyses of the meaning of a "Jewish state" in Palestine see the Israeli Jewish scholar Uri Davis's *Israel: An Apartheid State* (London: Zed Books, 1987). Also see: Sabri Jiryis, *The Arabs in Israel* (New York: Monthly Review Press, 1976); Elia T. Zureik, *The Palestinians in Israel: A Study in Internal Colonialism* (London: Routledge & Keegan Paul, 1979); and Ian Lustick, *Arabs in the Jewish State: Israel's Control of a National Minority* (Austin: University of Texas Press, 1980).

24. For the texts of the armistice agreements see John Norton Moore, editor, *The Arab-Israeli Conflict III: Documents*, American Society of International Law, (Princeton, New Jersey: Princeton University Press), pp. 380–414. For an analysis of the armistice agreements see Fred J. Khouri, *The Arab-Israeli Dilemma* (Syracuse: Syracuse University Press, 1985), pp. 68–101.

25. Zionist leaders and Emir Abdullah of Transjordan conspired to divide western Palestine between them and prevent the establishment of the independent Palestinian state that was stipulated in U.N. Res. 181, the November 1947 resolution that partitioned Palestine and legitimized the existence of Israel. See Segev, *1949*, p. 14; Yaniv, *Dilemmas of Security*, p. 68; and Michael J. Cohen, *Palestine and the Great Powers 1945–1948* (Princeton, New Jersey: Princeton University Press, 1982), pp. 313, 318, 320–23, 325–35, and 374.

26. Cobban, *The Palestine Liberation Organization*, pp. 165–67 raises the question of why Fateh "elected" to allow all the resistance groups into the PLO structure as *organizations*, rather than simply dominating the organization by itself. She presents a comment from Khaled Hassan who says he opposed that idea from the outset. I would dispute her inference (and Hassan's) that there was any real choice involved.

27. The major instances of groups splitting from the PLO include the 1974–77 "Rejection Front"; the 1983 Fateh "dissident" movement; the post-1982 "Democratic Alliance" and the "National Alliance"; the short-lived "Palestinian National Salvation Front"; and even Fateh's 1985–86 "marriage" to Hussein. For analyses of the 1974–77 "Rejection Front" see Gresh, *The PLO: The Struggle Within*, pp. 184–87 and Cobban, *The Palestine Liberation Organization*, pp. 149–152. For an analysis of the post-1982 splits in the PLO see "The PLO Split," *MERIP Reports*, no. 119, (November-December 1983). The issue contains pieces by Eqbal Ahmad, Rashid Khalidi, Helena Cobban, and others and is devoted entirely to this question. Also see Sahliyeh, *The PLO After the Lebanon War*, who presents much solid factual information though his judgments and analysis are sometimes incorrect.

28. For an analysis of Arab state treachery and duplicity *vis-à-vis* the Palestine national movement see Cheryl A.Rubenberg, "Conflict and Contradiction in the Relations between the Arab States and the Palestine National Movement," in *Palestine: Continuing Dispossession*, Glenn Perry, ed. (Belmont, MA: Association of Arab-American University Graduates, 1986), pp. 121–45.

29. For a good analysis of the Lebanese situation and the relationship between the PLO and Lebanon see P. Edward Haley and Lewis W. Snider, eds., *Lebanon in Crisis: Participants and Issues* (Syracuse, New York: Syracuse University Press, 1979), passim but especially John K. Cooley, "The Palestinians," pp. 21–54.

30. This is not to say that the resistance had no power capabilities of its own in dealing with the Arab regimes. It did; for instance, the existence of large Palestinian communities living within the Arab states, the strength of mass sentiment throughout the Arab world in support of the cause of Palestine, and the opportunity, which Fateh leaders skillfully mastered, of playing one Arab government off against another. Still, the Arab states retained ultimate power because of the absence of a Palestinian territorial base.

31. For an excellent analysis of the shift in the locus of power to the conservative regimes led by Saudi Arabia resulting from the massive new oil wealth generated in the post-1973 period, see Abbas Alnasrawi, "The Arab Economies: Twenty Years of Change and Dependency," *Arab Studies Quarterly*, Vol. 9, no. 4 (Fall 1987).

32. The new order was evident as early as the 1967 Khartoum Arab summit conference which called for "unified efforts at international and diplomatic levels to . . . assure the withdrawal of the aggressive forces . . . from Arab lands." This resolution (despite the better known—in the West—call of the conference for "no recognition, no negotiation, no peace") sought a political solution and implied recognition of Israel within the pre-1967 borders. And, indeed, the diplomacy of the Arab states in the following years gave clear indication of their willingness to accept Israel, at least *de facto* if not formally, within the pre-1967 boundaries. On the meaning of the Khartoum Conference see Khouri, *The Arab-Israeli Dilemma*, p. 313. Also see Mahmoud Riad, *The Struggle for Peace in the Middle East* (New York: Quartet Books, 1981), pp. 71–80. In addition, Rubenberg, *Israel and the American National Interest: A Critical Examination* (Champaign: University of Illinois Press, 1986), passim illustrates the willingness of the Arab world to accept the existence of Israel in the aftermath of 1967.

33. See the analysis in Fouad Ajami, *The Arab Predicament: Arab Political Thought and Practice Since 1967* (New York: Cambridge University Press, 1981), passim.

34. Ibid., p. 9.

35. The idea of the PLO as the "sole, legitimate representative" of the Palestinians had been proposed at an Arab summit conference a year earlier (in Algiers) but (primarily because of Jordanian opposition) the proposal did not receive unanimous support and therefore was not made "public" until its unanimous adoption at Rabat in 1974. Nevertheless, the PLO knew full well of the debate at Algiers, and the prospect of receiving such a "blessing" from the Arab states hung over Palestinian politics during the ensuing year.

36. While this discussion emphasizes Fateh's dominance of the PLO, the reader should bear in mind that there was a significant amount of democracy in the PLO—more, certainly, than in any Arab state, and more, probably, than in any other liberation movement. The existence of the various factions that had either popular Palestinian constituencies, or Arab government backing, or both, and possessed armed militias, meant, by definition, that Fateh could not just impose its will on the PLO. Thus there has been within Palestinian politics a dialectic between centralism and the diffusion of power, between democracy and authoritarianism, between hierarchical vs horizontal authority, and so on. The interested reader should look at Gresh, The PLO: the Struggle Within, passim, which gives a very vivid picture of the democratic processes within the PLO. Also see Cobban, The Palestine Liberation Organization, passim; Rashid Khalidi, Under Siege: P.L.O. Decisionmaking During the 1982 War (New York: Columbia University Press, 1986); and Aaron David Miller, The PLO and the Politics of Survival, (Washington, D.C.: The Center for Strategic and International Studies, Georgetown University, and New York: Praeger Special Studies, 1983), pp. 40–64.

37. Gresh, The PLO: The Struggle Within, pp. 141–46, which includes a text of the November statement and an analysis of Fateh's position.

38. Formally Fateh maintained a rough parity or a minority position in some institutions but, as noted above, individuals identified as "independents" were typically Fateh supporters, and at least de facto, Fateh controlled each institution.

39. See Cobban, The Palestine Liberation Organization, pp. 152–53.

40. To speak of the Fateh leadership as having a "conservative" world view is actually misleading since within Fateh one finds individuals with a range of political perspectives including respectable "left" positions.

41. The PLO developed a highly sophisticated set of civilian institutions in the camps in Lebanon, including a complex health care system with hospitals and clinics, a factory system, schools, cultural and artistic organizations, a research center, and much more. See Rubenberg, The Palestine Liberation Organization.

42. The post-1982 splits in the PLO included the Democratic Alliance (i.e., PFLP, DFLP, PLF, Palestine Communist Party), the National Alliance (i.e., Fateh dissidents, Saiqa, PFLP-GC, PPSF), and the subsequent Palestine National Salvation Front (in which all the above participated except the DFLP and the Palestine Communist Party). Also see note 14, above.

43. Meir's famous quotation appeared in the Sunday Times (London), June 15, 1969 and is quoted in Noam Chomsky, Fateful Triangle: The United States, Israel and the Palestinians (Boston: South End Press, 1983), p. 51.

44. Quoted by Amnon Kapeliouk in Le Monde Diplomatique, August 1982, from Ma'ariv, December 5, 1975, cited in Chomsky, Fateful Triangle, p. 70.

45. Davar, November 11, 1982, interview in Trialogue (journal of the Trilateral Commission), Winter 1983, cited in Chomsky, Fateful Triangle, p. 112.

46. David K. Shipler, Arab and Jew: Wounded Spirits in a Promised Land (New York: Times Books, 1986), p. 235.

47. For an analysis of the "international conference" issue see Rubenberg, "U.S. Policy Toward the Palestinians."

48. Peled's views are widely known and available in many sources. See for example American Friends Service Committee, *A Compassionate Peace: A Future for the Middle East* (New York: Hill and Wang, 1982) and Chomsky, *The Fateful Triangle*. In addition, see Yehoshafat Harkabi, *The Fateful Choices Before Israel*, Essays on Strategy and Diplomacy, Number Seven, The Keck Center for International Strategic Studies (Claremont, CA.: College Press, 1987).

49. Yaniv, *Dilemmas of Security*, pp. 52, 53, 67, 68, 90. However, Yaniv disingenuously attributes Israel's unwillingness to deal with the PLO as being based on security concerns.

50. Rodinson's *Israel: A Colonial-Settler State* is relevant here. On the British and Palestine see Walid Khalidi, editor, *From Haven to Conquest: Readings in Zionism and the Palestine Problem Until 1948* (Beirut: Institute of Palestine Studies, 1971), especially Part II, "The British Shield 1920-1939," pp. 227-480. For another view see W. Roger Louis, "British Imperialism and the End of the Palestine Mandate," in W. Roger Louis and Robert W. Stookey, editors, *The End of the Palestine Mandate*, (London: I.B. Tauris & Co., Ltd., 1986), pp. 1-31.

51. The imposition of the Phalange Party (the party of the Gemayel clan) as the dominate power in Lebanon was one of the reasons for the 1982 Israeli invasion of Lebanon. (Of course, destroying the PLO infrastructure and driving the PLO from Lebanon as a means of weakening Palestinian nationalism in order to facilitate the extension of Israeli sovereignty over the West Bank was the most important reason for the invasion.) On Israel's objectives in Lebanon see Ze'ev Schiff and Ehud Ya'ari, *Israel's Lebanon War* (New York: Simon and Schuster, 1984); Jacobo Timmerman, *The Longest War: Israel in Lebanon* (New York: Vintage Books, 1982); Jonathan C. Randal, *Going All the Way: Christian Warlords, Israeli Adventurers, and the War in Lebanon* (New York: The Viking Press, 1983); and Rubenberg, *Israel and the American National Interest*, pp. 254-328. Israel had a long interest in establishing exclusive Christian dominance in Lebanon and as far back as 1948 made financial contributions to the Phalange. In 1954 David Ben-Gurion (in temporary retirement from the prime ministership) and Moshe Dayan discussed the appropriateness of then "bringing about" a Maronite state in Lebanon using every means available. On this point see: Livia Rokach, *Israel's Sacred Terrorism: A Study Based on Moshe Sharett's Personal Diaries and Other Documents*, second edition (Belmont, MA.: Association of Arab-American University Graduates, 1980).

52. For an analysis of Soviet-PLO relations see Galia Golan, *The Soviet Union and the Palestine Liberation Organization* (New York: Praeger, 1980) and Galia Golan, "The Soviet Union and the PLO since the War in Lebanon," *The Middle East Journal*, Vol. 40, no. 2 (Spring 1986), pp. 285-305. Also see Oles M. Smolansky, "The Soviet Role in the Emergence of Israel," in Louis and Stookey, *The End of the Palestine Mandate*, pp. 61-78.

53. See Lillian Craig Harris, "China's Relations With the PLO," *Journal of Palestine Studies*, Vol. 7, no. 1 (Autumn 1977), p. 136 and pp. 123-54 passim.

54. *Ibid.*, p. 124 and 127-31. In part this was because the PFLP was associated in the Chinese mind with "international terrorism" while the DFLP was considered too "pro-Soviet." In part, it was also pragmatic since Fateh was the most powerful group within the PLO.

55. Cobban, *The Palestine Liberation Organization*, pp. 216-221.

56. Kissinger's first trip to China was in July 1971 followed by another in October 1971. See Kissinger, *Years of Upheaval*, pp. 7, 46, 49 and 692-93. Of interest is a

comment by Harris, "China's Relations with the PLO," p. 154 who writes "China is said to have sought Israel's vote on seating China at the United Nations in exchange for a more favorable Chinese posture toward Israel."

57. Cobban, The Palestine Liberation Organization, p. 219 citing Hashim S.H. Behbehani, China's Foreign Policy in the Arab World, 1955-75: Three Case Studies (London and Boston: Kegan Paul International, 1981), p. 98.

58. Cobban, The Palestine Liberation Organization, pp. 221-28.

59. Golan, "The Soviet Union and the PLO," p. 285.

60. Golan, The Soviet Union and the Palestine Liberation Organization, passim; Gresh, The PLO: The Struggle Within, pp. 154-55; and Cobban, The Palestine Liberation Organization, p. 224.

61. See "The Soviet Attitude Toward the Palestine Problem," Journal of Palestine Studies, Vol. 2, no. 1 (Autumn 1972), pp. 187-212. Parts of one document—a discussion among Boris Ponomarev, Mikhail Suslov, and the Syrian Communist Party leader Khaled Bekdash—are also printed in Cobban, The Palestine Liberation Organization, p. 224. Both make the Soviet position very explicit.

62. Cobban, The Palestine Liberation Organization, p. 224 and Golan The Soviet Union and the Palestine Liberation Organization, p. 53.

63. For an analysis of the United States' inherent antipathy to Palestinian nationalism see Rubenberg, "U.S. Policy Toward the Palestinians."

64. The key policy planning groups—the elite private institutions that develop policy recommendations for implementation by the government—have repeatedly advocated a resolution of the Palestine/Israel conflict based on some form of Palestinian self-determination. See for example Report of a Study Group, Toward Peace in the Middle East (Washington D.C.: The Brookings Institution, 1975), which made the following proposal on U.S. policy concerning the Palestinian question: "There should be provisions for Palestinian self-determination, subject to Palestinian acceptance of the sovereignty and territorial integrity of Israel within agreed boundaries. This might take the form either of an independent Palestinian state accepting the obligations and commitments of the peace agreements or of a Palestinian entity voluntarily federated with Jordan but exercising extensive political autonomy." (p. 2) In addition, see Harold H. Saunders, The Middle East Problem in the 1980's (Washington, D.C.: American Enterprise Institute for Public Policy Research, 1981); Joseph N. Green, Jr., et. al., The Path to Peace: Arab-Israeli Peace and the United States: Report of a Study Mission to the Middle East (Mount Kisko, New York: Seven Springs Center, 1981); Harold H. Saunders, The Other Walls: The Politics of the Arab-Israeli Peace Process (Washington, D.C.: American Enterprise Institute for Public Policy Research, 1985); and William B. Quandt's Camp David: Peacemaking and Politics (Washington D.C.: The Brookings Institute, 1986).

65. See Rubenberg, Israel and the American National Interest, the major thesis of which is that Israel does not fulfill the strategic role that it is generally given credit for. For another analysis that disputes the thesis of Israel as a strategic asset see: Harry J. Shaw, "Strategic Dissensus," Foreign Policy, No. 61 (Winter 1985-86), pp. 125-41.

66. For detailed analyses of the Israeli lobby see Rubenberg, Israel and the American National Interest, pp. 329-76; Paul Findley, They Dare to Speak Out: People and Institutions Confront Israel's Lobby (Westport, Conn.: Lawrence Hill, 1985); and Edward Tivnan, The Lobby: Jewish Political Power and American Foreign Policy (New York: Simon & Schuster, 1987).

67. For an excellent analysis of the ways in which pro-Israeli forces impact on Congress and influence the policy making process see Quandt, Camp David.

68. The analysis of the institutionalization of the perception of Israel as a strategic asset is derived from a sociological analysis of how "knowledge"—itself defined as a product of human creation—about the social order is constructed, transmitted, and institutionalized in Peter L. Berger and Thomas Luckmann, *The Social Construction of Reality: A Treatise in the Sociology of Knowledge* (New York: Anchor Books, 1967). It was first applied to U.S.-Israeli relations in Rubenberg, "U.S. Policy Toward the Palestinians."

69. The best analysis of the intelligentsia's role as the state's "secular priesthood" is Noam Chomsky's *Towards A New Cold War: Essays on the Current Crisis and How We Got There* (New York: Pantheon Books, 1979). See especially the chapters "Intellectuals and the State" and "Foreign Policy and the Intelligentsia," pp. 60–114.

70. See Rubenberg, *Israel and the American National Interest*, passim for thorough documentation of the statement that Israel's survival was never in danger.

71. Nadav Safran, *Israel: the Embattled Ally* (Cambridge, Mass.: The Belknap Press of Harvard University Press, 1978). Another typical example of such "scholarship" is Bernard Reich's *The United States and Israel: Influence in the Special Relationship* (New York: Praeger, 1984).

9

The PLO in Retrospect: The Arab and Israeli Dimensions

Aaron David Miller

Twenty years after the 1967 war, the Palestine Liberation Organization (PLO) is confronting yet another crisis, yet another fork in the road. More than two years after the Arafat-Hussein agreement promised to open a new chapter in the Jordanian-PLO relationship, the diplomatic possibilities it created have soured. At the same time Syrian President Assad's personal vendetta against Arafat and tensions with Jordan and Egypt have complicated the PLO's position in the Arab world. In Lebanon, where Arafat hoped to reestablish a major base, Israel, the Shia militia Amal, and Syria continue to hammer away at any gains. Indeed, the PLO remains in limbo—dangerously dependent on its allies and highly vulnerable to its adversaries.

That the PLO—the current institutional embodiment of Palestinian nationalism—finds itself once again treading water in the deep end of the Middle East pool is hardly a new development. As its own spokesmen readily concede, the PLO has been down before. And even its most bitter enemies admit that since the late 1960s the PLO has demonstrated a remarkable resilience and ability to serve as a credible symbol for Palestinians and a dynamic factor in Middle Eastern and peace process politics. Despite its fecklessness, over the last two decades the PLO has become for many Palestinians the institutional expression of a powerful idea—Palestinian nationalism.

That the PLO still enjoys this status and leverage but is unable to accomplish its avowed goal—the establishment of a Palestinian state—is more than a passing observation. Since 1967, it has been at the heart of the PLO's and Palestinians' predicament. The PLO's greatest achievement over the past twenty years is its claim to represent Palestinians and its ability to prevent others—be they Palestinians, Arab states, or Israel—from

---

The views expressed in this chapter are the author's alone and do not necessarily reflect those of the Department of State or any other U.S. Government agency.

playing this role; yet, the organization is unable to find a way into negotiations. Since the 1970s, the PLO's rise on the international stage has been dramatic, yet its fortunes in the region have fluctuated dramatically. Why, despite all of its success at home and abroad as a symbol of Palestinian national identity and as the chief spokesman for the Palestinian cause, has the PLO remained so vulnerable? And why, two decades after the 1967 war, are the Palestinians still so far away from regaining an inch of historic Palestine?

The answers to these questions go well beyond the Israeli invasion of Lebanon, the PLO's current organizational muddle, Arafat's confrontation with Assad, or his continuing maneuvers with King Hussein. These are important developments. But they are only symptoms of more fundamental problems that cut to the core of the Palestinian movement and the environment in which it has operated. Although the PLO of today differs radically from earlier organizational incarnations—the Arab Higher Committee of the 1930s or Ahmed Shukairy's 1964 PLO—the challenges it faces today have remained strikingly similar. These challenges are as relevant today as they were at any stage of the Palestinian national movement's development.

For almost half a century, and especially since 1967, the Palestinian national movement has had to contend with three formidable challenges. The first challenge, its own organizational structure, is a subject dealt with in another chapter [by Cheryl Rubenberg]. Second, its relations with Arab states: how can Palestinians hope to achieve their objectives when they are dangerously dependent on Arab regimes that do not necessarily share their goals? And third, the Palestinian-Israeli relationship: How can Palestinians hope to win a political and military conflict with an established and powerful state that regards the PLO as a mortal enemy? These latter two challenges are the focus of this essay. Together they raise serious questions about the future of an independent and cohesive Palestinian national movement and about its ability to accomplish any of its avowed goals.

Ambivalent Allies

Since 1967 the PLO has never had a great deal of room to maneuver in the highly volatile world of inter-Arab politics and the Arab-Israeli conflict. Although Palestinians have provided the catalyst for triggering important events in the Middle East and the PLO has used what little leverage it possessed remarkably well to survive, the PLO has been forced by and large to react and adapt its tactics to circumstances beyond its control. It is ironic that the PLO has rarely been able to control or turn to its advantage the consequences of events that it helped to set in motion.

To some extent the 1967 war proved to be an exception to this trend. Out of the Arab states' humiliating defeat came important benefits for fledgling Palestinian national groups that had already been operating for over a decade. The war opened new opportunities for a more militant, ideological Palestinian leadership which seemed less willing to adhere to

Arab state tactics and timetables in the struggle against Israel. The traditional Palestinian leadership—some of which was embodied in the Egyptian-dominated PLO—was discredited as were many of the "progressive" Arab regimes which had based much of their credibility on waging a successful war against Israel. By contrast, the unconventional, if amateurish, attacks of the fedayeen together with their new inspiring ideology raised their prestige in the Palestinian community and forced key Arab states to take them seriously.

At the same time, however, these new successes generated serious risks and challenges. The emergence of an independent Palestinian movement determined to create an independent Palestinian state represented a major change in the status quo inimical, for different reasons, to the interests of both Israel and some Arab states. Thus, after 1967, established states wary of dramatic changes in the status quo were faced for the first time with a highly volatile movement trying to change it. Although the objectives of some PLO groups would become more moderate over the years, even the less grandiose goal of a Palestinian state in part of historic Palestine would be adamantly opposed by Israel and contested by Jordan and Syria who, while supportive of Palestinian rights, were determined to see that their own interests were protected.

Nowhere was this conflict of interest more evident that in the PLO's relationship with its Arab allies. Without a secure base of operations and independent access to military, political, and financial resources, the Palestinians naturally looked to their Arab brothers as their major source of support. From the 1930s when the early Palestinian nationalists appealed to Arab kings and presidents for political support against the British and the Zionists to the 1948 war in which refugees and guerrillas relied almost entirely on their Arab neighbors to redeem their cause, Palestinians saw the Arab nation as their first line of defense.

Even after 1967, when it became clear to a new generation of Palestinians that they would have to rely on themselves to set the direction of their struggle against Israel, they could not escape their dependence on Arab regimes. The larger the resistance movement became, and the more so-phisticated their tactics, the more resources were required. The importance the PLO still attaches to the Arab decision to confer on it the mantle of sole legitimate representative of the Palestinians reflects how vital Arab support continues to be.

This support, however, has come at an enormous price. The ability of the Palestinians to carry out their struggle against Israel depends primarily on the Arab commitment to their cause. It is this bond that gives the Palestinian problems its resilience in Middle Eastern politics. Yet the Arab commitment has from the beginning been extraordinarily ambiguous. Es-tablished Arab states, while supportive of "the Palestinian cause" in the ideal, have looked first to the protection of their own particular national interests. It is not so much that Arab regimes do not share a desire to help Palestinians fulfill their national aspirations, but they are determined to ensure that the process of achieving a homeland and the homeland itself do not conflict with their own security and political interests.

The 1967 war only exacerbated these tensions. The emergence of an independent Palestinian national movement posed serious problems for those Arab regimes that had traditionally considered themselves champions of the Palestinian cause or who hosted large Palestinian populations. Already torn between genuine support for the Palestinian cause and a desire to use it to foster their own political and territorial ambitions, these regimes became even more concerned about an independent Palestinian organization they could not control. Conflicts between the Palestinians and established states intensified dramatically in the period after the 1967 war. In fact, with the exception of Egypt, all of the states along the confrontation line with Israel (Lebanon, Syria, and Jordan) had major military confrontations with the PLO.

The sources of this new tension are not difficult to discern. First, the emergence of a credible, popular Palestinian movement created real problems for Arab regimes such as Jordan, Lebanon, and Syria that hosted large Palestinian populations. For Jordan, with a resident population at least half Palestinian, the appearance of a dynamic, militant Palestinian movement, some of whose groups actively pushed for the overthrow of the Hashemite monarchy, represented a major problem. No matter how well assimilated East Bank Palestinians, there was bound to be tension between their identity as citizens of Jordan and their affinity with the Palestinian people. Similarly, for Lebanon, where thousands of Palestinians looked to the PLO to protect them against a variety of Christian and Muslim groups, armed Palestinian elements would disturb an already precarious internal balance and provide a catalyst for civil war.

Second, what had seemed relatively manageable for Lebanon and Jordan before 1967 suddenly seemed unmanageable as PLO groups quite naturally looked to these countries to provide sanctuary and support in their struggle against Israel. Not only did these Palestinian groups exacerbate tensions inside the country, and in the case of Jordan, directly challenge the Hashemite regime, but their attacks against Israel courted military retaliation. As the 1982 Israeli invasion of Lebanon and Israel's 1985 attack on PLO headquarters in Tunis demonstrated, the problem of hosting a PLO presence remains an acute one for those Arab states who share borders with Israel and even those who do not.

Third, the PLO's determination to guard its independence and the Arab states' need to ensure that their own interests remained predominant guaranteed perennial conflict, particularly on Arab-Israeli issues. Whether in the case of Syria, which sought to dominate the Palestinian national movement, or Jordan, which had tried to co-opt it, the Arab state-PLO rivalries run like a continuous thread through the fabric of regional politics. In the five years after the Israeli invasion of Lebanon these tensions have been especially bitter. The Assad-Arafat rift reached a new level of personal bitterness over the Lebanon war and the PLO's accommodation with Jordan.

And what promised to be a new start in PLO-Jordanian relations after the February 1985 agreement between Arafat and Hussein lost momentum as Palestinian and Arab agendas once again diverged.

It is in this precarious world of Arab interests and designs that the PLO was created and is still forced to maneuver. For Arafat the primary challenge over the years has been how to guarantee the broadest possible Arab support and still maintain his leadership over a relatively independent PLO. Being all things to all regimes has produced an ambiguous strategy that tries to accommodate states like Syria which see no urgency in any deal with Israel and those such as Jordan that see more immediately the need for a negotiated settlement. The end result for the PLO, indeed the trademark of its Arab diplomacy, is a strategy based on the kind of calculated ambiguity that prevents a full-fledged commitment to either option.

Nowhere is the PLO's predicament more evident than in the Jordanian-Syrian-Palestinian triangle that has emerged in recent years. The Israeli invasion of Lebanon, the Reagan initiative, the Hussein-Arafat dialogue, and Syrian supported Fateh mutiny only exacerbated the PLO's dilemma and sharpened the difficulty of maintaining relations with Amman and Damascus. On the surface it seemed that Arafat with his fighters out of Syrian control, with Damascus humbled by the Israelis in Lebanon, and with Jordan interested in a deal, now had more room to maneuver. But the Palestinians, now negotiating with Hussein from a position of weakness, were unwilling to deputize the King to negotiate on their behalf in the context of the Reagan initiative or to settle for anything less than a state led by the PLO. The Hussein-Arafat negotiations and the February 1985 agreement only exacerbated tensions within Fateh, with other PLO groups, and with Syria and pointed up Arafat's continuing dilemma. Moreover, Arafat's unwillingness to agree to the King's demands that he accept United Nations Resolution 242 resulted in a serious rift with Jordan. These differences may be papered over as both Hussein and Arafat perceive limited benefits in maintaining a dialogue. But the fundamental tensions in the relationship will likely remain.

Thus, after two decades the PLO is still caught—trapped between Arab states whose price for cooperation in a negotiated settlement is too high for the PLO to pay and others, particularly Syria, determined to block any accord that ignores their interests and does not give them a primary role in resolving the Palestinian issue. The PLO's "Arab dilemma" is not new but it is in many respects more acute than ever. For the first time since the late 1960s, the PLO has no independent base of operations which can be described as even relatively secure. More to the point, the PLO's access to the confrontation line with Israel has been severely restricted by Jordan, Syria, and various Lebanese groups. Even those PLO groups closely aligned with Syria have found greater problems in operating in Lebanon. Similarly, the PLO's access to the West Bank has been further curtailed since the February 1986 break with Hussein. And operating from bases once thought secure, such as Tunis, now entails serious risks. For the moment, the PLO is confined to working from places such as Baghdad and Sanaa, not particularly relevant or close to core Arab-Israeli issues.

The Israeli Challenge

Since 1967, the PLO's dependence on its Arab allies has severely weakened its ability to deal with its most formidable challenge—Israel. Although many Palestinians have defined this challenge in military terms and cast it in the language of liberation and armed struggle, it is also a problem of political and diplomatic persuasion. If Palestinians cannot take what they want by force, and it is obvious they cannot, then attempting to convince Israel that Palestinian nationalism can coexist with political Zionism or to persuade others to force Israel to concede territory might be considered equally worthwhile goals. The Palestinian national movement has yet to demonstrate that it can succeed in either area.

From the beginning Palestinian nationalism dealt with Zionism and Israel from a position of weakness. Palestinians were slower to develop a national identity and much more confused and uncertain about their "national" origins than the Zionists. Political Zionism, despite its divisions, was a determined yet pragmatic force willing to make tactical compromises with the Turks, Germans, and British. Palestinian nationalism was divided, prone to radicalism by the 1930s, and maximalist in its goals—boycotting cooperation with the mandatory authorities while the Jews were using the British to help create the foundations of institutions that would form the basis of their state. Indeed, the Palestinian nationalists' most successful enterprise, the 1936–1939 rebellion, left the Palestinian community leaderless and exhausted at a time when the Zionists were mobilizing to confront Nazism in Europe.

For the next twenty years the Palestinians, more dispirited and divided than ever, struggled to redefine their national movement while Israel developed at a remarkable pace. In 1964, the year the Egyptian-sponsored PLO was created, Israel was in the process of developing, with French support, a nuclear reactor at Dimona. Nor was the Palestinian effort to narrow the gap in their struggle against Israel more encouraging after 1967. Paradoxically, the tactics that brought the Palestinian issue to world attention—military and terrorist activities—only retarded the movement's efforts to get what it wanted, hardened Israeli attitudes, and reinforced Israel's inclinations to deal with the Palestinian issue as a military problem.

Nowhere has this fact been more clearly apparent than in Palestinian activities on the West Bank. The PLO has raised local consciousness and mobilized support to block any separate West Bank, Jordanian, or Israeli initiatives on the area's final status. But in a decade and a half of Israeli occupation, the PLO has not been able to thwart Israeli settlement or economic policies, let alone make the costs of its stay too high for Israel to bear.

Faced with a divided and passive West Bank community from which it was separated and confronting an Israeli government that sought to co-opt and control West Bank elites, the PLO has not succeeded in creating a unified national leadership able to forcefully resist occupation policies. In fact, the PLO's constant fear has been that West Bankers would allow themselves to be "rescued" by either Jordan or an Israeli government committed to giving them more political control over their own affairs. Although Arafat's stock in the occupied territories is still high, West Bankers are increasingly frustrated by his endless vacillation and tired of the revolutionary slogans they know can never "save their land" or improve the quality of their lives. Despite this frustration, however, West Bankers are unlikely for the foreseeable future to consider other options for a settlement that bypass the PLO. Such an outcome would depend on fundamental changes in Israeli and Jordanian policy as well as a major trauma within the PLO that would further weaken or discredit its leadership.

In one area the Palestinian national movement has made progress in their campaign against Israel. It is paradoxically the arena least relevant to the Palestinians' ultimate goals. Since the early 1970s, largely under Arafat's direction, the PLO has pursued a strategy on the international stage designed to accomplish three basic objectives: keep the Palestinian issue high on the international agenda; link the PLO with a solution of the problem; and isolate Israel. Capitalizing on Arab oil power and the sympathies of many Asian, Africa, and European countries for what they believed to be its anti-colonial struggle against Israel, the PLO was able to gain diplomatic recognition abroad and to promote its cause at the United Nations and other international forums.

The image of peripatetic Arafat taking the Palestinian issue to Mali, however, conflicts with some harsh but simple political realities. International sympathy and support is of little consequence unless it can be focused and converted into political power on behalf of Palestinian goals. Otherwise the quest for recognition becomes an end in itself, enhancing Arafat's personal status and maintaining the illusion of momentum and activity but ultimately leading nowhere. No matter how many times Arafat meets with a president or foreign minister or how many UN resolutions condemning Israel are floated in New York, the Palestinians will be no closer to the achievement of their territorial aims. And isolating Israel diplomatically will only reinforce its belief that the PLO is a mortal enemy committed to its destruction.

The Past as Prologue?

What the future will bring for the PLO is uncertain. What is clear is that the Arab and Israeli challenges facing the PLO are likely to become even more formidable in the years ahead. Palestinians are correct in claiming that their national movement has faced crossroads and suffered defeats before and survived. But the environment today is radically different than in the past. For the first time since 1970 the PLO does not possess even a relatively secure and independent base of operations. And it is unlikely that any of the Arab states, let alone those bordering Israel, will ever again permit the PLO to establish the independence it achieved in Jordan or Lebanon. The "time is on our side" argument is based on the assumption that sooner or later there will be a political-strategic shift in the balance of power that will catapult the PLO to center stage or somehow tip the advantage to the Arabs or Palestinians. Or that somehow a *deus ex machina* will appear to make the choices for the PLO less difficult and risky. Unfortunately for the Palestinians, most of these kinds of dramatic changes have resulted in a weakening of their position. The remainder the Palestinians were either unwilling or unable to exploit.

The most recent example of this kind of process occurred in the aftermath of the Israeli invasion of Lebanon. In the wake of Arafat's second exit from Lebanon in late 1983, there were those who believed that he was on the verge of rethinking his strategy and ready to turn the PLO's military defeat in Lebanon into a political victory. According to some, Arafat was now convinced that Syria's support for the Fateh rebels left him no choice but to cut a deal with Jordan and ignore Damascus and his more radical colleagues. And events over the past several years, including Arafat's decision to convene the Palestinian National Council in Amman in November 1984 and his February 1985 agreement with King Hussein, seemed to confirm this view.

Events over the past two years have demonstrated that the story is not so simple. Indeed, there is more business as usual in Palestinian politics than the optimists would care to acknowledge. The Arafat-Assad rift has not pushed the PLO into the arms of Hussein; the Hussein-Arafat relationship came apart not as a result of failed American promises but from underlying tensions between the PLO and Jordan; and Arafat's terms for a settlement— though they appear to be just from a Palestinian perspective—do not coincide with those of Jordan, Syria, Israel, or the United States.

However justified Palestinians may feel in supporting the PLO's position on the peace process, there is little doubt that their national movement is trapped in a vicious circle made of its own blunders and circumstances beyond its control. This circle remains tight and unbroken—reinforced by four powerfully appealing assumptions that all but guarantee the continued frustration of Palestinian national aspirations:

Time is on our side. However stark the realities of their current predicament, PLO spokesmen continue to take the long view and insist that time is on their side and that the strategy of the revolution will ultimately triumph. This kind of rhetoric may well be for public consumption, but it is just possible that some Palestinian leaders believe it. Political Department head Faruk Quaddumi once compared the Palestinian movement to an olive tree—difficult to uproot and capable of bearing fruit for many years. Drawing upon images of the Crusades and of Israel's impermanence, Palestinian strategists push the line that no historic compromises should be made. They insist that the Palestinian demographic advantage inside Israel and an Arab demographic advantage outside will eventually exacerbate the internal contradictions of Israeli society and lead to the collapse of the Jewish state. No island, many predict, can withstand the force of the sea forever.

This kind of thinking, of course, is problematic at best. The fact that the PLO has been able to veto a peace settlement does not mean that the Middle East or Israel is inevitably headed for the kind of Armageddon-like end which some Palestinian politicians prophesy. States, once established, do not disappear overnight. And it is simply not relevant now to speak of a strategy based on a millennium. Moreover, it is becoming clearer that key Arab states are no longer willing to sacrifice their own political, economic, and security interests in a futile crusade to destroy Israel and help achieve Palestinian national rights. The bitter conflicts between Arab regimes and the Palestinian national movement evident two decades ago have not dissipated, and if anything have intensified. In the end, the PLO may well find that it has few allies in any long-term or determined struggle against Israel.

The organization is the state. In the absence of a guaranteed role in a peace process along the lines it prefers (international conference with a co-equal Soviet-American role), Arafat will take no steps, such as acceptance of UN Resolution 242, that splits Fateh or forecloses the possibility of reconciliation with other PLO groups and Syria. In a very real sense the PLO as an organization has become a surrogate homeland—complete with a functioning bureaucracy, diplomatic corps, military apparatus, and broad sense of national identity and purpose. Those who believe that the *sine qua non* for the emergence of a moderate pragmatic Arafat is a formal split in the PLO and a further fracturing of Fateh underestimate the importance these men attach to the institution. It guarantees their prestige and livelihood, and provides them with the leverage to remain central to the negotiating process. Like the PLO's commitment to the armed struggle, the organization can only be abandoned after territorial goals are realized or at the very least on the verge of being achieved. Given Israeli and Jordanian opposition to the PLO, such a *quid pro quo* is unthinkable in any negotiating framework. Indeed, since the PLO is unlikely to get an ironclad guarantee for either participation in the negotiating process or for involvement in any final outcome down the road, organizational interests will remain paramount.

All things to all regimes. The Palestinian movement is today trapped between an idealized vision of its past ("armed struggle," a strategic relationship with Syria, and the Soviets) and its future (a pragmatic diplomatic strategy and a close link with Jordan and ultimately accommodation with the United States and Israel). Arafat is both unable and unwilling to make a clear-cut choice between them. He is as usual keeping his options open. He knows that the road to Damascus leads nowhere but is unable and unwilling to take the King's highway because the risks (splitting the PLO and perhaps losing it all) outweigh the benefits (the prospects of allowing Hussein to enter into a two-way deal with Israel and West Bankers from which Arafat would most likely be excluded). Nor would accepting UN Resolution 242, Israel's right to exist, and abandoning violence—conditions essential for a dialogue with the United States and beginning a long process of accommodation with Israel—necessarily guarantee PLO participation in negotiations or in the final settlement that emerges. Thus, fence-sitting guarantees survival but it also ensures paralysis.

Diaspora dreams and West Bank realities. To put it simply, the PLO is working to achieve a solution of the Palestinian problem that accords it a central role. On the other hand, its most important constituency—West Bankers and Gazans—who deal with the realities of the Israeli occupation are committed to "saving their land" and would likely settle for something less than an independent Palestinian state run by the PLO. In any case, Israeli and Jordanian opposition to such an entity will make the PLO's dreams nearly impossible to realize. The only way *Palestinians* on the *West Bank* and *Gaza* will ever have any hope of fulfilling any of their national aspirations is by cooperating with Jordan and ultimately with Israel in some kind of shared role over the future of the West Bank. This fact may seem cruel and unjust to Palestinians both in the occupied territories and throughout the Arab world who are convinced of the moral and ethical correctness of their cause, but it appears to be their only hope for any kind of negotiated settlement. Holding out for an independent and sovereign state, let alone for the liberation of Palestine, will preserve the "pursuit of the revolution" but is unlikely to lead to the achievement of any of their territorial goals.

Twenty years after the Six Day war the PLO is no closer to actually regaining an inch of Palestine than when it spoke of the liberation of Palestine in the 1960s. Although the PLO's own miscalculations and blunders explain much of its failure, the harsh environment in which it has operated goes a long way toward explaining its current predicament. In short, the entire Palestinian national movement is far too dependent on its Arab allies and far too vulnerable to its Israeli adversary to have much hope of accomplishing its *territorial* objectives.

After 1967 the Palestinian issue really became two separate sub-conflicts: one between key Arab states and the Palestinian leadership and the second between Israel and the PLO. In both of these contests, the PLO had some leverage and was able to score significant gains. But overall, the Palestinian movement has dealt with its friends and its enemies from a position of weakness. Indeed, it has already lost the military/political struggle with Israel and is in the process of losing the political battle with some important Arab states.

The PLO has never really had a credible military option against Israel and never will. Whatever other purposes the armed struggle served, it did little to better position the Palestinians in their confrontation with Israel. Nor have the PLO's efforts to isolate Israel in the international community, despite some success, really amounted to much. The Palestinians have never come close to marshalling the kind of political power necessary to force the great powers to pressure Israel into territorial concessions or even to drive a wedge between Israel and the United States. Banking on another war or an upheaval in Israel to accomplish this goal is a silly policy.

How the PLO is faring in the second sub-conflict with its Arab allies is less clear. It has been commonly assumed since the 1974 Rabat summit that no Arab state would dare end-run the PLO into negotiations with Israel. Egypt, of course, was viewed as idiosyncratic and no others have subsequently followed Sadat's lead. To a great extent, the Rabat syndrome still pertains. And Syrian and Jordanian efforts to undermine or co-opt Arafat's PLO have failed.

Nonetheless, the PLO's ability to frustrate Arab designs and veto unilateral Arab bids for peace does not mean that the Palestinians can marshal Arab support to achieve its own political and territorial goals. The fact that no Arab state can enter into a formal peace treaty with Israel while the Palestinian issue remains unaddressed does not mean that the same Arab state will not acquiesce in *de facto* arrangements with Israel or accept an informal state of no war/no peace. And even should another war erupt, would it put the Palestinians in a better position to accomplish their goals? Have the cumulative effects of the 1967, 1973, and 1982 conflicts benefitted the PLO or Palestinians? Indeed, is the PLO in 1987 any better equipped to deal with the Arab states and Israel?

Palestinians often claim that there is an inherent and self-sustaining logic to their cause: that the forces of history and the politics and demographics of the Arab-Israeli conflict will ultimately assure them of victory. This sense of the inevitable is supported by the popular notion that a people has a moral right to determine its own future and that sooner or later through war or diplomacy the Palestinian people, led by the PLO, will determine theirs.

There are no sure bets in history. In the Middle East, as elsewhere, the environment is a cruel one. And even those groups with drive and determination do not necessarily succeed. In any event, it is not moral conviction alone that guarantees the success of national movements and nations. It is a combination of *political skill, military power,* and *luck* that determines whether a people can acquire and hold on to territory. The PLO has no military option and lacks an effective political strategy beyond perpetuating its own survival. In the end, whatever support it enjoys among Palestinians, the PLO will have to be judged not by its popularity, but by its ability to accomplish its avowed goal—the establishment of a Palestinian state. More than two decades after it emerged as a force in Middle Eastern politics, the PLO seems further away than ever from achieving this goal.

The Arab States

10

The June 1967 War:
A Turning Point?

L. Carl Brown

On June 5, 1967 Israeli troops poured across the Egyptian border, beginning a war that was destined to last just six days. By the end of that time Israel's forces had reached the Suez Canal, the Jordan River, and the Golan Heights.

Before those six days in June, Israel confronted only one group of Arab irredentists—the Palestinians. After the June war Israel occupied three significant territories previously held by Egypt, Jordan, and Syria.

Before that crushing defeat the Arabs, except the specialists who knew the military realities, could nurse the illusion that they had never been defeated by Israel. The 1948 war could be seen as having been more nearly lost by the Arabs—with divided command, mismanagement, and at times worse—than won by Israel.

Likewise, the Suez war of 1956, which was clearly a major political victory for Egypt's Gamal Abdul Nasser, could easily be remembered (incorrectly) as a military triumph. In less than a week the June war destroyed all such illusions.

The speed and magnitude of the Israeli victory over its Arab neighbors was immediately seen by victors and vanquished alike as a decisive turning point in modern Middle Eastern history, a perspective fully shared by outside observers. This stark appraisal has been the received wisdom ever since.

Rethinking the Impact of the Six Day War

Writing contemporary history necessarily involves, with the passage of time, a shifting of the camera eye from the "close-up" to the increasingly wide-angle focus. Dramatic events seen in cataclysmic terms by contemporaries become subject to reinterpretation. Sometimes they seem to fade into the historical background, losing their sharp edges. In other cases, the importance

133

of the earlier event is confirmed and becomes an accepted milestone in human history.

As the June war recedes into the past (roughly half of the population in the countries involved were born after that war), a reinterpretation may be useful. Here it will be argued that although the Six Day War will continue to stand out as a dramatic event in modern Middle Eastern history, it did not usher in a significant systemic change. That is, the events of June 1967 are not to be compared, say, to the American, French, or Russian Revolutions, the early Arab-Muslim conquests, the fall of Constantinople to the Ottomans, the Louisiana Purchase, and other such events that radically changed fundamental arrangements of political life.

Instead, those few days of June twenty years ago are to be compared to certain military confrontations that impressed contemporaries but did not alter the basic group alignments. Thus, whereas a crushing defeat of one side and the overwhelming victory of the other might well be expected to engender a clear change in the relationships among the parties concerned, the 1967 confrontation between Israel and the Arabs merely brought into bold relief the pattern of Middle Eastern diplomacy that has existed for generations. The basic "givens" of the Arab-Israeli confrontation remain today as they have been since 1948, and the June war can be seen as but one more somber link in the historical chain of international relations known as the Eastern Question.

On the one side of the conflict is a territorially minute but militarily and technologically powerful state—Israel. On the other is a large cluster of peoples—the Arabs—organized into more than twenty different states sharing a sense of grievance concerning the fate of Arab Palestine and the Palestinians. Notwithstanding this common concern, the Arabs, spread as they are over a vast territory twice the size of the continental United States and extending from the Atlantic to the Gulf and from the southern border of Turkey to the Indian Ocean, have been and remain divided according to countless different problems and perspectives.

Thus Israel, seeing itself as surrounded by actual or potential enemies, responds ambivalently with both bristling aggressiveness and poignantly stated yearning for peace with its neighbors. On the one hand, it insists on being militarily stronger than any conceivable combination of its foes and acts preemptively to maintain that military dominance. On the other hand, even while continuing a policy of keeping its neighbors off balance and at tactical disadvantage it seeks an idyllic peace not merely of Arab resignation but of positive acceptance. Yet, Israel is reluctant to lower the stick and offer the carrot.

As for the Arabs, they continue to advance unqualified support for the Palestinian cause as the touchstone of political rectitude even while never agreeing consistently on the tactics to be pursued, much less the burdens to be borne. To many Arab leaders today, as in the past, the Palestinian cause can be unhesitatingly supported only to the extent that the Palestinians themselves do not seek to determine the modalities and pace of regional politics. The Arabs, even those most directly affected (i.e., the Palestinians organized into the Palestine Liberation Organization), hesitate between entering into negotiations immediately and holding out for a position of strength presumed to be attainable at some indeterminate future time. Those Arabs who look back in pain at half-a-loaf compromise solutions missed since 1947 (if not since 1917) are counterbalanced by other Arabs who invoke the image of the Crusaders and their eventual retreat from their Middle Eastern foothold leaving only a few architectural traces as forlorn reminders of their once-dominant position.

Overlaying the regional politics is the jockeying for Middle Eastern position on the part of the great powers, a global diplomatic game which since at least the 1950s has been largely—but not exclusively—defined in terms of the superpower rivalry between the United States and the Soviet Union. These two powers continue to rise and fall in their Middle Eastern standings. Such was the case before the Six Day War. Such has been the case since then.

The question of whether the June war offers a decisive turning point in Middle Eastern politics and diplomacy is of more than antiquarian interest. If the Six Day War brought in its wake a radically changed diplomatic environment, then policy-makers inside and outside the region would be advised to concentrate their analyses and their search for solutions on events of the last twenty years. If, on the other hand, the war only served to exacerbate preexisting circumstances of confrontation then those seeking solutions must go back further in time and focus their attention on what emerges as a stubbornly durable Middle Eastern approach to regional and international politics.

This paper argues for the second hypothesis. A good way to begin testing it might be to pass in review certain of the sharp changes generally believed to have been ushered in by the June war, that is, the decline of Nasserism, the rise of Islamic radicalism, and the emergence of the Palestine Liberation Organization (PLO).

The Decline of Nasserism

It is often suggested that the June war brought to an end the previously dominant influence of General Abdul Nasser. There can be no doubt that in Arab politics, and to a considerable extent in Third World politics, the label "Nasserism" identifies an age.

Nasser, with a handful of his fellow "Free Officers" from the Egyptian military, had toppled the almost 150-year-old Egyptian monarchy and sent King Farouq into ignominious exile. For the first time in some 2,500 years, Egypt's political leadership was clearly and categorically of native stock. But from the time of the epoch-making Bandung Nonaligned Conference in 1955, Nasser led not just Egypt but the entire Arab world toward Afro-Asian solidarity and the sense of unity that was meant to bind together the Third World. He also popularized in his own country and throughout the Arab world a heavy dose of state-directed populism that came to be called Arab socialism.

On another front, Nasser shattered the illusion still cherished by British, French and American leaders that the Arab world, for all its internal divisions and disputes with the West, remained a Western preserve. His daring step in negotiating the purchase of Soviet arms in 1955 (cautiously camouflaged at the time as a Czech-Egyptian arms deal) enabled the Soviets to become a major player in the ongoing diplomatic game involving the Arab world and Israel. More than any other Middle Eastern leader, Nasser exposed the limitations of John Foster Dulles's strategic fence mending according to which those Middle Eastern states bordering the Soviet Union (Turkey, Iran, and Pakistan) would form, in recognition of the Soviet threat, a barrier behind which Arab squabbles and the Arab-Israeli confrontation could continue, and perhaps even ultimately be resolved, under Western stewardship. Instead, Nasser gave the Soviets the opportunity to leapfrog over Mr. Dulles's "Northern Tier."

Nasser assured Egypt the leadership of pan-Arabism and succeeded in convincing friends and foes alike that he might well do for the Arabs in the twentieth century what Bismarck had done for the Germans in the nineteenth.

Thus, if a single event such as the Six Day War could be shown to have quelled the Middle Eastern groundswell we call "Nasserism," that alone would be sufficient to isolate June 1967 as a crucial turning point. A closer look, however, suggests that the war delivered the *coup de grace* to the already ebbing Nasserist political fortunes.

Consider, for example, the movement toward Arab political unity: the United Arab Republic (UAR), created in 1958 with the union of Egypt and Syria, fell apart in September 1961, almost six years before the outbreak of the June war. Later, the on-again, off-again unity proposals involving Egypt, Syria, and Iraq came to be viewed with appropriate cynicism by all parties, perhaps most of all by Nasser himself.

Exactly a year after the breakup of the UAR, a revolution in Yemen overthrew the centuries-old Imamate rule. Egypt was soon involved militarily on the side of the Republicans against Saudi Arabia, which supported the Imam and his followers. Arabs were locked in combat with other Arabs, while two outside Arab states chose their different "client." This inter-Arab military confrontation, coming on the heels of the dramatic set-back to Arab unity hopes, reveals a Nasserist Arabism that had already peaked.

The months and weeks leading up to the June 1967 war further revealed Nasser's weakness within the Arab world. Indeed, the most persuasive interpretation of Nasser's acts and statements throughout May and early June of 1967, which set the pace of events leading to warfare, is that Nasser felt obliged to recoup his position there. Malcolm Kerr put it crisply in his classic study on the Nasser period:

> It was not hard to imagine, early in May 1967, that the mounting tension in the Arab world would lead to some sort of violent outbreak. The conflict to

which all signs seemed to point, however, was between Arab revolutionaries and conservatives. The old quarrel with Israel seemed irrelevant: the Arabs were preoccupied not with her but with one another.[1]

This recollection of inter-Arab developments countering Nasserist political leadership after 1961 is not to imply that Nasserist pan-Arabism had gone unchallenged by Arab leaders beforehand. The roll call of those who challenged Nasser's leadership includes Iraq's Nuri al-Said and then even Abd al-Karim Qasim who overthrew the Iraqi monarchy, Camille Chamoun in Lebanon, Habib Bourguiba in Tunisia, and, intermittently, King Hussein of Jordan and King Saud of Saudi Arabia, both of whose relations with Nasser fluctuated violently. Even so, until roughly the early 1960s Nasserist pan-Arabism seemed to be an expanding force. Thereafter, it appeared merely as one of several forces in a multilateral Arab field.

There is, of course, no doubt that Egypt's defeat in the Six Day War had an immediate catalytic effect, bringing about developments within weeks that might otherwise have required years. These included Nasser's acceptance of a settlement in Yemen with Saudi Arabia, essentially on King Faisal's terms, and his willingness thereafter to work within an Arab consensus much closer to the domestic and foreign policy preferences of the Arab conservatives. Even the later diplomatic revolution effected by Sadat when he switched from the Soviet to the American "alliance" may be seen as prefigured by Nasser in 1969 and 1970, the last two years of his life. Nasser's acceptance of the Rogers initiative in July 1970 symbolized a closing of the door in his ambitious two-part strategy aimed, first, at providing revolutionary or at the very least progressive leadership and strength-in-unity to the entire Arab world, and second, at championing an Arabism based on neutralizing great power influence in the area. But that grand strategy was already in the process of winding down well before June 1967.

It is true that Nasser might have been able to maintain Egyptian troops in Yemen had he not been defeated in the Six Day War. He might have been able to achieve other short-term victories here and there (although the overthrow of Libya's King Idris and the rise to power of Qaddafi suggests the volatility of such seeming victories). He might have been able to better orchestrate his informal working alliance with the Soviet Union to achieve greater maneuverability in the region (although the tough public exchanges between Khrushchev and Nasser in 1959 or the way in which the Soviet Union was clearly hedging its Middle Eastern bets in the mid-1960s by supporting Syria as much as, if not more than, Egypt should not be forgotten). He might have been able to so manage his regional politics as to appear to lead Arab forces against Israel even while avoiding a military confrontation. Any of these alternatives could have taken place, but their very enumeration suggests the unlikelihood of his managing, much less mastering, all of them concurrently.

Seen in this light, the sudden, dramatic convergence of Arab hopes and militancy on the person of Gamal Abdul Nasser from mid-May until the outbreak of war on 6 June can be seen as Nasserism's "last hurrah." In socio-psychological terms, what took place throughout the Arab world reveals much about an entire society's sense of insecurity and impotence, its fears and aspirations and its subconscious desire to achieve catharsis by violently breaking the bonds that would seem to bind them. In terms of sheer power, it was a poignant but unrealistic effort to revert to the 1950s, when the heady challenges to what was seen, and not without cause, as an oppressive system appeared to succeed or at worst to provoke only manageable losses.

In both regional and international terms, Nasserist Arabism has earned an important niche in history. Seen, however, in terms of the entire eighteen year Nasserist period from 1952 to 1970, a stronger case can be made that Nasser's own brand of Arabism had reached its attainable limits by the early 1960s. The June war hastened a decline already well underway.

Islamic Radicalism Before and After the June War

The January 1979 overthrow of the *Pahlavi* dynasty in Iran followed by the October 1981 assassination of Egypt's Presiden Anwar al-Sadat focused world attention on the phenomenon of Muslim religio-political radicalism. To many observers, the Arab defeat in the June war signalled the arrival of Islamic fundamentalism as a major force, for it spelled the defeat of an entire generation of leaders and left the political field clear for the Muslim radicals uncompromised by previous follies and failures.

According to this interpretation, the leadership of the Arab world at the time of the June war shared a generalized political orientation: However much they might differ among themselves in domestic or foreign policies they were all wedded to a confused array of alien, Western notions including nationalism and the idea of a strong, centralized nation state; Marxism in varying forms; and in general the notion of a society based on universal, rational, and "scientific" principles, rather than on unchanging religious norms.

The crushing defeat of the Arab armies and the accompanying disgrace of the Arab regimes—so this argument goes—brought about the downfall of the alien, non-Islamic (if not, indeed, anti-Islamic) ideas that this generation of political leaders had so rashly borrowed. The way was open for a return to the authentic Islamic political community, a community based on God's immutable Law, the *Shari'ah*, which required the creation not of nation states based on ethnic or linguistic or cultural identity but of the single Islamic polity—the *Umma*.

That a major military defeat can trigger a sharp delegitimization of the defeated governments and bring in its wake movements of political reaction characterized by a revivalist, nativist, religious coloration is not to be denied. Clearly, the June war was an especially traumatic defeat, destroying not only the Arab armies but also the popular illusion of a new-found Arab unity and strength almost miraculously welded together in the last days before the war began. Nor is there need to discount the plummeting prestige of all Arab establishment leaders and institutions following the June war or to deny that Muslim religio-political radicalism became an increasingly important force during these years. Even so, a few by no means insignificant reservations are in order, both with regard to timing and context and to the depth of genuinely systemic change.

First, the two major examples today of states controlled by those who would create uncompromising Islamic polities are Iran and Pakistan. Neither is an Arab state, and neither was directly affected by the Arab defeat in June 1967. In both cases, the forces creating the Islamic governments were fed by entirely different circumstances. The links binding Pakistan's Zia and Iran's Ayatollah Khomeini to the June war are tenuous, at best.

In fact, the influence has more nearly gone in the other direction, from the Islamic East westward to the Arabs. Although Iran is overwhelmingly Shi'ite while the Arab world is overwhelmingly Sunni, the rise of Ayatollah Khomeini's Islamic Republic clearly struck a responsive chord among Arabs, Sunni as well as Shi'a, including many who had previously worn their religious affiliation rather lightly. And while Pakistan has never had as strong a following in the Arab world as their shared religion might suggest, the Indo-Pakistani Muslim fundamentalist, Abu al-Ala Mawdudi (1903–1979) has had an ideological impact on Sunni Muslim radicalism in the Arab world that is probably greater than anyone's since Hasan al-Banna, the Egyptian founder of the Muslim Brethren. Since the early 1950s virtually all of Mawdudi's many books and tracts have been translated into Arabic and widely disseminated.

All of which is to say that the wave of Islamic religio-political radicalism today can be traced to many different sources, not simply developments taking place in the Arab world.

Moreover, to depict Arab polities before June 1967 as embracing alien secularism and positivism is to engage in historical myopia. Saudi Arabia is based on a scriptural-literalist and rigorously fundamentalist religious program labelled Wahhabism by the outside world. The power base of Libya's King Idris was that of a modern religious brotherhood, the *Sanusiyya*. The mass support for Sudanese politics until independence and beyond was split between two rival religious brotherhoods, the *Khatmiyya* and the *Mahdiyya*. The ruler in Yemen held what can only be called a combined religious and political office (as the title imam indicates). A major influence in preparing Algerians for the bitter, eight-year struggle for independence (1954–1962) against the French was the Muslim reformist Algerian Association of *Ulama*.

Nor have religion and politics been far from the surface in modern Egyptian history. Indeed, in this matter as in so many others, Egypt stands out as the bellwether of the Arabs. Among the many twentieth century examples of this intermingling in Egypt are: the effective political unity of Muslims and Copts in Saad Zaghlul's *Wafd* Party; King Fuad's informal alliance with the *Azharite ulama* in his quest for the title of caliph; the scandalized reaction to the publication in the 1920s of Ali Abd al-Raziq's

Al-Islam Wa Usul Al-Hukm (Islam and the Bases of Governing), as well
to Taha Husayn's book on pre-Islamic poetry; and finally, the important
role of the Muslim Brethren from its founding by Hasan al-Banna in 1928
to this day.

As with later Muslim religio-political radicalism, the activities of the
Muslim Brethren transcended Egypt in ideological influence and in deeds.
The Muslim Brethren were deeply involved in both propaganda and guerrilla
activities against the continuing British presence in Egypt as well as against
Zionist aims in Palestine. They were also intimately involved with certain
of the Egyptian "Free Officers" who overthrew King Faruq in 1952 (including
Anwar al-Sadat); in the early months of the post-revolutionary period
observers wondered if the Muslim Brethren were, or might become, the
real power behind the new regime. The break came when Nasser's government
signed an agreement with Britain that the Brethren attacked as not securing
all of Egypt's demands (the incident, thus, being a classic example of a
practical confrontation pitting extremist all-or-nothing politics against the
politics of piece-meal pragmatism).

Then, in October 1954, following a failed assassination attempt by a
Muslim Brother against Nasser, the Egyptian government moved against the
organization. Six of their leaders were hanged in December following well-
publicized trials, and hundreds of others were tried and imprisoned. Both
Egypt and the Arab world were stunned and in most cases disapproving.
(It is worth recalling that Nasser's great popularity in the Arab world did
not evolve until after he had secured undisputed leadership of Arabism
and the struggle against outside domination through such acts as signing
the arms deal with the Soviets, nationalizing the Suez Canal, holding out
against the Anglo-French-Israeli invasion of 1956, and uniting Egypt with
Syria to form the United Arab Republic in 1958.)

In the years just prior to the Six Day War, Egypt witnessed yet another
major confrontation between Islamic fundamentalism and established political
order with the harsh crack-down by Nasser's government on Muslim dissidents
in 1965. The following year the movement's chief idealogue, Sayyid Qutb,
was executed—an event that had a somber precedent in the assassination
of Hasan al-Banna, widely believed to have been carried out by the Egyptian
police. The June war was thus not needed to give these dissidents either
their motivation for action or their ideology.[2] Indeed, in Egypt as in the
Arab world, all the essential doctrinal points and at least the cadres for
Muslim fundamentalism were in place well before June 1967.

It is entirely too soon to suggest that the present wave of religio-political
radicalism in the Arab part of the Muslim world will produce the significant
systemic change that the earlier wave associated with Egypt's Hasan al-
Banna did not. Sadat is dead, but the state apparatus associated with his
policies survives. The Arab world's hesitant and contradictory reaction to
the essentially religious communal warfare in Lebanon can hardly be
interpreted in terms of lining up with religious radicalism. Adamantly
secularizing Arab nationalist regimes exist in both Syria and Iraq, not to

mention the Peoples' Democratic Republic of Yemen. Indeed, the only significant recent regime change associated with radical religious politics in the Arab world has been the April 1985 overthrow of Gaafar Nimeiry in Sudan. A major factor leading to his ouster was his rash attempt to impose an Islamic republic and the strict application of the *Shari'ah* on a country that contains large non-Muslim minorities.

Muslim fundamentalism is an important religio-political current in the Arab world, and its importance has grown significantly since 1967. At the same time, those who observe that the Egyptian masses seem increasingly attached to radical Islamic politics might wish to recall that the Egyptian masses of thirty years ago lionized Gamal Abdul Nasser and roared their approval as he lashed out against Arab rivals who attempted to clothe themselves in Islamic symbolism.

The Palestinian Movement and the Arab State System

It has been said that the only victors of the Six Day War were Israel and the PLO. This jeeringly paradoxical statement highlights an important truth: as soon as the dust of battle settled, it seemed clear that the Arab state system was no longer in a position to successfully champion the cause of Palestine. This was an opportunity, bleak as it appeared in mid-1967, for the PLO.

Formally, the PLO had come into existence in 1964 at the behest of the Arab states. The signal for its creation was given at the first Arab Summit Conference in January 1964, organized by Nasser. It was likewise Nasser who more or less hand-picked Ahmed al-Shuqayri, a Palestinian lawyer and flamboyant orator, to put together the Palestine Liberation Organization. This Shuqayri did by May of that year, and the Arab states approved the new entity at the second Arab Summit in September.

The above summary account is not to suggest that the PLO emerged, Athena-like, full-grown from the head of Nasser. This would be to overlook the rich, complex history of the Palestinian national movement both before 1948 and after. More precisely, it would be to overlook the prior creation of the Palestine National Liberation Movement (Fateh), and a significant number of other organizations, not to mention names that have now become household words, such as Yasser Arafat or George Habash.

What can be said, however, is that the formal creation of the PLO in 1964 was a Nasser-led maneuver by the Arab states to direct and thus to control the Palestinian national movement. It was intended to ensure that any Palestinian diplomatic or military initiative would be yoked to an overall Arab strategy. But the Arab leaders who had been able to set aside their many other political differences in pursuit of this strategy were, quite literally, *hors de combat* following the June war. The PLO moved into the breach.

Ahmad al-Shuqayri was soon dropped, and Yasser Arafat assumed the PLO leadership that he has maintained to this day. In 1968, less than a year later, the PLO stand against a punitive Israeli raid at the Jordanian village of Karameh was hailed by Palestinians everywhere as proof of Palestinian organization and will not to be defeated, even less to be disregarded.

What, then, can be said concerning the argument that the June 1967 war set in motion a significant, irreversible development in Palestinian nationalism and thus in the Arab-Israeli confrontation? Given the widespread American tendency to distrust, indeed to disparage, Palestinian nationalism in general and the PLO in particular, one must proceed with care to avoid inadvertently contributing to existing American misperceptions. But while the efforts of the Palestinian leaders after Shuqayri and the staying power of the reconstituted PLO in the face of multiple threats and temptations is impressive by any objective criterion, the many activities on several different fronts in the two decades between 1967 and 1987 do not offer definitive evidence of a systemic change in the nature of the Arab-Israeli confrontation. Moreover, certain other events since 1967 may well stand out as more decisive in shaping the ongoing Arab-Israeli confrontation than the June war.

In the larger temporal context, the Arabs of Palestine have experienced a number of cyclical changes in their relations with the larger Arab world, fluctuating from almost total reliance on outside Arab support and leadership to the other extreme of virtually going it alone. Golda Meir's inexcusably harsh and inept dismissal of the Palestinians as having no existence was based—as are most crude political insults—on a half-truth. Throughout the long period of Ottoman rule the Arabs of Palestine identified themselves not as Palestinians or even primarily as Arabs, but rather on the basis of religion or locale or way of life. This, properly understood, is an unexceptional statement. The same could be said about most peoples everywhere (including Europe) before the age of nationalism and the nation-state.

As the Western-imported virus of nationalism spread throughout the Middle East, the Arabs of Palestine—just as Arabs elsewhere and especially in the Fertile Crescent—faced possible nationalist options, such as Otto-manism, before settling on Arabism firmly in this century. It is indeed a historical fact that the Arabs of "Greater Syria," which includes Palestine, were first and most fervent in their support for Arab nationalism. Thus, in the post-World War One settlement the Palestinians championed not a Palestinian nationalism as such but the creation of a larger Arab state to include Palestine. This sense of attachment to the greater cause of Arabism has never been lost.

At the same time, political borders necessarily dictate the daily arena of most political confrontations. Since 1917 Palestinians have confronted a double challenge in the form of a rival nationalist claim (Zionism) for the same territory and direct or indirect political domination by an outside power (Britain), for that year brought not only the Balfour Declaration but also General Allenby's wresting of Jerusalem from the Ottomans. Add to this that other parts of the Arab world necessarily confronted different political challenges based on different political borders, and it can be seen how naturally a sense of Palestinian identity has evolved over the past seventy years.

This Palestinian political spectrum, ranging from narrowly Palestinian nationalism to broad Arab nationalism, can be partially adumbrated in the following summary time line: (1) the early insistence (c. 1915–1936) on a solution within the framework of a larger Arab state, including Palestine; (2) the impressive but ill-fated "Arab Revolt" in Palestine from 1936 to 1939, during which the major political stimuli came from the Arab Palestinian countryside; (3) a period of disarray and the passing of the initiative from the now-scattered Palestinian leadership to outside Arab leadership, institutionalized from 1945 on in the Arab League; (4) the defeat of the Arab armies in the 1948 Arab-Israeli war followed by a period of even greater despair and dispersal accompanied, however, by the early stirrings of more strictly Palestinian efforts—the gestation period of the later groups such as Fateh; (5) Nasserism from the mid-1950s to the early 1960s, yet another period during which Palestinianism was absorbed into a greater Arabism; and finally, (6) the discrediting of what remained of a declining Nasserist Arabism by the Arab defeat in June 1967.

Continuing the chronology from June 1967 onward, however, uncovers similar shifts on the Palestinian political spectrum. The strict limitation imposed on a nationalist movement-in-exile lacking its own state and its own territory was revealed in the 1970–1971 civil war pitting the Palestinian organization against the state of Jordan. Nor was it lost on the Palestinians that no other Arab state was prepared to put Palestinian interests first. The limits to PLO initiative and PLO autonomy were sharply etched. Seemingly, the Palestinians could not rely on, but also could not do without, the other Arabs.

There soon followed yet another cycle at the state level: the Arab-Israeli war of October 1973 appeared to repair the Arab state system's failure in June 1967 to face up to the challenge from Israel. In the following year, 1974, another Arab summit designated the PLO as "the sole legitimate representative of the Palestinian people." Another Palestinian effort to achieve an acceptable resolution of the conflict with Israel within the framework of the larger Arab unity seemed imminent.

When peace came, however, it was partial—the March 1979 Egyptian-Israeli peace treaty brokered by President Jimmy Carter. Whatever solace the PLO could take in finding that most other Arab states chose to scorn Egypt for having made a separate peace with Israel was soon to be dissolved in the Lebanese tragedy.

It was in Lebanon following the outbreak of the Lebanese civil war that the Palestinians received their cruelest lessons: first, that the constellation of political forces in Lebanon was, on balance, no more prepared to accept an essentially autonomous PLO on their soil than Jordan had been; and second, that no Arab state was prepared to offer more than rhetorical opposition, if that, to anti-PLO activities in Lebanon.

Most traumatic of all were the Israeli interventions, first for a season in 1978 and then bringing full warfare beginning in the summer of 1982.

Surely, from the Palestinian perspective, the ultimately successful Israeli military-diplomatic campaign to force the PLO out of Lebanon brought the matter back to June 1967. The only difference was that this time, instead of Arab armies suffering defeat at the hands of Israel, the Arab state system remained on the sidelines while Israel directly took on a hopelessly mismatched PLO.

One more tragedy remains to be chronicled—the massacres at Sabra and Shatila. While still absorbing the bitter lessons of Arab ineffectiveness in challenging the Israeli invasion, the PLO, militarily ousted from the last territorial refuge that had permitted some degree of political and military autonomy, discovered that the formal and informal commitments of the outside world (especially the United States) and of the invading Israeli forces could not be counted on to protect Palestinian men, women, and children living in the refugee camps. The Palestinian-PLO political cycle had surely reached its nadir.

And yet, six years later, the PLO can demonstrably lay claim to being, as the Rabat Arab Summit stated, "the sole legitimate representative of the Palestinian people." It has also recouped much of the organizational and quasi-military strength it possessed in Lebanon before the 1982 Israeli invasion. Since that time, the PLO has continued to have its ups and downs *vis-à-vis* other Arab states. For somewhat more than a year it pursued a common negotiating front (since broken off) with its old neighbor-enemy King Hussein of Jordan. The PLO has also survived, or so it now seems, a determined effort by President Hafez al-Assad to topple Yasser Arafat and to bring the organization under Syrian control. Moreover, the April 1987 meeting in Algiers of the Palestinian National Council (the Palestinian "parliament-in-exile") seems to have restored PLO unity around Arafat. An increased Soviet commitment to the PLO also appears to have emerged from the Algiers meetings.

On the other hand, while those who over the years have cried after this or that crisis "Bye bye PLO" have been proven wrong, this nationalist organization is no closer to even its minimal goal of statehood in some part of the former mandated Palestine. As in the past, the PLO remains able to secure enough support from Palestinians, other Arabs and the outside world to make its claim to being a necessary player in any Arab-Israeli settlement stick. It cannot be defeated. It cannot be dismissed. Even so, as in the past, the likelihood of its being able to orchestrate things so as to achieve a breakthrough leading to a genuine settlement remains remote. For this reason, it is difficult to claim that the June 1967 war brought about a significant systemic change for the Palestinians.

Instead, it may now be appropriate, twenty years later, to modify the old post-June war aphorism that the only victors were Israel and the PLO. Perhaps there were no victors at all.

Conclusion

The question of how the Six Day War may have changed reality or perceptions in Israel is not within the scope of this paper. Nonetheless, it may be relevant to record the recent reflections of Israel's preeminent diplomat, Abba Eban, known to millions throughout the world for his defense of the Israeli position in the United Nations debates immediately following the June war.

In an interview with *New York Times* correspondent Thomas L. Friedman almost exactly twenty years after the war, Eban noted:

> Although the Six Day War was a tremendous military salvation and political gain, and enabled us to get the peace with Egypt, we went a little bit crazy intellectually as a result of it. We interpreted the war as not just a victory, but as a kind of providential messianic event that changed history permanently and gave Israel the power to dictate the future.[3]

The reality was quite different, Eban told the *Times*. The Arab world remained intact, with the "power of refusal" largely untouched.

June 1967 will always be a significant milestone marking Middle Eastern history. No doubt, things will never be quite the same following those six days of warfare, especially for those peoples and nations directly involved and more particularly the Israelis and Palestinians. Nothing in the above interpretation is intended to discount that manifest truth.

Even so, the regional diplomatic-military system stubbornly survives. Worse, it might well be argued that the stakes in the ongoing game have been raised while the balance of forces has not been sufficiently altered to provoke major change. Six years and four months after the June war, the second largest tank battle in world history took place in the sands of Sinai (the first being that between the Nazis and the Soviets during the second World War). Then, somewhat less than nine years after the October 1973 war, the world watched an Israeli army beseige an Arab capital, Beirut.

In the civil war that has been tearing Lebanon to pieces since 1975, a conservative estimate would total some 47,000 dead. That is more than the dead on both sides in all four Arab-Israel wars of 1948, 1956, 1967, and 1973.

During recent years, of the twenty countries world-wide devoting more than 10 percent of the gross national product to military expenditures, ten are located in the Middle East, with Israel and the confrontation states at the top of the list. The Middle East has for some time now been receiving over 40 percent of the total world arms exports. And from the selling side of the world arms bazaar, Israel, with a population smaller than the state of Maryland's, is the world's ninth leading arms exporter. The proportion of armed forces per 1,000 people worldwide is 6.1. In the Middle East, the figure is 14.5.

To point out that the June 1967 war did not radically change the regional diplomatic-military system is thus not an argument of complacency. It is not to suggest that time will heal these wounds. The situation is getting worse in the Middle East, all within the framework of a tenaciously durable system.

From this perspective, the June war, rather like Black September in Jordan, or the October war, or the Camp David accords, or the Israeli invasion of Lebanon, stands out as yet another would-be turning point that ends up more nearly just spinning in place.

If this bleak analysis is correct then it follows that those who would make peace in the Middle East should study how that system itself might be changed.

Notes

1. Malcom Kerr, *The Arab Cold War: Camal Abd Al-Nasser and His Rivals, 1958-1979* (New York: Oxford University Press, 3rd Edition, 1971), p. 126.

2. Examples from the writing of Egyptian dissidents are given in Emmanuel Sivan, *Radical Islam: Medieval Theology and Modern Politics,* (New Haven: Yale University Press, 1985), pp. 16-18.

3. *New York Times*, (14 June 1987), p. A3.

11

Structural and Ideological Change in the Arab Subsystem Since the Six Day War

Bassam Tibi

Wars are not merely military events. History reveals that the non-military dimensions of war constitute the most important part of their legacy. Wars bring to light other existing conflicts. The military effects of war shape ensuing historical developments in favor of one of the various existing options, either supporting an existing order or breaking new ground for an alternative to it. War can also undermine a prevailing setting without promoting an alternative to it. The June war of 1967 seems to have produced a follow-up development to which the latter case applies. The salient feature of the Middle East since June 1967 is disarray.

Twenty years after June 1967 is time enough to make more than an instant assessment. Yet in the academic literature on the Middle East we find mostly judgments about the June war which scarcely go beyond generalities. Alan Taylor points out that the war "profoundly changed the foundering Arab system,"[1] and he emphasizes that it "irreversibly altered the structure and character of the Arab system."[2] No analysis follows this statement to reveal the alleged change of the "structure and character" of the system. Furthermore, the reader is left on his own to make guesses about the "system." Another author, Cheryl Rubenberg, draws our attention to the fact that the June war "shattered the prevailing stasis" of the major conflict in that area to such an extent that "the Middle East has never

This paper reflects in a summary fashion some of the working hypotheses and preliminary findings of my DFG (Deutsche Forschungs-gemeinschaft) sponsored research project, "Conflict Linkages in the Middle East Since the Six Day War." (That project was carried out at Princeton University in the academic year 1986/87 with an appointment as a Visiting Research Fellow.) The findings of the project will be published in German as a book under the title *Der Nahe Osten seit dem Sechs-Tage-Krieg: Regionale Eigen-dynamik und Grossmachtinteressen*.

been the same."[3] She, too, leaves us without specific knowledge about what Middle East we are dealing with after the events of June 1967.

Carl Brown suggests a reinterpretation of the effects and of the historical background of the June war. On this basis he argues that the Six Day War did not usher in a significant systematic change.[4] To Carl Brown, the basic features of the Arab-Israeli conflict after June 1967 are still the same and Nasser's weakness did not start with the crushing defeat of June 1967 but occurred earlier. Moreover, Brown argues that Islamic religio-political radicalism cannot be attributed to the de-legitimization triggered since that defeat. He is of the view that religion and politics have always been related to one another in the order of the day in the Middle East. Brown is right in insisting that the June war "must not be pushed forward to explain everything." In my view, however, he failed to consider the importance of the spin-off effects of that military event which contributed to developing a historical turning point structurally and ideologically.

The major concern of a reassessment is not to confirm or to refute those who exaggerate the overall importance of the June war or to reject those who deny it was a real turning point. It is rather the historical scope of that war, within which it should be placed as a crucial event. In my view, Moroccan historian Abdallah Laroui grasps the ultimate meaning of June 1967 in viewing the date of that war as the beginning of a completely new historical period in the modern Middle East.[5] He characterizes previous periods as follows: 1) From 1850 to 1914 Middle Easterners went through the *nahda*, a period during which they sought to revive their classical culture and simultaneously assimilate modern Western achievements, 2) Following the *nahda*, the Arabs, now subject to colonial rule, fought for the decolonization of their territories, 3) Decolonization resulted in building up the modern state. Looking at this sub-divided Arab entity as a colonial legacy, the Arabs of the post-colonial period committed themselves to a pan-Arab unionist movement which took on different forms. To Laroui, June 1967 marked a process of "moral crisis," which "culminated in a period of anguished self-criticism, a searching reappraisal of post-war Arab culture and political practice. The principal victim of this process has been Nasserism."[6]

In dealing with the "crisis of Arab intellectuals," Laroui focuses on the ideological and cultural consequences of the Six Day War. There are, however, also systematic changes to deal with, provided we accept the Middle East as a regional system of its own. Taylor and Rubenberg, and to a certain extent also Carl Brown, look at the Middle East from outside, though the latter scholar is—at times—critical of such a way of looking at regional development. On the other hand, Laroui, living in the region and belonging to it, views the region in a completely different way. This author once participated most intensely in the Arab debate of "anguished self-criticism"[7] after June 1967, but he shares with the quoted scholars the fact of being a part of Western (in his case, West European) scholarship in the Middle East.

In this chapter I want to make an effort, in a modest way, to combine the views of the people of the region itself with the scholarly manner of analyzing the impact of the June war. In addition to the contrasting views of the "insiders" and "outsiders," we are at the very outset confronted with the diverging schools of thought of "regionalism" and "globalism." They provide different ways of looking at political development in a region like the Middle East. There exists no clear separation between insiders and outsiders and globalists and regionalists, since insiders tend to be globalists when they blame outside powers for their own problems while outsiders, being mostly globalists, fail to see the regional dynamics of events.

The June War: Between Globalism and Regionalism

In dealing with the Middle East since the June war,[8] without repeating the historical events easily accessible in a wide range of books and articles,[9] there is a need to make an effort at conceptualization. The June war shattered the societies of the geographical area of the Middle East profoundly. (We still incorrectly call that geographical area "Middle East" in a Euro-centric manner, despite the fact that the historical period of Europe being the center of the world has come to an end.[10] Looked at from another geographical perspective, say from West Africa or Latin America, China or California, the area that we are talking about is not the "Middle East," and it is geographically simply wrong to employ this term from such a perspective. However, the superpowers, who have now inherited the old power position of Europe, adopted this term. I use it in my presentation for reasons of easy comprehension.)

The very name "Middle East," which originated in the colonial past, draws our attention to the fact that this area of the world is part of a world order. On the one hand, we cannot deal with the micro-structure without referring to the overall structure. But, on the other, we cannot deduce regional developments from this macro-structure that we call world order or world society.[11] This leads us to discuss, in a very brief way, regionalism and globalism as a conceptual frame of reference for studying the historical importance of the June war, and the developments it has triggered.

The debate between globalists and regionalists is of long standing in the academic discipline of international relations. Since the end of World War II particularly, the school of thought represented by the "globalists" has sought to interpret world politics within a frame of reference that reduces the complex structures of world order, or as some say the international system, to a simple bipolar structure. This bipolarity refers to the East-West conflict.[12] Even scholars dealing with area studies have been strongly affected by this bias. In our field of inquiry, Middle East studies, the poison of Cold War ideologies made the scholarly character of many publications of the 1950s and 1960s questionable. In my view, the concept of the regional subsystem, first outlined by Leonard Binder in 1958 and further developed in the following two decades by other scholars,[13] was and still is a viable methodological option for analyzing political, social, and economic change in regions of our world, and it is free from bipolar bias.

I try to employ this concept in my study of the historical period in the Middle East between 1967 and 1982. In this study, I deal with the regional international relations of the Middle East. The year 1967 refers to the Six Day War. I, however, am interested not in this war but rather in its repercussions, as well as the new period it has launched. In my view, the year 1982 marks an end to that period not because of Israel's invasion of Lebanon, but because it tentatively marks the end of the oil age in the Arab subsystem of world order. Students of oil issues are aware that the international phenomenon of the "oil glut," with the concomitant dropping of oil prices, started in that year. The oil price slide later became even more dramatic.[14] Since December 1986 oil prices have been rising again. But dealing with this lies beyond the scope of my study. The underlying concern in beginning my study with the year 1967 is the assumption that the events of June 1967 were a turning point in the contemporary history of the Middle East.

The very first question that arises when subscribing to a conceptual approach for analyzing historical developments subsequent to the June war refers to the regional actors and to their relations with external actors. Global models dealing with this issue are preoccupied mostly with superpower rivalries. Peoples of the region are ignored or perceived in a distorted way. One distortion is to look at regional actors as allies or proxies of one or the other superpower. Seen from this angle, they can only be perceived as friends or as enemies. If they are neither allies nor proxies, then they seem to be "nativists" or fundamentalists. U.S. foreign policy decision-makers generally subscribe to this view. The so-called "nativists" are perceived as reactionaries by the Soviet foreign policy experts, who view events in a way reversed, yet similar to their American counterparts. Afghanistan is a case in point. Superpowers have always tried to fit the Middle East, as well as other non-Western regions, into their schemes.

A more fruitful way of dealing with the Middle East since the June war can be pursued with the help of the framework of regional subsystems, developed during the 1970s and since neglected.[15] In so doing, we should look at the Middle East as a regional subsystem, with interstate relations in that region composed of interaction taking place within that subsystem. However, we have to take into consideration that these states are very different in their structures and in their outlooks. The standards of their development, their natural resources, as well as their military, economic, and political capabilities are so different that it is simply wrong to talk about a single "Arab society," al-mujtama' al-'Arabi, as many Arab writers do, or about an Arab world, as many Western analysts do. We should rather talk about a system with a regional setting, a system with a great exposure to those external powers seeking allies or proxies to impose and promote their interests with the assistance of local actors. The reference to the superpowers' interests in the Middle East should, however, not mislead us to adopt viewpoints implied in the global models, which we have just criticized. Viewing the role of the superpowers should not distract us from recognizing the dynamics of the interstate relations in the area. Analysts focusing on the superpower involvement in the Middle East generally overlook this regional dynamic, and if they do not, they believe it derives from outside forces. This notion is unfortunately equally true for American scholars, aiming to sell their Middle East expertise to foreign policy decision-makers, and for those Middle Easterners who exclusively explain the problems of their region as merely the effects of its penetration by the superpowers.

There exists another extreme, opposed to the global models and to the views of those who put the blame on outside powers. It is the extreme of a pure regional analysis. Analysts working within regional confines tend to be shortsighted because they cannot view the problems in a full-scale context. It is not my aim to provide here a fully elaborated methodological essay. I merely want to emphasize the need for a comprehensive analysis, combining both regional and international aspects, in order to attain a proper conceptual understanding of the interstate relations in the Middle East since the June war.

Another issue must be raised before addressing some of the effects of the June war. In arguing that the war triggered substantial regional political processes, we implicitly assume and consequently accept the notion of the regional system or subsystem. We then cannot escape the question concerning the delimitation of the subsystem: which countries are members of the system, and to what extent do they constitute a system? If we focus on socio-cultural and linguistic criteria in talking about the Arab states when we deal with the Middle East, we exclude three active and most important regional actors, Turkey, Iran, and Israel. Indeed, the criterion of cultural identity for identification with the region is problematic. Views about it—whether this identity is Arabism or Islam or whatever—are divided. In other words, it is questionable to restrict the Middle East to an ideological entity (a pan-Arab region[16]) or an Islamic one (the Muslim *umma*[17]). A scholarly analysis has to leave such ideological concepts aside and deal with the region as a whole, including Turkey, Iran, and Israel.[18] *Structural interconnectedness* and the *density of interaction* (cooperation and integration as well as discord) are the criteria that I employ to define and delimit the Middle East as a regional subsystem. In my presentation, I want to focus on the political, military, and strategic formations of the region. In restricting my analysis to the Arab states, I merely focus on inter-Arab state relations.

The Arab Part of the Subsystem and Its Center: A Shift from Cairo to Riyadh?

Regional subsystems are, to a certain extent, regionally autonomous. They have regional dynamics which cannot be directed by the global powers. They are, however, subordinate systems since they are part and parcel of the global system. Internally, these subsystems have a regional hierarchy of power and social stratification.[19] In the Middle East, Egypt was (and to a certain extent still is, notwithstanding its limited resources) the most developed Arab state. It is in this sense that Egypt has been considered the center of the Arab part of the subsystem. Nasser added to the real structural weight of Egypt an ideological claim.

Prior to the June war Egypt itself claimed to be the center of the Arab entity in the Middle East.[20] Ideologically, Nasserism was the mainstream. The analysis of social-structural constraints shows, however, that the Nasserite ideology of pan-Arabism did not correspond with real underlying structures. Little structural interconnectedness and little interaction existed. Ideologically, the Arabs condemn the barriers of the nation-states as an outcome of the colonial legacy. These condemnations were part and parcel of the foreign policy pronouncements of most of the Arab states. In reality, these barriers were nevertheless jealously preserved and protected. Egypt under Nasser was the center in terms of ideology, but not in terms of political and structural hegemony. The scarcity of resources in Egypt was a great impediment in translating the pronouncements of the pan-Arab ideology of Nasserism into real foreign policy performance, beyond the well-known rhetoric. The involvement in the war in Yemen and the serious negative effects it had on the Egyptian economy clearly indicated Egypt's limits. If Nasser's Egypt had had the required resources to back its claim to be a regional superpower, it would have been a real center of the Middle Eastern regional subsystem. It is true that Egypt under Nasser had the strongest army and the greatest skills of all the Arab states, and this reality reflected the arrogant saying that "the Arabs are nothing without Egypt." Among the Arab states Egypt is, however, a country with very scarce resources and therefore lacks the needed leverage for a hegemonic regional policy. In the regional stratification of the subsystem, Egypt belongs to the poor and not to the rich states.[21]

The June war did not lead merely to the crushing of Egyptian military power. The Israeli blitzkrieg-like destruction of the Egyptian air force on the ground stood symbolically for other destruction, most notably of the Nasserite experiment as such. The subsequent Arab summit at Khartoum in August 1967 was indicative of this. Egypt withdrew even its verbal claims. Symbolically, it withdrew its military forces from Yemen. Egypt's adversaries among the Arabs began to show courage. It was fortunate that Nasser died only three years after the crushing of his experiment, for he was spared witnessing further damage. For some, he has survived historically as an innocent hero, victimized by the event.[22] We know, however, from the outstanding research of John Waterbury, that the Nasserite experiment failed as a model of development. The failure was related to structural constraints, as well as to inadequate policy performance and planning.[23] This happened prior to the June defeat, which was, in this respect, merely an eye-opening event.

On the regional level, greater interstate rivalries were the result of Egypt's withdrawal from leadership in the Arab arena. The rich Arab oil states started to lay the foundation of the new "oil age" in Arab politics.[24] To describe this process, an Arab saying became widespread: *min markaz al-thawra ila markaz al-tharwa* (from the center of revolution to the center of wealth). Accordingly, the *markaz* (center) has become Saudi Arabia, which seemingly started to replace Egypt in the Arab system.[25]

Unlike Egypt, the newly acclaimed center-state Saudi Arabia is not poor in resources by any means.[26] A transfer of resource possession into hegemonic position, however, presupposes a certain level of structural development, which is not assured by the availability of "wealth" as such. In fact, it is lacking in Saudi Arabia, despite the great efforts in developmental planning in the past years. Not surprisingly, Saudi Arabia itself has never claimed to be a center. William Quandt is right when he argues that this role has been imputed to the Saudis by foreigners.[27]

An author in the prominent Egyptian foreign policy periodical *al-Siyassa al-Duwaliyya* (issued by al-Ahram Center for Political and Strategic Studies) describes the retreat of Egypt since 1967 in the following way: "New centers of power and of political leadership have come into being in the Arab region. They emerged from the wealth of oil which started to be an alternative source to that of pan-Arabism. . . . the conservative state . . . became victorious, and it is the one which now prevails in the Arab East. Ever since the Arab summit at Khartoum in August 1967 this tendency has become clear."[28] However, in the same Egyptian journal the director of the al-Ahram Center, Sayed Yassin, warns against overemphasizing the new Saudi role. For him it is true "that Saudi Arabia has acquired a central role in Arab politics. . . . It is, however, wrong to assume that Egypt's role has been taken over by Saudi Arabia."[29] Yassin draws attention to the structural weakness of Saudi Arabia that render the nation unable to assume the role of a hegemonic power. Saudi Arabia lacks the needed leverage for the practice of such a hegemonic policy. We know that the Saudi foreign policy is based on "pursestrings."[30] Checks cannot replace such needed leverage as military and economic power. A bank account or oil in the ground is not economic leverage; nor is modern weaponry, without the needed skills and technical infrastructure, military leverage.

In sum, Saudi Arabia has advanced since 1967 to become a central state in the Middle Eastern regional subsystem, but has not replaced Egypt. Until the Camp David accords Saudi Arabia sought to make use of the structurally more developed Egypt to serve its own ends.[31] During the 1970s the Arab part of the Middle Eastern regional subsystem no longer had a center of its own. Competing rival centers emerged (Syria, Iran, Libya, Algeria) since none of the Arab countries had either a strong basis of power like Egypt, or the uncontested political leadership that Nasserism once possessed. The region ever since has been a "fragmented system"[32] characterized at times as polycentric and at other times as being in complete disarray.[33]

Political Petrolism
as an Alternative to Nasserism?

In an interesting article Bahgat Korany coined the term "political petrolism" to denote the main feature of Arab politics since the crushing Egyptian defeat in June 1967. The shift from Nasserist Egypt as a base to Saudi Arabia as a center of politics based on oil wealth marks the emergence of political petrolism. In fact, two different models of development were competing: Nasserism and petrolism. In the words of Korany, "Nasserism seemed to embody the Arabs' urge for liberation and their insistence on a distinct identity. As well, Nasserism expressed a new type of leadership . . . Nasser talked directly to the Arab masses over the heads of their traditional leaders . . . "[34] (The competing options are substantially a regional variety of the overall competition in our modern age that Reinhard Bendix analyzed most clearly on a world historical level in his masterfully written book, *Kings or People*.[35])

The problem with Nasserism is that it was based on rhetoric rather than on a consistent strategy of development. It is true that Nasser provided a model for overcoming underdevelopment. In the previously cited, extremely well-grounded work of John Waterbury there is strong evidence for the assessment that the model was ill-planned and lacked consistency.[36] Jean Lacouture is correct in calling Nasser an "orator." The Nasserist period, he says, "can perhaps be summed up as a time of poetry, and it must be said that poetry and politics do not always have very close relations, and poetry can lead to political difficulties and disappointments. . . . The orator has given way to the manager, the banker or the technician . . . Egypt is outclassed by massive oil producers like Iraq and Saudi Arabia and Iran. It seems to me that in some ways *the time of the canal is past and the day of the Gulf has dawned*."[37]

The rivalry between the Egyptian and the Saudi model, that is between Nasserism and political petrolism, has a historical parallel. Mohammed Ali began in 1805 to establish a modern Egypt,[38] while the Wahhabis of Arabia were fighting for a return of pristine Islam.[39] The Wahhabis viewed innovations as *bid'a*, (deviation) from true Islam, whereas Mohammed Ali aimed at introducing modernity and at adopting Western achievements.[40] He had overall regional claims as Nasser did. Both failed for internal and external reasons. Salafi (backward oriented) Islam in its Wahhabi variety was the response both to Mohammed Ali and to Nasser. The former was able to overcome the warriors of pristine Islam and the latter failed.[41] Political petrolism proved to be a powerful force. Can we truly speak of a combination of Islam and oil as do some biased authors such as Daniel Pipes in his widely read book, *In the Path of God: Islam and Political Power*?[42] An answer requires a closer examination of the issue.

Political Petrolism and Political Islam Since June 1967

In his article, "The June War: A Turning Point?" Carl Brown rejects the idea that political Islam emerged from the crushing 1967 defeat. Indeed, Islam is not an oil-related issue, for it has always been the heart of the religio-culture and of the religio-polity of the Middle East. Brown is right when he draws our attention to the fact that Islam has never been far from politics even during the earlier liberal period and the time of Nasser. It is true that Nasser deferred to Islam, as have many other secular Arab political leaders. Their recourse to Islam served secular ends, however. Morroe Berger showed this clearly in his book *Islam in Egypt Today*.[43]

It was utterly clear that, notwithstanding all references to Islam, the legitimacy of Arab political systems which suffered the crushing defeat of June 1967 was secular. In this sense we can talk about a legitimacy crisis or the de-legitimization of the secular Arab regimes.[44] The reference of Carl Brown in his paper to two non-Arab countries promoting political Islam, Pakistan and Iran, should not distract us from the fact that the current re-politicization of Islam started in Egypt.[45] (The writings of Khomeini were absolutely unknown in the Arab East prior to the emergence of the Iranian *mullacracy*.) In the early 1970s Egyptian and Lebanese authors started to offer *al-hall al-Islami (the Islamic solution)*[46] as an alternative to such "imported solutions" as liberalism, nationalism, socialism and Marxism.

The re-emergence of political Islam, or what Carl Brown terms "religio-political radicalism," was due to the June defeat as far as the Arab East is concerned. Since the leading theological writers are Egyptians generally, and since the Arab East is considered to be the core of Sunni Islam, the spill-over of political Islam came from Cairo to non-Arab countries in Africa and also in Asia. It did not happen the other way around.

Many non-Shia Muslims in Arab and non-Arab countries admired Khomeini at the outset for toppling the mighty Shah. There were, however, no noteworthy attempts at copying the Shia version of political Islam in Sunni countries.[47] It was the June defeat and not the spill-over of the Iranian revolution that has been behind the emergence of political Islam in the Arab East. The advancement of the "Gulf" at the expense of the "Suez Canal" coincided with the re-politicization of Islam. Oil is, however, not the background of political Islam, notwithstanding the obvious Saudi attempts to employ politicized Islam in the service of their political ends. It is therefore completely wrong to allege that the "great oil boom" explains political Islam.[48] It is sad to see how some authors confuse oil and the religio-cultural constraints of politics.

Two Decades in the Shadow of the 1967 Defeat: Pax Saudiana, De-Legitimization, and Political Islam— Disunity and Fragmentation

In my view, the most adequate characterization of the impact of the June war on the entire Middle East, and of ensuing developments, is the one offered by the Moroccan historian Laroui in the word "crisis." The Middle East has never experienced such a difficult period in its modern history. Even the colonial conquest of the Middle East did not cause the disarray that has characterized the Middle East and its people during the two decades since June 1967.

The new central actor-state in the region, Saudi Arabia, did not offer any new options other than political petrolism. Despite the widespread consensus, Saudi Arabia did not aggressively promote political Islam. Although it has used Islam for security reasons, it has cared little about *al-hall al-Islami* propagated by the Islamic neo-fundamentalists, notwithstanding the fact that they received oil money to the extent that this was convenient to the Saudis.

Saudi Arabia has always been preoccupied with its own internal stability, tending to consider foreign policy issues only as they affect inner security of the Saudi state.[49] It is true that Saudi Arabia has been promoting political Islam, but its paramount concern has been its own security.

Political Islam, however, has been a double-edged sword in domestic and regional Middle Eastern politics.[50] It is like Pandora's box: once you open it, you never know what will come out. Those who opened it unleashed forces they could not command. Sadat was assassinated by an Islamist, and the Saudis who promoted the concerns of political Islam are now becoming victimized by their own proteges.

Prior to the June war the ideology of pan-Arabism was the ideological device of Arab interstate relations. Nationalism was accepted as an ideology. The reality is that we live in nation-states in accord with the order that originated in Europe[51] and then spread worldwide. It is sad to see the esteemed Carl Brown calling this process "the Western-imported *virus* of nationalism." It was not only the ideology of nationalism that spread in the Middle East. It was the new institutional structure of the system of international relations, in which the nation-state constitutes a unit of action and interaction. The nation-state—and not the ideology it fosters—is an actor in the international system. Muslim fundamentalists (traditionalists) and neo-fundamentalists (Islamic militants, mostly laymen without a traditional educational Islamic background) despise the nation-state, which has replaced the universal Islamic order of caliphate. They view the emergence of the nation-state as a Western conspiracy against Islam. Islam and nationalism have always been at odds.[52] Islam is a universalism that aims at uniting all Muslims in a comprehensive *umma* (community), whereas Arab nationalism merely aims at a pan-Arab state on the already existing basis of the nation-state. Pan-Arabism is a future-related utopia aimed at uniting the existing Arab nation-states in one pan-Arab state, whereas political Islam aims at restoring the Islamic past of universal glory.

The question arises of how both ideologies are related to the post-June 1967 political development in the Middle Eastern subsystem. One can talk in a rhetorical manner of the "end of pan-Arabism" as Fouad Ajami once did.[53] But this cannot replace a serious scholarly analysis. Pan-Arabism was the hope of the peoples of the Arab part of the Middle East. It was not merely an ideology of its own; it symbolized hope for a better future based on unifying the Arabs in their efforts to harness their available structural resources and transform their societies into developed ones, free of external hegemony. This ideology symbolizing the Arab hope for a better future has, nevertheless, been employed in intra-Arab disputes. Most of the Arab political conflicts prior to June 1967 were related to this regional preoccupation in interstate relations.

The years 1967–1970 were clearly characterized by a vacuum in Arab leadership. They were also characterized by a search for other options. The hitherto prevailing strategies and options had proved unsuccessful with the defeat in the June war. In the aftermath of the period of uncertainty, the rise of political Islam characterized the 1970s and culminated in the Iranian Revolution of 1979. Khomeini sought to export his clerical vision into the Arab environment. Without belittling political Islam or the spill-over effects of the Iranian Revolution, I have shown in my article the limits of a "revolution for export" claimed by Iran.[54] The upheaval in Iran clearly revealed, however, that in terms of structural interconnectedness and interaction, the Middle East is not reducible to the Arab states system, as I have indicated earlier. Long before the Iranian Revolution, political Islam had become a salient feature in the domestic policies and in regional interstate relations.

One of the declared objectives of the Islamists has been reduce external hegemony in the region. Ironically enough, it was the Islamic Revolution in Iran that has contributed to intensifying the penetration of the region by the middle-range powers and the superpowers in their role as arms suppliers. The destructive and never ending Iraq-Iran war contributes to a hitherto unprecedented degree of superpower involvement in the region. Huge arms shipments to Iran and Iraq from the superpowers, and also the Soviet intervention in Afghanistan, are indicative of this and support this observation. To be fair, we have to add to this statement that it is not political Islam which has contributed to this end; it was the June war which launched a further militarization of the entire Middle Eastern subsystem. Figure 11.1 shows that the Middle East increased its percentage share of the Third World's import of major weapons from 31.6 percent to 43.4 percent in the period after the June war. This trend accelerated after the October 1973 war and reached a peak of 54.3 percent of all Third World military imports. These military expenditures menace the economic and social development of the sadly underdeveloped countries of the region, for they waste resources that could have been employed for better ends. Among the twenty largest Third World weapon-importing countries, the eleven Middle Eastern states rank at the top. (See Table 11.1.)

In drawing conclusions, I want to characterize the inter-Arab state system relations as a system without a center, or in other words, a body without a head. Egypt, the most advanced Arab society, lost its leading position after the June war. Instead of recovering and returning to the system in better shape as a result of having learned from the bitter experience of the past, Egypt involved itself in a separate peace treaty with Israel. No prudent person would dispute the idea that peace between Israel and the Arab states is the primary precondition to better development of the Middle East. But only a comprehensive peace based on mutuality could contribute

158

FIGURE 11.1   Percentage Shares of Imports of Major Weapons,
              Third World by Region, 1963-1982

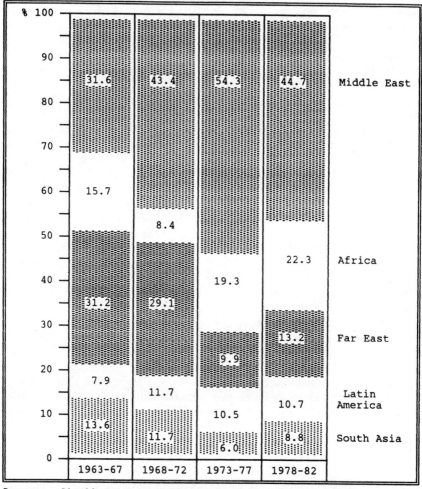

Source: Stockholm International Peace Research Institute,
          World Armaments and Disarmament, SIPRI Yearbook 1983
          (London and New York: Taylor & Francis Ltd., 1983),
          p. 271.   Reprinted by permission of the publisher.

TABLE 11.1 Rank Order of the 20 Largest Third World Major
Weapon Importing Countries, 1978-1982

Percentages are based on SIPRI trend indicator values, as
expressed in U.S. $ million, at constant (1975) prices.

Importing Country	Percentage of Total Third World Imports	Importing Country	Percentage of Total Third World Imports
1. Syria	9.4	11. Morocco	2.4
2. Libya	9.2	12. Algeria	2.4
3. Saudi Arabia	8.2	13. Jordan	2.3
4. India	6.5	14. S. Yemen	2.1
5. Egypt	5.8	15. Argentina	1.8
6. Iraq	5.2	16. Peru	1.5
7. Israel	4.9	17. Indonesia	1.4
8. S. Korea	4.1	18. Taiwan	1.3
9. Iran	3.5	19. Cuba	1.2
10. Viet Nam	2.5	20. Thailand	1.1
		Others	22.1
		Total	100.0
		TOTAL VALUE	47,710

Source: Stockholm International Peace Research Institute,
World Armaments and Disarmament, SIPRI Yearbook 1983
(London and New York: Taylor & Francis Ltd., 1983),
pp. 270-271. Reprinted by permission of the
publisher.

to this end. Camp David could have become a positive turning point if it had been, as envisaged by President Carter,[55] based on a comprehensive peace settlement. Instead it turned out to be a separate peace treaty paving the way for further, limited regional wars. The Lebanon war of 1982 was a case in point.[56]

If we define stability not by simply referring to the frequency of violent political changes, but by referring instead to the accepted legitimacy of political regimes, then we cannot fail to describe most of the Middle Eastern political regimes as unstable, based primarily on coercion. Their superficial stability is deceiving, since it lacks durable bases. The current Middle Eastern state system can be characterized on the one hand as domestically unstable and regionally diffuse and, on the other, as a regional subsystem with a great deal of international penetration. No serious short-term analysis can show a light at the end of the tunnel. The "age of oil" during the period of 1967-1982 was characterized by lack of hope and despair. The resort to political Islam was not an expression of hope but rather a sign of the desperation of the hopeless.[57] One could describe it as a "bedouinization"[58] of Arab politics. This age has been coming to an end since 1982 in the sense that oil prices are falling and the Arab oil states are loosing their "pursestrings," but it is not an end in the sense that a light at the end of the tunnel has become foreseeable. If we avoid self-deceit and naive optimism, we cannot fail to see how sad and how unpromising all future prospects for the Middle East really are.

Notes

1. Alan R. Taylor, *The Arab Balance of Power* (Syracuse, NY: Syracuse University Press, 1982), p. 43.

2. Ibid., p. 47.

3. Cheryl A. Rubenberg, *Israel and the American Interest* (Urbana and Chicago: Illinois University Press, 1986), p. 88.

4. L. Carl Brown, "The June War: A Turning Point?" delivered at the American University Conference on twenty years after the Six Day War, and published in this volume. The references to Carl Brown are quotations from this paper. See also Carl Brown, *International Politics and the Middle East: Old Rules, Dangerous Game* (Princeton, NJ: Princeton University Press, 1984), in which he views the current problems of the Middle East in historical continuity with the "classical Eastern question."

5. Abdallah Laroui, *The Crisis of the Arab Intellectual: Traditionalism or Historicism?* (Berkeley, CA: University of California Press, 1976), pp. VII–XI.

6. Ibid., p. VIII.

7. The most important contribution on this Arab "anguished self-criticism" is the book by Sadiq al-Azm, *Al-Naqd al-Dhati Ba'd al-Hazima* (Beirut: Dar al-Tali'a Press 1968). The debate to which this author also contributed was published mainly in periodicals, among which were *Mawaqif, Dirasat Arabiyya, al-Adab.* For an overview of this debate, including the contributions of al-Azm and my own, see Fouad Ajami, *The Arab Predicament: Arab Political Thought and Practice since 1967* (Cambridge: Cambridge University Press, 1981), Chapter one, pp. 28–29, 30–37.

8. The military part of the Six Day War is best described by Edgar O'Ballance, *The Third Arab-Israeli War* (London: Faber & Faber, 1972). See also the historical survey of Egyptian historian Abdulazim Ramadan, *Tahtim al-Aliha: Qissat harb yunio 1967 (The Destruction of the Gods: The History of the June War 1967)*, two volumes (Cairo: Maktabat Madbuli Press, Vol. I 1985, Vol. II 1986). The term "destruction of the Gods" refers here to the de-legitimization of the Arab leaders after June 1967.

9. See, among others, *The Arab-Israeli Confrontation of June 1967*, Ibrahim Abu-Lughod, ed. (Evanston, IL: Northwestern University Press, 1970).

10. See Roderic H. Davidson, "Where is the Middle East?" in Richard Nolte, ed., *The Modern Middle East* (New York: Atherton Press, 1963), pp. 13–29, and Nikki Keddie, "Is There a Middle East?" *International Journal of Middle East Studies* Vol. 4 (1973), pp. 255–271 (Focus on Iran). The best political geography of the Middle East so far is provided by Alasdair Drysdale and Gerald H. Blake, *The Middle East and North Africa, A Political Geography* (Oxford: Oxford University Press, 1985).

11. See the works of Hedley Bull, the Anarchical Society, *A Study of Order in World Politics* (New York: Columbia University Press, 1977), and Hedley Bull/Adam Watson, eds., *The Expansion of International Society* (Oxford: Oxford University Press, 1984).

12. Morton A. Kaplan, *System and Process in International Politics* (New York: Wiley, 1957).

13. Leonard Binder, "The Middle East as a Subordinate International System," in *World Politics*, Vol 10: 3 (1958), pp. 408–429. The early scholarly debate on "subsystems" is documented in the books of Louis J. Cantori and Steven Spiegel, *The International Politics of Regions* (Englewood Cliffs, NJ: Prentice Hall, 1970) and in Richard A. Falk/Saul H. Mendlovitz, eds., *Regional Politics and World Order* (San Francisco: W.H. Freeman, 1973). The debate has ever since taken place mostly in scholarly periodicals. Among the many recent articles with reference to the Middle East are William R. Thompson, "Delineating Regional Subsystems: Visit Networks and the Middle Eastern Case," in *International Journal of Middle East Studies*, Vol. 13 (1981), pp. 213–235, and James H. Lebovic, "The Middle East: The Region as a System," in *International Interaction*, Vol. 12: 3 (1986), pp. 267–289.

14. See the briefing in the monthly journal *Petroleum Economist*, (London); see also B. Tibi, "Der Oelpreis-Sturz und seine Opfer," in *Anno 86, Bertelsmann Jahrbuch* (Gutersloh: Bertelsmann Press, 1986), pp. 91–95.

15. Some of the main issues of this debate, referred to in my introductory remarks, are summarized in the article by William R. Thompson, "The Regional Subsystem: A Conceptual Explication and a Propositional Inventory," in *International Studies Quarterly*, Vol. 17 (1973), pp. 87–117.

16. This is the argument of Jamil Matar and Ali Eddin Hillal in *al-Nizam al-Iqlimi al-Arabi* (Beirut: Center for Arab Unity Studies, Third edition, 1983).

17. Such arguments can be found in Asaf Hussain, *Political Perspectives on the Muslim World* (New York: St. Martin's Press, 1984); see my critical review in *The Middle East Journal*, Vol. 40: 1 (Winter 1987), pp. 105–106.

18. The author follows the delimitation of Michael Hudson, "The Middle East," in James Rosenau, ed., *World Politics* (New York: The Free Press 1976), pp. 466–500.

19. For a social stratification of the Middle East see the valuable contribution of John Waterbury in John Waterbury and Ragaei El Mallakh, *The Middle East in the Coming Decade* (New York: Council on Foreign Relations, McGraw-Hill, 1978), esp. pp. 27ff.

20. See B. Tibi, "Aegypten und seine arabische Umwelt," in *Beitraege zur Konfliktforschung*, Vol. 12,4 (1982), pp. 33–60.

21. See Malcolm H. Kerr and El Sayed Yassin, eds., *Rich and Poor States in the Middle East* (Boulder. CO: Westview Press, 1982), esp. part 3.

22. Most of the articles of the special issue of the periodical *Qadaya Arabiyya* (ed. Anis Sayigh/Beirut): *Abdul Nasser wa ma ba'd* (Beirut, 1980) subscribed to such a view.

23. John Waterbury, *The Egypt of Nasser and Sadat: The Political Economy of Two Regimes* (Princeton, NJ: Princeton University Press, 1983), pp. 99–100.

24. See Saad Eddin Ibrahim, *The New Arab Social Order: A Study of the Social Impact of Oil Wealth* (Boulder, CO: Westview Press, 1982); see also the contribution of S.E. Ibrahim to the volume of Kerr amd Yassin cited in note 21 above.

25. See B. Tibi, "Vom Zentrum der Revolution zum Zentrum des Petro-Dollars. Aegypten und Saudi-Arabien in der Neuen Arabischen Sozialordnung," in *Beitraege zur Konfliktforschung* Vol. 14: 2 (1984), pp. 101–128.

26. Tim Niblock, ed., *State, Society and Economy in Saudi Arabia* (New York: St. Martin's Press, 1982). This volume includes many interesting contributions.

27. William B. Quandt, *Saudi Arabia in the 1980s: Foreign Policy, Security, and Oil* (Washington, DC: The Brookings Institution, 1981), p. 135.

28. Hassan Abu-Talib, "Azmat siyasat al-tadamun al-Arabi," in *al-Siyassa al-Duwaliyya* (Issue no. 68, 1982), pp. 359–361.

29. El Sayed Yassin, editorial in *al-Siyassa al-Duwaliyya*, (Issue no. 62, 1980), p. 929.

30. L. Turner and J. Bedore, "Saudi Arabia, the Power of the Pursestrings," *International Affairs*, Vol. 54 (1978), pp. 405–420.

31. See the article by Paul Jabber, "Oil, Arms, and Regional Diplomacy: Strategic Dimensions of the Saudi-Egyptian Relationship," in the volume by Kerr and Yassin cited in note 21 above, pp. 415–447.

32. Tareq Y. Ismael, *International Relations of the Contemporary Middle East* (Syracuse, NY: Syracuse University Press, 1986), pp. 59ff.

33. See the interpretation of Paul C. Noble, "The Arab System: Opportunities, Constraints and Pressures," in Bahgat Korany and Ali Hillal Dessouki, eds., *The Foreign Policy of Arab States* (Boulder, CO: Westview Press, 1984), pp. 41ff.

34. Bahgat Korany, "Political Petrolism and Contemporary Arab Politics, 1967–1983," in *Journal of Asian and African Studies*, Vol. 21: 1–2 (1986), pp. 66–80; here p. 69.

35. Reinhard Bendix, *Kings or People: Power and Mandate to Rule* (Berkeley: California University Press, 1978).

36. See the outstanding book by John Waterbury cited in note 23 above.

37. Jean Lacouture, "The Changing Balance of Forces in the Middle East," in *Journal of Palestine Studies*, Vol. 2: 4 (1972/73), pp. 25–32; here p. 26, italics my own.

38. More details about this period are provided by Afaf Lutfi al Sayyed-Marsot, *Egypt in the Reign of Muhammed Ali* (Cambridge: Cambridge University Press, 1984).

39. For more details about the Wahhabis see the classic article by Richard Hartmann, "Die Wahhabiten," in *Zeitschrift der Deutschen Morgenlandischen Gesellschaft* (ZMG), Vol. 78 (1924), pp. 176–213.

40. The historical clash between Mohammed Ali's modernization and Wahhabi Islam as contrary models of development is shown in B. Tibi, *Arab Nationalism: A Critical Enquiry* (New York: St. Martin's Press, 1981) chapter 4, esp. pp. 53ff., 62ff.

41. See the historical overview of the Saudi-Egyptian link provided by Daniel Crecelius, "Saudi-Egyptian Relations," *International Studies*, Vol. 14: 4 (1975), pp. 563–585.

42. Daniel Pipes, *In the Path of God: Islam and Political Power* (New York: Basic Books, 1983.

43. Morroe Berger, *Islam in Egypt Today* (Cambridge: Cambridge University Press, 1970).

44. An in-depth analysis of the legitimacy issue in the Middle East is to be found in Michael Hudson, *Arab Politics: The Search for Legitimacy* (New Haven: Yale University Press, 1977), esp. pp. 1–30.

45. See the case study on Egypt in the comparative country studies chapter in B. Tibi, *Der Islam und das Problem der Kulturellen Bewaeltigung Sozialen Wandels* (Frankfurt: Suhrkamp Press, 1985), pp. 173ff.

46. See, for instance, Yusuf al-Qurdawi, *al-Hall al-Islami farida wa darura* (Beirut: al-Risala Press, 1974).

47. B. Tibi, "The Iranian Revolution and the Arabs," *Arab Studies Quarterly*, Vol. 8: 1 (1986), pp. 29–44.

48. Daniel Pipes, *In the Path of God: Islam and Political Power* (New York: Basic Books, 1983), chapter 10.

49. See the very interesting article by Ralf Hoppe, "Saudi-Arabiens Aussenpolitik als Versuch einer eigenstaendigen kriseneindaemmenden Regionalpolitik im Nahen Osten," in *Orient* Vol. 26 (1985), pp. 205–227.

50. For a cross-regional conceptual interpretation see B. Tibi, "Die gegenwaertige politische Revitalisierung des Islams: eine religionssoziologische Deutung," *Revue Suisse de Sociologie*, Vol. 9: 3 (1983), pp. 657–675.

51. For more details see Charles Tilly, ed., *The Formation of National States in Western Europe* (Princeton, N.J.: Princeton University Press, 1975), particularly chapter one by Tilly. See also chapter I of my book, *Arab Nationalism* (cited in note 40) in which I deal with the origin of the national state in Europe itself.

52. See B. Tibi, "Islam and Arab Nationalism," in Barbara Freyer Stowasser, ed., *The Islamic Impulse* (London: Croom Helm, 1987), pp. 59–74; see also my book on Arab Nationalism cited in note 40 above.

53. Fouad Ajami, "The End of Pan-Arabism," in *Foreign Affairs*, Vol. 57: 2 (1978/79), pp. 355–373. Reprinted in Tawfic E. Farah, ed., *Pan-Arabism and Arab Nationalism: The Continuing Debate* (Boulder, CO: Westview Press, 1987), pp. 96ff; see also the interesting evaluation by Elie Chalala, "Arab Nationalism, A Bibliographic Essay," in this volume by Farah, pp. 18–56.

54. See my article cited in note 47 above. On modern Islam and its re-politicization see also my articles "Islam and Modern European Ideologies," *International Journal of Middle East Studies*, Vol. 18: 1 (1986), pp. 15–29; and "The Renewed Role of Islam in the Political and Social Development of the Middle East," *Middle East Journal*, Vol. 37: 1 (Winter 1983), pp. 3–13.

55. One should be sensitive to the important difference between the highly respectable intentions of President Carter during Camp David and the actual consequences of the separate peace treaty between Egypt and Israel. President Carter always envisaged a comprehensive peace and has considered Camp David to be a part of such an endeavor. See the very interesting retrospective of Jimmy Carter, *The Blood of Abraham* (Boston: Houghton Mifflin Co., 1985), esp. pp. 1–20 and 193ff.

56. In my view the Israeli invasion of Lebanon could not have come about without the separate peace treaty between Israel and Egypt. An elaboration of this view is included in my article "Aegypten und seine arabische Umwelt," cited in note 20 above.

57. See my books on Islam in which I show that contemporary political Islam is based on "defensive-cultural responses" to the present sociopolitical and economic situation, arousing this desperation in the hopeless: B. Tibi, *Die Krise des Modernen Islams* (Munich: Beck Press, 1981), reviewed in the *Middle East Journal* by B. Stowasser, Vol. 37: 2 (1983), pp. 284–285; and most recently B. Tibi, *Der Islam und das Problem der kulturellen Bewaeltigung sozialen Wandels* (Frankfurt: Suhrkamp Press, 1985).

58. The term "bedouinization" has been coined by Nazih Y. Ayubi in many publications; see his contribution in Kerr and Yassin cited in note 21, pp. 349ff; here p. 359.

12

The Dialectics of
Inter-Arab Relations, 1967–1987

Bahgat Korany

Introduction

Compared to global systems with their heterogeneity and complexity, regional systems with their functional and/or geographical delimitation might be thought easy for the analyst to understand, although still posing problems for the policy maker. And the analyst searching for the structure and processes of the Arab system might be justified in assuming his task would be more simple than that of other Third World specialists working on the African, Asian or Latin American systems. Do not all Arab policy makers affirm the existence of a single Arab nation bound by language, history, geography, and culture? Have not theoreticians and historians traced the evolution of this single Arab nation and predicted, as early as the 19th century, the inevitability of its translation into a concrete political reality— presumably a unified state? The analyst of inter-Arab relations is thus led to expect to rely not on the concepts and methodology of international relations but rather on a domestic political analysis characteristic of the study of internal systems.

Such an analyst, however, soon has to reconcile himself to some imposing facts: that the Arab nation is divided into twenty-one existing states as well as an aspiring one, Palestine; that the number of these states has been increasing rather than declining since the end of the second World War with its wave of political decolonization; and that Arab behavior has manifested more than its share of inconsistencies and shifting alliances. After being presumed disarmingly simple, the Arab system becomes inextricably complex. Baffled by this complexity, analysts have differed in their approach to it.

Some wrote off the inter-state dimension as artificial, and continued to evoke history and geography, culture and destiny to reiterate the oneness of the Arab nation, without dealing with the practical problems of how a nation could be translated into a political authority, be it a unified state, a federation of states, a supra-national authority or something less. It was this lacuna that doomed the experience of the United Arab Republic, which was launched in 1958 with all the odds on its side, yet ended after a mere three years with mutual recriminations among the most established unionist forces and amid the disenchantment of their bewildered masses.

Other analysts overreact by going to the other extreme of writing off the Arab nation as a hollow slogan or pure demagogy and conceive of the Arab system as a "normal" state system, whatever "normal" means in this respect. Many non-specialists of the region approach the Arab world in this way. Moreover, in 1978 Fouad Ajami gave credence to this thesis by forcefully arguing its merits in the influential *Foreign Affairs:*

> . . . an idea that has dominated the political consciousness of modern Arabs is nearing its end, if it is not already a thing of the past. It is the myth of pan-Arabism, of the *umma Arabiyya wahida dhat risala khalida,* "the one Arab nation with an immortal mission." Now, however, . . . slowly and grimly, with a great deal of anguish and violence, a normal state system is becoming a fact of life.[1]

The problem with these two schools of thought is that they avoid confronting the complexity of inter-Arab relations by concentrating on one part of the Arab equation: *raison de la nation* or *raison d'état.* The dilemma of inter-Arab relations is that these two cannot be dissociated, and there are occasional ups and downs in the fortunes of each. Neither has completely disappeared, even when one of them has achieved ascendancy. This accounts for the misty image of inter-Arab politics, the inconsistencies and oscillations. It is as if the *raison d'état/raison de la nation* contradiction is beyond the limited capacity of Arab regimes to handle or to control. The result of such role-conflict for existing regimes is to compartmentalize behavior into a verbal aspect that emphasizes *raison de la nation* and an action aspect that gives pre-eminence to *raison d'état.* Thus the contradiction between "say" and "do" adds to the misty image of inter-Arab politics and baffles the observer.

Contrary to the thesis of the death of Arab nationalism as of the late 1970s, the *raison d'état* aspect of inter-Arab politics had already been accepted and codified in the 1945 Charter of the Arab League. My content analysis of the Charter shows that the word "state" (in the sense of "mini-state"— *dawlat qutriyyat,* or "territorial state") is mentioned forty-eight times in the Charter's twenty articles, that the establishment of the League is based on the "respect for the independence and sovereignty of each state," and that the decisions of the League's Council are *not* enforceable or obligatory in cases where differences between member states concern "a state's independence, sovereignty, or territorial integrity."

Historically, then, the third round of Arab-Israeli wars in 1967—the focus of this volume—did not create the *raison d'état/raison de la nation* conflict. Rather, it acted as a watershed to differentiate two phases in the evolution of the Arab system and to determine the way the system is based and directed in each phase. It thus shaped the fortunes of each part of the equation in the *raison d'état/raison de la nation* dialectics.

To state the thesis succinctly, the pre-1967 phase of inter-Arab relations was characterized by a) a strong base, Egypt, and b) charismatic leadership, Nasserism; the post-1967 phase has seen the loss of status of the base and the questioning of the leadership role. The decline of both the system's base and charismatic leadership transformed it from a self-guided, mono-centrist system generally stressing *la raison de la nation* in word and act to a form of polycentrism bolstering the *raison d'état* (sometimes tribe- or family-based). The result is a predominantly egocentric pattern of inter-Arab relations, leading to the decline of central direction and the proliferation of centrifugal forces, a process one might label the Lebanonization of inter-Arab relations.

The Year 1967 as the Watershed

The past twenty years have been rich in crucial events: the 1973 war, the oil embargo, Sadat's visit to Jerusalem, the Camp David agreements and the establishment of full diplomatic relations between Egypt and Israel, the Iraq-Iran war, the 1982 Israeli invasion of Lebanon, and the general consolidation of Israel's military hegemony in the region (the 1981 attack on Iraq's nuclear reactor, and the 1985 attack on PLO headquarters in Tunisia). But it is argued here that these milestones—important as they are—seem to be consequences of 1967, not only in terms of chronology, but also and especially in terms of the impact of that war.

At a certain time, the events of 1973 seemed even more crucial than those of 1967 since the Egyptian-Syrian attack on the cease-fire lines demonstrated brilliant Arab military coordination and minute planning. This Arab initiative did indeed put in question Israel's proclaimed military invincibility and exposed the limits of any security based purely on garrison or warfare state. Last but not least, the long-awaited mobilization of Arab resources by the use of the oil weapon added to the manifestation of a strong and unified Arab will, and managed to make Arab concerns world concerns.

With the benefit of hindsight, however, we can see that the 1973 events constituted—for various reasons that cannot be dealt with here—but one major point in the chain of events that have marked the evolution of the Arab regional system since 1967, an evolution conditioned by that watershed. What Nasser said at that time is still valid. "After this great catastrophe," he stated in November 1967, "we were like a man who went out in the street to be hit by a tram or a car and lay both motionless and senseless on the ground." Six months later (25 April 1968) he described himself as "a man walking in a desert surrounded by moving sands not knowing whether, if he moved, he would be swallowed up by the sands or would find the right path." Indeed, on 23 November 1967, Nasser had admitted that his country's direct losses—at the hands of a state with one-tenth

Egypt's population—were 11,500 killed, 5,500 captured, eighty percent of Egypt's armor and 286 of its 340 combat aircraft destroyed. The chaotic collision between two divisions of the Egyptian army in their disorganized race to withdraw to the mountain passes showed that the army as a military corps had ceased to exist. To add insult to injury, Israel's casualties were comparable proportionally to yearly road accidents in any industrialized country or even in Israel itself.

Worse still, there was no diplomatic victory (as in the 1956 Suez war, for instance) to compensate for this military disaster. On the contrary, to this Arab military defeat was added political humiliation, as observers noted:

> The pre-war picture of Israel as a beleaguered fortress . . . had earned the Israelis wide international sympathy . . . By the discrepancies between their threats and their performance, the Arabs had invited the world's derision. This had been skillfully encouraged by Israeli psychological warfare and propaganda which stressed the cowardice rather than the lack of skills of the Arabs and took every opportunity of showing the Arab and especially the Egyptian armies in a humiliating light—for example, by photographing Egyptian prisoners stripped to their underwear or in other unheroic situations.[2]

Arab speeches of the time are crammed with the themes of the "ordeal," "cruelty of our situation," "our great pains," "the greatest test and crisis of our modern history." These expressions are in fact reminiscent of the first wave of writings by Constantine Zureik and others after the first so-called "catastrophe," that of 1948. Similarly, the so-called "setback" in 1967 led to a second wave of lamentation literature.[3]

In an atmosphere of tightening political control by the existing regimes, it seemed that mass protest and lamentation could be expressed only through novels and other literary forms, and thus publications of this genre increased noticeably. For instance, between 1961 and 1966 the number of novels published in the Arab world was ninety-two, but increased between 1968 and 1973 to one-hundred sixty-three; i.e., a yearly average of fifteen novels for the first period compared to twenty-seven in the second.[4]

The question posed in some Arab circles then should be recalled now: since it was Syria and Egypt—with Hussein's Jordan a very late and hesitant follower—that got involved in this war, and without consultation with other Arab countries, why does the defeat have to be considered an "Arab" one rather than simply the defeat of the "radical pole" in Arab politics? This brings us to the point of Egypt's centrality and its impact on the *raison de la nation/raison d'état* dialectics.

Inter-Arab Dialectics:
The Determinant Role of the Base

As is well-known, Egypt's population constitutes almost one-fifth of that of all twenty-two members of the Arab League. (In fact, at the height of their petro-power in 1975, the six countries that coalesced in the Gulf

Cooperation Council contained not more than one-quarter of the population of Egypt.) Historically, Al-Azhar Islamic University radiated enlightenment all over the Arab and Islamic world; Egypt's many famous authors, poets and journalists set the literary and intellectual pace; and Egypt's teachers flocked to socialize future Arab elites. Egyptian universities were the aim of promising Arab intellectuals, and the story goes that Arab high school students felt they had to work hard and earn high grades to get admitted to Cairo University, or otherwise they would be forced to accept admission to Cambridge or Oxford!

Egypt's multifaceted pre-eminence in the region was reflected in the Arab League. It was in Alexandria that the meeting was convened to establish the League and to approve its protocol. The minutes of this meeting are full of speeches affirming Egypt's accepted pre-eminence.[5] And it was in Cairo that the headquarters of the new regional organization were located. Until the late fifties, Egypt's share in the League's budgets was between forty and fifty percent,[6] and in 1974 of the two-hundred fifty-three permanent and non-permanent staff members of the League, one-hundred sixty-six were Egyptians.[7] Until the League was forced to move from Cairo to Tunis after Egypt's separate peace with Israel, the three Secretary-Generals had all been Egyptians.

Various quantitative indicators that span a long period in the evolution of the Arab system confirm Egypt's centrality. One study used the pattern of official visits for the period 1946–1975 to confirm Egypt's preeminence among Arab and other Third World countries.[8] Another, using as an indicator meetings between Arab leaders for the period 1966–1978, concluded that "Egypt is situated at the heart of the center."[9]

It was Egypt's centrality—with all that the country represented in state and intellectual infrastructure—that contributed to transforming Nasser's 1952 army movement into a revolutionary model to be followed. That army movement had initially been a classical coup d'tat, like so many in Latin America and the Arab world itself. (Syria experienced three coups in the year 1949 alone.) But by embarking on a program of political liberation and radical social transformation (e.g., the 1953 program of agrarian reform), the new Egypt set itself up as a matrix of radical political change under strong leadership. It is in this context that both the rise of Nasser's charismatic leadership and its pan-Arab appeal cannot be dissociated into separate cause and effect but must rather be viewed as two parts of an interacting and dialectical relationship. For it was during the 1956 battle against the Baghdad Pact and Nasser's insistence instead on nonalignment that his charisma and Arab-international status were established and he became the accepted *Arab* leader. An early analysis confirms it:

> Abdel Nasir's adoption and propagation of the new ideology of Arab-unity nationalism (Cairo-centered) as his own personal message brought about a substantial normative change in the belief system of Egyptians. Increasingly, Egyptians began to look at themselves as Arabs, thus sharing and adopting their leaders' belief system.[10]

There was thus an impressive reinforcing relationship between the state-base (Egypt) and the charismatic leader (Nasser), both bolstering the ideology of Arab unity with Egypt as its center. The leader's pan-Arab popularity reinforced Egypt's primacy in the Arab world, and both this primacy and the leader's charisma transformed Egyptian nationalism into Arab nationalism, thus adding the weight of this huge mass to the proclaimed Arab cause. As Fouad Ajami puts it:

> In having Egypt see it one's way, there is a tangible interest to be served—stability or revolution or a base in a turbulent region, depending on the viewer—and the intangible gratification of having an ancient civilization on one's side.[11]

Thus, Ajami devotes the second part of his three-part book, *The Arab Predicament*, to "Egypt as a State, as an Arab Mirror." Egypt's centrality, even now, is confirmed by yet another book, *Rich and Poor States in the Middle East*, by Malcolm Kerr and El-Sayed Yassin.[12] In this recent (1982) analysis of political economy, the four longest of the book's thirteen chapters, and the introductory and concluding chapters, focus on Egypt and the other chapters combine the Gulf countries with Egypt.

To conclude, the Arab system's fortunes were thus correlated with Egypt's. Did not Nasser, during a 1967 resignation speech, with his drawn and haggard features, his half-choking and uncharacteristically hesitant voice, symbolize the state of nervous and physical disarray of the post-1967 Arab system? Yet, inter-Arab politics are characterized not by the permanent ascendancy or decline of *raison d'état/raison de la nation*, but rather by their continuous dialectics. The fortunes of each depend on the nature of the state-base and on the type of leadership at the system's helm. Events of the post-1967 phase confirm this thesis.

Rising Petro-Power and the Decline of the Base

Unrelenting crisis brought Arab leaders together again in a summit at Khartoum in August 1967. Two issues dominated the talks: the economic and military ruin of the front-line states (Egypt, Syria, and Jordan) as a result of their military defeat; and the war in Yemen.

That war had been going on for almost five years and had put Egyptian and Saudi forces into direct confrontation, each supporting one faction in the civil war and each supported by one side in the Cold War (the USSR versus the United States, and also Britain). Indeed, the fact that about 70,000 Egyptian troops were tied down in Yemen was not unrelated to the outcome of the 1967 war. Yet repeated attempts before 1967 to end foreign intervention in the Yemen civil war and repatriate Egyptian troops had failed dismally. At the Khartoum conference, however, the crisis of the Arab system was so intense that agreement was the only way out.[13] There was also agreement to translate Arab support to the front-line states into financial reality. This double agreement made of the Khartoum summit an unexpected success, as Mohamed Heikal writes:

> . . . a formula for bringing the fighting in the Yemen to an end was concocted and the oil-producing countries agreed that, instead of cutting back their oil supplies to the West as advocates of the "oil weapon" had been urging, they would give financial support to the countries which had suffered from Israeli aggression—which meant in the first instance to Egypt and Jordan, since Syria was not represented at Khartoum. King Faisal opened the bidding with an offer of fifty million pounds.[14]

The Khartoum Arab Summit was crucial in legitimizing the change of political poles in the Arab systems.[15] It formalized the decline of the radical Arab order and its subservience to what can be termed "political petrolism" in at least two respects: withdrawal of Egyptian forces from Yemen and Egypt's financial dependency on subsidies from the oil-rich states. Moreover, the death of Nasser on 28 September 1970 (the ninth anniversary of Syria's secession from the United Arab Republic) removed the nationalists' symbol and the reference point. Their dispersion was rendered easier since neither Qaddafi's fervor in his fragile state nor the stateless Palestinian revolution could provide an alternative base. Consequently, the process of "deradicalizing" the system could continue unabated.

After the Egyptian base was tamed, it was to be captured. First, Nasserism had to be disavowed and liquidated in Egypt's socio-economic organization and in its foreign policy. As a result, specific political measures were institutionalized. Instead of a socialist model of development based on the public sector, infitah ("opening"—the policy of economic liberalization) encouraged the private sector and foreign investment, accelerating the desocialization of the economy. At the international level, close partnership with the West, especially with the United States and its regional allies, had the primacy over relations with the socialist countries and the Third World. What Kissinger had foreseen in 1973 as U.S.-Egyptian coordination at the national, regional, and Third World levels was becoming fact—to the delight of the conservative oil states.

Some quantitative indicators, such as the following, confirm the primacy of the oil states in inter-Arab politics:[16]

1. By 1979, 55 percent of the capital of inter-Arab economic joint ventures was contributed by oil-rich Saudi Arabia, Kuwait, the United Arab Emirates, Qatar, and Libya; and usually the country that contributes the most capital is the host country for the project's headquarters.
2. Thus, the oil states were becoming the locale of an increasing number of new Arab organizations. In 1970, Cairo was host to twenty-nine, or 65 percent, of these organizations, Iraq hosted none and Saudi Arabia only one. Eight years later, Baghdad had become the locale for twelve organizations, thus occupying the second place after Egypt, and Saudi Arabia was in third place with eight organizations.

FIGURE 12.1 Mobility of Labor and Capital

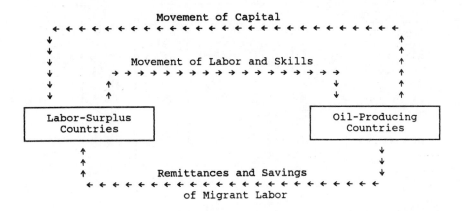

Source: Mahmoud Abdel-Fadil, <u>Oil and Arab Unity</u>, in Arabic
(Beirut: Center for Arab Unity Studies, 1979), p. 161.

3. Fewer Arab League meetings were held in Egypt and more in the oil states. The proportion of meetings held in Cairo decreased from 70.5 percent in 1977 to 42.2 percent in 1978.
4. Egypt's share in the Arab League budget dropped. That share was above 40 percent until the late 1950s but declined until in 1978—the year the Arab League moved to Tunis—it was only 13.7 percent, equivalent to the contribution of Kuwait.

Yet, the rise of oil states created a golden opportunity for a balanced, less monocentric Arab system to develop since the shortages of the new rich powers were offset by the "excesses" of the old, declining powers in that they created a demand for the surplus labor of those countries (see Figure 12.1). Moreover, the huge oil revenues were partially redistributed through remittances to the poor labor-exporting countries, with the result of more equal and widespread benefits to the system as a whole (see Table 12.1). What better basis for an integrated system could be asked for?

Seeming Arab Complementariness in the 1970s

With the exception of Algeria and Iraq, the so-called "rich" countries were lacking in everything from food to arms. There were huge deficiencies in infrastructure and in established bureaucracy as well as manpower. Once development projects were envisaged, both skilled and unskilled labor was acutely needed, and importing it was beneficial to the Arab system as a whole, for the problem of most Arab countries has been the reverse: a

TABLE 12.1   Remittances in Select Labor Exporting and
             Importing Countries (in millions of U.S. dollars)

Country	1973	1974	1975	1976	1977	1978
Export Labor						
Sudan	6.3	4.9	1.5	36.8	37.0	66.1
Egypt	123.0	310.0	455.0	842.0	988.0	1824.0
N. Yemen	NA	135.5	270.2	675.9	987.1	910.1
S. Yemen	32.9	42.8	58.8	119.3	187.3	254.8
Jordan	55.4	82.0	172.0	401.8	420.8	468.0
Import Labor						
S. Arabia	-391.0	-518.0	-554.0	-989.0	-1506.0	-2844.0
Bahrain	NA	NA	-227.6	-252.8	-300.5	-387.7
Oman	NA	-111.0	-208.0	-220.0	-222.0	-212.0
Libya	-273.0	-350.0	-260.0	-257.0	-856.0	-557.0
Kuwait	NA	NA	-276.0	-315.0	-370.0	-433.0

Country	1979	1980	1981	1982	1983	1984
Export Labor						
Sudan	115.7	209.0	322.7	107.1	245.8	275.3
Egypt	2269.0	2791.0	2230.0	2116.0	3315.0	3611.0
N. Yemen	936.7	1069.5	777.4	911.4	1084.4	995.5
S. Yemen	311.5	347.1	406.2	429.7	436.3	479.3
Jordan	509.0	666.5	921.9	932.9	923.9	1053.3
Import Labor						
S. Arabia	-3365.0	-4064.0	-4100.0	-5211.0	-5236.0	-5284.0
Bahrain	-278.8	-282.8	-317.6	-311.4	-300.0	-345.7
Oman	-249.0	-326.0	-452.0	-684.0	-692.0	-819.0
Libya	-371.0	-622.0	-1314.0	-1597.0	-2098.0	-1544.0
Kuwait	-532.0	-692.0	-689.0	-702.0	-906.0	-855.0

Source: IMF *International Financial Statistics Yearbook*, December
          1980, February 1983, December 1985, as adapted from Nazli
          Choucri, "The Hidden Enemy: A New View of Remittances in
          the Arab World," in *World Development*, 14/6 (1986), pp.
          697-712.

labor surplus. Thus, the complementariness between the factors of production, labor and capital, provided an excellent prod for integration and
thus a higher level of resource exploitation. Moreover, the acceleration of
the laborers' movement across state frontiers showed the fragility of legal
state barriers, and made the different strata of Arab society very aware of
their interdependence.

Why did this integrative process stop half-way despite the factors in its
favor? This question touches on one of the most nagging issues of recent
social analysis: the transformation of political systems. Although some studies
have addressed themselves successfully to the transformation of nation-state
systems,[17] analysis of the transformation of inter-state or international systems
is still in an embryonic stage.[18] Consequently, the discussion of the ups
and downs in the Arab system can shed light on the conceptual issues of

system transformation and can also provide information on this important region of the world.

Two preliminary explanations can be given in answer to the question: 1) the inability of oil states to act as an alternative system base; and 2) the absence of a pan-social project to give normative direction and hold the system together.

Fragility of the System's Petro-Based Hub

The oil states are neither powers nor even states in the conventional sense of these concepts. If they are powers at all, it is purely in the financial sense. They lack almost all other attributes of power: sizable population, solid administrative structures, well-trained effective military manpower, and pan-Arab political organizations. Even though Saudi per capita income is sixteen times that of Egypt, Saudi Arabia is basically poor in most indices of development. In 1975 Saudi Petroleum Minister Ahmed Zaki Yamani described his country in the following way:

> . . . We are still a poor country . . . we lack industry, agriculture . . . manpower . . . we have to import engineers, technicians, specialized workers that we don't know where to house because we lack hotels. To build hotels we need contractors, but the contractors themselves need hotels to live in. It is a vicious circle that exhausts us. Among other things we lack cement. We lack harbors because we lack cement to build them. Last, but by no means least, we lack water. We haven't a single river, a single lake. We depend on rainfall alone. For one hundred years, it has rained less and less frequently, for the last twenty-five years hardly at all.[19]

Even in purely financial terms, Saudi per capita income is comparable to that of Finland, which is not a particularly rich country, and has lent its name to the political term "Finlandization," indicating almost total marginality and dependence. Until the gigantic projects at Jubail and Yanbu' manage to give an industrial base to the Saudi kingdom, it remains dependent on the outside world. In fact, in all of the oil states, even basic infrastructure is still in the making, and that thanks to foreign labor. For instance, in 1975 the percentage of foreign labor was 81 percent in Qatar and 85 percent in the United Arab Emirates.

Another reason for the fragility of the "petro-based hub" is that historical patterns of social organization and the process of state-formation render those countries family-states rather than nation-states. The economist Hazem El-Beblawi is to the point when he writes:

> Though oil wealth has transformed them (the Gulf States) into advanced welfare states, they still remain patriarchal in a distinctly familial way. The Sa'uds, the Sabahs, the Al-Thanis, the Qasimis, the Al-Nahayans, the Al-Maktums, the Al-Khalifas, are not only the ruling families: they embody the legitimacy of the existing regimes.[20]

Pan-Arabism retreated in front of the *raison d'état*, which is now indiscriminately mixed with *raison de famille*. Two results follow from this situation: a) the leadership is characterized by a limited time horizon and an extremely personalized perception of national and international events; and b) inter-Arab relations are contaminated with the long history of inter-family feuds. In a word, family frictions impose extreme limitations on political coordination. Unfortunately, the rising technocratic elite has not been able to change this situation drastically. Consequently, Arab finance has not been up till now a complement to pan-Arabism. The oil states are unable or unwilling to devise an Arab strategy. If they seem in control, it is not so much that their achievements have won out, but that the outcome has been determined by the failure and exhaustion of the so-called "radicals."[21] Thus, the oil states' primacy in the Arab system represents victory by default.

This is not a strong base for a system. Even if Saudi Arabia, the crescent of Islam, is now armed with a barrel of oil and is increasingly becoming the site of secular as well as religious pilgrimage, it has not been able to keep the system together.[22] As has been said, "the hegemony of mere money unsupported by manpower, cultural attainments, military strength or industrial development may be something of a mirage."[23]

Grabbing for Dollars

The increasing labor-capital complementariness was not correlated—as the functionalist theory of integration insists—with equivalent political integration. All that could be achieved from 1971 to 1974 was a Cairo-Riyadh axis, based on a trade-off of Egyptian capabilities and Saudi money. And a predominant characteristic of a relationship based on money is constant haggling which could break the relationship at any time. A general mood of "affairism" rivaled nationalist commitment, penetrated the highest echelons of society, and even trickled down to the masses in former revolutionary centers like Egypt and Syria. Heikal summarized the change in his typically vivid style:

For a generation the men who directed the course of events in the Arab world had been ideologists or officers from the armed forces—or sometimes officers who turned into ideologists or ideologists who tried to behave as if they were officers . . . (for example, Sadat, Assad, Boumedienne, Qadhaffi, Michael Aflaq, Saddam Hussein) . . . Many of these were still there, but they were now being joined by the first installment of a new breed of power brokers, the middlemen, the arms dealers, the wealthy merchants who flitted between East and West, between royal palaces and the offices of royal companies . . . (for example, Kamal Adham, Mahdi Tajjir, Adnan Khashoggi) . . . and by royalty itself, for who in the Arab world now exercised more power than Prince Fahd or Prince Sultan of Saudi Arabia? Could not individuals such as these, it was argued, achieve more for the Arab world than mass movements and radical revolutions?

It is not surprising if in this changed atmosphere men and women in Egypt and Syria felt that the time had come for them, too, to see some improvement in their material circumstances. They had known hardship; now they looked for their reward—for more to eat and for better houses to live in. Of course, money would have to be found to pay for this, but who would dare to suggest that the Arabs were short of money? It was being said that the Arabs possessed the power to bring the rest of the world to starvation; surely they must have the power to feed themselves? So eyes turned to the oil-producing countries. Oil fields began to loom far bigger in the public mind than battlefields; *tharwa* (riches), it was said, had begun to take over from *thawra* (revolution).[24]

Although by the end of 1978 petro-dollars to Egypt amounted to some $15 billion, this was not enough to prevent Egypt's defection. Egypt's *infitah* elite did not find the Arab price right, and thus went off to the highest bidder: the United States and Israel at Camp David, sacrificing some nascent pan-Arab projects like the 1975 Arab Military Industrial Organization.[25] Briefly, the Arab system has become—in the words of the Arab poet Nizar Qabbani—a "large supermarket in which everything is for sale."[26]

"Unity of Destiny": The Persistent Search for a Midwife

The bases of the Arab system—language, history, geographical proximity, shared experiences, economic complementariness—are still there. It is the political manifestation and coordination of the system's will that are lacking. The result is that the system exists, without its strong base, as demonstrated by the reaction to Egypt's relations with Israel. Yet it is a system in disarray, out of joint, and in frenzied search for a new balance and *modus operandi* after the 1967 earthquake.

The Egyptian-Syrian-Saudi coordination in 1973 seemed to give a new base to the system, but despite brilliant cooperation between economic and political-military means, this axis was short-lived. The period 1975–1976 witnessed the cracks in this axis widening with the acceleration of Egypt's go-it-alone diplomacy toward Israel and Syria's go-it-alone Bismarckian policy toward Lebanon. The Saudis tried in 1976 to avoid the dilemma of choice between Syria and Egypt and continued power-brokerage and conflict-management to maintain a policy of consensus. But the Riyadh mini-summit meeting in October proved to be nothing but a truce. Then the break was made official with Sadat's separate peace with Israel. The 1979 departure of the Arab League from Cairo—stripped of most of its employees and infrastructure—made the state of disarray in the system manifestly clear and the continuation of the desperate search for direction even more necessary.

Agonizing as it is, this phase is not the end of the system since its other bases are still there almost untouched. It is rather another stage in the painful phase of transition. All international systems pass through different phases of evolution and the Arab system is no exception. One of its characteristics is that, in the face of the increasing legitimization and consolidation of the *raison d'état* in most of the Third World, it has not resigned itself to this fact and given up the search for collective policies or managed to eliminate constraint imposed by *raison de la nation*. This is why the Arab system has often been trapped in the policy of "quick fixes," of which there have been three since 1967.[27] The first was the rise of non-state actors, represented by the Palestinian movement, to give mass direction after the failure of charismatic leadership. This attempt failed, first in Jordan in 1970 and then in Lebanon in 1982. Then the dominant political order was based on "petro-power," characterized by consumerism, "affairism," and fragility, and this too finally failed. Now, the Arab system, in the search for collective identity, is facing the wrathful rebellion represented by Islamic fundamentalism. Different as they are, these "quick fixes" represent insistence on collective responses to the crisis of the system. At a more specific political level, the agony in passing the 1982 Fez plan for peace with Israel shows that the collective response can be painfully translated into a collective decision. Both the obstacles to and possibilities for a "system will" are thus manifested.

Additional evidence that the collective urge and the system's legitimacy have not surrendered to the thesis of *raison d'état* is the continued debate in Arab newspapers. Thus in order to provoke an all-Arab discussion of the Arab impasse, "Page for National Dialogue," was earmarked in *Al-Ahram*, the oldest of Arab newspapers, throughout 1985 for a debate. About a hundred Arab politicians and intellectuals commented on such issues as Arab national security, inter-Arab conflicts and the "Arab civil war," Arab dependency, absence of democracy, freedom, and human rights. They came from fourteen different Arab countries with a noticeable participation of Maghrebi nationals, thus breaking the traditional Mashreq monopoly over pan-Arab issues. They approached the topics from different angles, reflecting variations in political and social values but the same commitment to collective action.

Despite the strength of *raison d'état* and the continuing ebb of collective action, the commitment to *raison de la nation* shows noticeable persistence. Indeed, the participants in *Al-Ahram's* dialogue converged to identify various causes for the Arab crisis, with the 1967 defeat seen as the main one, and suggested over twenty solutions. A number of these cannot be carried out overnight (*e.g.*, a full modernization, revolution, change of all Arab regimes), while others were more operational and short-term (*e.g.* ending the Iraq-Iran war and the Western Sahara conflict, stopping the Lebanese civil war, modifying the charter of the Arab League, and planning Arab economic integration).

Whatever the solutions proposed, the importance of the pan-Arab dialogue is that it is taking place. If the pan-Arab ideal were dead and buried, the dialogue would not involve so much energy or arouse so much interest at the mass level. The confrontation between the *raison d'état* and *raison de la nation* continues unabated. Realization is increasing that return to the

Egypt-based, charismatic leadership system of pre-1967 might be romantic nostalgia, but there is also the realization that not every Arab state can go its own way.

Conclusion

Rather than breathlessly itemizing the many events that have characterized inter-Arab relations in the past twenty years, this paper has concentrated on the structure that determines the evolution of such events—that explains rather than describes them. The analysis has attempted to show that the present crisis does not mark the death of *raison de la nation* or the victory of the *raison d'état*. If this were the case, the crisis would have been limited to some states rather than being regional or pan-Arab in character. We would have seen less oscillation and fewer inconsistencies and ambiguities in inter-Arab relations.

Events of the last twenty years show that the Arab system is dominated by a state of transition in a continuous dialectic between the imposing and/or imposed *raison d'état* and the persistent *raison de la nation*. Since the system is dynamic and subject to penetration,[28] external influences[29] and such political earthquakes as the 1967 war are bound to intervene with the *raison d'état/raison de la nation* dialectic, pushing the system from one phase to another and provoking a crisis of transition. Crises may indeed put an end to a system, but they can also be a sign of growth.

An Arab system, then, will continue to be with us, reflecting the pains of the transitional phase and its persistent adaptation to the *raison d'état/raison de la nation* dialectic, characterized by the nature of the state-base and the type of leadership at its helm.

Notes

1. "The End of Pan-Arabism," *Foreign Affairs*, 57/2 (1978), p. 356.
2. Robert Stephens, *Nasser* (London: The Penguin Press, 1971), pp. 497, 504.
3. Sadek al-Azm, *Self-Criticism After Defeat* in Arabic (Beirut, 1968).
4. Shukri Maddi, *The 1967 June Defeat in the Arab Novel*, in Arabic (Beirut, 1978), pp. 26–35.
5. Abdel-Hamid Mwafi, *Egypt and the Arab League*, in Arabic (Cairo: El-Hayaa El-Amah Lil-Kitab, 1983), pp. 77–127.
6. Ibid., pp. 323–336; and Tawfiq Hasou, *The Struggle for the Arab World* (London: Routledge & Kegan, 1985), pp. 26–31.
7. Hasou, pp. 27–30.
8. William R. Thompson, "Center-Periphery Interaction Patterns: the Case of Arab Visits, 1946–1975," *International Organization* 32/2 (Spring 1981), pp. 355–73.
9. A. Diskin and S. Mishal, "Spatial Models and Centrality of International Communities," *Journal of Conflict Resolution* 25/4 (1981), pp. 655–76.
10. Richard Dekmejian, *Egypt Under Nasser* (New York: State University of New York Press, 1970), pp. 35–47.
11. *The Arab Predicament* (Cambridge: Cambridge University Press, 1981), p. 83.

12. *Rich and Poor States in the Middle East* (Boulder, CO: Westview Press, 1982).

13. This discussion is based on Bahgat Korany's "Political Petrolism and Contemporary Arab Politics, 1967–1983," *Journal of Asian and African Studies* 21/1–2 (1986).

14. *The Road to Ramadan* (New York: Ballantine Books, 1975), p. 45.

15. Ibid., p. 4; and Abdel-Mejid Farid, *From the Minutes of Nasser's Arab and International Meetings*, in Arabic (Beirut: Center for Arab Research, 1979), pp. 83–105.

16. See Ali Dessouki, "The New Arab Political Order," in Kerr and Yassin, *Rich and Poor States in the Middle East*, pp. 326–327; and also Mwafi, p. 336.

17. Barrington Moore, *Social Origins of Dictatorship and Democracy* (New York: The Penguin Press, 1966).

18. Evan Luard, *Types of International Society* (New York: The Free Press, 1976).

19. Quoted by Nazih Ayubi, "OPEC and the Third World: The Case of Arab Aid," in *The Arab Peninsula*, ed. Robert W. Stookey (Stanford: The Hoover Institution), pp. 23–24.

20. "The Predicament of the Arab Gulf Oil States," in Kerr and Yassin, *Rich and Poor States in the Middle East*, pp. 210–211.

21. Ajami, *Arab Predicament*, p. 155.

22. Bahgat Korany, "Dependence et comportement international," *Revue franaise de science politique* 28/6 (1978), pp. 1067–93.

23. Kerr and Yassin, p. 11.

24. *The Sphinx and the Commissar* (London and New York: Harper and Row, 1978), pp. 26–60.

25. See Amani Kandil, *Public Policy-Making in Egypt*, unpublished Ph.D. dissertation, Cairo University (1985); Raymond Hinnebusch, *Egyptian Politics Under Sadat* (Cambridge: Cambridge University Press, 1985); and Samya Said, *The Social Origins of the Infitah Elite in Egyptian Society*, unpublished M.A. thesis, Cairo University (1985).

26. Quoted by Fouad Ajami, "The World Beyond the Words," in *Pan-Arabism and Arab Nationalism: The Continuing Debate*, ed. Tawfic Farah (Boulder: Westview Press, 1987), p. 193.

27. Ajami, "The World Beyond Words," p. 199.

28. Bahgat Korany, "Unwelcome Guests: The Political Economy of Arab Relations with the Superpowers," paper presented to the symposium "The Arab World in the Next Decade," Center for Arab Studies, Georgetown University, Washington, D.C., 1985; and to be published in the forthcoming *The Next Arab Decade*, ed. H. Sharabi (Boulder: Westview Press).

29. See L. Carl Brown, *International Politics and the Middle East* (Princeton: Princeton University Press, 1984).

13

Egypt, Syria, and the Arab State System

Raymond A. Hinnebusch

Egypt and Syria are the core actors around which the Arab state system revolves. When Egypt and Syria are united they constitute a powerful axis which can impose a certain cohesion on the Arab state system; when they are divided, the Arab world is condemned to fragmentation. Historically, they occupied the geopolitical center of the Arab world, uniting Maghreb and Mashreq. An Egypto-Syrian axis has always been—from the New Empire of Ramses to the Fatamids, Ayyubids, and Mamluks—a major key to regional power. In the post-World War II era it has also been so, especially because other potential power centers have either been too marginal (Iraq) or insular and weak (Arabia) or, by reason of the rise of nationalism, disqualified to play a regional role (Turkey).

Egypt and Syria are the most culturally and politically developed Arab societies. But lacking oil wealth, they have a special common stake in an Arabism which would entitle them to a share of the resources of the oil-rich states. More important, they are central, and their union or division is decisive because they are the two major Arab military powers on the front line with Israel, the major foreign intrusion in the Arab world and the main obstacle to the aspirations of Arabism. When united, they give the Arabs leverage over and security against Israel; when divided, the Arab world is open to Israeli—and by extension Western—power. Indeed, the unfolding of the Arab-Israeli conflict has been intimately linked to the ups and downs of Egyptian-Syrian relations.

The most weighty consequence of the 1967 Arab-Israeli war on the evolution of the Arab state system has in fact been its changing impact on this relationship. It was a major shared disaster, and the elimination of its consequences a major common challenge which could, and for a while did, draw Cairo and Damascus together; but, ultimately, it split them and so shattered the precarious cohesion of the Arab world.

The Emergence and Eclipse of
the Egyptocentric Arab State System (1955–1970)

The nascent Arab state system which emerged in the Middle East after World War II was peculiarly fragile. While the Arab world constituted a cultural unit tied together by a dense network of communication, family ties, and a nascent common Arab consciousness, it was divided into a multitude of small weak states, still under the shadow of Western imperialism. The identification of citizens with these states was weak and political loyalties frequently cut across boundaries, preventing the consolidation of a system of national states on the European model; indeed, in their high level of permeability to both foreign and pan-Arab influences, the Middle Eastern states lacked the basic features of the prototypical European state system.[1] But weak states did not mean pan-Arab solidarity. Arab political elites, isolated from each other by imperial rule and preoccupation with their separate struggles for state independence, had developed little tradition of consensus formation or common action and lacked a leading center. Hence, they were powerless to prevent the major disaster of modern times for the Arab world—the colonization of Palestine and the establishment of the state of Israel. State elites shared no consensus on how to deal with this situation, disagreeing on whether or not close political ties to the West, which had sponsored the creation of Israel, were a desirable or efficacious way of containing its perceived threat.

The first major watershed in the development of this state system into a more viable autonomous entity was the emergence of Egypt as its center. This development resulted largely from the rise of a Cairo-Damascus axis growing out of the shared belief that the Israeli threat could best be contained and the common interest of the Arab states advanced only by a roll-back of Western influence in the area and through neutralism and pan-Arab solidarity as the principles of foreign policy. At this time, Arab nationalism was sweeping the region, as rising middle class political movements sought to liberate their countries from the remnants of Western control and confront the Israeli challenge. Nasser in Egypt began to challenge Western tutelage in the name of neutralism, contesting with pro-Western Iraq the proper course for the Arab world, and the positive response of Syria, where Arab national sentiment was uniquely intense, tilted the balance of power decisively in favor of Egypt and at the same time drew Egypt out of its insularity and into the Arab arena. Egypt and Syria thus became the joint centers of radical Arab nationalism, on the front line in the confrontation with Israel as was no other Arab state (save Jordan, a minor Western-dependent actor). To this partnership Egypt contributed its weight as the most populous, culturally advanced and militarily powerful of the Arab states while Syria contributed its intense Arabism and centrality in the Mashreq.

On the basis of this Syrian-Egyptian axis, Nasser's pan-Arab stature was built and crowned in the formation of the United Arab Republic. The ascendance of mass Arabism over state loyalties and Nasser's successful championship of this sentiment provided the key to Egypt's preeminence.[2] Because Nasser could galvanize Arab opinion regardless of state boundaries, Egypt was able to define certain standards of conduct first developed in Syria—neutralism, defense of Palestinian rights, pan-Arabism—as the norms of legitimacy for the whole state system which Arab rulers ignored at their peril.[3]

The first major blow to the Egyptocentric system was the collapse of the United Arab Republic, which had developed into Egyptian hegemony instead of partnership, shattering the Cairo-Damascus axis. Subsequently, traditional regimes found the resources to resist Nasserism, and in Syria and Iraq, Arab nationalist regimes challenged Cairo's authority, giving birth to a certain "revolutionary polycentrism." Thus, Egypt's drive for hegemony sparked the resistance which checked it and the unionist tide. In the end, the best that Nasser could manage was a precarious foreign policy consensus worked out in the various Arab summits of the sixties. Egypt did not become the Prussia of the Arab world. But to the end Nasser remained the paramount leader, the one credible acknowledged arbiter of inter-Arab politics to whom even his rivals often had to defer.[4] Moreover, Egyptian policy in concert with Syria played the major role in the rollback of Western hegemony over the Arab world, permitting the emergence of a relatively independent Arab state system.

The complexities of Syrian-Egyptian relations as they developed in the mid-sixties also led to the 1967 war, which shattered the Egyptocentric state system they had given rise to. Baethist Syria, seeking both to contest Nasser's tutelage over Arab nationalism and to draw him to its own more militant championing of Palestinian liberation, began, through support of the *fedayeen*, to challenge Israel. Nasser, attempting to maintain his credibility as a leader of militant Arabism and maintain control over events, reestablished his alliance with Syria, and hence set in motion the chain of events which would drag him, along with Syria, into the devastating 1967 defeat.[5]

The defeat was, of course, a watershed. On the one hand, Arab nationalism, as the dominant mass ideology, was shaken by the defeat of the two main nationalist states; it was never to recover, leaving a widening ideological vacuum. Nasser's leadership and particularly his ideology were also hurt to the point that when he died his successor felt no compulsion to continue his ways. On the other hand, the Arab cold war between conservative and radical states was buried, as the former, in exchange for an end to radical subversion, undertook to subsidize the rebuilding of the shattered Egyptian and Syrian armies. As a result, the legitimacy of these regimes was enhanced even as that of the radical states was eroding. The leadership succession of 1970, bringing Sadat and Assad to power, marked the end of an era. These new leaders, lacking both the charismatic power and ideological intensity of their predecessors, wanted and needed to adopt the more immediate goal of recovering the captured territories and to employ pragmatic tactics toward this end. The messianic dimension of Arab nationalism was dying. Nasser's death left a leadership vacuum that could not be filled by one man, only by a concert of leaders. It radically reduced Egypt's preeminence and set the stage for the emergence of a new Arab system.

The Arab Triangle:
An Aborted Arab State System (1972–1975)

In the early seventies a new Arab state system began to take form, and emerged full blown from the crucible of the 1973 war, a system best described in Fouad Ajami's words as the "Arab Triangle."[6] It was the direct result of the efforts of the new leaders in Egypt and Syria to cope with the consequences of the 1967 war. Egypt and Syria were driven together in a new close, and more equal, alliance by their common need to roll back the Israeli advance into their territories in that war and, after diplomacy failed, by the military attack jointly planned and undertaken against the Israeli occupation. The two front-line states were also driven by the need to rebuild their armies into an alliance with the conservative, oil-rich states. The third pole of the triangle was, of course, Saudi Arabia, the leading oil state which bankrolled the remilitarization and orchestrated the oil weapon that supported Egypt's and Syria's war effort and postwar diplomacy. As an outcome of the war and the energy crisis, it acquired unprecedented financial resources and prestige qualifying it, for the first time, for a major role on the Arab stage. A second major consequence of the war was the emergence of a consensus among this "big three" to seek a negotiated settlement of the conflict with Israel—peace in return for the lands captured in 1967— and to do so in concert. As long as Egypt and Syria stuck together and refused to settle separately, with Saudi Arabian support in the background, the leverage to achieve such a settlement potentially existed.

For a brief period the Arab world achieved an unprecedented cohesion, the benefits of which seemed incontestable. Israel had, for the first time, been seriously challenged militarily; this, together with the oil embargo, showed the potential costs to the West of failure to accommodate Arab interests. Israel was put on the global political defensive and could no longer attack the Arab states with the old impunity. The new constraints on Israel and unprecedented Arab power and solidarity translated into a level of security in the Arab world unknown since independence. The new oil wealth was shared with Arab states which lacked it and might have laid the foundations for Arab economic integration and complementary economic development. The recovery of lost national dignity and the unprecedented world recognition of Arab rights, interests, and power caused a resurgence of Arab pride and solidarity vanquishing the post-1967 malaise. The possibility of an honorable peace appeared, for the first time, to be in sight. This new system foundered, basically, on the rocks of Israeli intransigence: Israel preferred land to peace. This precipitated Sadat's decision to go it alone and break Arab ranks, setting Egypt and Syria at odds. In turn, Syria, obsessed by its vulnerability, was provoked into policies which further divided the Arab world. Thus, from Sadat's policies flowed a chain of consequences which have fragmented and rendered powerless the Arab world.

Egyptian Foreign Policy Under Sadat (1974–1981): The Unfolding of a Separate Peace

The origins of Sadat's separate peace can be traced back to the 1967 war itself. The defeat brought home to Egyptians the high costs of pan-Arab activism. Although in the short run the Israeli occupation of the Sinai further embroiled Egypt in the Arab-Israeli conflict, in the long run the costs of the struggle led Egyptians to look to their own special interests and identity. The success of American over Soviet arms in the war and the failure of the USSR to protect its Arab allies strengthened forces inside Egypt hostile to Moscow and favoring accommodation with the West. A growing portion of the Egyptian elite was convinced that America held the cards to a solution and that Egypt would have to come to terms with her. Nasser had believed the lost territories would probably have to be recovered by force of arms; but his acceptance of the peace proposals of 1969 known as the Rogers Plan had amounted to acknowledgement of the United States as a major arbiter in the Arab world and of the irreversibility of Israel, which paved the way for Sadat to take decisive strides toward a Western alignment and Israeli peace.

Sadat came to power obsessed with the need for American mediation. To obtain it, he was prepared to accept a partial, even separate settlement. His proposal to open the Suez Canal in return for partial Israeli withdrawal was step-by-step diplomacy before Kissinger, indicating a readiness to accept at least an interim separate peace. Fundamentally, Sadat's belief that America would keep Israel strong enough to prevent an Egyptian military recovery of the Sinai but alone could, if it wished, force an Israeli rollback anchored his policy from the outset. His conservative personal values inclined him toward Western accommodation and made him suspicious of the USSR. More Egyptocentric and less capable of pan-Arab leadership than Nasser, and un-handicapped by a history of personal frictions with the United States, Sadat had less to lose and a greater chance of success than his predecessor in seeking an American-sponsored peace. His need to court the Egyptian bourgeoisie and Saudi Arabia, both of which deeply distrusted the USSR and wanted American intervention, reinforced this orientation. So did conflicts with the Soviets over weapons deliveries. The Soviets, though unable to deliver a diplomatic solution, seemed unprepared to give Egypt the offensive military equipment which might offer a chance for a military one. They feared a new military round would end in a 1967-type disaster in which they would be asked to save Egypt and risk detente and confrontation with the United States—risks that did not seem worthwhile for a regime which had purged pro-Soviet leaders, was increasingly displaying anti-Soviet sentiment, and seemed prepared to chuck them for American help. Perhaps believing that punishing Sadat would halt his rightward course, they procrastinated on arms deliveries to the point that he took it as a personal snub. In a warning to the Soviets and as a bid to win American diplomatic help, Sadat expelled Soviet military advisors in 1972—a major step in burning his bridges to the East. Even when diplomacy failed, Sadat did not give up on the United States: his subsequent military strategy of seeking merely a foothold on the east bank of the Canal as a way of breaking the Israeli grip was aimed at preparing the way for American intervention and mediation. In practice, the unwillingness and inability of the Sadat regime to carry out a total war mobilization of Egyptian society and its deteriorating relations with its main arms supplier, the Soviet Union, probably made any other strategy unrealistic. But there could be little doubt that the outcome of such a limited war would inevitably dictate negotiations in which Egypt would have to make major political concessions.

In fact, the outcome of the military showdown—Israeli penetration of the Western side of the Canal—greatly increased Sadat's dependence on U.S. help, and he accepted Kissinger's intervention with alacrity. While politically Sadat had a strong bargaining hand, militarily his position was uncertain. Egyptian forces on the east bank of the canal appeared in jeopardy, and he feared a resumption of the fighting would go against him. The Soviets' failure in the face of American intimidation to enforce the cease fire convinced him he could not depend on them. His whole position as "Hero of the Crossing" was at risk if he lost his Sinai foothold. Anxious to commit the United States to his cause, Sadat underplayed his hand in the first disengagement negotiations. The 1974 agreement legitimized an Egyptian presence in the Sinai and removed the Israeli salient west of the Suez, but it also weakened the military option Egypt needed to play a credible hand in subsequent negotiations and, in defusing the immediate war-time crisis, it put an end to the conditions which might have forced a rapid superpower imposition of a comprehensive peace.

Once Sadat put all his eggs in the American basket, his prestige was staked on that policy and his relations with the USSR quickly withered. Cut off from Soviet support, Egypt's military capability rapidly deteriorated, its bargaining leverage with Israel consequently declined, and its dependence on American diplomacy increased. The obstacles to an overall settlement loomed suddenly larger: Israelis seemed determined to avoid one; the PLO, with whom they refused to deal, assumed the right to bargain for the West Bank; and the Americans seemed unwilling to impose a comprehensive settlement. This situation, plus the fact that Egypt badly needed promised Western economic aid, left Sadat little alternative but to accept the second Sinai agreement of 1975. But this agreement virtually took Egypt out of the Arab-Israeli war equation, and together with the massive American rearming of Israel which accompanied it, greatly reduced Arab military pressure on Israel and hence its incentive to make further concessions for peace. In satisfying the Americans that the conflict had been substantially defused, it also reduced the sense of urgency which had hitherto driven American diplomacy.

In both these respects, the agreement virtually destroyed Syrian diplomatic leverage and reduced immensely the prospects of an overall settlement. The agreement was also a first step in Egypt's withdrawal from the Arab world: it caused a decline in the Arab financial support Egypt had received as a front-line state and it alienated the Arab nationalist opinion which had long sustained Egyptian leadership of the Arab world. As against these costs, Sadat had concrete gains to show: the Suez Canal and Sinai oil fields won back, a significant withdrawal of the Israeli army, ending its threat to the Egyptian heartland, and the promise of a massive infusion of Western aid into the battered economy. Before long, however, Sadat would again be faced with the choice between sticking with the Arab world in pursuit of a comprehensive peace, made much less likely by his own actions, or taking the ultimate steps toward a separate peace.

Not surprisingly, the so-called "peace process" subsequently stalled. In principle, Egypt still rejected a separate peace. But the proposed all-party Geneva conference promised to be intolerably protracted, if not a dead-end road to a comprehensive settlement, for it was clear that Israel would not return the West Bank or the Golan except under pressure no American president was likely to bring to bear and that Syria and the PLO would not settle for less. Egypt and the Arabs in general had, owing to Sadat's own policies, no credible military alternative to diplomacy. Egypt was under intense economic pressures, and Sadat, for reasons of internal political stature, could not wait indefinitely. Moreover, if he stuck with the common Arab position he might regain no more of the Sinai. He knew that Israel was prepared to return the Sinai for a separate peace which would relieve pressures on it for a wider settlement and decisively break the solidarity of the Arab world. Thus, Sadat opted for his trip to Jerusalem. To be sure, he correctly expected the trip would revitalize the American commitment to a Middle East peace, and he hoped it would shift Israeli opinion in favor of a wider peace. But because Syria and the PLO refused to follow his lead and because the Israelis knew he was prepared to proceed without them, the trip in practice increased Sadat's leverage in bargaining for Egypt but further undermined the prospects for a wider settlement. At Camp David he found out how little Washington's apparent commitment to Israeli withdrawal would deliver: a separate Egyptian-Israeli peace, made more palatable by a mere promise of a cosmetic "autonomy" for West Bank Palestinians, was the most Israel could be brought to concede. The military and political balance was clearly in Israel's hands and Sadat had to accept what Begin was prepared to offer. Fully committed, whatever the cost, Sadat pressed ahead: his enormous personal stake in the peace process made any retreat, which would have conceded the initiative to his radical opponents, impossible. His sense of personal mission to bring peace to Egypt had been heightened by internal and external acclaim, and he would not tarnish his image as a far-sighted statesman by a returning to the "fear and hatred" he said characterized the Syrians and Palestinians. In the subsequent negotiations, an impatient Sadat went further and signed a treaty without any progress on West Bank "autonomy," in spite of its virtual nullification of Egypt's prior treaty obligations to the Arab states, and despite the failure to recover full sovereignty in the Sinai. The result was a final shattering of the Cairo-Damascus axis and the isolation of Egypt from the Arab world.

Sadat believed that the other Arabs had no choice but to acquiesce in his course because without Egypt they were militarily and diplomatically incapable of pursuing either war or a different kind of peace. But virtually the whole Arab world, including Egypt's conservative allies, closed ranks in warning that Egypt could not have both a separate peace and normal relations with the Arab world. Sadat was not, however, deterred and indeed the all-Arab opposition to his policy only increased Egyptian alienation from the Arab world: what right had the rich and ungrateful Arabs, for whom Egypt has spilled blood and treasure, to dictate her foreign policy? In turning away from the Arab world Egypt opened itself to massive American penetration: the country which had led the expulsion of Western influence from the Middle East now welcomed it back.

Sadat embedded his new foreign policy alignment in a web of interests and ties which would make it irreversible in the short run: an economic *infitah* to the West, in which the Egyptian bourgeoisie, enriching itself, acquired a strong stake; a massive economic dependency on American aid; and a burgeoning debt burden. He burned his last bridges to the USSR and, openly bidding to play the role of America's regional surrogate in place of Iran, forfeited any Egyptian claim to Arab nationalist leadership. The Arab world had lost its center. The 1967 war, in itself, was a disaster for Arab nationalism, but this, its ultimate consequence, appeared to be the last nail in its coffin.[7]

Syrian Foreign Policy Under Assad:
A Failed Bid for Arab Hegemony

Egypt's abandonment of Syria and the Arab world sparked a defensive reaction in Syria, which faced a radical decline in its diplomatic bargaining leverage and a worsened military security position vis-à-vis Israel. Assad still aimed for a comprehensive settlement through some combination of military and diplomatic pressures. But, burned by his dependence on Egypt, he now set out to mobilize the resources to go it alone and, in fact, over the next half-decade a multi-pronged Syrian strategy for doing so emerged.

Assad first tried to forge an Arab concert in the Mashreq, which would draw Jordan, Lebanon and the PLO under Syrian leadership. As they shared with Syria either the insecurities of a border with Israel (Lebanon, Jordan) or its stake in rolling back the Israeli occupation (Jordan, the PLO), such a concert was the most immediately realizable and natural alternative to the Egyptian alliance. The fact that Lebanon, Jordan, and Palestine were viewed by Syrians as "fallen away" parts of historic Syria made their incorporation into a Damascus-led alliance all the more appropriate. Militarily, the alliance would guard against Israeli flank attacks on Syria through Lebanon or Jordan, and politically, it would deter any Jordanian temptation to pursue separate negotiations over the West Bank. Lebanon was a special danger spot on Syria's soft western flank: because of its civil war and the Palestinian presence it was particularly vulnerable to Israeli military and political penetration and, after Camp David, such a weak and divided country was a natural target for Israeli and American efforts to promote another separate settlement. In establishing Syria as leader of a power bloc in the Arab East, Assad also sought to send the message to Washington that Syrian conditions would have to be satisfied if the "peace process" was to be carried further.

As Egypt's separate peace crystallized, as conditions for both successful diplomacy and military action declined, and as the balance of power increasingly tilted against the divided Arabs, Syria sought to block any further Middle East negotiations unless, as seemed unlikely, they promised to accommodate Syria's interests and Arab rights as Assad saw them. This meant Syria had to prevent the legitimation of Camp David, lest it open the door to further separate peace agreements leaving Syria out. At the Baghdad summits, Assad took the lead in isolating Egypt and rallying the Arab states around Syria as the main confrontation power. Indeed, a brief Syrian-Iraqi rapprochement provided the political weight to force a decisive Arab break with Egypt and commit the Arab states to a military build-up in the Arab East.

Assad has subsequently given priority to an effort to achieve military parity with Israel. The threat of an Israel strengthened and emboldened by the neutralization of its southern front had to be contained; and successful peace negotiations, Assad began to insist, depended on the restoration of a more favorable Arab-Israeli power balance.

Finally, it was crucial to Syria's strategy to acquire decisive and unique influence over PLO policy. Palestinian activity against Israel could easily provoke a confrontation with the latter when Syria could least afford it, but if such activity were under Syrian control, it could be kept of suitable scope and timing to demonstrate the costs of a failure to satisfy Palestinian and Syrian interests. With such control, Assad could veto any attempt to settle the Palestinian problem which left Syria out since without the blessing of the PLO, neither the West Bank "autonomy" plan nor Jordanian initiatives would be credible. On the other hand, Assad could promise to "deliver" the PLO if an acceptable overall settlement—full Israeli withdrawal to the 1967 lines—was in the cards. Moreover, as sole champion of the Palestinian cause, Syria would be uniquely situated to demand full support from the other Arab states for its strategy.

Generally, in its relations with other Arabs, Syria adopted the attitude that, as the only remaining important confrontation state and the last bastion against Arab capitulation to Israel, its own political and military needs were virtually identical with the higher Arab national interest. Syria argued, in effect, that "what's good for Syria is good for the Arab world" and that other Arab actors were obliged to fall in with its strategy. In claiming the right to define acceptable norms of Arab state conduct, Syria bid to take the place of Nasser's Egypt as the center of the Arab world.

Assad's effort failed, largely because the other Arab actors—the various Lebanese parties, Jordan, the PLO—were unwilling to cede their foreign policy autonomy to Syria, and Syria's efforts to make them do so only set off conflicts. Assad had some initial success in drawing Jordan, Lebanon and the PLO into a loose alliance, but the nearly simultaneous outbreak of the Lebanese Civil War greatly raised the stakes. It raised the threat that Israel would use the war to intervene and put Syria's western flank at risk, but it also offered the opportunity for Syria to insert itself as arbiter and hence draw Lebanon under its political-military wing. In practice, Lebanon became the morass in which Syria's bid for leadership in the Eastern Arab world foundered. In its initial intervention in 1975, Syria tried to establish itself as the balancing agent between the two rival communities, to sponsor some mild reforms, and to end the fighting. But as the conflict escalated, and the PLO-Lebanese left coalition, ostensibly Assad's closest allies, appeared intent on a military defeat of the Maronites, Syria's military security considerations quickly assumed priority, bringing Assad into conflict with his allies. Syria intervened again in 1976 to forestall a Maronite defeat that Assad feared would throw the latter into the hands of Israel and balkanize Lebanon. He also sought to prevent the emergence of a radical state, sponsoring guerrilla war against Israel and giving the latter an excuse for intervention. An Israeli drive through the Bekaa Valley to split Syria and encircle Damascus was the nightmare of the Syrian military command. Personal ties and animosities, fear that sectarian strife could spill across the border, and outrage at the defiance of its own allies were additional motives for the intervention which curbed the PLO-Left alliance and ended the fighting with Syrian forces entrenched on Lebanese terrain.

Syria briefly appeared to win hegemony in Lebanon but soon discovered that Maronite objectives were not compatible with its own. The Maronites resisted Syrian penetration and the reconstruction of a central government under its influence and bound to its diplomacy, preferring *de facto* partition to such subordination. They sought a total expulsion of the PLO as against Syria's desire for a controlled Palestinian presence in south Lebanon. After 1978, in increasing defiance of Syria, the Maronites entered into alliance with Israel and consolidated two mini-states, one in their traditional mountain homeland, and the other on the southern border, closely aligned with Israel. Syria's efforts to punish them only cemented the Israeli connection making Israel, as much as Syria, arbiter of Lebanon. This precipitated several Syrian-Israeli conflicts which threatened to draw Israel deep into Lebanon, ultimately opening the door to its 1982 invasion. In short, Syria's actions in Lebanon—first weakening its own allies, strengthening a Maronite "right" whose interests were incompatible with Syrian goals, and then pushing the Maronites into the Israeli embrace—helped bring about what it most intended to prevent.

The 1982 Israeli invasion, encouraged by the growing Arab fragmentation, almost led to what Syria feared most, yet another separate peace. Militarily,

Syria took a beating, although it extracted a price from the Israelis. In the wake of the war, the American-Israeli *combinazione* tried to impose a deferent Maronite client regime in Beirut and a peace treaty on Lebanon, which would open it to Israeli influence, threaten Syria's western flank, and undermine resistance to Camp David. Syria stood firm and was able, with the help of Lebanese allies, to deflect this threat. But it was a purely negative victory. In its wake, Syria has failed to put a fragmented Lebanon back together or to assert its hegemony there. Indeed, the policy of divide and rule which Syria pursued has contributed to the chaos which it finds impossible to manage, and has dissipated Arab energies to the benefit of Israel. Syria failed to restore Lebanon as a buffer between Israel and its vulnerable western flank, although it was able to fortify the strategic approaches to Syrian territory.

Lebanon also became the burial ground of the "strategic alliance" Assad hoped to forge with the PLO. The 1976 military intervention against the Palestinians opened an irreparable gap between Syria and the PLO, and certainly made it easier for Sadat to settle separately with Israel. While Camp David did throw Syria and the PLO together again for a while, the Israeli invasion of Lebanon widened the cleavage. Recriminations arising from the failure of the two to coordinate their resistance to the Israelis, the PLO's subsequent flirtation with diplomacy in concert with Jordan and Egypt—conducted after the organization lost its base in Lebanon—and Arafat's determination to retain his autonomy led Assad to attempt to split the PLO, depose Arafat and bring the organization under Syrian control. Arafat, in effect, not only stubbornly resisted Syria's pretension to be the prime patron of the Palestinian cause but also threatened to legitimize Camp David and to support separate peace initiatives which left Syria out.

The effort to oust Arafat, however, failed, and in its various phases, from the siege of Tripoli to the "War of the Camps," dissipated Syrian, Palestinian and Lebanese energies in internecine fighting which benefited only Israel. Given the very small likelihood that the Arafat-Hussein initiative would ever get off the ground, Assad seemed to be needlessly expending political capital in a personal vendetta with the man most Palestinians still considered their legitimate leader. Attacking Arafat only drove him into the arms of Syria's rivals, Jordan and Egypt, beginning the legitimation of the Camp David process, the very outcome Syria so feared. Moreover, fighting Palestinians largely vitiated Syria's claim to be champion of the Arab national cause, the role which was the basis for Assad's claim on the support and cooperation of other Arab states. The PLO-Syrian conflict seemed to replicate the earlier Egyptian-Syrian split: instead of bringing together the parties with the strongest stake in rolling it back, the common challenge of the Israeli occupation had, on the contrary, split them over the proper strategy for accomplishing this rollback.

In the upshot, Syria's attempts to assert leadership of the Arab world against Israel and Camp David badly faltered. Damascus failed to establish control over Lebanon and the PLO. The post-Camp David front against

Egypt rapidly collapsed in part because of Syria's own actions. Assad put matters of leadership rivalry and regime security above Arab solidarity in allowing his relations with Jordan to deteriorate, in failing to pursue detente with Iraq, and in supporting Iran against the latter. The Iran-Iraq war has further undermined Syria's stature and strategy. Indeed, if the Israeli Mossad had its own man in the Baghdad presidency, it could not have devised a more damaging blow to the Arab cause than the Iraqi attack on Iran. The attack diverted the latter from championship of the Palestinian cause and engrossed a major Arab army in a seemingly endless, enervating conflict far from the Israeli front. The threat of Iranian expansionism assumed a much higher priority than the Arab-Israeli conflict in Saudi Arabia, the Gulf states and Jordan. Syria's alliance with Iran therefore reduced its credibility in the Arab world and alienated Jordan, Saudi Arabia and the Gulf states whose political and financial support Syria needs. This alliance also encouraged the Iranian intransigence which has kept the war going. In giving the enervation of a rival Arab regime priority over the weight the Iraqi army must carry on the Israeli front, Syria's claim to championship of the Arab cause was again compromised. Syria has seldom been so isolated in the intra-Arab arena, more likely to be left to its own devices in case of an Israeli attack, and so lacking in the diplomatic leverage which would flow from its leadership of a wider Arab bloc. One sign of Syria's impotence was the annexation of the Golan, a deliberate provocation which showed that Israel considered the political-military balance sufficiently unfavorable to Syria to rule out, *a priori*, a negotiated settlement. Another dramatic indicator of Syrian and Arab vulnerability under conditions of fragmentation was the capitulationist sentiment in the Arab world in the face of Israel's invasion of Lebanon, its assault on the PLO and the Syrian army, and the devastation of Beirut.

Syrian policy has succeeded in two respects. Its military buildup has turned it into the main Arab military power and, while it cannot defeat Israel, it can make an Israeli attack on it extremely costly; the old days of overwhelming Israeli dominance seem gone. Syria has demonstrated more than once that if it cannot impose a peace to its liking, it can prevent any further settlements which damage its interests. But it has demonstrably failed to achieve the leadership which would enable it to rally other Arab states behind its strategy, and without such solidarity Syria has no hope of achieving an Israeli rollback to the 1967 lines or of sustaining its drive to establish a Syria-centric Arab world. While this failure is, in part, a result of factors outside Syria's control—such as Maronite particularism and the Iraqi attack on Iran—Syria's own policy is also to blame, particularly its insistence on the priority of its own immediate security needs over those of the Palestinians and other Arabs and its heavy-handed attempts to coerce its potential allies—a course bound to be self-defeating.[8] Syria's basic dilemma is that it alone cannot force an Israeli rollback to the 1967 lines and can only hope to prevail through Arab solidarity behind this objective. But Syria's efforts to force other Arab actors to fall in behind its strategy have largely proven counterproductive, leading to further fragmentation.

A Centerless Arab World:
The Consequences of Fragmentation

The current Arab state system is obviously in profound disarray. By all evidence there has been a radical decline in pan-Arab sentiment, which had appeared to be on the rebound in the wake of the 1973 war. At the mass level, disillusionment at Arab impotence and infighting has, without doubt, sharply eroded belief in the concept of an Arab community or nation, and turned many to other lesser, more particularist identities or to a broader Islamic one. At the elite level, preoccupation with narrow regime and state interests dominate as they always have, but the decline of mass Arabism has removed the restraints on this behavior that once existed. How else can one explain public tolerance of Syrian or Shiite attacks on Palestinians, of Egyptian and Maronite alignments with Israel and the United States against other Arabs, of Saudi Arabia's and Jordan's intimate links to the United States in spite of American complicity in the invasion of Lebanon, the U.S. use of guns against Lebanese, Syrians and Libyans, and Washington's manifest contempt for the interests of even its Arab "friends?" Moreover, the pursuit of narrow state and sectarian interests feeds on itself: Egypt's unilateralism inflated Syria's fears and self-serving heavy-handedness toward the Palestinians which, in turn, aggravated the Palestinians' fortress mentality, which, in turn, stimulated Shiite sectarianism, and on and on.

The most obvious manifestation of the decline of Arabism is the readiness of Arab actors to align with the enemies of other Arab powers; above all Egypt's peace with Israel, but also the Maronite alliance with Israel and Syria's and Libya's with Iran. Another sign of Arab disarray is that, for the first time, the Arab state system is under attack from two fronts, both west and east, and the Arab states are divided in their assessment of who the greatest threat is, Iran or Israel. Would a united Arab world have been so vulnerable to this?

The Arab system is now centerless, and no single state or axis can impose cohesion on it. Syria possesses military power but has frittered away much of its legitimacy in internecine fights with other Arabs; Saudi Arabia has wealth but, preoccupied with Iran, has abandoned any leadership role in the Arab-Israeli conflict; Egypt remains dependent on the United States, having virtually sold its foreign policy to the highest bidder. The insecurity of the Arab states has never been greater. Israeli power has been projected in the region with less restraint and against less resistance than ever before— witness the invasion of Lebanon and the attack on the Iraqi reactor, events virtually unimaginable in a cohesive Arab world. An Arab state, Libya, has been directly attacked by a great power—the first time since Suez—with no apparent cost to the U.S. position in the Arab world. And, the Gulf states and Iraq are threatened from the east. The prospect of inter-Arab economic cooperation has vanished; the oil states squander their wealth on the Iran-Iraq war, while impoverished Egypt falls into hopeless economic dependency on the United States, and Syria's military burdens threaten to crush her economy.

Inter-Arab fighting is more violent than ever. The civil war in Lebanon, the most obvious manifestation of such conflict, is the result of both foreign intrusions—Israeli and Iranian—and increasing sectarian particularism, especially among Maronites, but also among Shiites and Palestinians. Could intervention and particularism have reached such dimensions in a cohesive Arab world? Nor is there any precedent for the vicious intra-Palestinian fighting at Tripoli. Finally, the prospects for peace seem more remote than ever and the plight of homeless Palestinians, now victims of Arabs as well as Israelis, never more onerous. If this record is any indication, the decline of pan-Arabism is likely to end not, as some have imagined, in greater stability, but in growing inter-Arab conflict, increasingly opening the Arab world to outside powers.

Conclusions: Toward a Future Arab State System

Is this fragmentation a natural phenomenon, a manifestation of a gradual "Latin-Americanization" of the Arab world, an inevitable balkanization into separate nation-states? To accept this is to assume the Third World must necessarily replicate the historical model of the European state system. But there are other models, not least the golden age of Arab civilization itself. Is this process beneficial, that is, will it turn the separate states inward to their own affairs, bringing stability to the region? So far it would be hard to argue that the process has brought stability or any other benefit. Just the opposite; by contrast to the previous periods, the current position of the Arab world is one of unrelieved gloom. But what can be expected in the future?

An Arab resurgence is not impossible. It may be premature to believe that Arabism is dead, although it certainly appears to have reached a nadir. But deep wellsprings of Arab sentiment are rooted in a common culture, language and history—the stuff of nationhood–which could again at some future time be tapped. The Arab world may now be more interdependent— at least as regards transfers of labor and capital—than it was two decades ago and hence the economic bases of solidarity are firmer. Clearly, there seems to be a recognizable common Arab interest: as this survey has tried to show, when the Arabs act against each other in the long run "all fall down," and when they act together, all benefit. It would take little more than an end to the Iran-Iraq war and Egypt's reaffirmation of its obligations to collective Arab security, bringing together the much enlarged and increasingly professional Syrian, Egyptian, and Iraqi armies, to strengthen immensely the political-military power of the Arab world. It could be, too, that if another period of oil scarcity is in the cards, the Arabs may get one last chance to translate the oil weapon into diplomatic leverage. If this were to happen, the Arab world might gain the leverage to achieve an acceptable Middle East peace. One thing is certain: if the Arab world is to achieve cohesion, it will be on the basis of a concert of states and a growth of trans-state institutions. The weak governments once easily threatened or overturned by the pan-Arab appeal of a charismatic leader have been replaced by far stronger, less penetrable states. Thus, only if the Arab states, especially the two central powers, Egypt and Syria, begin to put common Arab interests above ties to foreign powers and narrow regime interests, is there much prospect that the fragmentation of the Arab world will be reversed and a new basis of solidarity achieved.

Notes

1. Paul Noble, "The Arab System: Opportunities, Constraints, and Pressures," in Bahgat Korany and Ali Dessouki, *The Foreign Policies of the Arab States* (Boulder: Westview Press, 1984), pp. 46–48.

2. Patrick Seale, *The Struggle For Syria* (London and New York: Oxford University Press, 1965) (Whole volume).

3. Noble, "The Arab System," pp. 48, 52–3, 56.

4. Malcolm Kerr, *The Arab Cold War* (London and New York: Oxford University Press, 1971), pp. 44–105.

5. *Ibid.,* pp. 106–28.

6. "Stress in the Arab Triangle," in *Foreign Policy* 29 (1977/78), pp. 90–108.

7. Raymond Hinnebusch, *Egyptian Politics Under Sadat: The Post-Populist Development of an Authoritarian Modernizing State* (Cambridge: Cambridge University Press, 1985), pp. 46–48, 54–57, 65–69.

8. Raymond Hinnebusch, "Revisionist Dreams, Realist Strategies: The Foreign Policy of Syria," in Korany and Dessouki, *The Foreign Policies of the Arab States,* pp. 283–322; "Syrian Policy in Lebanon and the Palestinians," in *Arab Studies Quarterly,* vol. 8, no. 1 (Winter 1986), pp. 1–20.

PART TWO

The Superpowers' Policies

The United States

14

American Middle East Policy
Since the Six Day War

Steven L. Spiegel

As late as November 1966, the President told a news conference, "We are increasingly interested in the African continent and the Middle East. Our reports give us a reason to believe that things are going as well as could be expected." By contrast, in a commencement address in May 1968, his earlier complacency had vanished. "Today in two areas of danger and conflict—the Middle East and Vietnam—events drive home the difficulty of making peace."[1]

As these contrasting comments by Lyndon Johnson shortly before and after the Six Day War suggest, the dramatic events of May and June 1967 had an immediate impact on American thinking about the Middle East. Previously, it was an area of minor concern, a backwater region only considered a top priority during the first years of the Eisenhower administration. Since the 1967 war, the problems of the area have been almost constantly at the forefront of discussion, from the halls of Congress to the Oval Office to the media. In the perspective of forty years since Israel's establishment, the Six Day War stands as the seminal event which led American policy makers to reassess the importance of the Middle East and, perhaps more importantly, the perils its instability holds for American interests—including the threat to oil supplies, the possibility of Soviet expansion, and the dangers of confrontation with the USSR.

On a wide dimension of American foreign and domestic concerns, the Six Day War can be seen to have led to prime changes in the U.S. approach to the area. In this paper, these changes are viewed from a variety of perspectives: the impact of the Six Day War on the Soviet-American competition, on public attitudes toward the region, on the handling of the Arab-Israeli issue by the Johnson administration and its successors, on the domestic political debate between conservatives and liberals, and on the role of key interest groups, the President, and Congress.

The Impact of the Six Day War
on the Soviet-American Competition

In order to understand the critical importance of the Six Day War to the competition between the United States and the Soviet Union, it is useful to consider briefly the prior history of superpower confrontation in the area. The Truman Doctrine, the basic American declaration of the cold war in 1947, was oriented to two nearby countries, Greece and Turkey. Yet, except for discussion of a Middle East Defense Organization in 1952, U.S. engagement in the region prior to 1953 had largely been economic—the product of American companies seeking expanded involvement, often at the expense of European competitors. From 1945 onward, Americans had progressively become uneasy involved observers in the Palestine question, but the policy had been inconsistent and contradictory. The uncertainties are reflected in alternative support for partition and trusteeship, in recognition of the fledgling State of Israel and the arms embargo which discriminated against the new state, in quiet participation on the United Nations Palestine Conciliation Commission with Turkey and France, and in sponsorship of the Tripartite Declaration supposedly limiting British, French, and American arms shipments to the area.

Eisenhower and Dulles entered office committed to a more active American policy in order to address the threat of expanded Soviet involvement and influence in the region. In order to block Moscow, they devised a multifaceted strategy: (1) Because the British could no longer be trusted to protect American interests in the area, America would take over; (2) the U.S. would try to encourage a group of states in the area to organize a "mini-NATO" to thwart potential Russian influence (later the Baghdad Pact); (3) arms sales would be stepped up to the Arabs (especially Iraq, hopefully Egypt); (4) the United States would keep its distance from Israel and would try to settle the Arab-Israeli dispute.

Eisenhower and Dulles had correctly identified the threat of Soviet involvement and they had developed a sophisticated strategy, but it did not work. Khrushchev, anxious to develop a strategy for challenging the West in the Third World, simply "jumped over" the Maginot Line the two American leaders had created in the form of the Baghdad Pact when he began selling arms to Nasser's Egypt and to Syria in 1955. During the Suez crisis the following year, the Russian leader was able to pose as the protector of the Arabs while threatening to punish the British, French, and Israelis. The United States pressured all three to cease their activity and eventually to withdraw; the Russians got the credit. By tying his fate to the nationalist Arab movement led by Nasser, Khrushchev had catapulted the Soviet Union into a central role in the area. When a radical coup overthrew the pro-Western government in Iraq in July 1958, the Russian role appeared to constitute an even wider menace. In response, Eisenhower intervened in Lebanon.

By the end of the 1950's, the Russians were pursuing large programs of arms transfers to Egypt, Iraq, and Syria; they were engaged in demonstrative aid projects like the Aswan Dam; larger numbers of Arab students were travelling to Moscow. The United States, though heavily involved in the region, had no effective means of countering Russian inroads and was attempting to bolster regimes still ready to align with the West.

In the 1960's, the Kennedy administration attempted to improve relations with Nasser, but was thwarted by the Yemen war which seemed to hold the prospect of Russian influence and Egyptian troops at the border of oil-rich Saudi Arabia. The Johnson administration, trying to develop a new program for containing Soviet expansion, began to expand arms sales to several conservative Arab states and Israel.[2] During this period, the Russians had gradually been increasing their involvement in the region, especially through continuing military aid. Yet they too were hindered by quarrelling Arab clients. Particularly after 1966, a new radical Syrian government began calling for a "national liberation campaign" against Israel and complained that Nasser's involvement in the holy campaign was marginal.[3]

In order to resolve these divisions, Moscow began warning Nasser of imminent Israeli plans to attack Syria.[4] This action was consistent with the Soviet pattern of stirring up local conflict in the hopes of gaining political benefits. All parties knew this accusation was false and Nasser at first ignored it. By May 1967, however, with his army bogged down in Yemen and his economy deteriorating, Nasser flirted with the tides of history by ordering a partial withdrawal of the United Nations Emergency Force which had been stationed in the Sinai since 1957. He thus set in place the events which led to the Six Day War three weeks later.

From Moscow's perspective, the consequences of the war were horrifying and indeed it has never fully recovered its former position in the region. The two Arab states most closely associated with the Soviet Union, Egypt and Syria, were roundly defeated. Both lost significant pieces of territory; their armies were decimated. As these defeats occurred, the Russians could do little but fulminate in support of their Arab clients at the United Nations and increase their presence in the Mediterranean. Even their confrontation with the United States in protection of Syria during the last hours of the war appeared to be little more than posturing.[5]

Yet in the immediate aftermath of hostilities, the balance did not appear totally negative from the Kremlin's perspective. Although the Israelis won their victory largely with French rather than American weapons, the United States was blamed. As a consequence, several Arab states broke off diplomatic relations with Washington and de Gaulle's abrupt snub of Israel forced America for the first time into the position of Israel's protector. Moscow's enormous resupply of weaponry to the Arabs compensated for the dismal showing of the USSR and its arms during the war. It forced the United States to step up its arms transfers to Israel in order to maintain the regional balance of power. By 1969, when Nasser started his War of Attrition along the Suez Canal, the Soviets could justifiably argue that the return of Arab power had begun under their sponsorship. They were also heavily engaged in training and support for the Palestine Liberation Organization (PLO), which intensified its terrorist attacks against Israel after 1967.[6]

The Six Day War certainly increased the immediate dependence of key Arab states on Moscow and of Israel on the United States. In more subtle terms, however, the nature of the Soviet-American competition was altered. For the first time the means of Russian involvement in the region had contracted and America's options had expanded. In frustration at the successful Israeli attack and its inability to reverse the outcome of the war, Moscow broke diplomatic relations with Israel. It was to prove a terrible blunder. Henceforth, the United States was the only superpower in close touch with both sides. Since the results of the war necessitated diplomatic discussions on conditions under which Israel might return the territories, a negotiated process of some kind was inevitable. The Soviets, always fearful of losing their Arab support purchased largely with arms transfers, continued to align with the radical ideologues. They thereby proved themselves irrelevant for serious negotiations.

The changed atmosphere could be seen immediately after the war. It was the United States which took the lead in trying to reach some kind of *modus vivendi*, a process that led to UN Security Council Resolution 242 in which an agenda for discussion was set. In 1969 it was the United States which promulgated the first major post-1967 peace plan for the area, the Rogers Plan, and the United States which arranged the ceasefire which ended the War of Attrition in August 1970. When Syrian tanks invaded Jordan the following month, the United States and Israel demonstrably maneuvered to strengthen King Hussein. The Syrians and their Palestinian allies were defeated.[7]

Nasser's successor, Anwar Sadat, was progressively frustrated in his attempts to regain the Sinai through reliance on Moscow. Indeed, in 1972 he expelled the large contingent of Russian advisors who had entered Egypt during the War of Attrition. His countrymen applauded. Following the Yom Kippur war, the supremacy of American diplomacy was epitomized by the Kissinger shuttle, Carter's diplomacy and the Reagan Plan.

Thus, the initial outcome of the Six Day War was confusing: America's client had won, but Washington's relations with the Arab world suffered severe setbacks to the advantage of the USSR. Viewed in perspective, however, it was the Six Day War which was the turning point: a consistent tide of frustration for Washington was transformed into a period when opportunities emerged. By contrast, Moscow's fortunes began to decline. While these developments were certainly not inevitable, Russian errors and clever American initiatives concretized advantages that the 1967 war had made possible.

The American Policy Response to the Six Day War

The opportunities created by the Six Day War, and their effect in particular on the Soviet-American competition, can only be seen in retrospect. At the time, Americans greeted the war with a combination of exhilaration, relief, and fear.

There had been earlier Arab-Israeli wars in 1948 and 1956 as well as the U.S. intervention in Lebanon. There had been previous attempts at peace efforts and at blocking the Soviet Union. But the national response to the Six Day War was unusual in its emotion and as an event which seemed to necessitate new policies and attention.[8]

The sudden onset of the crisis made it all the more compelling by comparison with other Mideast crises. The 1948 war had been evolving for years; the Suez Crisis was the culmination of a period of regional tension which began with the Soviet-Czech arms deal in September 1955. Despite its surprise beginning, the Yom Kippur war occurred in a period when Middle East issues were attracting prime attention in the United States. For Americans, easily jolted by shifting tides of mood and fad, the Six Day War struck like a bolt from nowhere.

The shock was intensified by America's preoccupation with Vietnam in 1967. By this time, dissension and self-doubt were emerging from an incubation period into a state of full-scale convulsion. The outbreak of hostilities in the Middle East challenged the administration's concentration on Southeast Asia. The Vietnam war had been sold to Americans by the Johnson administration as crucial to defining America's global role and the future of the conflict with international communism.[9] Yet the events in the Middle East reminded Americans that there was more to the world than Saigon. As several Senatorial critics pointed out, on various scales of determining the national interest, the Middle East appeared more significant than Indochina because of its crucial location astride three continents, the direct threat of Russian expansion, oil, the threat to a democracy (Israel), and the impact on the Suez Canal. By challenging the contemporary dominant worldview, the Six Day War contributed to the disintegration of the Vietnam-centered complex the Johnson administration had propounded.

Americans crave moral clarity in world affairs: good versus evil; democratic versus totalitarian; no grays. By 1967, the distinction between the communist oppressor and the democratic defender was blurring in Vietnam. At a critical moment the Middle East conflict appeared, and seemed to offer the contrast between hero and villain that Americans were losing in Southeast Asia. In the conventional perspective the Israelis were "minding their own business" when Nasser created a crisis, the Arab states encircled the Jewish state, and then threatened to destroy it. The public's impression was that Israel's survival was at stake. Suddenly, the Israelis attacked and vanquished all of their would-be conquerors in six short days.

These events seemed to imitate a Hollywood script, and they were accompanied by an emotional concentration heightened by the impact of television. Except for Vietnam itself and the Cuban missile crisis, the Six Day War was one of the earliest international crises when television operated as a factor in the political equation. It was an equation which aided the Israelis at the Arabs' expense, as suggested by the sudden rise of Israel's popularity in public opinion polls.

Mixed with the public exhilaration were other sentiments, especially within the Johnson administration. First, there was widespread relief that

Israel had successfully acted on its own, avoiding the need for American rescue. Second, there was concern at the sudden deterioration of U.S. relations with a large segment of the Arab world. Third, there was fear that the Arab-Israeli dispute could lead to a future Soviet-American confrontation, which made the Middle East even more dangerous than Southeast Asia.

The newfound responsibility for Israel, the search for ways to mend relations with the Arab world, and the danger of Soviet-American confrontation created contradictory requirements for American policy. This is illustrated by the approach to arms sales. Once de Gaulle terminated France's special relationship with Israel, Washington was deprived of flexibility, especially in the wake of Russian resupplies of the Arab belligerents. Since the United States wished to compete by rearming pro-American Arab regimes, especially Jordan, it was forced to assume major responsibility for maintaining the regional arms balance in Israel's favor. In subsequent years administrations attempted to protect the balance of power by selling Israel sufficient weapons to counter British, French, Russian and American arms sold to the Arabs. This policy has been controversial at home and often based on conflicting and inaccurate calculations. The frequent regional wars attest to the difficulty of managing an arms race in which the U.S. is only one of several suppliers and of preventing conflict by arming the participants on both sides to the hilt.

The Six Day War itself was a prominent example of this frustrating task. Although the Johnson administration, like all involved parties, was caught offguard and unprepared, it did work to prevent war. For the first time in a crisis the U.S. and Israel both tried to gain the other's confidence, but their immediate objectives were running at crosspurposes. Israel—mobilized and progressively encircled—wanted quick action. The Johnson administration—overcommitted and uncertain—stalled.[10] The result was a war which could only have been averted by an early major U.S. initiative, at least the contemplated multilateral fleet and perhaps an American or multination expeditionary force sent to the Sinai as a replacement for the recently deposed United Nations Emergency Force. In the light of Vietnam, these steps were unthinkable. Even had the U.S. not been at war, it is unlikely that the Johnson administration would have been prepared to act quickly and effectively.

The events of the war reinforced the need to do something about the Arab-Israeli dispute lest it result in another similar crisis. In comparison with arms sales and crisis diplomacy, there were few contradictions and many potential benefits in attempting to ameliorate the Arab-Israeli dispute. Israel's security would be enhanced, the Arabs could be coaxed into improved relations with Washington, the dangers of Soviet-American confrontation would be reduced.

In their approach to peacemaking, many American leaders, especially Lyndon Johnson, were influenced by the experience of 1957 when Israel had been forced to withdraw from the Sinai and the Gaza Strip on the promise of future Egyptian concessions, which was not fulfilled.[11] When Nasser unilaterally evicted the United Nations Emergency Force from the Sinai, he destroyed the last vestige of the 1957 agreements. Whatever Arab-Israeli compromise individual American officials might advocate after 1967, no principal figures urged unilateral withdrawals by Israel without an Arab commitment to some type of peaceful arrangement. Before the Carter administration, American officials disagreed with Israel's demands for complete normalization of relations with Arab states in return for withdrawals, but they were also not prepared to entertain withdrawals prior to a form of Arab recognition of Israel and commitment to non-aggression.

American officials differed markedly from Israel in their belief that in return for Arab commitments to peace the Jerusalem government should ultimately withdraw totally from the occupied territories with the possible exception of the most minor of adjustments.[12] Within weeks of the Six Day War, they were appalled at Israel's efforts to assume complete control of Jerusalem. They believed that Israel was making unrealistic demands for direct negotiations with Arab representatives and for ultimate normalization of relations as the price of withdrawal. Logically, therefore, it appeared that the occupied territories would become the source of deep division between Jerusalem and Washington. There were certainly frequent tensions between the two governments over the issue, but ironically the occupied territories became a source of agreement as well. The Arab states refused to accept publicly the argument that the Six Day War had altered irretrievably the Mideast balance of political forces. At Khartoum in August 1967 they declared defiantly that there would be no negotiations, no recognition, and no peace with Israel. They were thereby standing firmly in favor of the 1957 formula of unilateral Israeli withdrawals, which the United States would no longer support. Except for Sadat's diplomacy, this stance assured a minimal common Israeli-American perspective toward the peace process.

Vietnam was sufficiently all-consuming that Ambassador Arthur Goldberg at the UN was left to conduct American diplomacy. The result was UN Security Council Resolution 242, which called both for Israeli withdrawals "from territories occupied in the recent conflict" and for every state in the area to be acknowledged as sovereign and "to live in peace within secure and recognized boundaries."[13] Yet Johnson was content to entrust peace-keeping to UN mediator Gunnar Jarring, whose efforts did not result in major breakthroughs. This passive *modus operandi* was broken only by a fleeting approach to Egypt by Secretary of State Rusk in the fall of 1968 concerning possible discussions about a new peace process. In retrospect, the 1967 crisis occurred too late in the term for a major initiative. This administration's method for dealing with Mideast conflict resolution was too passive, its diplomatic skills too limited, its engagement in Vietnam too overpowering for it to sponsor negotiations.

In American politics, each new administration attempts to set out in new directions, especially in reaction to previous crises. Thus, Richard Nixon came to power determined to address the problems for the United

Nixon

States created by the Six Day War. He therefore sought to reestablish America's shattered image in the Arab world and to resurrect relations broken in 1967; to reduce the Russian role in the area; and to promote America's position by facilitating an Arab-Israeli settlement. He was less certain regarding how he might achieve these goals.[14] During the first term, when the Middle East took a backseat to Vietnam, China, SALT, and detente, Nixon was confronted by two competing strategies represented by his two warring national security aids, Henry Kissinger and William Rogers. The Secretary of State, who was at first given the prime responsibility for Mideast policy, favored a region-oriented approach popular at the State Department. The outcome of this strategy was the Rogers Plan of December 1969 which laid out a program by which Israel would withdraw from all but insubstantial territories captured in 1967 in return for the Arabs registering their "binding and specific commitment" to non-belligerency. Kissinger argued that the United States could not press for negotiations until the key Arab parties, particularly Egypt, first made a move toward the United States lest the Soviets receive the credit for any breakthrough which might occur. His arguments were strengthened by the poor reception of the Rogers Plan by both the Arabs and Israelis.

Rogers successfully achieved an end to the 1969–1970 war of attrition along the Suez Canal, but this ceasefire was controversial because of Egyptian violations. He was subsequently unable to arrange even a limited agreement between Egypt and Israel, but his efforts demonstrated that after the Six Day War the United States would no longer withdraw from peace efforts in the area, even if the President was primarily involved in other regions.

After the Yom Kippur war, the incentive to support conflict resolution was even greater. Kissinger's shuttle diplomacy followed by Carter's flirtation with a Geneva conference and then the Camp David accords and the Egyptian-Israeli peace treaty demonstrated that American engagement in the Arab-Israeli peace process had become a consistent pattern of Washington's policy toward the area. This pattern only reinforced the lesson decision makers believed they had learned in 1967—that it was the Arab-Israeli issue which was the perennial source of instability in the region. Zbigniew Brzezinski even suggested at one point that the energy crisis of the 1970s could be solved by a settlement of the Arab-Israeli conflict.[15]

This concentration on Arab-Israeli issues which was focused by the Six Day War and then concretized by the Yom Kippur war made it more difficult for policy makers to adjust to the changed circumstances raised by the fall of the Shah, the Iranian hostage crisis, the Iran-Iraq war, and the Soviet invasion of Afghanistan. If the Middle East is defined by the Arab-Israeli dispute and the Palestinian question in particular, then other issues are peripheral events, a part of another drama. Ironically, the Carter administration dreaded a second energy crisis, but anticipated that it would be caused by a new Arab-Israeli conflict. Instead, the 1979 crisis was precipitated by the fall of the Shah.

Thus, while in the public arena there was drama, emotion and excitement, the Six Day War intensified security concerns for decision makers vis-à-vis relations with the Arab world, the protection of Israel, and both the danger of confronting the Soviet Union and the necessity to block Soviet expansion. When combined with later events, these lessons were sufficiently powerful that policy makers had difficulty adjusting when the Arab-Israeli dispute became less central to ongoing Mideast developments.

Changes in the American Domestic Arena
Precipitated by the Six Day War

The domestic American reaction to the Six Day War was much deeper than temporary exhilaration. The press and media expanded their coverage of the area—establishing bureaus and stationing correspondents in places where they had not previously been located on a permanent basis. Until 1967, Israel had been pictured in America largely in mythical terms—as suggested by the novel and movie *Exodus* and the oft-repeated description that the Israeli pioneers had turned swamps into orchards. Progressively, with the news media exercising a microscopic examination of the Jewish state, a different picture emerged of a country like any other suffering internal tensions, contradictions, even corruption. The harsh realism conveyed by the intensified news coverage was to have a corrosive impact on Israel's image in America, especially during the 1970s.

Coterminous with a more balanced view of Israel, the Six Day War unleashed the Palestinian question on the American scene. Despite a series of airline hijackings and terrorist incidents in the years following 1967, the Palestinian cause, the PLO and its leader, Yassir Arafat, gained a degree of respectability, especially in liberal intellectual circles. The discovery of the Palestinians was closely tied to Vietnam. A segment of the war's critics argued that Israel, by relying on the military instrument, was demonstrating its identification with American imperialism. The Palestinians, according to this position, were victims suffering oppression analogous to the harm being inflicted on the Vietnamese people by the United States.

Regardless of the accuracy of these attitudes, they had a powerful impact on one segment of American intellectual and political thought. The Palestinian refugees had been a problem for Israel and her supporters since the 1948 war. Now, however, a vibrant moral argument developed to counter the moral claims of Israel represented by the holocaust and the Jewish state's democratic tradition. It was an argument which would come closest to official policy at the outset of the Carter era, by which time the Palestinians had come to symbolize for many American liberals identification with Third World aspirations and concerns.

Support for the Palestinian cause as a moral issue required ignoring or explaining away the PLO's resort to terrorism. This was accomplished by arguing that Israeli actions were either worse or had driven the Palestinians to desperation, or that the Palestinians were comparable to revolutionaries the world over. It was also achieved by the argument that Israel had been transformed from a David to a Goliath, using military means to subjugate the Palestinians.

The Palestinian cause never gained a following in America comparable to Europe. Yet, the Middle East question was important in weakening the left because it split opponents of the Vietnam War between backers of Israel and sympathizers with the PLO. Until 1967, Israel had been a unifying issue of the labor-liberal coalition which had been dominant in American politics since 1932. This coalition was itself disintegrating, divided between supporters and opponents of the Vietnam war. The process begun by the seminal events of 1967 meant that opponents of the war were themselves also divided over Israel, a factor which has quietly contributed to the weakness of the left in American politics ever since.

The crisis preceding the Six Day War conveyed in the most dramatic and emotional of terms to American supporters of Israel that the survival of the Jewish state could be threatened militarily. As liberals gained a reputation for reluctance to use the military option, the argument developed that no liberal administration could be relied upon to protect Israel in a crisis like the Six Day War in which Israel might not be so successful. The surprising support for Richard Nixon over George McGovern in some sections of the Jewish community in the 1972 presidential campaign was directly related to this fear (although McGovern still received a substantial majority of Jewish votes).[16] The faith of Nixon supporters was reinforced by the huge airlift of military supplies to Israel worth $2.2 billion during the Yom Kippur war. Although counterarguments could be made, the Carter administration's diplomatic pressure on Israeli leaders also seemed to confirm a suspicion of liberals which had first emerged after the 1967 war.

Thus, it is not surprising that several dominant members of the neo-conservative movement in America are Jewish. Before 1967, Israel received major conservative support, but it was the liberals who took the lead on behalf of the Jewish state. Afterward, liberals, especially in Congress, maintained their backing, but it often appeared that Israel's intense supporters were on the right—militant anti-communists epitomized by Ronald Reagan as well as religious fundamentalists. If some liberals were disillusioned by what they regarded as Israel's over reliance on the military for its survival, many conservatives admired Israel's "moxie" (as Richard Nixon liked to put it), opposition to the Soviet Union, and loyalty to America's anti-communist crusade. Once the Israelis became dependent on American weaponry after 1967, they also acquired the ability to assist the Pentagon and American corporations with the refinement of U.S. equipment. Their reliability and consistency eventually became much admired in Washington. The origins of a new view of Israel's importance can be seen after the Six Day War when the Israelis provided intelligence on Russian equipment used against them, equipment which was also employed by the North Vietnamese against the United States.

The events of 1967 also had a dramatic impact on the way that many conservative Christians interpreted contemporary Middle East history. Many conservatives, especially evangelicals, began to view the continued existence of Israel as a necessary precondition for the Second Coming of Jesus Christ.

Since 1967, the American evangelical movement has become a powerful force in support of Israel. From Rev. Billy Graham's friendship with Richard Nixon to Jerry Falwell's significant role in the Reagan coalition to the presidential candidacy of Pat Robertson, the evangelists have become a prime element in the pro-Israeli coalition. In such media as television's electronic church, a link is drawn between support for a theological millennial prophecy based on specific interpretations of the Bible and support for Israeli policies of the moment.

One publication which had a particularly strong impact in mobilizing religious conservatives in America toward a favorable perspective toward Israel was a book by Hal Lindsey. In *The Late Great Planet Earth*, originally published shortly after the war of 1967, he used biblical passages to substantiate his claims that the Bible predicts such factors in current international affairs as the Russian and Arab (and even Black African) threats to Israel which will "lead to the last and greatest war of all time," resulting in the Second Coming of Jesus.[17]

Thus an argument for support of Israel, which envisioned the ultimate destruction of Israel, paradoxically became a major factor after 1967 in popular lore about the Middle East. It is perhaps not surprising that theological interpretations should attach themselves to an event such as the Six Day War, so filled with trauma and emotion, and which resulted in the Israeli conquest of East Jerusalem with its holy shrines.

Both before and after the Six Day War, conservatives and liberals have been represented among American supporters of the Arabs and among those who sympathized with Israel. The impact of the war, however, was to alter the balance in favor of Israel even as it increased popular and official attention to Israel. Yet with respect to two very different groups, the international oil companies and the American Jewish community, the war had the effect of reinforcing old patterns.

From the perspective of the international oil companies, the events of mid-1967 were not good news. Nasser had falsely accused the United States and Britain of colluding with Israel in its pre-emptive attack against Egypt. These accusations led several radical Arab states to break off diplomatic relations with the United States. That could have meant attacks against petroleum installations in the area. As a consequence, the companies stepped up their efforts to gain a more "balanced" American policy toward the Middle East.[18] A Senate committee later uncovered briefing papers used by ARAMCO officials in the late 1960's to greet such dignitaries as visiting businessmen, Congressmen, educators. The papers instructed their readers to call for a more evenhanded policy by the United States, one less disposed toward Israel and more sympathetic to the Arab states.[19]

The increased insecurity of the oil companies after the Six Day War intensified their vulnerability to Arab pressure. This growing leverage led Saudi Arabia to encourage a campaign by company representatives to warn the Nixon administration that the key Arab oil producers, especially Saudi Arabia, might soon employ the oil weapon for political purposes. During the Yom Kippur war, the ARAMCO chairmen cautioned against sending military supplies to Israel during the war. In 1973 the oilmen performed as they were instructed.[20]

No one, including the Israelis, had to instruct the American Jewish community how to operate in the wake of the Six Day War. No American group was as deeply affected by the events of 1967, which were particularly important in the history of United States Jews. Of all major western Jewish communities, the Americans were the last to embrace the Zionist objective. Only the death of six million European Jews placed American Jewry at the forefront of the international effort outside Palestine to create a Jewish state in at least part of the British mandate.

From 1945 to 1949, in rallies, speeches, articles, and efforts to influence the American government, U.S. Jews became progressively more active in the Zionist enterprise. Following Israel's war of independence, however, such activity lessened, as many Jews turned to charitable contributions and social service organizations as means of expressing their support for Israel. Even the 1956 Suez war failed to change this pattern, because the survival of Israel was not at stake in that war and even many Jewish supporters of Israel had doubts about the wisdom of the Israeli-British-French campaign. Moreover, the 1950's was a period of emerging Jewish suburban life and rising socio-economic status, encouraging a more reserved expression of political action.

The events of May 1967, however, served to re-awaken American Jewry's interest. Israel's apparent vulnerability and the unwillingness of friendly countries such as France and even the United States to come to her aid left an indelible mark. Afterward, American Jewish life would never be the same. Travel to Israel increased dramatically as did the Israel-orientation of Jewish religious, cultural, communal, and political activity.[21] This focus sharpened as a result of increased attention to Israel in the American mass media and the succession of crises that occurred in the Middle East after 1967. These developments created ample opportunities for individuals and organizations to become engaged in political efforts on behalf of Israel. The war thus initiated an era in which much of Jewish life in America was defined by problems confronting the Jewish State. The preoccupation with Israel emerged as an important factor in American politics and a powerful constraint to be confronted whenever presidents sought to deal directly with the Arab-Israeli dispute. In the 1980's the pro-Israel lobby became more active and pro-Israel political action committees intensified contributions to political candidates they viewed as sympathetic. The major impetus for this activity was the defeats the lobby suffered in the Senate in 1978 and 1981, when it did not block major arms sales to Saudi Arabia proposed by the Carter and Reagan administrations.[22]

The intensified attention to the Middle East is reflected in the presidential campaigns which followed the 1967 war. In the two preceding elections of 1960 and 1964, the issue was barely mentioned, of interest only to the most committed partisans of Israel. Afterward, candidates increasingly found it necessary to issue policy statements on such issues as arms sales, the peace process, terrorism, aid to Israel, the Palestine question, even the location of the American embassy in Israel. The heightened priority of Mideast issues and the wider public interest led to pressure on Presidential candidates to reveal their plans and to identify their advisors.

The increased prominence of the problem was reflected each time a new Chief Executive assumed office. After 1967 presidents could no longer afford to leave the Mideast on the back burner, secured safely in the hands of trusted subordinates until occasional decisions might be required. Each president since has deemed it necessary to address the issue as a top priority early in his term.[23] Similarly, Congress has been more engaged in the problem since 1967. Formerly, the majority of legislators made traditional sympathetic statements on behalf of Israel and voted for aid. Symbolism was more significant than substance. Since 1967, however, aid to Israel and the Arab states—especially Egypt—has escalated, and the Mideast has become the central component of the foreign aid package. As part of the intensified involvement of Congress in the formulation of foreign policy, both houses have played a greater role in the determination of arms sales, and prominent legislators have expressed their views on major issues such as the peace process and terrorism. In this sense, Congress has reflected the increased attention by the media, key interest groups, and successive administrations. Major confrontations between the legislative and executive branches have occurred over such issues as the Mideast arms package of 1978 and the sale of AWACS jets to Saudi Arabia in 1981.

Congress has not taken the lead in Mideast policy, but has reacted to presidential initiatives while concentrating on areas of its special responsibility, especially relating to foreign aid. Yet presidents have known that Congressional attitudes represented an important constraint on policies they might consider, even while they maintained wide latitude for policy formulation and initiative. Since 1967, Congress has contributed to the strengthening of the American-Israeli relationship, although the critical decisions in Mideast policy have been made at the highest levels of the Executive Branch.

The U.S. and the Six Day War in Perspective

With the hindsight of twenty years, then, the Six Day War can be seen to have had a major influence on the United States and American policy in the Mideast. Changes have come about in five areas:

1. It created an opportunity for the United States to reverse the adverse direction of its competition with the Soviet Union in the region. Until 1967, the Russians had been on the advance. Although it was not clear at the time, the Six Day War created conditions which led to the emergence of the United States as the preeminent superpower in the area.

2. American policy makers' concerns about the implications of the Six Day War for the competition with the USSR, relations with the Arabs, and the security of Israel led to accelerated American involvement in efforts

to resolve the Arab-Israeli conflict. Though the Johnson administration increased America's involvement only gradually, the Nixon administration followed with a more active response to the events of 1967. In turn, the involvement in conflict resolution thrust the United States into the central position in Mideast politics.

3. In relations with Israel, the Six Day War created a new and symbiotic relationship. For the first time, Washington became primarily and directly responsible for Israel's security, leading eventually to the Jewish state's dependence on the United States for both economic and military assistance. The Six Day War also precipitated a cultural interdependence that was subsequently to have a far-reaching impact on Israeli politics and society, as the Americanization of Israel began. The United States, as the powerful partner, could have used Israel's new need for support as leverage to press for diplomatic concessions. At times after 1967, American leaders were tempted to exert pressure and even to consider imposing the conditions of peace. Yet Washington invariably retreated because of the difficulties of forcing Israel to undertake policies it rejected, the constraints imposed by domestic favoritism toward Israel, the rejection by the Arabs of most American initiatives, and the belief shared with Jerusalem that territory should be traded only for some form of peace.

4. The territories also created an Arab attraction to the United States. However many arms the Russians might ship to their Arab clients, only diplomacy seemed capable of dislodging Israel from the territories. The Arabs were largely unsuccessful in their military campaigns, but were almost always unprepared to deal directly with Israel. This peculiar combination of requirements brought several key Arab states to rely on Washington, since Moscow had no influence in Jerusalem. Despite America's sponsorship of the Arabs' chief adversary, an enemy which occupied territory they viewed as their own, several Arab states were gradually brought to increased dependence on Washington as the only available avenue for influence on Israel. Thus the results of the Six Day War led the Arabs–like the Israelis–to regard the United States with greater respect and awe.

5. Not only the American role in the Middle East, but domestic attitudes toward the Arab-Israeli dispute were eventually altered by the Six Day War. For America's liberals, the Israeli victory exacerbated divisions between supporters and opponents of the Vietnam war and even among opponents of American intervention in Southeast Asia. Henceforth, Israeli policy in the occupied territories and the Palestinian claims for independent statehood (non-existent when the Jordanians controlled the West Bank and the Egyptians ruled the Gaza Strip before 1967) became a source of concern and controversy on the left of the American political spectrum. Israeli dependence on military instruments and apparent Palestinian deprivations became powerful forces for sympathy with the new Mideast underdog, which Israel's liberal supporters constantly were forced to confront. On the other hand, both political and religious conservatives were fascinated with the determination of history in favor of the Israelis. As a beacon of eschatalogical

hope or a strategic asset to America's security concerns, the Six Day War opened a period of conservative flirtation with Israel. Meanwhile, oil companies active in the area revived efforts to gain a more evenhanded American policy in the wake of Washington's increased identification with the Jerusalem government, while the American Jewish community emerged from the crisis committed more than ever to engagement with Israel.

The net effect of this increased attention to the region has been a greater prominence for the Arab-Israeli issue in presidential campaigns and in the time and energy devoted to the problem both by Congress and the President. Each president has set the tone, devised policies, and pursued initiatives, while Congressional support has contributed to the growth of the American-Israeli relationship since 1967.

Any analysis concentrating on the impact of a particular event necessarily risks overemphasizing the importance of that development. In retrospect, patterns of history emerge. Yet the lessons and decisions we have discussed here were not inevitable. The Six Day War was a significant event which led to changes in American policy and a greater involvement by Washington in the area. As always, these policies were conceived and implemented by individuals at the pinnacle of power. If different presidents had been elected or if they had chosen different advisors, the policies the United States pursued might well have diverged dramatically. In this respect, the Johnson and Nixon administrations were particularly important in determining the lessons which would be drawn form the Six Day War. While strongly backing Israel's right to Arab concessions, their decisions to pursue the peace process provided a foundation on which subsequent administrations would build in the wake of later crises and challenges.

The peculiarity of the Six Day War was its sudden arrival, swiftly altering maps, assumptions, and the destiny of an entire region. The shock, emotion, and impact still linger, even after twenty years. Washington is still adjusting to the consequences of the events set in motion by three short weeks in 1967.

From the perspective of twenty years, American policy is nearly unrecognizable. A host of conditions have changed: the energy crisis, the Egyptian-Israeli peace treaty, U.S. disillusionment with Arab inability or unwillingness to aid in American peace initiatives, resentment at Arab terrorism. Compared with 1967, in 1987 the United States was closer to both Arabs and Israelis and stronger in its competition with the Soviets, though it had suffered a severe blow from the fall of the Shah and rise to power of a revolutionary fundamentalist and anti-American government in Iran.

In the 1980's a Reagan administration committed to a Soviet-oriented view of the Middle East has progressively celebrated the importance of Israel as a reliable ally. Few in 1967 would have considered the Jewish state in a similar light. Judging by Congressional reactions to this aspect of Reagan's Middle East policy, a bipartisan consensus has developed regarding the critical role of Israel to American concerns in the area—especially in the eastern Mediterranean. Moreover, the establishment of a close relationship

gypt stands in marked contrast to the tense relations with Cairo two
des earlier.

Yet at the twentieth anniversary of the Six Day War, the Reagan
administration seemed singularly unable to continue the sponsorship of an
Arab-Israeli peace process. Despite many apparent initiatives, it was unable
to promote negotiations based on the Reagan Plan, which envisioned
Palestinian "self-government" in the West Bank and Gaza in political
association with Jordan. Since no other acceptable formula had emerged,
the Palestinian question remained unresolved. As epitomized by the Iran
arms scandal, the administration was even more frustrated in attempting
to manage the Iran-Iraq war. Lebanon remained in turmoil. The Russians
under Mikhail Gorbachev were attempting to create a diplomatic challenge
out of these continuing instabilities. Presumably, new American initiatives
await the next administration.

Many critics have argued that America is stymied; her position dangerous
and her sun setting in the area. Yet the prognosis of these Cassandras is
distinctly premature. Twenty years of travail with a volatile and unpredictable
region has demonstrated to many Washington decision makers that patience
and caution can produce more effective results than hasty policies concocted
to thwart perceived imminent dangers. Many decision makers have learned
that the Middle East should not be ignored, but U.S. policy can also suffer
from too much nervous attention. After twenty years of struggling with
the outcome of the Six Day War, officials and analysts alike are still seeking
to discover an acceptable balance between impatience and complacency.

Notes

1. Lyndon B. Johnson, *Public Papers of the President* (Washington DC: U.S.
Government Printing Office), 13 November 1966, p. 1378; 4 June 1968, p. 680.

2. Komer memorandum on Harriman mission to Israel, 26 February 1965, State
Dept. doc. 4880, 1-7; Komer memorandum of conversation with Harriman, 25
February 1965, A.M. State Dept. doc. 4878, p. 3.

3. Theodore Draper, *Israel and World Politics: The Roots of the Third Arab-Israeli
War* (New York: Viking Press, 1968), pp. 36-37; Moshe A Gilbo'a, *Six Years-Six
Days: Origins and History of the Six Day War* (Tel Aviv: Am Oved Publications,
1969), p. 78 (in Hebrew).

4. Bernard Lewis, "The Consequences of Defeat," *Foreign Affairs* 46 (July 1967):
p. 322; Abba Eban, *An Autobiography* (New York: Random House, 1977), p. 318.

5. Earle G. Wheeler, Lyndon Baines Johnson Oral History Interviews, 7 May
1970, tape 2, 24.

6. Edward R.F. Sheehan, *The Arabs, Israelis, and Kissinger* (New York: Thomas
Y. Crowell Press, 1976), pp. 18-20, p. 85.

7. For complete discussion see Steven L. Spiegel, *The Other Arab-Israeli Conflict:
Making America's Middle East Policy, from Truman to Reagan* (Chicago and London:
University of Chicago Press, 1985), pp. 198-203.

8. For example, Nadav Safran, *Israel: The Embattled Ally* (Cambridge, Mass: Belknap Press, 1978), pp. 417–18; William B Quandt, *Decade of Decisions* (Berkeley and Los Angeles: University of California Press, 1977), p. 71.

9. Spiegel, p. 152; also author's interview with Dean Rusk.

10. For Johnson's lack of decisiveness, see Eban, p. 358; Lyndon B. Johnson, *The Vantage Point: Perspectives of the Presidency 1963–69* (New York: Holt, Reinhart and Winston, 1971), p. 293; also author's interview with Dean Rusk, 1 July, 1975. Discussion of Johnson administration vacillation also found in Spiegel, pp. 136–153.

11. Lyndon B. Johnson, *Public Papers of the President*, 19 June 1967, p. 633.

12. Author's confidential interview with a former CIA official. John P. Leacacos, *Fire in the Basket: The ABC's of The State Department* (Cleveland and New York: World Publishing, 1968), p. 334; Arthur S. Lall, *The UN and the Middle East Crisis, 1967* (New York: Columbia University Press, 1968), p. 213; Eban, pp. 442–45; Lawrence I. Whetten, *The Canal War: Four-Power Conflict in the Middle East* (Cambridge: MIT Press, 1974), pp. 47–48; Gideon Raphael, "UN Resolution 242: A Common Denominator," *New Middle East*, June 1973, 28–29; Theodore Draper, "Road to Geneva," *Commentary*, February 1974, pp. 25–27; Goldberg, Department of State Bulletin, 21 August 1967, pp. 262–65; Gideon Raphael, *Destination Peace: Three Decades of Israeli Foreign Policy* (New York: Stein and Day, 1981), pp. 177–82.

13. Lall, 255; Draper, "Road to Geneva," p. 27; Quandt, p. 55.

14. Henry Kissinger, *White House Years* (Boston and Toronto: Little, Brown and Co., 1979), p. 564; Richard Nixon, *RN: The Memoirs of Richard Nixon* (New York: Grosset and Dunlap, 1978), p. 477.

15. Zbigniew Brzezinski, "Recognizing the Crisis," *Foreign Policy*, Winter 1974–75, p. 67.

16. Stephen D. Isaacs, *Jews and American Politics* (New York: Doubleday, 1974), pp. 570–75; Richard Reeves, "McGovern, Nixon, and the Jewish Vote," *New York Magazine*, 14 August 1972, p. 26; see also "The Chosen Party" (30) and "Is Nixon Kosher?" (2) of the same issue; in an interview with the author, Leonard Garment emphasized Nixon's concern with the Jewish vote; also author's interview with Lawrence Goldberg.

17. For Biblical prediction of establishment of the State of Israel, see Hal Lindsey, *The Late Great Planet Earth*, (New York: Bantam Books, 1980), pp. 42–45; for repossession of Jerusalem, pp. 54–58.

18. Robert H. Trice, "Domestic Political Interests and American Policy in the Middle East: Pro-Israel, Pro-Arab, and Corporate Non-Governmental Actors and the Making of American Foreign Policy," PhD. Dissertation, University of Wisconsin, 1974, pp. 174–80; *New York Times*, 22 December 1969, p. 1; *Multinational Corporations and United States Foreign Policy*, (hereafter called MNC, hearings), 94th Congress, 1st Session, 1975, VII, pp. 510–511; telegram from Jungers of Aramco to McQuinn, Socal, Aramco, New York, Jan. 16, 1973; MNC VII, p. 534.

19. *Multinational Oil Companies and U.S. Foreign Policy*, (hereafter called MNOC), (Washington DC: U.S. Government Printing Office, 1979), VII, pp. 517–528.

20. MNOC, 144; MNC VII, pp. 546–547.

21. *Gallup Opinion Index*, Report 25, July 1967, p. 5; Spiegel, p. 158; Steven L. Spiegel, "U.S. Middle East Policy," *Journal of International Affairs*, Vol 36 #2, Fall/Winter 1982/83.

22. Edward Tivnan, *The Lobby: Jewish Political Power and American Foreign Policy* (New York: Simon and Schuster, 1987); Wolf Blitzer, *Between Washington and Jerusalem* (New York and Oxford: Oxford University Press, 1985); Steven Emerson, *The American House of Saud* (New York: Franklin Watts, 1985).

23. Kissinger, p. 564, p. 350; Zbigniew Brzezinski, "Recognizing the Crisis," *Foreign Policy*, Winter 1974-75, p. 67; Jimmy Carter, *Public Papers of the President*, 1977, p. 1006; *New York Times*, 29 September 1981, p. 1; 5 February 1981, p. 1; 6 September 1981, p. 16.

15

Entanglement:
The Commitment to Israel

Duncan L. Clarke

The American commitment to Israel assumes many forms: classified and unclassified written agreements, presidential statements, military and economic assistance, legislation granting Israel and its citizens unique privileges, and a variety of other diplomatic, economic and security-related U.S. government actions and policies supportive of the Jewish state. This chapter focuses principally, although not exclusively, on executive agreements concluded in 1975, 1979 and 1983. It also assesses the costs and benefits of the commitment and some of the factors that account for this "special relationship."*

Slide Toward Commitment:
Kennedy/Johnson Administrations

The policies of "friendly impartiality" toward both Arabs and Israelis, refusal to sell offensive arms to Middle East states and willingness to exert *significant, sustained* pressure (without an American *quid pro quo*) on an Israel that had acquired additional territory through war began to change when Dwight Eisenhower left office. Shortly after his election, President Kennedy made an oft-quoted remark to an incredulous David Ben-Gurion: "I know I was elected by the votes of American Jews. I owe them my election. Tell me, is there something that I can do for the Jewish people?"[1] In 1962, citing a need to offset Soviet arms transfers to the region, the Kennedy administration sold Hawk surface-to-air missiles to Israel. Although a defensive system, the Hawk transaction was noteworthy because it was the first substantial sale of a sophisticated U.S. weapon to Israel. Later that

---

*I will soon begin a long-term study on this subject. This chapter contains some preliminary observations, all of which require substantial further elaboration.

year Kennedy confided to then Israeli Foreign Minister Golda Meir, "I think it is quite clear that in case of an invasion the United States would come to the support of Israel."[2] Lyndon Johnson, and most Americans at the time, tended to see Israel and Israelis as did Leon Uris in *Exodus*: beleaguered, hard working, independent pioneers sharing a common religious heritage with America. This perception, plus the Bible stories of his youth and his many close Jewish friends, contributed to Johnson's deep attachment to the State of Israel. Not surprisingly, the administration was filled with Jewish and non-Jewish political appointees who shared this sentiment.[3]

In FY 1965–1966 the U.S. provided Israel with, among other things, M-48 tanks and A-1 Skyhawk attack aircraft, the first sale of offensive American arms to a Middle East nation. The $92 million in military assistance to Israel in FY 1966 exceeded the total U.S. military aid given that country since its founding in 1948. On the eve of the Six Day War Johnson refused to issue a pledge urgently sought by the Israeli government—that an attack on Israel would be considered an attack on the United States. The refusal was based partly on U.S. opposition to a surprise attack by either Israel or Egypt and the conclusion of a CIA Special National Intelligence Estimate that Israel would win the war quickly and decisively.[4] However, following the 1967 war, Johnson sharply augmented America's committal posture toward Israel. In January 1968 Johnson issued what theretofore was the strongest public statement by an American president. A joint communiqué declared that the U.S. would "keep Israel's military defense capability under active and sympathetic examination" and "make every effort to increase the broad area of understanding" between the two countries.[5]

Then, in 1968, just before leaving office and over the virtually united opposition of the national security bureaucracy, Johnson approved the sale of Phantom jets to Israel. No quid pro quo was asked of Israel. Executive branch analysts argued that Israel had no objective military need for Phantoms, that the sale would upset the regional military balance, would improperly reward Israel for lands seized in a war in which it struck first, and alarm the Arabs. But here, as so often in subsequent years, emotional and domestic considerations took precedence over working-level assessments of American interests in the Middle East. 1968 was an election year, Congress supported the sale, the American Israel Public Affairs Committee (AIPAC) lobbied vigorously, and Johnson's personal affinity for Israel overrode the best analysis.[6]

The Johnson administration was a watershed in U.S.-Israel relations. The U.S. acquired a firm, albeit largely unwritten and ill-defined, commitment to Israel. Washington became Israel's principal arms supplier. Israel was not pressured to return Arab territories acquired through the force of arms. And the post-1967 period marked the beginning of what proved to be an exponential growth in Israel's economic and military dependence on the U.S.

Formal Commitment

Memorandum of Agreement, 1975

Between December 1971 and March 1973 the Nixon administration agreed to sell additional Phantoms and Skyhawks to Israel, concluded a memorandum of understanding to transfer U.S. technical information to Israel, and President Nixon stated that the United States would assist in modernizing the Israeli Defense Forces (IDF) and "maintain [an] ongoing relationship of financial assistance and military supply." No quid pro quo was asked of Israel, although Nixon was impressed by Israel's actions during the Jordanian crisis in September 1970. In 1974 Nixon promised future American economic assistance and affirmed the long-term nature of the military supply relationship.[7] Then, in 1975, in the context of the peace process between Israel and Egypt in which the former agreed to the principle of withdrawal from "vital areas in Sinai," President Ford signed a memorandum of agreement (MOA-75) that constituted the first formal, written and public U.S. security commitment to Israel. Ford later justified this unprecedented gesture: "If we provided the [military] hardware, we could convince the Israelis that they were secure. Then they might be willing to accept some risks in the search for peace."[8] That is, Ford assumed that a unilateral U.S. commitment, plus the massive military and economic aid that flowed in its wake, would make Israel so strong—indeed, regionally predominant—that it would feel secure enough to negotiate peace with its neighbors.

MOA-75 (Memorandum E) contained, among other things, the following provisions:[9]

- The U.S. will be "fully responsive . . . to Israel's military equipment and other defense requirements, to its energy requirements and to its economic needs."
- "Israel's long-term military supply needs from the United States shall be the subject of periodic consultations" between the two nations and "the United States will view Israel's requests sympathetically, including its request for advanced and sophisticated weapons."
- [Under specified conditions], "if the oil Israel needs to meet all its normal requirements for domestic consumption is unavailable for purchase . . . , the United States Government will promptly make oil available for purchase by Israel . . . "
- If Egypt violates its September 1, 1975 agreement with Israel, the U.S. will "consult with Israel as to . . . possible remedial actions" by the U.S.
- The U.S. "will view with particular gravity threats to Israel's security or sovereignty by a world power." In such an event, the U.S. will

"consult promptly with Israel regarding what support, diplomatic or otherwise, or assistance it can lend Israel . . . "

- The U.S. and Israel will conclude a "contingency plan for a military supply operation to Israel in an emergency situation."
- The U.S. "will support Israel's right to free and unimpeded passage through" the Straits of Bab-el-Mandeb and the Straits of Gibraltar.

Memorandum E was accompanied by additional classified and unclassified agreements. Memorandum G, for example, committed the United States to provide Israel with F-16 aircraft and nuclear-capable Pershing I missiles, although Congress killed the latter transaction. Memorandum F stipulated that "The United States . . . will not recognize or negotiate with the Palestine Liberation Organization so long as the Palestine Liberation Organization does not recognize Israel's right to exist and does not accept Security Council Resolutions 242 and 338."[10]

Just six months after the U.S. ambassador was helicoptered off the roof of the American embassy in Saigon, MOA-75 launched the U.S. down a path that, by 1983, became one of its most sweeping and costly security commitments since the 1949 North Atlantic Treaty.

Not unlike Vietnam, it is difficult to make a persuasive case that an Israel still today officially at war with all but one of its Arab neighbors constitutes the kind of vital American interest justifying such a commitment. The general public was in 1975, and remains today, unaware of the specific nature and implications of the commitment. There was virtually no meaningful public airing of this issue in 1975, 1979 or 1983. And, despite sharp congressional criticism of presidential misuse of executive agreements for committal purposes—culminating in the passage of the Case-Zablocki Act of 1972—Congress here acquiesced in the Executive's use of this very instrument to conclude an agreement of much greater consequence than earlier executive agreements over which Congress was much exercised.

How deep and broad a commitment is MOA-75? The Office of Legislative Counsel of the U.S. Senate addressed this question in a memorandum for the Senate Foreign Relations Committee:

Because of the vagueness and numerous uncertainties of Agreement E . . . it is difficult to predict [its] ultimate impact . . . , [But] in assessing the . . . extent and desirability of the commitments made in Agreement E by the United States, the Committee may wish to view the Agreement in terms of the broadest reasonable construction to which it could be subjected either by Israel or [the] United States . . . , [T]he Agreement may be construed to provide . . . as follows.

1. The United States will introduce its armed forces into hostilities for the purpose of: (A) taking remedial action in the case of an Egyptian violation of any of the provisions of the Agreement; (B) defending Israel against threats by a world power; (C) maintaining Israel's right to free and unimpeded passage through the Straits of Bab-el-Mandeb and the Straits of Gibraltar; and (D) carrying out a military supply operation to Israel in an emergency situation.

2. United States economic and military assistance to Israel will be substantial and will include sophisticated systems . . .

3. The above obligations are undertaken *without* regard to: (A) the financial cost to the United States; (B) the aggressive nature of any act by Israel; (C) any . . . action by the United Nations against Israel, or the fact that the fulfillment of such commitments could under certain circumstances be in violation of the United Nations charter; (D) any lapse of time or change in the relationship between the United States and Israel; or (E) except [for necessary authorizations and appropriations] the absence of approval of the Congress.[11]

To be sure, this is a worst-case (or, for Israel, a best-case) analysis, one subject to critical questions. Yet it highlights MOA-75's possible ramifications.

Perhaps the central question is whether MOA-75 is legally binding on the United States. The Office of Legislative Counsel thought it was not because MOA-75 is neither a treaty subject to the advice and consent of the Senate nor an agreement otherwise formally sanctioned by Congress. That is, the Office asserted that because President Ford negotiated MOA-75 on his own, without formal subsequent (or prior) congressional authorization, the agreement is constitutionally flawed.[12] But this view contravenes or ignores the official State Department position,[13] historical precedent, established case law, and congressional actions since 1975. Executive agreements have been concluded by presidents since at least 1817. The Supreme Court has never held any executive agreement *ultra vires* for lack of senatorial or congressional consent. Indeed in *United States v. Belmont,* 301 U.S. 327 (1937), the Court specifically upheld the constitutionality of an executive agreement where such consent was absent. An executive agreement, like a treaty or statute, is the law of the land, although it would be superseded by a subsequent executive agreement, treaty or statute when they conflict with the prior executive agreement.[14] Moreover, since 1975, Congress— which was fully informed of MOA-75 and other memoranda and held hearings on them—has both acquiesced in and, through numerous actions and implementing legislation, repeatedly indicated support for these agreements. The Senate Foreign Relations Committee stated in 1975 that its "failure to signify approval does not connote disapproval."[15] The crucial provisions of MOA-75 concerning U.S. military and economic aid to Israel could not be implemented without legislation. Not only has Congress annually appropriated enormous sums for this purpose, but both the House and Senate have passed resolutions by wide margins expressly supportive of a strong U.S. commitment to Israel's security. There can be little doubt, then, that MOA-75 as well as the agreements of 1979 and 1983 are binding *de jure* commitments. There is no question whatsoever that they are firm *de facto* commitments.

Some might argue that MOA-75 is not as binding on the U.S. as the above assessment suggests since many of its artfully drafted and carefully qualified provisions leave it up to Washington to decide how to respond to, say, a threat to Israel by a "world power," an Egyptian violation of its

1975 agreement with Israel, etc. This line of reasoning is unpersuasive. All parties—the U.S., Israel, the Soviet Union, and the Arab world—know that in a crisis the U.S. will honor its commitment to Israel. MOA-75 sharply *reduces* American freedom of action in this regard. Indeed, that is why nations conclude formal security agreements at all—to enhance credibility by minimizing, through legally binding accords, the possibility that one party will not come to the aid of the other. In the post-World War II era the United States has never entered into a security arrangement with other states without hedging the instrument's language. Even Article 5 of NATO's charter, for instance, states that an individual alliance member may take "such action as it deems necessary" in the event of an armed attack on one or more NATO states (66 Stat. 2241).

The core American rationale for MOA-75, as noted above, was to provide Israel with sufficient assurances as well as an outpouring of military and economic assistance so as to compensate it for eventual withdrawal from the Sinai and to induce Israel to more confidently entertain peace proposals from a position of armed supremacy. Peace between Egypt and Israel was indeed formalized in the Camp David accords, and Israel did withdraw from the Sinai, which certainly serves Egyptian, Israeli and American interests—for as long as the accords last, that is. But query the wisdom of or need for *such* a strong formal U.S. commitment to Israel. Among other things, when deterrence again fails or when Israel takes unilateral aggressive actions as in 1982, it sharply increases the possibility of costly and dangerous American military involvement in an area whose intrinsic value hardly justifies the risk. Substantial American financial assistance to Israel (and Egypt) may have been a necessary and proper price to pay for a partial peace. But what is the rationale today for Washington's continued funding, at exceedingly generous levels, of a militarily superior Israel whose interest in pursuing peace initiatives is questionable and whose abject dependence on the U.S. is profoundly unhealthy for both countries?

The assumptions ungirding President Ford's decision to conclude MOA-75 have proven to be substantially erroneous. Prospects for a general Arab-Israeli peace settlement have been dim since 1979. This is so for many reasons, not the least of which is the internal balance of political forces in Israel. However, a central factor is Israel's predominant regional military power which, to be sure, has given it greater confidence. But it is a confidence to reject, not entertain, peace offers. This attitude was well put by Henry Kissinger: "I ask [Prime Minister] Rabin to make concessions, and he says he can't because Israel is weak. So I give him more arms, and he says he doesn't need to make concessions because Israel is strong."[16] Instead of pursuing a negotiated comprehensive peace settlement with Jordan, Syria, the Palestine Liberation Organization (PLO) and other appropriate actors, Israel has sought to "neutralize" its opponents through repeated military actions (and, via AIPAC, by thwarting proposed U.S. arms sales to moderate Arab nations). There is surely no warrant for supposing that an Israel which enjoys a firm U.S. commitment and an effectively automatic, unrestricted flow of American assistance—regardless of Israeli actions or policies or U.S. interests elsewhere in the region—will be inclined to make territorial concessions.

Beyond this, a case can be made that the Camp David accords, accompanied as they were by a renewed and expanded American commitment to Israel, reduced the prospects for a comprehensive Middle East peace settlement. The Accords failed to address any of the crucial issues of concern to Arab actors other than Egypt. At peace with Egypt, Israel has far less incentive to make additional territorial concessions. Since Camp David, Israel has formally annexed East Jerusalem, extended its sovereignty to the Golan Heights, and expanded its presence in the West Bank and Gaza. None of these actions can be reversed easily.[17] Moreover, the formal U.S. commitment to Israel, greatly solidified in 1983, makes it less likely that other Arab actors—virtually all of whom are more vulnerable to pressure from the Arab world than is Egypt—can safely seek peace with Israel. That commitment further alienates the United States from Arab countries and undercuts the ability of the U.S. to again act as a more or less "neutral broker" in Arab-Israeli negotiations. This state of affairs is what George Ball had in mind when he testified that, "We have sewed up the wound and left the infection inside."[18]

There is yet another legacy of the 1975 memoranda that impedes peace prospects and American interests. It may be unique in the annals of diplomacy for a superpower to accede to the wishes of a small state and formally agree not to recognize or negotiate with an important third party unless the small state agrees to such recognition or negotiation. That is what the United States did in Memorandum F, even though most American Middle East specialists and Arab states hold that there can be no meaningful peace without accommodating the interests of the Palestinian people through their most authoritative representative, the PLO. The substance of Memorandum F is reflected in the Framework for Peace portion of the Camp David agreements wherein Israel is granted veto power over PLO participation in future peace negotiations.[19] When American officials do attempt a dialogue with the PLO or even speak of a need for a Palestinian "homeland," as President Carter did in 1977, they incur the instant wrath of Israel and the American Jewish Community.[20]

Memorandum of Agreement, 1979

Two hours after the Treaty of Peace between Egypt and Israel was signed, the United States and Israel signed a Memorandum of Agreement (MOA-79) specifically reaffirming MOA-75 and all other prior agreements and assurances between the two countries. This executive agreement went beyond MOA-75. For example:

- In the event of "a violation or threat of violation of the Treaty of Peace, the United States will consult with the parties . . . and will take such remedial measures as its deems appropriate, which may include diplomatic, economic and military measures . . . " Military measures may include "the strengthening of the United States presence in the area, the providing of emergency supplies to Israel, and the exercise of maritime rights."

- The United States "will support" Israel's right to navigation and airspace through the Strait of Tiran and the Gulf of Aqaba.[21]

Israeli Prime Minister Menachem Begin declared MOA-79 "a beautiful document."[22] His elation is understandable. As with MOA-75, the executive branch considered MOA-79 legally binding on the United States.[23] There was virtually no dissent from this interpretation in subsequent congressional hearings. MOA-79 solidified and broadened the formal security commitment Israel had long and eagerly sought. For the United States, however, it suffers from all the flaws of its predecessor.

Strategic Cooperation Agreement, 1983

Since at least the 1973 Yom Kippur War, Israel and the American Israel lobby have exploited America's concern about the Soviet threat. No president was more receptive to this appeal than Ronald Reagan. And no president has proved a truer 'friend of Israel' (a phrase charged with meaning for the Israel lobby).

Just ten months after the Reagan administration entered office and one month after it narrowly turned back AIPAC's effort to defeat the AWACs sale to Saudi Arabia, the United States and Israel, on November 30, 1981, signed a Memorandum of Understanding (MOU-81) directed expressly "against the threat to peace and security [to the Middle East region] caused by the Soviet Union."[24] In addition to countering the Soviets, the administration apparently also hoped to assuage the concerns of Israel and its supporters over the AWACs sale and ease the annual game of political hardball all recent administrations have had to endure from AIPAC and Congress.

MOU-81 was unprecedented in several respects: it formally acknowledged the alleged importance of "strategic cooperation" between the two nations, specifically named the Soviet Union (instead of a "world power") as a principal threat, created a coordinating council and joint working groups to implement the agreement, provided for broad-based military cooperation, and called for extensive defense-related technology and arms transfers as well as joint planning and readiness activities and air and naval exercises.[25] When, two weeks after MOU-81's signing, Israel annexed the Golan Heights in contravention of U.S. policy, Reagan canceled MOU-81. But, as has always been the case since the Eisenhower administration, American sanctions/pressure against an Israel whose actions contravene U.S. interests were short-lived.

National Security Decision Directive (NSDD) 111 of October 29, 1983, which is classified, made close strategic cooperation an administration priority. The next month President Reagan and Israeli Prime Minister Yitzhak Shamir signed agreements sometimes called the Strategic Cooperation Agreement (SCA-83), that reinstated MOU-81 and then went well beyond it.

Israel's reason for wanting SCA-83 is evident. Despite its regional military superiority, Israel knew it could not sustain the costs of either another Arab-Israeli war that turned out to be of long duration, or perhaps even a protracted limited war, without solid American backing and across-the-board assistance.[26] But why would the United States believe yet another security commitment to Israel was necessary? The question is especially troubling as SCA-83 came in the wake of a highly counterproductive Israeli invasion of Lebanon—a country Reagan briefly and puzzlingly considered a U.S. "vital interest"—that later proved unpopular among most Israelis, greatly increased the threats to Israel and costs to the United States, caused thousands of civilian casualties, and triggered the introduction of U.S. troops into Lebanon (241 of whom died from a truck-bomb just six days before NSDD-111 was signed).

Among the many factors probably contributing to the decision were Reagan's long-standing personal attachment to the Jewish state and his receptivity to the 'Israel is a strategic asset' school of thought, particularly that school's assertion of Israel's utility in countering Soviet threats and influence.[27] Prior to 1983, several organizations and individuals had espoused the view that Israel was a U.S. strategic asset deserving of an intimate committal relationship. They included The Jewish Institute for National Security Affairs in Washington, AIPAC (and its Steven J. Rosen), some Jewish American analysts and academics like Steven L. Spiegel and Joseph Churba, and ardent congressional friends of Israel such as Senator Rudy Boschwitz and Congressman Jack Kemp.[28] But this view was, and remains, a distinct minority one among American national security and Middle East specialists within and without government. On the other hand, Congress, which seems instinctively disposed to saying yes to Israel and AIPAC,[29] held no public hearings on SCA-83 and acquiesced in it.

The case for SCA-83 within the executive branch was led by Secretary of State George Shultz. He was apparently joined by National Security Adviser Robert McFarlane (who later had a taste of strategic cooperation with Israel in the Iran-Contra scandal) and UN Ambassador Jeanne Kirkpatrick. In opposition were Secretary of Defense Caspar Weinberger, the Joint Chiefs of Staff (JCS) and, below the seventh floor, much of the State Department.[30] Even after the president announced his decision, General John Vessey, Chairman of the JCS, publicly voiced his opposition and argued that the goals of Israel and the United States differed sharply.[31] The military services have long opposed a deep security commitment to Israel[32] for several reasons besides the fundamental one cited by General Vessey: it could (as in 1973) dangerously draw down the U.S. arsenal, stretch already overextended American forces and divert them from other more critical missions, present immense logistical problems, and compromise American intelligence and state of the art weaponry.

The purpose of SCA-83, said President Reagan, was to "give priority attention to the threat to our mutual interest posed by increased Soviet

involvement in the Middle East." But Prime Minister Shamir described its
purpose differently: "to *strengthen Israel* and deter threats to the region."[33]
That the interests of the two countries in SCA-83 and throughout the
region differ is clear enough. Israel understandably seeks to ensure its own
security while the United States has diverse, complex, sometimes conflicting
interests throughout the entire region, including the countering of Soviet
influence. Henry Kissinger recognized what Ronald Reagan did not when
he said, "The strength of Israel is needed for its own survival but not to
prevent the spread of Communism in the Arab world. So it doesn't necessarily
help United States global interests as far as the Middle East is concerned.
The survival of Israel has sentimental importance to the United States
. . . "[34] Indeed, if thwarting Soviet influence in the Arab world is the
primary American interest, a case can be made (although not by the author)
for abandoning Israel. Reagan's first Secretary of State, Alexander Haig,
discovered far more Arab concern about an aggressive Israel than interest
in a "strategic consensus" against the Soviet Union when he visited the
region. An Israel made militarily superior by the United States, which
occupies Arab lands and launches military strikes far beyond its own borders,
provides compelling reasons for Arab states to turn to the devil himself
for protection, even if he resides in Moscow. "Israel," said Sheik Ahmed
Zaki Yamani, "is the opening through which the Russians creep into the
Arab world."[35]

Moreover, U.S. officials are skeptical of the feasibility and advisability of
using Israeli bases for Persian Gulf contingencies. And, while Israel has
alluded to the possible use of its air and naval forces against Soviet forces
in the eastern Mediterranean and elsewhere, few Israelis believe IDF ground
forces should engage the Soviets, except if Moscow attacks Israel directly
or if a Soviet proxy like Syria engages Israel.[36] It is distressing that the
American public, which must provide the taxes and quite possibly the
young men to honor SCA-83, remains unaware of its scope and cost. Public
ignorance is maintained through secrecy, the low-profile public announcement
of the agreement, fleeting press attention, the absence of open congressional
hearings, and the understandable disinclination of Congress, the president,
and the Israel lobby to spell out the costs. Yet some of SCA-83's provisions
are known.[37] They are here listed, accompanied by brief comments.

Joint Military Cooperation.[38] Perhaps the clearest manifestations of the
changed relationship engendered by SCA-83 are the activities of the Joint
Political Military Group (JPMG) and its joint working groups that were
authorized by the agreement. The JPMG has met regularly since its first
meeting in January 1984. It is co-chaired by a senior State Department
official and the Director General of Israel's Defense Ministry. The JPMG
has not served as a forum to discuss potential joint operations against the
Soviet Union throughout the region. Rather, it is a mechanism for reaching
agreements on the use of Israeli facilities in crises and the prepositioning
of U.S. military stocks in Israel. It also facilitates information exchange in
order to reach agreements on, among other things, joint military planning

and exercises.[39] A U.S. official commented: "Israel uses [the JPMG] to its advantage . . . But the JPMG is *not* the only area where this occurs . . . You have Israelis wandering around the Pentagon, picking up information here and there." He added that the process was exceedingly "lopsided," with Israel benefiting far more from it than the U.S.

Also created by SCA-83, but not publicly announced, was the Joint Security Assistance Planning Group (JSAPG), co-chaired by a senior State Department official and the same Israeli official who co-chairs the JPMG. JSAPG was designed to coordinate and, hopefully, reduce open political controversy over the level and terms of U.S. economic assistance to Israel. But according to a knowledgeable U.S. official, it has not worked out that way:

> The JSAPG is designed to discuss in private, in order to coordinate aid needs, funding, and terms. It is meant to keep emotion out, somewhat, . . . so that politics is removed. But Israel keeps working on congressional support to find new aid enhancements in ways that don't show good faith in what JSAPG is supposed to do. It is supposed to represent a bilateral commitment to eliminate controversial issues on aid. But Israel has *not* taken efforts to get its congressional supporters to withdraw legislation on enhanced financing and other obviously controversial matters. Israel says they can't stop the senators, and as a result it is a one-way relationship.

Prepositioning of Military Supplies. Under the agreement, U.S. military supplies have been prepositioned in Israel. They would surely be turned over to Israel if it was attacked. The U.S. thereby loses or substantially dilutes the kind of leverage over Israeli actions it had in 1973.

Military Assistance Grants and Related Privileges. Israel received a $425 million increase in U.S. military grants. In 1984 *all* foreign military assistance sales (FMS) to Israel were placed on a permanent grant (not loan) basis. Economic aid has been in the form of outright grants since FY 1981. For years, the U.S. has provided every Israeli citizen an average annual subsidy of approximately $1000, and this figure reflects only direct assistance. The actual amount is much higher when numerous special privileges accorded Israel are considered.[40] Such dependence is striking, even alarming. It cannot be in Israel's long-term interest. Nor, in a time of burgeoning American budget and trade deficits, should it be welcomed by the United States. The potential political implications of this situation, when understood by the American public, are evident.

SCA-83 affirmed and expanded upon a secret Memorandum of Agreement signed on March 19, 1979.[41] In that MOA the U.S. agreed to allow Israel to sell $200 million in military exports or services to the U.S. Defense Department and spend up to $200 million of its FMS assistance in Israel, rather than in the U.S. as would otherwise be required under the Buy American Act. In March 1984, the two nations signed a Memorandum of Agreement concerning exchanges of scientists and engineers in research, development, procurement and logistics support for selected defense equipment.[42] The latter agreement is, among other things, certain to open the door to protests from American firms who object to sensitive technology transfers to a foreign country with whom they must compete on the international market in various arms and arms related exports. The administration did not, in 1983, grant Israel's request to bid on U.S. defense contracts on an equal footing with NATO allies. But, true to form, Israel gained this privilege—one that could bring it hundreds of millions of dollars—in 1986 when Congress designated Israel a "major non-NATO ally." Only Japan, Australia and South Korea—who, unlike Israel, are all allied to the U.S. via mutual security treaties—were also so designated. This new policy was implemented and the March 1984 agreement was expanded in a memorandum of understanding signed on December 14, 1987.[43]

Finally, Congress and SCA-83 authorized Israel to use FMS funds to develop and procure the Lavi fighter despite vigorous opposition from the Pentagon, the intelligence community, most of the rest of the national security bureaucracy, and some defense firms. The Lavi—before Israel's cabinet, under intense Pentagon pressure, narrowly voted to cancel it in August 1987[44]—promised to be more costly and less effective than the U.S. F-16, strain Israel's chronically ill economy, compromise U.S. technology, cost American jobs, and possibly compete with American aircraft in the international arms market. Before terminated, the program's costs reached $1.5 billion, 90 percent of which was paid by the U.S. government. Total program costs, most of which would have been picked up by the U.S. taxpayer, could have exceeded $10 billion.[45]

Cluster Bombs. The IDF had repeatedly violated U.S.-imposed restrictions on the use of U.S.-produced cluster bombs. But SCA-83 apparently permitted Israel to purchase cluster bomb fuses, thereby enabling it to produce its own bombs.

Free Trade Agreement. SCA-83 called for negotiations leading to the creation of a free trade area between the U.S. and Israel that would eliminate all tariffs and other trade barriers. In 1984, Congress, in PL 98-573, authorized these negotiations to proceed and an agreement was subsequently concluded. This was apparently the first time in history that Congress permitted an executive agreement dealing with foreign economic policy to go into effect without further congressional action. AIPAC lobbied vigorously for the agreement over the objections of several American agricultural and industrial associations and even the usually pro-Israel AFL-CIO. These groups argued, among other things, that the free trade agreement gave Israel an unfair advantage since its industries and agricultural concerns were heavily government-subsidized and, moreover, there was no equity in affording Israel duty-free access to the $3 trillion U.S. market in exchange for U.S. access to the $8 billion Israeli market. But 1984 was an election year. Many members of Congress saw this as a relief measure for Israel's endemically beleaguered economy. Hence, Israel received another special privilege, one that not even our closest allies enjoyed (although ratification of a free trade agreement with Canada was pending in 1988).[46]

The United States neither asked for nor received anything of note in return from Israel for SCA-83—unless, that is, one subscribes to the myth that Israel is a strategic asset fully justifying an increased likelihood of American regional military involvement, the financial expense to the U.S. government, economic disadvantages to American firms and workers, alienation of the Arab world, and a heightened incentive for Arab nations to turn elsewhere for protection and arms. SCA-83 reminds one of the "balanced" U.S.-Israel relationship depicted in an Oliphant cartoon in the early 1970s which showed Golda Meir grasping an armload of U.S. Phantom jets while Richard Nixon held a large bowl of chicken soup.

Reduced prospects for peace in the Middle East constitute another serious cost. The Reagan administration claimed that SCA-83 was not directed against Arab states, but the Arabs should be skeptical. SCA-83 symbolizes a closing of ranks and a formal choosing of sides by Washington. The United States thereby moved closer toward forfeiting its role as "honest broker" in a peace process. But the Reagan administration did not seem to care much about this. For instance, Secretary Shultz, in an inflammatory address to an AIPAC audience in May 1987, asked:

Secretary Shultz: Is the PLO qualified [for peace negotiations]?
Audience: No.
Secretary Shultz: Hell, no! Let's try that on for size. PLO?
Audience: Hell, no!
Secretary Shultz: You got it! . . . They showed once again they don't want peace . . . [47]

Nine months later Shultz was in Israel on a peace mission while Israeli soldiers were shooting and beating scores of Palestinians in occupied Gaza and the West Bank. Needless to say, Shultz had difficulty finding "qualified" Palestinians who had the authority and legitimacy to negotiate a just and peaceful settlement.

Other Formal Commitments

The United States and Israel have numerous formal and informal security-related commitments beyond those already mentioned. Some are classified. Many implement provisions of MOA-75, MOA-79 and SCA-83. Only two additional agreements are here mentioned briefly; one that is in place, another that is a possibility.

When Israel withdrew from the Sinai in 1982, the 162 person U.S. civilian Sinai Field Mission was replaced with a 2700 person Multinational Force and Observers (MFO) to monitor the peace treaty between Egypt and Israel. The U.S. component of the MFO consists of a battalion of 808 men, a logistics support unit of 356 and 50 civilians. The commitment is open-ended, subject only to continued congressional authorization and appropriations.[48] Of the many indices of commitment, few are stronger than the stationing of ground forces. Should war again break out between

Egypt and Israel, it is quite possible that these troops, and therefore the U.S., would be quickly engaged.

An instrument entertained with varying degrees of interest by Israel since the 1950s, and by AIPAC in the 1980s, is a U.S.-Israel Mutual Defense Treaty.[49] It would put the icing on a cake whose ingredients include SCA-83 and its predecessors. But, apart from eliminating whatever legal ambiguity may surround a commitment by executive agreement and opening the relationship to much needed public debate when the treaty goes to the Senate for certain ratification, this would be another unwise step. Israel already enjoys a too intimate U.S. commitment. A mutual defense pact would compound virtually all the problems discussed above and narrow Washington's already limited diplomatic and strategic options in the Middle East. Only after a comprehensive regional peace settlement would it be advisable to conclude such an alliance.

Why the Deep Commitment?

Many factors contribute to the deep U.S. commitment to Israel,[50] but three stand out: the 'Israel is a strategic asset' perception, normative considerations, and the Israel lobby's activities within the American political process.

Strategic Asset Perception. Of the reasons commonly cited for Israel's purported strategic asset status,[51] only two—intelligence exchange and weapons-related technology transfers/weapons refinements—have some substance.

Israel gives useful human intelligence to the United States. But in return the U.S. provides a spectrum of intelligence, including sensitive signals and photo-reconnaissance intelligence, to a country long targeted by hostile intelligence services. Israel, probably knowingly, attacked the American intelligence collection ship, U.S.S. Liberty, in 1967; may have been implicated in illicit diversions of enriched uranium from a Pennsylvania nuclear reactor between 1957–1960 (and has since improperly obtained uranium from other sources); unlawfully received timing devices (krytrons) that can be used in manufacturing nuclear weapons from an American accomplice in the 1980s; and otherwise committed espionage against the United States long before Jonathan Pollard severely compromised U.S. security.[52]

Israeli defense industries, the country's largest employers, have provided the U.S. with useful technical innovations and weapons refinements, and the IDF has "battle-tested" American weapons to the benefit of the U.S. military. There is no semblance of balance, however, in technology transfer or research and development. The trickle from Israel is matched by a flood from the United States. Without this link to the United States and annual U.S. subsidies, Israel's defense industrial base would stagnate and probably collapse. While individual American firms benefit (others do not), there is no net economic gain for the U.S. because of the grant basis for FMS aid, forgiveness of outstanding loans, and numerous special privileges afforded

Israel. Moreover, Israel has sometimes "refined" American weapons by making minor alterations, claiming they are no longer American weapons, and reselling them to third parties in violation of U.S. law and policy. Israel has also contravened U.S. law and policy—and compromised U.S. advanced systems—by battle-testing these systems in risky attacks against Syria, Iraq and Tunisia. Israel's 1,500-mile bombing raid on the PLO in Tunisia in 1985, a country with which Washington had always enjoyed cordial relations and had pledged to defend against external threats, was (shockingly) excused by President Reagan as "a legitimate response and an expression of self-defense."[53] Secretary Shultz was forced later to "clarify" this misstatement. Finally, it should be noted that the U.S. has not been without ample opportunity to battle-test its own weapons in the post-1945 era.

Normative Considerations. A democratic political system and an avowed moral essence are at the core of the American public's image of and identity with Israel. Yet these vital elements are in danger of eroding because of, *inter alia:* repeated IDF military offensives; Israel's hold on Jerusalem, a city sacred to two other great religions; an occupation of Arab lands that is in some respects analogous to South African apartheid and contrary to the principle of self-determination—an ideal embedded in the American Declaration of Independence and the American psyche; the rise of what Ofira Seliktar calls "New Zionism" in Israel, growing incidents of Jewish terrorism against occupants of the West Bank, and scores of human rights abuses by *Shin Bet* (Israel's principal internal security service); and the decline of democratic values among segments of Israel's population.[54]

The Catholic Church and most mainline Protestant churches, while affirming ecumenical kinship with Judaism, have maintained or increased their distance from the State of Israel. For instance, the General Assembly of the Presbyterian Church (USA) in 1987 adopted the position that, "The State of Israel is a geopolitical entity and is not to be validated theologically."[55] What happens to the normative pillar of the American commitment when the above developments/perceptions seep down to the general public, as they surely will?

The Israel Lobby in the U.S. Political System. AIPAC's refrain is that a strong Israel serves American interests. But the Israel lobby exists for one purpose: to advance the welfare of a foreign country whose interests clash frequently with those of the United States. How effective is the lobby in furthering Israel's interests? What weight should be given to AIPAC and associated groups within the constellation of factors influencing the policy process?

As a rule, AIPAC and its supporters tend to argue *in public* that the Israel lobby differs little from other interest groups who petition the government, and, that its influence is regularly exaggerated, especially by "enemies of Israel" (who, inferentially, may be closet anti-Semites). So Steven Spiegel asserts that it is a "myth" that "the pro-Israel lobby . . . [has] great leverage," and when "taken to its logical extreme [the myth] erupts in antisemitism . . . "[56] In private, however, before receptive audiences or in one-to-one discussions, AIPAC officers often boast of their impact in Congress and the executive branch.[57] Those targeted for political opposition by AIPAC and Jewish Political Action Committees (PACs), like former Congressman Paul Findley, consider AIPAC "King of the Hill."[58]

There is no reasonable doubt among informed scholars, journalists and government officials that AIPAC, the almost 100 pro-Israel PACS, and other groups like the Conference of Presidents of Major American Jewish Organizations [Presidents' Conference] powerfully affect virtually every significant facet of American policy toward Israel.[59] But assessing the Israel lobby's relative impact against other factors influencing the American political system is a much more difficult task. Two such factors include the following:

• Congress and the President, in supporting Israel, may simply be reflecting the public mood. Since 1948, a majority, or at least a sizeable plurality, of the public has held favorable views of Israelis and Israel, especially when contrasted with Arabs and Arab states. Yet it is also true that most Americans object to military aid that may entail direct involvement on behalf of Israel in threatening situations, that a majority of the general public has always opposed sending troops to Israel's assistance, and that recent polls (unlike most prior ones) indicate majority support for reducing the level of Israel's economic and military aid.[60]

• Many members of Congress and some U.S. presidents have felt an emotional attachment to Israel and/or shared a belief that it is a strategic asset deserving of generous support wholly apart from AIPAC. However, it is very doubtful that the depth, scope and automaticity of support would be as great in the absence of AIPAC. In addition, legislators often vote pro-Israel on certain issues, not out of conviction, but out of fear of AIPAC and Jewish PAC retribution.[61] Some legislators do speak openly and critically about U.S.-Israel relations, but usually only after they have decided not to run for reelection. Thus Senator Barry Goldwater, then chairman of the Senate Select Committee on Intelligence, said in 1984: "We stand a better chance of going to war in the Middle East because of promises we've made to Israel without any treaties. . . . I don't like the way Israel has been playing around with our promises to come to her aid almost regardless of reason."[62]

Conclusion

For emotional reasons, to facilitate a possible peace settlement and (although a less persuasive rationale) to maintain American credibility, the United States should be committed to Israel's survival. But a more distant relationship is badly needed and the U.S. should not defend or acquiesce in the concept of Eretz Israel. The present intimate bond does not serve American interests and is a mixed blessing for Israel itself. Except perhaps for El Salvador and Honduras, no other nation is so thoroughly dependent on the United States. This dependence calls Israel's very sovereignty and national dignity into question. It invites mutual resentment, disrespect and, eventually, a backlash in both countries.

Without fundamental changes in American policy and in the forces influencing that policy, a backlash *will* occur. Americans will tire of subsidizing an Israel thought incapable of salvaging its own economy, resistant to making peace with its neighbors, and increasingly at odds with U.S. diplomacy in the Middle East. As has been said, even Sugar Daddies die. Also, unless Israel is the object of an unprovoked attack, when the risks of the present level of commitment become evident, the public will likely reject—as it probably always has—the notion that Israel is a "vital" U.S. interest (that is, worth going to war over).

The perceived "dual loyalty" of some members of the American Jewish community *is* an issue, one that the current U.S.-Israel relationship only exacerbates. It will not do to accuse those raising this point of antisemitism,[63] although anti-Semites will be quick to exploit it. As the issue gains salience it will surely spawn malign, corrosive attitudes.

The alarm within the Jewish community in 1985–1987 over the Jonathan Pollard affair highlighted this concern. Pollard explained his motive for conducting espionage against his country: "As far as I was concerned . . . there was no difference between being a good American and a good Zionist."[64] Just prior to the 1984 Israeli elections Kenneth Bialkin, chairman of the President's Conference, stated: "If the Alignment wins and changes Israel's policies, we will support them; if the Likud wins and pursues a strong line in the West Bank we will get behind them."[65] This sounds like Stephen Decatur's, "my country right or wrong," but with a difference— Decatur was speaking of America, not a foreign country.

AIPAC's practices closely parallel Decatur's words. Some distinguished members of the Jewish community have expressed concerns about AIPAC's and the community's single-issue focus. There are also signs that American Jews are becoming somewhat more accepting of open Jewish criticism of Israel and supportive, under certain conditions, of Israeli negotiations with Jordan and the Palestinians.[66] But above all, American society as a whole must openly and actively debate the implications of America's committal posture toward Israel. Failure to do so will cost the country dearly.

Notes

1. Melvin I. Urofsky, *We Are One! American Jewry and Israel* (New York: Anchor Press, 1978), p. 333.

2. Mordechai Gazit, "Israeli Military Procurement from the United States," in Gabriel Sheffer, ed., *Dynamics of Dependence: U.S.-Israel Relations* (Boulder, Colo.: Westview Press, 1987), pp. 98, 121.

3. Steven L. Spiegel, *The Other Arab-Israeli Conflict: Making America's Middle East Policy, From Truman to Reagan* (Chicago: University of Chicago Press, 1985), pp. 123, 128–29.

4. John Ranelagh, The Agency: The Rise and Decline of the CIA (New York: Simon and Schuster, 1986), p. 474; Stephen Green, *Taking Sides: America's Secret*

Relations with a Militant Israel (New York: William Morrow, 1984), p. 187; Donald Neff, *Warriors for Jerusalem: The Six Days that Changed the Middle East* (New York: Linden Press, 1984), pp. 136–37.

5. Lyndon Baines Johnson, *Public Papers of the President* (Washington, DC: Government Printing Office, 1968), pp. 20–21.

6. See Spiegel, *The Other Arab-Israeli Conflict*, pp. 160–63.

7. See generally Gazit, "Israeli Military Procurement . . . ," pp. 108–112.

8. Gerald Ford, *A Time to Heal* (New York: Harper and Row, 1979), pp. 308–309.

9. U.S. Congress, Senate, Committee on Foreign Relations [hereafter cited as SFRC], *Hearings: Early Warning System in Sinai*, 94th Congress, 1st session, 1975, pp. 249–51.

10. Ibid., pp. 252–53.

11. Emphases added, Ibid., pp. 71–72.

12. Ibid., pp. 65ff.

13. Ibid., p. 85.

14. Louis Henkin, *Foreign Affairs and the Constitution* (Mineola, NY: Foundation Press, 1972), pp. 177–86.

15. SFRC, *Report: Early Warning System in Sinai*, No. 94-415, 94th Congress, 1st session, 1975, p. 8.

16. Quoted in Richard R.F. Sheehan, *The Arabs, Israelis, and Kissinger* (New York: Readers Digest Press, 1976), p. 199.

17. See William B. Quandt, *Camp David: Peacemaking and Politics* (Washington DC: The Brookings Institution, 1986), pp. 330–31.

18. SFRC, *Hearings: Early Warning System in Sinai*, p. 19.

19. The Framework for Peace also refers to "the legitimate rights of the Palestinian people," a phrase Israeli Prime Minister Menachem Begin later said had "no meaning." Jim Hoagland, "Dispute on Israeli Settlements Snags Accord," *Washington Post*, September 20, 1978, p. A1.

20. Edward Tivnan, *The Lobby: Jewish Political Power and American Foreign Policy* (New York: Simon and Schuster, 1987), pp. 102, 132.

21. U.S. Congress, House of Representatives, Committee on Foreign Affairs [hereafter cited as HFAC], *Hearing and Markup: Supplemental 1979 Middle East Aid Package for Israel and Egypt*, 96th Congress, 1st session, 1979, pp. 257–58.

22. Stephen Rosenfeld, "The Language and the Chemistry," *Washington Post*, March 30, 1979, p. A23.

23. HFAC, *Hearings and Markup: Supplemental 1979 Middle East Aid Package . . .* , p. 29.

24. For the full text of the agreement see Nimrod Novik, *Encounter with Reality: Reagan and the Middle East (The First Term)* (Boulder, CO: Westview Press, 1985), pp. 86–88.

25. Ibid.

26. See Wolf Blitzer, *Between Washington & Jerusalem: A Reporter's Notebook* (New York: Oxford University Press, 1985), p. 69.

27. There is another, simpler explanation. The decision may have been a rash reaction by officials frustrated over events in Lebanon they could not control, who were desperately searching for something to demonstrate "resolve" and who were under domestic political pressure to move closer to Israel as the presidential election year approached.

28. Blitzer, *Between Washington & Jerusalem*, pp. 73–74.

29. The remark of a senior Senator about Israel is illustrative: "We [the Congress] are like wealthy parents of adolescents who can't resist giving our beloved too much." Robert Kaiser, "The U.S. Risks Suffocating Israel with Kindness," *Washington Post,* May 27, 1984, p. C1.

30. See Bernard Gwertzman, "Reagan Turns to Israel," *New York Times Magazine,* November 27, 1983, p. 63.

31. Interview, General John W. Vessey, Jr., *Meet the Press,* November 27, 1983, (Washington, D.C.: Kelley Press, 1983), p. 3.

32. Harry J Shaw, "Strategic Dissensus," *Foreign Policy* 61 (Winter 1985-1986), p. 136. Some military officers, however, take a contrary view. See Elmo R Zumwalt, Jr., *On Watch: A Memoir* (New York: New York Times Book Co., 1976), p. 442.

33. Emphases added. White House press release, November 29, 1983. It appears Israel never agreed with the Reagan administration's assertive, regional anti-Soviet orientation but went ahead with the agreement on the entirely realistic assumption that its own interests would eventually prevail. Leslie Gelb, "United States-Israeli Talks Said to Aim at Soviets," *New York Times,* July 20, 1984.

34. Quoted in Seth P. Tillman, *The United States in the Middle East* (Bloomington, Ind.: Indiana University Press, 1982), p. 52.

35. Quoted in Christopher Van Hollen, "Don't Engulf the Gulf," *Foreign Affairs* 59 (Summer 1981), p. 1068. Shortly after Israel (a nonparty to the Nuclear Non-Proliferation Treaty) flew U.S. supplied aircraft 600 miles to destroy an internationally controlled and inspected nuclear reactor in Iraq (a treaty party) in contravention of American law and policy, President Reagan remarked: "It is difficult for me to envision Israel as being a threat to its neighbors." *New York Times,* June 17, 1981, p. 26.

36. Much more can be said about this, but see Shaw, "Strategic Dissensus," pp. 129-33.

37. See Aaron S. Klieman, *Israel's Global Reach: Arms Sales as Diplomacy* (Elmsford, NY: Pergamon-Brassey's, 1985), pp. 177-78; Bernard Gwertzman, "U.S. Israeli Panel Will Coordinate Military Planning," *New York Times,* November 30, 1983, p. A1; George Ball, *Error and Betrayal in Lebanon* (Washington, DC: Foundation for Middle East Peace, 1984), p. 82.

38. Information and quoted passages in this subsection are drawn substantially from the author's personal knowledge and interviews conducted by Michelle Parks. Michelle Parks, "U.S.-Israeli Strategic Partnership: A Muddled Guide to Policy," The American University, unpublished paper, October 21, 1986 (mimeo).

39. See Steven L. Spiegel, "U.S. Relations with Israel: The Military Benefits," *Orbis* 30 (Fall 1986), p. 493.

40. See U.S. General Accounting Office [hereafter cited as U.S. GAO], *U.S. Assistance to the State of Israel,* GAO/ID-83-51, June 24, 1983; SFRC, *A Staff Report: The Economic Crisis in Israel,* S. Prt. 98-251, 98th Congress, 2nd session, 1984, pp. 25-28, 46; U.S. GAO, *U.S. Security and Military Assistance: Programs and Related Activities-An Update,* GAO/ID-85-158, September 30, 1985; Mohamed El Khawas and Samir Abed Rabbo, *American Aid to Israel: Nature and Impact* (Brattleboro, VT: Amana Books, 1984).

41. See "(U) Letter of March 19, 1979, from Secretary Brown to Minister of Defense Weizman, with SECRET attachment," in HFAC, *Hearings and Markup: Supplemental 1979 Middle East Aid Package . . . ,* p. 240. Terms of the agreement are found in Klieman, *Israel's Global Reach,* p. 177 and *Maariv,* February 26, 1982.

42. Klieman, *Israel's Global Reach,* pp. 176-78.

43. Larry Cohler, "Pro-Israel Community Pleased With Results," *Washington Jewish Week*, October 23, 1983, p. 3; Memorandum of Understanding between the Government of Israel and the Government of the United States of America Concerning the Principles Governing Mutual Cooperation in Research and Development, Scientist and Engineer Exchange, Procurement and Logistic Support of Defense Equipment, December 14, 1987 (mimeo); Larry Cohler, "Rabin, Carlucci Agree to Drop U.S.-Israel Military Trade Barriers," *Washington Jewish Week* December 24, 1987, p. 9.

44. The Lavi episode was a "win-win" experience for Israel. Following the program's cancellation, the U.S. promised to reimburse Israel handsomely in F-16s, foreign assistance, and special privileges.

45. U.S. GAO, *Foreign Assistance: Analysis of Cost Estimates for Israel's Lavi Aircraft*, GAO/NSIAD-87-76, January 1987; Duncan L. Clarke and Alan S. Cohen, "The United States, Israel and the Lavi Fighter," *The Middle East Journal* 40 (Winter 1986), pp. 16-32.

46. U.S. Congress, House of Representatives, Committee on Ways and Means, *United States-Israel Free Trade Area*, H. Report 1092, 98th Congress, 2nd session, 1984, p. 7; U.S. Congress, House of Representatives, Committee on Ways and Means, Subcommittee on Trade, *Hearings: Proposed United States-Israel Free Trade Area*, 98th Congress, 2nd session, 1984, especially pp. 107-108, 123-63, 342, 464.

47. U.S. Department of State, Bureau of Public Affairs, Secretary George Shultz, "Working for Peace and Freedom," *Current Policy*, No. 957, 1987, p. 3. In September 1987, under pressure from AIPAC, the State Department announced the closing of the PLO information office in Washington.

48. U.S. GAO, *U.S. Assistance to the State of Israel*, pp. 69-75.

49. Yair Evron, *An American-Israeli Defense Treaty* (Tel Aviv, Israel: Jaffee Center for Strategic Studies, 1981), p. 3.

50. See Cheryl A. Rubenberg, *Israel and the American National Interest* (Urbana, Ill.: University of Illinois Press, 1986), p. 8.

51. See, for example, Eugene V. Rostow, "The American Stakes in Israel," *Commentary* 63 (April 1977), pp. 32-46; Steven L. Spiegel, "Israel as a Strategic Asset," *Commentary* 75 (June 1983), pp. 51-55; Steven J. Rosen, *The Strategic Value of Israel* (Washington, DC: American Israel Public Affairs Committee, 1982).

52. Jeffery T. Richelson, *The U.S. Intelligence Community* (Cambridge, Mass.: Ballinger, 1985), p. 323; Ranelagh, *The Agency*, pp. 253, 571; Green, *Taking Sides*, pp. 157-74, 179; Charles Babcock, "Israel Uses Special Relationship to Get Secrets," *Washington Post*, June 15, 1986, p. A1; Charles Babcock, "Computer Expert Used Firm to Feed Israel Technology," *Washington Post*, October 31, 1986, p. A1; Steven Dryden, "Illegal Uranium Sales To Israel Discovered," *Washington Post*, July 12, 1985, p. A29. It seems that, in the Iran-Contra scandal, Israeli intelligence agents proposed the 'arms for hostages' deal to the U.S. and either originated or heartily endorsed the idea of transferring monies from this transaction to the Contras. *President's Special Review Board* [Tower Commission] (Washington, DC: Government Printing Office, February 26, 1987), pp. III-4, IV-12; U.S. Congress, "Report of the Congressional Committees Investigating the Iran-Contra Affair," H. Report 100-433, 100th Congress, 1st Session 1987, pp. 279-80. Glenn Frankel, "Israeli Contact Loses Duties," *Washington Post*, July 9, 1987, p. A1. Throughout, said the Tower Commission (p. IV-12), it was "clear . . . that Israel had its own interests, some in direct conflict with those of the United States, in having the United States pursue the initiative."

53. *Washington Post*, October 3, 1985, p. A1. See also Clarke and Cohen, "The United States, Israel and the Lavi Fighter," pp. 22, 25-27.

54. Ofira Seliktar, *New Zionism and the Foreign Policy System of Israel* (Carbondale, Ill.: Southern Illinois University Press, 1986); Tivnan, *The Lobby*, pp. 250–52; Glen Frankel, "Israeli Court Renews Debate Over Secret Policy Methods," *Washington Post*, May 26, 1987, p. A1.

55. John Bolt, "Presbyterians Back Jewish Faith, Stay Neutral on Mideast Politics," *Washington Post*, June 20, 1987, p. D6.

56. Spiegel, *The Other Arab-Israeli Conflict*, pp. 388–89.

57. Tivnan, *The Lobby*, pp. 138, 163, 198, 148–49; Douglas Bloomfield, "Israel's Standing in Congress: Will Foreign Aid Be Spared?" in Nimrod Novik, ed., *Israel in U.S. Foreign and Security Policies* (Tel Aviv, Israel: Jaffee Center for Strategic Studies, 1983), especially pp. 18–23.

58. Paul Findley, They Dare to Speak Out: People and Institutions Confront Israel's Lobby (Westport, CT: Lawrence Hill, 1985), p. 25.

59. See, for example, Tivnan, *The Lobby*; Rubenberg, *Israel and the American National Interest*; Charles McC. Mathias, "Ethnic Groups and Foreign Policy," *Foreign Affairs* 59 (Summer 1981), pp. 975–98; Tillman, *The United States in the Middle East*, pp. 54, 276; Charles Babcock, "U.S.-Israeli Ties Stronger Than Ever," *Washington Post*, August 5, 1986, p. A1.

60. Eytan Gilboa, *American Public Opinion toward the Arab-Israeli Conflict* (Lexington, Mass: Lexington Books, 1987).

61. Tivan, *The Lobby*, pp. 187–94; Rubenberg, *Israel and the American National Interest*, pp. 357–75.

62. Interview with Senator Barry Goldwater, "'Mr. Conservative' Sizes Up Challenges Reagan Faces," *U.S. News and World Report*, December 17, 1984, p. 53.

63. "A characteristic of the anti-Jew," according to Bernard Lewis, "as opposed to the pro-Arab is his tendency to harp on Jewish power and influence, which he usually greatly exaggerates, and to complain of Jewish double loyalty." Bernard Lewis, *Semites and Anti-Semites* (New York: W.W. Norton, 1986), p. 251.

64. Wolf Blitzer, "Why Did He Spy?" *Washington Jewish Week*, February 26, 1987, p. 1.

65. *The Jerusalem Post* (International Edition), July 8–14, 1984.

66. Steven M. Cohen, *Ties and Tensions: The 1986 Survey of American Jewish Attitudes Toward Israel and Israelis* (New York: The American Jewish Committee, 1987), especially pp. 89–90; Earl Raab and Seymour Martin Lipset, *The Political Future of American Jews* (New York: American Jewish Congress, March 1985), pp. 19–20.

16

Jewish and Arab Diasporas in the United States and Their Impact on U.S. Middle East Policy

Andrea Barron

The political environment of the United States, a nation of immigrants, has generally been receptive to attempts by ethnic diasporas to influence American foreign policy toward their country of origin or "homeland." The extent to which a diaspora is able to achieve its goals depends on a variety of factors including its size, economic status, level of political activity, and attachment to its "homeland" as well as on the attitudes of American policy makers and the American public toward the "homeland." (A "diaspora" will be defined here as "a minority ethnic group of migrant origins which has maintained sentimental and/or material links with its land of origin.")[1]

Greek-Americans, for instance, helped convince Congress to impose an arms embargo against Turkey in 1975 after it invaded Cyprus and displaced 200,000 Greek Cypriots. (The embargo was lifted in 1978 after Turkey—an important NATO ally—reacted by closing down twenty-six U.S. bases that had been used to gather intelligence on the Soviet Union.) And in 1977, Black Americans created Transafrica, a professional lobby which played a critical role in the decision by the Reagan administration to impose economic sanctions against the apartheid government of South Africa.[2]

This paper will examine the Jewish-American and Arab-American diasporas—two politically active ethnic communities with "homelands" in the Middle East—and their impact on U.S. policy in the region. Each community has recognized the important role played by the United States in the Arab-Israeli conflict and has sought to influence how the conflict is viewed by elected officials and the public. Since 1948, but especially since 1967, Jewish Americans have lobbied the executive and legislative branches of government

---

This chapter was updated in March 1988 in order to incorporate developments resulting from the Palestinian uprising in the occupied territories.

to provide Israel with economic and military support. Although they have objected to U.S. arms sales to Jordan and Saudi Arabia, most Jews have been relatively satisfied with America's Middle East policy and want to preserve the U.S.-Israel "special relationship." Arab-Americans, on the other hand, are trying to disrupt the foreign policy status quo. Since the 1967 war, they have argued for U.S. diplomatic recognition of the PLO and for a less Israel-centered foreign policy that would lead to better relations with the Arab world.

The Jewish-American Diaspora

The Jews have been viewed as the classic diaspora because they had no homeland for nearly two thousand years but were able to remain a separate ethnic-religious community in the countries where they settled. Even after Israel was founded, most of the world's 13,000,000 Jews continued to live in the diaspora. In 1984, only 27 percent resided in Israel. The world's largest Jewish community is in the United States, which has 5,705,000 Jews. There are other sizeable communities located in the Soviet Union (1,575,000), France (530,000), Great Britain (330,000), and Canada (310,000).[3]

Most American Jews or their ancestors arrived in the United States during the late nineteenth and early twentieth centuries from Eastern Europe and imperial Russia. (There had been a smaller wave of Jewish immigrants from Germany in the mid-1800s). Some of the Eastern Europeans were fleeing the pogroms which followed the assassination of Czar Alexander II. Others saw their own economic situation deteriorating and were attracted by the vision of a "Golden America" overflowing with opportunities. By the time Congress virtually closed the doors to immigration in 1924, almost three million Jews had arrived in the United States.

The Jewish immigrants were determined to become Americans as quickly as possible and to maintain their Jewish identities at the same time. They established a host of institutions to help new arrivals, including the Hebrew Immigrant Aid Society, Jewish hospitals, nursing homes, and free loan societies. German immigrants founded the American Jewish Committee in 1906 to influence the U.S. government on behalf of American and European Jews. Then in 1918 Russians established the American Jewish Congress to combat anti-Semitism, support civil rights for Jews and other minorities, and promote the Zionist goal of a Jewish homeland in Palestine.

By the outbreak of the Second World War and especially after the Nazi Holocaust, the majority of American Jews had been "converted" to Zionism. But that did not mean that they had any intention of leaving America for Israel. In fact, David Ben-Gurion, Israel's first prime minister, and the other founders of the Jewish state were disappointed when so few American Jews decided to "make *aliyah*" (immigrate or literally "ascend" to Israel).[4] Israeli government statistics indicate that only about 50,000 Jewish Americans, less than one percent of American Jewry, have immigrated to Israel. The state's new arrivals came mostly from displaced persons camps in Europe and from the Middle East, not from the technologically developed societies of North America. By staying in the United States, however, American Jews have ended up performing an invaluable service for the Jewish state. They have given it between $300 and $500 million a year through the United Jewish Appeal (UJA) and have loaned it approximately $500 million a year by purchasing Israel bonds.[5] But even more important, they created lobbies which can take much of the credit for the fact that Israel now receives more than $3 billion a year in U.S. aid and that it has a "special relationship" with America enjoyed by few if any other countries.

The official registered lobby is the American Israel Public Affairs Committee (AIPAC), which concentrates on convincing Congress to pass legislation which supports the policies of the Israeli government. AIPAC has three principal objectives—first, to pressure elected officials to provide Israel with military, economic, and diplomatic support; second, to prevent the U.S. government from selling arms to so-called "moderate" Arab states like Jordan and Saudi Arabia that are still technically at war with Israel; and third, to stop the PLO from communicating directly with the U.S. government or the American public. The *de facto* lobbies, which have basically the same goals as AIPAC, include about 80 pro-Israel political action committees (PACs) and the Conference of Presidents of Major American Jewish Organizations. The PACs make contributions to candidates running in federal elections. The Presidents' Conference functions as a kind of "community lobby;" it represents AIPAC and 44 other organizations in dealing directly with the executive branch, especially with the White House and the State Department.

There are no exact figures on how many Jews the various lobbies actually represent but the Presidents' Conference probably speaks for most of the community. It includes the congregational and rabbinical bodies of Reform, Conservative, and Orthodox Jewry (over 3,000,000 Jews);[6] mass membership organizations like the Women's Zionist Organization Hadassah (385,000 members); B'nai B'rith Women (120,000 members); and community relations agencies like the American Jewish Congress (50,000 members).

Despite the fact that they make up only 2.7 percent of the U.S. population, Jewish Americans have been able to influence U.S. policy toward their "homeland" more than any other ethnic diaspora. Just three years after Israel was established, I.L. ("Sy") Kenen, the journalist who later became the founder of AIPAC, was able to obtain $65,000,000 in economic aid for Israel by working with several members of Congress including Senator Hubert Humphrey of Minnesota. One year later, Kenan drafted pro-Israel planks which he had inserted into both the Republican and Democratic party platforms.[7] On the diplomatic front, in 1962 the Presidents' Conference succeeded in derailing a Mideast peace plan proposed by President Kennedy which would have allowed Palestinian refugees the choice of repatriation to Israel or resettlement elsewhere with compensation.[8]

Several factors can help explain the extraordinary political strength of American Jews. Over ninety percent of Jews vote, compared to only fifty percent of the general public,[9] and they are concentrated in strategic states such as New York, Pennsylvania, and California, which all have large numbers of electoral votes. Jews are relatively well-off financially and are willing to donate both their time and their money to political campaigns; fifteen of the twenty-one individuals who loaned Hubert Humphrey's 1968 presidential campaign more than $100,000, for example, reportedly were Jews.[10] Moreover, by working with and within non-Jewish organizations, Jews have built on the sympathy for Israel that already existed among the American public. The Jewish War Veterans, for instance, through its ongoing relationships with other veterans organizations, has been able to reinforce the generally pro-Israel sentiments of American veterans.[11] The leadership roles played by Jews in the labor movement, as well as what has been described as "an almost natural affinity and alliance between American labor organizations and the *Histradut*, Israel's national trade union federation," help explain why there is a statue of Golda Meir in the AFL-CIO headquarters in Washington, and why the Teamsters are "the largest single institutional holder of Israeli bonds in the world."[12]

The voting behavior of American Jews, their economic resources, geographic distribution and high degree of communal organization are all key variables which have to be considered when analyzing the impact Jews have had on U.S. Mideast policy. But the *sine qua non* of their success has been their political will—their determination to mobilize all their available resources on behalf of Israel. Jewish Americans feel strongly that Israel must be preserved both as a refuge for persecuted Jews and as an answer to the Holocaust. Many U.S. Jews who were adults during World War II share a sense of collective guilt for not having tried harder to save their brethren in Nazi-occupied Europe. Through active support for Israel, they can assuage their guilt and at the same time affirm their Jewish identity.

After the Second World War, Jews were rapidly assimilating into American society, enjoying the financial and social benefits of nearly full acceptance by their Gentile neighbors. At the same time, however, second and third generation Jews were attending synagogue and observing Jewish holidays less frequently than ever before. They desperately needed an "Israel" in order to survive as a distinct ethnic-religious community. Milton Himmelfarb, an editor of the American Jewish Committee's monthly magazine *Commentary* explained:

> If—which God forbid—Israel should cease to exist, do we not know in our bones that the Jews would cease to exist? We have not in us the stuff of our *galut* ancestors, and what they were able to do in the absence of a Jewish state we and our descendants will be unable to do; for we are barely able to do it in the presence of a Jewish state.[13]

Most American Jews were ardent supporters of Israel before the 1967 war. But the war strengthened their commitment and "Zionized"[14] the still uncommitted. Even members of the anti-Zionist American Council for Judaism jumped on the Zionist bandwagon.[15] M.J. Rosenberg, a former editor of AIPAC's weekly publication *The Near East Report*, wrote about watching on television as "President Nasser of Egypt massed 100,000 troops in the Sinai and pledged with King Hussein to fight Israel to the death." Rosenberg said Jews feared the "Holocaust was going to be completed, 22 years after Hitler's death."[16] Jewish Americans responded to the crisis by pouring money into the UJA's Israel Emergency Fund. Between May 22, when Nasser closed the Gulf of Aqaba to Israeli shipping, and June 10, the day the war ended, they gave over $100 million to the Fund—most of it in cash.[17]

Once the war was over, according to Rabbi Arthur Hertzberg, vice-president of the World Jewish Congress, "the American Jewish community cast itself very early for the role of chief priest of the temple of unqualified admiration of Israel."[18] The government that had prevented the second Holocaust could do no wrong. American Jews would do everything for Israel except move there. They gave more money than ever before—donations were seventy percent higher in 1968 than in 1966 (although contributions were twenty-five percent lower than in 1967, when Israel was at war). And they visited Israel more frequently too; 2,000 community leaders traveled there in 1968, compared to only 140 in 1964.[19] But that was not enough. American Jews assigned themselves the responsibility of making sure that Israel would never again be in danger of annihilation. They—and the U.S. government—would guarantee it.

Following the 1967 war, AIPAC, the Presidents' Conference, and even individual Jews acting on their own began to apply sustained pressure on U.S. policy makers. They wanted the U.S. to ensure Israel's defense by supplying it with sophisticated weaponry which would match any arms the Soviet Union gave the Arabs. They argued that arming Israel would also be in U.S. interests; Israel was a democracy like the United States—it had a stable government, regular elections, and a vibrant free press. If the Arabs destroyed it, that would be a loss for the United States and a gain for the Soviets. In 1968, AIPAC orchestrated a campaign to convince the Johnson administration to accede to Israel's request for fifty F-4 Phantom jet fighters. The Phantoms would give Israel a qualitative edge over the Arabs. The State Department and the President both opposed the sale, which they feared might result in an escalation of the arms race with the Soviet Union.[20] But with the assistance of other Jewish organizations and of stalwart allies like the AFL-CIO, AIPAC "delivered" both houses of Congress and, finally, the recalcitrant President.

In the 1970s the U.S. increased aid to Israel through loans and grants and provided the Jewish state with additional Phantoms, Skyhawk jets, F-15 and F-16 planes. Military assistance jumped from ninety million dollars in 1966 to $1.7 billion ten years later.[21] In 1986, Israel was awarded more than three billion dollars in non-repayable grants. Not all of this support can be attributed to the skills of the lobbies. Impressed by Israel's performance during the June 1967 War and with the intelligence it had gathered on Soviet equipment captured from the Arabs, the Pentagon started to view Israel as a barrier against Soviet expansionism in the Middle East. Moreover, the American public saw Israel as a small struggling democracy that had been minding its own business in 1967 when the Arabs were preparing to attack, and Americans had a highly favorable opinion of the Jewish state. Fifty-six percent of the respondents to a Gallup poll conducted during the 1967 war sympathized with Israel, compared to only four percent who sympathized with the Arabs. Even after the 1982 Sabra and Shatila massacres and the Palestinian uprising that began in December 1987, more Americans expressed support for Israel than for the Arabs.[22]

The lobbies probably *can* take credit for the conversion of all U.S. aid to Israel into grants and for preventing the U.S. from "disciplining" Israel on certain occasions. In March of 1975, for instance, AIPAC mobilized its Capitol Hill supporters to reverse a decision made by President Ford to delay a shipment of arms to Israel. Ford was angry at the Israelis for not cooperating with Secretary of State Henry Kissinger in the troop disengagement negotiations with Egypt then underway in the Sinai and had declared a "reassessment" of U.S. policy toward Israel. By May, with the help of AIPAC, 76 senators had sent Ford a letter threatening to veto his foreign aid request if he was not "responsive to Israel's urgent military and economic needs." That was the end of "reassessment." The lobbies were also responsible for the decision taken by the Reagan administration in September 1987 to close the PLO Information Office in Washington, D.C.

The pro-Israel lobbies have suffered a few defeats through the years. They failed to stop the sale of F-15 fighter jets to Saudi Arabia in 1978 and lost the "Battle of the AWACs" in 1981 to Ronald Reagan, who personally lobbied dozens of senators not to reject his proposed sale of five AWACs (airborne warning and control systems) to the Saudis. AIPAC refused to take its losses lying down, however, and set out to punish some of the errant senators, such as Republican Charles Percy from Illinois, who had voted with the president. Percy was defeated in 1984 by Paul Simon, who reportedly received three million dollars—forty percent of his campaign funds—from American Jews.[23] Following the election, AIPAC's executive director, Tom Dine, acknowledged his organization's role in defeating Percy. "All the Jews in America, from coast to coast, gathered to oust Percy," he told the Council of Jewish Federations in Toronto. "And the American politicians—those who hold public positions now and those who aspire— got the message."[24]

There has been an extraordinary expansion of Jewish political strength in the 1980's, as growing numbers of politicians have "gotten the message" and as the lobbies developed a more positive relationship with the State Department, once seen as a bastion of "pro-Arab bureaucrats." AIPAC has been called "the most powerful, best-run and effective foreign policy interest group in Washington" by *The New York Times*, and Jewish PACs have proliferated since the lobbies lost the AWACs battle in 1981. According to the Federal Elections Commission, eighty pro-Israel PACs, with names like the Chicago-based "Citizens for the National Interest," spent almost $7 million in 1985 and 1986 to elect candidates who support Israel's policies.

At least 51 of these PACs are said to be run by individuals associated with AIPAC, although AIPAC has denied that it has coordinated anything even resembling a "national PAC."[25]

In 1985, AIPAC helped push a bill through Congress banning any U.S. contacts with the PLO. Two years later, it was behind the legislation sponsored by the then presidential candidates Robert Dole (R-Kansas) and Jack Kemp (R-NY) to close the PLO observer mission to the United Nations and the PLO Information Office in Washington. The State Department, initially opposed to the closing of both offices, especially wanted to avoid a shutdown of the New York mission, which it thought would constitute a violation of the U.S. Headquarters agreement with the United Nations. Deputy Secretary of State John Whitehead and Richard Murphy, Assistant Secretary of State for Near Eastern and South Asian Affairs, decided to "make an offer"—the administration would close the Washington office if Congress would leave the New York mission alone. The offer, however, was not made to Congress but to Morris Abram, Chairman of the Presidents' Conference. According to an aide to Representative Don Mica (D-Fla), one of the bill's principal sponsors, State Department officials "essentially went to the source of the pressure on the members (of Congress), rather than dealing with the members" (themselves).[26] In other words, American Jewish leaders "represented" Congress at a meeting with the U.S. State Department!

While Jewish political muscle has increased dramatically in the 1980's, this decade has also witnessed the beginning of sustained Jewish criticism of certain Israeli policies—namely Israel's 1982 invasion of Lebanon and its handling of the Palestinian protests which broke out in December 1987. The Lebanon invasion, especially Israel's role in the Sabra and Shatila massacres, was the main catalyst which transformed American Jewry from a monolithic body willing to "rubber-stamp" virtually all Israeli actions into an increasingly independent-minded diaspora often troubled by events in the "homeland."[27]

Rabbi Arthur Hertzberg, Rabbi Alexander Schindler of the Union of American Hebrew Congregations (UAHC), and Philip Klutznik, past president of both the World Jewish Congress (WJC) and the World Zionist Organization (WZO) and a former U.S. Secretary of Commerce, criticized the Begin government for launching the invasion. This was a different kind of war, they said. Israel was not fighting for its survival but to achieve a political end—the destruction of the PLO's infrastructure in southern Lebanon. Hertzberg attacked Begin in the pages of the *New York Times*, accusing Israel's prime minister of "squandering Israel's fundamental asset: its respect for itself and the respect of the world."[28] Schindler appeared on Israeli television and called for the dismissal of Minister of Defense Ariel Sharon, the "architect" of the invasion. Klutznik went even further. He joined Nahum Goldmann—like him a former president of both the WJC and the WZO—and former French Prime Minister Pierre Mendes-France in calling for "mutual recognition between Israel and the Palestinian people" and "negotiations with the PLO leading to a political settlement."[29]

Hertzberg, Schindler, and Klutznik all broke one of the cardinal rules governing the relationship between Israel and the American Jewish diaspora. The rule had been articulated clearly in January 1967 by Dr. Emmanuel Neumann, once known as the "dean of American Zionists," to repudiate a statement made by Jacques Torczyner, then president of the Zionist Organization of America. (Torczyner had criticized an Israeli raid on the Jordanian town of Samu.) The rule was that "Israel's military and defense matters are beyond . . . discussion at all times," and that American Jews should "avoid personal reflection on, and certainly denigration of, people at the head of the state and government (of Israel)."[30]

But after the Lebanon war and the rise to power of Begin's right-wing revisionist brand of Zionism, more U.S. Jews were willing to break this rule, and to accept criticism of Israel from other Jews. In 1981, for instance, fifty-seven percent of the respondents to a nation-wide poll on Jewish attitudes conducted by Professor Steven M. Cohen for the American Jewish Committee disagreed with the statement: "American Jews should not publicly criticize the policies of the government of Israel." By 1986, this percentage had climbed to 63 percent.[31] A plurality of respondents (48 percent) to the poll also agreed that the Palestinians have a right to a homeland on the West Bank and Gaza, so long as it does not threaten Israel (compared to 21 percent who disagreed and 31 percent who were not sure).

Up until September 1987, the Jewish organizations which took positions opposing those of the Israeli government were mostly small groups with limited political clout such as New Jewish Agenda. The 4,000 member New Jewish Agenda supports the creation of a Palestinian state in the West Bank and Gaza and "negotiations between Israel and legitimate representatives of the Palestinian people, including the PLO."[32] (Israel refuses to negotiate with the PLO under any conditions.) In 1984, members from Agenda and a local group—Washington Area Jews for Israeli-Palestinian Peace—lobbied delegates at the Democratic Party's Platform Committee convention to back an amendment to the platform calling on the United States to encourage Israel to freeze Jewish settlements in the West Bank (eighteen percent of the delegates voted for the amendment).[33] Three years later, representatives from these two groups and from a third—the Chicago-based America-Israel Council for Israeli-Palestinian Peace—met with PLO Chairman Yasser Arafat to discuss the Israeli-Palestinian conflict and the need for the PLO to abandon all violence if it is serious about peace with Israel.[34]

In September 1987 the American Jewish Congress (AJ Congress), a member of the Presidents' Conference, surprised both Israeli Prime Minister Yitzhak Shamir and many U.S. Jews by issuing a statement endorsing the idea of an international peace conference on the Middle East. Israel's national unity government is split on the conference idea—Foreign Minister Shimon Peres of the Labor Party supports it while Shamir and his right-wing Likud bloc does not. The AJ Congress said it was concerned that if Israel holds on to the West Bank and Gaza Strip, populated by 1.5 million Palestinians, by the year 2000 it would have to choose between two unacceptable alternatives—"becoming a non-Jewish state or a non-democratic state." The Congress called on other Jewish organizations to follow in its footsteps. But the response from Morris Abram, chairman of the Presidents' Conference, was that *Israelis* (author's emphasis) must make these kinds of decisions through their democratic process.[35] The implication was that American Jews have no business taking an independent stand on a question related to Israeli security. Shamir agreed and denounced the Congress for interfering in internal Israeli affairs while Peres appeared to welcome the organization's statement.

Three months after this controversial statement was published, widespread Palestinian protests against the military occupation erupted in the West Bank and Gaza Strip. Over 70 Palestinians had been killed by March 1988 in the worst outbreak of violence in the territories since they were conquered by Israel in 1967. The army tried to quell the uprising by using live ammunition, tear gas and a systematic policy of beatings— all directed at mostly teenage stone throwers. Many American Jews agreed with Rabbi Schindler from the UAHC, who said the riots should shock Israel into negotiating a political solution to the Palestinian question.

The Jewish diaspora's relationship to Israel had changed through the years—more Jews were now willing to challenge the "rule" that discussion of Israel's policies towards the Arabs was off-limits to them. The Lebanon war, the Jonathan Jay Pollard spy scandal, and Israel's involvement in the Iran-Contra scandal all tarnished the Jewish state's once pristine image in the minds of many Jews. But news reports of Israel's response to the uprising astonished and saddened them even more. There were confirmed reports of Israeli troops burying Palestinians alive, of soldiers firing tear gas canisters into hospitals, and of the government closing off parts of the West Bank and Gaza to the news media.

The Israeli government could no longer count on full support from all quarters of the Jewish community. Morris Abram and the more conservative wing of the community, which included the Anti-Defamation League of B'nai B'rith, justified Israel's response to the riots as a necessary evil. But the more liberal groups from the Jewish establishment—the UAHC, the AJ Congress and the American Jewish Committee—no longer were willing to confine their criticism of Israeli actions to private consultations with Israeli leaders. Theodore Ellenoff, president of the American Jewish Committee, even went so far as to compare Israel to South Africa regarding the restrictions the Jewish state had placed on the press.[36]

Although Jewish criticism of Israel has grown during the eighties, until March 1988 there was little change in the *kinds of policies* the Jewish lobbies supported on Capitol Hill. In the eighties, as in the seventies, the lobbies have argued in favor of high levels of U.S. aid to Israel and against arms sales to Arab states officially at war with Israel. Virtually all Jewish dissidents— namely Jews willing to express public disagreement with Israeli policies— share these positions. But some dissidents have begun to let Congress know that they are disturbed by certain Israeli actions. In April 1983, 16 rabbis took the unprecedented step of travelling to Washington to express their opposition to Israel's West Bank settlement policy.[37] Much more significant, however, was a letter sent in March 1988 to Secretary of State George Shultz by 30 senators including Jewish senators Carl Levin (D-MI) and Rudy Boschwitz (R-MN) and other "good friends" of Israel. The letter criticized Shamir for refusing to cede territory in the West Bank and Gaza in exchange for peace, saying that "peace negotiations have little chance of success if the Israeli Government's position rules out territorial compromise."[38]

The American Jewish Committee and other liberal Jewish groups expressed approval of the letter, while the Anti-Defamation League of B'nai B'rith called it "premature and counterproductive." The conservative National Jewish Coalition, which has advised President Reagan on Jewish concerns, said the 30 senators had "operated in haste" and had no right to "insert themselves into the internal politics of Israel."[39]

American Jews are likely to maintain their considerable influence on United States Mideast policy as long as Israel remains the central focus of organized Jewish life and as long as they continue to actively participate in domestic politics. What may shift slightly is the *type* of influence they choose to exert. Liberal Jewish groups worried about "Israel's soul" as well as its security needs have started refusing to give their stamp of approval to the Likud's territorial policies, and have begun making their views known in Washington. If a Likud government replaces Israel's present National Unity coalition, American Jewish criticism of Israel will probably grow. If a Labor government is elected, however, criticism is likely to diminish. In any case, because of the political strength of U.S. Jews, "official Washington" will probably respond to some degree to any significant shifts in Jewish opinion.

The Arab-American Diaspora

Although there are no precise statistics on the number of Americans of Arab descent, scholars estimate that there are probably between two and three million Arab-Americans. According to the *Harvard Encyclopedia of American Ethnic Groups*, about ninety percent of the Arab-American community is Christian and ten percent is Muslim. (Some Arab-Americans say that the Muslim percentage has been increasing in recent years and is actually considerably higher than ten percent.)[40] Arab-Americans are concentrated in the urban areas of major industrial states such as California, New York, Illinois, and Michigan, with the largest community living in the Greater Detroit area.

Over half of all Arab-Americans came to the United States between 1885 and 1940. Most of them were poor, uneducated peasants from the area then known as Greater Syria, a province in the Ottoman Empire that included the administrative district of Mt. Lebanon. Like most other migrants who poured into America during the great waves of immigration, they were in search of economic opportunities. Peddling became their predominant occupation; before 1914, as many as ninety percent were said to have been peddlers at one time or another. Peddling brought the early immigrants financial success and allowed them to assimilate rapidly into American society. It forced them to adapt quickly to American culture and to learn English more rapidly than other immigrants who labored in factories and continued to communicate in their native language.[41]

These Arabic-speaking immigrants often identified themselves as Syrian-Lebanese rather than as Arabs. Their primary communal loyalties were to their villages of origin and to their religious communities. The Christians were Syrian Orthodox, Maronites, and Melkites. (Maronites and Melkites are both affiliated with the Roman Catholic Church, although Melkites follow the Eastern rite or liturgical tradition.) The Syrian-Lebanese were often willing to cross ethnic lines in order to marry their co-religionists. Some Syrian Orthodox, for instance, preferred to marry Greek or Russian Orthodox non-Arabs rather than Arab Maronites.[42] (Jewish Americans, by contrast, did not have to choose between their religion and their ethnicity.)

The Syrian-Lebanese did establish some Arabic-language newspapers in the late nineteenth and early twentieth centuries and an attempt was made to unify the community by means of a series of Syrian-American federations in the 1930s. The immigrants continued to eat home-cooked Middle Eastern meals and held on to what have sometimes been characterized as "Arab cultural values" such as generosity, hospitality, and the practice of placing family honor above the desires of individual family members.[43] But in their zeal to acculturate into the American mainstream, they gradually lost touch with their ethnic roots and their lands of origin. One Arab-American researcher wrote: "If political and economic events had not reactivated Arab immigration and an interest in Arab culture, Syrian-Americans might have Americanized themselves out of existence."[44]

After World War II, a second major wave of Arab immigrants arrived in the United States. Of the 216,000 Arabs who came between 1948 and 1979, 142,000 or sixty-five percent immigrated after the 1967 war.[45] They were not only from Syria and Lebanon but also from Egypt, Jordan, Iraq, and North Africa. Palestinians entered the country as refugees, as citizens of Arab countries, or with Israeli passports. Unlike the earlier Arab arrivals, a large percentage of the new immigrants were politically sophisticated, well-educated members of the middle class. Some were fleeing political unrest in their homelands, such as the Egyptians whose land had been expropriated by Nasser's socialist regime. The post-war immigrants tended to be more nationalistic than the older Arabic-speaking community and kept themselves informed about political events in the Middle East.[46] They were able to identify fully as Americans and simultaneously maintain links with the Arab world, just as Jews who consider themselves patriotic Americans have strong ties to Israel. They were an authentic diaspora community— ethnic Americans who were determined to remain connected to their historical roots.

The post-war Arabs revitalized the Arab community by constructing new mosques, teaching Arabic in their mosques and churches, and publishing books and articles on Arab-Americans. They reached out to the older Syrian-Lebanese immigrants and encouraged them to develop an interest in their Arab heritage. During the 1950s, the two communities started to come together. It was during that period that the concept of an *Arab-American*, as opposed to a *Syrian-* or *Lebanese-American*, first emerged. Then came the 1967 war; Israel's lightning victory and the American public's enthusiastic support for Israel shocked many Arab-Americans. The war "Arabized" second, third, and fourth generation Arab immigrants, just as it had "Zionized" American Jews. The Jews had felt proud to bask in the glory of Israel's triumph. But Arab-Americans felt the sting of a press that expressed overwhelming support for the Jewish state. *Time* magazine, for example, expressed sympathy with the "besieged and threatened" people of Israel who it said "faced the implacable hostility and cocked guns of fourteen Arab nations and their 110 million people."[47]

Some Arab-Americans, such as Jim Zogby, now executive director of the Arab American Institute in Washington, D.C., felt that they—along with the Arab states—were being attacked. "We felt insulted," Zogby later said, "when we heard Arthur Goldberg [the U.S. Ambassador to the United Nations] denounce Arabs on the floor of the world body. He seemed to be talking about me," Zogby later recalled.[48] The 1967 war created and reinforced ethnic awareness among Americans of Arab descent, helped to further unify the community, and led to the establishment of several major Arab-American organizations.

The first organization created in the aftermath of the war was the strongly pro-Palestinian Association of Arab-American University Graduates (AAUG). It was founded in 1968 by Professors Hisham Sharabi of Georgetown University and Edward Said of Columbia University, who both have close connections to the PLO. AAUG focuses on politicizing Arab-Americans and providing information on the Palestinian question through its publications and lectures. The theme of its first convention was to examine the political quiescence of Arab-Americans as compared to other ethnic groups. A year later, AAUG published *The Arab-Americans: Studies in Assimilation* (edited by Elaine Hagopian). The book, which consisted of profiles of Arab-American communities in cities like Boston and Detroit, was said to have "represented a major turning point in Arab-American studies."[49]

AAUG has frequently criticized the "anti-Palestinian bias" of U.S. policy in its educational and outreach work. But it prefers to leave lobbying up to other organizations like the National Association of Arab Americans (NAAA). NAAA was established in 1972 for the avowed purpose of influencing U.S. Mideast policy—specifically to challenge the power of the "pro-Israel" lobbies. Richard Shadyac, one of its founders, has acknowledged that NAAA wants to "emulate the Jews" and participate in the political system in the way they have.[50] While AAUG has tended to attract post-1948 Arab arrivals, especially Palestinians, NAAA has appealed more to descendants of the first wave of Arab immigrants. NAAA's 13,500[51] members are more likely to be businessmen than academics, Republicans rather than Democrats.

NAAA has lobbied hard for a reduction in U.S. aid to Israel and for arms sales to Arab countries. NAAA leaders have argued that weapons sales to Jordan and Saudi Arabia support U.S. security interests in the Persian Gulf, especially in light of the growing Iranian militarism in the area. But aid to Israel, according to NAAA, drains the U.S. taxpayer and inspires Israel to embark on militaristic adventures like the 1982 invasion of Lebanon. Executive Director David Sadd, a former investment banker descended from Lebanese Maronites, has told Senate and House subcommittees that awarding Israel a "disproportionate share" of foreign aid does not serve the cause of peace in the Middle East. Sadd also testified before the Senate Committee on Foreign Relations against moving the U.S. embassy in Israel from Tel Aviv to Jerusalem. He said the move could cause a serious deterioration of U.S. relations with the Arab and Islamic worlds.[52] More recently, NAAA has fought to prevent the closure of the PLO Information Office in Washington.

A political action committee was established by NAAA in 1984 to contribute to candidates competing in the 1984 congressional elections. The PAC raised less than $20,000 that first year, which it distributed to 22 Democrats and 24 Republicans.[53] One of the Republicans was Helen Bentley from Maryland, who was running against Clarence Long, chairman of the House Foreign Operations Subcommittee. Long had been a key figure in increasing aid to Israel year after year and had been targeted by NAAA in one-minute radio broadcasts which asked listeners whether the United States should continue to give Israel "twice as much [money] as Americans are loaned through the Small Business Administration."[54] Long was defeated, but not because of NAAA's PAC money; the Maryland congressman reportedly received $142,550 from "pro-Israel" PACs. But the some 70 Arab-Americans who volunteered in Bentley's campaign[55] probably did help her win the election.

With the exception of this 1984 Maryland congressional race, NAAA has not made any real headway in the direction of influencing U.S. policy. Aid to Israel has continued to rise and, as discussed earlier, it was during a "negotiating session" with the Presidents' Conference that the State Department decided to close the PLO's Washington office. The 1981 AWACs deal did go through but it was President Reagan's personal lobbying and not NAAA which made the difference. Still, Sadd claims his organization has had some important successes. "NAAA has become part of the policy making apparatus in Washington," he has stated. "We don't have any muscle yet, but we are being heard."[56]

According to Sadd, the "turning point" for NAAA was when ABC's *Nightline* news program broadcast clips of NAAA staff the day of the AWACs sale.[57] The *Nightline* report and testimony offered on Capitol Hill, along with meetings held with President Reagan and Vice President Bush, have all given the organization the kind of visibility it has been seeking. So has recognition from Arab heads of state like Jordan's King Hussein and from key members of Congress such as Robert Dole. In 1985, when he was Senate majority leader, Dole told the NAAA annual convention that he saw the organization "going up and up . . . "[58] That, however, was before he decided to run for president in 1988. Probably hoping to boost his popularity with Jewish voters, Dole introduced the anti-PLO legislation in the Senate and called the PLO "a terrorist group" with "an ideology of hate and violence . . . which has no place in America . . . "[59]

While NAAA has patterned itself after AIPAC, the American-Arab Anti-Discrimination Committee (ADC) was modelled after the Anti-Defamation League of B'nai B'rith. ADC was founded in 1980 by James Abourezk, a former Democratic senator from South Dakota, to combat "stereotyping, defamation, and discrimination directed against Americans of Arab descent."[60] The 1967 war and the negative depiction of Arabs in the media helped to turn Abourezk into a self-conscious "Arab-American." So did assaults leveled against his character by Jewish lobbies, which he said attacked him for demonstrating sympathy for the Palestinians during his term in Congress.[61]

ADC has focused its energies primarily on protecting the civil rights of Arab-Americans and on correcting derogatory references to Arabs in the media, not on trying to change Mideast policy. The 16,000 member organization has succeeded in getting a radio station to apologize for making offensive remarks about Arabs and a toy manufacturer to discontinue production of a "Nomad" doll ADC said could instill racist attitudes toward Arabs in children.[62] In November of 1986, ADC submitted an "amicus curiae" ("friend of the court") brief to the Supreme Court on behalf of an Iraqi-born professor who claimed a Pennsylvania college had violated his civil rights by denying him tenure because of his ethnicity. The brief was also filed on behalf of a Maryland synagogue which was suing eight youths for defacing the temple. The Court ruled in favor of both the professor and the synagogue, extending the protection of an 1866 civil rights law to non-black minorities such as Arabs and Jews, whose ethnicity had made them victims of discrimination. According to ADC president Abdeen Jabara, Arab-American organizations helped lay the groundwork for the Court's decision by "raising public consciousness about the existence of a distinctive Arab-American community."[63]

ADC has also been a outspoken advocate of Palestinian rights. In 1987, it complained to the State Department that Israeli authorities were preventing Palestinian and Black Americans from entering Israel and the occupied territories. Jabara told the State Department it should issue a travel advisory directed at American tourists to Israel.[64] The Department's decision to discuss the problem with the Israeli Embassy and Israel's subsequent agreement to monitor the situation may have been influenced by ADC's intervention.

ADC may be able to point to a greater number of concrete accomplishments than NAAA but that is because it has set more modest goals for itself.

Americans are more apt to object to discrimination against U.S. citizens because of their ethnic origin than they are to the level of aid to Israel or to the closure of the PLO office. In fact, when ADC *has* tried to effect policy on Mideast-related issues, it has not had any more success than other Arab-American organizations.

Jim Zogby, former executive director of ADC, has been attempting to create the kind of grassroots Arab-American constituency which he hopes can force elected officials to speak to Arab-American foreign policy issues like "Palestinian rights and peace in Lebanon."[65] The vehicle created to guide this effort is the Arab American Institute (AAI), founded in 1985 by Zogby and George Salem, a Palestinian- born Washington lawyer who headed Ethnic Voters for Reagan/Bush in 1984. Salem's strength is among Republicans, Zogby's among Democrats; Zogby was vice chairman and deputy campaign manager in Jesse Jackson's 1984 presidential campaign. Together, they want to "create a political climate where Arab-Americans—Republicans, Democrats, and independents—can run for political office and win, while wearing their ethnicity on their sleeves."[66]

AAI has been working to achieve its goals by carrying out voter registration drives and by coordinating the establishment of Arab-American Democratic and Republican clubs in cities with sizeable Arab-American communities like Detroit, Chicago, Los Angeles, and New York. In 1986, AAI assisted fifteen communities in developing local power bases and taught Arab-American activists election skills such as precinct analysis, canvassing, and fundraising. At its 1985 regional conference held in Chicago, AAI helped Chicago Arab-Americans galvanize the community to become heavily involved in the 1987 mayoral campaign of Harold Washington. The mayor acknowledged the community's contribution by putting on a kaffiyeh (Arab headdress) after he won the Democratic primary and by creating an official liaison between the Arab community and City Hall after his victory. AAI began gearing up for the 1988 election in mid-1987, getting 11,000 Arab-Americans to agree to join its "Vote '88" project. Besides registering voters, the project wants to help Arab-Americans become appointed to positions in the presidential campaigns and advises them on how to become delegates at party conventions.[67]

AAI seems to be the only Arab-American organization which has started to survey Arab-American voting behavior. The surveys it has conducted so far have not been scientific and have been administered to a small sample of Arab-American community leaders. Still, they do provide some preliminary data on the electoral preferences of Arab-Americans. In the poll taken at AAI's founding conference in 1985, fifty-two percent of the almost 150 conference attenders who responded identified themselves as registered Republicans, twenty-five percent as Democrats, and twenty-three percent as independents. The overwhelming majority—seventy percent—said they had supported Jesse Jackson for president in the 1984 Democratic primaries. But sixty percent ended up voting for Reagan in the general election, compared to only fifteen percent for Mondale. The results were similar for a survey carried out at a Chicago AAI conference; seventy-three percent of the leaders polled had been for Jackson. But then forty-eight percent voted for Reagan, and only three percent voted for Mondale; thirty-two percent didn't vote at all.[68]

At first glance, the survey results may look strange; Arab-Americans backed the Democratic presidential candidate who was farthest to the left on the party's ideological continuum, but they chose Reagan over Mondale in the general election. Jackson, however, has said that the Palestinians have a right to national independence and has welcomed Arab-Americans into his Rainbow Coalition. Mondale, on the other hand, strongly supported transferring the U.S. embassy in Israel to Jerusalem and had actually returned political contributions from five Arab-Americans to avoid being accused of accepting "Arab money."

By tapping the growing ethnic self-awareness of Arab-Americans, AAI appears to be on its way to creating a viable political organization with bases in several large metropolitan areas. The $250,000 raised by Arab-Americans to support fifty-three candidates in the 1986 elections[69] does not even begin to approach the seven million dollars "pro-Israel" PACs raised that same year, but it is a beginning. AAI has also been encouraged by the fact that key officials in both major political parties, political candidates, and the media have all begun to take note of the new Arab-American political activism.[70]

AAI's efforts may help to elect more Arab-Americans and their allies to positions in local, state, and national government. It is, however, questionable whether AAI can get the U.S. government either to reduce aid to Israel or change its policy toward the PLO. (The United States has said it will not recognize or negotiate with the PLO until the organization renounces terrorism and accepts U.N. Security Council Resolutions 242 and 338.) Poll results suggest that American public opinion is divided on the issue of negotiations with the PLO. Fifty percent of the respondents to a May 1987 *Los Angeles Times* poll, for example, said they supported talks with the PLO compared to thirty-nine percent who did not.[71] Except for a small, vocal minority, however, Americans who favor negotiations do not seem to feel as strongly about their opinions as those who oppose such talks.

Many Americans who view the PLO as a terrorist organization have taken the time to tell their elected representatives how they feel. By contrast, most people who support talks with the PLO probably do not consider themselves "pro-PLO" at all. They would not be very likely to write a letter, make a phone call, or donate money to bring about a change in U.S. policy. According to I.L. Lewis, director of the *Los Angeles Times* poll, this segment of public opinion probably "likes the idea of dealing with the other side. It really doesn't matter with whom."[72]

Arab-American leaders could perhaps do a better job of "selling" the PLO to the public if they were able to persuade it to completely abandon violence in favor of diplomacy. But the PLO is unlikely to be convinced by arguments from Arab-Americans since the organization must respond to Palestinians in the Middle East, not to Arabs in America. The PLO might, however, decide at some future date that it has no other option but to "play the American card." At that point, it might turn for advice to the newly-mobilized Arab-American diaspora, which might then be able to serve as a bridge between the Palestinians and the United States government.

Conflict and Cooperation

Since the 1967 war, both the Jewish and Arab-American diasporas have stepped up their activities in the domestic policy arena in order to increase their influence on foreign policy. With greater frequency and intensity, Jews have promoted Israel's interests and the idea that a close relationship between the United States and the Jewish state is beneficial to both countries. Arab-Americans have been transformed from a passive into an active diaspora and have started to become involved in the political system as ethnic Arabs rather than as individuals who just happen to be of Arab descent.

After the war, Jewish and Arab-American communities began to target not only policy makers and the public but also each other. AIPAC, for instance, published a "Who's Who" of "anti-Israeli organizations and personalities" in 1983 which accused Arab-American leaders like Jim Zogby, James Abourezk, and Abdeen Jabara (as well as some non-Arabs such as former Under Secretary of State George Ball) of being part of a "campaign to discredit Israel." AIPAC said the "campaign" was built on an "artificial constituency" consisting of a minority of Arab-Americans, radical Marxists, major corporations, foreign diplomats, and foreign agents.[73] There was no acknowledgement that the post-1967 politicization of Arab-Americans and the growth of organizations like NAAA and ADC could be part of a genuine political movement. During the 1986 elections, Arab-Americans and other candidates who expressed sympathy for the Palestinians were targeted for defeat by "pro-Israel" PACs and various other Jewish organizations. In New York State, for example, the Anti-Defamation League of B'nai B'rith stopped a local Democratic Party from endorsing an Arab-American candidate by falsely branding him a "Libyan agent."[74]

Arab-Americans have, in turn, accused some Jewish organizations of what one writer has called "political racism." Helen Hatab Samhan wrote in the *Journal of Palestine Studies* that Jewish efforts to protect Israel have at times threatened the civil liberties of some Arab-Americans and excluded them from the political process.[75] Arab ethnics have reacted by exposing this kind of pressure as "Arab-baiting" and by building alliances at the grassroots level that they hope will help shield them from such attacks in the future.

U.S. Jews and Arabs may appear to be locked in a zero-sum game where one party wins only if the other loses. Recently, however, there have been some encouraging signs of cooperation and improved communication. Smaller Jewish groups have reached out to Arabs, organizing Jewish-Arab dialogue groups and annual "Jewish-Palestinian Friendship Dinners."[76] There has even been some movement at the upper levels of power. In June, 1987, two Jewish Congressmen—Stephen Solarz (D-NY) and Ben Gilman (R-NY)—joined two Arab-American representatives—Nick Rahall (D-WV) and Mary Rose Oakar (D-Ohio)—in sponsoring a reception on Capitol Hill for two members of the Israeli Knesset. The reception, which honored Ran Cohen of the Citizens Right Movement and Abdul Wahab Darawsha of the Labor Party, was organized by the National Association of Arab Americans.[77]

Conclusion

Twenty years after the 1967 Arab-Israeli war, Jewish Americans appear to have mastered the political skills an ethnic diaspora needs to maximize its influence on foreign policy. Arab-Americans, on the other hand, have just started to learn how to play the game. The integration and acceptance of Jews into American society has given the community greater self-confidence. It is now more willing than ever before to flex its muscles to increase U.S. aid and diplomatic support for Israel. Arab-Americans were practically invisible as an ethnic group before 1967. Then in the years immediately following the war, they were seen as a "defeated, dejected, and despised minority."[78] In the 1980s, the community seems slowly to be making friends and gaining access to political power.

The level of political activity carried out by the Jewish-American and Arab-American ethnic lobbies will probably increase in the future as activists from both groups develop more sophisticated lobbying techniques and seek to involve more members of their respective communities in political work. There are no signs, however, of a narrowing of the enormous gap which exists between Jewish-American and Arab-American political strength; the greater visibility of Arabs in politics does not necessarily translate into foreign policy successes for them. Liberal elements in the Jewish community may, in fact, be more successful than Arab groups in convincing the U.S. government to pressure Israel into making territorial concessions, although Jewish liberals are likely to argue in favor of American pressure only if a Likud member is prime minister of Israel.

Notes

1. This definition is borrowed from Milton Esman, "Diasporas and International Relations" in *Modern Diasporas in International Politics*, Gabriel Sheffer, ed. (New York: St. Martin's Press, 1986), p. 3.

2. See *Ethnicity and Foreign Policy*, Abdul Aziz Said, ed. (New York: Praeger, 1977).

3. *American Jewish Yearbook 1986*, Milton Himmelfarb and David Singer, eds. (New York: The American Jewish Committee and the Jewish Publication Society of America), pp. 350–364.

4. Charles R. Babcock, "Israel has Complex Bonds with Jewish Americans," *Washington Post* (August 8, 1986), p. A1.

5. Wolf Blitzer, *Between Washington and Jerusalem: A Reporter's Notebook* (New York: Oxford University Press, 1985), p. 121. Also see Robert S. Greenberger,

"American Jews are Increasingly Divided in Stance Toward Israel," *Wall Street Journal* (July 7, 1987).

6. Will Maslow, *The Structure and Functioning of the American Jewish Community* (New York: The American Jewish Congress and the American Section of the World Jewish Congress, 1974), pp. 24–25.

7. Edward Tivnan, *The Lobby—Jewish Political Power and American Foreign Policy* (New York: Simon and Shuster, 1987), p. 35.

8. Cited in Tivnan, *The Lobby*, p. 57.

9. Tivnan, *The Lobby*, p. 54.

10. Tivnan, *The Lobby*, p. 84.

11. Robert H. Trice, *Interest Groups and the Foreign Policy Process: U.S. Policy in the Middle East* (Beverly Hills, CA: Sage Publications, 1976), p. 66.

12. Blitzer, *Between Washington and Jerusalem*, pp. 180–181.

13. Nathan Glazer and Milton Himmelfarb, "McGovern and the Jews: A Debate," in *Commentary* (The American Jewish Committee, September 1972), p. 48. *Galut* is the Hebrew word for exile. Himmelfarb was referring to how European and first generation American Jews were able to maintain their religious and cultural traditions while living among non-Jews.

14. See Arthur Hertzberg, "Israel and American Jewry," in *Commentary* (August 1967) and Tivnan, *The Lobby*, p. 63.

15. Charles Silberman, *A Certain People—American Jews and Their Lives Today* (New York: Summit Books, 1985), p. 194.

16. M.J. Rosenberg, "Six Day War Revolutionized American Jewish Community," in *Jewish Advocate*, Boston (June 18, 1987).

17. Silberman, *A Certain People*, p. 185.

18. Arthur Hertzberg, "The Tragedy of Victory" in *The New York Review of Books* (May 28, 1987, p. 14.

19. Silberman, *A Certain People*, pp. 195–198.

20. Tivnan, *The Lobby*, pp. 66–68.

21. Novik Nimrod, *The United States and Israel* (Boulder: Westview Press, 1986), Appendix A, p. 144.

22. Eytan Gilboa, *American Public Opinion Toward Israel and the Arab-Israeli Conflict* (Lexington, MA: D.C. Heath and Company, 1987), pp. 48 and 128. See also James L. Franklin, "U.S. Support for Israel Undaunted, Panel Says" in *The Boston Globe* (February 18, 1988).

23. Tivnan, *The Lobby*, p. 191.

24. Cited in Tivnan, *The Lobby*, p. 191.

25. John J. Fialka, "Political Contributions from Pro-Israel PACs Suggest Coordination," *Wall Street Journal* (June 24, 1987).

26. Larry Cohler, "Jewish Groups Hail PLO Office Shut-Down" in *Washington Jewish Week*, Washington, D.C. (September 17, 1987), p. 3.

27. See Steven M. Cohen, *Ties and Tensions—The 1986 Survey of American Jewish Attitudes Toward Israel and Israelis* (Institute on American Jewish-Israeli Relations, The American Jewish Committee, 1987), p. 58. Fifty-two percent of the Jews polled in 1983 by Professor Cohen said they were "troubled by the policies of the current Israeli government." In Cohen's 1986 poll, forty percent of the respondents said they were "troubled."

28. Arthur Hertzberg, "Begin Must Go," editorial in *The New York Times*, September 26, 1982, p. E19.

29. Philip Klutznik, "Negotiations with the PLO: When? Now!" in *Facing the PLO Question* (Washington, D.C.: The Foundation for Middle East Peace, 1985), p. 11.

30. Cited in Michael Brecher, *The Foreign Policy System of Israel: Setting, Images, Process* (New Haven: Yale University Press, 1972), p. 139.

31. Cohen, *Ties and Tensions*, p. 58.

32. See the National Platform of New Jewish Agenda (New York: New Jewish Agenda, November 1982).

33. Andrea Barron, "Democrats Reject Settlement Proposal Freeze" in *Israeli-Palestinian Peace* (Newsletter of Washington Area Jews for Israeli-Palestinian Peace, Washington, D.C., Fall 1984), p. 6.

34. Jerome Segal, "Arafat Assures American Jews a Negotiated Peace is Possible" in *The Washington Report on Middle East Affairs* (Washington, D.C.: The American Educational Trust, September 1987), p. 1.

35. Elaine Sciolino, "U.S. Jewish Group Urges Peace Talks on Arab-Israel Issue" in *The New York Times* (September 22, 1987) p. A1. According to 1987 figures from Israel's Central Bureau of Statistics, the country has an overwhelming Jewish majority with 3,590,000 Jews (82 percent) and 785,000 Arabs (18 percent). However, almost forty percent of the people living under Israeli control, including the Palestinians in the West Bank and Gaza, are now Arabs.

36. James L. Franklin, "U.S. Jewish leader Criticizes Israelis for Crackdown on Press" in *The Boston Globe* (March 5, 1988).

37. Andrea Barron, "Personality Profile of Rabbi Balfour Brickner" in *The Washington Report on Middle East Affairs* (April 1986), p. 10, and telephone interviews with Rabbi Brickner conducted in March 1986.

38. Neil A. Lewis, "2 in U.S. Senate Dispute Criticism of Shamir" in the *New York Times* (March 7, 1988).

39. Ibid and "Representative Frank Urges Israel to Withdraw from the Territories" in *The Boston Globe* (March 9, 1988).

40. Alixa Naff, entry on Arab-Americans in the *Harvard Encyclopedia of American Ethnic Groups*, Stephen Thernstrom, ed., (Cambridge: The Belknap Press of Harvard University, 1980), p. 180.

41. See Alixa Naff, "Arabs in America: A Historical Overview" in *Arabs in the New World: Studies on Arab-American Communities*, Sameer Y. Abraham and Nabeel Abraham, eds. (Detroit: Wayne State University, 1983).

42. See Philip M. Kayal, "Arab Christians in the United States," in *Arabs in the New World*, p. 54. The official name of the Syrian Orthodox Church in the United States is now the Antiochian Orthodox Christian Church of North America.

43. Naff, "Arabs in America," p. 15.

44. Ibid., p. 23.

45. Ibid., p. 24.

46. Ibid., and Yvonne Haddad, "Arab Muslims and Islamic Institutions in America: Adaptation and Reform" in *Arabs in the New World*, p. 66.

47. "Israel: A Nation Under Siege" in *Time* (June 9, 1967), p. 38.

48. Milton Viorst, "Building an Arab-American Lobby" in *The Washington Post Magazine* (September 14, 1980).

49. *The Arab-Americans—Studies in Assimilation*, Elaine C. Hagopian and Ann Paden, eds. (Monograph of the Association of Arab-American University Graduates: Wilmette, Illinois: Medina Press International, 1969).

50. Viorst, "Building an Arab-American Lobby."

51. Telephone interviews with David Sadd conducted in September 1987.

52. "NAAA Testifies on Foreign Aid Bill" in *VOICE*, (Membership journal of the National Association of Arab Americans, Washington, D.C., March-April, 1984),

p. 10 and "Jerusalem Embassy Legislation Stalls" in the same issue of VOICE, p. 4.

53. Telephone interviews with David Sadd (September 1987).

54. Nabeel A. Khoury, "The Arab Lobby: Problems and Prospects" in *The Middle East Journal* (Summer 1987), p. 390.

55. Ibid.

56. Telephone interviews with David Sadd (September 1987).

57. Ibid.

58. See VOICE (May/June 1985), p. 15.

59. News Release from the office of Senator Robert Dole (R-Kansas), May 13, 1987.

60. See *ADC Times* (Newsletter of the American-Arab Anti-Discrimination Committee, Washington, D.C.).

61. Viorst, "Building an Arab-American Lobby."

62. See "Coleco Halts 'Nomad' After DC Protest," *ADC Times* (January 1987), p. 1. Also see an article on p. 3 of the same issue of *ADC Times*, on a Los Angeles radio station which apologized to ADC after a disc jockey introduced a song "Walk Like an Egyptian" then added "smelling like an Arab."

63. "Supreme Court Hits Anti-Arab Bias" in *ADC Times* (May/June 1987), p. 1.

64. See "Harassment of Arab-Americans by Israel Hit" in *ADC Times* (July 1987), p. 1.

65. See Wayne King, "Arab-Americans Looking to Politics" in *The New York Times* (August 3, 1987).

66. "Building Tomorrow" in *Notebook* (Newsletter of the Arab American Institute, Washington, D.C., Spring 1985), p. 1.

67. See "A First Step in Politics," p. 8 in *Notebook* (Winter 1987) and "More Sophistication and Respect," p. 12 in the same issue of *Notebook*. Also see "Gaining Local Access," pp. 3–6 in *Notebook* (Summer 1987) and "Harnessing our Political Strength," p. 1 in the same issue of *Notebook*.

68. See "AAI Questionnaire Reveals Political Attitudes" in *Notebook* (Spring 1985), p. 12 and "A Profile of Chicago's Arab Americans" in *Notebook* (Winter 1986), p. 6.

69. Address by Mansour H. Mansour from AAI at a dinner honoring Chicago Mayor Harold Washington, published in *Notebook* (Summer 1987), p. 6.

70. Ibid. See also King, "Arab Americans Looking to Politics."

71. George Skelton, "The Times Poll—Return of Land, Talks with PLO Supported" in *The Los Angeles Times* (June 3, 1987). See also Gilboa, *American Public Opinion toward Israel and the Arab-Israeli Conflict*, p. 187. The results were similar for a poll conducted by Newsweek/Gallup in August 1982, where forty-eight percent of the respondents favored U.S. negotiations with the PLO and forty-two percent opposed them.

72. Telephone interview conducted with I.L. Lewis (October 6, 1987).

73. See "The Campaign to Discredit Israel," Steven J. Rosen and Amy Kaufman Goott, eds. (AIPAC Papers on U.S.-Israel Relations, by the American Israel Public Affairs Committee, 1983).

74. Jim Zogby and Helen Hatab Samhan, "Arab-Baiting in the 1986 Elections" in *The Washington Report on Middle East Affairs* (February 1987), p. 5.

75. See Helen Hatab Samhan, "Politics and Exclusion: The Arab American Experience" in the *Journal of Palestine Studies* (Washington, D.C.: The Institute of Palestine Studies and Kuwait University, Winter 1987).

76. Courtland Milloy, "Jews, Arabs Hold Dinners for Peace" in *Washington Post* (March 18, 1986), p. C3, and Kenneth Bandler, "Arab-Jewish Dialogue in America" in *Israel Horizons* (*Journal of Americans for a Progressive Israel*) (September/October 1987).

77. Telephone interviews with David Sadd and with legislative assistant to Congressman Nick Rahall (September 1987).

78. Speech by Jim Zogby to the AAI National Leadership Conference, published in *Notebook* (Summer 1987), p. 17.

The Soviet Union

17

Moscow and the Arab-Israeli Conflict Since 1967

Robert O. Freedman

To understand the nature of Soviet policy toward the Arab-Israeli conflict, it is first necessary to examine the Soviet Union's strategy in the Middle East, because Soviet policy toward the Arab-Israeli conflict has only been a part—albeit a very important part—of overall Soviet strategy toward the region. Yet in trying to determine Soviet policy toward the Middle East, an analyst must come to grips with two central questions about Soviet behavior in the region. First, are Moscow's primary goals in the Middle East offensive or defensive in nature; and second, do the Soviet leaders follow one underlying strategy as they pursue their goals in the Middle East or is their policy determined on a country-by-country basis? Different analysts have answered these two questions in different ways, and their answers often contain, whether openly or not, policy prescriptions as to how the United States should deal with Soviet activity in the Middle East.

As far as the question of Soviet goals is concerned, there are two major schools of thought.[1] While both agree that the Soviet Union wants to be considered as a major factor in Middle Eastern affairs, if only because of its propinquity to the region, they differ on the ultimate Soviet goal. One school of thought sees Soviet Middle Eastern policy as being primarily defensive in nature—that is, directed toward preventing the region from being used as a base for military attack or political subversion against the USSR. The other school of thought sees Soviet policy as primarily offensive in nature—as aimed at the limitation and ultimate exclusion of Western influence from the region and its replacement by Soviet influence. The policy implications of this debate are clear. If Moscow is basically defensively oriented, then it is not only possible but actually desirable for the United States to work with the USSR to bring about settlements of conflicts such as that between the Arab states and Israel, and between Iran and Iraq. Conversely, if Moscow's goals are seen as offensive in nature, then it is undesirable to try to bring it into the peace process because the Soviet leaders would only exploit the opportunity to weaken the United States position. In any case, it is the author's opinion that Soviet goals in the Middle East, at least since the mid-1960s, have been primarily offensive in nature; and in the Arab segment of the Middle East, the Soviet Union appears to have been engaged in a zero-sum game competition for influence with the United States.

The question as to whether Moscow follows one underlying strategy as opposed to functioning on a country-by-country (or sub-region by sub-region) basis is also hotly debated. Those analysts who see the Soviet leadership following one underlying strategy usually base their viewpoint on the belief that Marxist-Leninist ideology still holds some meaning for the decision-makers in Moscow, while those who see the USSR as moving pragmatically in the region, treat Moscow as just another great power, not unlike Czarist Russia of the 19th century. In the author's opinion Moscow does in fact pursue one underlying strategy in the Middle East, and that strategy, at least in part, is influenced by Marxist-Leninist ideology. Prior to examining overall Soviet strategy toward the region, however, it is necessary to analyze the tactics Moscow uses to expand its influence and the obstacles it faces.

In its efforts to weaken and ultimately eliminate Western influence from the Middle East, and particularly from the Arab world, while promoting Soviet influence, the Soviet leadership has employed a number of tactics. First and foremost has been the supply of military aid to its regional clients.[2] Next in importance comes economic aid; the Aswan Dam in Egypt and the Euphrates Dam in Syria are prominent examples, and Moscow also provides scholarship assistance to Middle Eastern students. In recent years Moscow has also sought to solidify its influence through long-term Friendship and Cooperation treaties such as the ones concluded with Egypt (1971), Iraq (1972), Somalia (1974), Ethiopia (1978), Afghanistan (1978), South Yemen (1979), Syria (1980), and North Yemen (1984), although the repudiation of the treaties by Egypt (1976) and Somalia (1977) indicate that this has not always been a successful tactic. Moscow has also attempted to exploit both the lingering memories of Western colonialism and Western threats against Arab oil producers, and the USSR has, as in the case of the assassination of Indira Ghandi, deliberately used "disinformation" to discredit American policy.[3] The USSR has also sought influence through the establishment of ties between the CPSU (Communist Party of the Soviet Union) and such Arab ruling political parties as the Syrian Ba'th and the Algerian FLN. Yet another tactic aimed at gaining influence has been the provision of security infrastructure assistance to countries like the People's Democratic Republic of Yemen (South Yemen) and Ethiopia, although the South Yemeni crisis of January 1986 may raise questions as to the value of such assistance.[4] Finally, Moscow has offered the Arabs aid of both a military and diplomatic nature against Israel, although that aid has been limited in scope because Moscow continues to support Israel's right to exist both for fear of unduly alienating the United States, with whom the Russians desire additional strategic arms agreements and improved trade relations, and because Israel serves as a convenient rallying point for potentially anti-Western forces in the Arab world.[5]

While the USSR has used all these tactics, to a greater or lesser degree of success, since the establishment of Israel in 1948, it has also run into serious problems in its quest for influence. The numerous inter-Arab and regional conflicts (Syria-Iraq; North Yemen-South Yemen; Ethiopia-Somalia; Algeria-Morocco; Iran-Iraq, etc.) have usually meant that when the USSR has favored one party, it has alienated the other, often driving it over to the West. Secondly, the existence of Middle Eastern Communist parties has proved a handicap for the USSR, as Communist activities have, on occasion, caused a sharp deterioration in relations between Moscow and the country in which the Communist party has operated. The Communist-supported coup d'état in the Sudan in 1971, Communist efforts to organize cells in the Iraqi army in the mid and late 1970s, and the activities of the Tudeh party in Khomeini's Iran, are recent examples of this problem.[6] Third, the wealth which flowed to the Arab world (or at least to its major oil producers) since the quadrupling of oil prices in late 1973 has enabled the Arabs to buy quality technology from the West and Japan, and this has helped weaken the economic bond between the USSR and such Arab states as Iraq. Fourth, since 1967 and particularly since the 1973 Arab-Israeli war, Islam has been resurgent throughout the Arab world, and the USSR, identified in the Arab world with atheism, has been hampered as a result, particularly since the Soviet invasion of Afghanistan in 1979 where Moscow has been fighting against an essentially Islamic resistance force. Fifth, in the diplomacy surrounding the Arab-Israeli conflict, Moscow is hampered by its lack of diplomatic ties with Israel, a factor which enables the United States alone to talk to both sides of the conflict. Finally, the United States, and to a lesser extent France and China, have actively opposed Soviet efforts to achieve predominant influence in the region and this has frequently enabled Middle Eastern states to play the extra-regional powers off against each other and thereby prevent any one of them from securing predominant influence.

In the face of these problems, Soviet strategy in the Middle East has gone through two stages since World War II. In the late 1940s and early 1950s, it was essentially defensive since at that time the primary Soviet goal was to prevent the region's being used as a base of attack against the USSR. By the mid-1960s, however, the Soviet goal had shifted to an offensive one as the Soviet leadership sought to oust the West from its positions of military, political, and economic influence in the region and to substitute Soviet influence. This strategy helped precipitate the 1967 Arab-Israeli war and has characterized Soviet policy since 1967, as it has sought to unite the Arab states in an "anti-imperialist" alignment directed at Israel, which it characterizes as the "linchpin" of Western imperialism in the Middle East, and against the United States as Israel's primary backer.

The major Israeli victory in the 1967 war seemed at first to be a significant defeat for the Soviet drive for influence. Soviet military equipment and training had proved of little value, and the Soviet leaders' failure to aid their client states while they were being soundly defeated also served to lower Soviet prestige in the Arab world. Yet, paradoxically, the aftermath of the war was to see major Soviet gains in the region, although they were to prove temporary. One of the major results of the war was the radicalization of the Arab world and a concomitant weakening of the U.S. position. Egypt, Syria, Algeria, and Iraq all broke diplomatic relations with the United States because of alleged U.S. aid to Israel during the war, and in 1969 there was a further deterioration of the U.S. position, as a left-wing regime came to power in the Sudan and the pro-Western regime of Libya's King Idris was overthrown.

Meanwhile, by quickly resupplying Egypt and Syria with the weaponry that restored their military credibility, and championing Arab demands at the United Nations, the Soviet Union was able to restore its position in the Arab world. Nonetheless, the Soviet position was not without problems, since the Arab-Israeli conflict, which had been relatively subdued in the 1957–66 period, now became a central issue not only in the Middle East but also in world politics. In selecting its policy for this now highly salient issue, the Soviet leadership was faced with a dilemma. On the one hand, they wanted to continue to weaken Western influence in the Arab world while enhancing Soviet influence. On the other hand, with the main Arab interest now in regaining the lands lost to Israel in the 1967 war, the Soviet Union risked the possibility of direct confrontation with the United States, which by now was sending Israel advanced weaponry (hitherto France had been Israel's main supplier) and had taken a more overtly pro-Israeli position. The dilemma may have appeared particularly serious for the Soviets after the March 1969 border clashes with China signaled a further escalation of the Sino-Soviet conflict.

Yet another Soviet dilemma lay in the fact that, given the previous history of U.S. success in securing Israeli withdrawal from conquered Arab territory, the Soviet leadership had to be concerned with a possible turn by the Arab leaders toward the United States. Therefore, after neither U.N. Resolution 242 of November 1967 nor the two-power or four-power talks that followed it had succeeded in getting an Israeli withdrawal, which would have enabled the Soviet Union to demonstrate its ability to champion the Arab cause, Moscow decided to back Nasser as he launched his war of attrition against the Israelis in the spring of 1969.[7] The Soviet leadership followed up its decision by sending Soviet pilots and surface-to-air missile crews to Egypt in early 1970, when the war of attrition led to major Israeli retaliatory strikes against Egypt's heartland. Having gained control over a number of Egyptian military and air bases in the process, the Soviet leaders evidently considered the strategic gains worth the political risks, particularly when the Nixon administration, immersed in the Vietnamese War and a new conflict in Cambodia in the spring of 1970, took little action to prevent the consolidation of the Soviet position in Egypt. While the Soviet leaders were later to endorse Nasser's agreement to the U.S. ceasefire efforts in the summer of 1970, their move seemed primarily aimed at completing the emplacement of surface-to-air missiles along the canal at no further loss of Egyptian (or Soviet) lives. The subsequent Soviet/Egyptian violation of the ceasefire agreement, by moving more missiles up to the canal, further underlined both the Soviet commitment to Egypt and Soviet willingness to enhance Egyptian military strength against Israel, since the emplacement of the missiles gave Egypt the capability of launching an attack against Israel using the missiles as an umbrella against Israeli air attacks—as, indeed, it was to do in October 1973.[8]

Aiding Egypt in its war of attrition, however, was not the same as assisting the Arabs in a full-scale attack on Israel—something the Russians saw at the time as beyond the Arabs' military capability. While Nasser had mortgaged a good deal of Egypt's sovereignty to the Soviet Union in the form of bases in return for rebuilding his army after 1967, Anwar Sadat, who came to power in October 1970 after Nasser's death, was to adopt a different policy. When diplomatic efforts to bring about a Middle East peace plan stagnated, Sadat became increasingly disenchanted with the Soviets, whom he saw as unable to get the Israelis to withdraw by diplomatic means, unwilling to use military force for this purpose, and hesitant to supply the Arab states with the weaponry they needed to fight effectively.

The Soviet reluctance, which became increasingly evident during the 1971–72 period, may have resulted from three factors. In the first place, the strong U.S. reaction to what was at least a tacitly Soviet-supported Syrian invasion of Jordan in September 1970 seems to have indicated to the Soviets that the United States was more willing to take action in the Middle East than it had been in January 1970, when the Soviet Union sent its pilots and missile crews to Egypt. Second, the long-feared Sino-U.S. entente against the Soviet Union seemed suddenly on the horizon following Kissinger's surprise trip to Peking in July 1971 and the subsequent announcement of Nixon's visit to the Chinese capital. Finally, the long-delayed strategic arms talks, the centerpiece of Soviet-U.S. detente, were nearing conclusion. In sum, the Soviet leaders clearly did not wish—at that time— to jeopardize the benefits of detente to aid a rather fickle Arab ally such as Sadat, who had not only openly flirted with the Americans (U.S. Secretary of State Rogers was invited to Cairo in May 1971), but who had also opposed Soviet policy in the Sudan as well, particularly at a time when the United States, after the events in Jordan, was significantly strengthening its relationship with Israel.[9]

For his part, Sadat saw the emerging Soviet-U.S. detente as taking place at Arab expense, and soon after the Soviet-U.S. summit of May 1972 in Moscow, the Egyptian leader expelled the Soviet military advisers from his country while also ending Soviet control over Egyptian air, naval, and army bases. While the Egyptian action was a serious blow to the Soviet Union's strategic position in the eastern Mediterranean, the subsequent Soviet pullout, not only of advisers but also pilots and missile crews, lessened the chances of any direct Soviet involvement in a future Egyptian-Israeli war, and this factor must have softened the impact of the exodus, which was clearly a major blow to the Soviet Union's Middle East position.[10]

Sadat's Limited War Against Israel

While Sadat may have hoped that his ouster of the Soviets would lead to action from the United States in the form of pressure on Israel to withdraw from the Sinai, such pressure was not to be forthcoming—at least, not for more than a year and a half. Therefore, having sought to mobilize both U.S. and Soviet support for his policies, and having failed in both quests, Sadat moved to rally the Arabs, and particularly oil-rich Saudi Arabia, to his cause. By the spring of 1973 he had also secured a resumption in the flow of Soviet weapons, enough to enable him to launch a limited war against Israel, and by September he had achieved a general coordination of military planning with Syria. While the Soviet Union almost certainly knew about Sadat's plans for war, they did little to prevent it, and once both Egypt and Syria had demonstrated their military ability in the first days of the war, the Soviet leadership reinforced the Arab war effort with a major airlift and sealift of weaponry, as well as diplomatic support in the United Nations.[11] In taking such actions, the Soviet Union was stepping back from its policy of supporting detente, which had reached its highest point at the time of the Moscow summit of 1972, and which seemed to be reconfirmed by the Washington summit of June 1973. The change in Soviet behavior may be explained by several factors. First, the Sino-U.S. entente, which the Soviet Union had initially feared, had not come to fruition. Second, the Nixon administration, badly beset by Watergate, was in a weakened position vis-à-vis the Soviet Union. Indeed, by this time, one of the few positive achievements the Nixon administration could show was detente with the Soviet Union—a policy to which the administration was now wedded. These factors combined to give the Soviet Union more leverage vis-à-vis the United States and the Soviet leadership was not slow in taking advantage of the situation.[12]

The Arab coalition that Sadat had formed on the eve of the 1973 war fit neatly into the overall Soviet plan of forming an "anti-imperialist" alliance of Arab states. The fact that this Arab coalition included not only such "progressive" Arab states as Syria and Iraq but also such conservative ones as Kuwait and Saudi Arabia may have been perceived as an added bonus, because the oil embargo imposed by these countries against the United States and its NATO allies seemed to be a major step on the road to ousting Western influence from the Arab world—the Soviet goal since the mid-1960s—as well as weakening the overall Western position in the world balance of power. For this reason, Moscow gave extensive military aid to Syria and Egypt during the war, and pressured the United States to halt a major Israeli advance as the war came to an end.[13]

Unfortunately for the Soviets, however, the aftermath was to see not only the collapse of the "anti-imperialist" Arab coalition they had so warmly endorsed but also a serious deterioration of the Soviet position in the Arab world—despite all the military and diplomatic support the Soviet Union had given the Arab cause during the war. While the Arab-Israeli conflict remained the most salient issue in Middle East politics, it was the United States that was to take an active role in working toward a diplomatic settlement, earning for itself in the process a greatly enhanced status in the Arab world. Under the mediating efforts of U.S. Secretary of State Henry Kissinger, Egypt and Israel reached a disengagement agreement in January 1974 that led to the withdrawal of Israeli forces from both banks of the Suez Canal. Then, at the end of May 1974, Kissinger secured a disengagement agreement between Syria and Israel that led to a withdrawal of Israeli forces not only from territories captured in 1973 but also from the city of Kuneitra, captured in 1967. Yet another disengagement agreement was reached in late August 1975 between Israel and Egypt whereby the Israelis withdrew to the Mitla and Giddi passes in the Sinai Desert.[14]

While the United States was taking these initiatives, the Soviet Union was, essentially, sitting on the sidelines, although in the aftermath of the 1973 war a Geneva peace conference was convened under the co-chairmanship of the United States and the Soviet Union. It was quickly adjourned, however, and Kissinger, not the Geneva Conference, became the main instrument in working toward a settlement of the Arab-Israeli conflict. For their part, the Soviet leadership was clearly unhappy with the disengagement agreements—particularly the Sinai II agreement of 1975, which the Soviets denounced—but they proved incapable of influencing the course of events.

In an effort to directly affect the diplomacy surrounding the Arab-Israeli conflict in the aftermath of the 1973 war, the Soviet leadership tried a variety of tactics. Thus, at the Geneva Conference, Gromyko made a point of underlining Soviet support of Israel's right to exist and met privately with Foreign Minister Abba Eban to suggest Moscow's willingness to reestablish diplomatic relations with Israel once an Arab-Israeli settlement was reached.[15] (At the same time Moscow allowed a then record number of Soviet Jews to leave for Israel.) Several months later, however, in the face of the first Egyptian-Israeli disengagement agreement and Kissinger's efforts to work out a similar agreement between Syria and Israel, Moscow took the opposite course by sending arms to Syria and supporting the war of attrition Syria was waging on the Golan Heights.[16] In taking this action, the Soviet leadership may have hoped to torpedo the negotiations or, at least, prevent the lifting of the oil embargo then being considered by the oil-rich Arab states. At the very minimum, the Soviets may have felt that their aid would strengthen Syria's hand in the bargaining process and thereby preserve the Soviet position and prevent Syria's slipping into the pro-U.S. camp.

Another tactic used by the Soviet leadership during the Kissinger disengagement process was to urge the rapid reconvening of the Geneva Conference, although the Soviet calls did not meet with success. Even during the period from March to May 1975, when the Kissinger shuttle had been temporarily derailed and U.S. Middle East policy was going through one of its periodic "reappraisals," the Soviet Union's efforts to seize the diplomatic initiative proved ineffectual. Despite dispatching Kosygin to Libya and Tunisia, and sending a number of signals to Israel of continued Soviet support of the Jewish state's existence (these included sending several Soviet officials to Israel), the Soviet leadership proved unable to even coordinate Arab positions on a settlement let alone work out the details of an Arab-Israeli agreement.[17] A fourth tactic used by the Soviet Union, as developments began to move in a way unfavorable to Soviet interests in the aftermath of the 1973 war, was a fundamental policy change toward the Palestinians. With Egypt moving toward the U.S. camp, with the Saudi Arabian- Egyptian axis, tacitly supported by the Shah's Iran, now the dominant one in Arab politics, and with Syria still wavering despite large amounts of Soviet military aid, the Soviet leaders began to openly back the concept of an independent Palestinian state in the West Bank and Gaza regions.[18]

Following the Sinai II agreement and a U.N. meeting between Gromyko and Israel's new Foreign Minister Yigal Allon on September 24, 1975, Soviet plans for an overall settlement of the Arab-Israeli conflict, one facet of which would include an independent Palestinian state, became increasingly explicit, and the Soviet proposals were published, amid great fanfare, in April and October 1976. In their statements, the Soviets also came out for the immediate reconvening of the Geneva Conference with the full participation of the PLO, but this ploy proved ineffectual since neither Israel nor the United States would accept the PLO as a negotiating partner so long as it continued to call openly for Israel's destruction. In addition to U.S. and Israeli opposition, the Soviet peace proposals, which included offers of Soviet guarantees, were not greeted with much enthusiasm by the Arabs, and the growing civil war in Lebanon further reduced the efficacy of the Soviet plan.[19]

Indeed, the civil war in Lebanon, while temporarily sidelining both U.S. and Soviet efforts to settle the Arab-Israeli conflict, also posed a very serious problem for Soviet diplomacy. By June 1976 Syria had mounted a major invasion of Lebanon, and battles took place between Syrian and PLO forces. Since the PLO, despite its disparate elements, was now a close ally of the Soviet Union in the Middle East, while Syria remained the key swing country the Soviet Union wanted to prevent from joining the Egyptian-Saudi Arabian axis, it was inevitable that the Soviet Union's relations with one or both would suffer no matter which position the Soviets took toward the Lebanese fighting. The end result was that the PLO complained about insufficient Soviet aid, while Syria was clearly unhappy with both the negative Soviet comments about Syrian policy in Lebanon and a slowdown in Soviet arms deliveries. Nonetheless, the Soviets were saved further diplomatic embarrassment when a settlement of the civil war was reached in October 1976 that preserved the PLO as an independent force in Lebanon, although the fact that the settlement had been worked out under Saudi Arabian mediation and that it also included a reconciliation between Syria and Egypt could not have been happily received in the Kremlin, which continued to fear the adhesion of Syria to the Egyptian-Saudi axis.[20]

President Carter's Efforts

In the aftermath of the Lebanese civil war came the U.S. presidential elections. With a new president in office, albeit one relatively inexperienced in foreign affairs, all sides expected new U.S. initiatives to bring about a Middle East settlement. The Soviets, whose relations with the United States had hit a new low as a result of their involvement in Angola, but who hoped for a new SALT agreement and new trade agreements nevertheless, sent a number of signals to the incoming Carter administration that it would be willing to cooperate with the United States in bringing about a Middle East settlement.[21] The Soviet reasoning appeared to be that given the sharp diminution of Soviet influence in the Arab world due to U.S. diplomatic successes and the establishment of a large pro-U.S. camp in the Arab world (the only strongly pro-Soviet elements at this time were Libya, Algeria, and South Yemen—countries with relatively little influence in the area), Moscow would do well to have an overall settlement to consolidate the Soviet position in the region, even if the Soviets were not yet at the point where they could resume their offensive efforts to weaken and ultimately eliminate Western influence.

Fortunately for Moscow, Carter initially decided to jettison Kissinger's step-by-step approach and embarked on an effort to achieve a comprehensive Middle East peace settlement. In doing so he decided that Moscow could be a suitable partner in this endeavor. The end result of this process was the joint Soviet-American statement on the Middle East of October 1, 1977 which called, among other things, for the reconvening of the Geneva Conference by December 1977, thereby guaranteeing the USSR a principal role in the Middle East peace-making process.

Yet in bringing Moscow back into the center of Middle East peace-making—a major gain for Moscow—Carter made three serious misjudgments. Despite the clash between Moscow and both Syria and the PLO during the Lebanese civil war, Carter assumed Moscow could deliver both to the peace table. Secondly, Carter seemed to believe that unless Moscow was brought into the peace process, it would successfully sabotage it.[22] Finally, Carter erred seriously in failing to recognize that the Soviet conception of a Middle East peace settlement was very different from that of the United States. As it has evolved since 1973, the Soviet peace plan has been composed of three major components: 1) Israeli withdrawal from all territory captured in the 1967 war; 2) establishment of a Palestinian state on the West Bank and Gaza; and 3) acknowledgement of the right to exist of all states in the region, including Israel.

In assessing the Soviet peace plan, it is clear why Moscow finds it to its advantage. In the first place such a plan would preserve the State of Israel, whose existence has become an important part of Soviet strategy.

As discussed earlier, the Soviet Union has sought to consolidate "anti-imperialist" Arab unity around Arab enmity toward Israel. The mere fact of an Israeli withdrawal to the pre-war 1967 lines would not remove the potential threat of a future Israeli attack on the Arabs (or vice versa) or the memories of the generations-long Arab-Israeli conflict. Indeed, by supporting the concept of a limited peace (and opposing the concept of a more extensive peace, in which Israel would have trade, cultural, and diplomatic relations with its neighbors[23]) the Soviet Union would hope to keep at least a certain amount of latent hostility alive in the Arab-Israeli relationship, thereby forcing the Arabs to retain at least a modicum of unity to confront the putative Israeli threat. The Soviet leaders evidently hoped they could then exploit that unity to enhance their own position in the Middle East and weaken the position of the United States. In any case, by ensuring that tension would remain in the Arab-Israeli relationship, Moscow's importance as an arms supplier to the Arabs would be reinforced; it should not be forgotten that the provision of arms has been the Soviet Union's most important means of influence in the Arab world for many years, as well as an important source of hard currency for the USSR.

A second benefit of such a plan for the Soviet Union would be the termination of the American role as mediator in the Arab-Israeli peace process. This role has been a key to American influence in the Arab world since the 1973 war, for it demonstrated to the Arabs that it was the United States, and not the Soviet Union, that was able to secure Israeli territorial withdrawals. Once a final, as opposed to another partial, agreement was reached, the necessity for American mediation would be ended; and the Soviet leaders may have reasoned that this would lead to a drop in U.S. prestige and influence in the Arab world, as well as an end to the quarrels between the Arab states over the making of peace with Israel, quarrels that have impeded the Soviet drive to help create the "anti-imperialist" Arab unity.

Yet another benefit of such a plan would be that, by preserving Israel, the United States would not be alienated. Given the strong emotional and political ties between the United States and Israel, which have been reiterated by successive American presidents, the Soviet Union, if it sought to destroy Israel, would clearly jeopardize the chances for a Senate ratification of another strategic arms agreement. For this reason, the Soviet leadership in speeches to Arab leaders as well as in its peace plans has endorsed Israel's right to exist as an independent state. Concomitantly, the establishment of a limited Arab-Israeli peace would also lessen the possibility of a superpower conflict erupting from an Arab-Israeli war.

The establishment of an independent Palestinian state, if it were accepted, might well benefit the Soviet Union. The Soviet leadership obviously hoped in 1977—and still seems to hope—that such a state, whose creation Moscow began to advocate in late 1973, would be an ally of Soviet policy in the Arab world and would help combat U.S. influence in the region. Indeed, the Soviet Union would clearly gain from having another ally in the very center of the Middle East. In addition, the Soviet leadership appeared to believe that a Palestinian state on the West Bank and Gaza would be dependent on Soviet support because it would be sandwiched between a hostile Israel and a suspicious Jordan.

While Moscow may have hoped for a number of benefits for its Middle East position to emerge from the acceptance of its peace plan, and may have believed that the momentum for such an acceptance would be created by the convening of the Geneva Conference in December 1977, such was not to be the case. Indeed, the joint Soviet-American peace statement became moot, as the surprise visit of Anwar Sadat to Jerusalem in November 1977 and the subsequent Camp David agreements changed the face of Middle East diplomacy. Moscow was again thrown on the defensive by Camp David, and quickly expressed its concern that other Arab states would follow Egypt's example and sign what the Soviet media decried as a "separate deal" with Israel. Indeed, throughout the entire period from September 1978 until the present, Moscow has been preoccupied with the dangers of an expanded Camp David process, and one of the central thrusts of Soviet Middle Eastern policy has been to try to isolate Egypt and prevent any expansion of Camp David.

Fortunately for Moscow in the period immediately after Camp David, there was almost universal Arab antipathy toward the Camp David agreements and the subsequent Egyptian-Israeli peace treaty of March 1979. Indeed, Moscow had hopes that the large Arab coalition which had come together at Baghdad in November 1978 to denounce Camp David—a coalition highlighted by the rapprochement between Syria and Iraq—might form the "anti-imperialist" Arab bloc the USSR had sought for so long.

While the formation of the anti-Camp David Arab alignment at Baghdad and the fall of the Shah of Iran were clearly bonuses for Moscow in its zero-sum influence competition with the United States in the Middle East, the USSR was subsequently to run into serious difficulties because of two major events that were to have a very negative effect on the Soviet Middle East position: its invasion of Afghanistan and the outbreak of the Iran-Iraq war. Space does not suffice to properly evaluate the various theories offered to explain the Soviet invasion of Afghanistan in December 1979.[24] In my view, however, there were two overriding causes. In the first place the Communist regime that had seized power in an April 1978 coup had quickly alienated the Afghan people, and even the steadily increasing numbers of Soviet advisers could not prevent the regime from nearing the point of collapse (in this respect, Soviet policy toward Afghanistan from April 1978 to December 1979 was not unlike U.S. policy in Vietnam from 1962 until the major U.S. troop commitment in 1965). Secondly, Moscow probably thought it was a low-risk operation. Given the fact that the United States had done virtually nothing in Iran, first when the Shah fell and then when its diplomats were taken hostage—in a country where the United States had major interests—how much more unlikely it must have seemed to Moscow that the United States would take action in Afghanistan where there were almost no American interests.

Whatever the cause of the Soviet invasion, it was to have a very negative effect on its Middle East position. First, the Gulf Arabs, seeing the Soviet move, again turned to the United States as a counterbalance, despite Camp David. Secondly, the anti-Camp David coalition, already weakened by renewed hostility between Iraq and Syria, now fell apart. By January 1980 what had emerged in the Arab world were three major groupings. On the one hand was the pro-Western camp led by Egypt and including the Sudan (until April 1985), Oman, and Somalia. This Arab grouping supported Camp David, opposed the Soviet invasion of Afghanistan, and cooperated with the United States in joint military exercises. On the other side of the Arab spectrum was the so-called Front of Steadfastness and Confrontation, led by Syria (which increasingly had taken a pro-Soviet line and in October 1980 had agreed to sign a Treaty of Friendship and Cooperation with the USSR) and including Libya, the People's Democratic Republic of Yemen (South Yemen), the PLO, and Algeria.[25] This Arab grouping opposed Camp David and, with the exception of Algeria, supported Soviet activity in Afghanistan. In the center of the Arab spectrum was the group of Arab states composed of Saudi Arabia, Jordan, Kuwait, the UAE, Morocco, Iraq, North Yemen, Tunisia, Bahrein, and Qatar. These "Centrists" opposed Camp David but also opposed the Soviet invasion of Afghanistan. From the Soviet viewpoint, the diplomatic goal was now to move the Centrist Arab grouping back to the Steadfastness Front as at the Baghdad Conference so as to isolate Egypt and the other members of the pro-Western Arab bloc. While Moscow sought to exploit Israeli Prime Minister Begin's construction of settlements on the West Bank to achieve this goal, the outbreak of the Iran-Iraq war made this task far more difficult. Indeed, in many ways, the Iran-Iraq war was the wrong war at the wrong time at the wrong place for Moscow as it has caused Moscow major problems.[26]

Moscow, which could ill-afford to alienate either Iran or Iraq, remained neutral during the first two years of the conflict, but the fall-out from the war negatively affected its Middle East position. In the first place, while Syria and Libya backed Iran, both the Centrist Arabs and the Egyptian bloc of Arab states backed Iraq, with Egypt herself selling Iraq large amounts of weaponry. Under the circumstances, and as the Iraqi invasion first bogged down and then reversed into a retreat, a certain amount of rapprochement between the Centrist Arabs, who feared Iran, and Egypt became almost inevitable. This momentum accelerated after the formation of the Gulf Cooperation Council (GCC) in 1981, a group of five Centrist Arab states (Saudi Arabia, Kuwait, Bahrein, Qatar, and the United Arab Emirates) and one Arab state in the Egyptian camp, Oman. In addition, as the war intensified, Arab attention was diverted from the Arab-Israeli conflict, another blow to Moscow.

A third negative result of the conflict for Moscow was the strengthening of the U.S. position in the Gulf. The stationing (and eventual sale) of U.S. AWACS aircraft and the positioning of American ground radar personnel in Saudi Arabia following Iranian threats to close the Straits of Hormuz seemed to demonstrate American willingness to help defend Saudi Arabia and other Arab states in time of need, a development that made the American military buildup in the Indian Ocean more diplomatically acceptable, thereby refuting Moscow's charge that the U.S. buildup was a threat to seize the oil of the Arab world. Indeed, the AWACS move appeared to reverse the decline in Saudi-American relations caused by both Camp David and U.S. inactivity during the fall of the Shah, and Moscow became concerned that Saudi Arabia might even be enticed to join the Camp David process.

Moscow's response to the negative trends emerging from the Iran-Iraq war was threefold. In the first place, Brezhnev, on a December 1980 visit to India, issued a declaration calling for the neutralization of the Persian Gulf, a call he repeated at the 26th Soviet Communist Party Congress in February 1981.[27] Second, Moscow repeatedly called for a rapid end to the war, with Brezhnev stating at the 26th CPSU Congress that the USSR was taking steps in that regard. Finally, Moscow began to woo two key Centrist nations, Kuwait and Jordan, in an effort to slow the rapprochement between the Centrist Arab states and Egypt. In the case of Kuwait, the most neutralist of the GCC states, Moscow had some success; the Kuwaiti Foreign Minister, Sheikh Sabah al Sabah, was willing to give lip-service to some Soviet policy positions (including neutralization of the Gulf) in return for at least the appearance of Soviet support against a possible Iranian invasion. In the case of Jordan, King Hussein, now worried about the growing influence of Ariel Sharon on the Israeli government (Sharon had repeatedly stated that Jordan should be the Palestinian state), also drew somewhat closer to Moscow.[28]

Nonetheless, despite small gains with Kuwait and Jordan, Middle Eastern trends continued to move against the USSR, and Moscow, which had put an arms embargo against Iraq when the war broke out in September 1980, resumed shipments in late 1981, initially at a low level, as the USSR appeared to lose hope that the clerical regime in Iran, which had released the U.S. hostages in January 1981, and which was stepping up its pressure against the Tudeh party, would reciprocate Soviet efforts to improve relations with it. At the same time, tension remained high between Israel and Syria as a confrontation over the moving of Syrian missiles into Lebanon took place in the spring of 1981, and Moscow moved carefully to avoid being dragged into a war.

In addition, things appeared to be going from bad to worse for Moscow in Egypt where Anwar Sadat expelled the Soviet ambassador and a number of other officials in early September 1981. Three weeks later Sadat was assassinated, but any Soviet hope that Egypt would rapidly reorient its foreign policy seemed dashed as Sadat's successor, Hosni Mubarak, affirmed the continuity of his regime's policies with those of Sadat's, albeit with a somewhat more neutralist tone. Nonetheless, Mubarak's Egypt, like Sadat's, remained a major recipient of American military and economic aid and regularly carried out joint military exercises with the United States. Indeed, several consequences of the assassination were to have negative implications for Moscow. With Sadat gone, the heavy propaganda carried on by Egypt against its anti-Camp David Arab neighbors ceased, and Mubarak sought to accelerate the reintegration of Egypt into the Arab world while at the same time maintaining Egypt's peace treaty with Israel. Yet another negative result was that Britain and France agreed to provide troops to man the multinational force in the Sinai provided for in the Egyptian-Israeli treaty, thus demonstrating the first example of multinational NATO cooperation on a Middle East issue since the Suez crisis of 1956.

In sum, on the eve of the Israeli invasion of Lebanon, the major Middle East trends seemed to be going against Moscow as the Iran-Iraq war continued unabated, the United States improved ties with the Gulf Arabs, and the Centrist Arab states were slowly moving toward a reconciliation with Egypt. The Israeli invasion, at least initially, was to cause further problems for Moscow.[29] In the first place, Soviet credibility suffered a major blow because its frequent warnings to the United States and Israel during the course of the war proved to be ineffectual. Second, the quality of Soviet military equipment and, to a lesser degree, the quality of Soviet training were called into question by the overwhelming victory of U.S.-supplied Israeli weaponry over the military equipment supplied by Moscow to Syria. Finally, the Soviet leadership had to deal with a situation where the United States, having mediated the PLO withdrawal from Beirut (and having deployed Marines to Beirut to achieve this goal despite Soviet warnings), had the clear diplomatic initiative. On September 1—the eve of a long delayed Arab summit conference—President Reagan announced his plan for a Middle East peace settlement. In a clear effort to gain Centrist Arab support for his plan, Reagan called for a stop to Israeli settlement activity on the West Bank and announced U.S. refusal to accept any Israeli claim to sovereignty over the West Bank. To satisfy the Israelis, Reagan emphasized U.S. concern for Israel's security, asserted that Israel's final borders should not be the pre-1967 war boundaries, called for the unity of Jerusalem and direct Arab-Israeli negotiations, and reaffirmed U.S. opposition to a Palestinian state on the West Bank. In his most controversial statement, and one also aimed at obtaining Centrist Arab support, Reagan called for a fully auton- omous Palestinian entity linked to Jordan.[30] Moscow, while denouncing the Reagan Plan, and denigrating Israeli Prime Minister Menachem Begin's rapid rejection of it, was concerned that the plan might prove attractive in the Arab world.[31]

Given this situation, Moscow seemed pleased by the outcome of the Arab summit at Fez, Morocco, which not only indicated that the Arab world had regained a semblance of unity but also brought forth a peace plan which, except for its lack of explicit clarity as to Israel's right to exist, was quite close to the long-standing Soviet peace plan, in that it called for an Israeli withdrawal to the 1967 boundaries but no normalization of relations.[32] Moscow also was pleased that the Sudanese proposal to formally readmit Egypt to the Arab League was rejected. Nonetheless, the Fez conference did not reject the Reagan Plan, thereby leaving it, along with the Fez Plan, as one of the solutions which the Arabs would consider to resolve the post-Beirut diplomatic situation in the Middle East. With both the Reagan and Fez Plans now being considered, Moscow evidently felt that it too had to enter the diplomatic competition, and in a speech on September 15, Brezhnev announced the Soviet Union's own peace plan.[33] While a number of its points were repetitions of previous Soviet proposals, the new elements seem to have been added to emphasize the similarity between the Fez and Soviet plans. Thus Moscow called for the Palestinian refugees to be given the right to return to their homes or receive compensation for their abandoned property, for the return of East Jerusalem to the Arabs and its incorporation into the Palestinian state, with freedom of access for believers to the sacred places of the three religions throughout Jerusalem, and for Security Council guarantees for the final settlement—all provisions, almost word for word, taken from the Fez declaration. Brezhnev also took the opportunity to repeat the long-standing Soviet call for an international conference on the Middle East, with all interested parties participating, including the PLO, which the Soviet leader again characterized as "the sole legitimate representative of the Arab people of Palestine."

In modeling the Soviet peace plan on Fez, Brezhnev evidently sought to prevent the Arabs from moving to embrace the Reagan Plan. Nonetheless, with the United States clearly possessing the diplomatic initiative in the Middle East and both Jordan's King Hussein and PLO leader Arafat, along with other Arab leaders, expressing interest in the Reagan Plan, Moscow was on the diplomatic defensive—despite the massacres in Sabra and Shatilla which Moscow sought to link to the United States.

The Post-Brezhnev Era

It was at this point, in mid-November 1982, that Brezhnev passed from the scene. His successor, Yuri Andropov, had the task of rebuilding the Soviet position in the Middle East which had suffered a major blow during the Israeli invasion of Lebanon.

Under Andropov, Moscow's Middle East fortunes began to rise again, not so much because of Soviet successes as mistakes by the United States in the region. To be sure, Andropov moved to restore Soviet credibility in January 1983, two months after he took power, by sending Syria SAM-5 anti-aircraft missiles, weapons which had never before been deployed outside the Soviet bloc, and he followed these up with a shipment of SS-21 ground-to-ground missiles in September following the first U.S.-Syrian confrontation in Lebanon. On the diplomatic front, the Soviet Middle East position was aided by two major developments which severely weakened U.S. diplomatic efforts in the Middle East—the challenge to Arafat's position in the PLO and the collapse of the U.S. position in Lebanon.

Arafat, who in November 1982 had publicly stated that he was resigned to dealing with the United States as the dominant superpower in the Middle

East,[34] indicating thereby his willingness on negotiate on the Reagan Plan, had clashed with Andropov in Moscow during a visit in January 1983, in which the PLO leader called for a Palestinian-Jordanian confederation. While Moscow was in favor of the creation of an independent Palestinian state, the linkage to Jordan, a Centrist state, not only seemed to associate the PLO at least partially with the Reagan Plan, but also appeared to mean its defection from the Steadfastness Front, already badly weakened by the Israeli invasion. Consequently, the USSR only expressed its "understanding" of the PLO position—a diplomatic way of demonstrating its opposition.[35]

Fortunately for Moscow, Arafat's position was soon to weaken, as the Soviet interest in preventing a PLO turn to the United States was shared by both Syria and Libya, which actively moved to undermine Arafat's position. The efforts of the anti-Arafat forces were to prove successful as the Palestine National Council, which after a number of postponements finally convened in mid-February 1983 in Algiers, formally stated its refusal to consider the Reagan Plan "as a sound basis for a just and lasting solution to the Palestine problem and the Arab-Israeli conflict."[36]

One month later, despite Arafat's public renunciation of the Reagan Plan, Syrian President Assad moved to undercut his position within his base of power in the PLO, Fateh, by engineering a split in the organization. Subsequently, Arafat was expelled from Syria, and his loyalists in the Bekaa Valley came under increasing pressure. Ultimately, most of his troops were forced to move overland to Tripoli, Lebanon, and although Arafat was to join them in the early fall, he and his men were to suffer another humiliating forced withdrawal from Lebanon in December, this time after battles with Syrian-supported forces. For its part, Moscow, which sought to maintain good ties with both Arafat and Assad, found itself once again in the quandary of being caught between two Arab forces it was seeking to influence.[37]

Meanwhile, the United States had successfully mediated a troop withdrawal agreement between Israel and Lebanon which was signed on May 17, 1983. But Syrian opposition to the agreement, U.S. inability to mobilize the support of other Arab states such as Saudi Arabia on behalf of the accord, and major political mistakes by Lebanese President Amin Gemayel, who alienated both the Lebanese Shiites and the Druze and drove them into the arms of Syria, doomed the Lebanese-Israeli agreement. For its part, the United States, by coming out strongly in support of Amin Gemayel, became a party to the renewed Lebanese civil war and by September found itself in a military confrontation not only with the Druze and Shiites but with Syria as well. The September crisis, precipitated by the Israeli withdrawal from the Chouf Mountains, was ended by a ceasefire with no direct military conflict between Syria and the United States. Nonetheless, the attack on the U.S. Marine headquarters in October led to a rise in Syrian-American tensions and in early December to a military confrontation as two U.S. Navy planes were shot down by Syrian anti-aircraft fire.[38]

Interestingly enough, during this entire period, Moscow kept a very low profile, as it indicated it wished to avoid a superpower conflict over Lebanon which, by itself, was only tertiary to Soviet interests. Nonetheless, it sought to exploit the Syrian-American confrontation by tying the U.S. attack on the Syrian positions in Lebanon to the strategic cooperation agreement concluded between Reagan and Israel's new Prime Minister, Yitzhak Shamir, a week earlier, and claiming that by its attack the United States no longer qualified as an "honest broker" in the Middle East. Moscow also again appealed for Arab unity on an "anti-imperialist" basis in an evident attempt to exploit the Syrian-American clash to slow the rapprochement between the Centrist Arabs and the pro-American Egyptian camp in the Arab world.[39] Moscow's failure to aid its Arab ally during the confrontation must have raised questions of credibility in the Arab world, however.

Fortunately for Moscow, two months after the Syrian-American confrontation came the collapse of the U.S. position in Lebanon, a development highlighted by the "redeployment" of U.S. Marines to their ships. This was perceived throughout the Middle East as a major victory for Syria, Moscow's principal Arab client, and a major defeat for the United States and for the Reagan Plan as well. The U.S. redeployment was accompanied by naval shelling of anti-government positions in the vicinity of Beirut, although the rationale for the shelling was never clearly explained by the Reagan Administration. Indeed, the general course of U.S. policy during this period seemed confused at best, and whatever the mistakes the United States had made in backing the Gemayel government up until this point, the hurried exodus of the Marines from Beirut, coupled with what appeared to be indiscriminate artillery fire into the Lebanese mountains, could only hurt the U.S. image, not only in Lebanon but in the Middle East as a whole, something Moscow clearly welcomed and sought to exploit, despite the death of Andropov in February.[40]

Moscow was to achieve another success for its Lebanese policy when Amin Gemayel, now virtually bereft of U.S. military support, could only turn to Syrian President Assad for help in staying in power. Assad, at least in the short term, proved willing to do so—for a price. The price was the abrogation of the May 17 Israeli-Lebanese agreement, and Gemayel announced its abrogation on March 5. Yet even as Moscow was hailing this development (Soviet commentators called it a major blow to the entire Camp David process), there were a number of Middle Eastern problems which the new Soviet leader, Konstantin Chernenko, had to face despite the collapse of the U.S. position in Lebanon. First, a power struggle had erupted in Damascus over the successor to Assad, who apparently had not fully recovered from his November 1983 heart attack. Secondly, despite its victory in Lebanon, which the Syrian media was hailing as equivalent to Nasser's nationalization of the Suez Canal, Syria remained in diplomatic isolation in the Arab world, while Egypt continued to improve its ties to Centrist Arab states. Egypt's rapprochement with the Centrist Arabs was reinforced by the surprise visit of Arafat to Cairo after his expulsion from Lebanon in December 1983 (Arafat later went to Jordan where he resumed discussions with King Hussein), and the rapprochement was highlighted by the decision of the Islamic Conference to readmit Egypt to its ranks in mid-January, a development attributed by Moscow to the "pressure of conservative Moslem regimes".[41] Soviet concern could only have increased with Mubarak's visit to King Hassan of Morocco—the first official visit to an Arab country by the head of the Egyptian state since the 1979 peace treaty, as Moscow TV unhappily noted[42]—and by Mubarak's meeting with King Hussein in Washington in mid-February as the two Arab leaders prepared for talks with President Reagan.

King Hussein stated in late March that a victory by Israel's Labor party (which opposed annexation of the West Bank and advocated territorial compromise with Jordan, and whose leader, Shimon Peres, had spoken favorably about the Reagan Plan) in the just-announced Israeli elections of July 23, would be a healthy change.[43] Soviet concern was heightened, and during the spring and summer of 1984, Soviet diplomacy had a special Jordanian focus. Moscow assiduously wooed King Hussein, hoping to keep Jordan from embracing the Reagan Plan in the event, as the polls predicted, that the Labor party scored a major victory in the Israeli elections.[44] In addition, the Soviet leadership prepared a new variant of its peace plan, one that might prove more amenable to King Hussein than previous Soviet peace plans had been. While the Jordanian monarch had long shared the Soviet goal of an international conference to settle the Arab-Israeli conflict, he also had long desired a link between any Palestinian entity or state on the West Bank and Jordan, whose population was more than 60 percent Palestinian. The Soviet peace plan of July 29, which mentioned such a link, can be considered a major gesture to Hussein.[45]

Modeled on the Brezhnev peace plan of September 15, 1982 which, as will be recalled, had combined the basic three-point Soviet peace plan with the major components of the Arab program announced at Fez, the new Soviet plan had one additional key element—acknowledgement that the new Palestinian state could decide to form a confederation with a neighboring country. Given the previous clash with Arafat over this issue during the PLO leader's visit to Moscow in January 1983, the Soviet leadership's inclusion of this element may also be seen as a gesture to Arafat.

In addition to the new content in the Soviet peace plan of July 29, its timing is also significant. Apparently prepared to coincide with the July 23 Israeli elections, Moscow evidently hoped to use it to help keep King Hussein from joining the Reagan Plan. Contrary to expectation, the Labor victory was so narrow that it did not appear as if Peres, even if he could manage to form a narrow parliamentary majority, would be able to make the concessions that the Reagan Plan would require. This was a bonus for the USSR, as it now sought to use the plan as a rallying point for Centrist and Steadfastness Front Arabs to draw them together and away from the United States and its Egyptian-camp allies.

While Moscow got verbal support from most of the Arab world for its peace plan, the pace of Middle Eastern events once again seemed to confound Soviet strategy. In late September, soon after President Reagan addressing the United Nations had again emphasized the Reagan Plan as U.S. policy in the Middle East, and a Peres-led National Unity government had taken office in Israel, King Hussein, whom Moscow had been courting, suddenly reestablished full diplomatic relations with Egypt. This move, the final stage of a steady improvement of Jordanian-Egyptian relations since December 1983, appeared to be a major step in the rapprochement between the Centrist Arab camp and Egypt. To be sure, Moscow may have hoped that given the continuing tension in U.S.-Jordanian relations (due, among other things, to congressional opposition to U.S. arms sales to Jordan), and the steady development of Soviet-Jordanian relations, Jordan might pull Egypt away from its close ties to the United States instead of being pulled by Egypt toward the Reagan Plan. Nonetheless, despite resuming relations at the ambassadorial level with the USSR in August, Egypt continued its close military and economic relationship with the United States, as exemplified by the joint military exercise "Sea Wind" carried out by the two nations in early November.

The low-level treatment in Soviet media for the resumption of Egyptian-Jordanian diplomatic relations seemed to indicate that Moscow was trying to play down the development while continuing to cultivate Jordan. Yet resumption of diplomatic relations with Egypt was not the only move by King Hussein that discomfited the Soviet Union, not to mention Moscow's chief ally, Syria, which bitterly attacked Hussein for reestablishing ties with Egypt. In November, King Hussein agreed to convening the Palestine National Council in Jordan. Arafat was eager to convene the meeting in a friendly capital (he had been turned down by Algeria and South Yemen), and he managed to achieve a quorum in Amman despite boycott of the session by the Syrian-backed Palestinian National Alliance, and the Marxist Democratic alliance, which included the pro-Soviet Palestinian Communist Party. Moscow's displeasure with the meeting was exemplified not only by the absence of the Palestine Communist Party, but also by the failure of the Soviet Ambassador to Jordan to attend and by the pro-Soviet Israeli Communist Party's opposition.[46] In addition, both PFLP leader George Habash and DFLP leader Naef Hawatmeh announced their opposition to the PNC meeting after hurried visits to Moscow. While the PNC meeting, which was orchestrated by Arafat to demonstrate his control over the PLO while also offering a renewed tie to both the Democratic and National Alliances, did not, for precisely that reason, make any dramatic moves toward peace (in fact, Arafat emphasized the need for armed struggle), the very fact that the meeting took place when and where it did, held out the possibility of a final split in the PLO between Arafat's backers and those of Syria. Indeed, the chances of such a split seemed even greater in February 1985 when Hussein and Arafat signed an agreement on a joint negotiating position in the peace process.

Not surprisingly, the Soviet reaction to the Hussein-Arafat agreement, and its rapid endorsement by Mubarak, was a very negative one, as the Soviet leadership (which was to undergo yet another change with the death of Chernenko and the rise to power of Mikhail Gorbachev) became concerned about the formation of an Arab alignment consisting of Jordan, Arafat's wing of the PLO, and Egypt.[47]

Given this problem, Gorbachev evidently decided that if Moscow were not to once again be on the sidelines when a major Middle East peace effort was underway, he had to make some gestures to Israel. To be sure, the USSR and the United States had met in February for high-level talks to discuss the Middle East (the first such superpower meeting on the Middle East in seven years), but President Reagan gave no indication of wanting to include the USSR in the peace process.[48] Indeed, the most a U.S. official would concede was that the talks were "merely an exchange of thoughts in the hope of reducing misunderstandings. Even to call them explorations would be an exaggeration."[49] Not unexpectedly, therefore, no agreement was achieved in the talks, and the U.S. representative, Assistant Secretary of State Richard Murphy, noted that the USSR lacked credibility as a mediator because of its refusal to resume diplomatic relations with Israel and because of its treatment of Soviet Jews. He also stated that while the USSR was pressing for an international conference involving Security Council members and interested parties in the Middle East including the PLO, the United States felt that such large meetings would be counterproductive and called instead for direct talks between Israel and its neighbors.[50]

While signals about the possibility of the resumption of diplomatic relations had been sent from Moscow to Israel almost from the time relations were broken off during the 1967 war,[51] the signals increased in intensity soon after Gorbachev took power. Interestingly enough, Soviet gestures to Israel were to come despite a series of Israeli actions that bound the Jewish state even more tightly to the United States, including the signing of strategic cooperation and free trade agreements and Israel's willingness to allow the construction of a Voice of America transmitter on Israeli territory and to enter into the American Star Wars defense scheme. Indeed, it should not be ruled out that the Soviet gestures to Israel were aimed not only at gaining entry into the Middle East peace process, but also at winning favor in the United States with which a summit was on the horizon. Given Moscow's tendency to overestimate the influence of American Jews on American policy-making vis-à-vis the USSR, gestures to Israel could thus also be seen as part of Moscow's pre-summit maneuvering.[52]

In mid-July, with Arafat and Hussein calling for an Arab summit, and with a review session commemorating the 10th anniversary of the signing of the Helsinki agreements due to open at the beginning of August—a session that was likely to see the issue of Soviet Jewry raised—Gorbachev apparently decided that a major discussion between Soviet and Israeli diplomats on both renewing diplomatic relations and increasing the emigration of Soviet Jews to Israel was in order. The meeting took place in Paris at the home of Israeli pianist Daniel Barenbaum between the Israeli Ambassador to France, Ovadia Sofer, and his Soviet counterpart, Yuli Vorontsov. Sofer's description of the meeting was leaked to Israeli radio, which promptly broadcast it.[53] The most interesting aspect of what Vorontsov reportedly said is that he seemed to indicate that diplomatic relations could be restored if there was at least a partial Israeli withdrawal on the Golan Heights, and that large-scale emigration of Soviet Jews could take place if they emigrated to Israel and not the United States, and if Israel ended the anti-Soviet propaganda it was undertaking in the United States and Europe.

Yet the Soviet hint of renewed relations, while welcome in Israel, was received in a highly negative way by Moscow's Arab allies, especially Syria. Syria, the USSR's main bastion in the Arab world, was incensed that the USSR would consider renewing ties with Israel while even part of the Golan Heights seized during the 1967 war remained in Israeli hands. As a result, the USSR in both official visits and radio broadcasts to the Arab world repeated the old Soviet position that diplomatic relations would not be restored until Israel gave up all the land conquered in 1967.[54] At the same time, however, Moscow continued to hint to Israel that relations could be restored if Israel agreed to Moscow's inclusion in a peace conference.[55] For his part, Israeli Prime Minister Shimon Peres expressed a keen interest in improving ties with the USSR, much as his predecessor Yitzhak Shamir had done, and Moscow made yet another gesture to Israel in October, this time in the form of an agreement between Poland and Israel, whereby the two countries agreed in principle to establish "interest sections" in foreign embassies in each other's capitals—the first stage in the process of reestablishing diplomatic relations.[56] While Moscow was not yet resuming diplomatic ties itself, this was a clear gesture that it was prepared to so do, and Gorbachev, during his visit to Paris in early October, noted that "as far as reestablishing relations [with Israel] is concerned, I think the faster the situation is normalized in the Middle East, the faster it will be possible to look at this question."[57] The announced resumption of low-level diplomatic relations with Poland, World Jewish Congress President Edgar Bronfman's visit to Moscow carrying a message from Peres, Peres' meeting with Soviet Foreign Minister Edward Shevardnadze at the United Nations in October, and Gorbachev's visit to Paris reinforced the rumors circulating in Israel that Moscow was about to release 20,000 Soviet Jews and allow them to be flown directly to Israel on French planes.[58]

The momentum toward even a partial Soviet-Israeli rapprochement—if that indeed was Gorbachev's goal—was slowed and then stopped, however, as the peace process fell by the wayside in the face of an escalation of Middle East terrorism. While Moscow itself was to suffer both embarrassment and physical loss as a result of the terrorism (one of its diplomats was murdered and two others kidnapped in Beirut), the end result was that the peace process, centered around negotiations between Israel and a Jordanian-Palestinian delegation, was halted, a development from which Moscow would profit diplomatically.

The root of the problem lay in the fact that Arafat, in an effort to maintain credibility with the hard-liners in his organization, stressed the escalation of "armed struggle" (terrorism) soon after concluding the Amman agreement with King Hussein.[59] For his part Peres was vulnerable politically even for considering negotiations with Palestinians close to the PLO; he was frequently attacked by the opposition Likud party for being "soft on terrorism" and "soft on the PLO." As a result, when a wave of terrorist murders struck Israel during the spring and summer of 1985, Peres found it increasingly difficult to negotiate with any Palestinian closely linked to the PLO and also came under increasing pressure to retaliate. When three Israelis were murdered in Cyprus at the end of September by terrorists who proclaimed they were fighting for the Palestinian cause, Peres authorized an attack on PLO headquarters in Tunis on October 1, 1985, perhaps signaling to Arafat that if the PLO leader wished to fight while negotiating, Israel could play the same game.

Moscow lost little time in exploiting the Israeli attack to try to undermine the U.S. position in the Middle East, and once again appealed for Arab unity against Israel and the United States, as it sought to link Israeli action to the United States. In a radio broadcast in Arabic on October 2, the day after the attack, the Soviet commentator alleged not only that the United States had used its radar posts in the Mediterranean to direct Israeli planes to PLO headquarters in Tunis, but also that the Israeli bombers took off from a U.S. aircraft carrier—a classic case of Soviet disinformation.[60]

Even before the uproar over the Israeli attack had died down, another terrorist event from which Moscow would profit diplomatically took place. This was the hijacking of the cruise ship *Achille Lauro* and the murder of a Jewish passenger by a PLO faction headed by Mohammed Abbas, a hard-line PLO leader who was linked to Arafat because of their mutual opposition to Syrian leader Hafiz Assad.[61] The action of the United States in forcing down an Egyptian plane carrying the hijackers and Abbas inflamed U.S. relations not only with Egypt but also with Italy where the plane was forced to land, when Italian Premier Bettino Craxi allowed Abbas to leave his country. While subsequent U.S. aid to Egypt when one of its aircraft was hijacked to Malta somewhat smoothed over the strain in U.S.-Egyptian relations, serious diplomatic damage had been done, a development Moscow evidently hoped would lead to a weakening of U.S.-Egyptian relations.

Meanwhile, as the impact of the terrorist acts seemed to stymie the peace process, Peres sought to revitalize it by proposing talks with Jordan under "international auspices" (a clear change in Israel's former position on an international conference) and by stating that the resumption of Soviet Jewish emigration (*Aliyah*) from the USSR was more important than the restoration of diplomatic ties. "If they agree to renew *Aliyah*," he stated, "we shall waive our objections to their taking part in an international conference on the Middle East."[62]

Peres thus presented Moscow with an interesting choice. As far as its position in the Arab world is concerned, it is far less costly for Moscow to release Soviet Jews than to reestablish ties with Israel, and Moscow has long wanted to participate in an international conference on an Arab-Israeli settlement. On the other hand, it was doubtful whether the USSR would settle for just a symbolic role in an international conference—the most Israel seemed to be ready to concede—in return for sharply increasing the number of Jews allowed to leave the Soviet Union. Nonetheless, Israel clearly did not give up on the possibility, and the attendance of Israeli President Chaim Herzog at the National Convention of Israel's Communist Party in early December 1985, the first time an Israeli president had ever attended such a function, was a clear gesture to Moscow that Jerusalem was interested in continuing a dialogue with the USSR.[63]

For its part Moscow, while not immediately agreeing to Peres' terms, demonstrated its interest in keeping up the dialogue. Thus in August 1986 it agreed to public consular level talks with Israel in Helsinki, Finland. In part, of course, the Soviet action was also due to a desire to improve Soviet-U.S. relations. The nuclear disaster in Chernobyl, the precipitous drop in world oil prices (more than 50 percent of Soviet hard currency earnings come from oil and natural gas sales), Gorbachev's efforts to restructure the Soviet economy, and the major economic difficulties facing the USSR were all factors moving the Soviet leadership toward an arms control agreement that would prevent another expensive spiralling of the arms race. For this reason Gorbachev sought a second summit with the United States, and, given Moscow's tendency to overestimate Jewish influence in the United States, the new Soviet leader may well have felt that the gesture to Israel would help pave the way for the summit.

Nonetheless the Soviet-Israeli talks in Helsinki, the first such official diplomatic negotiations between the two countries since the 1967 war, did not immediately produce the results either side said it wanted, although the symbolic significance of the talks was probably much more important than their content. While the Soviets wished to send a team of officials to inventory Soviet property (primarily owned by the Russian Orthodox church) in Israel, Israel raised the issue of Soviet Jewry at the talks, and the meeting ended after 90 minutes.[64] Nonetheless, the very fact that the talks were held, and that one month later Israeli Prime Minister Peres and Soviet Foreign Minister Shevardnadze held detailed (and apparently cordial) negotiations at the United Nations, indicated that the Soviet Union was keeping alive its contacts with Israel.[65]

Moscow was to quicken the pace of its diplomacy in 1987. The Iran-Contra affair put the United States on the diplomatic defensive in the Middle East, and Gorbachev began actively to promote the Soviet peace plan once again, this time calling for a preparatory meeting of the U.N. Security Council's permanent members to arrange the conference. In addition, Moscow began tacitly to cooperate with Peres who had stepped down as leader of Israel's National Unity Government and was now foreign minister. It did so by sharply increasing the number of Jews being allowed to leave the USSR during the spring from an average of under 100 per month in 1986 to over 700 in April 1987 alone. This, together with highly publicized meetings between Peres and Soviet leaders like Karen Brutents, gave Peres the political ammunition he needed to try to bring down the National

Unity government and call for new elections on the grounds that Moscow
had sufficiently changed its policy to allow it to participate in an international
conference. Peres' efforts proved unsuccessful, however, as new Prime
Minister Yitzhak Shamir proved able to mobilize sufficient support in Israel's
Parliament in May 1987 to prevent new elections.[66]

Meanwhile, Moscow's activity in helping to at least partially reunite the
disparate factions of the PLO at the Palestine National Council meeting in
Algeria in April—a meeting which put a formal end to the Hussein-Arafat
peace initiative—raised questions in the minds of many Israelis as to whether
Moscow, despite Peres' protestations, was genuinely interested in peace. In
any case, the abortive attempt by Peres to include the USSR in an
international conference provides a useful point of departure for analyzing
Soviet policy toward the Arab-Israeli conflict since the 1967 war.

Conclusions

In the twenty year period since the 1967 war, there have been three
major areas of continuity in Soviet policy toward the Arab-Israeli conflict,
regardless of who was the leader in Moscow. First, Soviet policy toward
the Arab-Israeli conflict was always part of its larger policy toward the
Middle East as a whole. Second, a central factor of Soviet policy has been
its emphasis on Israel's right to exist as an independent state. Finally, in
dealing with the Arab-Israeli conflict, Moscow has never lost sight of its
impact on superpower relations and has frequently fashioned its policy
toward one element of the Arab-Israeli conflict, Israel, with an eye to the
effect of its policy on Washington.

In addition to these areas of continuity, there has been one significant
area of change, the development of an increasingly sophisticated Soviet plan
for settlement of the Arab-Israeli conflict, one that was carefully adapted
to changing circumstances within the Arab world.

In looking at Soviet policy over the last twenty years it is clear that
Moscow's policy toward the Arab-Israeli conflict can be seen as part of its
larger policy toward the Middle East as a whole. In the 1966–67 period,
Moscow encouraged (perhaps too strongly) an alliance of Arab states on
an "anti-imperialist" basis against Israel in an effort to weaken the U.S.
position in the region, but this policy backfired when it helped precipitate
the 1967 war. In 1973, after losing its bases in Egypt, Moscow supported
Egypt and Syria in their war against Israel in an effort to rebuild the Soviet
position in the Arab world while simultaneously weakening that of the
United States; and in the post-1978 period it opposed the Camp David
agreements and sought to isolate Egypt in the Arab world to prevent an
expansion of the Camp David peace process.

In each of the periods under consideration, Moscow was careful to
emphasize to the Arabs, as well as to Israel, that it supported Israel's right
to exist. Israel's existence was seen by Moscow as the "imperialist" element
in the Middle East against which the Arabs, in spite of their numerous

internecine quarrels, could rally, on an "anti-imperialist" basis. At the same time, given Moscow's overriding concern throughout the entire period with its relations with the United States, Soviet reaffirmations of Israel's right to exist and occasional hints about restoring relations with it after 1967 served both to reassure the American Jewish community, whose influence in the American policy-making process Moscow takes very seriously, and to avoid alienating the U.S. government from which Moscow sought additional SALT agreements, improved trade relations, and, after 1973, entry into the Middle East peace process via the convening of an international conference.

As far as the peace process itself is concerned, Moscow, since 1973, has used its peace plan as a tactical device to improve its position in the region and weaken that of the United States. If one examines the timing of the Soviet peace plans of 1976, 1982, and 1984, this becomes clear.

Second, not only the timing but also the substance of the Soviet peace plans indicate the tactical nature of Soviet peace efforts. By calling only for Israeli withdrawal to the 1967 borders, establishment of a Palestinian state on the West Bank and Gaza, and the right of all states in the region to exist, Moscow seeks to achieve a frigid peace (reminiscent of the North Korea-South Korea armistice agreement) where, although no war is in progress, the threat of war would be ever present and Moscow would be needed as a supplier of military aid and diplomatic support to the Arab side. While the United States has proposed a comprehensive peace complete with diplomatic, trade, and cultural relations between Israel and her Arab neighbors, Moscow has opposed the U.S. peace plan because it might lead to a diminution of tensions in the area, and thereby to a diminution of Soviet influence.

Finally, in the period since the Israeli invasion of Lebanon, with the Centrist Arab states continuing to gravitate toward Egypt, Moscow has used its peace plan to try to arrest this most unwelcome development. By modeling many of the components of its September 1982 peace plan on the Arab plan agreed to at Fez one week earlier, and then by acknowledging the Palestinian state's right to form a confederation if it so chose in the 1984 Soviet peace plan, Moscow has sought to rally the Centrist and Steadfastness Arab camps together on a document they could both agree on, while isolating Israel, the United States, and Egypt as opponents. Clearly Moscow continues to be concerned about the Reagan Plan, or another variant of Camp David, being accepted by a number of key Arab states. Indeed, despite the Soviet peace plan, such events as the resumption of diplomatic relations between Jordan and Egypt, the holding of the Palestinian National Council meeting in Jordan, and the now abortive Hussein-Arafat agreement indicate that Moscow has grounds for its concern, particularly if a final split within the PLO takes place.

In sum, therefore, since 1967, and especially since 1973, Moscow has sought to exploit the Arab-Israeli conflict to weaken the U.S. position in the Middle East while strengthening its own, primarily by encouraging a limited amount of tension in the Arab-Israeli relationship which would prevent U.S.-sponsored peace initiatives from gaining acceptance in the Arab world, a development which would enhance U.S. prestige in the region. Yet, in retrospect, one must ask if Soviet policy has been successful. Ever since the conclusion of the Egyptian-Israeli peace treaty in March 1979, the Arab-Israeli conflict has been transformed into a series of conflicts between Israel and her immediate neighbors (Syria, Jordan, Lebanon, and the Palestinians), with the other Arabs, increasingly preoccupied by other conflicts (the Iran-Iraq war since September 1980 and the Morocco-Polisario conflict in North Africa since the late 1970s), essentially looking on. The problem for Moscow has been that two of Israel's neighbors, Syria and the Palestinians, have been in almost constant conflict with each other, while another, Jordan, has both flirted with the possibility of peace with Israel and engaged in an on-again, off-again confrontation with Syria. Under the circumstances it has been almost impossible for Soviet leaders to orchestrate a single policy acceptable to Jordan, Syria and the Palestinians at any one time. In addition, Moscow has run the serious risk of armed conflict with Israel, or the United States, or both, because of the actions of its primary Arab ally, Syria, which has shown no hesitation in exploiting Soviet support in pursuit of Syria's objectives whether or not they coincide with those of the Soviet Union.

Indeed, possibly because its policy toward the Arab-Israeli conflict has not met with a great deal of success in recent years, the USSR, under Gorbachev, has begun an open flirtation with Israel in an effort to get it to agree to Moscow's participation in an international conference on the Middle East that would enable the USSR to play a major role in the peace process. It remains to be seen, however, whether given American hostility and Israeli suspicion (albeit a suspicion laced with the hope of getting Moscow to agree to allow more Soviet Jews to leave the USSR), the new Soviet policy will be any more successful than past Soviet policy.

Notes

1. For recent studies of Soviet policy in the Middle East, see Robert O. Freedman, *Soviet Policy Toward the Middle East Since 1970*, third edition (New York: Praeger, 1982); Jon D. Glassman, *Arms for the Arabs: The Soviet Union and War in the Middle East* (Baltimore: Johns Hopkins, 1975); Galia Golan, *Yom Kippur and After: The Soviet Union and the Middle East Crisis* (London: Cambridge University Press, 1977); Yaacov Ro'i, *From Encroachment to Involvement: A Documentary Study of Soviet Policy in the Middle East* (Jerusalem: Israel Universities Press, 1974); and Adeed Dawisha and Karen Dawisha (eds.), *The Soviet Union in the Middle East: Policies and Perspectives* (New York: Holmes & Meier, 1982). See also Yaacov Ro'i (ed.), *The Limits to Power* (London: Croom Helm, 1979), and Efraim Karsh, *The Cautious Bear: Soviet Military Engagement in Middle East Wars in the Post-1967 Era* (Boulder, Colorado: Westview Press, 1985). For an Arab viewpoint, see Mohamed Heikal, *The Sphinx and the Commissar* (New York: Harper and Row, 1978). For a Soviet view, see E.M. Primakov, *Anatomiia Blizhnevostochnogo Konflikta* (Moscow: Mysl', 1978).

2. For studies of Soviet military aid, see Glassman, *Arms for the Arabs,* and George Lenczowski, *Soviet Advances in the Middle East* (Washington: American Enterprise Institute, 1972). See also Amnon Sella, *Soviet Political and Military Conduct in the Middle East* (New York: St. Martin's, 1981); Bruce D. Porter, *The USSR in Third World Conflicts* (New York: Cambridge, 1984); and Efraim Karsh, *Soviet Arms Transfers to the Middle East in the 1970s* (Tel Aviv: Tel Aviv University Jaffee Center for Strategic Studies Paper No. 22, 1983).

3. See Richard H. Shultz and Roy Godson, *Dezinformatsia: Active Measures in Soviet Strategy* (New York: Pergamon-Brassey's, 1984).

4. For a discussion of the 1986 crisis, see Mark N. Katz, "Civil Conflict in South Yemen," *Middle East Review* Vol. 19, no. 1 (Fall 1986) pp. 7–13.

5. For a view of the role of Israel in Soviet Middle East strategy, see Freedman, *Soviet Policy,* chapter 8.

6. For studies of Soviet policy toward the Communist parties of the Arab world, see Robert O. Freedman, "The Soviet Union and the Communist Parties of the Arab World: An Uncertain Relationship," in Roger E. Kanet and Donna Bahry (eds.), *Soviet Economic and Political Relations with the Developing World* (New York: Praeger, 1975), pp. 100–134; John K. Cooley, "The Shifting Sands of Arab Communism," *Problems of Communism,* Vol. 24, no. 2, 1975, pp. 22–42; and Arnold Huttinger, "Arab Communism at a Low Ebb," *Problems of Communism,* Vol. 30, no. 4 1981, pp. 17–32.

7. For analyses of the diplomatic and military aspects of the War of Attrition, see Lawrence L. Whetten, *The Canal War* (Cambridge: MIT Press, 1974) and Alvin Z. Rubinstein, *Red Star on the Nile: The Soviet-Egyptian Influence Relationship Since the June War* (Princeton: Princeton University Press, 1977).

8. For an analysis of the ceasefire violation, see Robert O. Freedman, "Detente and Soviet-American Relations in the Middle East During the Nixon Years" in *Dimensions of Detente,* ed. *Della Sheldon* (New York: Praeger, 1978), pp. 89–92. See also Mohammed Heikal, *The Road to Ramadan* (New York: Ballantine Books, 1975), pp. 89–94.

9. Freedman, "Detente and Soviet-American Relations," pp. 92–101.

10. For an analysis of the Soviet exodus from Egypt, see Galia Golan, *Yom Kippur and After,* pp. 23–26.

11. Ibid., chapter 3.

12. Cf. Freedman, "Detente and Soviet-American Relations," pp. 101–109.

13. For a thorough analysis of Soviet policy during the Yom Kippur War, see Galia Golan, *Yom Kippur and After.*

14. For accounts of Kissinger's efforts, see William B. Quandt, *Decade of Decisions: American Policy Toward the Arab-Israeli Conflict 1967–1976* (Los Angeles: University of California Press, 1977), chapter 7; Matti Golan, *The Secret Conversations of Henry Kissinger* (New York: Bantam Books, 1976); and Edward R.F. Sheehan, *The Arabs, Israelis and Kissinger* (New York: Reader's Digest Press, 1976).

15. Cf. Matti Golan, *Secret Conversations,* pp. 137–142.

16. For an account of Soviet aid to Syria during this period, see Freedman, *Soviet Policy,* pp. 163–167.

17. Ibid., pp. 198–203. For a discussion of many such Soviet signals to Israel, see Yaacov Ro'i, "The Soviet Attitude to the Existence of Israel,"ed. Yaacov Ro'i *The Limits to Power,* (London: Croom Helm, 1979), pp. 232–253.

18. For an analysis of Soviet policy toward the PLO, see Galia Golan, *The Soviet Union and the Palestine Liberation Organization* (New York: Praeger, 1980).

19. For an analysis of the evolution of Soviet peace efforts up until this point, see Robert O. Freedman, "The Soviet Conception of a Middle East Peace Settlement," in Ro'i, ed., *The Limits to Power*, pp. 282–327.

20. For a discussion of Soviet policy during the civil war in Lebanon, see Freedman, *Soviet Policy*, chapter 7.

21. Ibid., pp. 271–273.

22. For a discussion of the events leading up to the October 1, 1977 joint statement, and for an evaluation of it, see Freedman, *Soviet Policy*, pp. 307–311.

23. The Soviet foreign policy weekly, *New Times*, asserted in an editorial in 1977: "It is no secret that by 'real peace' the Tel Aviv expansionists mean the notorious 'open borders' between Israel and its Arab neighbors, the 'free movement of peoples and goods' and even 'cooperation in respect of security'—all of which would make Tel Aviv the center of a huge neo-colonialist 'empire' in the Middle East." (*New Times* no. 36, 1977, p. 1).

24. For very competent studies of the invasion, see Henry S. Bradsher, *Afghanistan and the Soviet Union* (Durham: Duke University Press, 1983) and Thomas T. Hammond, *Red Flag over Afghanistan* (Boulder, Colorado: Westview Press, 1984).

25. The Steadfastness Front, which initially included Iraq, had come into existence in response to Sadat's visit to Jerusalem in 1977.

26. The origins of the war are discussed in Stephen R. Grumman, *The Iran-Iraq War*, Washington Paper No. 92 (New York: Praeger, 1982).

27. For the text of Brezhnev's statement, see Freedman, *Soviet Policy*, p. 398.

28. Ibid., pp. 403–405 for a discussion of Soviet policy toward Kuwait and Jordan in 1971.

29. For a detailed discussion of the Soviet reaction to the Israeli invasion, see Robert O. Freedman, "The Soviet Union and the Middle East," *Middle East Contemporary Survey 1981–82* (ed. Colin Legum, Haim Shaked and Daniel Dishon) (New York: Holmes and Meier, 1984), pp. 40–49.

30. The Reagan Plan is discussed in Barry Rubin, "The United States and the Middle East," in *Middle East Contemporary Survey 1981–82*, ibid., pp. 30–33.

31. Cf. *Izvestia*, September 10, 1982.

32. For the text of the Fez Plan, see *The Middle East Journal*, Vol. 37 no. 1 (Winter 1983), p.71.

33. *Pravda*, September 16, 1982.

34. Cited in report by Loren Jenkins, *Washington Post*, November 13, 1982.

35. *Pravda*, January 13, 1983.

36. Cited in report by Thomas L. Friedman, *New York Times*, February 23, 1983.

37. Moscow's quandary in dealing with the Assad-Arafat conflict is discussed in Robert O. Freedman, "The Soviet Union, Syria and the Crisis in Lebanon: A Preliminary Analysis," *The Middle East Annual—1983* (ed. David H. Partington) (Boston: G.K. Hall, 1984), pp. 103–157.

38. Ibid., for a discussion in detail of these incidents.

39. Ibid.

40. See reports by E.J. Dionne, *New York Times*, February 12, 1984; David Hoffman, *Washington Post*, February 12, 1984; and David Hoffman, *Washington Post*, February 15, 1984.

41. Tass, January 20, 1984 (*Foreign Broadcast Information Service Daily Report: Soviet Union* [hereafter FBIS:USSR], January 23, 1984, p. H-5).

42. Moscow T.V. service, February 8, 1984 (*FBIS:USSR*, February 9, 1984, p. H-6).

43. Cited in *FBIS:ME*, April 2, 1984, p. ii.

44. Numerous Jordanian delegations visited Moscow and many Soviet delegations visited Jordan, and the Soviet press was full of praise for Jordan's "independent" position.

45. For text of the peace plan, see *Pravda*, July 30, 1984. An English translation may be found in *Current Digest of the Soviet Press*, Vol. 36 no. 30, 1984, pp. 9–10.

46. *Jerusalem Post*, November 20, 1984.

47. Cf. *Pravda*, February 20, 1985 and Tass report, in English, February 27, 1985 (*FBIS:USSR*, February 28, 1985, p. H-1).

48. Cf. Reagan press conference, *Washington Post*, February 22, 1985.

49. Cited in an article by Henry Trewitt, *Baltimore Sun*, February 20, 1985.

50. Cited in report by Bernard Gwertzman, *New York Times*, February 22, 1985.

51. For an excellent survey of Soviet-Israeli relations, see Arthur J. Klinghoffer, *Israel and the Soviet Union: Alienation or Reconciliation* (Boulder, Colorado: Westview Press, 1985).

52. This is particularly true on the issue of Soviet Jewry. On this point, see Freedman, "Soviet Jewry and Soviet-American Relations" in *Soviet Jewry in the Decisive Decade 1971–1980* (ed. Robert O. Freedman) (Durham, North Carolina: Duke University Press, 1984).

53. Jerusalem Domestic Service, in Hebrew, July 19, 1985 (*FBIS:USSR*, July 19, 1985, pp. H-1, H-2).

54. Cf. comments by the Soviet charge d'affairs in Kuwait, Vladimir Zentchner, as reported in KUNA, July 23, 1985 (*FBIS:USSR*, July 26, 1985, p. H-1) and comments by Leonid Zamyatin, head of the International Information Department of the Communist Party Central Committee, as reported in KUNA, July 27, 1985 (*FBIS:USSR*, July 29, 1985, p. H-1).

55. Cf. *Novosti* report, cited in *New York Times*, August 7, 1985. See also Moscow Radio Peace and Progress, in Hebrew, July 22, 1985 (*FBIS:USSR*, July 23, 1985, p. H-3).

56. For a background analysis of this developmment, see the report by Thomas Friedman, *New York Times*, October 18, 1985. (A preliminary version of the agreement was broadcast over Israel radio on October 5, 1985.) Of course, Poland, which also wished to influence U.S. Jewish opinion, had its own reasons for making this move, but it could not have done so without Moscow's approval.

57. Cited in *Jerusalem Post*, October 6, 1985.

58. Cf. reports by Michael Eilan and Joshua Brilliant, *Jerusalem Post*, October 31, 1985 and Judith Miller, *New York Times*, October 26, 1985. The rumor was renewed after a December 1985 Bronfman visit to the Soviet capital (see the reports in the *Washington Post*, December 23 and 24, 1985).

59. For a background analysis of the rise in terrorism, see the report by Thomas L. Friedman, *New York Times*, October 3, 1985. A major seaborne attack on Israel in late April, authorized by Arafat's deputy Khalil Wazir (Abu Jihad) was prevented when the Israeli Navy sank the PLO ship carrying the terrorists. (See reports by G. Jefferson Price, *Baltimore Sun*, April 23, 1985 and Reuters, *Jerusalem Post*, May 10, 1985).

60. Moscow International Service in Arabic, October 2, 1985 (*FBIS:USSR*, October 4, 1985, p. H-3). The disinformation was at least partially successful as Arafat was quoted as claiming that the United States helped the Israelis refuel. (Cf. report by Jonathan C. Randal, *Washington Post*, October 3, 1985). Arafat also claimed the United States was out to kill him.

61. Cf. report by David Hirst, *Manchester Guardian Weekly*, November 3, 1985.

62. Cited in report by Asher Wallfish, *Jerusalem Post*, November 19, 1985.

63. Report in *Jerusalem Post*, December 4,, 1985. The head of the Soviet delegation to the Israeli Communist Party Conference, Mikhail Menashev, however, said Herzog's attendance at the convention would not influence Russia's policy on the exit of Soviet Jews or hasten the renewal of diplomatic ties. (Cited in *Jerusalem Post*, December 8, 1985).

64. For the Soviet view of the talks, see the Tass report, in English, August 19, 1986 (*FBIS:USSR*, August 20, 1986, p. CC-1). For the Israeli view, see Helsinki Domestic Service, in Finnish, August 18, 1986 (*FBIS:ME*, August 19, 1986, p. I-1) and Tel Aviv, IDF Radio in Hebrew, August 18, 1986 (*FBIS:ME*, August 19 1986, pp. I-1, I-2).

65. See the report by Bernard Gwertzman, *New York Times*, September 23, 1986.

66. For a detailed description of these events, see Robert O. Freedman, "Soviet Policy Toward Israel in the First Two Years of the Gorbachev Era," *Soviet Jewish Affairs*, forthcoming.

18

The Soviet Union and
the Arab States Since 1967

Yahia H. Zoubir

There seems to be a consensus among scholars that in the last fifteen years or so Soviet policy in the Middle East has been quite unsuccessful.[1] It is argued that despite a persistent Soviet offensive, Moscow has been unable to extend its influence in the region.[2] While these observations contain some truth, they fail to highlight not only some important Soviet successes, but also the potential gains Moscow could achieve in the near future.

Moreover, this consensus does not give much weight to the dialectical relationship which exists between long-term Soviet objectives and internal developments and contradictions existing in the Arab states. If viewed in a zero-sum perspective, while it may be argued that the Soviet Union has not made major gains, a reply can be safely made that the other contending superpower, the United States, has not fared much better. In fact, it may be argued that U.S. influence in the region is declining even faster and that U.S. policy failures have opened tremendous opportunities for Moscow to exploit.

The contention in this paper is that Moscow, despite the losses it has experienced in the Middle East over the past fifteen years, has greater objective possibilities of success in the region than has been argued by many analysts of the Soviet Union. It can be said at the outset that potential Soviet gains are the result of several factors: 1) Total U.S. alignment with Israel; 2) Consistent pro-Arab positions on Moscow's part regarding the Palestinian question and other issues; 3) Arab perceptions of the respective role of the two superpowers in the region; 4) Fluidity of political realities in the Middle East; and 5) Soviet flexibility and consistency in adjusting to new situations.

The analysis in this paper will extend to a part of the Arab world which has often been neglected, namely the Maghreb, i.e., Algeria, Tunisia, and Morocco. The purpose is twofold: first, to show that the Arab-Israeli conflict is not limited to the immediate zone of hostilities but extends beyond that region; and second, to demonstrate that the Soviet policymakers are aware of the bonds that link the Maghreb (Morocco, Algeria, Tunisia) to the Mashreq (Libya eastward). The Soviets understood this reality during the June 1967 war.

The June 1967 War

The so-called Six Day war was a watershed in the history of the Middle Eastern peoples and the relationship of the states in the region with the superpowers. Among the major long-term results of the war was a definitive U.S. alignment with Israel on the one hand, and firm, although qualified, Soviet support for the Arabs on the other. In addition, and this is a point never raised in scholarly discussions, the war brought the Maghreb and the Mashreq much closer together. The conflict altered the relationship between Maghrebi and Mashreqi states (e.g., reconciliation between Egypt and Tunisia), and between the Maghrebi states and the superpowers.

The June war had traumatic effects on the Maghrebi people, governments, and political parties. In Algeria, in particular, where the regime's position converged with that of the masses, the Arab-Israeli conflict was taken as a personal affair. It should be remembered that in 1956 France intervened in Egypt to punish Nasser for the support he gave to the Algerian movement of liberation. Now that they had attained independence, the Algerians wanted to show their gratitude and to make sacrifices as needed. Algerians expected that Moscow undoubtedly would side with and give total support to the Arabs in their "anti-imperialist" struggle until final victory. Moreover, there was a genuine fear that Algeria itself was the next target of "U.S. imperialism and Zionism."[3]

The defeat of the Arab armies shocked the Maghrebis. They felt that the war, in addition to its imperialist character (American and British forces were believed to have participated in the combat against the Arabs) was also a Judeo-Christian conspiracy against the Muslims. The Algerian government and masses alike were reminded of their own colonial experience.[4] The domestic implications of this perception are obvious and partly explain the increasing appeal of Islamic fundamentalist ideas.[5] More importantly, this also has bearing on Maghrebi perceptions of the Soviet Union. The latter's great support for the Palestinians became and remains the determining factor in the Maghrebis' attitude vis-à-vis the Soviets. In other words, the Kremlin's identification with the Palestinian cause cannot but be viewed positively in the region.

While Soviet prestige was not necessarily enhanced during or immediately after the war, the wave of anti-Americanism[6] throughout the Maghreb was a clear indication that the Soviets were certainly not the losers. In fact, even pro-Western monarch King Hassan II of Morocco thanked the Soviets for the support they gave the Arabs and for warning Israel to stop its expansionist moves.[7] In Algeria, however, there was great disappointment with Moscow. Algerians accused the Soviets of having sacrificed their Arab friends for the sake of peaceful coexistence with the United States. The semi-official newspaper bluntly declared in its editorial that "if peaceful coexistence becomes the general and constant policy of the Socialist states, it will represent a fatal blow to their solidarity with Third World countries."[8] Anti-Soviet feelings grew in the country, as witnessed by the demonstrations that took place in Algiers on June 9.[9]

Like other Arabs, Maghrebis expected more military support from the Soviets during the war.[10] However, the rearming of the defeated Arab armies by Moscow helped the latter regain its position of influence in the Arab world and restore the prestige it had just lost.

In the war's aftermath, certain aspects of the new situation were clarified:

(1) The war had brought to light the role played by the Maghreb in the Arab-Israeli conflict. The result was an extension of the region in which Moscow could turn anti-American and anti-Western feelings to its own advantage.

(2) Although Soviet military support was questionable during the war, realism dictated to all Arab states that in the context of the Arab-Israeli conflict Moscow was and still is the most reliable ally. Despite their rhetoric, the Chinese are distant and lack the required capabilities to support the Arabs. The United States was and remains too closely aligned with Israel to play the role of a broker in the conflict.

(3) Algeria emerged as one of the most credible Arab countries. Even though the Soviets were not quite ready to drop President Nasser[11] following Egypt's embarrassing defeat, developments in the Middle East made Algeria's position one to be always reckoned with by the U.S.S.R. Algeria's prestige, resulting from its war of liberation and its consistently radical and anti-imperialist positions, made the country an ideal partner of the Soviets. Algerian President Boumedienne's trip on June 12, 1967 as the emissary of the Arab countries, is a clear indication of this fact.

(4) The war radicalized the Palestinian movement, with which the Soviets now expressed greater solidarity and to which they provided more support.[12] Algeria's unconditional and consistent support for the PLO and Moscow's desire to see a unified Palestinian movement brought Algiers and Moscow closer together in coordinating their efforts to solidify a movement which most Arab states have attempted to divide and control.[13]

(5) More importantly, Arab and Soviet positions began to be measured by their respective determination on the Palestine question. Moscow's progressive and consistent support for what it considers legitimate Arab claims has helped the Soviets maintain their image as friends of the Arab peoples. Moscow has capitalized on that support to guarantee its presence in the Arab world, and it has understood that despite their usual disunity the Arab states would unite on the fundamental issue: Palestine and opposition to Zionism.

Additionally, the June war revealed an important aspect of Soviet policy in the Middle East. In spite of their support for the Arab states, the Soviets were not then, and are not now, willing to jeopardize detente with the

West or to adopt postures which might result in a direct, possibly nuclear, confrontation with the United States. Thus, it has become clear since 1967 that Moscow prefers a negotiated settlement to the Arab-Israeli conflict.[14] The Soviet task has been not only to reconcile the necessity of achieving these objectives while backing Arab claims, but also simultaneously to support the existence of Israel, which it has asked its Arab allies to recognize. All this suggests that the Soviet Union is interested in a peaceful settlement of the Arab-Israeli dispute.[15] However, the Soviets have made it plain that no settlement can be achieved without their participation.

The 1973 Ramadan war highlighted the dilemmas of Soviet policy in the Middle East. Moscow's support for the Arabs during the war—which it had unsuccessfully attempted to prevent[16]—revealed definite limitations. While the Arab armies' performance was considerably better than during the previous war, the Soviets refused to jeopardize detente with the United States by taking steps which could have led to a direct confrontation, although Moscow did not question the Arabs' right to liberate the Israeli-occupied territories.[17] From an Arab perspective, this was obviously not enough. While the letter sent by Brezhnev to Algerian President Boumedienne on October 8 asking Arabs to give their full support to Cairo and Damascus and urging them to unite was endorsed by most Arab states, it also created the impression that Moscow had partially abandoned its commitment to the Arabs.

Whatever the Arab perception and the limitations of Soviet support, however, the Arabs would certainly have faced another humiliating defeat without Moscow's political support and airlift—which, it is true, was prompted by Boumedienne's cash payments for arms on behalf of Syria and Egypt.[18] Soviet backing for the Arabs was minimal only when compared with the huge U.S. support for Israel. The Arabs no doubt understood that the United States was much more committed to the Jewish state than the Soviet Union was to the Arab states—creating the illusion for some Arab leaders that they could turn to the West, meaning the United States, to find a solution to the Arab-Israeli conflict. Sadat's alignment with the United States resulted from his conviction that the latter could exert influence on and wrest concessions from Israel.[19] This might have looked like a realistic assessment of the situation following Dr. Kissinger's initiatives after the Ramadan War. Unfortunately, the tremendous influence exerted by Israel and its friends and supporters in the United States over America's Middle Eastern policy made any balanced, long-lasting settlement of the Arab-Israeli conflict difficult.[20]

Unquestionably, in the 1970s, or at least until the Camp David Accords, Soviet influence in the Arab world seemed to have declined. The lifting of the Arab oil embargo, the partial Israeli withdrawal from the Sinai and from the Golan Heights (arranged by Dr. Kissinger), as well as Egypt's alignment with the United States all seemed to corroborate such an analysis. And yet, the Soviets did not appear to be embittered by these events.[21] While their attention had shifted toward another region where they could extend their influence, namely Africa, their policy in the Middle East concentrated on the most critical issue in the region, the Palestinian problem. This problem, which is the *only* rallying point of the Arab states, is also what guarantees Soviet influence in the Arab world.

The Soviets and the Palestinian Question

In order to ensure a permanent presence in the region, the Soviets have acted on two fronts: 1) formulation of peace proposals—acceptable to moderates as well as to radical states—to solve the Palestinian issue within the framework of an international peace conference; 2) improving relations with moderate Arab states in order to obtain support for Soviet initiatives, while also attempting to reduce these states' alignment with Washington. At the same time, Moscow has consistently called upon all Arabs to unite in order to put pressure on the United States and Israel to come to an agreement.

Until 1973, the Soviet position on the Arab-Israeli conflict was based on UN Resolution 242, which contains three major principles for peace: Israeli withdrawal from Arab territories occupied in June 1967; the right to all states to live peacefully within the recognized borders, including Israel; and "a just settlement of the refugee problem." This resolution, which was accepted by Egypt and Jordan, was rejected by many Arab states and the PLO because it did not acknowledge the legitimate rights of the Palestinians.[22] The Soviets, whose ties with the PLO were not very close before the Ramadan war, added a new element to their proposal which brought them closer to the PLO, namely, the creation of a Palestinian state. Although the PLO's and Moscow's conceptions of such a state diverged, the Palestinian leadership has come to accept the Soviet idea of a Palestinian state on the West Bank and Gaza rather than the previous Palestinian demand for a democratic state in historic Palestine.[23] Despite the differences that still exist between the Soviets and the PLO on tactics and objectives, Moscow endorsed the PLO as the sole legitimate representative of the Palestinian people in 1978, thereby accepting its participation in the peace process. Whatever the reasons that have motivated the Soviets,[24] their position has allowed them to maintain not only a consistent policy, but one accepted by all Arabs.

Support for the legitimate rights of the Palestinians has also helped the Soviets improve their image as the true friends of the Arab nations against its enemies, "Zionism and U.S. imperialism." The tactical importance of such a position should not be underestimated. In spite of its continued public support for the existence of the state of Israel, Moscow has succeeded in maintaining its image as a state opposed to Zionism. The United States' opposition to the PLO and its antagonism to Palestinian nationalism has been beneficial to Moscow. There is enough evidence to argue that the Soviets are quite aware of this fact and that they are convinced that caution and patience will pay off. All they have to do is to "wait for U.S. policies to fail,"[25] and there are good reasons to believe that U.S. policies will fail. Unlike the United States, which categorically refuses to deal with the PLO, Moscow, despite the absence of diplomatic relations with Israel, talks to both Israel and the PLO.

Camp David and After

The early Carter administration correctly understood that cooperation with the Soviet Union was necessary in order to produce a comprehensive settlement of the Arab-Israeli conflict. The Soviet response to such an American approach was positive and surprisingly moderate. Hence the October 1, 1977 U.S.-Soviet Communiqué, which constituted an excellent basis for a peace process:

> The United States and the Soviet Union believe that, within the framework of a comprehensive settlement of the Middle East problems, all specific questions of the settlement should be resolved, including such key issues as withdrawal of Israeli Armed Forces from territories occupied in the 1967 conflict; the resolution of the Palestinian question, including insuring the legitimate rights of the Palestinian people; termination of the state of war and establishment of normal peaceful relations on the basis of mutual recognition of the principles of sovereignty, territorial integrity, and political independence.[26]

Opposition to such an approach, mainly from Israel, undermined this process.[27]

Sadat's trip to Jerusalem in November 1977 marked the beginning of new developments in the Middle East. His rapprochement with Washington and his trip to the holy city which Muslims the world over consider to be illegally occupied by Israel could not but meet with negative reactions in the Arab world. One of the results of the Camp David Accords of September 1978 and the Egyptian-Israeli peace treaty in 1979 was the creation—albeit a temporary one—of a united stance by nearly all Arab states against what was perceived as a Washington-Cairo-Tel Aviv axis.[28] The agreements contained and/or lacked elements which united radical and moderate Arab states and led them to a position very similar to Moscow's.

One of the outcomes of the Camp David initiative was the exclusion of the Soviet Union from any Middle East peace process—this was a logical result of Kissinger's diplomacy—and to divide the Arab world by attempting to isolate the radical states (Syria, Algeria, Libya, PDR Yemen, and the PLO). While the Camp David Accords might have been appealing to some Arab states (Morocco, Saudi Arabia, and Jordan), their acceptance by the leaders of those countries would have been suicidal because the accords failed to offer a solution to the major issue, the Palestinian question. The Soviets, who captured the essence of Arab objections to the accords, rejected them on more or less the same grounds. According to a Soviet Middle East specialist, the Camp David agreements must be rejected for the following reasons: 1) only the Sinai would be returned while the West Bank, Gaza, and the Golan Heights would remain under occupation. 2) The Egyptian-Israeli treaty makes no mention of the legitimate rights of the Palestinians to self-determination, including the establishment of an independent state, nor does the treaty recognize the PLO as the sole legitimate representative of the Palestinian people or the PLO's right to participate in peace negotiations. 3) Egypt's sovereignty over the Sinai will be limited even after the territory is returned because the treaty guarantees Israel's "military-strategic control" over it, thanks to the air bases in the Negev Desert. 4) Egypt is neutralized by the treaty, which will obviously diminish Arab power against Zionism and help divide Arab ranks. 5) Egypt becomes a proxy of the United States against progressive Arab regimes.[29]

This analysis was congruent with Arab objections to the Egyptian-Israeli treaty, but the Soviets did not succeed in creating an "anti-imperialist" front since the Arabs failed to agree on and unite around a common platform. Boumedienne's 1978 proposal for a "strategic alliance" between the Arab states and Moscow to counter the U.S.-Israeli-Egyptian axis found support only among the Palestinians. Even the Syrians, who were now reconciled with the PLO[30] and, for a brief period, with Iraq, limited their understanding of such a "strategic alliance" to the military area, one that did not apply to the political or multilateral fields.[31]

The internecine conflicts within the Arab world came as no surprise. Moreover, the Arabs could not even agree on the type of sanctions that should be applied to Egypt. But the hesitancy shown in the decision to impose sanctions on Egypt only reflected the deep respect that the Arabs have for Egypt and for its past sacrifices on behalf of the Arab nation. Undoubtedly, both the Arabs and the Soviets were convinced that Egypt would reintegrate into the Arab world.

Even if Soviet influence seemed to be at a low ebb, the U.S. peace initiative proved to be not only unsuccessful, but also alienating for the Arabs. The perception of a U.S./Israeli threat to divide them pushed some Arabs to seek rapprochement with Moscow to counter that threat. Clearly, even the most pro-Western Arab states were, and still are, suspicious of the United States' peace-keeping role.[32] The fact that the Saudis, Kuwaitis and other conservatives participated, along with the radical states, in the Baghdad Conference of Arab States, held in November 1978, to condemn Egypt was in itself a victory for Moscow. The latter developed a new tactic for dealing with the Arab-Israeli conflict. Since Moscow clearly understood that the Arabs could unite on only one issue, it decided to stake on that understanding to denounce and effectively obstruct any attempt to produce another Camp David. This, I think, has been Moscow's trump card in the Middle East. Any Arab leader who tries to reach a separate peace agreement—which would obviously exclude the Soviet Union—will not only be reminded of Sadat's fate, but also of what the United States and Israel do against the Arabs in Lebanon and elsewhere.[33] In fact, the United States' one-sided relationship with Israel has made it impossible for any Arab state to pursue such a path or to openly align itself with Washington.[34] Interestingly, even the most conservative Arab regimes are now seeking to improve their ties with the USSR in order to reduce their dependence on the U.S.

Soviet Policies in the 1980s

Undoubtedly, the main beneficiary of the Egyptian-Israeli peace treaty was Israel. Having neutralized its major contender in the Arab world Israel now had a free hand in the region. Moreover, the treaty led to the formalization of the strategic alliance between the United States and Israel. Following the fate of the Shah of Iran and the Soviet invasion of Afghanistan, the U.S. increased its economic and military aid to Israel. While Egypt also received military and economic assistance as a result of the treaty, its position has been one of dependence vis-à-vis the United States rather than of relatively equal partnership.

Viewing the Middle East in the context of East/West confrontation, the Reagan administration attributed to Israel the major role among the countries designated as part of the 'strategic consensus' aimed at 'containing Soviet communism' in the region. The result of this conception was the strength-ening of the Soviet presence in the Middle East rather than its containment or exclusion. The policy of a 'strategic consensus' was bound to fail, for how could one realistically conceive of an alliance in which Arab states would unite with Israel to fight the Soviet Union? In Arab eyes, the Soviet Union *is not* the enemy.

The loss of Egypt in the 1970s represented a severe blow to the Soviets. However, it did not end their presence or their interest in the Middle East. Soviet relations with Syria—a key actor in the Arab-Israeli conflict—improved dramatically. In October 1980, the two countries concluded a Treaty of Friendship and Cooperation. Syrian President Assad's fear of isolation, his country's greater exposure to Israel after Egypt's defection from the Arab camp, as well as growing tension with Iraq, and domestic unrest prompted him to sign the treaty.[35] Syria's support for Iran in its war against Iraq led to rapprochement between Iraq and Jordan and, subsequently, to tension between Jordan and Syria. Despite its close ties with Syria, however, Moscow sought to develop better relations with conservative states throughout the Arab world.[36] While it has consistently urged Arab unity and sought to establish a "progressive" front against the West, in the last decade Moscow has engaged in bilateralism, i.e., the cultivation of closer state-to-state ties with Arab regimes irrespective of their political and ideological inclination.

This policy has been developed to guarantee a Soviet presence in the region should Moscow's experience in Egypt and Iraq be repeated in Syria and elsewhere. In addition, the Soviets want to gain broad approval for their comprehensive peace proposals,[37] to reduce U.S. influence, and to establish economic and diplomatic relations with moderate Arab states.[38] In fact, despite the invasion of Afghanistan—which damaged the Soviet image in the Arab and Islamic world—relations with conservative regimes have improved.[39] Clearly, in addition to other reasons, such as Iranian threats, the Gulf countries' acceptance of the Soviet role in the region stems from Moscow's positive position on the Arab-Israeli conflict. The Israeli attack on the nuclear reactor in Iraq in 1981, the continual U.S. refusals to sell arms to moderate, pro-American Arab states, the disastrous U.S. involvement in Lebanon in the wake of the Israeli invasion, the U.S. raid on Libya, U.S. endorsement of the Israeli raid on Tunis, and secret U.S. arms sales to Iran, could only fuel anti-American feelings and strengthen the Soviet image as a friend rather than an enemy of the Arabs. The Soviets have skillfully exploited this perception by strongly denouncing U.S. and Israeli acts against the Arab states and by giving the latter support in international forums and in public statements.

Moreover, the Soviets have intensified their use of Islam to further their policy goals in the conservative states. Moscow's organizing of Islamic conferences on its territory[40] and the sending of Islamic delegations to countries such as Saudi Arabia, Egypt, Sudan, Morocco, Jordan, and Kuwait helps dispel the USSR's image as an atheist, untrustworthy state. In fact, progressively, the perception grows that the Soviet Union is a better partner than the West.[41] Whether the Soviets have the capabilities is another question.

In spite of a setback in Lebanon in 1982, Moscow was able to rebuild its credibility among the Arabs. During the Israeli invasion of Lebanon, the Soviets were criticized for not acting with more determination on behalf of the Arabs and for basically abandoning the PLO. Suffice it to say that the Soviets avoided any moves that would have escalated the conflict to a level which might have led to a direct confrontation between the superpowers. However, Moscow made it known that an attack on Syria would have grave consequences. Undoubtedly, this was enough to deter any Israeli or U.S./Israeli attack on Syrian territory. Moreover, in order to repair the damage to its prestige caused by accusations that the Syrian defeat against Israel in Lebanon was the result of poor quality weapons provided by the Soviets, the Kremlin decided to upgrade Syria's military arsenal.[42]

Two points should be made here. First, while it is true that the Soviets did not do much during the war in Lebanon, Arab apathy was even more embarrassing. Unless it had intervened directly in the conflict—which is inconceivable—there was not much Moscow could do. Secondly, and perhaps more importantly, Soviet inaction could be explained by

> a feeling in Moscow that in the long-run the Israeli invasion of Lebanon would become a major embarrassment for the U.S. . . . The Soviet leaders may have reasoned, let the Arabs see for themselves how little they could expect from the United States; sooner or later they would realize that while the Soviet Union might not be able to deliver them military victory, the United States was unable to bring them peace on minimally acceptable terms.[43]

This analysis does indeed capture the essence of Soviet expectations in the Middle East. Moreover, assuming that the Soviet Union no longer considers the Middle East as part of a zero-sum game,[44] the Arabs, whatever reservations they might have about the Soviets, have no alternative but to turn to Moscow. Consequently, Karen Dawisha's argument that "a loss for the United States is no longer an automatic gain for the Soviet Union"[45] is not valid because it does not take into account the long-term negative consequences of U.S. policy in the region.

The constant humiliation suffered by the conservative regimes (U.S. refusal to sell them sophisticated weapons, U.S.-Israeli strategic pact, etc.) cannot but produce a change in attitudes in those countries. Recent developments in the Middle East should be seen in this context. The more even-handed approach adopted by Kuwait, the UAE, Oman, and, lately, Egypt seems to corroborate this point. And so do Kuwait's and Jordan's decisions to buy weapons from the Soviet Union. The re-establishment of diplomatic relations between Cairo and Moscow and the latter's recent decision to supply spare parts for Soviet weapons which are still part of the Egyptian arsenal[46] also follows this evolution. Primakov's observation that "the countries of the Middle East, irrespective of their social and political setup, are interested in maintaining relations with the Soviet Union and do not want a one-sided orientation to the U.S."[47] seems, therefore, well-founded. While the loss of American credibility in the Middle East has become a reality, Gorbachev's rise to power has coincided with an era of Soviet opportunities in the region.

Soviet Prospects in the Middle East

Soviet opportunities in the Middle East have, undoubtedly, increased in the last few years. While the September 1, 1982 Reagan peace plan could have represented an important advantage for the United States over the Soviet Union in the region, Israel's rejection of the plan was a blessing for Moscow. In spite of the absence of reference to a Palestinian state (or to self-determination), Reagan's proposal looked attractive to the Arabs. Israeli leverage over the U.S. made it possible for the Soviets to draw up their own peace proposal (September 15, 1982 and updated in July 1984) which contained all the elements that would be applauded by the totality of Arab states: reconvening of the Geneva Conference, Israeli withdrawal from occupied territories, creation of a Palestinian state, etc. Except for a few details, the Soviet plan contained basically the same propositions as the ones presented in the Arab Fez/Fahd peace proposals.[48] For obvious reasons, the Soviet plan has more credibility, not only because it includes all the Arab and Palestinian desiderata but mainly because the U.S. refuses to (or cannot) go beyond the Camp David formula. Moreover, as indicated earlier, the U.S. has ruled out the idea of a Palestinian state and denies any role for the PLO in any negotiations process.[49]

In addition to its peace proposal, the Soviet Union has constantly put pressure on Syria to stop its efforts to divide the PLO and encourage factional fighting among the Palestinians. At the same time, Moscow has successfully prevented any Camp David type of agreement from being undertaken. The Kremlin's tactic has been to denounce any moves that may lead to such a result. Hence Soviet denunciation of the Hussein-Arafat Amman agreement because "it ignores such important demands as equal participation by the PLO in all stages of a Middle East settlement and the establishment of an independent Palestinian state."[50] King Hussein broke the agreement a year later—a victory for the U.S.S.R. since the rupture also ended U.S. efforts to work out a separate Israeli-Palestinian-Jordanian peace agreement.[51]

In the last few years, Soviet policy in the Middle East has been more aggressive. Soviet strategy has consisted in cultivating relations with all Arab states regardless of their ideological orientation. No longer do the Soviets seem to concentrate on one or two "progressive" countries. The "Sadat syndrome," i.e., the fear of being thrown out after having made substantial investments in a given country, has dominated Soviet thinking. The new Soviet policy has been quite successful. Most Arab states have endorsed the Soviet proposal for an international peace conference—which would allow them to play a role in the Middle East peace process from which they have been excluded since 1973.

Moscow is well aware, however, that obtaining Arab support for the conference is not sufficient. This is why overtures have been made toward Israel to re-establish diplomatic relations and to get Israeli endorsement for the conference. The Soviets seem convinced—probably correctly—that if Israel accepts, the United States will agree as well. Whether the Soviets will renew diplomatic relations with Israel without the latter making territorial concessions to the Arabs remains to be seen. What is certain, however, is that Moscow will avoid allowing a massive Jewish emigration from the Soviet Union. Such a move would obviously damage the Kremlin's relations with most Arab states.

One can safely argue that Soviet recent success in the Middle East stems mostly from a sound policy toward conservative regimes (support for Iraq in its war against Iran since 1982, protection of Kuwaiti ships in the Gulf, selling of arms to Jordan and Kuwait, etc.)[52] and radical states (helping to restore the unity of the Palestinian resistance, attempting to bring reconciliation between Iraq and Syria, Morocco and Algeria, etc).[53] However, Washington has offered Moscow golden opportunities. America's blind support for Israeli actions and positions has created adverse effects for U.S. interests in the region. For instance, President Reagan's reaction to the Israeli raid on the PLO headquarters in Tunis as "a legitimate response and an expression of self-defense"[54] not only offended pro-Western Tunisia and embarrassed its government, but it allowed the Soviets to demonstrate to Tunisians and to most Arabs who their real enemy is.[55] The U.S. attack on Libya on April 15, 1986 corroborated the Soviet accusation. In fact, the Israeli bombing of Tunis and the U.S. raid on Libya have already led to an improvement of relations between the traditionally anti-Communist Tunisia and the Soviet Union.[56] Algeria, a staunch nonaligned nation, has tilted a little more toward Moscow after the two raids on two Maghrebi states.

Conclusion

The Soviet Union is back in the Middle East. The predominant position the United States established for itself in the 1970s is quickly fading away. The Soviet Union has been able to establish fairly good ties with almost all Arab states. While it cannot offer the highest quality technology or weaponry, the Soviet Union represents a solid counterweight to and perhaps a shield against the United States. The close U.S. identification with Israel has seriously damaged the United States' credibility as a broker in the Arab-Israeli conflict. Any Arab state that identifies itself with the U.S. too closely will undermine its own position in the Arab nation.

The argument that Moscow has not succeeded in creating a puppet state in the Middle East is to the credit of the Arab states rather than a Soviet failure. In fact, this fact destroys the foundation of the argument that a U.S.-Israeli strategic pact is required to stop Soviet advances in the region; the effect would be the reverse.

The notion that the Soviet Union is a superpower in eclipse in the Middle East is more applicable to the United States. An Arab observer is probably right when he argues that:

> The American movement in the Middle East is ending. The pro-Western Arab countries have learned a lesson they will not soon forget: It is very dangerous to follow the late President Sadat's advice and put ninety-nine percent of your cards in Washington's hands. Washington may play them in the wrong game, or just fail to play them at all.[57]

The United States is correct to emphasize the fact that the Middle East is vital to its interests. However, viewing the Middle East simply as a strategic area without taking into account the grievances of the people that constitute it will inevitably have disastrous effects. Unconditional U.S. support for Israel at the expense of the Palestinians and the Arab States has alienated the people in the region and created more hatred toward America. The reawakening of Arab nationalism and the spread of Islamic fundamentalism are only two obvious results of U.S. and Israeli policies in the Middle East. The Soviets need only be patient to reap the fruits of America's mistakes. Only a more even-handed policy toward the Arab-Israeli conflict could help the United States strengthen its position in the Middle East.

Notes

1. See for example, Adeed Dawisha, "Soviet Policy in the Arab World: The Limits to Superpower Influence," Adeed Dawisha and Karen Dawisha, eds. *The Soviet Union in the Middle East: Policies and Perspectives* (New York: Holmes and Meier Publishers, 1982); Karen Dawisha, "The USSR in the Middle East: Superpower in Eclipse?" *Foreign Affairs* 61 (Winter 1982/83).

2. Robert O. Freedman, "Soviet Policy toward the Middle East Under Gorbachev," Paper presented to the Annual Conference of the International Studies Association, Washington, DC. April 17, 1987. p. 2.

3. *Le Monde,* June 27, 1967. President Houari Boumedienne stated that the Sixth Fleet was cruising in Algerian territorial waters and that after Egypt and Syria were totally defeated, Algeria would be attacked. *Le Monde,* June 21, 1967.

4. Richard Roughton, "Algeria and the June 1967 Arab-Israeli War," *Middle East Journal* 23 (Autumn, 1969): 437–38.

5. On this point, see Yvonne Haddad, "The Arab-Israeli Wars, Nasserism, and the Affirmation of the Islamic Identity," in *Islam and Development,* John Esposito, ed. (Syracuse, NY: Syracuse University Press, 1980), pp. 107ff.

6. *Le Monde,* June 7, 17, 28 1967. See also *L'Annuaire de l'Afrique du Nord* 1967 (Paris: Centre National de la Recherche Scientifique, 1969), pp. 340ff.

7. *Le Monde,* June 13, 1967.

8. *El Moudjahid,* June 12, 1967, cited in Nicole Grimaud, *La Politique Exterieure de l'Algerie* (Paris: Khartala, 1984), p. 126.

9. *Le Monde,* June 11–12, 1967.

10. Robert O. Freedman, *Soviet Policy Toward the Middle East Since 1970,* (New York: Praeger Publishers, 1982), pp. 29ff.

11. Henri Pierre, "Moscou cherche a renforcer la position du President Nasser," *Le Monde,* June 22, 1967.

12. Galia Golan, "The Soviet Union and the PLO since the War in Lebanon," *The Middle East Journal,* 40 (Spring 1986): 285.

13. The policy of the two countries was crowned with success at the last Palestinian National Congress (PNC) meeting held in Algiers in April 1987.

14. See Dimitri Simes, "The Soviet Approach to the Arab-Israeli Conflict," in Michael Hudson, ed. *Alternative Approaches to the Arab-Israeli Conflict: A Comparative Analysis of the Principal Actors,* (Washington, DC: CCAS, Georgetown University, 1984), p. 144.

15. The Soviets have consistently supported UN resolution 242; they also backed the 1970 cease-fire agreement despite Syrian and Iraqi opposition. See Freedman, op. cit., p. 41.

16. See Galia Golan, *Yom Kippur and After: The Soviet Union and the Middle East Crisis* (New York: Cambridge University Press, 1977), pp. 63ff. Again, the Soviets favored a political settlement of the problem. The reason might also be their doubts about Arab capabilities to fight even a limited war successfully. See Karen Dawisha, "Soviet Decision-Making in the Middle East: The 1973 October War and the 1980 Gulf War," *International Affairs* (London) 57 (Winter 1980/81): 48.

17. *Ibid.*

18. The figure given is $100 million for each country. Golan, p. 101.

19. This belief was strengthened by the fact that the USSR had no diplomatic relations with Israel (they were broken in June 1967), and that, consequently, Moscow had no access to or leverage over the Israelis.

20. See Cheryl A. Rubenberg. *Israel and the American National Interest: A Critical Examination,* (Chicago: University of Illinois Press, 1986), pp. 175ff.

21. Lawrence Whetten, "The Arab-Israeli Dispute: Great Power Behavior," in Gregory Treverton, ed. *Crisis Management and the Superpowers in the Middle East* (New Jersey: Allenheld, Osmu and Company, 1981), p. 85.

22. Fred Khouri, "Palestinian Issues and Options in the Current Middle East Political Context," in Philip Stoddard, ed. *The Middle East in the 1980's* (Washington, DC: The Middle East Institute, 1983), p. 131.

23. On this evolution of positions, see Golan, "The Soviet Union and the PLO," p. 286; Khouri, pp. 131ff.; Mohammed el Sayed Selim, "The Soviet Role: Conceptions, Constraints, and Prospects," in Michael Hudson, *Alternative Approaches*, op. cit., pp. 155ff. It is not certain, however, how serious the Soviets are about the creation of a Palestinian state. In the joint U.S.-Soviet Statement on October 1, 1977, for instance, the Soviets made no mention of such a state. Freedman, *Soviet Policy*, pp. 308-9.

24. Golan argues that they are not based on ideological considerations, but on global-regional ones and in order to counter the U.S.. "The Soviet Union and the PLO," p. 286.

25. John C. Campbell, "Soviet Strategy in the Middle East," *Arab-American Affairs* 8 (Spring 1984), p. 81.

26. Quoted in William B. Quandt, *Camp David: Peace Making and Politics* (Washington, D.C.: The Brookings Institution, 1986), pp. 122-3.

27. Rubenberg. *Israel and the American National Interest*, p. 255.

28. Robert D. Freedman, "Soviet Policy Toward the Middle East Since Camp David," in Robert D. Freedman, ed., *The Middle East Since Camp David* (Boulder, CO: Westview Press, 1984), p. 13. Only Oman, Somalia, and the Sudan supported Sadat's initiative.

29. Y. Primakov, "A Dead End Middle East Settlement," *International Affairs (Moscow)* 2 (1979): 42-44.

30. Syrian-PLO relations were damaged when Syria intervened in Lebanon on behalf of the Christian forces against the Palestinian resistance in 1976. The intervention also caused strains in Soviet-Syrian relations. For a good discussion, see Pedro Ramet, "The Soviet-Syrian Relationship," *Problems of Communism* 35 (September-October, 1986): 37ff.

31. This analysis draws heavily from Rashid Khalidi's excellent *Soviet Middle East Policy in the Wake of Camp David* (Beirut: Institute for Palestine Studies, 1979), pp. 22-24.

32. Rashid Khalidi, "Arab views of the Soviet Role in the Middle East," *Middle East Journal* 39 (Autumn, 1985): 726-7.

33. See, for example, V. Konstantinov, "A Middle East Settlement and its Opponents," *International Affairs (Moscow)* (January, 1986): 105-109; O. Fomin, "Trying to Revive the Camp David Deal," *New Times* 18 (May, 1985): 14-15.

34. Rubenberg, *Israel and the American Interest*, p. 6.

35. Ramet, p. 40; Freedman, "Soviet Policy Toward the Middle East," p. 23.

36. For instance, in March 1978, Morocco became the Soviet Union's largest trading partner in Africa. The relationship has not ceased to improve despite the monarchy's close ties with Washington.

37. Larry Napper, "The Arab Autumn of 1984: A Case Study of Soviet Middle East Diplomacy," *Middle East Journal* 39 (Autumn, 1985): 734.

38. Yevgeny Primakov, "The Soviet Union's Interests: Myths and Reality," *AEI Foreign Policy and Defence Review* 6 (1986): 29, 31.

39. For an excellent discussion, see Stephen Page, "The Soviet Union and the GCC States: A Search for Openings," *Arab-American Affairs* 2 (Spring, 1987).

40. Following the Soviet invasion of Afghanistan, however, Moscow experienced a serious setback in the Arab and Islamic countries. In September 1980, many Islamic countries such as Pakistan, Saudi Arabia, Jordan, Algeria, Iran, etc. responded to the call by the secretary-general of the World Muslim League to boycott the Islamic conference to be held in Tashkent. See Rasma Karklins, "The Nationality

Factor in Soviet Foreign Policy," Roget Kanet, ed., *Soviet Foreign Policy in the 1980s* (New York: Praeger Publishers, 1982), p. 70.

41. On Moscow's Islamic policy see Helene Carrere d'Encausse, *Decline of an Empire: The Soviet Socialist Republics in Revolt* (New York: Harper Colophon, 1981), pp. 278ff; Alexandre Bennigsen, "Soviet Muslims and the World of Islam," *Problems of Communism* 29 (March-April, 1980): 43ff.

42. For an extensive account, see Cynthia A. Roberts, "Soviet Arms-Transfer Policy and the Decision to Upgrade Syrian Air Defenses," *Survival* 25 (July-August, 1983).

43. Simes, "Soviet Approach," p. 149.

44. Dawisha, "The USSR in the Middle East . . ." p. 444.

45. *Ibid.*

46. *Foreign Bulletin Information Service, Middle East/Africa* (FBIS/MEA), April 20, 1987.

47. Primakov, p. 30.

48. Freedman, p. 45.

49. Rurenberg, p. 46.

50. Fomin, "Trying to Revive the Camp David Deal," p. 14. Note that the Soviets did not attack the agreement directly; instead, they used comments by "Arab national patriotic forces."

51. Freedman, "Soviet Policy Toward the Middle East Under Gorbachev," op. cit., p. 22.

52. *Middle East Economic Digest* (MEED), April 18, 1987.

53. *MEED*, May 2. 1987.

54. *Washington Post*, October 3, 1985.

55. On the Soviet commentary on the attack, see *FBIS/MEA*, October 4, 1985, p. Q2. The effect that the Israeli attack on Tunisia has had on the Maghrebi population—and the subsequent emergence of a strong fundamentalist wave and anti-U.S. feelings in the region—can hardly be overestimated. See my "Soviet Policy Toward the Maghreb," *Arab Studies Quarterly* Vol. 9, No. 4 (Autumn, 1987).

56. See the statement of the Tunisian president of the National Assembly in *FBIS/Soviet Union*, April 18, 1986, p. H2.

57. Ghassan Salame, "Moscow's Moment in the Mideast," *Washington Post*, June 21, 1987.

19

The Economic Factor in
Soviet Middle Eastern Policy

Walter G. Seabold

In his well-known address to the 24th CPSU Party Congress in 1971, Soviet Foreign Minister Andrei Gromyko served notice that the Soviet Union intended to play a role in any negotiations of major international significance or of importance to Soviet interests anywhere in the world. Despite this assertion, Soviet activity and policy in the Middle East since the 1967 Arab-Israeli War has not yielded results nor influence in the region or in the overall Arab-Israeli peace process commensurate with Soviet perceptions or projections of their own stature as a global superpower.

Along with ideological, military and diplomatic factors, several economic factors and conditions in the Soviet Union tended, over time, to isolate and exclude it from active participation in the Arab-Israeli peace process in the post-1967 period. The dramatic downturn in the Soviet economy at the beginning of the 1970s and the oil price shocks of 1974 and 1979 (with the Western recessions that followed) led Soviet policymakers to lean toward a more cautious, calculating costs-and-benefits mode, especially regarding aid and trade with non-communist less developed countries. In the Middle East, this caution led to an almost exclusive reliance on military sales and services to Arab clients as the vehicle for expanding Soviet influence and power projection in the region. With the military reversals among clients in 1967 and 1973, changing diplomatic fortunes in key countries with Soviet support, and partly as a consequence of an acknowledged consideration of detente with the United States in the 1970s, the Soviet Union became increasingly cut off from the more moderate elements working to forge a lasting Arab-Israeli peace. As a result, a combination of factors— the militarization of the conflict by the Soviet Union, risk-aversive behavior, and a lack of clearly defined or operationalized goals in the Middle East— prevented the Soviet Union from playing the role in the region it had (or has) envisioned for itself.

The emphasis that the Soviet Union has placed on military sales and arms transfers to the third world is well known. During the period between

TABLE 19.1 Deliveries of Major Weapons Systems to the Middle
           East and North Africa by the Soviet Union

Year	Total Deliveries to Third World (millions 1975 US$)	Share of OPEC and Syria in USSR Deliveries to Middle East (Percent)	Share of OPEC and Syria in USSR Deliveries to Third World (Percent)
1970	1,136	27	16
1971	1,515	33	19
1972	1,225	26	11
1973	1,537	52	42
1974	1,930	99	78
1975	2,160	76	66
1976	1,554	102	63
1977	2,156	100	39
1978	3,526	100	44
1979	4,565	89	62
1980	5,265	83	58
1981	2,785	95	69
1982	2,904	97	65
1983	2,372	93	50
1984	2,856	98	58
1985	2,651	99	52

Source: Adapted from R. Cutler, L. Despres, and A. Karp, "The
        Political Economy of East-South Military Transfers,"
        in International Studies Quarterly, vol. 31 (3), 1987,
        p. 276. Used by permission.

Greater than 100 percent due to Nigeria, an OPEC member not
in the Middle East or North Africa

1955 and 1978, the Soviets concluded nearly $32.9 billion worth of military
and security agreements with at least three dozen countries in the third
world. They trained nearly 50,000 foreign military personnel in the Soviet
Union or Eastern Europe, and by the late 1970s, the Warsaw Pact had well
over 12,000 military advisers and technicians based in third world countries.
Over the years, nearly seventy per cent of this aid was concentrated in the
Middle East.[1] Even prior to the mid-1950s, the Czechs, among others, were
used as intermediaries for arms sales to such diverse clients as the Israelis
in the late 1940s and to Guatemala in 1954.

Indeed the Soviet Union has taken good advantage of the fact that the
transfer of military weaponry and services has been an accepted foreign
policy transaction practically since the inception of the nation-state system.
By the late 1960s, the Soviet economy came into a position to accommodate
growing demands, from the third world especially, on Soviet defense industry
resources. The research, development, diffusion, and deployment of new
and sophisticated military technologies took place in all the key sectors of
Soviet weapons production. Substantial investments in capital equipment
and in qualified military staff and technicians insured a steady output of

TABLE 19.2   USSR and Eastern Europe: Military Technicians in
             the Middle East and North Africa, 1984

Total (All LDCs)	21,335
Algeria	790
Libya	2,800
Egypt	20
Iraq	1,300
North Yemen	510
South Yemen	1,100
Syria	5,300
Other	80

Source: U.S. Department of State, 1986, p. 20.

TABLE 19.3   USSR and Eastern Europe: Training of Military
             Personnel in Communist Countries, 1955-1984,
             Middle East and North Africa

Total (All LDCs)	78,445
Algeria	3,555
Libya	7,360
Morocco	145
Egypt	6,340
Iran	845
Iraq	8,140
Kuwait	170
Lebanon	15
North Yemen	4,130
South Yemen	1,485
Syria	8,115

Source: U.S. Department of State, 1986, p. 21.

military goods and services capable of meeting the new and increasing
demands. In terms of sheer quantity at least, the Soviet Union had achieved
by the end of the sixties a comparative advantage in military hardware and
economy vis-à-vis the West, especially the United States. The achievement
of strategic parity with the United States formed the basis for Soviet foreign
policy in regard to the United States as well as the rest of the world. The
Soviet Union had gained, at least in one crucial area, superpower status.

Meanwhile, the gap between arms sales and arms transfers and non-
military economic aid increased dramatically. Although economic aid and
trade comprised about half the amount of military assistance in the early
1970s, the proportion dropped to only thirty-five percent of military aid
by 1979. The Soviet Union has been increasingly relying on military and
security packages in its relations with the Third World, but pressures on
the Soviets to adjust their traditional policies to the changing world market
environment are not likely to abate as new arms suppliers enter the market
and buyers become more demanding.[2]

Before 1967, and indeed beginning around 1955, the Soviet Union had
demonstrated a clear, long-term commitment and interest in bringing about
a transition in the domestic policies of the countries of the Middle East.

TABLE 19.4   Middle East and North Africa: Economic Credits
             and Grants from the USSR (millions of U.S.
             dollars)

Total	15,080
1958--1970	3,015
1971--1979	8,200
1980	525
1981	160
1982	NEGL
1983	1,910
1984	1,270

Source: U.S. Department of State, 1986, p. 6.

The number one priority on the Soviet agenda seemed to be the utilization
of the external policies of the Arab regimes to aid and increase Soviet
influence and power in the area. While the Soviets furnished arms principally
to their political clients in the region, by the late 1960s arms purchases
from the USSR were a clear sign of the Arab opposition to both Israel
and the West. Arms transfers were becoming the primary vehicle for Soviet
power projection and influence in the region. Prior to the 1967 Six Day
War, the Soviets certainly acknowledged but were no great supporters of
Israel, and similarly the United States never greatly supported the radical,
"progressive" Arab regimes favored by the Soviets. Nonetheless, both
superpowers had better, more normal relations with both sides of the Arab-
Israeli conflict before the war than after it. The political consequence of
the unqualified Soviet military support for Syria and Egypt after the Six
Day War was the exclusive identification of the USSR with the Arab cause.
The polarization of the conflict in superpower confrontational terms was
additionally reinforced by the decrease in non-military economic aid in the
Middle East. It was in the aftermath of the Six Day War that the process
began whereby the Soviet Union aided in militarizing and globalizing the
conflict so that a multilateral web of complex and divisive relations developed
between the Soviet Union, the United States, the Arabs, and the Israelis.
This set of relationships has become so tangled and unamenable to superpower
influence in terms of productive peaceful solutions that neither side seems
able to keep from digging diplomatic holes from which it can barely escape.

As a result of the Six Day War, the Arab defeat, and the cutting of
relations with Israel, the Soviet Union found itself becoming primarily an
arms supplier to the Arab side. As a conveyor of arms, the Soviets found
themselves increasingly cut out of many of the more important, long term
aspects of Soviet interests in the region. They stopped being effective in
economic or cultural spheres, and their policy in the region declined steadily
into a complete shambles by 1976. The Soviets were not seen as an even-
handed authority in the Middle East, and they were not able to follow up
short-term gains in influence with deeper, lasting roots.

That the Soviet Union became the principal arms supplier to the Middle
East is not surprising when one considers that the Six Day War of 1967

took place during the greatest military buildup the Soviet Union had ever undertaken in peacetime. The Arab states were certainly beneficiaries of the expansion of Soviet defense capabilities. Soviet defense policy developed continuously throughout the 1960s, but it was "after 1965 [that] the Soviet military budget rose annually, reaching a figure of 17.9 billion rubles in 1969."[3] As a result of their growing capabilities in the armaments sectors of their economy, the Soviets were able to swiftly replace the vast Egyptian and Syrian losses of equipment, and to assure themselves a place in the policy plans of the Arab states.

Yet on the diplomatic front, between 1967 and 1973, the Soviet Union clearly preferred a political solution to the Arab-Israeli conflict and continued throughout the period to try to persuade the Arabs to take this path. Nonetheless, the Soviets were susceptible to the Egyptian lure as the showcase for their Middle East policy from 1967 through the 1969–1970 War of Attrition; Nasser obviously wanted and felt he needed a superpower shield to cover his own defenselessness. While the USSR was accommodating enough, its failure to supply enough armaments to allow Nasser to launch a full-scale attack on Israel led to the War of Attrition in the first place. When Sadat assumed the presidency, he continued to press the Soviets to make good the deficiencies.[4] The Soviets did not deliver on their assurances to supply defensive and tactical as well as strategic weapons in the quantities the Egyptians wanted and considered essential until February 1973. This situation and attitude prevailed on the Soviet side despite the mounting evidence of an impending crisis in Soviet relations with Egypt.

At least part of the reason for Soviet caution and prudence with regard to the Middle East situation in the 1967 to 1973 period can be attributed to the downturn in the Soviet economy at the end of the sixties and early seventies. The size of the resources committed to the defense sectors of the economy in the late 1960s contributed heavily to the overall Soviet economic dilemma and interfered with the realization of Soviet objectives to globalize their foreign policy, particularly in the third world. The Kosygin Economic Reforms of 1965 were modest in scope, limited in success, and in any case, were not fully implemented until 1973. The notorious ineffi- ciencies and waste of the Stalinist economic system came to a head at the end of the 1965–1970 Five Year Plan, when many key Soviet industrial and agricultural production sectors failed to achieve their planned target goals, even though the industrial output plan as a whole was fulfilled. The main factors contributing to the downturn can be noted as follows: 1) the growing technological gap between East and West; 2) the managerial gap that accompanied the technological shortfalls. These two factors served as obstacles to renewal and modernization of Soviet production and economic man- agement; 3) the inability of Soviet planners to change over to more qualitative as opposed to quantitative approaches to economic production and man- agement; 4) a declining reserve labor pool which could be concentrated in key economic sectors to improve production; 5) the Soviet consumer's increased demands for goods and services, demands that could no longer be ignored either by the Soviet planners or the leadership.[5]

The delicacy and sensitivity with which the Brezhnev leadership approached this economic crisis, coupled with the wish to avoid a military confrontation with the United States, and particularly from 1969 on to develop and preserve a basis for detente with the West, helped to form the Soviet policy of restraint in the Middle East between 1967 and 1973. They needed to keep as many options open as possible to try to insure their place in the Middle Eastern scheme of things. It is possible that the only economically sustainable relationship the Soviets were willing and/or able to support was the military one, and this relationship was pursued with caution so as not to adversely affect the growing detente with the United States prior to the Soviet achievement of strategic military parity or superiority with the United States. Those in the Soviet hierarchy (including Brezhnev himself, most likely) who viewed superpower cooperation in the Arab-Israeli conflict as an essential element of the detente process were obviously active and successful in promoting political solutions and policies to their Arab clients between 1967 and 1973.[6] This is not to say, however, that the more hardline elements of the Soviet elite were quiescent. With the Egyptians and the Syrians both pushing very hard for more active Soviet military participation in the region anyway, those in the Soviet hierarchy (especially the military) who viewed the Arab-Israeli conflict in antagonistic, confrontational, East-West terms continually pushed the leadership to take advantage of increased Soviet military capabilities to provide the weaponry and support for a decisive military projection of Soviet influence in the Middle East region, despite the faltering of the economy in general.

As a partial result of the growing detente with the West and the United States in particular, Soviet restraint with regard to competition with the West for influence in the third world lessened remarkably. Much of this had to do with the Soviet interpretation of detente, which considered this competition to be outside the realm of superpower relations; the latter, it was felt, were qualitatively different from each side's relations with the rest of the world.

Soviet military involvement with the third world escalated markedly in the 1970s, beginning with the 1973 Yom Kippur War. The Soviet Union came to rely more and more on military intervention to project Soviet influence in the third world than in the pre-1973 period.

> Pressure for a policy shift . . . became much more intense after the expulsion of Soviet advisers from Egypt in July 1972. . . . the expulsion had dealt a major blow to the USSR. It had deeply embarrassed and humiliated the Soviets, demonstrating to the entire world the fragility of the Soviet position in the Middle East.[7]

The Soviet expulsion from Egypt created a new set of circumstances that effectively prevented the maintenance of any sort of more moderate Soviet position with regard to the Arab-Israeli conflict; the new militancy of the Soviet position was equally at odds with the initial priorities and goals of Soviet third-world policy in general. The Soviet decision to militarize the Arab-Israeli conflict and to actively support the Arab use of force by supplying the needed weapons took place in February 1973. In an effort to deal with and address the needs of the Soviet economy, the Politburo instituted new terms of trade for armaments and military assistance. The Soviets unleashed the Arabs in 1973 "on the condition that the Arabs would no longer be given easy credits and allowed to pay in local goods and produce, but would be required to pay in cash for what they received. Such payments would provide the hard currency eagerly sought . . . to finance the purchase of western technology and consumer goods."[8] This reversal of policy led to a general escalation of the Soviet military role in third-world disputes during the 1970s and new, harsher terms of trade to help provide the wherewithal to ease the internal economic troubles as detente failed to live up to expectations. Soviet Middle Eastern policy shifted dramatically along with Soviet foreign policy generally, commensurate with the "downward revision in the Soviet assessment of risk of superpower confrontation in the third world, and the shift in the conventional and strategic military balance in favor of the USSR."[9]

In the aftermath of the 1973 Yom Kippur War, the Soviet Union's loss of influence was almost total by 1976. The war created an unpredictable and uncontrollable fluidity in the political relations of the Arab world. After the war, "Sadat's decision to pursue a 'political option' greatly lessened the significance and diplomatic weight of arms shipments into the region, undercutting the Soviet Union's main lever of influence over the Arabs."[10] The results were a blow also to detente with the United States and to Moscow's position in the Arab world generally, as Western leaders tended to accuse the Soviets of violating detente and many Arab leaders accused them of knuckling under to it. Soviet influence tended to become confined to the more militant Arab countries after 1973. "Libya, Syria and Iraq received large quantities of Soviet arms, and Soviet influence remained strong."[11] However, this identification only with militant Arab states and the lack of relations with Israel effectively cut the Soviets out of the developing Arab-Israeli peace process. Even though the Soviet Union was still considered a major actor in the Middle East, the consequences of the 1973 war represented a major regional foreign policy setback.

Following the 1973 war, Soviet policy and intentions in the Middle East took a back seat to other adventures in the third world, most notably in Africa, where the Soviet Union enjoyed considerable success in projecting itself into third-world areas where opportunities presented themselves to expand Soviet influence and presence at the expense of the West. Interestingly, it has been in the economic sphere that Soviet Middle Eastern policy has found a basis for revival. An indirect benefit to Soviet global interests was triggered by the Arab oil embargo of 1974 and the emergence of OPEC as a powerful economic cartel in the last half of the 1970s. The benefits to the Soviet Union have proven to be somewhat of a double-edged sword both in terms of again expanding Soviet influence in the Middle East and the concomitant need to revitalize the Soviet economy to support the new third-world policies.

Soviet satisfaction with the 1974 oil embargo and the quadrupling of oil prices that followed and which wreaked havoc on Western economies was an unexpected outcome of the 1973 Yom Kippur War. It seems to have formed the basis of the new Soviet approach to the Middle East after 1976, although the direction of that policy and approach has not been made clear even today. Certainly, in the 1970s, the strain placed on NATO and the EEC as a result of the new-found Arab oil power helped to ease the setbacks of the 1973 war as well as to raise Soviet expectations concerning their Middle East policy. The Soviets were able to amass large sums of hard currency by exporting their own oil at the higher world market prices. But the political cost of this development was detente with the United States as well as the inability of the Soviet Union and the Eastern Europeans to make economic headway and reforms under the provisions of detente.

Soviet energy production, which seems by most estimates to be satisfactory for the time being, has become subject to the same volatility that world energy markets have experienced over the last ten to twelve years. In the course of the 1970s, the Soviet Union was forced to reduce its oil exports to Eastern Europe. The production goals set for the end of the tenth Five Year Plan (1976–1981) were revised as costs escalated and the returns diminished. Outlays for fuel rose at a much greater rate than cost increases in the economy as a whole. Falling rates of production forced the Soviet Union to increase the intra-CMEA (Council for Mutual Economic Assistance) price of oil and to revise the terms of trade and subsidization policies.

> Given the huge increase in the world market price for oil, as well as large increases in the market prices, the Soviets pressed the CMEA into accepting a new price setting formula in 1975, [the] Bucharest formula. Until then the price of oil had been held constant during [Five Year Plans] based on the average of world market prices during the preceding five years. In 1975, the Soviet Union more than doubled the price of its oil exports to Eastern Europe.[12]

Soviet oil production and subsidies also fell in 1980–81 in response to the oil price shock in 1979, again in 1983, and the subsidies may soon disappear altogether.

While the Soviet Union possesses enough oil and gas to meet its own domestic needs and therefore does not seem to be in a position to use much Middle Eastern oil, they may have in mind to guarantee future supplies to Eastern Europe, as well as to interdict Western supplies when possible. The bulk of Soviet hard currency earnings have come from arms and oil sales, and two thirds of current Soviet oil exports go to communist countries. In Eastern Europe, price rises and lowering of subsidies have not stimulated Eastern European ability to successfully seek alternative primary energy sources. The scaling-down of economic ambitions in the late 1970s and early 1980s in the USSR and Eastern Europe has proved to be economically and politically disastrous as the need to save energy has been added to the list of economic priorities in the centrally planned economies. The need to conserve energy and the effectiveness of implementation of conservation measures in the Soviet Union and Eastern Europe depends on the rate of renewal of capital stock and the replacement of high cost energy plants with energy-efficient plants and machines. Under the Gorbachev administration, this has apparently been worked into Soviet economic planning (or has at least begun). The true consequences though will be paid most heavily by the other CMEA members, especially in Eastern Europe. The Soviets have undertaken to do no more than maintain oil supplies and are anxiously prodding Eastern Europe toward greater energy independence from the Soviet Union. At present, Eastern Europe does not have the financial power to accomplish this goal, and the Eastern European economies are paying dearly both for Soviet oil and for Soviet stringency in primary resources in terms of supply as well as in terms of trade.[13]

The Soviets appear to be seeking a new basis for relations in their Middle East policy. They appear most recently to be offering themselves as moderates in the region. Very little is heard about reformulating the bankrupt policy of militarization and radicalization of the Arab-Israeli conflict, the Palestinian issue, Lebanon, or even the Iran-Iraq War. "Soviet authorities [have] referred to the need for more even-handed access to Middle East oil supplies. They meant that they would like more of it to go in their direction, amongst others . . . they do not seem to be in a position to use much of it themselves, and it is a reasonable guess that they have in mind particularly to supply the Six."[14] Such a policy, if successful, would certainly ease the growing burden on the Soviet and CMEA economies, and would also partially fulfill the goal of competing effectively with the West in a crucial economic area. On the other hand, from the military point of view, the Soviets do not seem to have an ideal-typical policy of military versus economic cooperation in the Middle East. There is no indication that they will voluntarily adopt a policy of restraint in arms sales to the region, as indicated by their refusal thus far to participate in an international arms embargo against Iran in hopes of putting an end to the eight year old Iran-Iraq War. General economic factors at the very least would impel the Soviets to seek to export the maximum amount possible under current conditions, since the hard currency they receive for their arms continues to constitute a significant input into the Soviet foreign trade economy.

The Soviets appear to have recognized that if they are to again be a significant presence in the Middle East they will need to modify their views on the foreign economic policies of developing countries, as well as those of the centrally planned economies. The gap between ideological formulas and reality has grown dramatically since the early 1970s. "Unable to build an alternate system, the Soviets have been forced to concede the inescapable condition of global interdependence."[15] The Soviet Union has a vital interest in insuring that the Eastern European economies have a stable economic environment in which to trade in Middle East oil markets. With political developments as uncertain as ever in the Middle East, the Soviets cannot afford the economic dislocation another oil embargo might cause. "The predisposition to seek disengagement from risky ventures is likely to be reinforced by Gorbachev's goal of concentrating on economic reforms and performance at home."[16] It would seem that the Soviet Union is currently preparing the way for a significant reassertion of presence and influence in the Middle East, but this move is not based on ideological, revolutionary expectations, but rather on a moderate, even-handed, principled approach that recognizes economic interdependence and the changing nature of superpower influence in the third world.

Notes

1. U.S. Department of State, Bureau of Intelligence and Research, *Warsaw Pact Economic Aid to Non-Communist LDCs*, Publication 9345, May 1986. See also, Paul R. Gregory and Robert C. Stuart, *Soviet Economic Structure and Performance*, Third Edition, (New York: Harper & Row Publishers, Inc., 1986).

2. See Elizabeth K. Valkenier, *The Soviet Union and the Third World: An Economic Bind*, (New York: Praeger Publishers, 1985). sk. 2,3. Robin Edmonds, *Soviet Foreign Policy: The Brezhnev Years*, (New York: Oxford University Press, 1983), p. 40.

3. Jon D. Glassman, *Arms for the Arabs*, (Baltimore: The Johns Hopkins University Press, 1975), pp.108–110.

4. Edmonds, *Soviet Foreign Policy: The Brezhnev Years*, pp. 82–83.

5. Dina Rome Spechler, "The USSR and Third-World Conflicts: Domestic Debate and Soviet Policy in the Middle East, 1967–1973," *World Politics*, XXXVIII, Number 3, April 1986, pp. 445–452.

6. Spechler, Ibid., p. 453.

7. Spechler, Ibid., p. 454.

8. Spechler, Ibid., p. 458.

9. Bruce D. Porter, *The USSR in Third World Conflicts*, (New York: Cambridge University Press, 1984), p. 143.

10. Porter, Ibid., p. 144.

11. Christopher Coker, *The Soviet Union, Eastern Europe, and the New International Economic Order*, The Washington Papers, Vol. XXII, 111, (New York: Praeger Publishers, 1984), p. 24.

12. Anthony Stacpoole, "Energy as a Factor in Soviet Relations with the Middle East," in Adeed Dawisha and Karen Dawisha, eds., *The Soviet Union in the Middle East: Policies and Perspectives*, (New York: Holmes & Meier Publishers, Inc., 1982).

13. See Joint Economic Committee, U.S. Congress, *East European Economies: Slow Growth in the 1980's*, Vol. 1, Economic Performance and Policy, (Washington: USGPO, 1985), pp. 299–382, and Ed A. Hewett, *Energy, Economics and Foreign Policy in the Soviet Union*, (Washington: The Brookings Institution, 1984), esp. ch. 5.

14. Stacpoole, "Energy as a Factor in Soviet Relations with the Middle East," p. 97.

15. Elizabeth Kridl Valkenier, "Revolutionary Change in the Third World: Recent Soviet Assessments," *World Politics*, XXXVIII, Number 3, April 1986, p. 422. See also relevant discussion in Valkenier, *The Soviet Union and the Third World: An Economic Bind*, (fn. 2).

16. Valkenier, "Revolutionary Change in the Third World," p. 432.

PART THREE

The Peace Process

20

The "Peace Process" Twenty Years Later: Failure Without Alternative?

Johan Galtung

The "Peace Process": Failed from the Beginning

The basic point should be made clear from the very beginning: there is no "peace process" in the Middle East. There has never been any peace process, and there was probably no intention of having one.

In saying this I refer to the core conflict, in the core area, not to the subsidiary conflicts that may also exist in or over the core area. I take the core area to be mandated Palestine as it was created after World War I by the Treaty of Versailles, for the administration of the former overseas possessions of Germany and parts of the Turkish Empire. According to Article 22 of the Covenant of the League of Nations certain communities that had belonged to the Turkish Empire had made substantial advances toward "existence as independent nations." Examples were Palestine, Iraq, and Syria. The first two were to be administered by Great Britain and the third by France; mandates for Iraq and Syria were to end in 1932 and 1936 respectively, whereas the mandate for Palestine (roughly corresponding to pre-1967 Israel and Jordan today) was to serve for the establishment of a national home for the Jewish people in accordance with the Balfour Declaration of November 2, 1917. However, in accordance with Article 25 of the mandate, only the territory west of the River Jordan was designated as a national home for the Jewish people; Transjordan was severed from the territory already in 1922.[1] I perceive the core area to be mandated Palestine, both Israel and Transjordan.

The core conflict is between Jews and Arabs in this area, more particularly between Israelis and Palestinians, over the exercise of the type of territorial rights associated with national sovereignty. And in this core conflict I see no peace process. There is *no image of peace* even in the sense of something conceivably acceptable to both parties, *nor any peace process.* There was a process associated with the name Camp David, but that was a "peace process" imposed by Egypt and Israel (and the United States) on the Palestinians, with no Palestinians present. By that process the Palestinians were fragmented and their unity denied. The Accord mentions Palestinians living in the West Bank and Gaza, those displaced in 1967, and the refugees as three separate groups to be dealt with in three different manners; the Accord does not even mention those deported since 1967, those displaced in 1948 (and later), or the Palestinians inside Israel.[2] Moreover, the procedural rules given in the accord are of such a kind as to give Israel a *de facto* veto on all essential points in any future process. The 1973 defeat of Egypt was transformed into a form of collusion to further crush those lower down.

In other words, there is neither an image of peace nor any peace process, if for no other reason than the nonrecognition of the Palestine Liberation Organization (PLO). Instead of a peace process there has been a war process, with the concomitant of war: occupation of Palestinian territory, harassment and repression, censorship, control of all other kinds of political expression, ransacking, arrests, expulsion, Palestinians defending themselves through acts of destructiveness and terrorism, reprisals—in short, the full panoply of the evils of occupation as known, for instance, to a Norwegian like myself from the German occupation of Norway in 1940–1945. That occupation was relatively mild if one ignores its specific Nazi content, leading to the extermination of more than half of Norway's 1,800 Jews. On the other hand, there was no German plan to expel the Norwegian population into a neighboring country such as Sweden, reserving Norwegian territory for the Germans alone.

Then there are two subsidiary conflicts in the area between Israel and the Arab/Muslim states, and these involve everybody with the superpowers and the United Nations. For the conflict between Israel and the Arab/Muslim states there has been at least a scenario for a "peace process." The image of peace is traditional, which in itself is unobjectionable: inter-state relations regulated by international law in general and specific (peace) treaties in particular. There was also the idea of a process, "peace by pieces," dealing with one Arab/Muslim state at a time. Egypt was to serve as the model, turning the 1973 defeat into reconciliation, with Sadat's journey to Jerusalem in 1977 as paradigmatic. The process would end with a treaty (Camp David) as the model for all of them. Next in line were Jordan and Lebanon, providing a setting for the more recalcitrant Syria and Iraq to follow suit, and ultimately the whole Arab world regardless of how distant from the core area. The problem was, of course, that any Arab/Muslim leader engaging in this process would be doomed to live in perennial fear of his own people, and by the time the "peace process" had reached Arab/Muslim country N the process would have already backfired, if not in N-1 or N-2 at least in N-3 and N-4. However this may be, the entire "peace process" died in Sabra-Shatila in 1982 in the eyes of much of the world when Israel was seen as a nation that had sunk to the level of the oppressors, condoning genocidal actions.

There are also the subsidiary conflicts involving the superpowers in the area. I think it is fair to say that there are two types of conflicts involved here. One is traditional superpower interference and intervention in what they see as their "interests." They invoke an age-old theory to make a wrong look like a right: the "sphere of interests," bolstering it with an even older theory that makes two wrongs look even more right—"if he has a sphere of interest in this area I am also entitled to one." There is an image of peace in this connection: the United States has Israel in its sphere of interest, the Soviet Union has Syria, with all this implies in terms of rights and duties on either side. As to the process, any reading of the history of the last forty years or so in the area would be sufficient.

Then there is that second type of conflict, which has to do with *conflict management*. That there is a conflict in the area is certainly not in doubt. But this is a peculiar conflict; a conflict not between right and wrong, nor between wrong and wrong, but between right and right—both Jews and Arabs in the core area having a right to settle—which makes it even more intractable. A conflict of that type calls for a manager. Whoever is able to manage the conflict successfully would be greeted with considerable gratitude not only by the inhabitants but also by a world desperately short of miracles. The key competitors for the position are the United States (Camp David) and the United Nations (Security Council Resolutions 242 and 338). But if these two are front runners the Soviet Union cannot afford to be far behind, so another major factor holding up any progress in the area is the refusal to give the Soviet Union a meaningful role as participant in the conflict-management process.

In this particular conflict there is also a possible peace image: a management directorate of the superpowers operating within a framework set by the United Nations. And for the process there is the machinery, slow but well-defined, of the United Nations. There is no guarantee, however, that this machinery will deliver an outcome totally satisfactory to either superpower. For that reason the stronger of them will certainly try to do without it.

In summary, at the periphery of the extremely complex and intractable conflict in the area there are both images of peace and processes; at the core there is neither. On the contrary, what goes on in the area is not a peace process, nor exactly a war process, except for certain periods at certain places, but the traditional way of clearing a territory for one's own use—disturbingly similar to what Americans have done to native Americans since the founding of the Plymouth Colony in Massachusetts. There is a combination of extermination, expulsion to other countries as refugees, internal expulsion to reservations, and the conversion of human beings into second-class citizens politically, economically, culturally, and/or militarily. Of course, there is also a fifth possibility, that of transformation into first-class citizens, but in a Jewish state with clearly theocratic features this would demand a conversion in so many senses as to be unacceptable.

Of course, we are not quite in the seventeenth, eighteenth, or nineteenth centuries; there is less focus on extermination, more on external and internal expulsion. Moreover, Palestinians in the core area accepted more willingly the role of second-class citizen than native Americans have done; they may have preferred exile in the internal reservations to very marginal participation in the American social structure. But the general philosophy of the "Chosen People" with a "Promised Land" on the one hand, and those on the other hand who "just happen" to live there, in what was defined as a sparsely populated territory, is disturbingly similar: a travesty of any idea of peace.

An Image of a Peace Process

For a peace process to take place there has to be one or several images of peace, in other words some kind of *goal* or goals, and some idea of a *process*—possibly even some mutually agreed *indicators* of whether the process is, roughly speaking, heading in the right direction or not. The crucial point here is probably the image of the goal; if that image gains some kind of acceptance a process can possibly be devised.

There are three rival images of some importance in this connection, given a general consensus that the present state of affairs is intolerable to Israelis and Palestinians, to Jews and Arabs alike—although the intolerable has now lasted for quite some time. The three images are: a one-state solution with the absorption of the Palestinians as first-class citizens within Israel; a two-state solution with the creation of an independent Palestinian state anchored in the West Bank and Gaza; and a confederate solution based on some kind of Israeli/Palestinian partnership. This writer does not believe in the first, has grave doubts about the second, but retains some faith in the third alternative. I fail to see how the idea of a Jewish national home, Judaism being a religion, is compatible with first-class citizenship for non-Jews, even if such citizenship is enshrined in some bill of rights. If Jews, Christians, and Muslims in the area could reconcile their differences by joint allegiance to an overarching system of belief, such as the Baha'i faith, then something might perhaps be worked out. But the proposition is absurd given the nature of the myth underlying the creation of the state of Israel, not to mention the unspeakable realities of the Holocaust perpetrated by a Christian nation on the Jews of Europe.

A Palestinian nation-state based on pre-1967 conditions might make more sense within the ancient code of nation-state building: one country per nation, all members of that nation inside that country, the construction of a state organization within that country controlled by members of that nation. But the objections are equally obvious: Palestinians have a rightful claim to territories within the pre-1967 borders of Israel; the territorial polarization in the two-state solution is a way of stripping for violent action; and the states would be so small that economic viability would be doubtful. To this some might object that since Jordan is viable, and a majority of its population is already Palestinian, why not "put" the rest of the Palestinians there by driving them out of the West Bank/Gaza areas, which could then be settled by Jews? Needless to say, any such follow-up to the 1967 territorial expansion would only make things worse, driving the Palestinians even further from their rightful homeland.

The confederate solution would have as its point of departure the core area, mandated Palestine, possibly accepting the River Jordan as the eastern border for Jewish settlement. The territory west of that river would then have Israeli and Palestinian cantons, possibly even exchanging some Israeli settlements on the West Bank for Palestinian settlements (Nazareth?) within pre-1967 Israel. Jerusalem would be the federal district in this configuration, open to all, ruled by them in conjunction, not by one or the other, nor by others.

Needless to say, formulations such as these are not satisfactory to those who believe in the sanctity of pure nation-states. Put differently, it would be satisfactory only to those who, like the Swiss, believe in a certain linguistic and religious contiguity and purity but at the same time can also think in overarching terms, comprising an identity as Swiss. Such a mentality would take a long time to develop in this particular area. The set of Jewish cantons would think of themselves as Israel for a very long time to come, and the set of Palestinian cantons would continue to think of themselves as Palestine. But through a process of shared experience, in as equitable a manner as possible, with neither secondary to the other, nor expelled by the other, an overarching identity might sooner or later emerge. Consequently, these are images that could be satisfactory to moderates in either camp, and there are many of them. There are perhaps more moderates on the Palestinian than on the Israeli side, as there is some ambiguity as to where the Peace Now forces are located politically. When they say "peace," does that mean continuation of the status quo with no belligerent adventures such as Lebanon in 1982? Continuation of the suppression of the Palestinians with no basic change in either direction? A two-state solution? A one-state solution?

For a fruitful discussion to emerge between the moderates of both sides the two basic problems of geographical borders and institutional arrangements would have to be addressed directly. For this to happen not only one but several maps should be produced; not only one but several institutional arrangements for a confederation should be elaborated. Time, perhaps years, would be needed for these matters to be discussed and processed. A confederation presupposes some limitation on Palestinian and Israeli sovereignty; somewhere between none (the two-state solution) and 100 percent limitation of one but not the other (the one-state solution, with the other side integrated as first or second class citizens, or expelled in accord with those haunting political cliches of "Jews into the sea" and "Arabs into the desert").

Although these extreme positions are to be avoided, any realistic image should be dynamic, starting, for instance, with images of a two-state solution plus a process of gradual integration and fusion, to come closer to a viable confederation. The presence and possible inclusion of Jordan in the core area has led to some thinking in the direction of Benelux, possibly with

Jordan as Belgium, Israel as the Netherlands, and Palestine as Luxembourg, not to press the analogy too far. This way of thinking is different from the Swiss model indicated above, but not incompatible if a more dynamic perspective on confederation formation is adopted.

So much for the image, what about the process? In one sense the process has already started. All over the world, but perhaps particularly in the United States, Jews and Arabs, Israelis and Palestinians of less purist persuasions are meeting in small groups,[3] with or without third parties, to discuss the core conflict. Very few of these discussions ever center on the confederate solution, which does not mean that such correlated images cannot be brought into the picture in the future. There is a people's diplomacy going on in this field of considerable proportions, a natural concomitant of the near total breakdown of meaningful discussion at the top level, between Israeli governmental parties and the PLO. (It will be remembered that I am not talking here about the subsidiary conflicts, where quite a lot of secret contact exist.) Familiarity with an image of a peaceful future in geographical and institutional terms, even with some concrete details, would be a necessary but not a sufficient condition for further progress.

Further progress can only take place if both parties recognize the right of the other to exist, in the sense of the right to a homeland in the core area, including the area west of the River Jordan. But this is not the same as recognition of the right of an Israeli state or a Palestinian state to exist. As is well known, these are exactly the rights that each side would not want to guarantee to the other. A confederate solution would obviate that problem by opting for a softer definition of "homeland." As a matter of fact, insistence on preconditions for talks is a signal that no talks are really wanted, since such preconditions tend to focus on the most, not the least, sticky issues. Talks, presumably, are about the intractable, not about the immediately feasible—hence, no preconditions.

Each side will have to accept, however, that the other decides who represents it in serious negotiations. The Jews, having had the privilege of building a nation-state with the usual executive organs, will have the traditional state machinery to build on the government in general and the ministry of foreign affairs in particular. The Arabs, not having a corresponding construction in the form of a Palestinian state (and for that reason possibly being reluctant to engage in the peace process unless more symmetry is established by moving closer to a West Bank/Gaza formation), will have to rely on their organization. This means the PLO, which seems to enjoy considerable support among Palestinians whether Israel likes it or not.[4] Any reference to Palestinian terrorist tactics by a state like Israel, certainly itself based on terrorism, is deeply inappropriate, a point that should be understood by the Israeli side. And these are the two parties to the discussions, ideally in need of nobody else. The future of both depends on their ability to meet, alone.

But there are subsidiary conflicts that also will have to be dealt with, and any Israeli/Palestinian solution will have to be acceptable to other actors on the scene. Hence a two-tiered or three-tiered process could be envisaged: one for the core conflict involving only Israelis and Palestinians; one for the subsidiary conflicts involving all other Arab/Muslim states in the area; and one involving the superpowers, partly with, partly without the United Nations. A general conference for the whole area has been discussed for a long period and might be useful. In that case it should take place under the aegis of the United Nations, possibly with the two superpowers as co-presidents, but preferably with no such arrangement (the important point being that if one is present the other should be).

The process is then open to other parties to be represented in the way they deem appropriate. In other words, a recognition of the PLO and the Soviet Union as discussion and negotiation partners is an absolutely necessary condition, which should be easier to agree on as the Soviet Union comes closer to the opening of diplomatic relations with Israel. The United Nations, on the other hand, might consider opening a new office or agency to serve as a setting in which this important process—not only for peace in the area but also for peace in the world—might take place.

The terms of reference for the process would be individual human rights and the rights of peoples rather than the rights of states. It is the right of the Jewish people to settle in (some parts of) their homeland. But the right of Palestinian Arabs to settle in (some parts of) their homeland must also be recognized. All of these are rights of peoples, not rights of states. The appropriate institutional arrangement should flow from the rights of individuals and peoples, rather than being built into the process from the beginning as all peoples' inalienable right to have a state. The question should always be asked: are we really convinced that the construction of the modern state, with its concomitant in terms of the right of the state to wage wars and to have unlimited internal jurisdiction, is such an unmitigated success?

As mentioned above, several maps, not only one, and several institutional arrangements, not only one, should be produced to provide a variety of images and processes, leaving it to the participants in the process to limit the range. This would certainly include mechanisms for review. There would be ideas about how to weaken a confederation in the direction of separate state formation if that should seem to be a better solution, and about how to strengthen a confederation, reducing the autonomy of other sovereign actors. Flexibility, not rigidity, would be the basic formula.

It is important to note that historically Muslims have been considerably more hospitable to Christians and Jews than Christians have been to Muslims and Jews, or Jews have been to either—but then it may also be said that historically Jews have not been given much of a chance. Today, enmity between Jews and Muslims is the rule, although that need not be a lasting condition. This enmity is strong enough, in my view, to make a one-state secular solution with Jews and Muslims (and some Christians) living side by side rather unlikely, but not strong enough to make it impossible for cantons to live side by side under some overarching administrative umbrella, jointly run.

Thus, I favor the confederate solution as a peace image. The one-state solution—born out of a conflict between the inalienable *rights* of two peoples—is incompatible with the principle of symmetry between Jews and Arabs, Israelis and Palestinians. The two-state solution is on the surface compatible, but denies Palestinians access to much of their land, gives them too little—and is too dangerous. The confederate solution gives access, keeps them apart, yet weaves them together in an equitable manner—as they must be—given how tightly they are woven together historically and geographically.

Conclusion: Some Trends to Consider

Today, twenty years after the 1967 war, the prospects for peace in the Middle East are certainly very far from good. Israel and the United States look strong and united, Palestinians and the Arab states weak and disunited. Most important of all, the Iraq-Iran conflict continues. Various processes— some strong, some weak, some hardly to be disputed, others highly con- troversial—in the course of time (and I am thinking here of periods not more than five to ten years) may change the picture considerably in favor of a peaceful solution.

First of all, there is the moral degradation of Israel symbolized by Sabra- Shatila. This moral degradation is confirmed almost every day by the suppression of human rights in the occupied territories. This is extremely important to Israel, as its political power in the past has derived from moral power, more particularly the guilt that Israel as an exponent of the Jewish people has exploited successfully (and to a large extent rightly so), especially in Europe. The United States is in a different situation, being *the* place in the world that has opened itself (and for that the United States deserves the gratitude not only of the Jewish people but of the world as a whole) as a home where Jews can be Jews, and Christians and many others can be themselves. Europe was never that generous. As moral power declines, the power of the carrot (economic power) and the power of the stick (military power) will have to increase, and there are limits to how much sympathy Israel can buy and how much terror she can instill in a numerically superior nation. There are also limits to United States support.

Second, Israel is an increasingly divided country. There is no need here to review internal divisions and the general move toward the right, toward the self-righteous, nationalist, orthodox line. But that move will increasingly be accompanied by counter-moves, as brilliantly put forward and analyzed by the former head of Israeli intelligence, Yehoshafat Harkabi, in his various writings.[5] There will increasingly be groups in Israel impatient with the current impasse, demanding more radical solutions such as the expulsion of Palestinians into Jordan and the transformation of the conflict into an interstate conflict that can be treated in a more conventional manner, using the military as military and not as police troops. But there will also be opposite demands, created by the dialectic of the process.

Third, I do not think the United States-Israeli alliance can remain as unbreakable as it looks today. There are limits to how far a tail can successfully wag a dog. The recent spy case (Pollard, Spring 1987) is less important than what I sense as an increasing irritation in the United States at the degree to which its position in a vast area of the world is dictated by Israeli logic. This will put limits on Israeli behavior. Those limits are likely to be overstepped by the more intransigent forces inside Israel, and ruptures may appear, particularly if the United States should get an administration less subservient to a numerically small minority inside its own borders, regardless of how strong that minority is as intelligentsia and managers of United States foreign policy debate in general, and in connection with Israel in particular.

Fourth, there seems to be a Palestinian awakening. Occupation with no prospect of any acceptable solution is intolerable to any people. Of course, there is the temptation to accept the condition and make the best of it, particularly in economic terms—going shopping in Tel Aviv, tilling the soil for Israeli masters. But the reactions, violent and nonviolent,[6] seem to be more numerous every day. Important in this connection would be the ability of the Palestinians in the diaspora to organize as well as the Jews in the diaspora have been able to do.

Fifth, there is, indeed, a new Islam coming. It is fundamentalist and dialectically created by, among other things, the pressures from Christian nations and from the Jewish nation in the middle of the Arab world. If the Christians are able to go everywhere and make all peoples their disciples (if not necessarily in the religious sense at least economically, militarily, and politically), and the Jews are able to fulfill their religious dream, *Eretz Israel*, why should not the Muslims also prove to be fundamentalists capable of realizing some of their dreams? And why should this be limited to Shiite Islam? Why not Sunni Islam as well? Not in the sense of the Sunnis becoming Shiites, as is the typical uni-centric model so frequently found in the United States—always looking for a "Center of Evil" and never able to see itself as a part of the problem, indeed the cause. Why should there not also be a genuine Sunni fundamentalism? It might take other forms, might even be opposed to the Shiite version, but an awakening there could and probably will be.

Sixth, there is a growing pan-Arabism. An institution like the Arab Thought Forum[7] would hardly have been possible some years ago. Many people in many Arab countries are well off, dedicated to Arabism as a cause, in religious and/or secular terms. This proposition is not very popular with Egyptians; maybe the fact that Egypt has been dethroned or has dethroned itself by participating in the infamous "peace process" has contributed to the pan-Arabic cause! Maybe Egypt loomed so high, was so dominating because of its geographical position, its centuries as a viable, relatively autonomous nation-state, that it served to demobilize other Arab states which now, separately and together, will have to take up the cause and carry it further. Egypt will sooner or later be reintegrated into the

Arab fold, but will never quite be able to rid itself of the suspicion of being pharaonic first and Arab second, with all that implies in terms of separateness—in an unequal manner.

Seventh, and dominating all of this: there is some kind of United States-Soviet appeasement going on. There is a *glasnost* in the Soviet Union, so far none in the United States, but it may come. The current administration in the United States and its attitude of extreme self-righteousness cannot last forever. But this is accompanied by one dangerous sign on the horizon: the United States always seems to need an evil and powerful enemy. Who can be the successor to the Soviet Union? Who would be more ideally suited than "Muslim Terrorists," religiously adequate, sufficiently menacing politically? And if that is the case there might be even less likelihood of the United States agreeing to the rights of the Palestinian people in any form—unless, the Palestinians are somehow seen as separate or separable from "Muslim Terrorism" in general. Or unless a wave of rationality should sweep over the American mainland and wipe away some of the paranoia haunting the United States.

Anybody can make projections and predictions. But there is now a dynamism in the Middle East that was absent for some years, and my general contention is that this dynamism does not favor the type of ironclad rule associated with an Israeli politician like Sharon. It may not play into the hands of Palestinian terrorists either. Sharon and most terrorists need each other for mutual survival. This should be increasingly clear to more moderate forces in either camp, and by moderate I mean "people in general." Thus, there is a hope that something might start moving in a more positive direction.

A confederate solution is problematic.[8] Any other solution is even more problematic, in the sense of being worse in human terms, and for that reason less viable.

Notes

1. In other words, this process has been going on for the better part of this century and can by no means be seen as a post-holocaust policy only. The Palestinian resistance has also been going on for the better part of the century.

2. For a good analysis from a moderate Arab point of view see Fayez A. Sayegh, Senior Consultant, Ministry of Foreign Affairs, Kuwait, *Camp David and Palestine, A Preliminary Analysis*, (New York: Americans for Middle East Understanding, 1978).

3. One example is actually the very conference in which this paper was presented, with all kinds of smaller dialogues going on in many different settings, formal and informal.

4. For an example see Sammy Smooha and Don Peretz, "The Arabs in Israel," *Journal of Conflict Resolution*, September 1982, for a survey reporting 64.3 percent supporting a Palestinian state in West Bank/Gaza, 20 percent only under certain circumstances, and 15.7 percent opposed; 68 perecent approved the PLO as the representative of the Palestinian people, 22.9 percent accepted the PLO with reservations, and 9.1 percent rejected it entirely. According to the survey undertaken 28 July to 8 August 1986, 93.5 percent see the PLO as the only legitimate representative

of the Palestinian people, with 78.8 percent endorsing Arafat as the Palestinian leader. (*Klassekampen*, Oslo, 18 March 1987, p. 12).

5. A general and director of intelligence turned professor of international relations, but a hawk turned dove? Harkabi denies this: "My country has moved so far to the right that by standing still I come out at the left." (In a discussion, Hebrew University, Jerusalem, January 1986).

6. See, for instance, Deena Hurwitz, "Nonviolence in the Occupied Territories," *I&P*, July 1986, p. 22.

7. ATF organized a very successful conference on nonviolence in the Middle East in Amman, Jordan, in November 1986.

8. For my own exploration of the theme of confederation in the Middle East, see "The Middle East and the Theory of Conflict," *Essay in Peace Research*, (Copenhagen: Ejlers, 1980), Vol. V, Chapter 3.

21

The Palestinianization of the Arab-Israeli Conflict

Herbert C. Kelman

The Six Day War of 1967 has had three significant consequences that have become increasingly apparent over the past twenty years:

First, among the Arab states, it initiated a process (accentuated by the 1973 war) of reassessing their conflict with Israel, leading to a gradual acceptance of the reality of Israel and a search for ways of disengaging from the conflict. Israeli occupation of the Sinai, the Golan, the West Bank, and the Gaza Strip created bilateral issues for Egypt, Jordan, and Syria in their conflict with Israel. It thus provided these Arab states the opportunity to redefine their goals, shifting from the demand for the dismantlement of the State of Israel to some version of the formula of "territory for peace."

The process of reassessment and redefinition produced the Egyptian-Israeli peace treaty in 1979. Jordan has indicated for some time its interest in settling on terms based on the "territory for peace" concept. Syria has signaled its readiness to make peace with Israel within its pre-1967 borders and—despite Israel's formal annexation of the Golan Heights—the bilateral territorial issues between Syria and Israel can probably be negotiated successfully. What remains as the major obstacle to a Syrian-Israeli agreement and (for different reasons) a Jordanian-Israeli agreement, as well as to normalization of Egyptian-Israeli relations, is resolution of the Palestinian problem.

Second, within the Palestinian community, the 1967 war accelerated the development of an independent Palestinian nationalism, expressing itself through a national liberation movement. Between 1948 and 1967 Palestinians

A somewhat different version of this chapter has been published in the *Jerusalem Quarterly* and is reprinted here by permission of the editor. This chapter was updated in March 1988 and a postscript has been added in order to incorporate developments resulting from the Palestinian uprising in the occupied territories.

looked primarily to the Arab states—and, from the late 1950s, to Gamal Abdel Nasser in particular—as champions of their cause. Arab failures in the 1967 war contributed to Palestinians' increasing disillusionment with the Arab states, to the growth of Fateh and other guerrilla organizations, to their takeover of the Palestine Liberation Organization (which was originally a creature of the Arab League), to the demand for an independent Palestinian decision, and to the general revival of a separate Palestinian nationalism (apart from pan-Arabism). The occupation of the West Bank and Gaza created a new set of grievances against Israel as a focus for national mobilization. The occupation also renewed the contact of Israeli Arabs with the West Bank/Gaza population, contributing to their increasing Palestinian identity.

All of these developments have strengthened the sense of unity among the various segments of the Palestinian community. The emphasis of the Palestinian movement since 1967 has been on liberation of Palestine through armed struggle. Over the years, however, its political positions have become more pragmatic, in part because of the increasing influence of Palestinians from the occupied territories. As a result, the political goal of the Palestinian movement has gradually shifted to the establishment of an independent Palestinian state in the West Bank and Gaza as the political expression of nationhood.

Third, in Israel the 1967 war reopened the question of Israel's borders, which had not been an active political issue since the 1948 armistice agreements. Possession of the occupied territories created a new sense of opportunity within Israel. For some, it was seen as an opportunity to trade territory for peace. For others, however, it was seen as an opportunity to establish a Greater Israel (*Eretz Yisrael ha-Shlemah*, which literally means "the complete Land of Israel"), with borders corresponding at least to those of mandatory Palestine. Although public opinion remains fluid, there is now a significant constituency within Israel that favors holding on to the territories—either out of commitment to an ultranationalist ideology (in some cases reinforced by religious messianism) or out of security concerns. Even political leaders who favor "territorial compromise" share some of the security concerns and are further constrained by the domestic political costs of territorial concessions.

Israeli settlements on the West Bank—originally in the form of ideological outposts designed to establish so-called "facts on the ground," and later in the form of attractive exurban housing projects for people working in Jerusalem and Tel Aviv—have complicated the decision to withdraw. The settlements and numerous other features of twenty years of occupation have increased both the level of tension and the sense of permanence of the Israeli presence in the territories. As a result, the Arab-Israeli conflict has been internalized by Israel: that is, increasingly transformed from an interstate conflict between Israel and its neighboring states to an intercommunal conflict within the post-1967 borders of Israel.

Palestinianization of the Conflict

What these developments over the past twenty years—in the Arab states, in the Palestinian community, and in Israel—have in common is that they all point to the increasing Palestinianization of the Arab-Israeli conflict. For the Arab states, the conflict has become Palestinianized in the sense that they seem ready to disengage from it and to come to terms with Israel on bilateral issues, provided a suitable formula for dealing with the Palestinian question can be devised. It is probably fair to say that the Arab regimes would be ready to settle in pursuit of their own interests, but that they cannot ignore the Palestinian issue out of concern for their own legitimacy, security, and standing in the Arab and Islamic world. For the Palestinians, the conflict has become Palestinianized in the sense that they have developed a national movement—representing their various, dispersed communities— which has taken over the primary responsibility for pursuing their cause. For Israel, it has become Palestinianized in the sense that the conflict has returned, in large measure, to its pre-state origin as a struggle with the Palestinian Arab community over the control of Palestine.

The evolution of these trends over the past twenty years has created both new opportunities and new necessities for an Arab-Israeli peace process. On the one hand, there are now opportunities for resolving the conflict in ways that satisfy the basic needs of all parties—opportunities that were not available as long as the Arab and Palestinian goal was the dismantlement of the State of Israel. On the other hand, it has also become increasingly evident that there can be no satisfactory termination of the Arab-Israeli conflict without seriously addressing its Palestinian dimension. A resolution of the Israeli-Palestinian conflict that is likely to be durable and to open the way to reconciliation and cooperation between the two peoples must be based on some formula that allows the two peoples, as peoples, to share Palestine/*Eretz Yisrael*. Such a formula must assure the continued secure existence of Israel as an independent Jewish state. At the same time, it must assure Palestinians the right to self-determination—their opportunity to give political expression to their national identity—within the land.

A formula that appears to meet these requirements is some version of a two-state solution: that is, the establishment of a Palestinian state on the West Bank and Gaza, committed to peaceful co-existence with the State of Israel. In order to meet the security concerns of Israel as well as of Jordan, this Palestinian state would probably have to be established in the context of a Jordanian-Palestinian confederation. Most Palestinians seem to be prepared to accept this limitation as long as their state retains the minimal characteristics of sovereignty. A more visionary version of such a formula is what has been called the "Benelux model," proposed by Abba Eban and endorsed by Yasser Arafat, among others. According to this model, a sovereign Palestinian state would be integrated in an economic and political union with both Jordan and Israel. An additional advantage of the two-state solution, in any of its variations, is that it is favored by a broad international consensus, which views it as a fair historic compromise to the conflict between the two communities.

What are the chances that some such compromise can in fact be negotiated? I shall argue that this type of solution is in fact consistent with the interests of the relevant parties, as these have evolved over the past twenty years, but that its implementation faces major barriers. I shall conclude with some remarks on the requirements for overcoming these barriers and setting an Israeli-Palestinian peace process in motion.

Does a Two-State Solution
Meet the Interests of the Parties?

The establishment of a Palestinian state in the West Bank and Gaza would meet the current interests of the Arab states in that it would permit them to settle their bilateral differences with Israel and disengage from the conflict without opening themselves up to the charge that they are abandoning the Palestinian cause. A Palestinian Arab state in part of Palestine can be seen as an honorable conclusion to this protracted conflict. Egypt, for obvious reasons, is enthusiastic about such an outcome, since it would provide retrospective justification for its peace treaty with Israel. For the states more distant from the fray, such as Iraq and Saudi Arabia, it would also represent a satisfactory basis for disengaging from the conflict. For Lebanon, it would offer some relief by defusing one of the sources of its domestic tension.

However, the key Arab parties in this context, Syria and Jordan, have considerable ambivalence toward the establishment of an independent Palestinian state. Each, for its own reasons, wants to maintain control over the Palestinians: Jordan, because of its fear that an independent Palestinian state might become a threat to the stability of its regime; Syria, because it views "ownership" of the Palestinian problem as a source of its own legitimacy and influence as a regional power. A Jordanian-Palestinian confederation would help to reassure Jordan, although the problem would be to limit Palestinian sovereignty sufficiently to meet Jordanian (and Israeli) security concerns, yet maintain sovereignty sufficiently to satisfy Palestinian national aspirations. From a Syrian point of view, of course, excessive Jordanian influence would be undesirable. Negotiations will have to take account of both Syrian and Jordanian interests and concerns.

In the final analysis, however, neither Syria nor Jordan is likely to stand in the way of the establishment of some form of Palestinian state on which the Palestinians and Israelis can agree. From the perspective of the Arab states, such a solution is the logical outcome of the Palestinianization of the conflict, in that it would permit them to settle outstanding bilateral issues and make peace with Israel while maintaining that the original conflict over Palestine has been resolved through a fair and honorable historic compromise in which the Arab side did not suffer defeat.

For the Palestinians themselves, the Palestinianization of the conflict over the past twenty years has also made the establishment of an independent state in the West Bank and Gaza a viable solution, congruent with their evolving perception of their national interests. A West Bank/Gaza state, particularly one with constrained sovereignty, is certainly not all the Palestinians had hoped for or feel they are entitled to. But the indications are that the mainstream PLO leadership and most of the Palestinian community—inside and outside the occupied territories—are now prepared to accept such a state as the only realistic option available to them.

Psychologically, this option was not available prior to 1967. The polemical question as to why Palestinians and other Arabs failed to call for a Palestinian state in the West Bank and Gaza when these territories were under Arab jurisdiction is quite irrelevant. Before 1967, Palestinians tended to approach the conflict from the perspective of either their Arab identity or their local identity. From the Arab perspective, the issue was recapturing the Arab territory on which Israel was established and placing it under Arab sovereignty—in other words, dismantling the State of Israel. From the local perspective, the issue for Palestinians was returning to the *specific* towns or villages, within Israel, from which they had come. Only as Palestinians began to adopt a *Palestinian national* perspective did a West Bank/Gaza state became a psychological option.

The establishment of an independent state—even though it would cover only part of Palestine and exclude the specific towns and villages from which most diaspora Palestinians originate—would achieve a meaningful goal for a national movement and represent a reasonable end to the national struggle. It would allow the Palestinians to exercise their right to national self-determination, to establish national sovereignty, and to obtain a territorial base for expressing their nationhood. At the same time, it would contribute concretely to the welfare of many Palestinians by ending the occupation for those living in the territories, by offering a haven to those who desperately need one (such as the inhabitants of refugee camps in Lebanon), by providing citizenship and passports to those who are now stateless, and by enhancing the Palestinians' sense of dignity and the feeling that at least minimal justice had been done.

It may appear paradoxical, but I believe it is correct to say that only as Palestinian nationalism grew and the conflict became Palestinianized did the compromise option of a West Bank/Gaza state emerge as a possibility. Many Palestinians, of course, reject this compromise. If and when such a state is actually offered to the Palestinians, however, there is good reason to predict that it would be widely accepted, even among many who are now in the rejectionist camp.

In Israel, the option of a Palestinian state, even in confederation with Jordan, is generally rejected. Israelis who favor territorial compromise more often than not want to return territory to Jordan, not to the Palestinians. They accept the need for Palestinian representation in a joint Jordanian-Palestinian negotiating team, but they insist that the Palestinian representatives not be PLO members. This position ignores the reality of Palestinian nationalism and the Palestinianization of the conflict by treating the West

Bank and Gaza as an issue between two states rather than one between two national communities. Current realities are such that neither Jordan nor West Bank/Gaza Palestinians are willing and able to enter into negotiations without PLO approval. The exclusion of the PLO, therefore, amounts to a continuation of the status quo.

Some observers argue that this is precisely what Israeli leaders want—that the military and diplomatic costs they incur by maintaining the status quo are negligible, while the domestic political costs of seriously pursuing negotiations would be enormous. This analysis, in my view, is based entirely on short-term calculations of interest. To be sure, short-term considerations often play the decisive role in political decisions. But in calculating Israeli interests, it is important to keep in mind the long-term effect of maintaining the status quo: consolidation of the *de facto*, if not *de jure*, annexation of the territories.

Many Israelis are deeply concerned about the consequences that incorporating the territories into Israel would have for the Jewish and democratic character of the state, as well as for its internal stability, and its international standing. Writers like Abba Eban and Yehoshafat Harkabi, among others, have described these consequences as disastrous for Israel. Harkabi, in fact, speaks of the continuation of the present policies as tantamount to national suicide. He goes on to draw the logical conclusion that Israel must be prepared to negotiate with the PLO over the establishment of a Palestinian state if it is to forestall the greater danger inherent in annexation of the occupied territories. Harkabi describes the real choice before Israelis as "either that Israel will withdraw and the West Bank will become a Palestinian state, probably confederated with Jordan, or that Israel itself will eventually become a Palestinian state."[1] In sum, from Israel's perspective, the Palestinianization of the conflict—that is, its transformation from an interstate to an intercommunal conflict as a result of the occupation of the West Bank and Gaza twenty years ago—makes a Palestinian solution the only viable option. Establishment of a Palestinian state, with appropriate security guarantees and a commitment to peaceful coexistence with Israel, may be the best way for Israel to maintain its own integrity.

Barriers to the Two-State Solution

The widespread resistance to this conclusion within Israel can be traced to many factors, including the ideological and political divisions in the population, which impose severe constraints on the political leadership and thus inhibit creative initiatives toward peace. But there is a more profound source of resistance to the idea of a Palestinian state, which suffuses Israeli attitudes almost across the board. It is directly linked to what I have described elsewhere as the psychological core of the Israeli-Palestinian conflict for both sides: the conflict "is perceived by the two parties in zero-sum terms, not only with respect to territory but also, most significantly, with respect to national identity and national existence. Each party perceives the very existence of the other—the other's status as a nation—to be a threat to its own existence and status as a nation. Each holds the view that only one can be a nation: either we are a nation or they are. *They* can acquire national identity and rights only at the expense of *our* identity and rights."[2]

Within this framework, Palestinian nationalism, the PLO as the embodiment and agent of Palestinian nationhood, and the establishment of a Palestinian state are seen as inherently threatening to Israel because of the conviction that a PLO-dominated state would of necessity be irredentist and ultimately committed to the destruction of Israel. Acknowledging the Palestinians' right to an independent state—indeed acknowledging their status as a nation—is viewed as placing Israel's own rights and status into question and into jeopardy.

Since the Palestinians widely share this zero-sum conception of the conflict, they have been unable to reassure Israelis and assuage Israeli fears of Palestinian intentions. It has been difficult for Palestinian leaders to say clearly and unambiguously that they accept Israel's right to exist and that they are prepared to accept a West Bank/Gaza state as the final settlement of the conflict. Palestinians mirror the fears of the Israelis: they see acknowledgment of Israeli rights and Israel's status as a bona fide nation as placing their own rights into question and their own national existence into jeopardy.

One of the consequences of the zero-sum view of the conflict is that the parties engage in systematic efforts to deny each other's identity and right to exist as a nation and to delegitimize each other's movement. Extreme forms of such delegitimization are the equation of Zionism with racism and of Palestinian nationalism, as represented by the PLO, with terrorism. Such rhetoric and the often violent actions consistent with it have the effect of reinforcing each party's fears and distrust of the other and confirming the image of the other as intransigent and committed to one's own group's destruction. The interactive nature of this process of delegitimization creates self-fulfilling prophecies that impede any moves toward negotiation.

If Israelis and Palestinians are to draw each other into a negotiating process that envisages a two-state solution, they must find ways of reassuring one another. Each must be persuaded that the process is safe, that participating in it will not endanger its national existence. Israelis must be convinced that the long-term survival of their state is assured. Palestinians must be convinced that their right to self-determination, including the establishment of a state of their own, is not precluded. Neither will enter into negotiations that leave their right to national existence in doubt, that define it as an item to be negotiated. In effect, then, recognition by the other—Palestinian recognition of Israel's right to exist and Israeli recognition of the Palestinians' right to self-determination—becomes a precondition for negotiation.

But recognizing the other presents a real dilemma for both Israelis and Palestinians for reasons already described: each side views recognizing the other as fundamentally dangerous because of the fear that in doing so it would be relinquishing its own rights and compromising its own legitimacy.

Recognition becomes even more dangerous in their eyes when it involves an open-ended commitment: that is, when there is uncertainty or ambiguity about the endpoint of the negotiations that the act of recognition is designed to set in motion. Because of each side's profound distrust of the other's intentions, both view open-ended commitments as irreversible steps that might leave them with nothing to show for their concessions and with their national existence severely compromised.

This concern about open-ended commitments accounts for the PLO's reluctance to endorse unconditionally U.N. Resolution 242 as a way of signalling its recognition of Israel. Resolution 242 itself is a highly problematic document from the Palestinian point of view. It represents, in essence, a "pre-Palestinian" formula, which treats the conflict as an interstate affairs and does not refer to Palestinian nationhood at all. From a Palestinian perspective, endorsing 242 unconditionally would be a major concession, casting doubt on their own claims without any assurance that this step would bring them closer to achievement of their political goals. They would, in effect, be acknowledging Israel's right to exist without reciprocal acknowledgment of their own rights, and they would be entering into a process whose outcome is uncertain and potentially fatal to their cause. It is not surprising that Chairman Arafat has been unwilling to endorse Resolution 242 unless the Palestinians' right to national self-determination is simultaneously recognized.

For Israelis, endorsement of the concept of a Palestinian state presents similar difficulties. From their perspective, such an endorsement would represent a dangerously open-ended commitment. They are not convinced that Palestinians would in fact accept such a state as the endpoint of their struggle, and they can point to numerous Palestinian documents and pronouncements that, in fact, describe a West Bank/Gaza state as an interim solution. Thus, in accepting negotiations that envisage a Palestinian state— and, indeed, in accepting the PLO as their negotiating partner—Israelis feel that they would be committing themselves to a process whose final outcome is at best unpredictable and at worst fatal. It is not surprising that even Israelis who are prepared to negotiate with the PLO over the establishment of a Palestinian state have been unwilling to do so without an unambiguous Palestinian commitment that such a state would represent a final settlement of the conflict and an end to the struggle over Palestine.

Conclusion

The escalatory dynamic of the Israeli-Palestinian conflict that I have described must be reversed if there is to be any progress in the Middle East peace process. If I am right in my view that the next step in a peace process must address the Palestinian dimension, then a way must be found to bring Israelis and Palestinians to the negotiating table. To this end, the two parties must engage in a prenegotiation process, aided by a mixture of official and unofficial diplomacy that allows them to develop a language of de-escalation and a strategy of mutual reassurance. Both sides must learn what they can do and say to reassure each other and how each can make it easier, rather than more difficult, for the other to reassure them in turn. Through direct interaction they can best help each other in this learning process.

In short, the prenegotiation process that I am proposing requires thoughtful and systematic efforts on the part of the Israelis and Palestinians to persuade one another that negotiations are safe, that they do not represent an uncertain path that might end up in disaster. Each side needs explicit or implicit recognition from the other in order to move to the negotiating table. But the recognition each asks must be such that it does not weaken the other or raise the other's fears. Recognition of the other should not be experienced as relinquishing one's own rights or placing one's own national existence in jeopardy. It should not commit either party to an open-ended process that leaves its political survival in doubt—that raises the question: Will we still exist when this process is over? Israelis should not see it as a process in which they might be asked to bargain away the state they have managed to create, nor should Palestinians see it as a process in which they might be bargaining away their struggle for a state. Rather, they must see it as a process that clearly assures them of an acceptable future.

A prenegotiation process that succeeds in opening the path to such negotiations is one that brings about simultaneous and mutual recognition by both parties of the other's right to national self-determination in the land they both claim and must ultimately share. Only in the context of mutual recognition can each party acknowledge the other's national identity and national rights without thereby compromising its own identity and rights. Mutual recognition—in the psychological sense, with the reciprocal assurances it entails—can then provide the framework for starting Israeli-Palestinian negotiations in earnest.

Postscript

The recent events in the occupied territories, starting in early December 1987, provide strong support for the proposition that the Arab-Israeli conflict has become Palestinianized in all three of the senses discussed in this chapter. In fact, these events both reflect and contribute to an intensification of the process of Palestinianization.

One of the many factors that precipitated the uprising in the West Bank and Gaza was the Arab Summit conference in Amman in the Fall of 1987, in which the Arab states went further than they had gone before in their attempt to disengage from the Arab-Israeli conflict and, in effect, to leave it to the Palestinians. Those who interpreted this development as a sign that the Palestinian problem had now become defused and could be safely ignored had totally misread the nature and meaning of the Palestinianization process that had been under way for the past two decades. First, they (and probably the Arab leaders themselves) overestimated the extent to which the Arab states could disengage from the conflict—much as they might want to—without some movement on the Palestinian issue. Second, they underestimated the extent to which the momentum of the Arab-Israeli conflict had already shifted from the Arab states to the Palestinians themselves. Further signs of Arab disengagement only strengthened this trend and, moreover, made Palestinians anxious to demonstrate that they had not been marginalized.

On the Palestinian side, the recent events represent a new phase in the Palestinianization of the Arab-Israeli conflict. As noted earlier, the occupation in 1967 contributed to the development of the Palestinian national movement and that the Palestinians from the territories have played an important role in redefining the goals of the movement. Throughout, however, Palestinians in the territories have tended to leave the initiative to the outside leadership. But with the recent events they have accelerated the process of Palestinianization of the conflict by taking the initiative themselves and placing the occupied territories in the vanguard of the movement. Thus, the Arab-Israeli conflict is now not only being pursued under the leadership of the Palestinian movement, but it is being acted out on the soil of Palestine/ *Eretz Yisrael.* It would be a mistake, however, to assume that West Bank/ Gaza leaders are now ready to present themselves as an alternative to the PLO and to negotiate a separate agreement for the territories. All indications are that the Palestinians in the territories see their recent activities as part of the Palestinian *national* struggle. It is very likely that West Bank/Gaza leaders will gain increasing influence in the internal politics of the PLO and will play a crucial role in setting the movement's future agenda. I doubt very much, however, that they will want or be able to pursue a separate course.

A further word needs to be said about the Palestinianization of the Israeli Arabs, which was mentioned earlier in this chapter. The recent events gave Palestinians in Israel an opportunity to demonstrate their increasing identification with the Palestinian nation (a process that began with the renewed contact between the Israeli Arabs and their West Bank/Gaza compatriots after the 1967 war) and their support for the Palestinian political consensus. Both they themselves, however, and the Palestinians in the territories recognize and accept their distinct status as Palestinians with Israeli citizenship.

On the Israeli side, the recent events have made the Palestinianization of the conflict and the consequences of that development dramatically clear. Israelis are painfully aware of the extent to which the conflict has been internalized by the country and transformed from an intermittent war with enemies across the border to daily confrontations within Israel's post-1967 borders. The implications of this transformation for Israel's international image and self-image, for the country's values and institutions, are now not merely the subject of conjecture and prediction, but the stuff of everyday experience.

These recent developments have not changed my view that the Palestinianization of the conflict has created new possibilities for a mutually satisfactory solution, along the general lines outlined in this chapter. I strongly disagree with the argument that the conflict has now become (or again become) a dispute over the whole of Palestine rather than over the territories. Recent events have perhaps revealed and reinforced trends in this direction, but it is premature and dangerous to conclude that the conflict has already reached that hopeless stage. Such a conclusion ignores the other and still powerful trends toward a historic compromise and thus contributes to self-fulfilling prophecies of disaster.

Among Palestinians, there is no evidence so far of any large-scale abandonment of the consensus that seems to have been achieved in wide segments of the community, both in the territories and in the diaspora: acceptance of a solution based on the establishment of a Palestinian state in the West Bank and Gaza *alongside of Israel*. Participants in the recent demonstrations have been calling for an end to occupation and for Palestinian independence without advocating a particular formula for a political solution; there has been no indication that as a group they are rejecting the consensus for a two-state solution that has been evolving in Palestinian circles. It is this same consensus, rather than the establishment of Palestinian rule over the whole of Palestine, that Palestinians in Israel have been supporting in their sympathy strikes and demonstrations.

Among Israelis, the internal debate over the future of the territories continues and will probably intensify once the initial shock of the recent events is absorbed. No doubt these events have strengthened the resolve of the annexationist elements in the society and created a greater responsiveness to their hard-line, anti-compromise message among the general population. However, the events have also strengthened the profound concerns of many Israelis about the consequences of Israeli rule over the territories. These concerns now focus not just on future possibilities, but on present realities. They have not yet been transformed into effective efforts to educate the Israeli public about the nature of Palestinian nationalism and the difficult choices that will have to be made in order to accommodate it along with Israel's own security needs. If a firm leadership communicates to the Israeli public the necessity of a historic compromise in order to insure the security and integrity of the country, it may well gain the support of the majority of the population, which at the moment can go either way.

Both Palestinian and Israeli leaders favoring a compromise have not faced up to the requirements of educating their respective publics. Once they decide to take the risk of informing their own constituencies about the realities of the situation, they will also be able to deliver to each other the reassuring messages that are now more essential than ever. The concern about appearing weak inhibits each side from communicating to the other that the actions and reactions on the ground do not preclude a mutually satisfactory solution of the conflict. The main message of the uprising is that Palestinians will not accept continued occupation and insist on exercising their right to self-determination. The main message of the Israeli response is that Israelis are prepared to pay any price in order to insure their national survival, which they see as threatened by the uprising. Both sides now need to communicate, in unambiguous fashion, that if the other is prepared to recognize and accommodate *their* fundamental needs for independent and secure national existence, they are prepared to negotiate a historic compromise that assures the *other's* independent and secure existence.

Notes

1. Y. Harkabi, "The Fateful Choices Before Israel," Discussion Paper 8, International Center for Peace in the Middle East, Tel Aviv (based on a lecture given at Claremont College in April 1986), p. 8.

2. Herbert C. Kelman, "The Political Psychology of the Israeli-Palestinian Conflict: How Can We Overcome the Barriers to a Negotiated Solution?" *Political Psychology,* 1987, Vol. 8, No. 3, p. 354.

22

Paradigms of Reality:
The Art and Science of Evaluating
the Middle East Peace Process

Ofira Seliktar

Introduction

The Six Day War of 1967 has created an enormous momentum in the Arab-Israeli conflict. Yet the initial expectations that the territories could be quickly exchanged for a comprehensive peace have not been borne out. Two wars and twenty years later, the record remains mixed. In 1979, Israel and Egypt signed a historic peace agreement, but Israel has not reached an accord with either Syria or Jordan. The Palestinian problem seems even less tractable today than it was in 1967. Two decades of occupation have not produced the necessary conditions for a mutually agreeable solution; on the contrary, they have added new and more complex dynamics to the issues involved.

The mixed record is clearly reflected in the differing evaluations of the peace process. Some hail the Israeli-Egyptian struggle and optimistically predict that it will ultimately pave the way towards a comprehensive settlement. Others view the peace treaty as a partial but terminal step that will allow Israel to evade negotiations with the other Arab states and the Palestinians. Still others argue that the apparent failure to solve the Palestinian problem will eventually doom the entire peace achievement and plunge the Middle East into terrible violence.

This gamut of visions, which ranges from exuberant optimism to doomsday pessimism, reflects the underlying difficulties in analyzing a conflict. Any such endeavor poses numerous and critical questions. How long can we expect a conflict to last? Are conflicts solved incrementally, or through sudden breakthroughs? Does time facilitate, or complicate, the resolution of conflicts? Are ideological conflicts more difficult to solve than territorial ones? Do solutions tend to follow the principle of justice, or of power? Moreover, answers to these questions hinge upon assumptions that influence our thinking. Some of these assumptions are visible, while others are so deeply embedded in our normative and cognitive structures that they are virtually unrecognizable. Yet these different assumptions act as "conceptual lenses"; they emphasize select aspects of the peace process, magnify certain explanatory dimensions, and blur or neglect others.

This chapter has two objectives. First, it will try to identify some of the major paradigms that have been used in evaluating the peace process. Then, after analyzing several representative case studies in each paradigm category, it will discuss the explanatory and predictive powers of these paradigms. Second, the concluding section will use this critique to develop a model whereby the Middle East conflict is conceived of as a discrete sequence of situations exhibiting both equilibrium and disequilibrium. The model metaphor can help us identify conditions that move the equilibrium into either war or peace. This device is also useful in constructing a broad overview of the entire process of conflict resolution, rather than presenting only partial paradigmatic explanations. Even though a broad systemic discussion of the peace process is a difficult goal toward which to strive, any suggestions of conflict resolution require that they keep in mind the extreme complexity of the Middle East struggle.

The Theoretical Paradigms:
From Normative Heavens to Empirical Groundbreaking

The complex, puzzling, and interminable phenomenon of the Arab-Israeli conflict has attracted enormous attention. Most of it, as exemplified in academic literature, political polemics, policy papers, press coverage, or even literature, tries to explain the origin and the duration of this epic struggle. In spite of the significant differences in interest and focus, this literature invokes a certain pattern of inference. The analyst either "explains" a certain chain of events by showing what set the chain in motion or describes the mechanics of their occurrence.

Studies that have attempted to provide a more systematic understanding of the process of conflict resolution and to predict outcomes are few and far between. The logic of explanation in these studies requires that the analyst choose the relevant dimension of the occurrence. The logic of the prediction requires that he weigh large quantities of factors known to be relevant to the outcome. Allison described the explanatory model in which the analyst builds a net. The model not only fixes the mesh of the net that the analyst drags through the material but also directs him "to cast his net in select ponds, at certain depths, in order to catch the fish he is after."[1]

This perspective suggests that our evaluation of the peace process in the Middle East is based on the expectations and predictions generated by the various theoretical paradigms. The term *paradigm* denotes the commonality of perspective that binds a group of social scientists together in the sense that they share certain assumptions. Although there is no complete unity of thought among scholars who work within a certain paradigm, the unity of that paradigm is derived from a certain view of reality. In order to illustrate how different types of paradigms influence our thinking, three broad approaches are used here. The choice is based on self identification of the scholar as working within a certain paradigm.

Normative Heavens: The Peace Studies Paradigm

The philosophical tradition of peace studies is as long as the history of humanity. The two major premises of the peace school cannot be disputed: Striving for peace should be the supreme normative goal of human beings; failure to secure peace leads to war that destroys lives and property. Peace studies offer a wealth of suggestions on how peace can be attained. They range from utopian schemes of how to order the world (legally, politically, and psychologically) to practical suggestions of conflict resolution and maintenance of peace. In spite of its long history, the peace perspective is a relative latecomer to Middle East studies, which have traditionally been dominated by the conflict perspective. Responding to the urging that scholars should engage in a "definition of peace—that is, something more than a lack of collective, organized violence,"[2] the number of studies that use the peace paradigm has increased. The paradigm was strongly influenced by the school associated with the International Peace Research Institute in Oslo, and it has been adopted by scholars and political activists such as Peace Now and the New Outlook circle in Israel.

Johan Galtung, a distinguished peace scholar, was one of the first to use the peace paradigm to analyze of the Middle East conflict. In his article, "The Middle East and the Theory of Conflict,"[3] Galtung admitted that a theoretical approach is inherently limited, because no coherent theories of conflict exist. Instead, he proposed structural reasoning as a way of creating an adequate language of conflict. Such language needed, he said, to broaden the concept of reality by suggesting potential rather than empirical reality.

The normative nature of the peace paradigm calls for making an attribution judgment on the causes of the conflict. The author opts for an asymmetrical presentation of the causes, a procedure is derived from his early work on imperialism and the topdog-underdog metaphor of international relations. Accordingly, the Jews, the British, and the United Nations are blamed for the conflict. Galtung states that the Balfour Declaration of 1917 and the U.N. Partition Proposal of 1947 belong to "the more tragic mistakes of recent history." Likewise, he blames the continuation of the conflict on Israel, which in the author's words "was conceived in sin, was born in sin, and grew up in sin." The conflict has been perpetuated because Israel is an expansionist state that moves along a territorial axis with six values: nothing, statelet, 1947, pre-June 1967, Suez-Jordan, Nile-Euphrates.[4]

The asymmetrical presentation of the origins of the conflict supplies the logic for the list of conditions the author recommends as a short-term effort to start the peace process. Since Israel bears the blame for the conflict, Galtung calls upon Israel to make some huge sacrifices. Among them is giving up the claim to legitimacy, giving up the idea of secure and defensible borders, and retreating to the pre-June line in exchange for an Arab promise of *de facto* recognition. The Arabs are called upon to enter into more direct negotiations, develop a more future-oriented position, and entertain the idea of a *de facto* recognition of Israel. The disparity between the demands upon Israel and the Arabs is especially evident in the tactical nature of the Arab concessions. The Arabs are urged to acknowledge a singularist Israel, i.e., a Jewish state, but to think about a pluralistic Israel-Palestine, a euphemism for a secular democratic state in Palestine.

Galtung's paradigmatic thinking is a prime example of what Sowell called an unconstrained vision.[5] Such a vision is not a hope, a prophecy, or a moral imperative. Rather, it is a "pre-analytic cognitive act," an almost instinctive sense of what human society is and how it functions. Unconstrained visions are useful for guiding us through the bewildering complexities of reality, but Galtung's paradigm is difficult to use in explaining the peace process or predicting its future. Since the solution to the conflict is predicated upon normative imperatives, the conditions for peace depend upon the absolute principles of justice as imputed by the author. These principles require that the Palestinians be compensated, through the creation of a confederated Greater Palestine, for the injustices done to them. The paradigm does not recognize the justice of the Jewish moral imperative or the reality of the conflict in the last fifty years.

A more systematic effort to apply the peace studies paradigm involves an early project of the International Peace Academy that resulted in the publication of *The Elusive Peace in the Middle East*, edited by Malcolm Kerr.[6] In a key contribution to the volume, George Haddad uses the method of historical exposition to trace the contours of the conflict. In this perspective, a peaceful solution can be achieved only if the historical-normative roots of the problem are identified and addressed.

Haddad adopts the asymmetrical attribution view whereby the Jews, the Big Powers, and subsequently the international organizations are held responsible for initiating the struggle. The author does not recognize the legitimacy of the Jewish rights to Palestine because neither religious feelings nor the historical plight of European Jews entitles them to a homeland. The normative evaluation of the origins of the conflict calls for a fairly passive representation of the Palestinian Arabs. They are described as the victims of the machinations of the Big Powers and of the League of Nations and its successor, the United Nations, which through a succession of "resolutions, declarations and challenges," conspired to deprive the indigenous population of its homeland.[7]

Israel, whom he calls the illegal successor of the illegal Jewish community in Palestine, is blamed for the continuation of the conflict because of its policy of "total colonialism." Unlike the classical colonial models where the European settlers coexisted with the natives, Israel removed the Palestinians from the land in 1948 and did not allow the refugees to return. No progress towards peace was possible because the Arabs were neither able to "wrest from Israel what it usurped" nor "willing to submit to injustice and coercion." The author does not elaborate on the territorial nature of the usurpation, but the subsequent discussion implies that he refers to the fact that Israel went beyond the boundaries of the 1947 U.N. Partition Proposal.[8]

Although Haddad resembles quite closely the paradigmatic thinking of Galtung in identifying the source of the conflict, he deviates from them in his suggestions regarding the peace process. Haddad does not view the peace settlement as being totally predicated upon redressing the moral injustice to the Palestinians that is derived from the "total colonialism" model. His lengthy discussion about the history of the various wars makes it clear that the author assumes that the balance of power between Israel and the Arab states would make it difficult to demand a total redress of Palestinian grievances. Stated differently, Haddad recognizes that any conflict resolution involves not only the claims of morality, but also the realpolitik of military strategic considerations. Even if he rejects all Jewish claims to. a legitimate and moral existence in the region, he recognizes that a compromise may provide for a workable peace solution.

These assumptions form the basis of Haddad's proposed suggestion for the peace process. Put briefly, it includes the recognition of the PLO as the sole representative of the Palestinian people and the creation of an independent Palestinian state in the West Bank and Gaza Strip. Jerusalem, it says, should either be internationalized or returned to its pre-1967 status. The Palestinians would be completely sovereign and free to choose their rulers. Israel would be required to admit an unspecified annual quota of refugees, and the remaining refugees would be compensated for their losses in 1948.[9]

The author does not make it clear whether these conditions are the absolute minimum for creating a just peace as defined by the peace studies paradigm, or just a bargaining position. It is equally not clear whether a functional compromise forced upon the Palestinians by the political, economic, and military strength of the Israelis is a basis for a permanent and just peace. For if, as the peace studies paradigm assumes, just peace is contingent upon rectifying the real source of the conflict, then a solution is less than permanent. A hint that this may indeed be the case comes in the author's conclusion that the "Arabs are determined not to abandon their rights and would continue to fight for them while time is on their side." Whether Haddad is aware of the far-reaching implications of his statement or not, the tension between pragmatic prescriptions and his normative concerns limits its usefulness for analyzing the Middle East reality.

A variant of the peace studies approach has been developed by Israeli peace activists and academies. One prominent practitioner of this approach is Simha Flapan. A prolific writer, Flapan contributed to both the academic study of the conflict and the polemic debate. In his two most recent books, *Zionism and the Palestinians* and *The Birth of Israel: Myths and Realities*,[10] and in other writings, Flapan traces the origins of the conflict to the claim of the Palestinian and Jewish peoples to the same territory. Flapan does not fix the blame on one or the other people. Rather, he argues that the struggle was perpetuated because of the dynamic association and interaction of the Arab and Jewish/Israeli elites and masses.

In searching for a peace solution, the nature of the interaction should be addressed. The author raises two important questions about the interaction process. The first is derived from the ontological query as to whether the "reality" under investigation is external to the actor, or is generated by individual consciousness. The second one is epistemological: i.e., it deals with how one can distinguish between what is "truth" and what is "myth." In answering these questions, Flapan takes the interesting stand that "reality" in the conflict can be both objective and the product of the individual consciousness. This leads to a variety of epistemological problems in the Arab-Israeli conflict. The most serious issue is the myths about the origin of the conflict and its subsequent conduct. Indeed, Flapan considers the myths disseminated by both the Arabs and the Israelis to be a major obstacle to peace in the region.

A major part of Flapan's work aims at dispelling the myths of the Israelis. The author feels that most Israelis, "intoxicated by their astounding victories," are not capable of cutting through the "web of myth and distortion" created by the "propaganda machine."[11] He identifies six central myths: 1) Zionists accepted the UN partition proposal and planned for peace; 2) Arabs rejected the partition and launched war; 3) Palestinian Arabs fled voluntarily, intending reconquest; 4) all Arab states united to expel the Jews from Palestine; 5) the Arab invasion was inevitable; and 6) defenseless Israel faced destruction by the Arab Goliath.[12]

The central assumption of Flapan's work is epistemological. If these myths were dispelled, there would be an increase in the peace consciousness of the Israelis and the conflict could be settled. This approach implies that a peaceful resolution of the Arab-Israeli conflict is not predicated upon a strict interpretation of the peace paradigm, i.e., Just Peace. Morality (as defined by the author) is still acknowledged as the major organizing principle, but it differs markedly from the paradigmatic presentation of Galtung and Haddad. Flapan does not apportion the blame for the origin of the conflict, but he calls upon the Israelis to assume an asymmetrically larger moral responsibility for its solution, mainly through acknowledging of the myths.[13]

The most attractive feature of Flapan's advocacy is the argument that moral obligations should be assumed by the victorious actor in the conflict, but the approach creates two problems in evaluating the peace process. One stems from the methodological difficulty in documenting the myths. Since Flapan embarked upon a major rewriting of history, he is often short on clear-cut evidence for his thesis. Some of his data are circumstantial, tenuous, or subject to different interpretations.

At times, there are contradictions and inconsistencies between earlier and later writings of Flapan.[14] At other times, Flapan buttresses his conclusions with dubious "popular psychology" speculations.[15] Another problem is caused by the fact that Flapan writes mostly about Israeli leaders; Arab

attitudes and policies are only marginally represented. The author acknowledges that this asymmetry may create the impression that only the "Zionist
movement is responsible for the absence of peace." Yet his writing is not
forceful enough in supporting the thesis that the Palestinian-Arab leadership
was not realistic enough and that this led to the "perpetuation of the
conflict and to national calamity."[16] On the contrary, most of the time
Flapan seems to present the Palestinians, elites and masses, as weak, confused,
manipulated, and lacking in will and resolve. Though subconsciously so,
this portrait of the Palestinians as simple and immature natives, given to
byzantine cultural habits, is fairly patronizing. However, unless the Palestinians
can be expected to assume a co-equal moral responsibility for their interaction
with the Israelis, the peace process would be stalled.

Yehoshafat Harkabi is another prominent Israeli advocate of the peace
study paradigm. Like Flapan, Harkabi recognizes that the reality of the
Middle East conflict is being continuously interpreted through an epistemological process of narration and legitimization. In his numerous works,
including the conclusive *Fateful Decisions*, Harkabi strives to contribute to
the peace process by analyzing interpretations of the conflict.[17]

As the author sees it, there is a universal tension between what different
societies regard as their normative ideology, i.e., their "grand design," and
the realities of their environment, i.e., "policy."[18] Regardless of its origin,
a just resolution of the conflict will occur only when both Palestinians and
Israelis reconcile their "grand designs" to more realistic "policy" lines. In
other words, a morally just solution must be based upon mutual compromise.

This interpretation of the peace paradigm sets the framework of a just
solution. It calls upon the Israelis to abandon their "grand design" of *Eretz
Israel* and give up the occupied territories, including the settlement policy.
Such a policy is not only just, but given the demographic size of the
Palestinians, politically prudent. This peace paradigm admonishes the Palestinians to recognize Israel and abandon their "grand design" of Greater
Palestine. Drawing on historical analogies, Harkabi warns that a failure to
abandon "grand designs" will lead to an existential war between the two
actors.[19]

Unlike Flapan, Harkabi assumes that the two sides are morally obligated
to make an equal effort to compromise. On the whole, the author finds
the Israelis slightly more realistic than the Palestinians. In particular, he
describes the PLO as being afflicted with the same spirit of rejectionism
that caused Palestinians in the past to misperceive reality. To complicate
matters, this spirit has been imparted to the new generation of PLO
leadership and has increased its dogmatic stand. Rejectionism and the use
of terror have in turn strengthened the Jewish right wing that is bent on
a Greater Israel.

Harkabi's work is highly useful in illustrating how the vicious circle of
conflict operates. In dwelling on the dynamics of the circle, Harkabi forges
a theoretical perspective on what is likely to happen when actors cling
rigidly to mutually exclusive "grand designs." Unfortunately, the work does

not offer a prescription for curing a national addiction to "grand design" policies. This failure is especially evident in Harkabi's discussion of unrealistic Palestinian expectations. The author admits that it would be useful if the Palestinians repudiated the PLO charter, which conjures up images of Greater Palestine. Since he sees no realistic chance for such a development, Harkabi is forced to argue, against his own theory, that the fact that the PLO has "forgotten" to mention the Charter in its recent meetings should be construed as a growing sign of realism.[20]

Ultimately, Harkabi's use of the peace paradigm is limited by the subjective vision of the author as to what constitutes reality and progress in the Middle East conflict.

The Practitioner-Scholar: Bargaining as a Form of Conflict Resolution

The practitioner-scholar idea is derived from the negotiation and bargaining literature. Like the peace studies paradigm, the negotiation literature holds that peace is preferable to war, but it does not make normative judgments about the origin of the conflict or speculate on new beginnings that require the transformation of humans or of the political system. Instead, the scholar uses bargaining theory to generate practical suggestions for conflict resolution. As a rule, the scholars who work within this paradigm do not use empirical survey data. Instead, they tend to rely on occasional and nonstructured observations of the conflict, including some interviews with elites. The literature adopts what may be termed the engineering approach to policymaking. Two major convictions underlie this approach: 1) any problem can be solved if given sufficient expert treatment; 2) problems should be treated as discrete rather than connected issues so that they can be solved "on their merits."

Herbert Kelman, a leading social psychologist, has adopted this approach to the Middle East conflict.[21] His writings are not derived from some absolute principles of justice but are dictated by what may be termed the symmetrical benevolence of his paradigm. His underlying assumptions are: 1) regardless of the moral and historical origins of the conflict, the continuous dynamics have created a certain new reality; 2) any solution to the conflict has to take into account the new reality; 3) the rights and legitimacy of both the Israelis and the Palestinians should be based on their cumulative achievements; 4) the best negotiating strategy is a symmetrical approach to the rights and legitimacy of both sides.[22]

The scholar plays a major role in apportioning symmetrical legitimacy. As Kelman says, "I try to understand the parties' needs and concerns, their hopes and fears, their blind spots and vulnerabilities, their rigidities and flexibilities."[23] Such a view of the conflict makes it more manageable for the scholar, and as Galtung remarked, "by invoking a plague on both your houses" the outsider emerges with an "aura of objectivity."[24]

Because of the requirements of symmetrical benevolence, the reality of the conflict has to be filtered through the self-described understanding of the author. Kelman explains that this understanding is not based on "standardized interviews with representative samples of Israelis and Palestinians yielding percentage distribution." Rather, it is a "composite view" based on interviews with a variety of respondents, Israeli and Palestinian, from various walks of life. The author does not explain why such a procedure is preferable to representative techniques, but he admits that "moderates," that is, Israelis and Palestinians who are willing to consider mutual accommodation, tend to be overrepresented in his sample. Moreover, such a sampling procedure is highly compatible with what Kelman describes as a bias "towards parallelism and optimism" in his analysis.[25]

The search for symmetry leads to some further filtering of reality. The major problem, as Kelman admits, is that the reality of the conflict is not always symmetrical in the moral or empirical sense. To bring the reality close to the requirements of the paradigm, the author uses functional parallelism. "I focus on these functional parallelisms because they help us understand the interaction process in the conflict" and "can serve as a basis for de-escalation and negotiation." These functional parallelisms are then defined as the author's hypotheses of conflict are presented with "persuasive intent." Their validity is derived from the paradigm and will be strengthened if they can serve to "move the parties towards the negotiating table."[26]

The resulting representations of the major dimension of the conflict are all structured to fit the requirements of parallelism. For instance, the author acknowledges that the Israelis have accepted the reality of Palestinian nationalism but refuse to grant legitimacy to the PLO. The Palestinians, and especially the PLO, whom Kelman sees as the present repository of Palestinian legitimacy, have thus far refused to recognize that Jews are a national group residing in the state of Israel. In spite of the asymmetry of these positions, Kelman does not view them as such.

Perhaps the best manifestation of the constrained reality of the symmetrical parallelism is not in the topics chosen for analysis, but in the issues omitted. Although the issue of terrorism has always been a major problem in Israeli-Palestinian relations since 1967, there is little discussion of armed struggle except in passing.[27] The author admits that the Palestinian National Covenant calls for the liquidation of Israel, but he describes it as a statement of principle rather than a specific program of action. The fact that Israelis view Palestinian terrorism/armed struggle as a first step towards implementing the principle of the Covenant that calls for the liquidation of the Jewish state may undermine the credibility of the author's analysis.

The reality of the symmetrical paradigm serves as a basis for recommending the conditions for negotiation. They involve: 1) direct communication between the Israelis and the Palestinians; 2) development of a formula for sharing land between the two peoples; 3) recognition of the national and international legitimacy of both parties. In other words, Israel is called upon to enter into direct negotiations with the PLO over the West Bank and Gaza Strip. To improve the probability of the paradigmatic scenario, Kelman suggest a number of ways to create the "psychological conditions" for negotiations. They range from mere technicalities to comprehensive reordering of the systemic properties of the two societies and the individual psychologies of their members.[28]

The usefulness of Kelman's approach for explaining and predicting the peace process in the Middle East is limited for two major reasons. First, the paradigm tends by definition to perceive (and exclude) particular ranges of alternatives. Second, the principles employed in estimating the consequences of the given alternatives extend only to a certain range within which choices must be located. For all practical purposes, the author advocates negotiation of a Palestinian state in the West Bank and Gaza Strip under the current leadership. In line with the negotiation theory, the paradigm does not discuss the final stage of the conflict, but it implies that the vision of a Greater Palestine cannot be ruled out in the true peace era. Whether this is a realistic prospect in the Middle East peace process is difficult to assess because the paradigm declines to consider alternative views of reality.

An interesting variation of the bargaining paradigm was adopted by Ralph White, a leading authority on the psychology of conflict.[29] Based on the integrative bargaining theory, i.e., a technique aimed at increasing the size of the joint gain, the approach concentrates on the immediate psychological obstacles to bargaining rather than on tackling historical complexities or the political-structural prerequisites to peace. The suggestions for peace resolution are based on "rational" concessions that would most likely have emerged from an intelligent, open-minded process of negotiations, if it were possible to have such a process. In its absence, the scholar generates proxy propositions.

White cautions that merely generating such "rational" propositions is not enough to achieve a breakthrough in the peace process. He points out that many academics or diplomats who assumed that they could persuade the protagonists to accept solutions that looked reasonable were time and again disappointed. To minimize such disappointments, the author provides a list of suggestions that, though "rational," are extremely hard for the Israelis and the Palestinians to accept. The list was submitted to both Israeli and Palestinian elites, and White used their reactions to isolate the major underlying misperceptions of the protagonists.

Among the more prevalent misperceptions of the Arabs were the view that Israel is "spreading like cancer," that Zionism is a monstrous evil, and that Israelis were the aggressors in all four wars. The common misperceptions of the Israelis were based on the fear that the Arabs want to destroy them, that Arabs engage in and condone terrorism, and that the Arabs were the aggressors in all four wars. Since the integrative bargaining approach does not assume that reality has to be expressed in parallelism, White does not try to argue that these perceptions are equally justified by actual experience. For instance, he finds that the "militant Palestinians in the PLO and a good many others are more reconciled to the prospect of war" and also that "there is great hostility and a commitment to violence" in the PLO

Covenant. Rather than prove that the Israelis are similarly disposed, the author simply points out that the Palestinians constitute only three percent of the Arab population and that not everyone in the Arab world is closely identified with the PLO.[30]

Since the misperceptions of the two sides about each other are so insidious, White does not find any comprehensive peace proposal realistic. Neither is it realistic, he finds, to demand that each side should act upon the promises of the other protagonists or the promises of a third party that guarantees such a peace settlement. Such a mistrust is not unique to the Middle East but is derived from a general lack of morality in international relations that, in the author's opinion, makes nations act mostly upon their own perceived national interests. To help build up some measure of trust between the Arabs and Israelis so that they can rely on mutual assurances and promises, the source of some of the most threatening perceptions and misperceptions should be eliminated, says White.

As White sees it, the Arabs can improve the atmosphere of peacemaking by clarifying the present ambiguity surrounding the "rights of the Palestinians." Since the Arab states declare that only the Palestinians can determine these rights, and since the Palestine National Covenant declares that it will use "armed struggle" to establish a "secular democratic state" in what is now Israel, Israeli fear of a new holocaust would continue. The Israelis on the other hand should dispel any misperceptions of militancy against Egypt. Quite significantly, White, who wrote before the beginning of the peace process between Israel and Egypt, correctly predicted that Israel's willingness to compromise would open major peace opportunities. Likewise, he pointed out that the Israeli-Egyptian accord can subsequently serve as a role model for other peace breakthroughs.[31]

Although modest, compared to other types of paradigmatically derived peace suggestions, White's approach seems to be more useful in evaluating and predicting the peace process. The proposal does not involve large-scale changes in the psychological makeup of the protagonists or a priori assumptions that the peace process is deterministically predicated upon the recognition of the PLO or of any other political entity, either Israeli or Palestinian. Rather, it emphasizes some key psychological elements that can break the peace impasse, such as removing the threatening intentions of the PLO's Covenant. Moreover, since the author is not bound by the strictures of parallelisms, he does not advocate *quid pro quo* bargaining concessions. Some of the psychological confidence-building measures can be carried out unilaterally in the hope that they can be reciprocated later. Perhaps the greatest contribution of White's work is that it succeeds in rising above the pitfalls of rationality-as-attributed-by-the-scholarly view of the peace process that identifies a series of functional imperatives for conflict resolution.

The notion of bargaining is also associated with the work of Noel Kaplowitz, who has attempted to apply the model of competing versus cooperative approaches to conflict by the Middle East elites.[32] The data were gathered through in-depth interviews with 50 Arabs and 28 Israeli elites. These data were analyzed for latent attitudes that make up the competitive and cooperative stands. The three categories among the Arabs are overt acceptors of Israel, totalists, and latent acceptors. The first two categories are clear. The overts, a small group of marginal Arab elites, view Israel as legitimate and accept its existence. The totalists perceive Israel as illegitimate and refuse to accept or negotiate with her—a view clearly reflected in the Rejectionist Front, a wing of the PLO.

The latent acceptors are more complex. They share the rejection of the totalists but are more open to compromises in two ways. For some elites, and most notably the bulk of the PLO leadership, compromise with Israel is a short-run tactical solution that they hope to abandon for total rejection at a more opportune time. But for others, compromise is a grudging stand stemming from the conviction that the cost of eliminating Israel may outweigh the benefits, especially since it might involve a nuclear conflagration in the Middle East.[33]

The Israeli response falls into the category of annexers, conciliators, and hard bargainers. The annexers view the occupied territories as part of the Jewish patrimony, a stand that corresponds to the position of the right wingers in Likud and National Religious circles. The conciliators are marginal left-wing groups, willing to declare prior to negotiations that Israel would withdraw from the territories. The hard bargainers are functional in the sense that they are in principle open to the final disposition of territories. The group, which comprises the majority of Israelis, demands maximum returns from territorial concessions: border adjustments and a full peace treaty.[34]

The author uses these latent dispositions of competitiveness and cooperation in order to speculate on some realistic scenarios for peace that are extrapolated from interactions between different Arab and Israeli responses. The two obvious peace oriented patterns are between Arab overt acceptors and Israeli conciliators, as well as between Arab overt acceptors and Israeli hard bargainers. However, they are not empirically likely because Arab overt-acceptors are marginal. A more promising interaction between Israeli hard bargainers would not guarantee a peace option unless the hostility and ambivalence of the latents can be replaced by an unambiguous acceptance of Israel. Drawing from socio-psychological theories of attitudinal and behavioral adjustment, the author suggests that this change can be effected when the "gains from a hostile orientation [are] so great as to outweigh the difficulties of acceptance." More specifically, Kaplowitz sees this kind of change among the Palestinians who become reluctant to support the PLO because of the high costs and low return of the guerrilla/terrorist activities. At the same time, the punitive, quid-pro-quo approach of the Israeli hard bargainers must be relaxed in order to promote an attitude change of a hostile adversary.[35]

The bargaining-interaction patterns dictate the range of territorial solutions that can range from the PLO-preferred "Greater Palestine," i.e., a uninational, nonsectarian Palestinian state where Israelis would become Palestinians of Jewish faith, to a Greater Israel, i.e., a unitarian Jewish state with or without a large Palestinian population. In-between options include a Palestinian state in the West Bank and a Jordanian-Palestinian federation. Given the distribution of attitudes within each category, Kaplowitz feels that the most realistic options include a Palestinian or a Palestinian-Jordanian state alongside Israel. Which of the preceding options will actually come to prevail cannot of course be predicted, but the author's innovative use of the interaction pattern of bargaining demonstrates that the outcome is predicated on a mix of idealist and realistic elements as they are internalized by the protagonists.

The Behavioral Research Paradigm: Empirical Groundbreaking

The behavioral science paradigm focuses on the inherent limitations of human knowledge in its quest for overarching social theories. The paradigm recognizes that theories and hypotheses do not blossom from intellects liberated from values and preferences. Social research views hypotheses and assumptions as similar to other artifacts of human behavior: a composite of intentions, concerns, learning, and values. Since values are an integral part of one's orientation, the social science paradigm strives to design rules of inquiry, to test thought and impressions against reality. To minimize this inherent bias, the social scientists working within the paradigm have tried to use stringently constructed surveys in order to generate empirical data.

Daniel Heradstveit was one of the first scholars to use the empirical approach to study the Middle East conflict. In his classic study *Arab and Israeli Elite Perceptions*, he set out to elucidate the possibilities of a peaceful settling of the conflict by interviewing large groups of Arab and Israeli elites.[36] The author justifies the choice of elites on the grounds that they actually shape public policy and engage in decision making. The elites chosen for the interviews were active politicians, civil servants in the Ministries of Foreign Affairs, editors and journalists, professors and students, and (on the Palestinian side) guerrilla leaders.

Heradstveit uses the data to probe the mutual perceptions of the protagonists in the conflict. These perceptions were arranged into categories that form the various dimensions of the conflict. One of the key findings is that both sides tend to adjust the origin and development of the conflict to their respective advantage. The Arabs view Zionists as a dangerous, expansionist phenomenon linked to colonialism and imperialism. Israel is an "artificial fragment" that has to be ejected from the Middle East. The Israelis blame "Arab irrationality" for the lack of peace. Both sides choose extremist groups as indicators of intention, whereas moderate indicators are often written off. Both protagonists feel that past events justify their faith in present strategy that in turn will ensure that the "future is on our side."[37]

The author then analyzes the perceptions of the protagonists with an eye to discerning possible solutions. He notes that on the Arab side the two competing strategies are 1) a political solution, i.e., negotiation, and 2) a military solution, i.e., war. The Palestinian guerrillas predominate in the military solution, since their goal is not to reach a new relationship with Israel but rather to dissolve the state in order to create another. Egyptian, Jordanian, and Lebanese elites opt for negotiations, whereas Syrians are for a mixed strategy. The Israelis indicate a preference for negotiation, with a strong element of status quo thinking. Significantly, these strategies are not strongly correlated with orientations towards territorial retrieval, which indicates that the desire to regain territories does not automatically lead to a preference for the military option.[38]

Heradstveit turns his analysis into a more predictive direction when he argues that any successful peace negotiation is predicated upon the actors' perception of the utility of the outcomes of their most preferred strategy. Some paired preferences can produce a deadlock, whereas others can prompt the protagonists toward negotiations. His major theoretical conclusion, therefore, is that neither resistance points nor goals nor targets can be evaluated statically; they should be evaluated dynamically, that is, in the context of the political situation at any given time. Heradstveit illustrates this position when he states that the Egyptian declaration that "they will not cede an inch of Arab territory," a major resistance point, has changed. Conversely, when the expected utilities are minimal, a party may not engage in negotiations, but may instead opt for the *status quo*. For instance, the author found that the preference for the *status quo* is by and large the utility calculus of the Israeli elite in his sample. As a result, he predicts that the conflict between Israel and Palestinians may come to resemble the pattern of Cyprus (or Northern Ireland), where there is tolerance for sporadic and terrorist activity, and wide acceptance that there are no solutions.

Another empirical study of the Middle East elites was conducted by John Mroz.[39] The Task Force that he headed held private discussions in 1978–79 with more than 175 government and other elites in Israel and the Arab states. Like other scholars who adopt the behavioral science paradigm, Mroz does not start with any specific assumptions about the origin of the conflict or the identity of the initial "aggressor." Rather, he acknowledges that the Arab-Israeli struggle is one of the most complex conflicts to resolve because of the web of "events and values and emotions" that have been exacerbated by outside influence. At the same time, the protagonists in the conflict, like other people in the Middle East, have developed "skills and procedures for coping with regional rivalries"—strategies that include complex alliances, intrigue and underground violence.[40]

Unfortunately, these rather byzantine practices have made the understanding of the conflict difficult not only to a "rational" Western observers but also to the various regional actors, thus complicating the already-tangled communication process. The major goal of the project is to sort out the different perceptions and misperceptions about concrete and esoteric threats as expressed by the various elites and to put them into a rational and mutually understandable categories. In the author's view, without a better understanding of this cognitive tangle no meaningful progress towards peace can be achieved.

Mroz identifies three cognitive dimensions of the conflict: perceptions, threats, and special concerns as expressed by six protagonists—the elites of Israel, Jordan, Syria, Lebanon, Egypt, and the Palestinians. These cognitions are sorted into three categories: primary military threats, secondary military threats, and nonmilitary security threats. The author uses the data to generate peace options that have a reasonable probability of being accepted by the majority of the protagonists. Among the options identified through the use of this procedure was a neutral Palestinian state in the West Bank and Gaza—based on the Austrian model of neutrality. Such a state would be run by a Palestinian elite willing to accept certain limitations on its sovereignty, such as a restriction on offensive weapons and an international supervision. Other options include a Jordanian and Palestinian federation and a federal structure for Lebanon.[41]

A major advantage of Mroz's approach is that the options are derived from extant realities and that their implementation does not therefore require large-scale changes in these realities.

The study, conducted in the late 1970s, is also predictive. For instance, the author suggested that the Palestinian problem would generate another war in the 1980s and that any peace settlement should include a federal solution to Lebanon, a need born out of the disintegration of this country. On the negative side though, the study does not clearly identify its sample or elaborate on its representativeness. Hence it is not always obvious whether the peace options are equally acceptable to all elites or whether they should be ranked according to the preferences of the main protagonists.

Ephraim Yuchtman-Yaar and Michael Inbar, two leading social psychologists, have the empirical perspective to study mass attitudes involving respondents from Egypt, Israel, the West Bank, and Gaza Strip.[42] This study also has a number of valuable features. Yuchtman-Yaar and Inbar call attention to the fact that the assessment of political conflicts, traditionally the domain of politicians and experts, involves a "complex pattern of information and inference." Because of the character of political analysis, this assessment consists of "covert processes of selection, weighting and linkage of information according to assumptions and rules not always made sufficiently explicit for scientific replication." The authors are aware that it is not always possible to explicate these assumptions, but their commitment to open empirical scrutiny is exceptional in a field which Azar described as too often featuring "scholarly literature" that is "little more than ideological argument couched in academic terms and academic style," bolstered by carefully selected data to fit the ideological content.[43]

Moreover, the study tries to find an appropriate balance between the normative and power dimensions of the conflict as they inform reality and translate into the objective perspectives of the respondents. Since Yuchtman-Yaar and Inbar argue that in the final analysis, "international conflicts derive from tangible factors" rather than from psychological ones, the search for a balance is problematic because the subjective dimension is a "difficult one to investigate" at any time, "let alone in an international conflict." Yet, as the authors prove, a failure to attempt an empirical investigation may lead to biased accounts of the conflict. Some of the more common forms of bias include an overemphasis of either the normative or the power perspective or a disregard for either objective or psychological factors.

As is dictated by the behavioral science paradigm, the authors focus the inquiry on perceived factors that determine the outcome of the conflict rather than on the more traditional concerns with its causes. Here some interesting national differences emerged. The Israelis tend to emphasize such items as "military strength," whereas the Arabs are more likely to put their trust in "God's will," "population size," or "Arab unity." In fact, the items "military strength" and "God's will" are diametrically symmetrical: the former has a mean score of 4.74 and a rank order of 1 among the Israelis, whereas the latter has the same mean score and rank among the Egyptians. Yuchtman-Yaar and Inbar explain that this structure reflects the tendency of each group to emphasize its perceived assets and to de-emphasize its liabilities. Their more general conclusion that "people tend to overestimate the value of available means and to underestimate unavailable ones" makes a good empirical illustration of the web of misperceptions that forms around any conflict. Whether a different structure of evaluation would be more or less conducive to conflict resolution is largely a matter of conjecture. The only hypotheses that the author would venture on the basis of the data is that "a normative orientation predisposes persons to a relatively rigid, non-compromising inclination, whereas instrumentality facilitates flexibility and pragmatism."

It is interesting to note, though, that in both Arabs and Israelis, there are age-related differences in the perception of normative and tangible factors. The younger people in both groups tended to overemphasize the clearly normative and abstract factors such as justice, whereas the older overemphasize more tangible political resources such as military power and economic development. The authors' conclusion that such a structure of cognition reflects the "pragmatic construction of reality by old people vis-à-vis the idealistic outlook of the youth," can have important implications for conflict resolution. As most of the radical demands on both sides of the conflict are articulated by younger persons, it is assumed by the authors that they may have less public support among their older cohorts.

The analysis of the perceived resources also reveals the importance which both groups attach to the United States as a mediator. United States influence is the only item where there is no difference between the two groups. The Israelis give it a mean score of 4.13 and a ranking of 4; the Egyptians rank it 6th with a mean score of 4.20. Russian and European influence as a resource in conflict resolution commands a much lower mean score and ranking from both groups. The authors argue that such a showing reflects the strong and continuous involvement of the United States in the Middle East. It is even more notable that its image as "honest broker" has not suffered in spite of the Israeli-American friendship. On the other hand, the anti-Israeli stand of the Soviet Union has done nothing to bolster Moscow's image as a resource. In fact, the Egyptians ranked it last of the 14 factors, even lower than the Israeli placement of 10 (the mean scores were 2.56 and 3.24 respectively).

A follow-up field study carried out in the West Bank and Gaza in 1985 probes the possible conditions for solving the Arab-Israeli conflict.[44] Since the authors are not restricted by any *a priori* assumption about the territorial solution, they include the entire spectrum of possible options. The questionnaire lists solutions ranging from the PLO-preferred secular, democratic state in Palestine (with and without the expulsion of the Jewish population) to the Israeli annexation of the West Bank (with and without the expulsion of the Arab population).

The support of the two extreme visions is not symmetrical. Whereas 65 percent of the Palestinians opt for the Greater Palestine solution, only 43 percent of the Israelis support annexation. The Jordanian-Palestinian federation was chosen by up to 38 percent of Israelis and 19 percent of the Palestinians. Thus the territorial issue remains a formidable barrier to the peace process.

Conclusions: Theories and the Reality of the Peace Process

In the preceding sections we have discussed a number of paradigms that have been used to evaluate the reality of the peace process and to predict its future. The normative paradigms, by forcing a stringent framework of explanation, have not been successful in evaluating the peace process or in predicting the required conditions for peace. For instance, Galtung's theoretical treatment, written in 1971, could not be used to predict anything as dramatic as Sadat's initiative. Flapan and Harkabi's efforts to tackle the epistemology of the peace process is more innovative and hopeful in charting new ways of breaking the stalemate. At the same time, the requirements of moral responsibility, conceived either symmetrically or asymmetrically, make it clear that any progress in the peace process entails tremendous changes in both the Israeli and the Palestinian societies.

The symmetrical benevolence of Kelman has been equally unsuccessful because it conditions the peace process too much on the acceptance of the PLO. The war in Lebanon, the fragmenting of the organization, and the appearance of indigenous leadership in the West Bank demonstrate that matters of legitimacy are not as easily settled as the paradigm asserts. Kelman's assertion that the PLO should be considered a government in exile is neither theoretically warranted nor empirically borne out. At best, it should have been viewed as one of the options, along with such other alternatives as the growth of local leadership in the West Bank.

Other variations of the negotiation paradigm have proved more successful in highlighting some crucial dimensions of conflict resolution. White's suggestions that the peace process can profit from psychological dramatics was borne out in Sadat's trip to Jerusalem. Kaplowitz's sophisticated analysis of interactive bargaining, which predicts that Arab latent acceptors can negotiate with Israeli hard bargainers, was confirmed in the peace treaty with Egypt.

The behavioral science paradigm, which informs the studies of Heradstveit, Mroz, and Yuchtman-Yaar and Inbar are more flexible in explaining reality and provide a more balanced view of the normative and power elements in creating and solving conflict. Yet, as Yuchtman-Yaar and Inbar caution, this paradigm can depict only one part of an extremely complex reality. Moreover, even if a study can identify the conditions for conflict resolution, they inevitably involve such psychological factors as perceptions of the normative, the instrumental, feelings of possession, and aggression which are difficult to control. Thus the absence of any normative postscript in the Yuchtman-Yaar and Inbar study stems from the recognition that even if conflict reality is analyzed with the best of scientific integrity, policy recommendations may involve a fair amount of wishful thinking. Likewise, Heradstveit's finding that the Middle East conflict may follow the pattern of Northern Ireland is a somber empirical reminder that some conflicts are interminable, regardless of our commitment to peace.

Recognizing the limits of our analytical powers should not discourage but rather should redirect the focus of paradigmatic thinking on conflict resolution. One useful avenue would be to depict the conflict in terms of a model with a known starting point but an unknown duration. The peace process with Egypt took some thirty-two years and four major wars to accomplish. Neither the number of wars nor the number of years is indicative of the time needed to effect the next breakthrough. However, the process should be treated as illustrating of the dynamics through which peace was achieved.

These dynamics can best be described as working through two simplified dimensions of the conflict. One dimension represents the different levels of aggregation: supranational organizations, nations, subnational organizations, other groups, and individuals. The other dimension represents different patterns of activity: routine behavior, purposive actions, extraordinary initiatives. The dynamics have produced a great number of incremental changes coupled with a few major disequilibrating events such as wars. To reduce the danger of a future disequilibrium, after each war there have been many actions designed to negotiate peace based on incremental measures such as international conferences and mediation. The failure of these actions can be explained in terms of the systemic properties of the model that can tolerate great amounts of incremental activity without producing a breakthrough change. Indeed, it took the sweeping drama of Sadat's extraordinary activity to disequilibrate the system and move toward peace.

It is not entirely clear whether the same conditions for a breakthrough exist in the current stalemate between Israel, Syria, and the Palestinians. Israel, which is in the process of being granted the status of a NATO-equivalent country, has increased its power standing in regional terms. As such, it would be less susceptible to activities such as Arab military threats or Big Power pressures. The Palestinians have yet to evolve a credible leadership which can engage in negotiation. Even if some progress is achieved through a Middle East conference, it is doubtful that the dynamics would be strong enough to move the system into peace. Alternatively, it is doubtful that the Palestinians and the Syrians can produce enough of a dynamic to swing the system into war.

The model paradigm suggests that the central questions of conflict resolution are quite different from the questions asked in more traditional research. Indeed, the crucial questions seem to pertain to equilibrium and disequilibrium management: what kinds of actions are needed to move the process toward peace? At what level of aggregation should the desired action arise? What various groups of actions, action-conduits, and feedbacks of action-conduits are needed to produce the desired actions? Can new actions and conduits be created? Which actors will have to agree on what? What means are available at what aggregation level to effect conflict resolution?

More systematic and rigorous ways of pursuing these questions should not only increase our ability to propose conditions for conflict resolution but should sharpen our effectiveness in evaluating the feasibility of the proposed solution. The model paradigm makes it clear that the argument is not simply that we have to identify steps conducive to conflict resolution that can be implemented. It also demonstrates that we have to consider power and normative factors in the selection of preferred solution alternatives and integrate them into dynamic, all-encompassing scenarios.

Notes

1. Graham Allison, *The Essence of Decision* (Boston: Little, Brown, 1971), p. 4.
2. J.D. Ben Dak, "Some Directions for Research Towards Peaceful Arab-Israeli Relations: Analysis of Past Events and Gaming Simulation of the Future," *Journal of Conflict Resolution* 16, no. 2 (1972), p. 284.
3. Johan Galtung, "The Middle East and the Theory of Conflict," *Journal of Peace Research* nos. 3-4 (1971), pp. 173-205.
4. Ibid., p. 176.
5. T. Sowell, *Conflict of Vision* (New York: W. Morrow, 1987).
6. G.M. Haddad, "Arab Peace Efforts and the Solution of the Arab-Israeli Problem," in M.H. Kerr (ed.), *The Elusive Peace in the Middle East* (Albany: State University of New York Press, 1975), pp. 166-248.
7. Ibid., pp. 167-168.
8. Ibid., pp. 189, 203.
9. Ibid., pp. 236-239.
10. Simha Flapan, *Zionism and the Palestinians* (London: Croom Helm, 1979); *The Birth of Israel: Myths and Realities* (New York: Pantheon, 1987); "Israelis and Palestinians: Can They Make Peace?" *Journal of Palestine Studies*, 15, no. 1 (1985), p. 20.
11. *Birth of Israel*, pp. 1, 2.
12. Ibid., pp. 7-8.
13. "Israelis and Palestinians," p. 21.

14. For instance, in *Birth of Israel*, p. 6, Flapan asserts that Ben-Gurion represented Palestinians Arabs as "pupils of Hitler" because of propaganda needs, but in "Israelis and Palestinians," p. 24, he acknowledges that the Palestinian leader Amin al Husayni decided to "stake the future of Palestine on the victory of Nazi Germany."

15. One of his most notable contentions is that Israel "projected onto the Arabs the wrath and vengefulness that they felt towards the Nazis." (*Birth of Israel*, p. 96).

16. *Zionism and the Palestinians*, p. 13.

17. Yehoshofat Harkabi, *Fateful Decisions* (Tel Aviv: Am Oved, 1986).

18. Ibid., p. 12.

19. Ibid., p. 45.

20. Ibid., p. 31.

21. H.C. Kelman, "Israelis and Palestinians: Psychological Prerequisites for Mutual Acceptance," *International Security* 3, no. 1 (1978), pp. 162–185 and "Creating the Conditions for Israeli-Palestinian Negotiations," *Journal of Conflict Resolution* 26, no. 1 (1982), pp. 30–75.

22. "Creating the Conditions," p. 42.

23. "Israelis and Palestinians," p. 183.

24. Galtung, p. 183.

25. Kelman, "Israelis and Palestinians," pp. 164, 165.

26. Kelman, "Creating the Conditions," p. 43.

27. "Israelis and Palestinians," p. 172.

28. Ibid., pp. 176–185.

29. Ralph White, "Misperception in the Arab-Israeli Conflict," *Journal of Social Issues* 33, no. 1 (1977), pp. 190–221.

30. Ibid., pp. 199, 204.

31. Ibid., p. 218.

32. N. Kaplowitz, "Psychological Dimensions of the Middle East Conflict," *Journal of Conflict Resolution*. 20, no. 2 (1976), pp. 279–317.

33. Ibid., pp. 284–292.

34. Ibid., pp. 292–295.

35. Ibid., pp. 303–304.

36. Heradstveit, D. *Arab and Israeli Elite Perceptions* (Oslo: Universitetsforlaaget, 1974).

37. Ibid., pp. 101–102.

38. Ibid., pp. 126–135.

39. J.E. Mroz, *Beyond Security: Private Perceptions Among Arabs and Israelis* (New York: Pergamon Press, 1980).

40. Ibid., pp. 21–26.

41. Ibid., pp. 136–183.

42. M. Inbar and E. Yuchtman-Yaar, "Some Cognitive Dimensions of the Arab-Israeli Conflict," *Journal of Conflict Resolution* 29 no. 4 (1986), pp. 699–725, and E. Yuchtman-Yaar and M. Inbar, "Social Distances in the Arab-Israeli Conflict. A Resource Dependency Analysis" *Comparative Political Studies* 19, no. 3 (1986) pp. 283–316.

43. E.E. Azar and J.W. Burton, *International Conflict Resolution Theory and Practice* (Boulder: Lynne Rienner Publishers, 1986).

44. E. Yuchtman-Yaar and M. Inbar, *The People's Image of Conflict Resolution: A Comparative Survey of Israelis and Palestinians* (Tel-Aviv: Institute for Social Research, Tel Aviv University, 1987).

23

Psychological Considerations in the Peace Process

Joseph V. Montville

There is some irony in the fact that this paper is written by a professional diplomat. It is only minimally concerned with current or proposed traditional diplomatic and political approaches and suggestions. Rather, it addresses the underlying psychological tasks of any peace-making strategy for Israel, the Palestinians and other involved Arab parties. In fact, it is concerned with the psychological tasks in any approach to resolving or managing a protracted ethnic or sectarian conflict.

The basic theme of this paper is that when addressing ethnic conflict, traditional diplomacy and statecraft are routinely frustrated by some of the iron laws of human nature. And unless would-be mediators address the fundamental psychological tasks in the resolution of protracted ethnic conflict, traditional political strategies alone have very little chance of succeeding.

Among the iron laws of human nature are the fact that all peoples have basic, non-negotiable needs for identity, security and self-esteem. Self-esteem comes from a capacity to value oneself as an individual and as a member of an identity group. One feels valued and valuable, for example, as a hypothetical Robert Smith might feel good about himself as a person and as an Englishman. Self-esteem is eroded when the individual feels unvalued or degraded or marginalized through no apparent fault of his own. This form of devaluation is especially depressing and hurtful when it appears that the individual's identity group—race or nation—is unvalued and degraded. He/she is disadvantaged or despised simply for being a member of a race, religion or nation.

When people, as individuals or groups, are denied their basic needs for identity, security—for themselves, their families, their futures—and for self-esteem, they become enraged and defensive. Sometimes their rage is self-

---

The views expressed in this chapter are the author's alone and do not necessarily reflect those of the Department of State or any other U.S. Government agency.

destructive, perhaps through depression, alcohol and/or drug abuse. But more often, they become aggressive in their own defense. They become violent. At some point, initial, spasmodic, defensive violence becomes routine and can be expected to continue until there is some basic resolution of the situation of degradation. This phenomenon can be traced in the European Zionist experience leading up to the establishment of the Jewish state in 1948. And it can be traced in the activities of Palestinians starting in the 1950s, at least, and continuing to this day. In this and many other cases of protracted ethnic and sectarian violence, we are dealing with the psychology of victimhood. In the Israeli-Palestinian case, it is the psychology of *competing* victimhoods.

Victimhood in ethnic conflict is an individual and collective state of mind that occurs when traditional structures which provide security and a sense of worth through membership in a group are shattered by aggressive, violent political outsiders. It can be characterized by either an extreme sense of mortal vulnerability or simply a consistent, low-level sense. It has at least three components:

- It results from personal experience. Some episode of physical or psychological violence occurs at the hands of an adversary that stuns the victim or those close to the victim.
- The violence against the victim or victim group is unjustifiable by almost any standard. The victim is aware that his civil and human rights are being violated and that most people would agree with him.
- And, the assault is part of a continuous threat posed by the adversary which nourishes a basic, if unarticulated, fear of annihilation in the victim or victim group.

This last element is critically important in the definition. It is always characteristic of victims that they are afraid of further challenges or attacks, that more attempts to destroy them lie in the future.

The late political psychologist, Jeanne Knutson, conveyed the mind-set of the victim vividly in an unpublished manuscript she sent the author in 1983. She wrote that a victim's identity is never erased. The first blows make the victim permanently on guard for the attack by the victimizer. Even if the latter—a tribe, another ethnic group or nation—loses power or the ability to mount a credible threat, the victim's fear continues, although perhaps diminished. A life-preserving primitive belief in personal safety having been breached, the victim, once terrorized, simultaneously mourns the past and fears the future. This intense anxiety over future loss is driven by the semi-conscious knowledge that passivity ensures victimization. The genesis of political violence is the belief that only continued activity in defense of one's self, or one's group, adequately serves to reduce the threat of further aggression against the self.

A very powerful declaration of ethnic victimhood is found in the early memoir of Menachem Begin entitled, *The Revolt* (1950). The reader may object that what follows is not necessarily representative of majority Jewish or Israeli thinking either at the time or at present. However, from the psycho-political perspective, the statement effectively reflects the concept of victimhood, and it also foreshadows a good deal of the emotion Mr. Begin would bring with him to the prime ministership of Israel in 1977.

> Step by step, stage by stage, the German butcher had turned our people into a panic-stricken, disunited mass striving only to live and forgetting that sometimes the only hope of living is to be ready to risk one's life. At the same time he was testing the reactions of the world, which he assumed, for the purposes of this experiment, was largely indifferent to the shedding of Jewish blood. He was not mistaken. . . . [But] a new generation grew up which turned its back on fear. It began to fight instead of to plead. For nearly two thousand years, the Jews, as Jews, had not borne arms and it was on this complete disarmament, as much psychological as physical, that our oppressors calculated. . . . When we launched our revolt against the yoke of oppression and against the wanton shedding of Jewish blood we were convinced that our people truly had nothing to lose except the prospect of extermination. . . . Only when you are prepared to stand up to Zeus himself in order to bring fire to humanity can you achieve the fire revolution. . . . When Descartes said: "I think, therefore I am," he uttered a very profound thought. But there are times in the history of peoples when thought alone does not prove their existence. A people may "think" yet its sons, with their thoughts and in spite of them, may be turned into a herd of slaves—or into soap. There are times when everything in you cries out; your very self-respect as a human being lies in your resistance to evil. *We fight, therefore we are!*[1]
>
> Themes are clear. Being marginal, being despised. Not being able to count on help from outside the group—the people—for defense of the most elementary right to life. And, in particular, the need to fight to protect the existence of an entire people.[1]

There is a competing perspective. In a study by the Group for the Advancement of Psychiatry of the psychodynamics of the Israeli-Palestinian conflict, the researchers interviewed a Palestinian Christian named Youssef, who was well educated abroad and at age twenty-three became a teacher of refugee students in the pre-1967 West Bank. In the following exerpts from the study, Youssef describes the development of his own sense of victimhood:

> I was slow in developing political consciousness; I was committed to ideas of reconciliation. . . . When I taught refugees . . . my anger grew. Exile is a terrible condition. . . . It is a condition of being in a place that is not my country. . . . It is the foreign way of seeing one's self and one's homeland—it destroys one's person, one's identity. [After the 1967 war, Youssef found that he could not sustain his lifelong opposition to all human violence. He began to feel that violence against oppression is sometimes morally justified.] . . . I read Fanon and I agree with him; being in exile is in itself a kind of violence; being in refugee camps is even worse—personal, direct, oppressed violence. Some Palestinians became paranoid, developed terrible personal

problems. Some solved their dilemma by becoming super-Arabs or super-Americans; racists—that's even worse.

The GAP study concludes, "Youssef came to believe there was no other way for a people threatened with obliteration—that sooner or later they must fight back and the only possible way involved assertion; the only possible assertion was violence even though such action required willingness to give one's life."[2]

There is an obvious parallelism in the sentiments expressed by the Jewish victim and the Palestinian victim. And even though the historical record of Christian persecution of Jews is infinitely longer than that of Palestinian victimhood resulting from the establishment of the Jewish state, there is no lessening of the intensity of the Palestinian emotion by the comparison.

There is some analytical help available to understand the phenomenon of competitive victimhood. John E. Mack, a Harvard psychiatrist and theorist in political psychology, was writing of Greek and Turkish Cypriots at the time, but this fact only underscores the universality of the iron laws of human nature referred to above. Mack wrote:

> It is remarkable how little empathy is felt by national groups for the suffering of their traditional enemies, even if the victimization on the other side is palpably evident and comparable to or greater than one's own. . . . Certainly the feeling of justification for hatred because of past grievances buttresses the hostility among individuals within the group and for the group collectively. The experience of traumatization has an additional effect which I would call the *egoism of victimization*. This is the tendency, which severe hurt and grief seem inevitably to bring about, to direct all investment, all empathy and love, toward those of one's immediate circle of fellow sufferers, defined generally in no broader terms than oneself and one's own afflicted people. Conversely, any investment of caring in the other side is withdrawn.[3]

Mack goes on to underline the point made in the three-part characterization of victimhood suggested above, noting that the fear that one's people will once again become victims perpetuates a hostile vigilance and an unwillingness to take risks. "It is for this reason," he continues, "that intervention of third-party groups, whose members are able to appreciate the ambiguities of the situation and the humanity and worth on both sides, may be essential if the cycle of repeated wars between two ethnic groups caught in a web of hostility is to be interrupted."[4]

The present writer has dealt at some length with the mechanisms of third party intervention, notably the problem-solving workshop, as an aspect of track two diplomacy in the resolution of ethnic conflict, in a volume entitled *Conflict Resolution: Track Two Diplomacy*.[5] What is important to emphasize here is that there are enormously difficult tasks of rehumanization of the adversary relationship between the parties in any ethnic conflict, and most emphatically that of the Israelis and the Palestinians. And as we have seen, an understanding of the psychology of victimhood goes a long way to explain the degree of difficulty.

To reverse the dehumanization process requires that Israelis and Palestinians, preferably with the help of third parties, breach the wall standing
between them created by their tragic experience and reinforced by the
dynamics of victimhood we have been discussing. Each people will have
to teach the other that they are worthy and valuable as a people, sharing
the universal desire for security, identity and respect and capable of recognizing
and respecting this right in the other.

Small, frequently scheduled, facilitated workshops which bring together
various leadership elites from the Israeli and Palestinian sides will be crucial
to this effort. There will also have to be major campaigns through schools,
media, and public education events of all kinds to communicate the humanity
of each side to the other. Collaborative economic development schemes
may contribute to the process. Whatever the mix of strategies in these
track two diplomatic efforts, it seems clear that no traditional diplomatic
or political peace plans will have a chance to succeed unless the psychological
obstacles to conflict resolution are removed.

As difficult and abstract as the foregoing task may sound, there have
been at least some modest attempts to begin it. (See *Conflict Resolution:
Track Two Diplomacy*.) It is with some trepidation that I suggest that there
are perhaps equally complicated and abstract parallel challenges which must
be confronted, if the Israeli-Palestinian process is to truly succeed.

John Mack referred to the reluctance of victims to take risks. In the
case of Israel this is true not only in the case of the Palestinians and other
Arabs, but also with Gentiles in general and Western Christians in particular—including Russian/Soviet "Christians." Modern Israel might not
even exist if European Jews had been able to establish secure and trusting
relationships over the centuries with the monarchies, empires and republics
of Europe, especially with their Christian subjects and citizens.

Christians have yet to understand the enormity of the moral debt they
owe to European Jewry for their unconscionable history of persecution.
The victimhood Menachem Begin so powerfully articulated in *The Revolt*
was rooted in the Jewish experience in Europe. The wariness of Israelis
toward various Western Middle East peace plans is also rooted in a basic
distrust of Gentiles earned the hard way over the centuries. There is a
great deal of healing in this relationship to be accomplished before a secure,
confident Israeli-Western alliance in the interest of establishing a just and
lasting peace with the Palestinians and other Arabs can be established.

Also difficult is the parallel challenge: reconciliation between the West
and the Palestinians in particular and the Muslim world in general. It is
obvious that for a variety of reasons in addition to the lack of a resolution
to the Israeli-Arab conflict, there has been a steady deterioration of the
relationship between Western Europe and the United States and the Muslim
world, especially the Arab states and Iran. Arabs and Iranians resident in
the West complain bitterly of heightened discrimination and abuse, and if
Muslims in the Middle East believe they have been deprived of their needs
and rights, they can be expected to act defensively, and at times violently,

just like the rest of humankind, to protect their sense of self-hood and dignity.

A peace-making strategy that does not integrally take these facts into account and does not provide for a reconciliation process on this level has minimal chance of lasting success. And for the healing process to be effective, political leaders at the highest levels must involve themselves and be seen to be involved by the target group or nation. For, above all, the psychological tasks of conflict resolution must ultimately be recognized and carried out by political leaders.

Notes

1. Menachem Begin, *The Revolt*. (Jerusalem: Steimatsky, 1950), p. 27 seq.

2. Group for the Advancement of Psychiatry (GAP), *Self-Involvement in the Middle East Conflict*. Vol. X, Publication No. 103. (New York: Mental Health Materials Center, 1978), pp. 465-79.

3. John Mack, "Foreword" to V. Volkan, *Cyprus: War and Adaptation*. (Charlottesville: University of Virginia Press, 1979), p. xvi.

4. Ibid., p. xvii.

5. Joseph Montville, "The Arrow and the Olive Branch: A Case for Track Two Diplomacy," in *Conflict Resolution: Track Two Diplomacy*, J. McDonald and D. Bendahmane, eds. (Washington, D.C.: Government Printing Office, 1987).

24

Arabs and Israelis: Changing Perceptions and Political Attitudes

Erika G. Alin and Abdul Aziz Said

Since the Six Day War, several plans for a peaceful settlement of the Arab-Israeli conflict have foundered. Many of these proposals appeared to have the potential for reconciling the conflicting interests of Arabs and Israelis. Yet the focus on tangible dimensions of interaction, such as military, political, and territorial assets, has resulted in a tendency to underestimate the role of perceptions and political attitudes in perpetuating the conflict. It is, therefore, necessary to analyze how Arabs and Israelis view one another and how changes in beliefs over the past two decades affect the course of a peaceful settlement of the conflict.

Public opinion surveys have reflected changes in perceptions and political attitudes. They have been available for Israeli Jews (hereafter Israelis) throughout the post-1967 period. Among the Arab states, few surveys have been conducted and most have been confined primarily to the political, professional, and intellectual elite, and to Egyptian political attitudes. In the 1980s there have been a few serious attempts to survey opinions among the West Bank Palestinian public.

Perceptual Context of the Conflict

The emergence of the state of Israel represents the institutionalization of an effort to guarantee survival for the Jewish faith through territorial sovereignty. As a result of the Arab threat, Israeli policies, since 1948, have been oriented toward survival and security. Concern with survival develops solidarity and an intense attachment to the country as well as an integrated population while security ensures survival as a nation. For the Arabs, Israel represents an intrusion into the "Arab nation," an indefensible affront and challenge to Arab dignity and sovereignty. Alien to the region, Israel is perceived as a constant political and military threat to Arab aspirations of security, unity, and development.

Throughout the post-1967 period, Arab and Israeli perceptions of one another as hostile and aggressive and of one's self as vulnerable and threatened have continued to determine policy.[1] Arabs and Israelis have generally remained pessimistic regarding the prospects for a political settlement. Real peace requires communication and at least a limited mutual understanding, which can emerge only in a political and psychological atmosphere in which perceptions and attitudes can change. Unfortunately, historical experiences, the potentially high cost of miscalculating the intentions of the opponent, and the uncertainty of how the other will respond to one's moves have strengthened resistance to change among Arabs and Israelis.

Yet over the past two decades several important modifications in political attitudes have occurred. Among the Arabs, there has been increasing recognition that Israeli will continue to exist in the region and that ways of coexisting must be found. The conflict has moved from the military to the political arena; from destruction of the Zionist entity to political accommodation with the Israeli state. Among Israelis, some have realized that most Arabs are no longer actively committed to destroying Israel. Israelis, furthermore, have moved from perceiving the conflict as involving only their relations with the Arab states to recognizing that a political settlement will require finding a solution to the Palestinian problem. There has been a convergence of perception among Arabs and Israelis on the need for a political settlement and some of the principal issues that need to be resolved.

Changes in beliefs and political preferences have occurred primarily in response to major events in Arab-Israeli relations, in particular the 1967 war; the 1973 war; the Sadat initiative of 1977 and the subsequent Camp David accords and Egyptian-Israeli peace treaty; and the Israeli invasion of Lebanon. Limits to change remain. Much has been either temporary or confined to minority segments of Arabs and Israelis.

1967–1973: Israeli Perceptions and Attitudes

Following the 1967 victory, Israelis felt a sense of euphoria and full confidence that their military superiority would succeed in perpetuating the status quo. This self-confidence and disdain for the Arab threat was reinforced by previous successes in the conflict. At the same time, there was an increasing sense of frustration and insecurity. The initial belief that victory would bring the Arabs to the negotiating table proved unfounded, and in the early 1970s Israel found itself vulnerable to the increasing militancy and guerilla raids of the PLO. Confidence in military superiority combined with the inability to attain peace reinforced the pre-war national consensus on relatively inflexible policies toward the Arabs.

Throughout the early 1970s, the Israeli public overwhelmingly supported the aggressive approach of the Labor Government toward the Arab states and many sought even more hardline policies.[2] On the question of the occupied territories, in the late 1960s, the majority agreed with the official policy of exchanging most of the territories for peace. However, opinions soon diverged as a growing segment of Israelis began to object to any territorial concessions while others continued to consider territorial compromise critical to prospects for peace. In 1971, 56 and 31 percent of Israelis refused to compromise on the West Bank and Sinai respectively, while the remainder favored the return of all or parts of these territories.[3] Thus in the early 1970s an increasing tendency for Israelis to disagree on territorial issues became apparent.

A combination of factors contributed to the hardline approach of many Israelis to the territories. As the peace process remained stalemated, many Israelis began to feel that territorial concessions would not bring the Arabs to the negotiating table. Israeli confidence in their ability to hold onto the territories through force increased following the victory, in 1970, over Egypt in the war of attrition. Finally, as a result of Palestinian militancy, many began to consider the territories to be vital to national security.

Throughout the 1967 to 1973 period, Israelis remained convinced that the Arab states intended to destroy Israel and were unwilling to make peace. Many, however, felt that the Arab public was more moderate in its approach to the conflict than the Arab governments. Over 75 percent of Israelis, in 1971, believed that Arabs interested in a peace acceptable to Israel could be found.[4] In late 1970, furthermore, many Israelis responded positively to the ceasefire with Egypt. The number of Israelis believing that the Arabs in general did not want peace dropped significantly (from 89 to 65 percent).[5] Yet in contrast to the more durable shift in attitudes that followed Sadat's visit to Jerusalem in 1977, in 1970 the increase in optimism regarding the prospects for peace was temporary. Since the ceasefire was not accompanied by fundamental changes in Egyptian policies toward Israel, most Israelis continued to perceive Egyptians and other Arabs as hostile and not wanting peace. Nonetheless, a significant minority (38 percent) in early 1971 believed that Egypt was interested in peace on terms acceptable to Israel.[6]

During the 1967 to 1973 period, Israelis continued to perceive Arab intentions as hostile and aggressive. As a result of military victory, there was a feeling of contempt for the challenge posed by the Arabs. As the peace process remained stalemated and Palestinian resistance increased, a general shift occurred toward more uncompromising positions on the occupied territories and more pessimistic orientations toward the prospects for peace. However, public opinion indicated that some Israelis were receptive to specific changes in relations with the Arab states and believed that there were Arabs who were interested in peace.

1967–1973: Arab Perceptions and Attitudes

In the period 1967 to 1973, the overwhelming majority of Arabs believed that Israel was an aggressive and expansionist state that presented a high level of threat to the Arab world. Opinions among middle and upper-class professionals and university students can be considered indicative of broader political trends. Seventy-five percent of this elite, between 1968 and 1972, perceived Israel as harboring expansionist designs and two thirds wanted the conflict to continue until the defeat of Israel.[7] Only a small minority of Arabs relatively peripheral to the conflict at the time (primarily Tunisians, Egyptian Copts, Lebanese, and some West Bank Palestinians) expressed a clear readiness for a political settlement with Israel.[8]

The overwhelming majority of Arabs opposed any acceptance of or compromise with Israel. Iraqi, Saudi Arabian, and Kuwaiti elites held the most hardline positions in the conflict, an average of 70 percent unambiguously supporting the destruction of Israel. Members of the Egyptian, Jordanian, and especially Lebanese professional and educated classes displayed slightly less aggressive attitudes toward Israel.[9] As among Israelis, Arab attitudes, at this stage, were shaped almost exclusively by ideological and emotional factors and were generally unrelated to socio-economic status or educational levels. Younger Muslim Arabs, however, expressed greater militancy toward Israel than their elders, and Christian Arabs were more likely than Muslims to believe that Israel wanted to negotiate peace.[10]

Following the 1967 defeat, Arab leaders tended to perceive developments in a negative light, as Israel had the upper hand in the conflict. Arab governments, in principle, rejected any recognition of or political settlement with Israel and generally expressed a determination to continue the struggle. However, as a result of the vast strategic gap that separated them from the Israelis, some Arab political and intellectual elites began, in the late 1960s-early 1970s, to recognize that Israel would probably continue to exist in the region.[11]

Egyptian and Jordanian political and intellectual leaders indicated an openness to political solutions through displaying flexibility on Security Council Resolution 242, which recognizes the right of all states in the region to live within "secure and defensible borders," and on the idea of a Palestinian state alongside Israel.[12] About 40 percent of the Egyptian elite was ready to consider a political compromise provided that Israel withdrew from all the territories occupied in 1967.[13] The willingness to compromise, however, was ambiguous and conditional. Egypt and Jordan continued to oppose direct negotiations with Israel and insisted on prior Israeli withdrawal from the occupied territories as a precondition to negotiations of any sort. Given traditional suspicions, Israelis feared that indications by Arab leaders of possible political compromise were intended primarily to camouflage the ultimate goal of destroying Israel. Positions favoring negotiations, furthermore, were not usually expressed publicly and were confined to a minority of Arab political leaders, professionals, and university students.

1973–1977: The Arab States and the PLO— A New Political Environment

As a result of their relative victory in the 1973 war, the Arab states tended to interpret subsequent developments in a manner consistent with

their perception that events were taking a favorable turn. The strategic gap
between the Arab world and Israel appeared to have narrowed, and the
Arab states perceived their influence relative to that of Israel as on the
rise. The war had demonstrated the inability of Israeli military power to
impose peace. The result was a new sense of confidence and a slight increase
in optimism regarding the prospects for peace. Following both the 1967
and 1973 wars, the side that had successfully demonstrated its military
strength grew more optimistic concerning the possibility that the opponent
would accept a political settlement on its conditions.

The October war eased the psychological barriers among some Arab
states, especially Egypt, to accepting the reality of Israel's existence. The
recognition of the need for a political settlement that had surfaced in an
ambiguous manner among some Arab leaders, in the late 1960s and early
1970s, grew clearer and more consistent. A new regional political environment
emerged as states such as Egypt, Jordan, and Syria indicated a readiness to
pursue the conflict with Israel through diplomatic channels.

Most Arabs did not believe that the new political and strategic environment
would lead to changes in Israeli policy. They, therefore, did not modify
their perceptions of Israeli intentions and continued to view Israel as an
aggressive and expansionist state.[14] Basic attitudes regarding the opponent
generally remained unchanged.

Trends among the Arab states influenced political developments within
the Palestinian community. The 1967 Arab defeat had spurred the PLO
into pursuing a strategy of total armed confrontation with Israel in order
to establish a "democratic state" in all of Palestine. Political and military
setbacks in the early 1970s made Palestinian leaders aware of the formidable
obstacles to achieving their maximum objectives. Following the October
war, some PLO leaders recognized the need to adjust their policies to the
emerging trend toward political compromise among key Arab states in order
not to be excluded from the diplomatic process.

Political change among the Palestinians, as among non-Palestinian Arabs,
was ambiguous and its evolution gradual. Historical experiences had made
Palestinians deeply suspicious of political solutions to the conflict with Israel
and reluctant to relinquish their reliance on the military struggle. Although
the 12th Palestinian National Council (PNC) in 1974 indirectly endorsed
the notion of a West Bank-Gaza state, for most Palestinians this represented
a tactical step toward liberating all of Palestine. Yet even if the apparent
move toward political moderation within key segments of the PLO leadership
was a cover for maximalist Palestinian aspirations, it was important for it
corresponded to the general trend in Arab politics in the mid-1970s.

1973–77: Changing Israeli Attitudes
Toward the Conflict

Following the October war, Israelis generally felt that developments were
taking a negative turn. The apparent increase in concerted Arab military

and political strength reinforced perceptions regarding Arabs as aggressive and seeking to destroy Israel. The number of Israelis that perceived Arabs as threatening rose, from 75 to 92 percent, between 1972 and 1976. Over the same period there was a significant drop in optimism regarding the prospects for positive changes in relations with the Arabs, from 45 to 25 percent.[15]

At the same time, however, international pressures increased to induce sufficient Israeli concessions to bring key Arab states into a diplomatic process. In the mid-1970s, these factors contributed to strengthening the belief of some Israeli leaders that political disengagement if not a peace agreement with the Arab states was necessary and that this would require moderation in Israeli policy, possibly including a change in the territorial status quo. This political approach, in which the minimum quid pro quo for territorial concessions was a formal peace treaty, had been the unofficial platform of the Labor Party in the post-1967 period.[16] In the mid-1970s, indications that Israel would seriously explore this political option came with the Sinai II agreement with Egypt and culminated in the Israeli-Egyptian negotiations following Sadat's visit to Jerusalem.

Following the 1973 war, there was in Israel an unprecedented, though limited, recognition of the Palestinian issue as a separate dimension to the conflict with the Arabs. The existence of the Palestinians had been increasingly recognized as a result of the 1967 occupation of the West Bank and Gaza and Palestinian guerilla raids. In 1970, however, Golda Meir's statement that "there is no such thing as the Palestinians" had reflected the consensus in Israel that the conflict involved only Israel's relations with the Arab states and that no Palestinian problem existed.[17]

Indications that a change was underway appeared in the 1973 electoral program of the Labor Party which stated that there was a need for a solution to the problem of the "Palestinian identity." However, in 1974, an overwhelming majority of Israelis continued to regard the "Arab Palestinian people" as an artificial concept[18] and believed that the Arabs equated "fulfillment of the legitimate Palestinian rights" with the destruction of Israel.[19] The public supported the government's position that there was no need for a Palestinian state in the West Bank and Gaza, Jordan being the homeland of the Palestinians.[20] Significant changes in Israeli public opinion on the Palestinian issue did not appear until following the Camp David Accords.

1977: Egyptian Attitudes Toward Peace with Israel

Following the 1973 war, a more "national" as opposed to pan-Arab approach to the conflict dominated among those Arab states that had, over the previous decades, assumed a significant proportion of the costs of the struggle against Israel. Meanwhile, in the mid-1970s, the initial post-1973 optimism among many Arabs regarding the prospects for peace gave way to pessimism as the political process stalemated.[21] Against this background, Egypt took an initiative toward peace.

Surveys have been conducted among Egyptian university students and Western-educated middle and upper-class Egyptian professionals and government employees on the assumption that their opinions generally reflect trends in national politics. This group, furthermore, represented the core of Sadat's constituency. During the 1970s, the focus of many of these Egyptians had shifted from ideological to national political and economic concerns, and this was reflected in their marginal commitment to the Palestinian cause.[22] By the mid-1970s, many among the Egyptian elite recognized the social and economic costs for Egypt of the conflict with Israel. Though uneasy at the idea of normalizing relations with a historical enemy, they recognized the advantages of a peace settlement.

Few (slightly over 10 percent) of the Western-educated Egyptian professionals and government employees objected to Sadat's initiative for peace in 1977. A minority of 21 percent, however, indicated mixed feelings at an early stage,[23] and over one-third ultimately opposed or were undecided on the treaty with Israel.[24] There were, therefore, significant differences in opinion among this group of Egyptians on the form of peace that Egypt should be prepared to accept. Though not primarily concerned with broader Arab interests, most recognized the importance to Egyptian concerns of achieving a comprehensive regional peace that took into consideration the political and territorial interests of other Arab states and of the Palestinians. Nearly half indicated unease at Egypt's break with the regional consensus and would have preferred closer coordination with other Arab states in the negotiating process. Only 25 percent approved of Sadat's "go it alone" strategy.[25] Sixty percent believed that peace with Israel should be conditional on the return of all occupied territories to the Arab states and a majority considered Palestinian participation and the establishment of a West Bank–Gaza Palestinian state to be critical to real peace.[26] The bilateral character of the treaty was clearly rejected as a vehicle for achieving the broader Arab and especially Palestinian rights that many considered necessary to the regional stability that Egypt ultimately sought.

Educated Egyptians preferred a comprehensive Arab-Israeli settlement and, therefore, appear to have been more sensitive than Sadat to the political dilemmas of a separate peace. Though over two-thirds supported the peace treaty,[27] most did not agree with Sadat's claim that only psychological barriers separated them from the Israelis.[28] Many perceived the government as having overstepped its mandate and gone beyond the national consensus.

1977: Israeli Attitudes Toward Peace with Egypt

Sadat's visit to Jerusalem in November of 1977 broke the public consensus that had existed in Israel during the previous decade on a number of core issues of the conflict, such as the refusal of the Arab states to make peace and the rather peripheral role of the Palestinian issue to a political settlement. Clear indications that a significant shift in Egyptian policies toward Israel was underway caused public opinion, after an initial surge, to stabilize around a level of optimism concerning the possibility of peace considerably higher than that of previous years. In early 1978, half the Israelis polled believed that there would not be another war with the Arabs, compared to only 24 percent prior to November 1977.[29] Overall faith in Sadat's intentions doubled. Israelis, therefore, generally responded positively to this concrete Egyptian initiative for peace. Yet this optimism was tempered by skepticism concerning whether Sadat's policies reflected a new Egyptian consensus or would be reversed by subsequent governments.

Many Israelis were uncertain concerning the principle of relinquishing territory in return for peace and the extent of territorial concessions Israel should be prepared to make under such a deal. Forty percent either objected to or were undecided on exchanging the Sinai for peace,[30] and slightly more than half objected to the government's initial suggestion of returning all of the Sinai.[31] However, over 75 percent of Israelis supported Camp David,[32] and once the treaty with Egypt became official policy in 1979 the public overwhelmingly supported its principles. This reflected a desire for peace and a lower commitment to the Sinai relative to the other occupied territories. However, an equally significant force in determining Israeli attitudes toward the peace with Egypt was public support for the government in dealings with the Arabs.

After a decade of ambiguity and stalemated relations with the Arab states under Labor rule, Israelis responded positively to the clarity and initiative of the new Likud Government. Most felt that the Government was doing more or less everything possible for peace and, in late 1978, over half expressed a readiness to support any compromise judged necessary to peace by Prime Minister Begin.[33] Following the October war, for many Israelis concern with the security threat had taken precedence over efforts to attain peace. The result was a general shift toward more hardline attitudes toward the Arabs, reflected in the 1977 electoral victory of the Likud, and a readiness to support limited concessions in order to eliminate the security threat posed by Egypt.

The Egyptian-Israeli Peace Process: Obstacles to Positive Relations and Assessments of the Peace

Egyptians and Israelis hold different perceptions of what peace should involve. Sadat intended the peace agreement as a first step toward a comprehensive Arab-Israeli settlement. It was anticipated that the treaty would indicate to Israelis that a significant change in Egyptian perceptions and policies had occurred and that a new form of cooperation would be possible. Israelis, however, doubted the permanence of the shift in Egyptian policies and were skeptical concerning Egypt's ability to deliver long-term changes among the Arab states. For Israel, the peace was to be a purely bilateral process that would neutralize the most powerful Arab state in the conflict and lead to formal recognition and specific tangible gains (such as trade and diplomatic exchanges). Although many Israelis believed that Egypt sincerely wanted peace, they were not interested in the "partnership" envisioned by Sadat. Furthermore, differences persisted among Egyptians and Israelis concerning security strategy, the occupied territories, and the Palestinian issue.[34]

As a result of the peace treaty, previous perceptions among Israelis and Egyptians have been challenged. Israelis no longer believe that Egypt is determined to destroy Israel and Egyptians are less inclined to perceive Israel as an aggressive and expansionist state. Yet in spite of the mutual pragmatic recognition of the benefits of peace, the failure of Israelis and Egyptians to live up to one another's expectations of the peace process has left both questioning the other's intentions and commitment to real peace. The peace process has both reflected and reinforced the considerable political and psychological barriers that continue to separate Arabs and Israelis.

Egyptians and Israelis have been divided on the achievements of the peace process. In the early 1980s, nearly half of the educated Egyptian elite felt that the treaty was inadequate to the securing of real peace and that its bilateral character jeopardized both Egyptian and Arab rights. An equal number displayed negative attitudes toward the process of normalizing relations.[35] Many Israelis had high initial expectations that peace would lead to substantial tangible benefits and improved relations with the Arab world as a whole. In the mid-1980s, however, nearly half felt that relations with Egypt had either remained unchanged or deteriorated.[36] Among many Egyptians and Israelis, therefore, there has been a general sense of disillusionment with the peace process.

The separation of Egypt from the Arab bloc left the other Arab states and the Palestinians with a sense of futility concerning the prospects for peace. Among Israelis, the fact of having neutralized Egypt, combined with disappointment with the normalization process and the failure of Jordan to join the autonomy talks, resulted in a feeling of security and lack of urgency in pursuing peace in the 1977 to 1982 period.

Post-1977: Political Change Among the Palestinians

The proposed autonomy talks associated with the Egyptian-Israeli peace treaty, and attempts to bring Jordan into this framework, caused Palestinians to fear that they would be excluded from the peace process. At the same time, many felt that the hawkish Israeli policies toward the West Bank would lead to annexation. Palestinian leaders, therefore, sought to adjust their policies to what appeared to be the international consensus on a political settlement: establishment of an independent Palestinian state in the West Bank and Gaza in return for Palestinian recognition of Israel's right to exist.

The endorsement, by the 13th PNC in 1977, of an "independent national state" (in the West Bank and Gaza) had indicated a fundamental moderation in the political attitudes of PLO leaders. Throughout the 1980s, Arafat has supported peace proposals that implicitly or explicitly recognize Israel's right to exist. On the West Bank, a group of relatively pragmatic Palestinian political leaders, consisting of pro-Jordanians and supporters of the PLO's mainstream Fateh organization, has emerged in the 1980s.[37] These leaders have had contacts with moderate Israelis with whom cooperation based on mutual understanding and common interests has proven possible. In the late 1970s and early 1980s, therefore, a shift occurred among PLO and West Bank political leaders toward increasing political realism and moderation in the conflict with Israel.

Pragmatic West Bank politicians have recognized the need to compromise on exclusive PLO representation and complete Palestinian national independence in order to arrive at a formula for negotiations and peace that will be acceptable to Israel. They have supported the idea of confederation with Jordan and joint Jordanian-PLO diplomatic initiatives and have, furthermore, displayed increasing flexibility in their relations with Israeli authorities.[38]

Less than a handful of public opinion surveys have been conducted in the West Bank. In spite of this and minor inconsistencies and methodological problems, the overall trend in public opinion is clear. Throughout the mid-1980s, the West Bank public has generally been more ambiguous and less flexible than its political leaders on issues related to peace. It is less supportive of possible Palestinian confederation with Jordan and of Jordanian-Palestinian political cooperation. In 1983, while the majority supported the Jordanian-PLO dialogue, barely a third favored forming a Jordanian-Palestinian team to negotiate with Israel.[39] The overwhelming majority, over 90 percent in 1986, consider the PLO as their sole legitimate representative, over 70 percent favoring Arafat as their leader as compared to only 3.4 percent favoring King Hussein.[40] Although many West Bankers have recognized the need to explore political coordination with Arab states, they are more insistent on exclusive PLO initiative and more suspicious of King Hussein's intentions than are many Palestinian leaders.

The overwhelming majority of the West Bank public is not prepared to accept any solution whatsoever in order to end the occupation but insists on the establishment of an independent Palestinian state. Although it is difficult to generalize from West Bank opinion surveys given the varying manner in which questions have been asked, Palestinians appear to retain the ideal of a state in all of Palestine as a permanent solution, while endorsing an independent Palestinian state in the West Bank and Gaza as acceptable under present circumstances. In 1986, less than one percent favored continued Israeli rule or any form of autonomy under Israeli control.[41] Though recognizing the need for concessions, West Bankers generally are somewhat less willing than most PLO and West Bank leaders to compromise on exclusive Palestinian representation and statehood. Survey results are ambiguous regarding the extent to which they are prepared to accept the fundamental concessions that are required in order to meet the minimal demands of the Israelis and others for Palestinian participation in the peace process.

The West Bank public, in the mid-1980s, may be undergoing a transition from more idealistic and inflexible to more realistic and pragmatic perspectives on peace. A similar shift occurred among segments of the Palestinian leadership in the late 1970s and early 1980s. However, should the *status quo* persist, or conditions deteriorate, a radicalization of public opinion should not be ruled out.

1977–1982: Stability and Change
in Israeli Political Attitudes

The peace treaty with Egypt did not cause most Israelis to change their perception that the West Bank, the Gaza, and the Golan were vital to national security. Most continued to feel threatened by the Arab states and by the possibility of a Palestinian state in the West Bank. Over 80 percent of Israelis felt that an independent Palestinian state would threaten Israeli security, and nearly as many (70 percent) expressed similar fears concerning a Palestinian confederation with Jordan.[42] As a result, throughout the late 1970s and early 1980s, opposition to relinquishing the occupied territories in exchange for peace, even with security guarantees, remained firm.

However, the proposed autonomy talks generated a permanent shift in Israeli public opinion on the Palestinian issue. A growing segment of Israelis, in the late 1970s-early 1980s, recognized that peace with the Arab states would require providing some form of political expression for the Palestinians. Those prepared to agree to Palestinian statehood in the West Bank and Gaza, if the PLO recognized Israel's right to exist and ended all hostile acts, increased from 10–15 percent in the mid-1970s to 30 percent following the peace treaty.[43] In 1980, around 40 percent felt that Israel should recognize the Palestinians as a nation.[44] An equal number believed that, in principle, the Palestinians were entitled to a state of their own.[45] Most Israelis, however, continued to reject the notion of an independent Palestinian state in the West Bank.

A majority of the Israeli public supported the Government's position that if any change in the political status of the West Bank Palestinians should be necessary, an agreement that preserved Israeli control over most of the area could be worked out with Jordan. Over 70 percent felt that Jordanian participation was vital to solving the Palestinian problem.[46] Over sixty percent, in 1981–1982,[47] opposed PLO participation in the autonomy talks (even if the PLO recognized Israel's right to exist) and considered such participation not a prerequisite to reaching an agreement on Palestinian autonomy.[48] Throughout the 1980s, the Israeli government and most of the public have believed that the PLO can (and should) be circumvented in the peace process. Most Israelis have sought to avoid dealing with Palestinian nationalist institutions and confronting the issue of Palestinian nationalism.

Post-1982: The Israeli Political Center and the "Fringes"

In the mid-1980s a solid political center can be found, consisting of over half of the Israeli public, that generally supports the hawkish policies of the government toward the occupied territories and the Palestinians. Most of these Israelis consider the territories to be vital to national security and, therefore, oppose territorial concessions. Around half would support limited Palestinian autonomy in the West Bank if necessary to perpetuating Israeli control. A minority is prepared to accept Israeli withdrawal from limited areas of the territories in exchange for an agreement with King Hussein or Palestinian self-rule in close association with Jordan.[49] This majority segment of Israelis generally opposes an independent Palestinian state in the West Bank and Gaza. Many believe that this option would not solve the Palestinian problem and that it would, consequently, present a threat to Israel's security.[50]

In 1987, most Israelis (61 percent) continue to oppose negotiations with the PLO even if the latter recognizes Israel.[51] The majority has been unable or unwilling to reconcile apparent transformations in PLO policies with firmly held beliefs regarding Palestinian aggression and hostility. Over 75 percent deny that positive changes have occurred within the PLO or are likely to do so in the future.[52] Israeli fears concerning Palestinian intentions are reinforced by the PLO's tendency to combine moderation with non-conciliatory pronouncements. The result has been that most Israelis defer to the government's hawkish policies toward the Palestinians.

In the post-1973 period, a minority of Israelis began to question official policy toward the Arabs. Following the treaty with Egypt, this segment grew in size as more Israelis began to fear that inflexibility on the Palestinian issue would deprive Israel of a unique opportunity to establish peaceful relations with the Arab states. The invasion of Lebanon, in June 1982, reflected the aggressive policies of the Government toward the Palestinians and the occupied territories. Growing concern with the impact of such policies on Israeli society and Israel's relations with Arab and other states stimulated the emergence of a solid political 'fringe' of about one-third of Israelis who perceive a sense of urgency regarding a political settlement and are prepared to make concessions for peace.[53]

These peace-oriented Israelis seek security through coexistence rather than military might and territory alone. Throughout the 1980s, about one-third of Israelis have been prepared to accept territorial concessions in return for peace and security guarantees.[54] Various options for the West Bank have been proposed: partition between Israel and Jordan, Palestinian autonomy in association with Jordan, and an independent Palestinian state. There has been a parallel increase in the number of Israelis recognizing the importance of legitimate Palestinian representation to a peace conference. Between 1975 and 1985, the number supporting the participation of a Palestinian delegation in a peace conference more than doubled, from 15

to 37 percent.[55] Throughout the mid-1980s, between 34 to 45 percent of
Israelis have favored negotiations with the PLO provided that it recognizes
Israel and refrains from terrorism. In late 1987, thirty-seven percent held
this position.[56] Israelis who are interested in a lasting peace that will be
upheld by all parties perceive a convergence of interests with the Palestinians
in seeking a negotiated settlement of the Palestinian problem and participation
of the PLO, as the legitimate Palestinian representative—provided the PLO
clarifies its position on a political settlement.

The prospects for a peace involving Israeli concessions, however, has
stimulated the emergence of an extreme right-wing fringe of anywhere
between 25 and 60 percent of Israelis depending on the issue. As a result
of security and/or emotional commitments, these Israelis oppose any form
of compromise on the occupied territories and reject Palestinian self-
determination and legitimate Palestinian participation in negotiations. Over
the past few years, support for extreme hardline positions has fluctuated
somewhat depending on the policies of the government in power.

The political center in Israel tends to support the government's position
in regard to the occupied territories and the Palestinian issue. It overlaps
with either of the political fringes depending on official policy and the
issue. From 1982 to the present, this core of the Israeli public has supported
the government's opposition to Palestinian statehood in the West Bank and
to negotiations with the PLO. Its political force has been reinforced by
the extreme fringe, which advocates more aggressive policies toward the
Arabs. Together, these segments comprise between 50 and 75 percent of
the public varying with the issue. The majority of Israelis, therefore, do
not presently appear ahead of their government with regard to a political
settlement. However, given the tendency of the political center to look
toward the government for direction, should a government emerge prepared
to compromise on the territories in return for peace, it is possible that
this majority segment would move closer to the peace-oriented political
fringe. The latter would, in such a case, reinforce the political influence
of the former.

Implications for a Future Arab-Israeli Peace

Among Arabs and Israelis, beliefs that have been shaped by historical
experiences continue to determine policy in the 1980s. Many Arabs still
fear Israeli aggression and expansionism. The majority of Israelis continue
to perceive the Arab states and the Palestinians as a security threat. However,
in the post-1967 period, important shifts in political attitudes have occurred
among the majority of Arabs and Israelis. Israelis have realized that the
conflict involves both their relations with the Arab states and with the
Palestinians and that peace requires providing some from of political
expression for the Palestinians. The treaty with Egypt, furthermore, demonstrated that peace with the Arabs is possible. Arabs have increasingly
come to accept that Israel will continue to exist and that coexistence is
possible and desirable.

While it used to be possible to speak of one Arab and one Israeli public stance toward the conflict, in the post-1967 period there has been a divergence of perceptions within each community. Significant minority segments have recognized that, alongside historical aspirations, a pragmatic accommodation to changed circumstances is underway within the other camp. Among these segments, there has been communication and cooperation based on a common perception of urgency and the real possibility of achieving peace. The shifts in policy stances among Arabs and Israelis over the past two decades and the mutual recognition of the need to coexist have created a theoretical possibility for peace.

The fundamental concessions that are needed for a real peace that resolves the major issues, which it may be assumed that both sides ultimately desire, will emerge not through technical agreements but only in a transformed political and psychological environment in which Arab and Israeli interests can be brought closer. This requires acceptance of one another and a readiness to communicate at official political levels. Important Arab and Palestinian leaders appear prepared to commit themselves to a political process. The Jordanian-Palestinian dialogue aimed at the possibility of entering into negotiations with Israel. Arab peace proposals have reflected the emergence of a regional consensus around a political settlement that provides for self-determination or preferably statehood for the Palestinians in return for recognition of Israel's right to exist.

Members of the Israeli Labor Party and other peace-oriented Israelis have been engaged in a dialogue with Palestinian political and intellectual leaders. An Israeli government willing and able to take initiatives toward a positive political settlement and engaged in constructive contacts with Palestinian and other Arab leaders could increase understanding and trust of Arab, and especially Palestinian, intentions among the Israeli public. In the 1980s, there exists a theoretical possibility for peace. What is required is a sequence of events that will broaden the psychological acceptance, communication, and mutual understanding that now exists among important segments of Arabs and Israelis.

During the past two decades, the strategic gap among Arabs and Israelis has narrowed. In the 1967 war, Israel impressed the reality of its existence on the Arabs. In 1973, the Arabs demonstrated to Israel that it could not impose its will on them. The strategic stalemate that emerged in the mid-1970s made possible a narrowing of the perceptual and political gap. Many Arabs and Israelis, however, do not recognize that changes in perceptions and political attitudes have occurred. Others have been unwilling or unable to act on their conclusions. Fundamental beliefs regarding the hostility of the opponent continue to shape political preferences. Yet the force of such beliefs has diminished somewhat as growing segments of Arabs and Israelis have accepted the need for some form of accommodation to political reality. This pragmatic recognition of the benefits of peace has made a political settlement a realistic option for the Arab states, the Palestinians, and the Israelis in the 1980s.

Notes

1. For discussions of the psychological bases and stability of perceptions see Daniel Heradstveit, *The Arab-Israeli Conflict: Psychological Obstacles to Peace* (Oslo: Universitetsforlaget, 1981); Herbert C. Kelman, "Psychological Prerequisites for Mutual Acceptance," *International Security*, 13/ 1 (1978); and Ralph K. White, "Misperceptions in the Arab-Israeli Conflict," *Journal of Social Issues*, 33, 1 (1977).

2. Abdel Jacob, "Trends in Israeli Public Opinion on Issues Related to the Arab-Israeli Conflict 1967–1972," *The Jewish Journal of Sociology*, 16, 2 (Dec. 1974), p. 198.

3. Jacob, p. 196.

4. Ibid., p. 202.

5. Ibid., p. 201.

6. Ibid., p. 202.

7. Michael W. Suleiman, "Attitudes of the Arab Elite Toward Palestine and Israel," *American Political Science Review*, 117, 2 (1973), pp. 484–485.

8. Noel Kaplowitz, "Psychopolitical Dimensions of the Middle East Conflict," *Journal of Conflict Resolution* 20, 2 (1976), p. 284.

9. Suleiman, p. 489.

10. Ibid., p. 484.

11. Kaplowitz, p. 206.

12. Ibid., p. 285.

13. Suleiman, p. 489.

14. Heradstveit, p. 82.

15. Ibid., p. 82.

16. Kaplowitz, p. 293.

17. Yoram Peri, "The Rise and Fall of Israel's National Consensus," *New Outlook*, 26 (1983), p. 26.

18. Murad A'si, *Israeli and Palestinian Public Opinion*, (Washington, D.C.: ICRPP, 1986), p. 7.

19. Ibid., p. 8.

20. Ibid., p. 7.

21. Heradstveit, p. 87.

22. Raymond A. Hinnebusch, "Children of the Elite: Political Attitudes of the Westernized Bourgeoisie in Contemporary Egypt," *The Middle East Journal*, 36, 4 (Autumn 1982), p. 535.

23. Ibid., p. 546.

24. Abdul-Monem Al-Mashat, "Egyptian Attitudes toward the Peace Process: View of an Alert Elite," *The Middle East Journal*, 37 (1983), p. 399.

25. Hinnebusch, p. 547.

26. Ibid., p. 546.

27. Al-Mashat, p. 399.

28. Hinnebusch, p. 547.

29. A'si, p. 9.

30. PORI, s/s 1202 (December 1977), *Index to International Public Opinion, 1978–1979* (Westport, CN: Greenwood Press: 1984).

31. Ibid., s/s 1203 (January 1978).

32. Ibid., s/s 1210 (October 1978)

33. Ibid., s/s 1198 (March 1978) and PORI, s/s 1215 (December 1978).

34. For a discussion of Egyptian and Israeli perceptions see Stephen P. Cohen and Edward E. Azar, "From War to Peace: The Transition between Egypt and Israel," *Journal of Conflict Resolution*, 25, 1 (1981).

35. Al-Mashat, p. 399.

36. PORI, s/s 1200 (October 1983).

37. Emile Sahliyeh, "The West Bank Pragmatic Elite: The Uncertain Future," *Journal of Palestine Studies*, 15, 4 (Summer 1986), p. 34.

38. Ibid., Saliyeh, pp. 39–40.

39. Abdul Satter Kassem, "Public Opinion Survey in the West Bank and Gaza Strip," in A'si, p. 21.

40. "The Al-Fajr Public Public Opinion Survey," *Journal of Palestine Studies*, 16, 2 (Winter 1987), p. 200.

41. Ibid., *Journal of Palestine Studies*, p. 201.

42. PORI s/s 1202 (January 1981) and PORI s/s 1200 (January 1983).

43. See A'si, p. 11 and PORI s/s 1201 (October 1985).

44. Sammy Smooha and Don Peretz, "The Arabs in Israel," *Journal of Conflict Resolution*, 26, 3 (1982), p. 459.

45. PORI s/s 1201 (October 1985).

46. Ibid., s/s 1200 (January 1983).

47. Ibid. (September 1981).

48. Ibid., s/s 1208 (April 1982).

49. Ibid. (September 1984).

50. A'si 11.

51. Israeli Mirror, 765, 24 September 1987, p. 4.

52. PORI, s/s 1212 (December 1981) and PORI, s/s 1199 (July 1980).

53. For discussions of the Israeli peace movement see: "Interview: Mordechai Bar-On: The Peace Movement in Israel," *Journal of Palestine Studies*, 14, 3 (Spring 1985); Simha Flapan, "Israelis and Palestinians: Can they make Peace?" *Journal of Palestine Studies*, 15, 1 (Autumn 1985); and Muhammed Miari, "The Making of a Political Movement," *Journal of Palestine Studies*, 14, 1 (Fall 1984).

54. Fouad Moughrabi, "Public Opinion and the Middle East Conflict," *The Link* 20, 3 (1987), pp. 11–12.

55. PORI, s/s 1201 (April 1985).

56. Israeli Mirror, p. 4.

About the Contributors

Erika G. Alin is a Ph.D. candidate in the School of International Service, American University, Washington, D.C. She received a B.A. in Political Science from the State University of New York at Stony Brook, New York, in 1986. She served as research assistant in the Department of Political and Security Council Affairs at the United Nations in New York in 1985.

Naseer H. Aruri is Professor of Political Science at Southeastern Massachusetts University in North Dartmouth. He is the editor of *Occupation: Israel Over Palestine; Middle East Crucible: The Arab-Israel Confrontation of 1973;* author of *Jordan: A Study in Political Development,* and numerous articles in scholarly journals including *Middle East Journal, Journal of Palestine Studies, the Muslim World, Arab Studies Quarterly,* and *Third World Quarterly.* He is a member of the Board of Directors of Middle East Research and Information Project (MERIP) and a frequent contributor to *Middle East International* (London) and several Middle Eastern newspapers.

Andrea Barron is a freelance journalist specializing in the Middle East. Her articles and book reviews have appeared in various journals and newspapers including the Israeli journal *New Outlook,* and the *Journal of Palestine Studies.* She has done graduate work in international relations and Middle Eastern studies at American University's School of International Service and Georgetown University.

Abdalla M. Battah is Adjunct Professor at American University's School of International Service. He is the recipient of the Karim Rida Said Dissertation Fellowship. During 1988–89, he will be a Post-Doctoral Fellow at the Institute of International Studies, University of Minnesota. His research and teaching interests include international relations theory, international political economy, politics of the Middle East, and conflict resolution. Dr. Battah is currently preparing for publication *Ibn Khaldun's Principles of Political Economy: Rudiments of a New Science* and *The Political Economy of Israeli Occupation: Implications on the Peace Process.*

L. Carl Brown is Garrett Professor in Foreign Affairs and Director of the Program in Near Eastern Studies at Princeton Unviersity. He is the author of *International Politics and the Middle East: Old Rules, Dangerous Game.*

Duncan L. Clarke is Professor of International Relations at the School of International Service, American University. He has been a Ford Foundation arms control Fellow, has testified often before congressional committees, and was Professor of Foreign Affairs at the National War College (1979–81). Clarke authored or edited *Politics of Arms Control; Decisionmaking for Arms Limitation; United States Defense and Foreign Policy—Policy Coordination and Integration;* and *Management Does Matter: Organizing America's Defense and Foreign Policy.* His articles have appeared in *Foreign Policy, Middle East Journal, Political Science Quarterly, Presidential Studies Quarterly* and elsewhere.

Robert O. Freedman is Peggy Meyerhoff Pearlstone Professor of Political Science and Dean of the Graduate School of the Baltimore Hebrew University. He is the author of two books, *Soviet Policy Toward the Middle East Since 1970,* now in its third edition, and *Economic Warfare in the Communist Bloc: A Study of Soviet Economic Pressure Against Yugoslavia, Albania and Communist China.* He is also the author of a monograph, *The Soviet Union and the Carter Administration,* and the editor of *Soviet Jewry in the Decisive Decade 1971–1980, The Middle East Since Camp David, The Middle East Since the Israeli Invasion of Lebanon,* and *Israel in the Begin Era.*

Johan Galtung, Professor of Peace Studies, University of Hawaii, Honolulu, is the founder of the International Peace Research Institute in Oslo and author of numerous books on peace and development issues, including *Essays in Peace Research,* Vols. I–VI, and *The True Worlds.* Galtung is currently working on Civilization Theory and a book on U.S. foreign policy.

Raymond A. Hinnebusch is Associate Professor of Political Science at the College of St. Catherine, St. Paul, Minnesota, and author of studies on Syria, Egypt, and Libya, including *Egyptian Politics Under Sadat.*

Herbert C. Kelman is Richard Clarke Cabot Professor of Social Ethics at Harvard University and chairs the Middle East Seminar at the Harvard Center for International Affairs. A social psychologist by training, he has worked extensively on the analysis and resolution of international conflicts. In recent years, he has been engaged in an action research program on the Arab-Israeli conflict, which has concentrated on the organization of problem-solving workshops with Israeli and Palestinian participants. His books include *International Behavior: A Social-Psychological Analysis; A Time to Speak: On Human Values and Social Reserach;* and, with V. Lee Hamilton, *Crimes of Obedience: Toward a Social Psychology of Authority and Responsibility* (forthcoming). He is past president of the Society for the Psychological Study of Social Issues, the Peace Science Society, the Interamerican Society of Psychology, the International Studies Association, and the International Society of Political Psychology.

Bahgat Korany is Professor of Political Science and Director of the Arab studies program at the University of Montreal. As a visiting professor, he has taught at Laval University in Quebec (1976), the Patterson School of International Affairs at Carleton University (1977, 1978), and the University of Dakar in Senegal (1977, 1978), and he has been a Fellow of the Center for International Affairs, Harvard University (1979–1980). His book *Social Change, Charisma and International Behavior* (1976) was awarded the Hauchman Prize for the Study of International Relations in Switzerland.

Yehuda Lukacs, born in Budapest, Hungary, lived in Israel for eighteen years before immigrating to the U.S. in 1981. He is Adjunct Professor at the School of International Service, American University. He is currently a Lady Davis Visiting Research Fellow at the Harry S. Truman Research Institute, Hebrew University, Jerusalem. In 1983–1984, he was the Projects Director for the International Center for Peace in the Middle East, Tel-Aviv, Israel. His publications include *Documents on the Israeli-Palestinian Conflict: 1967–1983*, Cambridge University Press, 1984 (forthcoming in 2nd ed.). His articles and book reviews have appeared in *Journal of Palestine Studies, The Middle East Journal, New Outlook*, and *Jerusalem Post*.

Aaron David Miller received his Ph.D. in Middle Eastern history from the University of Michigan in 1977. Since 1980 he has been employed as a Middle East specialist for the Department of State where he is now a member of the Secretary of State's Policy Planning Staff. His latest book is *The Arab States and the Palestine Question: Between Ideology and Self-Interest*. His articles have appeared in *The New York Times, Los Angeles Times, Washington Post, Orbis, The Jerusalem Quarterly, Current History*, and *Middle East Journal*.

Joseph V. Montville, a career Foreign Service officer, is currently Research Director at the Center for the Study of Foreign Affairs, Foreign Service Institute, Department of State. He has been Chief of the Near East Division and Director of the Office of Global Issues in the Bureau of Intelligence and Research, and has had diplomatic assignments in Iraq, Lebanon, Libya and Morocco. He is a founding member of the International Society of Political Psychology. His articles have appeared in *Foreign Policy* and *Political Psychology* and he is the author of a forthcoming article in the *Journal of the American Psychoanalytic Association*.

Ilan Peleg heads the Department of Government and Law at Lafayette College, Easton, Pennsylvania. He is the author of *Begin's Foreign Policy, 1977–1983: Israel's Move to the Right*, a co-editor (with Ofira Seliktar) of *The Emergence of Binational Israel*, and the author of numerous articles on the Middle East and different aspects of international relations.

Don Peretz is Professor of Political Science, State University of New York, Binghamtom. He has conducted research on Middle Eastern issues since 1952 and lectured extensively around the world. His numerous publications include *The Middle East Today*, entering its fifth edition, and *The West Bank, History, Society, Politics, and Economics*. His articles have appeared in *New Republic, Foreign Affairs, Middle East Journal, Progressive, Journal of Palestine Studies, New Outlook, Middle East Insight, Journal of Conflict Resolution*, and elsewhere.

Yoram Peri, Professor of Political Science, Tel-Aviv University and editor of the daily *Davar*, Tel-Aviv. He has been visiting Professor at Dartmouth College (1987) and Harvard University (1986). Former Political Advisor to Prime Minister Rabin; author of *Between Battles and Ballots: Israeli Military in Politics*, and other books and articles on Israeli politics, society and civil-military relations. He has written for several newspapers and publications and served as radio and television commentator.

Cheryl A. Rubenberg is Associate Professor of International Relations in the Political Science Department at Florida International University. She is the author of *Israel and the American National Interest: A Critical Examination; The Palestine Liberation Organization: Its Institutional Infrastructure* and numerous articles on the PLO, Palestinian human rights, and U.S. policy in the Middle East.

Emile F. Sahliyeh is Associate Professor of International Relations and Middle East Politics at the University of North Texas. Between 1978-1984, Dr. Sahliyeh taught at Birzeit University in the West Bank. In 1985, he was a Fellow at the Woodrow Wilson International Center for Scholars. In 1986, he was a Middle East Fellow at the Brookings Institution. In addition to numerous chapters and articles, he is the author of *The PLO After the Lebanon War* and *In Search of Leadership: West Bank Politics Since 1967.*

Abdul Aziz Said is Professor of International Relations at the School of International Service, American University, Washington, D.C. His numerous publications include *Concepts of International Politics*, (with Charles O. Lerche, Jr.), *Human Rights and World Order*, and *Ethnicity and U.S. Foreign Policy.* He has contributed to many journals and newspapers on current issues in global politics. Professor Said has served as a member of the White House Commission on Islamic Affairs and participated in many conferences and organizations dealing with human rights and global peace.

Walter G. Seabold is Adjunct Professor in the School of International Service, American University. He has research interests in Soviet foreign economic policy and in international political economy.

Ofira Seliktar is a research professor at the Department of Political Science, University of Pennsylvania, and an adjunct professor at Drexel University. She is the author of numerous scholarly articles, and *New Zionism and the Foreign Policy of Israel*, and the co-editor of *The Emergence of Binational Israel: The Second Republic in the Making.* Presently, she is working on a book entitled *Looking at an Everchanging World: Psychology of Political Risk Management.*

Steven L. Spiegel is Professor of Political Science at the University of California, Los Angeles. His latest book, *The Other Arab-Israeli Conflict: Making America's Middle East Policy, From Truman to Reagan*, received the 1986 National Jewish Book Award. Professor Spiegel has published widely on international politics and American foreign policy toward the

Middle East in such journals as *Commentary, Orbis, Middle East Review, International Studies Quarterly, International Organization,* and *Journal of International Affairs.* His other books include *Dominance and Diversity: the International Hierarchy, The International Politics of Regions* (with Louis Cantori), *The Middle East and the Western Alliance* (editor), and *The Soviet-American Competition in the Middle East* (senior editor).

Bassam Tibi, Professor of International Relations at Gottingen University, Federal Republic of Germany, recently worked at the Al-Ahram Centre for Political and Strategic Studies in Cairo on his research project, "Conflict Linkages in the Middle East Since the Six Day War." He was a Research Fellow at Harvard (1982) and Princeton (1986/87) and is currently a Rockefeller Fellow at Michigan, where he is undertaking research on Secularism and the Nation-State as Issues in the Arabic Literature of Islamic Revival 1970–1985. His books in English include *Arab Nationalism: A Critical Inquiry,* and the forthcoming *Crisis of Modern Islam.*

Avner Yaniv is Professor of Political Science at the University of Haifa, Israel. During 1982–83, and 1986–88 he was a visiting professor at Georgetown University. In addition to numerous articles, he is the author of: *Dilemmas of Security: Politics, Strategy and the Israeli Experience in Lebanon; Deterrence Without the Bomb: The Politics of Israeli Strategy;* and *Syria Under Assad* (co-editor with Moshe Maoz); and the forthcoming *Israel Among the Nations: The Foreign Policy of the Jewish State.*

Yahia H. Zoubir is Assistant Professor in the Foreign Policy Semester Program and the School of International Service at American University. His research interests include West European Politics, U.S. and Soviet foreign policies, and Maghrebi politics. His most recent publications include "Soviet Policy Toward the Maghreb," and "The Italian Communist Party, NATO and Social Democracy" (forthcoming). He is curently working on a book on Soviet-Maghrebi relations.

Index

AAI. *See* Arab American Institute
AAUG. *See* Association of Arab-American University Graduates
Abbas, Mohammed, 284
Abdullah, Emir, 114(n25)
Abourezk, James, 254
Abram, Morris, 244, 246
Achille Lauro, 284
ADC. *See* American-Arab Anti-Discrimination Committee
Aden-Algiers Agreement, 113(n14)
Afghanistan, 265, 273, 306(n40)
AFL-CIO, 228, 241, 242
African states, 18–20, 158(fig.), 314
Ahdut Ha'avoda, 56, 57
AIPAC. *See* American Israel Public Affairs Committee
Ajami, Fouad, 156, 165, 169, 182
Al-Ahram, 176
Al-Azhar Islamic University, 168
ALF. *See* Arab Liberation Front
Algeria, 111(n3), 139, 171, 264, 266, 294–295, 303, 305(n3)
Algerian Association of *Ulama*, 139
Ali, Mohammed, 154
Al-Islam Wa Usul Al-Hukm (Raziq, al-), 140
Allon, Yigal, 28, 31, 32, 270
Amalek, 63
Amal militias, 79
American-Arab Anti-Discrimination Committee (ADC), 251–252
American Council for Judaism, 241
American-Israel Council for Israeli-Palestinian Peace, 245
American Israel Public Affairs Committee (AIPAC), 218, 222, 225, 228, 231, 232, 233, 242, 243, 244, 254
American Jewish Committee, 239, 245, 246, 247
American Jewish Congress, 239, 240, 245–246
Amman accord, 80
Amnesty International, 76
Andropov, Yuri, 277

Anti-Defamation League, 246, 247, 254
Anti-Semitism, 62, 63, 97, 108, 109, 233, 239
Aqaba, Gulf of, 242
Arab American Institute (AAI), 252–253
Arab-Americans, 247–254, 255
  voting of, 252–253
Arab-Americans: Studies in Assimilation (Hagopian), 249
Arab and Israeli Elite Perceptions (Heradstveit), 356
Arab Higher Committee, 72, 121
Arab League, 143, 165, 167, 168, 171, 175
Arab Liberation Front (ALF), 94(table), 99
Arab Military Industrial Organization, 175
Arab Predicament, The (Ajami), 169
"Arab Revolt," 143
Arab states, 164–166, 177, 334, 368
  and Amman summit, 340
  and Arab Triangle, 175, 182
  Baghdad Conference of, 299
  and Camp David, 273, 274, 298
  and compromise with Israel, 373
  conservative, 100, 101, 170, 300
  and Egyptian-Israeli relations, 89, 273, 298, 299
  and Fateh, 101
  and Fez summit and peace plan, 79, 176, 276–277
  groupings of, 274
  and *infitah*, 170
  and international peace conference, 303
  and Iran-Iraq war, 274
  Khartoum summit, 115(n32), 152, 169–170
  and labor imports/exports, 171–172, 171(fig.), 172(table)
  lamentation literature of, 167
  Maghreb vs. Mashreq, 176, 294
  and nationalism, 23, 168, 181
  and oil prices, 19
  and Palestinians, 73–74, 333
  and Pan-Arabism, 23, 24, 83, 136, 191–192. *See also* Nasserism

392

perceptions/attitudes of, 353–354, 372–373
and PLO, 99, 100, 101, 110–111(n1), 122, 129–130, 141–144
Rabat summit, 2, 16, 76, 79, 100
and Reagan Plan, 277
and recognition of Israel, 100
rich oil, 152–153, 170–171, 171(fig.), 173–174
and Saudi financing, 30
and Soviet arms, 15, 302. *See also* Soviet Union, military assistance to Arabs
Sunni, 155
system of, 98–102, 180–182
and United States, 170, 212
See also individual states
Arab Thought Forum, 329
"Arab Triangle," 175, 182
Arafat, Yasser, 93, 95, 105, 141, 245, 291(n60), 331(n4), 334, 379
and armed struggle, 283–284
and Assad, 80, 123, 144, 189, 278
Cairo Declaration of, 97
and Fateh, 113(n4)
and Hussein, 96–97, 124, 127, 281
and Israel's right to exist, 379
and PNC, 127
and Reagan Plan, 277–278
and Resolution 242, 103–104, 339
and Soviet Union, 278, 280
and Syria, 278
United Nations address of, 76, 100
See also Palestine Liberation Organization
ARAMCO, 209
Arens, Moshe, 13
Argentina, 22, 23
Assad, Hafiz, 186–190, 284
and Amin Gamayel, 279
and Arafat, 80, 123, 144, 189, 278
and Mashreq, 186
See also Syria
Association of Arab-American University Graduates (AAUG), 249
Aswan Dam, 201, 264
Australia, 228

Bab-el-Mandeb, Straits of, 220
Baghdad Pact, 168, 200
Balfour Declaration, 142, 321, 346
Ball, George, 223, 254
Bandung Nonaligned Conference, 135
Banna, Hasan al-, 139, 140
Barenbaum, Daniel, 282
Bargaining theory, 351–356, 360
Barrah, Morris, 49

Ba'th Party, 83, 181, 264
Begin, Menachem, 13, 15, 27, 30, 52, 55, 56–57, 66, 224
comparison of Beirut to Berlin, 62–63
electoral victory in 1977, 59–71
and European terrorism, 45
and *Gahal*, 56
and Judea and Samaria settlements, 61, 68(n28)
and legitimate rights of Palestinians, 234(n19)
and National Unity Government, 57–58
and Neo-Revisionism, 61
peace plan of, 32–33
The Revolt, 365–366
Behavioral research paradigm, 356–360, 361
Bendix, Reinhard, 154
Benelux, 325–326, 334
Ben-Gurion, David, 55, 62, 239
Bentley, Helen, 250
Berger, Morroe, 155
Bialkin, Kenneth, 233
Binder, Leonard, 149
Birth of Israel, The: Myths and Realities (Flapan), 348, 363(n14)
Black September, 97, 105, 107
B'nai B'rith Women, 240
Boschwitz, Rudy, 225, 247
Boumedienne, Houari, 295, 299, 305(n3)
Bourguiba, Habib, 137
Brazil, 22
Brezhnev, Leonid, 275, 277, 280, 296, 313
Bronfman, Edgar, 283
Brookings Institution, 118(n64)
Brown, Carl, 148, 154, 156
Brutents, Karen, 285
Brzezinski, Zbigniew, 206
Buy American Act, 227

Cairo University, 168
Caliphates, 156
Camp David Accords, 273, 286, 321–322
autonomy plan, 2, 33–34, 185, 378
vs. comprehensive settlement, 223
and Framework for Peace, 223, 234(n19)
as model, 322
and Soviet Union, 286, 298–299
Canada, 239
Carter, Jimmy, 13, 17, 110, 143, 159, 163(n55), 206, 223, 271. *See also* Carter administration
Carter administration, 104, 206, 210, 271, 298. *See also* Carter, Jimmy
Case-Zablocki Act, 220
Catholicism, 53(n18)
CC. *See* Central Council

Central Council (CC), 93
Chamoun, Camille, 137
Chernenko, Konstantin, 279
Chernobyl, 285
Chile, 22, 23
Churba, Joseph, 225
Chuvakhin, 15
Cluster bombs, 228
CMEA. See Council for Mutual Economic
    Assistance
Cohen, Ran, 255
Cohen, Steven M., 245, 256(n27)
Commentary, 241
Conference of Presidents of Major Jewish
    Organizations. See Presidents'
    Conference
Conflict, 364
    management of, 323
    psychology of, 353, 354
    resolution of, 345, 348, 351-356, 362
    and third parties, 367
    victimhood in, 365-367
Conflict Resolution: Track Two Diplomacy
    (Montville), 367
Council for Mutual Economic Assistance
    (CMEA), 315, 316
CPSU. See Soviet Union, Communist
    Party
Craxi, Bettino, 284
Cyprus, 238
Czechoslovakia, 309

Darawsha, Abdul Wahab, 255
Dawisha, Karen, 302
Dayan, Moshe, 27-28, 29, 57
Day of the Land, 76
Defense Emergency Regulations (British
    Mandate), 65
de Gaulle, Charles, 12, 14, 201, 204
Democratic Front for the Liberation of
    Palestine (DFLP), 94(table), 101,
    111(n2)
Democratic Movement for Change (DMC),
    32
Deutsch, Karl, 41
DFLP. See Democratic Front for the
    Liberation of Palestine
Dine, Tom, 243
Disengagement agreements, 30, 31, 100,
    184-185, 269, 375
DMC. See Democratic Movement for
    Change
Dole, Robert, 244, 251
Dulles, John Foster, 136, 200

Eban, Abba, 67(n13), 145, 334, 337
EC. See Executive Committee

EEC. See European Economic Community
Egypt, 152, 170
    and Arab League, 168, 171, 175
    and Arab states, 167-169, 180-182, 329
    and "Arab Triangle," 182-183
    and Camp David, 175, 185-186, 273
    disengagement agreements of, 30, 31,
        184-185, 269
    and Gaza Strip, 98
    and Iraq, 180
    and Jordan, 281
    and Muslim Brethren, 140
    and oil states, 154, 170
    and Palestinian state, 335
    peace initiative of, 375-376
    peace treaty with Israel, 273, 300, 378
    perceptions of Israel, 378
    population of, 167-168
    and recognition of Israel, 79, 373, 374
    and Saudi Arabia, 153, 174, 175, 182
    and Sinai, 299
    and Six Day War, 166-167
    and Soviet Union, 16, 30, 105, 137,
        183-184, 200, 264, 266, 268, 286, 312,
        313
    and Suez Canal, 184
    and Syria, 175, 179, 180-181, 182, 186,
        270
    and United States, 186, 191, 211, 266,
        275, 281, 284, 300
    Wafd Party in, 139
    and Yemen, 152, 169
    See also Nasser, Gamal Abdul; Sadat,
        Anwar; United Arab Republic
Eisenhower administration, 12, 200
El-Beblawi, Hazem, 173
Eliahu, Mordechai, 77
Ellenoff, Theodore, 246
Elusive Peace in the Middle East (Kerr),
    347
Eshkol, Levi, 15, 26-27, 56
Ethiopia, 23, 264
Euphrates Dam, 264
European Economic Community (EEC),
    14, 79, 315
Executive Committee (EC), 93, 94, 95
Exodus (Uris), 207, 218

Faisal, King, 170
Falwell, Jerry, 209
Faruq, King, 140
Fateful Decisions (Harkabi), 350
Fateh, 93, 94(table), 96, 97, 99, 100-101,
    105, 111-112(n1, 2, 3), 116(n40), 141
Findley, Paul, 232
Flapan, Simha, 348-350, 360, 363(n14)
Ford, Gerald, 243

France, 12, 14, 15, 19, 201, 204, 239, 265, 276, 294
Free Center, 31, 59
Freij, Elias, 76
F-16 fighters, 228, 236(n44)
Fuad, King, 139

Gahal, 27, 30, 31, 56, 57, 58
Galilee, 72, 76
Galtung, Johan, 346–347, 348, 351, 360
GCC. See Gulf Cooperation Council
Geertz, Clifford, 42
Gemayel, Amin, 278, 279
Gemayel, Bashir, 36
General Assembly of the Presbyterian Church (USA), 231
General Syrian Congress, 71
General Zionists, 54, 56
Geneva conferences, 17, 105, 269, 271, 273
Gibraltar, Straits of, 220
Gilman, Ben, 255
Globalism vs. regionalism, 149–151
Golan Heights, 28, 35, 40, 59, 104, 190, 283
Goldberg, Arthur, 205, 249
Goldmann, Nahum, 244
Goldwater, Barry, 232
Gorbachev, Mikhail, 18, 282, 283, 302, 316, 317
Graham, Billy, 209
Great Britain, 239, 276
Greater Israel Movement, 58, 59
Greater Syria, 142, 247
Green Line, 33, 55
Gromyko, Andrei, 269, 270, 308
Group for the Advancement of Psychiatry, 366–367
Guatemala, 309
Gulf Cooperation Council (GCC), 167, 168, 274
Gush Emunim, 31, 32, 33, 49, 58, 60, 66

Habash, George, 101, 281
Habib, Philip, 36, 77, 96
Haddad, George, 347–348
Hagopian, Elaine, 249
Haig, Alexander, 107, 226
Halacha, 48
Harkabi, Yehoshafat, 62, 103, 328, 331(n5), 337, 350–351, 360
Hashemites, 123
Hassan, Hani, 93, 97, 111(n3)
Hassan, Khaled, 93, 97, 111(n3)
Hassan II, King, 39, 294
Ha'uma, 56
Hawatmeh, Naef, 281

Hebrew Immigrant Aid Society, 239
Heikal, Mohamed, 170, 174
Heradstveit, Daniel, 356–357, 361
Hertzberg, Arthur, 242, 244, 245
Herut, 27, 31, 54, 55, 57, 58
Herzog, Chaim, 285, 292(n63)
Higher Committee for National Guidance, 85
Himmelfarb, Milton, 241, 256(n13)
Histradut, 241
Holocaust, 62, 63, 97, 108, 109, 239, 241, 242, 324
Hormuz, Straits of, 274
Human rights, 327, 328
Humphrey, Hubert, 240
Hussein, King, 18, 30, 57, 124, 127, 137, 251, 275, 280, 281, 303, 379

Idris, King, 139, 266
Inbar, Michael, 358–360, 361
Indian Ocean, 275
International Peace Academy, 347
International Peace Research Institute, 346
Iran, 23, 138, 139, 265, 368. See also Iran-Iraq war
Iran-Contra affair, 79, 236(n52), 285
Iran-Iraq war, 157, 190, 274, 300, 316
Iraq, 14, 136, 170, 171, 179, 200, 264, 265, 266, 273, 314, 335. See also Iran-Iraq war
Irgun Zvai Leumi (IZL), 55, 59
Islam(ic), 88, 151
  fundamentalism, 138–141, 156, 176, 329
  vs. nationalism, 156
  political, 157, 159
  and Soviet Union, 265, 280, 301
Islamic Brotherhood. See Muslim Brethren
Islamic Conference, 279, 306(n40)
Islamic Supreme Council, 85
Islam in Egypt Today (Berger), 155
Israel, 11, 41, 334
  and Africa, 18–20, 21
  and Arab states, 372
  Ashkenazi in, 109
  and Asia, 20–21
  attack on Iraqi nuclear reactor, 35, 235(n35)
  and Camp David, 377
  colonialism of, 347
  Communist Party convention in, 285
  demographic changes in, 59
  and disengagement agreements, 269, 375. See also Disengagement agreements
  and Eretz Israel, 32, 49, 50, 56, 62, 333, 350
  espionage against United States, 230

extreme right in, 382
foreign policy shifts, 12
imperialism of, 104
and international peace conference, 39
and Iran-Contra affair, 236(n52)
Iron Fist policy of, 76, 79
and Jordan, 87, 374, 380
Labor party/government in, 30, 37, 39,
    47, 52, 59, 103, 372, 375, 383
and Latin America, 21-23
Law of Return, 44, 75
and Lebanon war, 2-3, 36-37, 104,
    117(n51), 144, 381
Likud party/government in, 30-31, 32,
    34, 37, 39, 40, 59-61, 66, 86, 103. See
    also Begin, Menachem
as major non-NATO ally, 228
and Maronites, 188
Military Order 949, 34
moral degradation of, 328
myths of, 349
National Coalition government in, 18
National Unity government in, 37, 38,
    57-58, 281, 285-286
"new facts" doctrine of, 28
occupied territories of, 13, 28, 29, 31,
    32-35, 38, 39, 49-50, 64-65, 212,
    296, 322, 328, 333, 342, 372, 381-382
"open bridges" policy of, 28-29
and Palestinian nationalism, 102-104,
    352, 380
and Palestinian state, 102, 103, 104,
    336-337, 375, 380
peace treaty with Egypt, 273, 300, 377
and People's Republic of China, 21
perceptions/attitudes of, 371-372, 374-
    375, 378, 380-382
and PLO, 36, 102, 103-104, 117(n51),
    144, 284, 336-337, 338-339, 380-382
and Poland, 283
populations in, 50, 257(n35)
and prenegotiation process, 339-340
and public opinion polls, 203
and Reagan Plan, 37-38
rejectionism of, 103-104
and religious symbols, 51
and Sabra and Shatila massacres, 66,
    322, 328
Second, 60
Second Republic, 66
and Sinai, 299, 375
and South Africa, 20
and Soviet Jews, 284-285
and Soviet Union, 15, 17-18, 104-105,
    202, 264-265, 282, 285
and Soviet weapons systems, 21
and Suez Canal, 269

and Syria, 3, 100, 332, 374
and terrorism, 326, 352
and Tunis attack on PLO, 123, 231,
    284, 303, 307(n55)
and United States. See United States-
    Israel relations
and uprisings in 1987-1988, 342-343
and West Bank, 84, 86, 87. See also
    West Bank/Gaza; West Bank
    Palestinians
Israel Emergency Fund, 242
Israeli Communist Party, 281
Israel the Embattled Ally (Safran), 109
Italy, 284
IZL. See Irgun Zvai Leumi

Jabara, Abdeen, 251, 254
Jabotinsky, Vladimir, 61
Jackson, Henry, 107
Jackson, Jesse, 252, 253
Japan, 228
Jarring, Gunnar, 58, 205
Jerusalem, 28, 35, 60, 104, 142, 205, 348
Jewish Institute for National Security
    Affairs, The, 225
Jewish War Veterans, 241
Jews, 43, 44, 45, 47-48, 60, 239, 327. See
    also United States, Jewish community
    in; United States-Israel relations, and
    U.S. Jews
Johnson, Lyndon, 199, 204-205, 218. See
    also Johnson administration
Johnson administration, 12, 201, 204-205,
    212, 213, 218, 242
Joint Jordanian-Palestinian Economic
    Committee, 87, 89
Joint Political Military Group (JPMG),
    226-227
Joint Security Assistance Planning Group
    (JSAPG), 227
Jordan, 18, 30, 55, 74, 202, 324, 325-326,
    380
    and autonomy talks, 378
    and Egypt, 281
    federation with Palestinians, 360
    and international peace conference, 80
    and Israel, 87, 374, 380
    and Palestinian state, 335, 373
    and PLO, 79, 86-87, 90, 99, 107, 123,
        143, 379
    and Syria, 74, 186, 202, 300
    and territory for peace, 332
    and West Bank, 83, 84-85, 86-87, 91,
        98
Jordan River, 325
Journal of Palestine Studies, 254
JPMG. See Joint Political Military Group

JSAPG. *See* Joint Security Assistance
    Planning Group

Kach, 48, 66
Kahane, Meir, 48
Kahan Report, 66
Kaplowitz, Noel, 354–356, 361
Katzir, 60
Kelman, Herbert, 351–353, 360
Kemp, Jack, 225, 244
Kenen, I. L., 240
Kennedy, John, 217–218, 240. *See also*
    Kennedy administration
Kennedy administration, 12, 201. *See also*
    Kennedy, John
Kerr, Malcolm, 136–137, 169, 347
Khomeini, Ayatollah, 155, 157
Khrushchev, Nikita, 137, 200
Kings or People (Bendix), 154
Kirkpatrick, Jeanne, 225
Kissinger, Henry, 30, 105, 106, 107, 170,
    206, 222, 226, 269, 296
Klutznik, Philip, 244, 245
Knutson, Jeanne, 365
Kook, Zvi Yehuda Hacohen, 60
Korany, Bahgat, 153
Kosygin, Alexi, 270

Labor Alignment party, 27, 31, 56, 60
Lacouture, Jean, 154
Land of Israel Movement, 31
Laroui, Abdallah, 148, 155
Late Great Planet Earth, The (Lindsey),
    209
Latin America, 22–23, 158(fig.)
Lavi fighters, 228, 236(n44)
League of Nations, 321, 347
Lebanon, 36–37, 76, 101, 104, 123, 145,
    186–187, 188. *See also* Lebanon war
Lebanon war, 2–3, 13, 36–37, 104,
    117(n51), 144, 301, 381. *See also*
    Lebanon
Levin, Carl, 247
Lewis, I. L., 253
Libya, 303, 314
Lindsey, Hal, 209
London Sunday Times, 76
Long, Clarence, 250
Los Angeles Times, 253

McFarlane, Robert, 225
McGovern, George, 208
Mack, John E., 367, 368
Maghreb, 176, 294, 303, 306(n55)
Maki, 27, 55
Mapai, 27, 54, 56, 57
Mariam, Mengistu, 23

Maronites, 188, 248
Marxism/Leninism, 88, 264
Mashreq, 176, 294
Mawdudi, Abu al-Ala, 139
Meir, Golda, 31, 102, 241, 375
Melkites, 248
Memorandum of Strategic Understanding,
    13, 17, 56
Menashev, Mikhail, 292(n63)
Mendes-France, Pierre, 244
MFO. *See* United Nations, Multinational
    Force and Observers
Mica, Don, 244
Milson, Menachem, 34, 35
Molet, Guy, 12
Mondale, Walter, 253
Morocco, 39, 79, 80, 288, 306(n36)
Moslem Brotherhood. *See* Muslim
    Brethren
Mroz, John, 357–358, 361
Mubarak, Hosni, 38, 275–276, 280
Murphy, Richard, 244, 282
Muslim Brethren, 83, 111(n3), 139, 140

NAAA. *See* National Association of Arab
    Americans
Nasser, Gamal Abdul, 88, 110–111(n1),
    133, 135–136, 140, 168, 180–181
    and Baghdad Pact, 168
    challengers of, 137
    death of, 170, 182
    resignation speech, 169
    and Rogers initiative, 137, 183
    and Six Day War, 166–167
    and Soviet Union, 136, 137, 266
    and UN Emergency Force, 201, 205
    See also Nasserism
Nasserism, 135–138, 148, 152, 154, 166,
    168, 170. *See also* Nasser, Gamal
    Abdul
National Association of Arab Americans
    (NAAA), 249–251, 255
National Guidance Committee, 76, 85, 89
Nationalism, 23, 42–45, 46, 48–49, 50, 51,
    52, 88, 106, 142, 156, 168, 181, 382
National Jewish Coalition, 247
National Religious Party (NRP), 27, 31. *See
    also* Gush Emunim
National Salvation Front, 80
NATO. *See* North Atlantic Treaty
    Organization
Nazareth Democratic Front, 76
Near East Report, The, 242
Neo-Revisionism, 61–63, 68(n23). *See also*
    Zionism
Neumann, Emmanuel, 245
New Jewish Agenda, 245

New Outlook, 346
New York Times, 107, 243, 244
Nicaragua, 23
Nightline, 250
Nimeiry, Gaafar, 141
Nixon, Richard, 205-206, 208. *See also*
    Nixon administration; Nixon Doctrine
Nixon administration, 12-13, 29, 212, 213,
    268. *See also* Nixon, Richard; Nixon
    Doctrine
Nixon Doctrine, 106-107
Nomad doll, 251
North Atlantic Treaty Organization
    (NATO), 222, 315
Norway, 322
NRP. *See* National Religious Party

Oakar, Mary Rose, 255
OAU. *See* Organization of African Unity
October 1973 war, 16, 30, 73-74, 166,
    206, 208, 210, 268, 296, 313, 315,
    373-374
Office of Legislative Counsel, 220-221
Oil, 19, 150, 159, 166, 182, 192, 209-210,
    213, 308, 314-315. *See also* Political
    petrolism
Organization of African Unity (OAU), 19
Ottoman empire, 34, 142, 247

Page for National Dialogue, 176
Pakistan, 139
Palestine Communist Party, 111(n2), 281
Palestine Liberation Organization (PLO),
    81, 86, 110-111(n1), 322, 327, 333,
    348, 379
    and Arab states, 78, 97, 99-100, 122,
        129-130, 141-144
    Beirut exodus of, 89
    cease-fire agreements of, 96
    Charter of, 351
    Communist party in, 80
    Covenant of, 352, 353-354
    creation of, 99
    and Democratic Alliance, 112-113(n14)
    and Egypt, 111(n1)
    and Fateh leaders, 93, 97, 100, 101. *See*
        also Fateh
    fragmentation of, 78, 116(n42)
    and Israel, 36, 102, 103-104, 117(n51),
        144, 284, 336-337, 338-339, 380-382
    and Jordan, 79, 86-87, 90, 97, 107, 123,
        143, 379
    and Jordan-Israeli cooperation, 87
    lack of territorial base, 97, 115(n30), 126
    and Lebanon, 143
    and Lebanon camps, 116(n41)
    moderation of, 379

objectives of, 95-98
and Palestinian state, 89, 96, 100, 338-
    339, 379
and People's Republic of China, 105
and PNC, 79-80, 286
and politics of unity and consensus, 99
and prenegotiation process, 339-340
raid on Karameh, 142
rejectionism of, 350
Rejectionist Front, 355
resistance groups under, 94(table)
and Resolution 242, 339
and Six Day War, 141-142, 144, 374
as sole representative of Palestinians, 2,
    16, 91, 97, 100, 116(n35), 122, 143,
    277, 297
and Soviet Union, 16-17, 97, 105-106,
    201, 270, 277, 297, 302
structure of, 93-95, 94(table), 99, 112-
    113(n14)
as surrogate homeland, 128
and Syria, 99, 123, 124, 186, 187, 189,
    270, 281, 306(n30)
and terrorism, 97, 207, 326, 338, 350
and United Nations, 100, 126. *See also*
    Arafat, Yasser, United Nations
    address of
and United States, 110, 220, 243, 253
and United States-Israel relations, 106,
    220
Washington office, 243, 244, 250
and West Bank/Gaza, 34-35, 85, 86-88,
    124, 125-126, 129
See also Arafat, Yasser; Palestinians;
    West Bank Palestinians
Palestine National Council (PNC), 79-80,
    93, 94-95, 95(table), 96, 100, 110,
    112(n4), 127, 144, 278, 281, 286, 374,
    378-379
Palestinian National Alliance, 281
Palestinian National Covenant, 352, 353-
    354
Palestinian National Front (PNF), 75, 85,
    87
Palestinian National Movement (PNM), 73,
    81, 121, 125, 341
Palestinians
    and Arab states, 73-74, 333
    and Arafat, 330(n4)
    diaspora of, 98, 248
    and EEC, 14
    federation with Jordan, 360
    and Greater Palestine, 360
    and Greater Syria, 142
    in Israel, 341
    and Jordan, 30, 74, 143
    in Lebanon, 72

misperceptions of, 353–354
and Nasser, 333
and Palestinian state, 330(n4), 335–336.
  See also Palestinian state
and PLO, 330(n4). *See also* Palestine
  Liberation Organization
political spectrum of, 143
refugee camps of, 98
and Six Day War, 72, 121, 142
and Syria, 74, 79
and United States, 77, 109
in United States, 248
and Yom Kippur war, 73–74
See also West Bank/Gaza; West Bank
  Palestinians
Palestinian state, 324–326, 327, 328,
  330(n4), 333, 334, 337–339, 342, 348,
  378, 380
Pan-Arabism, 23, 24, 83, 136, 152, 156,
  176, 181, 191–192, 329. *See also*
  Nasserism
Path of God: Islam and Political Power
  (Pipes), 154
Peace Now, 325, 346
Peace studies paradigm, 346–351
Peled, Mattityahu, 103
People's Republic of China (PRC), 21, 105,
  265, 266, 295
Percy, Charles, 243
Peres, Shimon, 13, 15, 18, 31, 32, 38–39,
  245, 280, 281, 283, 284, 285–286
PFLP. *See* Popular Front for the
  Liberation of Palestine
Phalangists, 36–37, 104, 117(n51)
Phantom jet fighters, 242
Pipes, Daniel, 154
PLO. *See* Palestine Liberation Organization
PNC. *See* Palestine National Council
PNF. *See* Palestinian National Front
PNM. *See* Palestinian Nationalist
  Movement
Poland, 53(n18), 283
Political petrolism, 154, 170
Pollard, Jonathan, 230, 233, 329
Pompidou, Georges, 14
Popular Front for the Liberation of
  Palestine (PFLP), 94(table), 101,
  111(n2)
PRC. *See* People's Republic of China
Presidents' Conference, 232, 240, 242

Qabbani, Nizar, 175
Qasim, Abd al-Karim, 137
Qatar, 173
Quaddumi, Faruk, 127
Quandt, William, 30, 153
Qutb, Sayyid, 140

Rabin, Yitzhak, 31, 32, 37, 102, 222
Rafi, 56
Rahall, Nick, 255
Rakah, 18, 27, 28
Ramadan war. *See* October 1973 war
Raziq, Ali Abd al-, 139–140
Reagan, Ronald, 208, 224, 231, 235(n35),
  243, 276, 282, 303. *See also* Reagan
  administration; Reagan Plan
Reagan administration, 13, 91, 107, 210,
  213–214, 243, 300. *See also* Reagan,
  Ronald; Reagan Plan
Reagan Plan, 77, 214, 276, 277, 278, 279.
  See also Reagan, Ronald; Reagan
  administration
Regionalism. *See* Globalism vs. regionalism
Revolt, The (Begin), 365–366
Rich and Poor States in the Middle East
  (Kerr and Yassin), 169
Robertson, Pat, 209
Rogers, William, 105, 206. *See also* Rogers
  Plan
Rogers Plan, 29–30, 183, 202, 206. *See
  also* Rogers, William
Rosen, Steven J., 225
Rosenberg, M. J., 241–242
Rubenberg, Cheryl, 147–148
Rusk, Dean, 205

Saad Haddad, 104
Sabah, Sabah al, 275
Sabra and Shatila massacres, 37, 66, 144,
  243, 244, 322, 328
Sadat, Anwar, 16, 32, 105, 138, 140, 156,
  182, 183–186, 212, 267, 268, 273, 275,
  377
Sadd, David, 250
Safran, Nadav, 109
Said, Edward, 249
Said, Nuri al-, 137
Saiqa, 99, 101
Salem, George, 252
Samhan, Helen Hatab, 254
Sanusiyya, 139
Sapir, Pinhas, 29
Saud, King, 137
Saudi Arabia, 30, 80, 100, 136, 137, 153,
  156, 169, 170, 173, 174, 175, 182, 191,
  209, 335
SCA-83. *See* United States–Israel
  relations, Strategic Cooperation
  Agreement
Schindler, Alexander, 244, 245, 246
Schmidt, Helmut, 52
Schneerson, 61
Sea Wind, 281
Seliktar, Ofira, 231

Shadyac, Richard, 249
Shah of Iran, 155
Shamir, Yitzhak, 38, 39, 77, 224–225, 245, 279, 283, 286
Sharabi, Hisham, 249
Shari'ah, 138, 141
Sharon, Ariel, 13, 17, 36, 37, 59, 64, 66, 244, 275
Shevardnadze, Edward, 283, 285
Shin Bet, 231
Shultz, George, 225, 229, 231
Shuqairy, Ahmed, 111(n1), 121, 141
Simon, Paul, 243
Sinai, 59, 104, 184, 185, 201, 205, 222, 299, 375
Six Day War, 26, 42, 54, 134–135, 166–167, 199, 294–297, 332–333
    and annexation, 64
    and Arab-Americans, 248–249
    and Egyptian-Syrian relations, 179
    and Islamic fundamentalism, 138
    and Israeli political system, 64–66
    and Israeli populations, 50
    and Likud, 59, 61
    and Neo-Revisionism, 61–63
    and Palestinian nationalism, 72, 121, 142
    and PLO, 141–142, 144, 374
    and Soviet-American competition, 202, 213
    and Soviet Union, 15, 201–203, 265–266
    and television, 203
    and territorial nationalism, 49
    and United States, 202–214, 266
Siyassa, al-Duwaliyya, al-, 153
Socialism, 136
Socialist International, 52
Sofer, Ovadia, 282
Solarz, Stephen, 255
Soloveichik, 60–61
South Africa, 19, 20
South Korea, 228
South Yemen, 264
Soviet Union
    and Afghanistan, 273, 306(n40)
    and Africa, 314
    and Algeria, 294–295
    and Arafat-Hussein agreement, 281–282, 303
    bilateralism of, 300
    and Camp David, 286, 298–299
    Communist Party (CPSU), 264
    and conflict management, 323
    economic credits and grants of, 311(table)
    economic downturn of, 308, 312–313
    and Egypt, 16, 30, 105, 137, 183–184, 200, 264, 266, 268, 286, 312, 313
    Friendship and Cooperation treaties of, 264, 300
    and international peace conferences, 284–285, 286, 288, 297, 303
    and Iran-Iraq war, 274, 275, 303
    and Islam, 265, 280, 301
    and Israel, 15, 17–18, 104–105, 202, 264–265, 282, 285
    and Israel's right to exist, 264, 271–272, 286, 296
    and Jewish emigration, 284
    Jews in, 17, 239
    and Lebanon war, 276, 301
    and Middle East Communist parties, 265
    Middle East strategy, 265–268
    military assistance to Arabs, 15, 272, 308, 310(tables), 311–312, 314, 316
    military buildup of, 312
    as moderate, 316, 317
    and Nasser, 136, 137, 266
    and oil embargo, 314–315
    and Palestinian state, 105–106, 270, 272–273, 280, 297
    peace plans of, 271–272, 277, 280, 285, 287, 297, 302
    and People's Republic of China, 266
    and PLO, 16–17, 97, 105–106, 201, 270, 277, 297, 302
    and Reagan Plan, 276, 280, 287
    as resource in Middle East conflict, 360
    and Sino-U.S. entente, 267
    and Six Day War, 15, 201–202, 265–266, 295–296
    and Syria, 137, 200, 264, 268, 277, 288, 300, 302, 314
    and Third World, 308–310, 309(table), 313, 314
    and United States, 202, 211, 267, 282, 287, 296, 313, 315, 330
    and U.S.-Syrian confrontation, 279
    and War of Attrition, 312
    and Yom Kippur war, 268, 296
Spiegel, Steven L., 225, 231–232
State Department Reports on Human Rights Practices, 76
State List, 31, 59
State vs. nation, 44–45. *See also* Nationalism
Steadfastness Front, 274, 278, 280, 290(n25)
Sudan, 23, 139, 141, 265, 266
Suez Canal, 16, 30, 184, 185, 269. *See also* Suez war
Suez war, 133, 210. *See also* Suez Canal

Syria(n)
and Arab world, 187, 190, 191
and Camp David, 187
coups in, 168
and Egypt, 179, 180–181, 186
and Egyptian-Saudi axis, 175, 182, 270–271
and Iran, 190, 300
and Iraq, 273
and Israel, 3, 100, 332, 374
Israeli disengagement agreement, 100.
    See also Disengagement agreements
and Jordan, 74, 186, 202, 300
and Lebanon, 186–187, 188–189, 270, 301, 306(n30)
and Maronites, 188
and Palestinians, 74, 79
and Palestinian state, 335
and PLO, 99, 123, 124, 186, 187, 189, 270, 281, 306(n30)
and Soviet-Israeli relations, 283
and Soviet Union, 137, 200, 264, 268, 277, 288, 300, 302, 314
and United States, 266, 278
See also Assad, Hafiz; United Arab Republic

Talmon, Ya'akov, 42, 49
Tamir, Shmuel, 59
Taylor, Alan, 147, 148
Teamsters Union, 241
Tehiya, 45, 65–66
Terrorism, 17, 43, 97, 108, 201, 207, 231, 283–284, 326, 338, 352
Third World, 157, 158(fig.), 159(table), 192, 308–310, 309(table), 313, 314
Time, 249
Torczyner, Jacques, 245
Total colonialism, 347, 348
Transafrica, 238
Transjordan, 321
Treaty of Rome, 15
Truman Doctrine, 200
Tunis, 123, 303, 307(n55)
Turkey, 23, 179, 238

UAHC. *See* Union of American Hebrew Congregations
UAR. *See* United Arab Republic
UJA. *See* United Jewish Appeal
Umma, 138, 151
UN. *See* United Nations
UNIFIL, 96
Union of American Hebrew Congregations (UAHC), 246
United Arab Emirates, 173, 180–181
United Arab Republic (UAR), 136, 165

United Jewish Appeal (UJA), 240, 242
United Nations (UN), 327, 347
Arafat address to, 76, 100
Emergency Force, 201, 204
Multinational Force and Observers (MFO), 229
Partition Proposal (1947), 346, 348, 349
Resolution 242, 14, 29, 37, 58, 105, 124, 202, 205, 297, 323, 339
Resolution 338, 105, 323
Resolution 425, 96
UNIFIL, 96
"Zionism as racism" resolution, 20
United States
Arabs in, 247–254
church groups vs. Israel, 231
and Egypt, 186, 191, 211, 266, 275, 281, 284, 300
and Indian Ocean, 275
and Iran, 213
and Israel. *See* United States-Israel relations
Jewish community in, 91, 208, 209, 210, 213, 233, 238–239, 239–247, 254–255.
    See also American Israel Public Affairs Committee
Jewish lobbies in, 240. *See also* *individual groups*
and Libya, 303
Marines in Lebanon, 278, 279
as mediator, 359–360
moral power of, 328
and native Americans, 323
and Palestinian nationalism, 77, 106, 207
and People's Republic of China, 105
and PLO, 110, 220, 243, 253
and PLO Washington office, 243, 244, 250
pro-Israeli forces in, 107–108, 109, 231–232
and Saudi Arabia, 210, 211, 243, 274
Senate Foreign Relations Committee, 221
and Six Day War, 202–214, 266
and Soviet Union, 202, 211, 267, 282, 287, 296, 313, 315, 330
strategic consensus policy of, 300
Supreme Court, 221
and Syria, 266, 278
and Third World nationalism, 106, 207
and Turkey, 238
See also United States-Israel relations
United States-Israel relations, 13–14, 16, 30, 184, 201, 304, 329
and Cold War, 77
and *Eretz Israel*, 232
and formal treaty, 13

and free trade agreements, 228
and international peace conference,
   245–246
and Israel as strategic asset, 106–109,
   225, 229, 230
and Israeli dependence, 22
and Israeli intelligence, 208
and Jordan, 202
and Lebanon war, 244, 278
and Memoranda of Agreement, 219–224
and Memorandum of Understanding,
   224
and military assistance grants, 227, 230
and mutual defense pact, 230
National Security Decision Directive
   111, 224–225
and occupied territories, 29, 205
and PLO, 106, 220
and resale of U.S. weapons, 231
and Sinai withdrawal, 222
vs. Soviet Union–Syria, 323
Strategic Cooperation Agreement (SCA-
   83), 224–229
and Tunis PLO attack, 231
and uprisings in 1987–1988, 91
and U.S. aid, 30, 211, 218
and U.S. church groups, 231
and U.S. evangelicals, 208–209
and U.S. Jews, 210, 213, 233, 238–239,
   239–247
and U.S. liberals, 212
and U.S. public opinion, 232, 243
and Yom Kippur war, 208
See also Israel; United States
United States v. Belmont, 221
Uruguay, 22
Uris, Leon, 218
U.S.S. Liberty, 230

Venezuela, 22
Versaille, Treaty of, 321
Vessey, John, 225
Vietnam war, 203, 207, 208
Voice of America, 14, 282
Vorontsov, Yuli, 282

Wahhabism, 139, 154
War of Attrition, 201, 202, 206, 266–267,
   312
Warsaw Pact, 209
Washington, Harold, 252
Washington Post, 107

Waterbury, John, 152, 154
Wazir, Khalil, 105, 111(n3), 291(n59)
Weapons, imports of, 157, 158(fig.),
   159(table)
Weinberger, Caspar, 52, 225
West Bank/Gaza, 33, 40, 72, 98
   and autonomy, 185
   Day of the Land in, 76
   de facto annexation of, 50, 65, 66
   and Jewish underground, 50, 66, 67
   and Jordan, 83, 84–85
   and Likud, 59, 60
   and Moshe Dayan, 27–28
   and "new facts" doctrine, 28
   and Palestinian state, 88, 89, 96
   and PLO, 34–35, 85, 86–88, 124, 125–
      126, 129
   public opinion surveys in, 379
   settlements in, 31, 68(n29), 103, 104
   universities in, 35
   uprisings in 1987–1988, 90–91, 243, 246,
      340–343
   and Village Leagues, 35, 76
   See also Israel, occupied territories of;
      Palestinians; West Bank Palestinians
West Bank Palestinians, 83–91, 243, 246,
   324, 341, 379–380. See also Israel,
   occupied territories of; Palestinians;
   West Bank/Gaza
West Germany, 62
White, Ralph, 353–354, 360–361
Whitehead, John, 244
Women's Zionist Organization Hadassah,
   240
World Muslim League, 306(n40)

Yamani, Ahmed Zaki, 173, 226
Yaniv, Avner, 103
Yassin, Sayed, 153, 169
Yemen, 136, 137, 139, 152, 169, 201
Yom Kippur war. See October 1973 war
Yuchtman-Yaar, Ephraim, 358–360, 361

Zaghlul, Saad, 139
Zayyad, Tewfiq, 76
Zionism, 41, 43, 47–48, 61, 74–75, 97, 104,
   107, 109, 125, 142, 210, 231, 239, 241,
   297, 338, 353. See also Neo-
   Revisionism
Zionism and the Palestinians (Flapan), 348
Zogby, Jim, 249, 252, 254
Zureik, Constantine, 167